MW01201883

Thank you!
Garage Band Theory: Tools The Pros Use To Play By Ear

Congratulations are in order! You've made a wise investment in your musical education, one that I trust will serve you well for a long time.

I hope you'll learn as much from this program as I have in the process of developing it. Truth is, I'm still learning and I know the information in this book is a great platform to begin building your musical knowledge, expand on what you already know or help another student get a good start.

And when you've been through GBT, not only will your practice time be more productive and focused, you'll be able to discuss any aspect of music with anyone!

If you'd like to help others learn about GBT the best thing you can do is to contribute a positive comment on Amazon.

Here are two things you can do that will help spread the word most effectively:

1) I would be very grateful if you would visit Amazon.com and rate the book, honestly … the good the bad and the ugly … according to their system of stars.

 A brief review is a great help, but for those of you that really like it, please tell readers about the value you see in the book.

*Please note that Amazon's policy on posting reviews is that you must have an Amazon.com account that has successfully been charged for the purchase of any physical or digital item.

Also important is that you are NOT required to have purchased the product you are reviewing from Amazon. Anyone who has an 'active' Amazon account can review products.

2) If you've never shopped at Amazon but would like to contribute a positive comment that I can post on the book's website or include in marketing, send your comment to ds@garagebandtheory.com (about 15 words would be adequate and greatly appreciated!)

Be sure to go to GarageBandTheory.com to download all the supplemental content … there's a lot. I'll be adding stuff periodically and will notify you when I do.

Have fun with this, that's what music is for...

Thanks again,
Duke Sharp
Cowboy Heaven Publishing
P.O. Box 248
Gallatin Gateway, MT 59730

TOOLS THE PROS USE TO PLAY BY EAR

"Don't be put off by this giant book— Duke's got the secrets of the universe in here.
Quite simply, this is the most comprehensive book on music theory I've ever seen."
Bill Payne, Little Feat

"Garage Band Theory is a must for any musician."
Rodney Crowell
Time Grammy Award Winner

"Something for every musician at any level.
Especially helpful is the musical notation and tablature for a variety of instruments.
This book inspires me to learn and practice more."
Sam Bush
Americana Music Association Lifetime Achievement Award
International Bluegrass Music Hall of Fame

"Garage Band Theory offers you everything you need to know to understand, play and make your own
music. Because he is both an accomplished musician and teacher, Sharp's Garage Band Theory is an
excellent guide for beginners and more advanced players alike."
Sam Barry, author, musician

"A great resource for musicians young and old no matter what your training.
Garage Band Theory is a veritable encyclopedia of useful tools and tips.
This book lifts the lid off the "black box" of music theory and let's the light shine in—and in a fun, practical
way. This is a book which should be left handily lying around the living room, bedside, studio, classroom,
(restroom?)—ready to be dipped into at any time for reference purposes or just to improve or refresh one's
fluency in the language of music. For less than the price of a single lesson, GBT offers a lifetime of learning."
Alasdair Fraser
Scotland's premier fiddle ambassador

"Garage Band Theory let me know how little I know... but in a good way. It's a great book!"
Sterling C Ball CEO, Ernie Ball Inc.

"This book is written in the people's key."
Kostas
Nashville Songwriter Hall of Fame

©2015 Duke Sharp

Editors: Sam Barry, Kathy Kamen Goldmark, Brant Robey

Proof Readers: Karen Bovee, DeAn Krey, Debbie Olsen, JoAn Reichart,
Leif Routman and Janice Watson and Alexander Opitz

Technical Editors: Craig Hall, Shawna Lockhart, Rich Robiscoe, Kris Ellingsen, Kyle Brenner,
Ron Schmipf, Eddie Tsuru, Gloria Thiede and Ryan Karlin and Kimolisa

Index: Diane Eherenberger

Front Cover: concept, photography and design Lib Caldwell
Front Cover Design: Brian Murphy, Dana Aaberg
Back Cover Design: Brant Robey, Tammy Stone, Jonathan Gullery, Dana Aaberg Cover
photography: Lib Caldwell
Illustrations: Duke Sharp

Author photo: Tammy Stone

Gallatin Gateway, Montana, USA

Duke Sharp, Nong Khai, Thailand, © Tammy Stone 2010

The author wishes to thank Craig Hall, Jerry Sharp, and Greg Sharp for their incalculable assistance in the development of this book.

Compiling and filtering the information in this book took just about eight years. During the process, I probably asked every musician with whom I'm acquainted at least one question about something with which I was struggling, and nearly all provided useful answers.

I was also teaching private lessons in a busy music store, and nearly all of my students were subjected to various drafts and finished chapters, many found errors and made useful suggestions. It would require another volume to list everyone, and I'd certainly forget some people, so I'll just have to say thanks to so many for your assistance.

The individual who is essentially responsible for the existence of this book is Craig Hall. Craig is an extraordinary player and teacher. When I first started taking students, Craig recommended that I make copies of the lessons I created. He said that over the years there were countless times he would sketch out a lesson and sometimes he really "got something just right" and then it went away with the student. So I took his advice. After about a year, it occurred to me that I had the framework of a book.

I would write a chapter or two with everything I knew about a topic and then take it to Craig. Many of the things I knew about music theory simply weren't so and Craig very patiently pointed out each and every error. All of the advanced jazz information came from Craig—and most of the good jokes.

While Craig did most of the technical proof reading to make sure I got the musical facts straight, Rich Robiscoe, Kris Ellingsen, Kyle Brenner, Ron Schmipf and Eddie Tsuru also made important contributions and observations.

Other editors who helped enormously with basic grammar stuff and copy editing include The Author Enablers, Sam Barry, Kathy Kamen Goldmark, Karen Bovee, Debbie Olsen, Brant Robey, DeAn Krey, JoAn Reichart, Janice Watson and Leif Routman. All made significant contributions to this work and I'm grateful.

Alex and Jerry Sharp, my parents, sang in a performing choir into their eighties and the fact that they always supported and encouraged my musical inclinations is probably the reason I have pursued music as a career.

In addition to his extensive knowledge of music theory which he so generously shared with me throughout this process, Ron Schmipf saved my bacon more than a couple of times when my computer was doing its best to kill the book.

My partner in Two Grass Crew, Mike Parsons, teaches fiddle, mandolin, banjo and guitar and he helped "road test" a lot of the things in GBT on his students.

Lib Caldwell, a longtime friend and gifted guitarist, came up with the idea for the cover and took the photos. (WMC Photography, Livingston, Montana) The fellow sitting at the piano is a terrific keyboard player, Rich Ruggles. We call Rich "Pinky" these days, and you'll encounter him in a few places in the book. Fortunately, he has a good sense of humor. Lib, Rich and I moved to Montana together in 1976 to play music and we've never outgrown the habit. You can hear both of them playing on one of my CDs, Yucca Pie, on a song called "Formica Fandango," which they co-wrote, along with Johnny Regan.

Sincere thanks to other obliging friends, family and acquaintances who contributed to the project: Dean Anderson, Sterling Ball, Larry Barnwell, Michael Blessing, Duke Brekhus, Sam Bush, Rodney Crowell, Fred Decker, Paul Decker, Andy Dena, Kris Ellingsen, Diane Ehrenberger, Kyler Ernst, Mark Fife, Alasdair Fraser, Joanne Gardner, Tom Garnsey, Michael Gillan, Adam Greenberg, Roper Greene, Geno Kreis, Cynthia Logan, John Lowell, Michelle Madeline, Nancy McKaskey, Scott McMillion, Jerry Mullen, Tom Murphy, Stacey Olsen, Bill Payne, Polly Payne, Andy Petrov, Dan Poynter, Jim Reichart, Paul Rose, Andrea Sharp, Toni Tease, Eddie Tsuru, Debra Wahlberg, Stuart Weber, and Craig Wishniewski.

Front Cover—concept, photography and design: Lib Caldwell
Front Cover—Brian Murphy, MurphyWorks
Back Cover—Dana Aaberg, Jonathan Gullery, Brant Robey, Tammy Stone, Duke Sharp
Photography—Lib Caldwell
Index—Diane Ehrenberger, Ryan Karlin, Shawna Lockhart

Despite all the contributions of so many, in the end, any mistakes are mine. What a long strange trip. Thank you all.

Duke

Table of Contents

Go to www.garagebandtheory.com and get your free stuff!

Music Theory, Mathematics and Playing By Ear

The phrase "Music Theory" seems to intimidate lots of people. It sounds a little bit scary and difficult. Quantum Theory and Einstein's Theory of Relativity come to mind. I suspect that both are quite a lot more difficult than Music Theory.

The "Music Theory" that I've described is intended to define the words, phrases, and concepts that will enable you to communicate with other musicians and allow you to think clearly and conceptually about music.

A two-word definition of Music Theory that I like is this: music vocabulary. It's all relatively simple, factual stuff, not abstract theories. When the meanings of musical words and symbols are understood, it's relatively easy to understand the processes and concepts that are relevant to most back-porch pickers and many levels of pro and semi-pro gigs.

An interesting paradox is the fact that I never intended to write about Music Theory. The original idea was to explain the process many people use to play popular music by ear. I play "by ear" as do most of the people I play with.

Much to my surprise, I discovered that the only sensible way to explain the process is to use the conventional structure and the vocabulary associated with it, which is thought of as Music Theory. So, even though this book deals almost exclusively with topics that definitely fall under the heading of Music Theory, everything is intended to help you play by ear.

The range of emotions that music can evoke is nearly limitless. Listening to music can inspire visual imagery as well as other creative art forms. It is truly a magical art form, with apparently infinite variations. Volumes could be written describing music and all of the ways it permeates our lives.

As a direct contrast, on a page, the language of music is a simple written language.

Consider… when this system of conveying musical information was invented the vast majority of the population was not literate. They couldn't read anything because they had never seen a page with writing on it. There was no *New York Times* being delivered to any doorsteps. For most people associating a physical action with instructions on a page was about as common as a flying toaster. Well, maybe not quite that rare, but you get the idea.

In addition, everything had to be drawn by hand, starting with drawing the lines on a page. One line at a time and one note at a time. No copy machines, just feathers and little bottles of ink. "Like, wow, Mister Beethoven, how many guys in the band need a copy of this?"

The physical and social realities of the age necessitated a simple system. It works so well that there have been no major structural changes for a few centuries, and a lot of really clever people have been using it. If it really needed revising, someone would have done it by now. At different places in this book I'll poke fun at certain aspects of Music Theory that seem odd and confusing, but overall the system is very well-designed and a relatively simple solution to some really complicated communication issues. That's what it's for… communication.

There is a group of lines and a handful of symbols that correspond to notes on your instrument. There are a couple of number substitution codes that let us think about musical ideas in general terms. There are names for most of the musical patterns that we are accustomed to hearing.

I've acquired a dislike for the phrase "play by ear." In my opinion, "play by ear" is misleading and actually discourages people from developing a skill they already use unconsciously and naturally every single day. "Play by ear" implies that there is some sort of physical requirement or magical quality inherent in the ability to recognize musical sounds.

It seems to me that on most levels, a better description is "playing by memory" because it is a learned process. No one is born instinctively knowing which sound is connected with whatever caused it.

If you'll pause and think for a moment, you'll realize that you can identify dozens, if not hundreds of different sounds without having to see whatever it is that is making the noise. A dog barking, a clap of thunder, wind in the trees, a car door slamming, or a passing train… the list is long. Many of the distinctions you commonly make between different sounds in the course of a day are quite subtle.

When your favorite song comes on the radio, do you have to wait for the DJ to tell you who is singing? Probably not. Can you identify who is walking down the hall from the sound of the footsteps? Can you tell whether it's your dog or the neighbor's dog making the racket?

Chances are good that you know what a duck is, something you probably didn't know when you were two years old. Today, when you hear one quacking, even if you can't see it, you automatically associate the name "duck" with the sound, and these separate images—one visual, one auditory—plus the word "duck" somehow become almost a single entity. The process of identifying sounds and communicating about those sounds is possible partly because you can associate a name with the sound you hear.

The same is true for musical sounds. When you have names to associate with the sounds that you hear, locating those sounds on an instrument, any instrument, becomes much easier.

A fellow named Ludwig van Beethoven wrote Symphony #5 minor op. #67 in about 1806. His tools were a piano, paper, pencils, and a head full of music. He wrote it one note at a time… every note for each instrument. He was well on his way to becoming deaf at the time he commenced writing this symphony.

Symphony #5 was not the only thing he wrote after his hearing began to fail, not by a long shot. Try Symphony #9. Although the first performance of Beethoven's Ninth Symphony was far from perfect (only two rehearsals), the audience loved it and the applause was heartfelt and thunderous.

Mr. Beethoven was about as deaf as an old boot by this time, and apparently oblivious to the response. Can you imagine this highly emotional artist/composer standing with his back to the audience, head down, probably wondering if anyone liked it? Karoline Ungar, who sang alto, gently tugged his sleeve so he'd turn and see the clapping hands and waving hats. Wow.

Beethoven is regarded by many as one of the greatest composers to have lived on this planet. I happen to agree and I do enjoy listening to his music occasionally, but those are not the reasons I decided to mention him. There are other great composers who are nearly as well known. Mozart might have been more gifted and Bach was certainly more prolific, to name two.

The fact of Beethoven's deafness presents an interesting context in which to consider the phrase "play by ear." Beethoven played and composed on a piano. His ears did not work, yet he wrote for orchestras of thirty instruments (or more) plus vocalists, and obviously he "heard" every instrument, every voice, every note, and subtle nuance. Did he "play by ear?"

I think so. What else could you call it? To say that Beethoven played by ear might be a little like saying that Michael Jordan played basketball or M.C. Escher could draw. Obviously true, but certainly not anywhere near a complete description of the extent of their abilities.

My point is that the "ear" part of the phrase "play by ear" is to a large degree about "memory." Beethoven heard his music inside his head, not through his ears.

I don't think that it's possible to learn the sort of extraordinary, magical skills and talents that Beethoven or Michael Jordan brought to their respective art forms. But it is absolutely possible to develop and enhance your own natural abilities to find the chords and melodies for popular tunes without needing any written clues.

Are you able to distinguish between the sounds of a piano and a trumpet and a bass drum and a violin? Of course. Probably, if you close your eyes and imagine the sound of any of those instruments, you can sort of "hear" it.

Can you sing along when everybody sings "Happy Birthday to You" or "Jingle Bells" or "The Star Spangled Banner?" Can you sing "Twinkle, Twinkle Little Star" and "Mary Had a Little Lamb?" Have you ever seen music for those songs or did you learn them "by ear?" Can you sort of imagine "hearing" those songs without singing out loud?

There is a prevailing myth that a fortunate few are recipients of this "gift"… "a good ear"… and "either you have it or you don't." Although musical memory does come more easily to some people than others, as is true of nearly all things, I am certain that identifying sounds is a natural ability that most of us use daily. With patience and practice this common ability can be developed into useful musical skills. This ability is not the same as the "inexplicable power" that possesses the musical magicians.

An important element of playing by ear is learning to listen. It's something that many people forget to include as an essential part of practice time: listening time.

Hearing musical details is a result of listening, and there is a different between the two. You can hear a stream flowing without ever listening to it closely. When you pause and listen carefully, you can begin to hear all the small sounds that make up the sound of the creek. Every little pour-over and every wave has a distinct, individual voice and it is possible to distinguish between them. But you do have to listen closely.

Undoubtedly, you are able to recognize the difference between a snare drum and a piano. But the difference between a violin and a viola is much more subtle. You really have to listen to tell which is which.

An important aspect of the "play by ear" process is correctly identifying what it is that you're hearing. That is what most of this book is about—naming the musical events you're likely to hear and describing the structure they inhabit. All of the exercises and examples are intended as listening exercises. One way to hear them is to play them, obviously; but in many instances the objective is not so much about acquiring the physical ability to produce the sound as it is to hear the noise, so you can identify and name it. Most of the examples throughout this book were created in a software program called Finale but after finishing converted the files to MuseScore which I like better. You can download the files at **www.GarageBandTheory.com** so you can hear them play.

Obviously, this process of hearing and accurately identifying musical sounds can't be mastered overnight. It isn't as easy as instantly distinguishing between a crowing rooster and a doorbell. But most of the time it is easier than being able to distinguish between the sound of rain and the sound of sleet.

On the other hand, if you find yourself answering the telephone at the sound of your neighbor riding by on her Harley, you may want to consider a different hobby.

There seems to be an unspoken belief that musicians who play and compose music, but who have no formal training, are somehow more "gifted" or "soulful" than those who are "classically trained" because everything the unschooled musician plays is somehow "pure, untainted, free."

I think that the main difference between talented musicians who have no formal training and talented musicians who understand theory is that those who have no formal training have greater difficulty expressing certain ideas to other musicians.

There is nothing in my experience that leads me to believe that absence of musical knowledge in any way contributes to the quality of the music. Associating names with sounds does not restrict creative, soulful, musical inspiration. Some people seem to be so wrapped up in the intellectual aspects of music that they forget about the actual sounds, but mostly, knowledge is good.

I remember kids in school who were forced to play band instrument, who dutifully learned which key on the clarinet would produce the tone that was associated with a dot on a page. You would see a troop of them at school performances, playing these odd arrangements of pop tunes, and it never sounded very musical or looked like much fun. Those of us who were fooling around learning guitar "by ear" thought there was nothing quite as ridiculous or hilarious as the version of "Purple Haze" rendered by the marching band at a football game. We thought it was mainly because they were reading music and playing horns.

Later, I discovered that there's nothing ridiculous or hilarious about how Tower of Power could lay down the same tunes. Those guys are serious readers and there's a bunch of horns. They could read "Row, Row, Row Your Boat" straight off a page and make the dead want to dance. It's not about the tunes or the instruments or the paper. It's what the musicians do with the music that makes you want to jump up and down and shake your bones.

I have encountered accomplished players who are resistant to the idea of learning theory, or learning to read music for fear that their fluid musicality will somehow be impeded by knowledge. It's my impression that many people who have learned to "play by ear" are afraid that if they learn to read what's on the page they will somehow lose the "creative juice" and their music will begin to sound like those uninspired kids in high school.

We've all seen those books that have a detailed line drawing with every space numbered, and all you have to do is match the colors to the numbers and… "you too can paint the Mona Lisa." Occasionally, I've overhead conversations between a blues guitar "teacher" and different parents saying that he didn't teach students music theory or scale exercises, and that he wouldn't learn to read music for the same reasons he wouldn't paint by numbers. "That's just like being a jukebox or a photocopy machine, and it isn't creative. All that stuff does is interfere with "feeling" the music… is the general theme of his story.

There seems to be this perception that if you learn to paint by numbers, or learn to read music, then somehow that's all you will be able to do.

First, is that necessarily bad?

There are talented artists in all genres whose art lies in interpreting the scene rather than creating it. Neither Ella Fitzgerald, nor Frank Sinatra ever composed a tune. How many actors are expected to write their lines? Ansel Adams photographed landscapes and Albert Bierstadt painted them, and obviously, neither created the scenes they were viewing. I think it's safe to say that if both artists had rendered the same landscape there would be very few similarities in the individual interpretations.

These people are interpreting something that they did not create, but certainly could not be considered a "paint by numbers" artist in a derogatory sense.

Why then, is reading and interpreting a written piece of music considered by some to be "less creative" than writing a simple tune or "figuring songs out by ear?"

I, for one, don't see it that way. They are two different skills, two different art forms, two sides of the same coin.

If you want to learn a difficult tune, you can spend hours finding all the notes by ear. Or, you can spend $2 and have all the difficult passages figured out for you and you can spend the hours practicing the tune instead of searching for the notes. In addition, learning to interpret music from a page or painting by numbers can allow intuitive leaps, and be a platform for developing techniques and skills that might take 20 years to discover otherwise.

If you're messing around with your own ideas while you use written clues as an integral component of your studies, you can learn to apply ideas and techniques that people like Ludwig van Beethoven, Duke Ellington, and Miles Davis developed, to your own creations. I don't think that knowledge impeded these guys' creativity or "feel." Knowledge and good listening skills combine to make the best of both worlds, I think.

It seems to me that "playing music by ear" can be described as a process that involves normal, everyday, intellectual skills that most of us take for granted.

Identifying sounds is one part of the "play by ear" process. Another part of the process is learning to anticipate what's coming next, what is likely to occur in certain situations. Again, this is something we all do on a regular basis.

When you walk into a restaurant there is a sequence of events that is fairly predictable. Different restaurants have different procedures, but after you've been to 20 of them, the surprises are few and far between. Maybe there is a host or hostess who will show you to a seat. Maybe there's a sign that says "Please Seat Yourself." Maybe there is a buffet and a menu. Maybe there is just a cafeteria-style line. Maybe you just get in line and ask for a taco. But as soon as you've identified the type of restaurant, the events are predictable, with slight variations for which you adjust. The details are different, but the structure is very similar. Once you're in the door, you'll have no difficulty finding your way around and getting a burger. This is not information you were born with, it is information that you have learned.

When you become familiar with different styles of music, events are just as predictable. The types of chords and harmonies, the feel or the beat, the choice of instruments, and the general structure are consistent within genres to a large degree. Bluegrass songs are similar to other bluegrass songs, jazz songs are similar to other jazz songs and rock songs are similar to other rock songs. And they are all similar to each other.

The fact is, in most popular music, the number of patterns that occur are fairly limited. You'll learn that certain chord combinations and sequences are used over and over in nearly all genres. This knowledge is at the core of anticipating the flow of the song. You can learn to recognize and identify musical phrases and events just as you have already learned to identify other sequences like lightning and thunder.

An idea that seems to have a somewhat negative impact on many students' perception of their own musical capability is the idea that "music is very mathematical, and I'm not good at math."

It is absolutely true that there are loads of numbers associated with music, and that many musical ideas are expressed using numbers.

But it is never the sort of "math" that requires addition and subtraction. You will not need a slide rule or a calculator.

Nearly all of the numbers that you will encounter in this book are used to identify and sort musical objects. It can be helpful to think of these musical objects for a moment as if they were boxes of apples, oranges, and bananas. In the apple box there are seven slightly different varieties of apples, labeled 1 though 7. The box of oranges has seven different types, labeled 1-7, and the banana box contains seven different bananas, numbered 1-7. As soon as you can recognize the difference between an apple, a banana, and an orange, then you'll never confuse the apple called "1" with the orange or banana called "1," even though the number is the same.

At first the musical objects you'll learn about are not as distinctly different as apples and oranges, but the analogy is valid. Most of the musical numbers are part of a system for identifying "objects" and you don't add, subtract, divide or multiply them.

It's completely logical to suppose that these identification numbers are related to the "music is mathematical" concept. However, it's not true. Most musical numbers in this book are labels that help with identification and communication. Many "musical objects" could have been labeled with colors, or the names of exotic swamp creatures and would still serve essentially the same function.

The majority of math in music that I've been able to discern is the sort of math that is evident in the symmetry of bead work, weaving and other visual art forms. It's very easy to see geometric patterns on a page or a Navajo blanket, but difficult to express those patterns accurately with words. It's easier to express them numerically. If you assign each line and each space a number, and assign numbers to horizontal distances, then these patterns can be expressed using those numbers.

Humans are good at recognizing patterns, and we tend to find symmetry pleasing and satisfying. There are loads of symmetrical patterns in music. An enormous percentage of music in all genres consists of repetitive patterns. There are mirror images and circles and phrases that repeat. It's difficult to describe these musical patterns using words, but they are easy to see on paper, and numbers can be a convenient means of describing the components. We also hear the patterns, but it's much more difficult for most people to recognize symmetry when it's aural and not visual.

Even though we hear the symmetry and can see it on a page, the same patterns don't usually look symmetrical on an instrument so it can be difficult to recognize them when you're playing. Their existence does not depend upon your ability to see them.

Using a ruler to measure a distance involves numbers and is undeniably a math-based idea, but does not require what most would think of as "mathematical ability" to correctly identify a span of four inches on a ruler. Measuring time, recognizing that three seconds pass quicker than 11 seconds involves some sort of math awareness. Numbers are used to measure time, and to identify musical distances and objects. It is math-based stuff, expressed numerically, but it is certainly not arithmetic. Don't be intimidated by the numbers.

I'm not suggesting that everyone who can read a ruler, or see that a painting on a wall is a little bit crooked can instantly recognize musical patterns and symmetry. But pattern recognition, which can be thought of as "applied mathematics" is closer to what we musicians do with numbers than applying math skills to balance a checkbook.

It seems that perhaps the mathematical relationships that exist in music became evident *after* people began drawing representations of music on paper. The idea that "music is mathematical" sort of implies that music is derived from equations that will predict the sort of patterns you can see in a Bach fugue, but that's backwards, I think. For me, the math doesn't exist until I visually examine the music. Pictures show it and numbers help describe it.

I can see it, hear it, recognize it, and reproduce it without needing any ability to add 2+2. You don't need a degree in calculus to recognize patterns. As you go through this book, be aware of patterns that are visually obvious, look for patterns that aren't obvious, and don't worry about having to find the diameter and circumference of the Circle of Fifths. It's not that kind of math.

You can learn to recognize the structural components of songs, too. Most songs have an underlying structure that will be similar from song to song… intro, verse, chorus, bridge, verse, chorus, outro, or some variation. These songs parts contain musical phrases just like a kitchen will contain a refrigerator and stove. You can walk into 25 houses and all will have kitchens, bathrooms, bedrooms, etc. No two kitchens will be identical, but chances are that you'll know which room is the kitchen the instant you see it. There are likely to be bathrooms near the bedrooms and closets in the bedrooms. Again, this is something you have learned. Understanding song structure allows you to anticipate when musical events are likely to occur, and realize they are not spontaneous, unpredictable phenomena like earthquakes.

Those of us who learned to play "by ear" spent thousands of hours experimenting with note and chord combinations. Finding things that sound good. Finding things that sound bad. Learning to recognize patterns and shapes. Listening to our favorite bands and songs over and over, trying to play along and learn the riffs, digging divots in vinyl albums.

Learning to play "by ear" we memorized patterns and shapes and sounds and then repeated them, without learning the names. What we learned, while trying very hard not to, is basic music theory, without the associated vocabulary. Each one of us individually re-invented the wheel… again… and then couldn't talk to each other about what we learned. We even thought we invented a new system. Way to go, guys. You might say we took the long way around.

You don't have to know all of this vocabulary to be able to play really well. Many of my friends don't, and some of them are truly great players.

But if you learn the stuff in this book, you'll save yourself lots of hours. I wish I'd had something like this 35 years ago. Here's to a lifetime of good pickin'. Have fun.

How to Use This Book

Most people who own an instrument (or several) have no intention of being a "professional musician." Nearly everybody is a hobbyist. Playing music is mainly a means of relaxation and recreation and a creative outlet. Bluegrass jams abound, worship groups are using guitars instead of pipe organs, and it's fun just hanging out somewhere and playing music.

One thing that these musical gatherings have in common is that musical complexity is not usually the objective of the exercise. Another is that most of the people you'll see playing in these situations are not reading music. It's reasonable (and accurate) to conclude that playing music by ear can't be all that hard to do.

It seems that there are two distinct aspects of this process commonly known as "playing by ear."

One is the coordination required to produce sounds on the instrument, which is essentially a physical thing.

The other is comprehension of what it is you're doing, or the intellectual side of it.

The experiences I've had teaching have convinced me that the intellectual concepts that are useful "play by ear tools" for the recreational player can be acquired more easily and quickly than the physical playing skills. I'll present exercises to help you grow in both areas.

To get the most from this book, I recommend you begin with a couple of hours and skim the whole thing. Ten or 15 minutes in each chapter is probably enough. Read a little, look at the exercises, and just get an idea of the direction of the book and where it winds up.

One of the main differences between this book and other theory books is that I began with a particular target, which was to answer the question, "How do you figure songs out by ear?" Begin with the awareness that absorbing this process takes time, and accept that you won't completely "get it" the first time through. Nobody does.

This book is written and arranged with the intent that a person with no musical knowledge can work through it alone. But I do assume the reader has a little bit of experience with an instrument. I don't tell you how to hold a pick or any of the basic "this is how to make noise on the instrument" things. If you are starting from absolute zero and the instrument is awkward and uncooperative, a few lessons would be useful.

I do recommend taking lessons with a good teacher. The vocabulary and exercises I've presented here are intended to help students of any level to make better use of certain aspects of lesson time. A teacher can illuminate any ideas that I haven't presented in a way that is clear to you, and can help with the playing exercises and tunes. Applying these concepts to an instrument and turning them into music is different than understanding the concepts and a teacher can help with that.

I've arranged the information in such a way that each chapter presents information that serves as a foundation for the following chapter(s). I've been pretty successful at keeping things in sequence and not assuming previous knowledge on the part of the reader, but occasionally there are instances of words being used in some of the early chapters without a complete definition having been provided. Usually, a definition is soon to appear, or a precise definition isn't needed at that point.

You will become familiar with a written page of music. When you consider that people have been using this system of writing music for several hundred years, you'll realize that there are literally millions of musical ideas written down. This book is intended to be the key that will allow anyone to open the door and explore that vast musical library.

I have been playing music in public for pleasure and wages for over 30 years. I don't read music fluently, and neither do most of the people I play with. But I can decode anything that's on paper and I understand the system well enough that I can figure out nearly anything I can hear. Many of the tools and skills I use to do that are what I have described in this volume.

Most of the intermediate to advanced musicians I've encountered who want "some lessons" have found themselves "in a rut" and need some new ideas. One reason they have to hire someone to suggest some different approaches is that they (usually) have no idea how to interpret a page of music. The library is locked up tight. A few dozen focused hours with this book will allow players who already have good dexterity to study any style of music. Knowledge is power.

That is not to suggest that I have discussed and explained every detail associated with music theory and reading music on a page. This book is not intended to answer all of the questions that a person might have about music theory. The topic is enormous and could conceivably occupy an obsessed, insomniac fanatic for 100 years or so. I have not only condensed and abbreviated some of the ideas; I have also completely ignored some areas. And I'm certain there is a ton of stuff that I simply don't know about.

In spite of the fact that Garage Band Theory is not "complete," it does provide answers to the questions most commonly asked by the students I've encountered and will allow anyone to continue their musical education with a solid background in the fundamentals.

A criticism I received from an editor at a major publisher was that the book is not targeted at a specific ability level. She felt that because some of it is for beginners and some of it is for advanced players marketing the product would be difficult, and she suggested I split it into three or four volumes.

Something I've noticed is that when a beginner practices, after a while, they are no longer a "beginner." In addition, for the most part, people with "beginner playing skills" can easily understand concepts that are beyond their physical abilities. A major publisher wants you to run out and buy a new book on a regular basis. My students find it very useful and more economical to have basic concepts and advanced ideas contained within a single book.

I have always wondered why all of the books contain such a small slice of useful stuff. My believe is that the publisher's interest has much less to do with the convenience of students and teachers than their interest in selling a student several books at $20 to $30 a whack.

Another publisher suggested that I focus specifically on guitar and not mention how the same concepts apply to all instruments. Then I could have several books with basically the same information.

I've noticed that most people enjoy seeing the relationships between the different instruments. Many of my students who started as guitar students are now multi-instrumentalists, and they appreciate the fact that they did not need several additional books. As you apply these exercises to your main instruments, you'll see how the ideas transfer to other instruments. If you should decide to try another instrument, you'll begin with a solid foundation.

I hope you'll find this book useful for a long time.

Bandstand theory (i.e., Garage Band Theory) began to evolve when classically trained players and composers started jamming with the jazz and blues players who had no formal training. Its roots are in classical theory, and a substantial percentage of what is presented here is in fact "classical theory."

Bandstand theory works very well, but is it not as refined and precise as classical theory. This is partly due to the fairly haphazard way that this vocabulary developed "in the streets." One result is that some of the shortcuts that I've illustrated that are commonly used by lots of players will not be a sufficient explanation of some topics for many serious classical theorists.

You wouldn't want to use this book exclusively to study for your University Music Theory 101 class; but there is nothing here that is in serious conflict with anything that would be presented in a conventional theory course. In fact, if you understand the contents of this book *before* you get to Music Theory 101, you'll have a big head start on the class. It was written for those musicians who want to understand and apply relevant concepts to their favorite tunes without slogging through the muddy depths of academic theory.

The information here will help bridge the gap between all of those musicians who have played in school marching bands and orchestras who understand classical theory and can play their instruments, but find that they don't know how to jam with their friends who have guitars. The classically trained player speaks a different language than the blues guitarist, but they're thinking about the same stuff. The words are a little different, but the music is the same.

It is not uncommon for a student to fully understand the basic concepts presented in this book after… a few hours in each chapter.

That is not to suggest that you can master this information in a few weeks—it does take time for it to become second nature—but basic theory is certainly not as abstract and difficult as many people seem to imagine.

One of the main challenges that many private music teachers face, especially considering beginning guitar, banjo, and mandolin students, is the issue of providing relevant, useful, and practical information to a student while their hands are learning the first moves. Even though none of the concepts are especially difficult, it's nearly impossible to articulate any of them sensibly in the context of 30-minute lessons separated by seven days.

For example, most beginning guitar/banjo/mandolin students will learn a few chords right away, because it's a good place to start. Physically, it's not real hard and it isn't long before you can sort of play a handful of chords. However, acquiring that level of skill does tend to occupy most of the time allotted for the first several lessons. Then, quite sensibly, one of the questions beginners ask is often something like, "So, Mr. Professional Musician, what makes this chord an A minor and this one a C major?"

And even though they may be playing both chords perfectly, it's remarkably difficult to answer that "simple" question clearly, accurately, and completely when the student has no previous experience or vocabulary, regardless of the student's age or intelligence. Pointing at the fretboard and saying, "This note, right here, that's the difference"… doesn't really explain anything.

Strumming two or three chords in a row is not a terribly difficult thing and that is enough to "play" loads of songs. At the same time, a vocabulary that describes enough ideas to define chord qualities and chord progressions is fairly advanced. The fact that a person is often unable to accurately explain what they are doing does not prevent them from doing it correctly and musically. A lot of the people I play with regularly are in this category, and they're good players.

This sort of mixed up physical/intellectual business that is inherent in the process of learning to play many musical instruments means that you'll get the most from this book by skipping around a bit.

Explaining music theory is a little like trying to unravel a long rope that is all tangled up into a big knot. Everything is connected to everything else. There isn't really an absolutely correct starting point, you just sort of start picking at it, and after a while it starts coming undone.

For instance, with regard to the sequence in which the topics are presented, deciding where the information in **"Reading the Road Map"** works best (from the perspective of a beginner) presented a problem for me, for a few reasons.

We all listen to songs, so nearly everyone has a lot of experience with this subject, even if you can't play a note and can't verbally identify the things that are occurring. It isn't particularly difficult to understand how a song is represented on paper, and that is what this discussion is about. The reading/listening exercise suggested in **"Reading the Road Map"** requires zero familiarity with any instrument, and you don't even need an instrument for this one. It can be practiced by anyone and can be useful from day one. A lot of the things in **"Reading the Road Map"** can be understood almost immediately. In some ways, it's an ideal place to start.

The problem lies in the vocabulary. There are just enough instances of words and phrases in that chapter that require foundational knowledge that prevent it from being first, and it doesn't fit in between any of the other chapters. So, it's near the end.

It contains most of the "road map" information that will enable you to read and play through the exercises in all of the preceding chapters if you have no experience with a written page of music. There are things in every chapter that a beginner can (and should) play, but unless you have some understanding of how a page works, it can be difficult to apply what is on the page to your instrument. If you have little or no experience with traditional musical symbols, I suggest that when skimming the book for the first time, spend a bit more time there, and return occasionally.

Although my primary errand is to address the vocabulary and structure of music, I'm aware that the desire to actually *play* music is usually the reason a person might look at this book. Making the noise is what it's all about, not the definitions.

Most people begin playing by learning a few chords. Typically, I have beginning students practicing basic scales and chords right away, even though both exercises are relatively advanced concepts, from a theoretical standpoint. "Play this, you'll understand what it is you're doing soon" is the approach I take.

So, even if you are a beginner, I suggest that you start playing the Intro to Major and Minor Scales starting right away. Won't hurt you a bit. The same goes for the exercises in the chapters on chords. You don't have to know the technical explanation for a scale or a chord to be able to play one. There are some easy three-note chords in **"Major and Minor Chords"** and in **"Chord Progressions."** There is no reason you shouldn't be fooling around with anything you're able to play, even if you don't fully understand the names.

There are sight singing exercises that don't require an instrument at all. If you can hum the tune for "Oh Susannah," "Auld Lang Syne," and a couple of other familiar tunes, you can do these right away.

If you've been playing for a while and have a good grip on the basic open position chords you might want to skip right to **"Chord Progressions"** and try "Doing the Two-Five-One" and "Eleven Variations on the Twelve Bar Blues."

Absorbing the information is different than playing with the sounds. Be sure to work through each chapter in succession, pencil n hand, and be sure you have a good grasp on the information in each chapter before moving to the next one. Play the examples, answer the questions, and check your answers. There's no reason to stop messing with the more advanced stuff that hasn't been explained yet, but go through the text systematically.

How to Use This Book

I'm often asked, "How long should this take?"

I'm happy to say that there is a simple, precise, correct answer.

I don't know.

This is something like a bottomless well, and there is no way that most of us will ever master every aspect of music theory. That is one of the things that I love about playing music. I can get up every day for the rest of my life and find something new and challenging. The same is probably true for you, too, even if today is only your seventh birthday.

Many of my students come once a week. Those who spend some time every day on these chapters seem to move along with no real trouble to a new chapter each week or two. That is to say, they understand the concept and the words well enough to continue on to the next chapter. Nothing is really very complicated.

This doesn't mean that they can play every exercise at bullet speed or score 100% on a pop quiz, but we can have a musical conversation about what they are trying to do, and they can ask questions and pretty much comprehend the answers.

It takes a while for those ideas to be absorbed and become connected to each other as part of your musical awareness. I highly recommend that first you should skim the whole book. Next take it one chapter at a time for comprehension. After you've read every page, touched every exercise, and filled in all the blanks, review the whole thing once again. Six or eight months is a realistic timeframe to develop an initial working knowledge of the material here. If you are a more advanced player in terms of coordination, then you'll probably move a bit more quickly. Think of it as two or three semesters of a college level music course.

There are lots of illustrations in each chapter. Some use a fretboard and some use a keyboard. In most cases there is tablature for guitar, banjo, and mandolin. You should try to play every one of them.

There is no need to learn to play every example perfectly. Be sure you understand the concept, play the illustration/exercise well enough to hear it, and move along. Since you're probably going to go through the book twice, you'll play them all a little bit better the second time around.

If at all possible, try everything in here on two or more instruments. This is not a requirement, but if you can apply the information to more than one instrument, it will probably absorb into your awareness sooner. No matter what your primary instrument is, it would be a great benefit to have access to some sort of keyboard while working through this book. It doesn't have to be a grand piano.

There are several places that I used "Twinkle, Twinkle, Little Star" as an example and exercise. With millions of songs to choose from, I chose "Twinkle, Twinkle, Little Star."

I'm aware that no sane person over the age of 10 has any compelling desire to learn to play "Twinkle, Twinkle, Little Star" or any of the other nursery rhymes I use for examples and exercises. Many of them are used in more than one chapter. Play them anyway. This book is not about presenting songs to learn, even though there are a bunch of them included. Tunes like "Twinkle" and other nursery rhymes are useful for illustrating ideas because most people know what the tune I supposed to sound like. You won't have to learn a new tune every time a new idea is illustrated, so you'll be able to play the exercise more quickly and move on.

On the liner notes of his album, *Q's Jook Joint*, Quincy Jones briefly tells a story about the days when he and Ray Charles were playing polkas in Seattle to pay the bills. Evidently, young Mr. Jones was having a bit of trouble being wildly enthusiastic about the material they were performing, and he quotes young Mr. Charles as advising him to "Be true to it. Every music has its own soul." In other words, if *you* can't find the soul in a piece of music, him to "Be true to it. Every music has its own soul." In other words, if *you* can't find the soul in a piece of music, it is probably not the fault of the tune. Be open minded, and don't let your musical preferences and prejudices demean music that is significant to someone else is advice offered by Ray Charles (**www.raycharles.com**) and Quincy Jones (**www.achievement.org/autodoc/page/jon0bio-1**). I don't think that Q ever recorded a version of "Twinkle, Twinkle, Little Star," but you really should check out Mozart's version.

At any rate, playing all of the examples and exercises is strongly recommended. Some are mainly a conceptual type of thing you'll play through once or twice and that will be plenty. Some of the exercises, particularly in **"Scales,"** are exercises I do nearly every day and may become part of your musical life.

There is a set of questions at the end of most chapters. They are mostly fill in the blanks, "yes or no" type of questions. I recommend that you don't skip any of these. I suggest that you use a pencil or a separate sheet of paper for your answers so you can check yourself more than once.

All the time I was in school I hated homework. Homework and quizzes and tests… I swear, I'd rather chew up an entire jumbo roll of aluminum foil than sit and do homework. And then, to my surprise, I found myself including the same sort of exercises I detested in school as part of my very own book. Misdirected, deranged revenge, perhaps?

The reason I included written tests is to help a student retain more of the information. Our memories have the capacity to remember images and sounds, among other things. Retaining thoughts is a much more difficult task for our brains. If you write the stuff down and say it or sing it out loud, you create a sound and an image for your brain to store. No matter how loudly you think, writing is a more effective memory device. Sing along with the exercises that you play, and fill in the blanks on the quizzes. It is definitely time well spent.

With regard to the written exercises, especially for those who have little or no previous experience with these topics, unless you're getting less than 50% of the answers correct, keep cruising through the book and plan to improve your scores the next time around. It's possible to get hung up on relatively insignificant details. As your comprehension of the whole system improves, the bits and pieces that seem confusing the first around begin to clear up on their own. Don't let questions about intervals prevent you from getting into the stuff farther along, for instance.

I am a believer in the idea that a picture can be worth 1,000 words. There are hundreds of diagrams and illustrations in this book, and whenever possible, I wanted any explanations of these diagrams to be visible while you are looking at the illustration. When there is an example to be played on one page and an explanation of the example on another page, I wanted you to be able to place the book on a music stand or lay it on the kitchen table, and refer to the explanation while you play the example.

In many chapters, I had to insert some sort of spacer page(s) so that written explanations and illustrations are not on opposite sides of a page.

I definitely did not want to leave blank pages in the places that I had to insert a spacer. It's pretty common to see a photograph or some other cute little drawing to fill pages like these in other publications, but to me, both of those approaches seemed like a waste of paper.

Thanks to my Dad, I have always enjoyed reading famous quotations. Throughout the ages, brilliant thinkers have made remarks that condense useful and inspirational ideas into a sentence or two. Music has always been an important aspect of the human experience and people like Aristotle, Plato, Confucius, and William Shakespeare have made comments that touch on aspects of music that are nearly impossible to convey in text of this nature.

So, to fill these spacer pages with something reasonably useful, I dug through my collection of quote books and several websites and I compiled a collection of thoughts, statements, and ideas that help convey some of the emotion and magic that I've not been able to express while describing the facts. In addition to the ancient ones, you'll find people like Carlos Santana, Jerry Garcia, Courtney Love, Yo-Yo Ma, and Elvis Presley.

These pages help to articulate some of the life, energy, and emotion that music can express. Some are serious and some are humorous. All are a reminder of how music touches and influences everyone, not only those of us who play. I hope you'll enjoy them as much as I do.

Many people are intimidated by the prospect of learning to play an instrument, especially adults over about 30; but years of working with all age groups has convinced me that it is a skill that can be developed by nearly anyone who will just stick with it.

So, along with the quotes that are specifically music related, I included reflections by people like Albert Einstein, Vince Lombardi, Isaac Newton, John Wooden, Zig Ziglar, Hannibal, and Harry Truman, that I hope will inspire readers to recognize that "ordinary" people can and do attain lofty goals.

I strongly recommend that you have at least one matching CD and songbook by your favorite artist (or artists) to use as a supplement to this book. You'll want to have access to recorded and printed versions of a bunch of tunes so you can look at what you're listening to. Each chapter illustrates things that you can find in most songbooks, and it's extraordinarily useful to analyze music that you're familiar with and enjoy.

In nearly every chapter I'll suggest things to look for in your other songbook (or books). Listen to the recordings while you look at the written music. I often use a Beatles songbook, *The Beatles Book, Easy Guitar*, (Hal-Leonard) because much of what they recorded is relatively complex and this book provides lots of learning opportunities in a small space. Plus, I really like a bunch of the tunes.

I've supplied a list of songs that I have mentioned or dissected in this book and nearly all are available on iTunes. It is not necessary for you to have recordings of all of these tunes, but since we're talking about "playing by ear" it is to your advantage to be able to listen to many of them. I highly recommend that you invest some dollars to add these songs into your music education library.

My primary instrument is guitar and most of my students are learning to play guitar. As a consequence, the examples and text are directed toward guitar more than other instruments, but nearly every concept applies to all instruments.

In the chapter **"Note Names,"** I have included staff and tab for bass, banjo, and mandolin, as well as guitar.

Guitar tabs actually work quite well for bass because the bass fretboard is the same as a guitar fretboard, with fewer strings. Same goes for a banjo in standard bluegrass tuning… three of the strings on a banjo match three of the strings on a guitar. The mandolin tabs also do double duty because they (basically) work for tenor banjo, mandola, violin and viola.

Using guitar tabs for bass and banjo, and mandolin tabs for tenor banjo, mandola, violin, and viola, require that adjustments be made by the player according to which instrument is substituted. There is absolutely no way to explain how those adjustments work at this point, but (hopefully) it will be clear after reading **"Note Names." "The Key"** also will provide clues. If you're learning to play mandola or bass and you're having trouble understanding how the tabs I included apply to your instrument, find someone to help.

You'll notice the shaded bands on many of the fretboard diagrams. Most guitars, basses, mandolins, and banjos have dots on the fretboard, and in most of the illustrations that use fretboard diagrams, I shaded the frets that correspond with the usual locations of the dots.

Lots of people have a desire to play an instrument and will often find plenty of encouragement from their friends who play. "It's really pretty easy, once you get a handle on a few chords," they'll say. And that much is absolutely true.

The part that frequently gets left out by these well-meaning pickers is that "getting a handle" typically takes a couple of years. There seems to be something resembling mass amnesia with regard to how hard the first couple of years of the process really are. Training your body to do a new trick takes a while. What we're talking about is muscle memory and that takes time.

I have heard the question, "How long does it take?" answered this way: "Anywhere from 2,000 to 2,500 hours." Everyone is different, of course, but as a general thing, that does seem to be a reasonably accurate assessment of how long it takes for an absolute beginner to develop the skills to be a "moderately advanced intermediate" player. An hour a day for five or six years, and you're right in there. Thirty minutes to an hour of practice, four or five days a week, is a guesstimate for the amount of time an "average" guitar student seems to practice. At that rate, accumulating 100 hours of practices takes a few months. If you practice four hours a day, then you accumulate 100 hours in a month. It's all about hours of practice time, not months on the calendar.

My experience teaching has convinced me that anyone who has desire, normal dexterity, patience, and a degree or two of self-discipline, can learn to play a bit. Woody Allen once said, "Ninety percent of success is just showing up," and it's a relevant thought. (Woody Allen is best known for his work in film, but he's also a pretty serious clarinet player.

On the same topic, Thomas Edison believed: "Genius is five percent inspiration and 95% perspiration. Accordingly, a 'genius' is often merely a talented person who has done *all* of his or her homework." (**www. thomasedison.com/quotes.html**) "Great works are performed, not by strength, but by perseverance," said Samuel Johnson. "Perseverance is a great element of success. If you'll only knock long enough and loud enough, you are sure to wake up somebody," Henry Wadsworth Longfellow.

Just practice every day. The hours add up. Allow yourself to become (and remain) fascinated by the endeavor. And, in those times when you find that it's trickier than it looks, don't get discouraged and wonder why *you're* such a dork.

"They *said* it was easy, it *looks* easy, what's wrong with *me*? I know this guy who's dumb enough to eat paint off a fencepost, and he *rocks*!!!" is a common lament among beginners of all ages.

It is easy, after a while. But for nearly everyone, at first it's hard. There are occasional "mutants" who just pick up an instrument and play, but they are rare individuals. It's not their fault, don't hold it against them.

Be aware that learning to play an instrument is different than learning other tasks. It is natural and normal to want to measure and gauge your physical progress, but it doesn't happen as quickly as anyone would like. Adults seem to have great difficulty with this part of the deal. We grow accustomed to a learning process where someone shows how to perform a task of some sort, you try it a couple of times, and then you pretty much have it.

Learning to play an instrument *does not work that way*. I don't know why, exactly, but I know it is true in 99.9 cases out of 100. If you don't get it right away, that means you're just like almost everyone else. Nearly everyone you have ever heard playing music anywhere struggled with it for hundreds of hours. After you do it 1,000 times, it's easy. Until then, it's not. Sorry. There are no shortcuts, you have to invest time.

I think that a reasonable timeframe for measuring incremental progress is about six months. An expectation of noticeable improvements each week is unrealistic and usually creates frustration. An evaluation every few months is plenty. This is a lifetime endeavor. Nothing will change very much from day to day or week to week. Be patient with yourself and have fun. I never heard anyone say, "I sure am glad I quit playing my guitar, just think of all the beer commercials I would have missed!" Remember Woody Allen and Thomas Edison.

When addressing the question of what is the best way to learn to write, a famous author by the name of Raymond Chandler once said, "Analyze and imitate. No other school is necessary."

This idea can be applied directly to the process of learning to play music. This book will supply the tools required to analyze your favorite musicians. "Imitate" is to a certain extent a physical thing, and there are plenty of exercises in this volume to aid in that aspect of your education.

A benefit of practicing an instrument not often discussed is that for most people, the rest of the planet seems to fade from awareness while practicing. It is possible to create an hour of peace in your day, regardless of your level of skill. This is an activity that does require concentration and I nearly always feel refreshed rather than taxed by the effort. I think that it's partly due to losing the worries for a while. I've heard it compared to meditation by people who study both music and meditation.

With regard to practice time, it has been my experience that those who practice about 45 minutes a day make steady progress. Those who practice for fewer than 30 minutes a day tend to quit after a few months. I can't really explain it, but I have observed it.

Of those who do practice 45 minutes consistently, students who do focused exercises for at least half of their practice session *always* make more progress than the ones who mostly jam on the songs they want to learn, but only occasionally do scales and other exercises. When a person gets into the range of about 90 minutes of daily practice time, with about 30 to 45 minutes of focused exercises in each session and maybe 45 minutes to an hour messing with songs, is when progress really starts to accelerate.

It has been my experience and is my firm opinion that any individual's rate of progress with a musical instrument is less connected to natural talent than it is dependent on the proven model of "pick up the instrument every day and play with it." I have seen more than a few students who initially seemed to have very little "natural ability" surpass more "talented" players because they were willing to consistently do the exercises required to get into shape.

An important aspect of my own study of music is that I don't intend to quit playing. Ever. So, if it takes me two hours or two weeks or two months to develop a technique or assimilate an idea, it really doesn't matter. I'm only interested in consistent progress, because *there is no finish line* in my game. Learning to play music is not a race, it is not a contest.

I try to divide my practice sessions roughly in half. I like to do my workout first, usually about an hour or so of scales and other focused exercise. The other part of my practice time is spent jamming, playing songs, and generally just fooling around.

If you're in decent physical condition, participating in a sport is fairly easy. Whether it's basketball, volleyball, or soccer, if you can run and jump, you can involve yourself at some level. The same principle works for musicians. A solid foundation in fundamentals will allow you to play rock, country, blues, classical, or jazz… whatever.

I really enjoy practicing with my instruments. "The only reason I book gigs is so I have an excuse to hang out and practice all the time," is a line I heard once and I love it. I wish I could recall who said it.

But for many people, the word "practice" conjures an image of struggling through pages of complicated, undecipherable code with an unsympathetic teacher pointing out every error.

That may be why the word "play" is used. Although I do "practice" skills, to me it feels like "playing." You may want to remove the word "practice" from your musical goals and think of the time you spend as "play" time.

When learning anything new, I recommend that you play it SLOWLY and CORRECTLY. And keep it slow until you can do the entire exercise at the same speed, perfectly, a bunch of times in a row. Then speed it up... a little bit. You *can* teach yourself to make mistakes, and if you repeatedly hack through a song or exercise that is exactly what you'll learn to do.

Don't play "the easy part" fast and then slow down to play "the hard part" all the time. You'll teach yourself to do that. If you repeatedly stumble through "the hard part" because of trying to play too fast, you will learn to stumble through that part. Then you'll have to unlearn the mistakes. Practice slowly... it's faster.

Listening exercises are important, too, and I consider that to be separate from the physical practice sessions. For beginners in particular, I think that listening exercises are at least as important as the hours spent developing physical skills.

For me, "listening" means sitting quietly and paying close attention to whatever it is that you choose to listen to. That is not the same as having the radio on while you drive or do the dishes or homework or exercise at the health club. There is nothing wrong with listening to music while you participate in other activities, quite the opposite. It's just not the same as listening with the intent of learning. I try to listen to something every day that I have no intent of ever playing. There is something quite magical in listening to "classical music" that might be 300 years old. I've included tabs for a couple of songs that are nearly 700 years old, and they're cool tunes. Magic.

I strongly recommend that you listen closely to recordings by your favorite artists every day, as an essential part of your continuing music education. "Playing by ear" implies that listening is involved. Learning to listen and recognize what other musicians do is a skill that can be acquired, and like any other skill, the more you do it, the more proficient you will become.

My intent with this book is to assist you in your goal of learning to play by ear. Listening to your favorite music, and learning to identify the things I'm presenting in that music, is an extremely important part of the process.

Obviously, I recommend that you play all of the exercises I've presented, but everything in this book is also a listening exercise. By that I mean that you'll want to learn the names of the sounds you're making. You want to hear the intervals, the scales, the chords, and the progressions and associate names with them.

Advanced coordination is not required to be able to play most of the examples. Remember that you can hear all of these things quite well, if you play them slowly.

It is also very helpful to sing along with the exercises. It's more like humming than singing. This is not about singing perfectly in tune. This is about connecting a sound on your instrument with a sound inside your head.

What we're trying to do is to get the sounds inside our head to somehow appear at the ends of our fingers and manifest themselves on an instrument. Music is invisible, it exists inside your head, it only *looks* like your hands are making it. It's an illusion.

One of the most important effects of playing for an hour is the multiple hours you subsequently spend turning that music around somewhere in the back of your mind. That's where the music is, not in your hands. Our minds have to help our hands develop the coordination that's required so they don't impede the expression of the music that's inside. Be aware that lots of very important "practice time' does not involve touching an instrument.

It you hum along with repetitive scale exercises while you play them, you are singing what you're playing. If you hum those same exercises while you drive, do the dishes, and exercise at the health club, you can add lots of practice time to your normal day. If you'll invest enough hours doing this, you'll find that after a while you can "turn it around," and play whatever you can sing. That ability can be thought of as the essence of playing by ear, and can be learned.

Those who practice repetitve exercises and consciously think about the exercises and tunes when they're NOT playing make even more progress. The last chapter, **"Putting It All Together"** is about using the ability to hum simple, familiar tunes to figure out the chords by ear.

There are good reasons to fool around with tunes like "Twinkle, Twinkle, Little Star," "Mary Had a Little Lamb," "Happy Birthday To You," and "Pop Goes the Weasel," etc. These are tunes that you probably know but probably have never seen the written music. Try to find where they are on your instrument.

At first it's slow. The first time you try to pick out Happy Birthday it might take two hours. So what? The only consistent, specific goal is to speed up the process. The more you try it, especially as you progress through this book, the easier it will become. It's not about learning these songs; it's about developing that connection between your head and your hands and learning to recognize a system that you can use to play by ear. Start with simple, familiar tunes and build on that base. If you're a beginning guitar/banjo/mandolin student and you have a keyboard, try picking out simple tunes there.

This book is not intended to answer every question a person might have about music theory.

This book is intended to allow you to access all of the musical information that is available.

The Internet has become an enormous source for musical education. You can do a Google search for any of the words and concepts I've presented here and find a list of sources. In the instances that my explanation or presentation is inadequate for you, I suggest that you dig around online and see what's available. Music dictionaries are available. There are exercises that can supplement the ones I've provided, and text that covers the same topics. Each author and teacher will bring something to the discussion that may be useful to you in your education.

I could never have written this book and made all of the examples without the use of a computer and a few software programs. There is one in particular that I use all the time and recommend to anyone who is interested, and the rest cause me endless headaches.

I'm confident that most of the software and hardware difficulties that I've encountered have much more to do with "operator error" than any deficiencies in the computers or software. I'm a person who finds working with a computer to be about as pleasant, natural, and intuitive as it might be to eat living, breathing tarantulas. Any negative opinions I have about software are heavily influenced by irrational fear and loathing for the tools in general, and are probably not fair representations of how someone else might interact with the products. OK?

Today, I know that Microsoft Word was never intended to be used to create a book of this nature. I didn't know it for a long time. Years. I spent countless hours raging against the machine, alternating between various combinations of confusion, anger, terror, frustration, and misery. I thought it was the software. Nope. It was the cyber-dummy who lives in my mirror.

All of the examples of musical notation and tablature were created in Finale (*www.finale.com*). It's a powerful program and can do loads more than I have ever attempted. I have friends who use it regularly and they use far more of this program than I ever have, or ever will. It can do nearly anything musical, and do it very well, they tell me. Several of them claim that it's easy.

The program that I really have fun playing with is called Jammer Pro. (*www.soundtrek.com*)

Inexplicably, after a fairly short learning period, I've had nothing but fun with this. Maybe that's because I've never attempted to use any of its more complex features, and I never will, although I suspect that it works quite well. I love this program. It creates full band backup tracks that I use for practicing and for writing. I work in a few bands and I use Jammer to make practice tracks of tunes so we can "rehearse" independently. I've spent hours just sitting and "jamming" with it. It's "computer generated midi files" which I generally dislike, but Jammer sounds and feels to me like the people who developed all of the styles, grooves, and things are players. There are lots of "humanize" functions that I'll never touch, because I just use it for practice, writing, and rough demos, not recording. You need a decent sound card to get the most of out of any midi file, but it will make the Jammer bands in your computer sound pretty good.

Even if your computer "skills" are similar to mine, I think that Jammer should be on your list as a supplement to this book. It is not required or necessary. You won't be able to fully apply it directly to the information in this book until you get to **"Chord Progressions,"** but at that point it's the best practice tool I've ever encountered, aside from the discipline required to actually practice.

One of the more difficult skills that I discuss in this book is developing the ability to hear all of the different instruments independently when you listen to a band play a song. A program like this allows you to plug in any song, in loads of different styles, and then individually select the bass, drums, keys, etc. in any combination, at any speed, and replay it as many times as you want. It will create music for you, so you can be pretty clueless when you start. See it on the screen while you listen to it play. I don't think that there could be a better way to practice that aspect of learning to play by ear. I bet I scratched 30 pounds of vinyl off of my 60's record collection trying to learn to do that.

The vocabulary you will be learning in this book will help you to understand how to make your own practice tracks and adapt them to your level of ability. Then, you'll be able to apply all the knowledge you've accumulated in the chapters **"Counting, Major & Minor Chords,** and **The Key,"** and you'll hear how they relate to music. Jammer doesn't show the midi files in traditional notation, but the way software shows midi notes is an extremely useful visual aid to understanding traditional notation. You'll be amazed how many fuzzy concepts clarify instantly as soon as you start to make your own tracks.

Jammer Pro is not available for Mac as of this writing, but if you use a Windows based machine and can work it into your budget for music education, buy it. My limited experience with support has been outstanding.

The phrase "lifetime endeavor" is a good one to consider anytime that you may feel discouraged by an apparent lack of progress, or overwhelmed by the fact that the possibilities are infinite. The bright side of those two issues is that anyone can improve, regardless of their ability, and there is always going to be a brand new frontier to explore, if you want to do it.

Just do it.

How to Use This Book

Note Names

Chapter 1

Are you ready? Here they are:

A B C D E F G

That's all of them. On a piano keyboard these are the white keys.

They are the same on a guitar or any other instrument, and they always occur in the same alphabetical sequence. Unfortunately, on most other instruments, they don't come "color-coded" like they are on a keyboard. Brass or wood, colors or not, notes are the same on all instruments.

There is a difference between a note and a tone.

A tone is a sound, something you can hear. A note is something you can see on a page that represents a tone. In a practical sense they are nearly synonymous. Throughout this book, I'll refer to the keys on a piano as "black notes and white notes," and frets on string instruments as notes, in spite of the fact they really aren't "notes."

Even though the number of different tones that exits is theoretically infinite, there are a total of seven different names used to identify all of the tones we use in Western music. These seven tones are known as the "naturals."

The number of different tones that any instrument can produce is due to the physical characteristics and structure of the instrument. A grand piano has 88 keys, so it can produce 88 different tones. A classical guitar has 18 frets and six strings. It can produce 43 different tones (128 if sufficiently out of tune… this is quite difficult and should not be attempted without adult supervision).

A clarinet uses a vibrating reed to produce a tone and a harpsichord uses a vibrating string, so the sound produced by each instrument is quite different. Whatever mechanical apparatus is used to create the sound, all of them use the same notes.

For our purposes in this chapter, what distinguishes one tone from another is the "frequency" of the vibration carried by a sound wave. This frequency of vibration is described by the term Hertz (Heinrich Rudolf Hertz 1857-1894). 100 Hz = 100 vibrations (cycles) per second.

The lowest A on a guitar is said to have a frequency of approximately 110 Hz. The next higher A has a frequency of 220 Hz, and the next higher A is approximately 440 Hz. They share the same name, sound very similar and are mathematically related (multiples of 2), but they are obviously different tones.

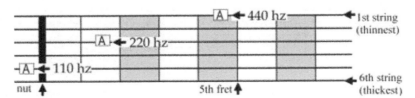

In spite of the fact that they are not identical, for most practical purposes in understanding basic theory any "A" is the same as any other A. Every B is the same as any other B, each C is the same as any other C, and so on. I'm excluding "transposing instrument" considerations here; we'll get to that in **"The Key."**

One way to visualize this concept is to think of a seedling pine tree and a fully-grown tree. Whether it is six inches in height or 60 feet tall, it is always a pine tree.

With this in mind, **A=A**, we can say that there are a total of 12 different tones that occur in a repeating pattern, and these 12 tones comprise nearly all the music you will ever hear. Here's a keyboard... it could be an accordion or a piano or any keyboard instrument.

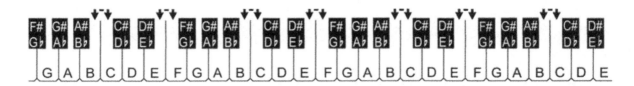

This represents a guitar neck... six horizontal lines are the strings, and the vertical lines represent the frets. The lowest notes are to the left, and the thickest string is at the bottom. This is how the notes might look on a single guitar string if they were color-coded black and white like they are on a keyboard.

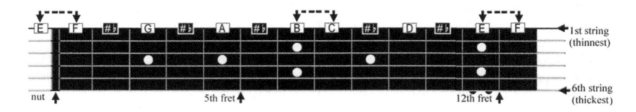

Notice that the pattern of black and white is identical to the pattern on the keyboard. There is a "black" note between **F** and **G**, between **G** and **A**, between **A** and **B**, between **C** and **D**, and between **D** and **E**.

There is no "black" note between **E** and **F** or between **B** and **C** on the keyboard or on the guitar, or the clarinet or any other instrument.

Each string on a guitar (or mandolin or banjo, etc.) can be visualized as a separate keyboard, each beginning with a different note, but having the same pattern of black and white notes.

Nearly all string instruments number the strings beginning with the thinnest string as the first string. One exception is the five-string banjo, details soon. The sixth string on a guitar is E. The first fret is F, the third fret is G, and the fifth fret is A (110 Hz). This is exactly the same note as the fifth string played open (110 Hz). The pattern repeats beginning at the 12th fret, which is E again.

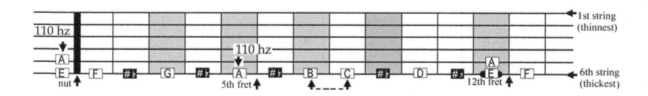

The fifth string played open is A, the second fret is B, the third fret is C, and the fifth fret is D, which is exactly the same note as the fourth string played open. The pattern repeats beginning at the 12th fret, which is A again, one octave higher.

It's easy to see the repeating octaves on any keyboard, not so easy to see on stringed instruments, invisible on horns. The pattern is there on all instruments whether or not it's easy to see.

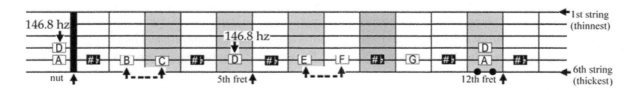

The fourth string played open is D, and the fifth fret is G, which is exactly the same note as the third string played open. I trust that you're beginning to see another pattern.

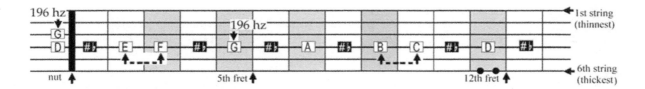

The third string played open is G, fourth fret is B.

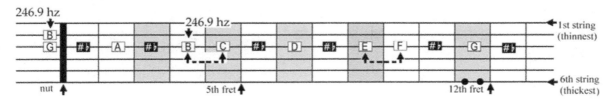

The second string played open is B, the fifth fret is E.

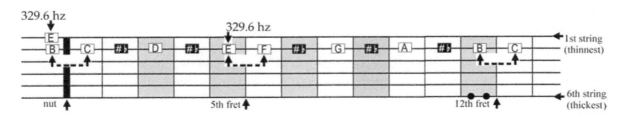

The first string played open is E. The pattern is identical to the note names on the sixth string.

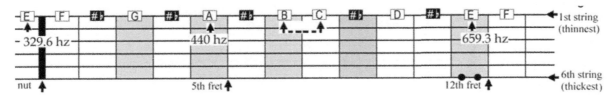

There's a bit of a bonus available here. When you learn the names of the notes on either the sixth string or the first string, you'll have learned 33% of the neck in one whack. At this point, I think it's safe to assume you already know the alphabet, so learning all seven note names on the E strings shouldn't present much of a problem. Why not start right now? Twenty minutes of study will take you a long way on this one. Play each one and say the name out loud. Then do it again. And again.

A bass has four strings, and the names of the notes are identical to the four lowest strings on a guitar, E-A-D and G. The diagram on page 17 of this chapter shows the names of the open strings for 11 instruments.

Notice that the alphabetical sequence and pattern of black and white notes are the same on each instrument. B always follows A, and A always follows G. The sequence is the same on trombones, tubas, and all the other instruments too, but there's no way to illustrate it here. Violins and violas don't have frets, but the note names correspond to the notes shown for the mandolin. Notes on the viola correspond to the notes on a mandola. When you've memorized this sequence you will have learned a fundamental concept that you can apply to any instrument you may care to play.

Brace yourself. Let's take a look at a bunch of G-strings.

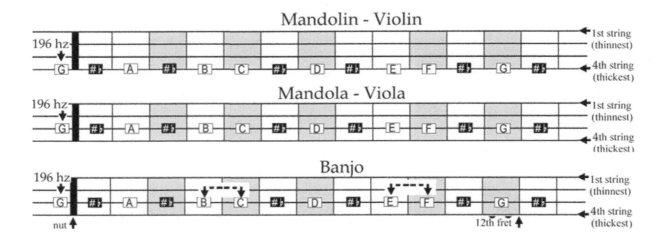

This seems like a good place to consider a couple of different methods of tuning a guitar.

First, a small battery powered tuner is the best option. They are relatively inexpensive and the chromatic tuners will tune any instrument, as well as any alternate tunings that you may like. For someone just learning to play, a tuner will help tune your instrument quickly and accurately so you will learn what the instrument is supposed to sound like. Highly recommended.

For those situations when a tuner is not available, most people use the method that involves matching the fifth fret of the sixth string (low E) to the A string open. Next, match the fifth fret of the A string to the D string open, and fifth fret of the D string to the open G string. Match the fourth fret of the G to the open B, and the fifth fret of the B to the first string open (high E). As long as the sixth string is somewhere in the ballpark when you begin, this method will get the guitar in tune with itself, but merrily ignores the rest of the planet.

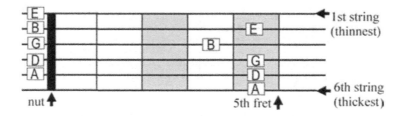

This works pretty well, as long as you get each one right. The catch is that if you miss one, even by just a little, the rest are going to be out of tune from that point forward.

A more reliable method is to tune all the strings to match the open A. Not only is each string not dependent on the previous one being correct, you will also learn a few locations for A, which can be a useful reference point.

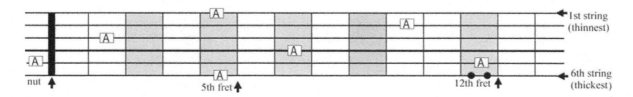

You can use any open string as a reference. Orchestras tune to what is called "concert A 440 Hz" produced by an oboe, which is an instrument that cannot be tuned once its reeds are in place.

This same method will work on all string instruments. Since a banjo doesn't have an open string tuned to A, you can use G instead. It really doesn't matter which note you use as your reference. Again, this only tunes the instrument to itself. If you use the fifth fret method and seem to still have a wanker or two, or you just want to check your results, use this method.

Notice that the seventh fret on the A string is E. You can match the low E to this one. Open A will tune to the seventh fret on the D string, open D to the seventh fret of the G string, etc. Whichever method used to tune your instrument, you should double-check your results with a second method.

This brings us to a point where we need to take a look at the way tones (i.e. sounds produced by instruments) are represented on a page.

These are some of the symbols used to indicate notes played on all instruments. Some are just a circle; some have a "stem" or a "stem and flag" attached to a circle or a dot. These variations indicate the duration of a tone, and that is discussed in the chapter on **"Counting."**

This chapter we're concerned with the pitch of the notes, or what tone is produced when you strike a key on a piano or pluck a string.

The note symbols are placed on a "staff" which is a group of five horizontal lines, and a space between each line. They are numbered from the bottom to the top. Visually, a space is thicker than a line, but either one is just a hook to hang a note on. A space serves exactly the same function that a line does, they just appear to be different. Here are some notes placed randomly on a staff.

We can surmise from this kind of illustration that some notes are higher than others, but until a line or space has been assigned a letter name, that's it… some are higher and some are lower.

All instruments produce variations of the same tones, and use the same five-line staff and the same symbols to represent the notes. There is a device called a "clef" that is placed on the staff. Different instruments use different clefs.

There are three commonly used clefs. They all look different, but all three do the same job. They name one of the lines.

Each line and each space represents one note name, and they are always in the same alphabetical sequence. Each of these three clefs indicates a certain line and names that line.

The funny looking contraption at the left of the staff is known as a "C clef" and it tells which line will be the note C. The clef is centered on the third line of the staff, so that line will be C.

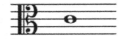

The lines and spaces on all staffs are always named alphabetically, and as soon as you know where C is you can find the others. No matter which clef is being used, there is always a B right below C, and there is always a D just above C.

The C clef is a movable clef, which means that it can be placed to relocate C to any of the five lines.

Here's some good news. The C clef is never used on music written for guitars, basses, banjos, mandolins, or pianos. If you play a viola or cello, this is a familiar companion, but almost nobody else sees one. Well, trombones, sometimes.

This clef is known as the G clef, because the curlicue circles the line that will be the note G. Another name for the G clef is "treble" clef. This is the one used for guitar, banjo, and mandolin. It doesn't move. Do the dance of joy! Hip hip hooray!

This clef is called the F clef because the two dots indicate the line that is the note F. This one is used for bass and is also called the "bass" clef. It can jump around like the C clef, but the F clef is not nearly as active. It usually appears exactly as shown here.

This is known as the "Grand Staff." This is used when you need to show a very wide range of notes for an instrument such as a piano.

Notice that the upper staff has an extra line below the staff and the lower staff has an extra line above it. These are called "ledger lines" and they are used to extend the staff.

Also notice that the notice on both ledger lines is named C. Although it would appear to be two different notes, those two C notes are the same note.

Even though there's enough room between those two staffs to add more lines, in reality there is only one line between them. The separation just keeps it from looking like a single staff with 11 lines.

The C that is in between the two staves is called… middle C. On a piano, there is one, and only one middle C, and that note is near the center of the keyboard. Middle C has a frequency of somewhere around 261 Hz.
On a guitar, Middle C (261 Hz) can be found in four convenient locations near you.

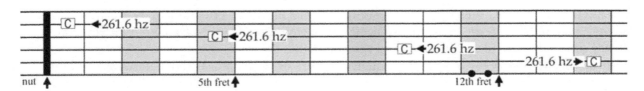

This shows how some of the notes between any middle C and the lowest E on the sixth string of a guitar appears when written on a staff with a G clef using ledger lines.

Someone somewhere decided that guitar music would not be written on the grand staff. Instead it would be written using a single staff using the G clef. In order to avoid using seven ledger lines below the staff, he decided that middle C for guitar (261 Hz) would appear near the center of the staff instead of in the middle of the grand staff. After relocating middle C only three ledger lines are needed to show the low E on a guitar.

If that unidentified someone had not taken it upon himself to relocate middle C for guitar music, it would be written like this, identically to piano music.

There are plenty of good reasons to shift the location of middle C on the staff, it happens a lot, and eliminating the bass clef for guitar music makes it easier to read for most people.

So… the frequencies (Hz) of the notes that are played on a guitar don't match the frequency of middle C (261 Hz) as written on the Grand Staff. There are other instruments that share this confusing quality, especially in the family of wind-powered instruments like clarinets and trumpets and saxophones. They are known as "transposing instruments" and we'll come back to that topic in **"The Key"** after you have enough information to understand the explanation. Right now, it may seem like a bad idea… to write something other than what is intended to be played. *"I wrote down the notes I want you to play. Only kidding. Ha Ha."* After you understand it, it still may seem like a bad idea. But, it's really a very good idea, it's just confusing at first. This is the appropriate place to introduce the concept, but you need quite a bit more information before you can understand why it's sensible to shift the notes around on the staff and how that shift is accomplished. Sorry.

Five lines and four spaces is a visually friendly layout. Adding more than two or three ledger lines to a staff makes things more difficult to read, so it's really quite helpful to be able to show notation for any instrument using as few extra lines as possible, and that is the idea behind relocating middle C for guitar notation, as well as the other transposing instruments. (**The Key**).

At the same time there are lots of instruments that can play notes that are more than three octaves higher than 261 Hz. Piccolos, violins, harmonicas, and mandolins all get way up there, and even a grand piano has a C that is four octaves above middle C. Indicating those notes on paper would involve about a dozen ledger lines above the staff, and it's just about impossible to read or write.

There is a way around this logistical inconvenience.

8va is a symbol that means that the notes played should be one octave higher than they are written.

The notes in example #1 sound identical to the notes in example #2, even though they appear at different locations on the staff.

8vb does the same thing, except it means to play an octave lower than written. The notes in example #3 are identical to the notes in example #4, even though they appear at different locations on the staff.

A guitar has six strings. This shows the six notes on the staff that correspond to the six open strings as written for guitar.

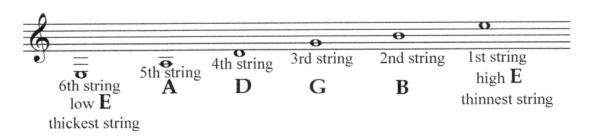

One of the properties of string instruments such as guitars, banjos, mandolins, basses, violins, and other similar instruments is that a single note on the page can be played in more than one place on the neck.

As shown earlier, the fifth fret played on the sixth string is the same note as the fifth string played open (both are about 110 Hz), the fifth fret played on the fifth string = the fourth string open, the fifth fret played on the fourth string = the third string open, etc.

The following fretboard illustration shows four different places to play the same G.

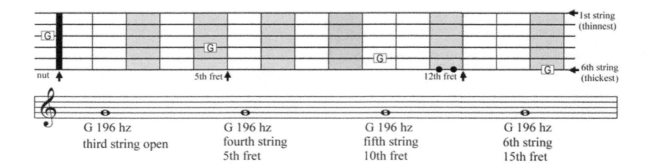

The mass (thickness) of each string is different so there is a subtle difference in tonal quality, but all four notes are the same pitch (about 196 Hz), and all four correspond to a single G note on the staff.

As you might imagine, there are times that this creates some difficulties in reading for the instrument.

Tablature (tab) neatly solves the problem by using a picture of the six strings (horizontal lines) on the neck, but instead of drawing frets (vertical lines), numbers are used to indicate on which fret the note is played on a given string. This shows the same four G notes as they appear in tablature.

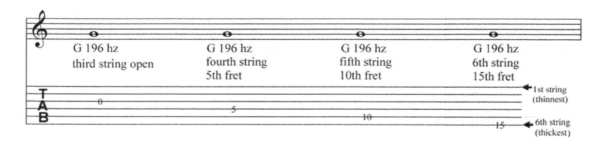

This is Twinkle, Twinkle, Little Star shown in standard notation and tablature.

This is exactly the same tune played on entirely different frets.

Same tune using yet another group of strings and frets.

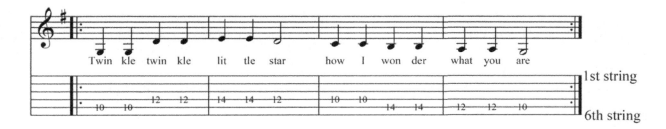

Here it is again shown very high on the neck using the lowest strings.

Tablature is just a different way to represent the same information that standard notation represents. There are advantages to both systems in different situations, but standard notation is much more versatile. Standard notation can be used for all instruments and tablature can't.

There is just one more type of clef that you should know about. It's used for showing percussion instruments of all kinds.

There are dozens of percussion instruments and they all can be shown on this clef. Woodblocks, tambourines, castanets, congas, triangles, and maracas can all be shown on this clef. A standard drum kit will usually consist of a kick drum, snare drum, high hat, high tom, mid tom, low tom, crash and ride cymbals, and all of them can be shown on a percussion clef.

Most percussion instruments don't produce definite pitches the way a piano or a flute does. In addition, they usually only produce a single tone. So to show a rhythm that a woodblock might play requires only a single stave instead of a five-line staff system. Vertical lines are still used to show measures.

In rhythmic notation, the stems and flags are the same as other notes, but the note heads can be a bit different. The rhythm clef can appear as a rectangle, as shown below. Sometimes it is shown with two parallel vertical lines, like this example.

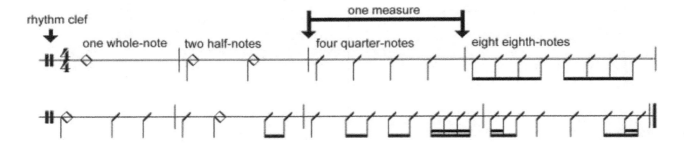

The drummers you see most often are sitting behind and in the middle of what is known as a "drum kit." As drum kits contain several instruments, it is convenient to use a five-line staff to accommodate more than one instrument.

Notice that the rhythm clef doesn't indicate a line to identify any notes. Instead, each line and each space on a rhythm clef are used to identify a certain instrument.

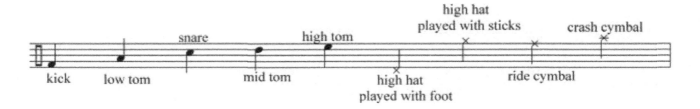

The note heads for the drums can be the little dots like usual, or slashes as shown above. In a five-line staff, usually dots work better.

The kick drum (a different name for the bass drum, same instrument) will always be shown on the bottom space. The snare will always be on the third space. Cymbals are usually shown with an "**X**" and are at the top of the staff, except when the high hat is played with the pedal, and then it's shown down low on the staff, usually in the first space below the bottom line.

Here is what a simple rock drum line might look like. Kick, snare and hat with a tom fill in measure four.

I bet you noticed that I said that there are 12 different notes, but I have only identified seven of them.

This could be considered a major omission.

On the other hand, if I could consistently get seven hits out of 12 at bats in the major leagues, I'd be guaranteed a prominent place in the Hall of Fame. Seven for 12 ain't bad.

OK. This isn't baseball and I don't play in the major leagues. Odds are excellent that I won't be pitching the opening game of the World Series this year. Next year… who knows?

Anyway. You have probably heard of sharps and flats.

Those words are used in conjunction with the seven natural note names, and they do serve to identify the missing five notes.

However, I haven't presented enough information at this point to sensibly discuss sharps and flats, so we'll come back to this topic in **"Intervals: Part Two."**

Go through a couple of the songs in your Beatles book, or whichever fakebooks / songbooks you're using and write the note names under/over/beside the notes on the staff. *Use a pencil*… you might make mistakes you'll want to correct. If you will do that for a dozen songs, you will know the staff well enough to be able to begin reading (decoding) any written piece of music. Why not start now?

Reflections

*"A determined soul will do more with a rusty monkey wrench
than a loafer will accomplish with all the tools in a machine shop."*
Robert Hughes

*"A few can touch the magic string, and noisy Fame is proud to win them;
Alas for those that never sing, but die with all their music in them!"*
Oliver Wendell Holmes

"A jazz musician is a juggler who uses harmonies instead of oranges."
Benny Green

*"A man may fulfill the object of his existence by asking a question he cannot
answer, and attempting a task he cannot achieve."*
Oliver Wendell Holmes

*"A man should hear a little music, read a little poetry, and see a fine picture every
day of his life, in order that worldly cares may not obliterate the sense of the
beautiful which God has implanted in the human soul."*
Johann Wolfgang von Goethe

*"A musician must make music, an artist must paint, a poet must write,
if he is to be ultimately at peace with himself.
What one can be, one must be."*
Abraham Maslow

*"A painter paints pictures on canvas.
But musicians paint their pictures on silence."*
Leopold Stokowski

*"A song has a few rights the same as ordinary citizens...
if it happens to feel like flying where humans cannot fly
or to scale mountains that are not there, who shall stop it?"*
Charles Ives

"After silence, that which comes nearest to expressing the inexpressible is music."
Aldous Huxley

"All the sounds of the earth are like music."
Oscar Hammerstein

"An archer cannot hit the bulls-eye if he doesn't know where the target is."
Unknown

Note Names, Hertz and MIDI Note Numbers

The range of human hearing is generally considered to be between about 20 Hz and 20,000 Hz. MIDI (Musical Instrument Digital Interface) is how computers communicate with each other about music, and each note has a MIDI number assigned to it… 0 through 127.

The lowest open E string on a bass corresponds to MIDI note #28 and the other three bass strings are #33 (A), #38 (D), and #43 (G). A cello's low C string produces the same frequency as MIDI note #36 followed by #43 (G), #50 (D) and #57 (A). The guitar's low E, the sixth string, is the same frequency as MIDI note #40, followed by #45 (A), #50 (D), #55 (G), #59 (B) and #64 (E). On a mandola or a viola, the low C is MIDI note #48, followed by #55 (G), #62 (D) and #69 (A). The lowest note on a mandolin and a violin is MIDI note #55 (G), followed by #62 (D), #69 (A) and #76 (E). The low D on a five-string banjo is MIDI note #50, followed by #55 (G), #59 (B) and #62 (D). Middle C is #60. These Hertz frequencies can be refined to have a lot of numbers to the right of the decimal. The values shown are approximations.

Instrument	Note	Hertz	MIDI
	C	16.4	12
	C#	17.3	13
	D	18.4	14
	D#	19.4	15
	E	20.6	16
	F	21.8	17
	F#	23.1	18
	G	24.5	19
	G#	26	20
	A	27.5	21
	A#	29.1	22
	B	30.9	23
	C	32.7	24
	C#	34.6	25
	D	36.7	26
	D#	38.9	27
Bass	E	41.2	28
	F	43.7	29
	F#	46.2	30
	G	49	31
	G#	51.9	32
	A	55.01	33
	A#	58.27	34
	B	61.72	35
Cello	C	65.40	36
	C#	69.30	37
	D	73.40	38
	D#	77.80	39
Guitar	E	82.40	40
	F	87.30	41
	F#	92.50	42
	G	98.00	43
	G#	103.80	44
	A	110.00	45
	A#	116.50	46
	B	123.50	47

Instrument	Note	Hertz	MIDI
Mandola	C	130.8	48
	C#	138.6	49
Banjo	D	146.8	50
	D#	155.6	51
	E	164.8	52
	F	174.6	53
	F#	185	54
Mandolin	G	196	55
	G#	207.7	56
	A	220	57
	A#	233.1	58
	B	246.9	59
Middle C	C	261.6	60
	C#	277.2	61
	D	293.7	62
	D#	311.1	63
	E	329.6	64
	F	349.2	65
	F#	370	66
	G	392	67
	G#	415.3	68
	A	440	69
	A#	466.2	70
	B	493.9	71
	C	523.3	72
	C#	554.4	73
	D	587.3	74
	D#	622.3	75
	E	659.3	76
	F	698.5	77
	F#	740	78
	G	784	79
	G#	830.6	80
	A	880	81
	A#	932.3	82
	B	987.8	83

Note	Hertz	MIDI
C	1046.5	84
C#	1108.7	85
D	1174.7	86
D#	1244.5	87
E	1318.5	88
F	1396.9	89
F#	1480	90
G	1568	91
G#	1661.2	92
A	1760	93
A#	1864.7	94
B	1975.5	95
C	2093	96
C#	2217.5	97
D	2349.3	98
D#	2489	99
E	2637	100
F	2793.8	101
F#	2960	102
G	3136	103
G#	3322.4	104
A	3520	105
A#	3729.3	106
B	3951.1	107
C	4186	108
C#	4434.9	109
D	4698.6	110
D#	4978	111
E	5274	112
F	5587.7	113
F#	5919.9	114
G	6271.9	115
G#	6644.9	116
A	7040	117
A#	7458.6	118
B	7902.1	119

Note	Hertz	MIDI
C	8372	120
C#	8869.8	121
D	9397.3	122
D#	9956.1	123
E	10548.1	134
F	11175.3	125
F#	11839.8	126
G	12543.9	127
G#	13289.8	na
A	14080	na
A#	14917.2	na
B	15804.3	na

This illustration shows standard tuning for several of the most common stringed instruments. (For standard and non-standard guitar tunings, see **"The Key."**)

Notice the similarities. The four strings on a bass are tuned to the same notes as the four lowest strings on a guitar. Electric bass or acoustic bass, both use the same tuning.

A baritone ukulele is tuned to the same four notes as the four highest strings on a guitar.

Three of the strings on a five-string banjo match three of the strings on the guitar.

The strings on a mandolin are tuned to the same notes a bass uses, but they're in the opposite order. They are also a couple of octaves higher in pitch but they are the same notes. Mandolins and mandolas actually have eight strings, not four as shown here. Each string as illustrated here is in fact a pair of identical strings, close together, and the pair is played as if it was a single string. This is also the way a 12-string guitar is strung. Six pairs of closely spaced strings, each pair played as if it was a single string. A 12-string guitar is tuned just like a standard six-string guitar.

Violin tuning is identical to a mandolin's tuning. Violins don't have frets like a mandolin does, but the notes are in the same basic locations.

Three of the strings on a mandola are the same as three of the strings on a mandolin.

Viola, cello, and tenor banjo are all tuned to the same four notes. The viola and cello don't have frets, but the notes are the same, with a cello being one octave lower than a viola.

A five-string banjo has a couple of features that make it different than most of the others. First of all, the fifth string is shorter than the other four strings and is attached to the side of the neck at the fifth fret. It I knew why, I'd tell you. I indicated the existence of that string with a dotted line on this illustration, since the drawings don't include a fifth fret.

When you hold most of these instruments facing toward you (right-handed instruments) the thinnest string (highest in pitch) is on the right.

A five-string banjo and ukulele are the same as the others, until you get to that last string. On a five-string banjo the fifth string, in standard tuning is a G note, an octave higher than the third string G.

On a ukulele, the fourth string is higher than the third string, but lower than the first string. There are several "standard" tunings for the ukulele and usually the pattern is the same, with the fourth string higher than the third string but lower than the first.

Bowing is quite difficult, for the violin, viola and cello, but there's no reason to let that stop you from playing with one. One of my musical heroes is David Lindley, and once I saw him play a violin just like it was a mandolin, flatpick and all. Mr. Lindley is the fellow who told me that the Persian scale has 43 tones. Mister Dave can make music on anything, and he plays an instrument from the Arab world called an ud, which looks sort of like an oversized mandolin with a real short neck that has 11 strings, grouped (I think) into four pairs and a set of three. (**www.davidlindley.com**) Like the instruments in the violin family, the neck on an ud has no frets. By playing in between the places that we're accustomed to hearing as "correct" notes, he is able to use the 43-tone scale. I wouldn't recommend using **any** of those additional 31 notes with a traditional bluegrass band, even if you *can* play them on your fiddle.

"Can you really distinguish between all those tones?" I asked Mr. Lindley.

"Yes… but it takes *a lot* of practice," he said, with a little twinkle in his eye. Absolute madness.

Dulcimer is a string instrument with frets that inhabits its own world. If you compare the frets on a dulcimer to the frets on all of these other instruments, you'll notice a big difference. The frets on guitars, banjos, mandolins, etc., are spaced symmetrically and evenly, and if you play every fret on a single string you'll play all 12 notes. They are farthest apart near the nut and gradually get closer together as you move up the neck toward the bridge.

The frets on a dulcimer are not consistently spaced that way. They are placed to create a scale or mode when played sequentially up the fretboard.

All of the string instruments are very similar and when you have learned something on a guitar, for example, it's not real tough to transfer it to a bass, banjo, or ukulele. You might as well experiment with all of them if you have the opportunity. After you've read the chapter on **"Scales,"** you'll probably even understand a dulcimer.

Stringed Instruments – Standard Tuning

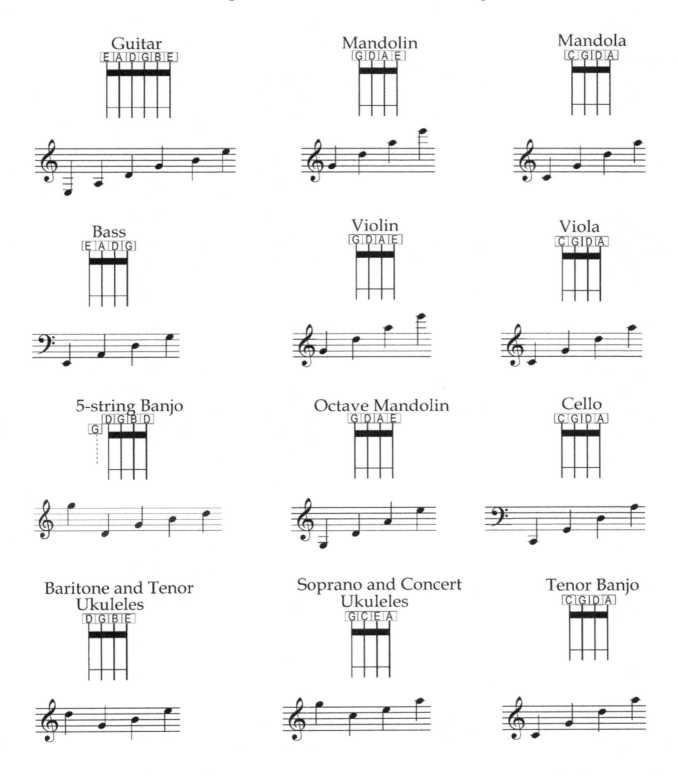

All of the exercises in this book are written using "repeat signs." It is one of the most common musical road signs.

A repeat sign replaces two regular bar lines. You'll see repeat signs in nearly every songbook. There are two parts to this symbol. The one on the left indicates the beginning of the part to be repeated and the one on the right shows the end.

beginning repeat   ending repeat

When you're reading through a piece of music and you see the beginning repeat sign, all you do is notice where it is, and continue reading. Just keep cruising until you get to the ending repeat sign. Then, you jump back to the first one and go forward from that point again. This example is shown repeating only two measures, but usually a section to be repeated is eight or more measures. No matter how close together or how far apart they are, it works the same every time.

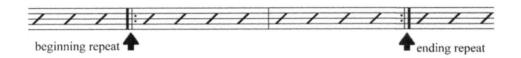

beginning repeat   ending repeat

If a section is to be repeated more than once, above the ending repeat sign there will be something written to tell you how many times you should repeat that phrase.

3 times

beginning repeat   ending repeat

It is also possible to show several adjoining sections that repeat. This the way I've shown many of the exercises in this chapter.

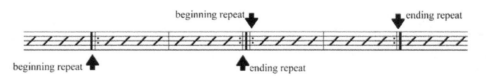

beginning repeat   ending repeat

beginning repeat   ending repeat

A line like this shows four separate exercises. Notice that this example is the first example on the next page. Since I usually included no indication of how many times you need to repeat exercises like these, you should probably think in terms of several million times. Well, maybe not that many.

NOTE NAMES ON GUITAR

Exercise #1
4 measures

Exercise #2
2 measures

Exercise #3
2 measures

Exercise #4
2 measures

         1 - Note Names

Notes on the Guitar

Notes on the Bass

1 - Note Names

Notes on the Banjo
Standard bluegrass tuning, 5th string not shown.

Notes on the Mandolin and Violin

There are no frets on a violin, of course, but the notes are in the same relative locations as a mandolin.

Notes on the Mandola, Viola and Tenor Banjo

Note Names

1. How many different letters are used for naming notes? _____

2. They are: _____

3. A tone is something you can _____, and a _____ is something written on a page that represents a tone.

4. 110 Hz, 220 Hz and 440 Hz all produce the note _____.

5. The sixth string of a guitar in standard tuning is called the _____ E string.

6. The fifth string of a guitar in standard tuning is tuned to an _____ note at approximately _____ Hz.

7. The fourth string of a guitar in standard tuning is tuned to a _____ note.

8. The third string of a guitar in standard tuning is tuned to a _____ note.

9. The second string of a guitar in standard tuning it tuned to a _____ note.

10. The first string of a guitar in standard tuning is called the _____ E string.

11. An oboe uses different notes than a piano.   **True   False**

12. Each string on any string instrument has the same sequence of notes as a piano.   **True   False**

13. The notes on a G string of a mandola are in a different sequence than the notes on the G string of a bass guitar.   **True   False**

14. Although the number of different tones is theoretically infinite, we use a total of only _____ different tones.

15. Notes are placed on a structure called a _____.

16. Each staff consists of _____ lines and _____ spaces.

17. A _____ is used to identify the name of one of the five lines on a staff.

18. There are three commonly used clefs, named the _____ clef, the _____ clef, and the _____ clef.

19. Identify these clefs.

_____ clef   _____ clef   _____ clef

20. Leger lines are used to _____ the staff.

21. Name the notes.

22. How many different notes are shown below on the grand staff? _____
    Write the correct name beside each note.

23. On a piano, middle C occurs in two locations.   **True   False**

24. One of the properties of string instruments such as guitars, banjos, mandolins, basses, violins, and other similar instruments is that a single note on the page can be played in more than one place on the neck.   **True   False**

25. The notes in example #1 of music would sound 1) **the same** 2) **different** than the notes in example #2.

26. The notes in example #3 of music would sound 1) **the same** 2) **different** than the notes in example #4.

27. In tablature each horizontal line represents a _____.

28. In tablature each number represents a _____.

29. In tablature, the low _____ string is at the bottom and the high _____ string is at the top.

30. The following line shows different instruments as they are represented on a _____ clef.

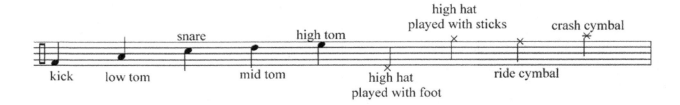

31. The rhythm clef doesn't specify any single line, because notes are not indicated as they are on the other clefs. **True   False**

32. Instead, each line and each space on a _____ _____ are used to identify a certain instrument.

Name The Notes

Counting

Chapter 2

"It's impossible to overstate the importance of learning to count in time."

Obviously, that's a load of B.S. It's easy to overstate the importance of learning to count in time. Check it out.

Not learning to count in time is the leading cause of slow, horrible, painful death in all known life forms. Professional politicians and energy executives, too.

See, it's easy to exaggerate. Anybody can do it. But, counting is important.

The question is, just exactly what is there to be counted? And why?

We'll start with *what* you're supposed to be counting.

In a way we're counting seconds, as in hours, minutes, and seconds. We're counting the time.

It can be useful to imagine a piece of music as a two dimensional object with height and length. It's easy to see those dimensions, height and length, on a line of written music.

You can see that these notes go up the page, which cleverly indicates that we're going to higher notes, then they go back down to lower notes. Height on the staff represents the relative "pitch" of a note. The notes go up and down on the page and the sound corresponds. The notes that are higher in pitch are higher on the staff.

These notes also go across the page… and that represents length.

What is being measured when counting is time. Not objects, but how long a certain event lasts. How long each note sustains and how much time passes between notes. Seconds and fractions of seconds. Like the guy holding the stopwatch at a race measuring how quickly (or slowly) a certain event occurs.

The words used to describe and measure this span of time are:
      Whole notes (and rests). A **whole note** lasts for four beats.

The names of these following notes are all derived from their relationship to the whole note.
      Half notes (and rests). A **half note** lasts for two beats.
      Quarter notes (and rests). A **quarter note** lasts for one beat.
      Eighth notes (and rests). An **eighth note** lasts for one half of a beat.
      Sixteenth notes, thirty-second notes, sixty-fourth notes, etc.

A **"note"** means make some noise. A **"rest"** means it's time to shut up. Rests are a part of music, not the absence of music. A quarter note takes up the same amount of time that a quarter rest does, an eighth note lasts exactly as long as an eighth rest, etc.

You probably remember when I said that "musical mathematics does not require basic math skills." Well... I lied and I did it on purpose. But this is the only area that we'll have to do arithmetic. We'll be dividing numbers that are smaller than 16 into equal pieces. Sorry, can't be avoided.

This illustrates the notes and their relationship to the whole note.

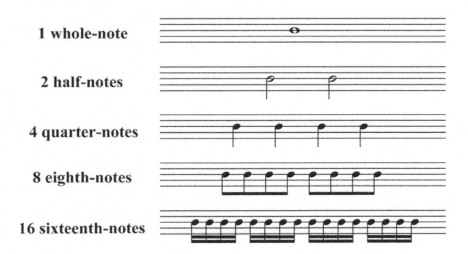

A measure of music can be thought of as a finite container, like a water glass. A glass can contain only a certain amount of water, a measure of music contains a certain number of beats.

Shown below are some measures of music. The measures are separated by "bars"... the vertical lines on the staff. The only thing a bar line does is show where the first beat in each measure is found... immediately to the right of the bar. A bar line is a little bit like a comma in a sentence. Just as a comma is not pronounced, you don't count differently as you pass from measure to measure. Bar lines and commas are visual references for easier reading. Often a measure of music is referred to as a "bar" of music. A 12-bar phrase is 12 measures of music.

The symbol at the left of the line... **4 over 4**... is called a **"time signature."**

In English, this symbol is pronounced "four-four" time.

The number on the bottom tells what kid of note is the basic unit of measurement. It's usually either a quarter note or eighth note. In this case, with a number of 4, it refers to a quarter note. The top number tells how many beats there are to be counted in each measure. There will be the equivalent of four quarter notes counted in each of these measures.

The top number in this time signature tells us that each measure contains exactly four beats. The note in each of these measures is a whole note. A whole note counts as four beats, so a single whole note fills one measure all the way up. That is all the room there is.

One whole note = one whole measure.

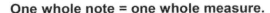

Arithmetic in music works just like arithmetic in the second grade. Cut a whole cheese into two equal pieces and you have *"cut the cheese."*

Sorry. I never quite got over second grade humor.

Divide one whole note into two equal pieces and you have two **half notes.**
Two halves = one whole. These measures are full.

Quarter notes are next and the arithmetic stays the same.
Four quarters = one whole. Two quarters = one half.

Notice the spacing of the notes on the staff. They are placed in positions roughly consistent with the amount of time they occupy in the measure. Even visually, a quarter note occupies ¼ of the measure, and a half note occupies ½ of the space in most printed music.

On occasions you encounter handwritten music, the writer probably tried to space the notes in the measure so they indicate time too, but don't depend on it.

A graph is another useful visual tool to represent and understand the way notes divide a measure lengthwise and how they are higher and lower relatives to each other.

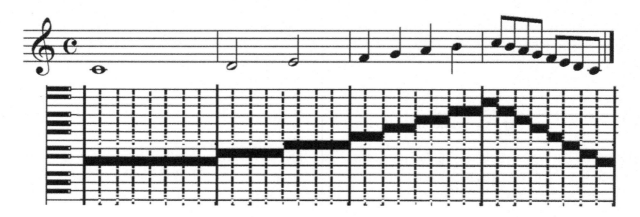

The little vertical keyboard at the left of the graph shows which note is being played, and the heavy horizontal bars show how long each notes lasts. (This sort of "graph and keyboard) is found in many music software programs. It's easy to drag the notes up and down, or change the duration by clicking and dragging.)

Another way to visualize this idea is to imagine that a measure of music is the equivalent of a single inch on a ruler. A whole note (or rest) is one full inch long, a half note (or rest) is a half inch, a quarter note (or rest) is a quarter inch, and so on.

Any combination of halves, quarters, sixteenths, etc. is OK. When it adds up to one inch, the measure is full.

A desirable quality in most popular music is a steady, consistent pulse, kind of like a heartbeat. Some songs have a fast pulse, and some songs have a slow pulse. Not all measures of music last the same length of time. We can do fast, we can do slow; but at whatever speed (tempo) a song is played, it usually remains basically the same from beginning to end. At least that is generally the plan.

You probably have heard someone "count off" a tune… "a one and a two and a one, two, three, four"… and then everybody starts playing and nobody is counting anymore. Just jammin'.

Wrong. It's not like saying, "On your mark, get set, go!" and then everybody takes off and plays at whatever speed they can manage.

It's more like synchronizing your watches so everybody gets to the same place at the same time. "I'll meet you a Pinky's at 11:30" means something specific. If your timepiece runs at a different speed than your friend's watch, then chances are you'll miss each other. Counting serves the same sort of function, keeping everyone synchronized all the way through the tune.

It only looks like they stopped counting. In fact, everybody is counting all the way to the end, but it happens internally. ***Everybody keeps on counting all the way to the end. At the same speed.*** Some people tap a foot, some nod their head. I know a guy who clicks his tongue. When an orchestra performs, the conductor standing in front waving his arms is counting time for each performer from the first note to the last with the baton in his right hand. It's not just random waving. When the baton goes down, that indicates the first beat… the down beat. A downstroke with the baton will mark the first beat of every measure of the song, beginning to end, even if it's two hours long.

Regardless of what you use to keep track, you do keep on counting, all the way to the end, at the same speed.

The third beat, 11th measure refers to a specific location in a song, in the same way that "Pinky's in Livingston, Montana" referred to a specific spot on the planet that was frequented by a pleasantly eccentric, humorous and talented keyboard player. Pinky is on the cover of this book. Mr. Lib Caldwell, who is also a great guitarist, took the photos and designed the cover. They're both playing on a song they wrote with another fine musician, Mr. Johnny Regan, called "Formica Fandango" on my *Yucca Pie* CD. (**www.dukesharp.com**) Try the Lib-a-Richie Sandwich when you go to Pinky's. Mighty fine. Lib designed the *Yucca Pie* cover, as well as the "Pickin' After Midnight" cover.

OK, sorry for the digression, I'll get back to counting music now. The goal with counting is to be able to arrive at the same place at the same time as everyone else in the band does. Pinky plays in time, he's a great groove player, *and*… he *also* usually arrives at the gig about 20 minutes later for load-in than the rest of us. Ask Lib, if you think I'm fibbing. Pinky has perfect timing, always.

When playing a song by ear, part of the process is predicting *what* is going to occur. Another part is anticipating *when* to do it. That's what counting is all about. Timing is everything.

Here are two measures of music for five different instruments.

You don't count faster when there are more notes to be played. The tempo stays the same. You just squeeze more notes into the same space. You can put dozens of marbles in a glass, or four eggs in that same glass. A measure that contains one whole note goes by at exactly the same pace as a measure that has sixteen 16th notes in it.

Everyone is counting **one and two and three and four and** at the same speed, so they all play at the same speed. The banjo plays more notes, but arrives at the beginning and end of each measure at the same time the bass does, who is only playing one note. All five musicians play the first note of each measure (the downbeat) at precisely the same instant. Togetherness.

How do you know what speed to play?

If you are looking at a sheet of music, frequently there will be an illustration close to the first measure of the song… a quarter note with a number beside it as shown below. It's a metronome setting.

That number indicates how many beats will be played in one minute. A quarter note is usually what is counted as one beat. When I see the symbol "quarter note = 120" what I say is "one hundred twenty beat a minute." It's kind of like setting the cruise control on your car. Or maybe it's like the speed limit signs on the highway. How fast are we going? Set your metronome to 120 beats per minute.

What does this mean to us? This is where we figure out how long each "beat" lasts. How fast does this song go?

First, we all know that there are 60 seconds in one minute. Right?

If you say "one potato, two potato, three potato, four potato" you can get an approximate feel for how long a second is. Each potato is about one second.

In this particular time, the composer/arranger says that in order to derive full spiritual benefit from this inspirational piece of music, there should be precisely 120 potatoes… I mean quarter notes or beats… counted in a single minute.

120 ÷ 60 seconds = 2 beats per second. Each quarter note is ½ of a second long in this particular piece of music.

So… we've got four measures of music, each measure has enough room in it for four quarter notes. Each quarter note will last for ½ of a second. Each measure would be two seconds long and the entire four measures will pass in eight seconds.

Compare this phrase to the previous one. There are two eighth notes written instead of a single quarter note, and two quarter notes replace one half note, but the speed remains the same. It still takes eight seconds to play this passage. One hundred twenty (120) beats per minute.

These are the same notes, played at the same tempo, there are just more notes in the same space. Instead of holding a single quarter note for ½ of a second, you would play two eighth notes, and each one would last ¼ of a second.

Here we go again… same tempo, 120 bpm, there are just a lot more notes. Four 16th notes replace a single quarter note. The whole thing still passes in eight seconds, just like the first one.

Here are the same four measures, but this time the "speed limit" indicates a tempo of 60 beats per minute.

At 60 bpm, each quarter note would last for one full second. Each measure will be four seconds long and the whole thing lasts 16 seconds.

Now let's speed it up. Here are the same four measures at 240 bpm, and it would be played in four seconds— approaching bluegrass speed.

I used numbers that conveniently coincide with a clock, but that's just to make the arithmetic easy. Any song can be played at any tempo that you choose.

Imagine that you are driving along with the cruise control set at 60 mph and there are telephone poles beside the highway. You'll pass one every couple of seconds. Whole notes. Then you come up on a barbed wire fence, and you pass those poles much more quickly (32nd notes), but you are still cruising at 60.

Next day, on the same stretch of road, you're driving your Hot Rod Lincoln on your way to see your sweetie, Maybeline, and you're doing about 197 mph. The telephone poles look like a picket fence. My papa said, "Son, you gonna drive me to drinkin' if you don't stop drivin' that Hot Rod Lincoln."

The poles are all in the same holes they were the day before… their relationship to each other is exactly the same, but you pass them much more quickly.

Today, you might want to play a song real fast and tomorrow play it slow. It's OK. You can play any piece of music at whatever "speed/tempo" you choose.

A quarter note is the one most often used in a metronome setting. It's the easiest one to translate into words that makes sense to me. "Quarter note = 125" I read as saying "one hundred twenty-five beats per minute."

But occasionally, you'll see an eighth note or half note used in the symbol. This is a little bit confusing for me, so I usually "translate" back to the quarter note symbol.

Look at these three lines. Although the metronome setting is different in all three lines, I still will think and pronounce all three as 60 beats per minute.

There are also lots of descriptive words used to provide some clues as to how quickly or slowly a piece of music is to be played. Most of the words are Italian, with an occasional German or French word. This abbreviated list of words is some that tell you how fast to go.

Largo (very slow, around 40-60 bpm), ***adagio*** (sort of slow, around 66-76 bpm), ***andante*** (still pretty slow, about 76-108 bpm), ***moderato*** (moderately, 108-120 bpm), ***allegro*** (kind of fast, about 120-168 bpm), ***presto*** (fast, 168-200 bpm), ***prestissimo*** (fast for sure, 200 bpm and up). These are some of the words that were used to indicate tempo in the days before metronomes became common.

Accelerando (often abbreviated to accel.) means gradually get faster and ***ritardando*** (usually abbreviated to rit.) means gradually slow down.

OK… time for some more information about **4-4**. This is known as the "time signature." Another word that is pretty much interchangeable with "time signature" is "meter."

It is really not a fraction at all. I know it sort of looks like one and we just finished dividing a whole note into a bunch of pieces. Since most people have heard that "music is very mathematical," it's natural for people to associate this symbol with a fraction, but it's not. There is not even a line between the numbers. OK? Forget pies are square, long division, and the cosine. None of that naughty stuff here, it's a family show.

The top number tells how many beats there are in each measure. This one says that each and every measure has just enough space in it to hold four **beats**. Not notes. **Beats**. Right??? Four beats, no more, no less. The top number tells *how many beats are contained in each measure.*

The bottom number tells which kind of note will be used to count one beat.

A **"4"** on the bottom means that a quarter note is one beat.

Some of these measures have four notes, some have three notes, **but they all have four beats**. You just continue counting steadily to four. Each measure could have thirty-two 32nd notes in it.

Each measure can contain any combination of quarter notes, half notes, eighths, 16th, and 32nd notes (and/or rests), so long as it all adds up to four beats.

If you have a metronome, set it at 60 bpm and try counting one-two-three-four out loud as it clicks. Try to say the numbers at exactly the same instant that the machine clicks.

It's kind of tough to do because there is quite a bit of space (one full second) between each click and it's hard to feel a rhythm.

Now set the metronome at 120, and count every other click as a number and the clicks in between as "and." I'll use the symbol "**&**" to replace the word. **&** = and.

It's much easier to feel a rhythm with that extra click. Even though there are no eighth notes to be played in this example, that's what we're counting by inserting **"and"** in between the numbers. You're still counting at 60 bpm. **One** and **two** and **three** and **four** and **one** and **two** and **three** and **four** and **one** and **two** and **three** and **four** and etcetera, etcetera, etcetera.

That works pretty well most of the time. But there are also times when it's useful to "sharpen the edge" just a bit more.

Turn the metronome back on at 120. And this time say "**one**-po-**ta**-to-**two**-po-**ta**-to-**three**-po-**ta**-to-**four**-po-**ta**-to-**one**-po-**ta**-to-**two**-po-**ta**-to-**three**-po-**ta**-to-**four**-po-**ta**-to" and say the number on a click and the syllable **"ta"** on a click.

The word "po-ta-to" has three syllables. The numbers each have one syllable. One-po-ta-to adds up to four syllables. Conveniently enough, there are four 16th notes in a quarter note, so you can use this phrase for measuring/counting 16th notes. I can't really recommend them for counting time. We use other syllables.

We have to continue using the numbers, because it's real important to know where **ONE** is. The first beat in each measure is frequently where chord changes and other relevant events occur, so we always want to identify **ONE**. If you hear somebody say, "Where's **ONE**? I can't find **ONE**," that's what they mean. First beat of the measure.

Next, we'll divide the quarter notes in half. The word "**and**" works well for a counting syllable, so we'll keep it as well. "**And**" marks the center point between the beats. 1-&-2-&-3-&-4-&.

Then, we need two more sounds for the next division. Frequently, the sounds that are used are "uh" and "eee," as in "**one eee and uh two eee and uh three eee and uh four eee and uh.**"

Each of these syllables represents a 16th note. It's a little tricky to get the **eee** sound after the word three (three-**eee**), but as a general thing this phrase works well after you get accustomed to it.

You can sill say "one-po-ta-to-two-po-ta-to-three-po-ta-to-four-po-ta-to" to yourself if you like. It really doesn't matter which syllables you use, so long as you learn to do it.

What seems to happen after a while is that all the syllables go away, and the clock just sort of ticks inside your head. But when you need to find a specific spot, you can do that by remembering the syllables. The numbers neatly divide a measure into four equal parts. The word *and* divides each of those spaces in half, and the other two syllables give us 16 equal divisions of a single measure.

In terms of counting, it's as if there is only one measure and it repeats itself over and over until the song ends. **1** - e - & - a - **2** - e - & - a - **3** - e - & - a - **4** - e - & - a - **1** - e - & - a - **2** - e - & - a - **3** - e - & - a - **4** - e - & - a - **1** - e - & - a - **2** - e - & - a - **3** - e - & - a - **4** - e - & - a **1** - e - & - a - **2** – etc.

 is the most commonly used time signature. This symbol 𝄴 has the same meaning as 4/4 and is pronounced "common time."

Common time is 4-4 time, and 4-4 is most common. Count to four using quarter notes as the counter.

is pronounced "two-four-time." It means there are two beats in each measure and a quarter note is one beat. Any time signature can be shown with any clef.

A rest is counted exactly the same way you count a note.

is pronounced "three-four time." It means there are three beats in each measure and a quarter note is one beat. Sometimes called "three-quarter time." Waltzes are in ¾ time.

The time signature lives between the clef sign and the first note. The Blue Danube Waltz (*www.mfiles.co.uk/scores/the-blue-danube-piano.pdf*) and The Tennessee Waltz are two famous examples of 3-4 time.

Notice that there is no arbitrary speed limit/metronome setting associated with any of these time signatures. Time signature only indicates how many beats are in each measure, not how quickly (or slowly) they are played. It tells how much water is in the glass; not how fast you drink it.

If there's no metronome setting indicated, ♩ = **88 (or whatever)**, you just play it at a tempo that feels right. Usually that is determined by how fast you might want to sing it.

Just because most songs use **2-4**, **3-4**, and **4-4**, don't think you're limited to these three choices. **5-4** and **7-4** are not as easy to play, but there is no real shortage of music written in other time signatures. "Money" by Pink Floyd is in **7-4**, "Black Dog" by Led Zeppelin moves around between **3-4**, **4-4**, and **5-4**, "Living in the Past" by Jethro Tull is **5-4**, several Beatles and Grateful Dead tunes use multiple time signatures, and "Take 5" by The Dave Brubeck Quartet is in **5-4**, to name a few.

The other note that is most often used as the basic counting unit is an eighth note.

 pronounced "six-eight" and most frequently seen that use an eighth note as the counter. (twelve-eight) are the two time signatures that are

 means that there is room for six beats in each measure and each beat is one eighth note.

Sometimes you'll find it most convenient to count **6-8** time just the way it's shown here. That kind of depends on the tempo of the song you're playing. Slower tunes work pretty well this way.

When you're playing something faster, saying one-two-three-four-five-six can be cumbersome, so you actually will use a different spoken phrase to keep track. Try counting like this instead…

When you count **6-8** time this way, one and a two and a, it starts feeling like there are only two beats in each measure.

Now here's a look at **12-8** time. To me, this is a lot like **4-4** time, with a **triplet feel**. Instead of dividing each beat in half, the beats are cut into three equal portions. In fact, whenever the top number is divisible by three, the writer probably expects you to lump the beats together into groups of three. There is a "rule" that says: Anytime the top number in a time signature is divisible by three, then you *do that* in order to decide how many beats are in a measure. But, like most rules, this one doesn't *always* apply. The topic is fairly awkward to discuss, and I can't explain all of the exceptions to this little "rule" mainly because I don't *know* all the exceptions to this little rule. I know it doesn't apply in **3-4** time… dividing the top number by three would turn it into **1-4** time, and would probably annoy those who enjoy waltzing. **3-8** time is also sometimes an exception. Tempo is also one of the factors involved. **As shown below, there are 12 eighth notes in each measure, which corresponds nicely to the time signature. However, there are only four beats.**

I think of 9/8 time as if there are three beats, each chopped into thirds.

Dividing something in half is pretty easy. Cutting the same thing into thirds can be a little bit tricky. There are a few different ways to count this.

I like to use the word **triple** because it reminds me that there are three parts to each beat. The catch is that **tri-ple** is only two syllables. So, I add the word "**it**," and it flows pretty nicely. **Tri-ple-it tri-ple-it tri-ple-it tri-ple-it.** 1-&-a-2-&-a-3-&-a-4-&-a.

Tri-ple-it it works real well when only two of the three notes are used. In a "shuffle" feel, you are playing triplets, but you skip the one in the middle. If you are accustomed to counting 1-&-a-2-&-a-3-&-a-4-&-a, at first it's a little bit tricky to leave out the "**and**" while keeping consistent time. 1- -a-2- -a-3- -a-4- -a.

But if I use **tri-ple-it tri-ple-it tri-ple-it tri-ple-it**, I can skip that middle syllable and still keep time. It turns into **trip- -lit trip- -lit trip- -lit trip- -lit.** If you play triplets like this real slow, about 60 bpm, it's a good, slow blues feel.

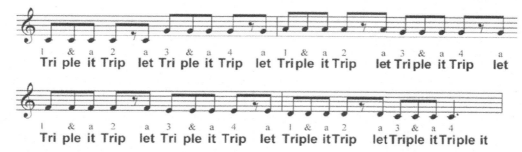

There are a couple of ways to lengthen the duration of any note on paper. One is called a "tie" and what it does is join two consecutive notes. The effect is that you play only the first note, but add the value of the two notes together. A tie is often joining the last note of a measure to the first note in the following measure.

In this example, you would count one beat each on the first three notes, but the fourth note would be held for two beats… the last beat in the first measure and the first beat in the next.

In the next example, you would play the first note (one beat) second note (two beats) and then play the fourth note on the fourth beat. That quarter note (one beat) is tied to a whole note in the next measure. A whole note gets four beats, so you would hole the last note in the first measure for five beats… the value of the first note plus the value of the note to which it is tied. A tie extends the length of a note, so the two notes joined are always on the same line or space. You can't tie a G note to an E note, for example.

The other way to extend the duration of a note is to place a "dot" after it. A dot makes the note longer by 50%.

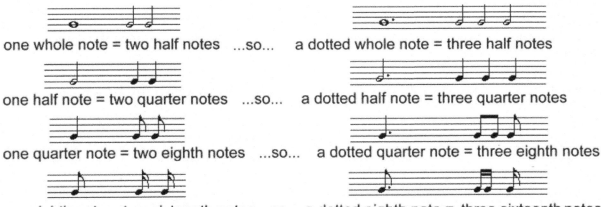

one whole note = two half notes …so… a dotted whole note = three half notes

one half note = two quarter notes …so… a dotted half note = three quarter notes

one quarter note = two eighth notes …so… a dotted quarter note = three eighth notes

one eighth note = two sixteenth notes …so… a dotted eighth note = three sixteenth notes

A "slur" is another line that is used to "connect" two notes, that looks similar to a tie, but it indicates something different. The name suggests the function of the symbol, you sort of slide from one to the other, but both notes are played, not just counted like they are when they're tied. A slur does not extend the duration of a note. This shows two slurs.

It's way beyond the scope or intent of this book to explain and illustrate all of the different time signatures and ways of counting. I've barely introduced some of the most common ones.

I have always felt that a few percussion/drum lessons can be a worthwhile investment for anyone learning any instrument. Even if you're learning to play a dulcimer or a bagpipe, six or eight sessions with a good drum instructor can help you understand things about rhythm that will be useful as long as you play.

There is a book called *Progressive Steps to Syncopation for the Modern Drummer,* written by Ted Reed, Alfred Publishing. Currently, it sells for $7.95 and has been a standard for drummers for quite a long time. This book is not about counting, really. It's a well-designed book full of exercises for learning to read rhythm. If you can read rhythm, you can count.

You can work through the book on your own with a metronome. At first, you don't want to use an instrument. Sixty (60) bpm is a good place to start, so set the metronome to 120. Just tap the rhythms on the page or on your leg. It's a really painless way to read rhythm. An investment of eight entire dollars, plus 100 hours, will pay big dividends.

I suggest that you find this book and have someone show you how to count through the exercises. It was written as exercises to be played on a snare drum, but it is also a nearly inexhaustible source of strumming patterns.

Using a CD of someone you enjoy listening to is another way of practicing counting. While you listen to the songs, count along in time. Initially, this is a bit more difficult than the Ted Reed exercises, but it does help bring this exercise into the realm of "real world usefulness." If you're doing the Ted Reed book too, you will hear those same patterns in the book on nearly any CD you might choose to work with.

If you can, choose a band or an artist that uses drums, because the drummer will often be playing the kick drum on the first and third beats of nearly every measure, and the snare will be in between on the second and fourth beats. At first, usually the snare is easier to recognize than the kick. If you're having trouble hearing the kick drum, try focusing on the bass guitar, because often the bass will match the rhythm that the kick is playing. In a four or five-piece band, the bass and drums are a team, known as "the rhythm section," and you definitely want to learn to hear how the two work together.

It takes time to be able to hear each instrument individually, but it is one of the most useful skills that you can develop. Listening for the snare drum is a good place to begin.

Bluegrass is also good for learning to count even though there is no drummer. Instead, the mandolin takes the place of the snare drum, and will often be found chunking chords on the second and fourth beats. Bluegrass bass is just as predictable, usually found on the first and third beats. The instruments in a traditional bluegrass band… bass, guitar, fiddle, mandolin, and banjo… have such distinct individual voices that it's a good place to practice listening for individual instruments in a mix. Choose a song and try to follow the bass all the way through while you tap your foot and count. Rewind, start it over, and follow the banjo. Rewind and follow the mandolin. Rewind and follow the fiddle. Rewind and follow the guitar. Start over.

I like to have my students use Beatles' songs to practice counting songs that change time signatures, because one of the many interesting things those guys frequently did was to use more than one time signature in a single song. There is a book called *The Beatles Book* (Easy Guitar, 100 songs) that has a bunch of good tunes in it. There are 10 tunes with time signature changes in this one publication, so it's a pretty economical tool. Plus, the recordings are easy to find and lots of people are familiar with Beatles' tunes.

This is a list of songs in that book that use multiple time signatures:

All You Need is Love
A Day in the Life
Blackbird
Everybody's Got Something to Hide Except for Me and My Monkey
Hello Goodbye
Here Comes the Sun
I Want You
Lucy in the Sky with Diamonds
Strawberry Fields
You've Got to Hide Your Love Away

Open the book, choose a song, turn on the CD, and count along. As always, if this is way too confusing on your own, don't be embarrassed to ask somebody for some help with it. Usually, if someone can show you how to get through one or two songs, you probably can figure out the others. We get by with a little help from our friends.

It really doesn't matter which artist's book you use. Look through all the songs and check the time signatures. Are there songs in several different meters, or do they tend to stay in "common time?" Do the songs change meters anywhere in the middle? Put on the CD and follow along in your book. Plan on listening 10 or 15 times through about a dozen songs before it starts to become easy.

Pop tunes are usually in the range of three minutes long. Ten songs, three times each, is about 30 minutes. Repeat it a dozen times and it's about six hours worth of practice.

Six hours doesn't seem like an excessive investment in this sort of enterprise to me.

Chapter 13, "**Reading the Road Map**" explains most of the symbols you're likely to encounter, so if these symbols are something you have no experience with, you may want to read it through a couple of times to get you started. If it's still not making sense for you, find someone to help.

Counting in time is one of the most useful skills that you can develop. It's not hard, it just takes a bit of practice. So practice.

Pickup Measures and Pickup Notes

I thought the song "You Are My Sunshine" would be a dandy song to illustrate an example of a pickup measure because so many people know the tune. Unfortunately, the licensing department at Hal Leonard Corporation refused to sell me a license to use that song… or any other songs you might know for that matter. So… here is my very own, original composition called, "You Are My Moonshine." It's remarkably similar to "You Are My Sunshine." The words and chords have been changed so we may forever preserve and protect my pal Hal's interest in "You Are My Sunshine." I didn't change the rhythm, so if you're familiar with "You Are My Sunshine" this will still be a good example. This is in the key of A minor, but since we haven't talked about chords or keys yet, I didn't include the chords here. Use two fingers to tap eighth notes and say the words in time.

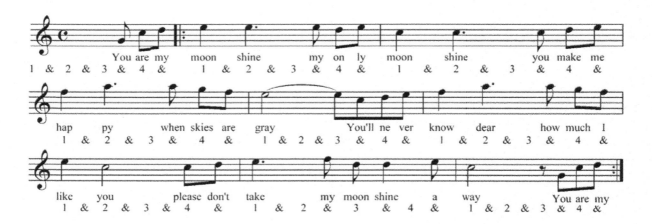

There is a treble clef and a time signature indicating that there should be four beats in each measure. Then, the very first measure has a grand total of three 8th notes in it. There is no way to make three 8th notes add up to four beats. I hope you're kind of wondering… "What's up with that?"

Notice that those first three notes are not included in the measures to be repeated. Those first notes are just a little "lead in" to a song, and it's very common.

You'll remember how players "count in" to the first beat of a song, and "one and two and three and four and," then the song begins on "one."

The notes in a pickup measure happen *during* the count in.

If you're counting a song in you'll say "one and two and three and four and." Beginning with the "the and of 3" (the eighth note between three and four) is when those few notes in the pickup measure are played or sung. The count "and four and" corresponds to the words "You are my."

Then you go past the beginning repeat sign, as far as the ending repeat sign. The word "way" is a half note for two beats, "one and two and." There's an eighth rest on three.

Notice the three notes in the last measure right before the ending repeat sign. Those three notes are identical to the three notes in the pickup measure and they lead you to the first note in measure two, the same way the notes in the pickup measure do. When there is a pickup measure, very often the notes in the pickup measure are identical to the last couple of notes that are at the end of the phrase to be repeated, like it's shown in "You Are My Moonshine."

I began this little discussion about pickup measures in the context of the lyrics, since that's how most of us initially connect with songs, and there are lots of songs that start with a vocal pickup, as shown here.

All My Lovin
Lennon and McCartney

Often a song starts with some sort of instrumental intro. The intro might be only a measure or two or they might play a whole verse before the singer jumps in. In the example below, the guitar starts the tune on 1, then the vocalist comes in with some "pickup notes." It's not really a pickup measure as shown above, since the song starts instrumentally on the first beat.

All I've Got To Do
Lennon and McCartney

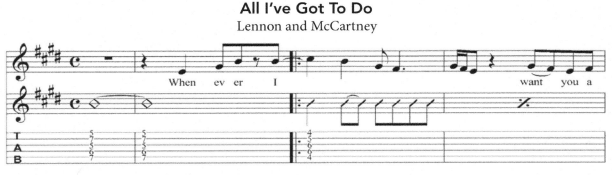

Here's another example, and notice that the guitar's first notes are the pickup measure and five bars later the vocal line starts on the AND of 1. Neither one clearly identifies the first beat.

And I Love Her
Lennon and McCartney

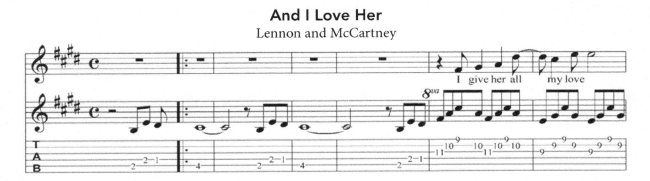

If you're sitting in a room and singing and playing songs, you'll notice that nobody has any trouble dealing with these pickup measures and pickup notes and the chances are good that nobody knows what a pickup measure is. It's a very natural thing, lots of songs have pickups of some sort. Notice that I didn't have to look through very many songs in the Beatles' book to find three examples of pickups.

But, my errand here is to show you things that can help you figure songs out by ear, and one of the most important things to figure out in that process is the location of 1… the first beat, the down beat. That's where tons of important musical events occur and take my word for it, you don't want to always miss the mark by three 8th notes, or whatever, just cause you didn't know about pickup measures and pickup notes.

It's reasonable to assume that the first sound made by an instrument or the first words sung will indicate that all-important first beat; however, very often it simply is not the case.

This is how the poem would probably appear on paper (except for the **bold**, of course).

> You are my **moon** shine
> My only **moon** shine
> You make me **hap**-py
> When skies are **gray**
> You'll never **know** dear
> How much I **like** you
> Please don't **take** my moonshine a-**way**

It is not logical to think that the musical beats do not occur anywhere near the beginning of each poetic line since poems are often quite rhythmic.

	&	4	&
	You	are	my
moon shine	My	on	ly
moon shine	You	make	me
hap-py	When	skies	are
gray	You'll	nev	er
know dear	How	much	I
like you		Please	don't
take my moon shine			a-
way.			

The first word is not on the first beat, but the last word is. Not intuitive.

Frequently, you have to make this kind of shift to get the first beat in the right place.

I provided a few familiar tunes so you can practice counting. If you know this one, it's a good place to start. There are examples in this chapter, as well as a few more in the last chapter, "**Putting It All Together**." At first just say the rhymes aloud while you tap in time with your finger or foot or whatever. Practice makes better.

Some of the examples have pickup measures, some don't. Being able to locate the first beat in a measure is a crucial skill for playing by ear. Don't rush through these exercises. Practice humming a tune while you tap in time and learn to become aware of "one"… the first beat in every measure. It's the landmark that all players use for finding the way around and through a tune.

Hum the tune for "You Are My Sunshine" but don't use the words. Instead, use "one and two and three and four and."

Instead of singing "You are my," sing the count as it's shown here and on page 42… "and four and." Instead of the word "sun" in the first measure, sing "one and." Replace the word "shine" with "two and three." "My on-ly" is "and four and."

Next measure, "sun" is "1 &." "Shine" is 2 & 3." "You make me" is "& 4 &."

For me, it's extremely useful to be able to sing tunes that way, replacing the poetry with the count and tapping along. Learn to find 1.

A "hands-on" counting technique

Remember that the lyrics to most songs are poems and they can be spoken in a way that is rhythmic.

When you're trying to learn to count in time, at first a good way to approach it is to forget all about the tune for a while. Say it as a poem. Repeat a single section, over and over, while tapping beats until you begin to feel the rhythm. Practice with any song or poem that you know well. I've supplied several familiar songs at the end of this chapter as well as at the end of the final chapter, "**Putting It All Together**."

Try tapping a finger, or your foot in a consistent rhythm and say the words in the same rhythm that they are sung. **Ma**-ry-**had**-a-**lit**-tle-**lamb**-whose-**fleece**-was-**white**-as-**snow**.

For me, the very easiest thing is to tap the first finger of my right hand while I say the poem. In this example, you're tapping on "1 and 3"... the first and third beats in each measure.

This one looks harder because it uses a lot more notes, but if you say the poem at the same speed as Twinkle, it's about the same. What you're trying to accomplish is to feel a rhythm and locate some reference points. In this one you're tapping all four beats in each measure.

Now, try the same thing, except tap on the second and fourth beats. When you listen to music, you'll often hear the second and fourth beats accented by the snare drum. It sort of feels like you're tapping in between the beats. If you tap your foot on the first and third beats, your finger on the second and fourth beats, you can begin to get a feel for something drummers do a lot... kick, snare, kick, snare, kick, snare, kick, snare.

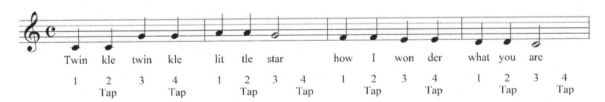

Tapping (or accepting) in between the beats... on **AND**... 1 & 2 & 3 & 4 &... is known as "syncopation."

Syncopation is a subject that is way too involved for me to get into here, and the definition I gave you is not really complete. It's not wrong, but there is quite a bit more to it than that. This might be a good subject to take up with a drum/percussion instructor… a few lessons with a good teacher can make a big difference.

Since we're on the subject of tapping the beats with your fingers, it's a good time to show you a simple technique that can make it easy to pinpoint some event in a measure of music. This is about using your fingers to pick stuff out by ear. It isn't as messy as it sounds.

Imagine that you're listening to a song (not looking at it like it is here) and you're trying to locate exactly which division of the beat the word "**his**" falls on in the tune "Yankee Doodle."

This is a "two-handed" operation. I'll start with my left hand. I stop the recording and I start staying the poem, over and over. As I say the poem, I tap each beat (quarter notes) with a different finger, beginning with my pinky.

My pinky taps when I say "**Yan**" on 1. My ring finger taps when I say "**doo**" on 2. My middle finger taps when I say "**went**" on 3, and my first finger taps when I say "**town**" on 4.

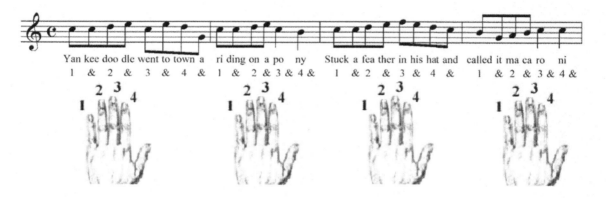

At the same time, I'm tapping eighth notes with my first and middle fingers, so that my first finger taps a beat on 1, "**Yan**," "**doo**" 2, "**went**" 3, and "**town**" 4. Middle finger taps &… kee-dle-to-a.

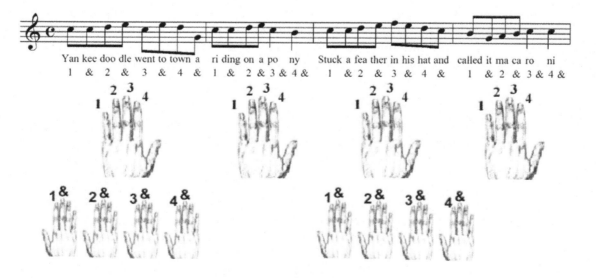

When I get to the word "his" all I have to do is look at my hands. My left hand tells me that it's the third beat and my right hand tells me that it's on the "**&**" of that beat.

If you're trying to find 16th notes, it works exactly the same way, except I use all four fingers of my right hand.

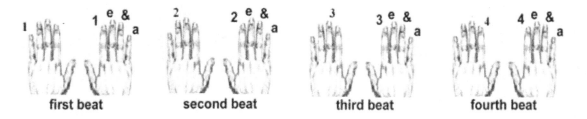

Of course, you can do the same thing with 3-4 time and triplets...

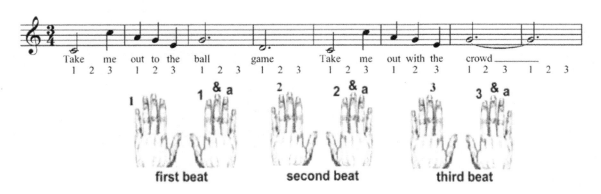

It's a pretty handy technique.

There is absolutely no way to resist that pun. You would have said it, too.

You may be wondering, "Where did you learn to do that?"

Watching Craig Hall write out a rhythmically complicated 16th note passage from memory in a studio session. It was about 14 bars long and it took him nearly two entire minutes. It was correct the first time. I went home and practiced.

Learning to count in time and developing the ability to identify the first beat in each measure is without a doubt one of the most important and useful skills that you can develop. You can know a jillion scales and chords, but if you can't play all of those things at the right time, most of the time it won't be very musical. It's just about impossible to play with other people when you can't agree on timing.

It's also something that you can practice anywhere. It doesn't even require an instrument.

I don't think it's possible to overdo this. Practice it a lot. When you're walking, pretend that your footsteps are the quarter notes, and you can be thinking **DA** da **DA** da **DA** da **DA** da for eighth notes. Do 16ths **DA** da la pa **DA** da la pa **DA** da la pa **DA** da la pa **DA** da la pa **DA**. I count triplets on my bicycle... every time my foot gets to the bottom of a stroke, that's a beat... **DA** da la **DA** da la **DA** da la **DA** da la **DA** da la **DA** da la.

Do it enough and it starts to become a natural thing. The numbers sort of go away and you just feel it. Eventually, you're sure to find someone looking at you kind of funny and you'll realize that you're doing it aloud in line at the grocery store. The good thing is at that point it's becoming an unconscious part of you and that's exactly what you're after.

Jingle Bells

James Pierpont

Happy Birthday To You

Mildred J. Hill and Patty Smith Hill

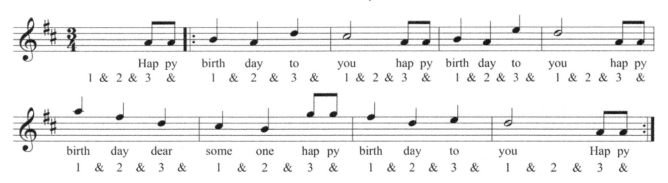

Yankee Doodle

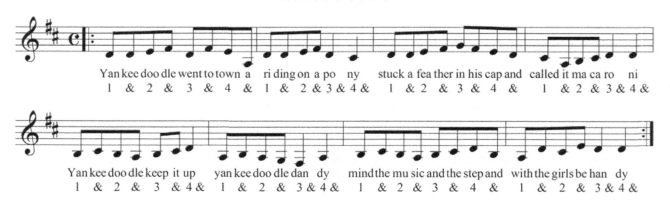

Home On The Range

Brewster Higley and Dan Kelley

Auld Lang Syne

Pop Goes The Weasel

Row Row Row Your Boat

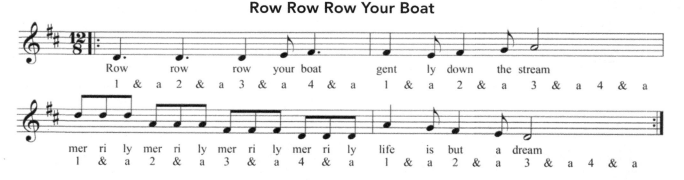

Are You Sleeping

Take Me Out To The Ballgame
Jack Norworth and Albert von Tilzer

Silent Night
Joseph Mohr

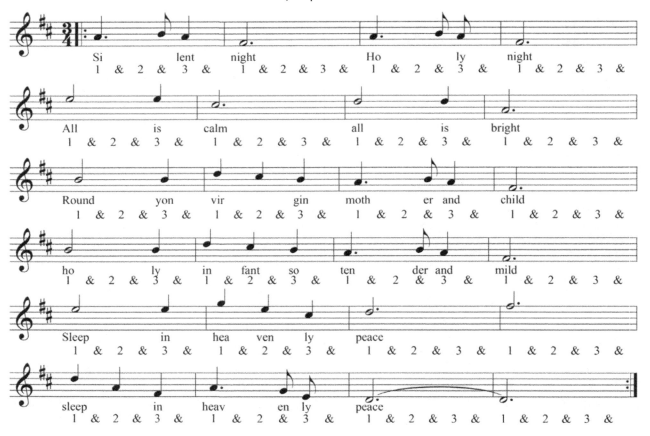

Scarborough Fair

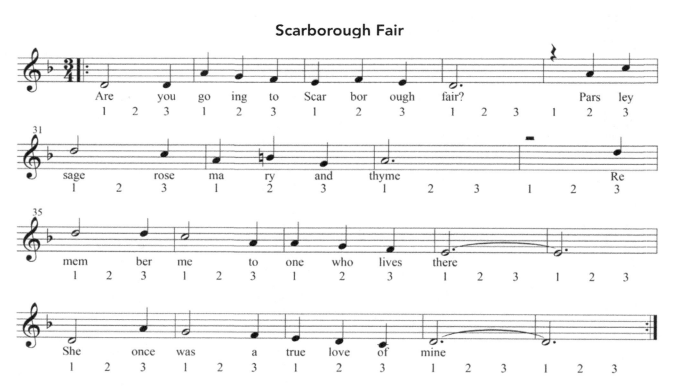

2 - Counting

Greensleeves

Many historians believe that these lyrics were composed by Henry Tudor, a.k.a. King Henry the Eighth. It was (and is) a common practice to use a familiar melody and compose a poem to fit the tune. You may be familiar with the Christmas carol "What Child Is This"… another poem set to this tune. I'm no historian, but my understanding of dear, old Henry's reputation of a scorned or dissatisfied lover leaves me a bit concerned about the fate of the young lady in the poem. I seem to remember that the lovely Anne Boleyn did not fare well when Henry tired of her. We'll never know for sure, but an appropriate subtitle for Henry's poem might be "Summon The Executioner."

Alas, my love, you do me wrong,
To cast me off discourteously.
For I have loved you well and long,
Delighting in your company.

Chorus:
Greensleeves was all my joy
Greensleeves was my delight,
Greensleeves was my heart of gold,
And who, but my lady greensleeves?

Your vows you've broken, like my heart,
Oh, why did you so enrapture me?
Now I remain in a world apart
But my heart remains in captivity.

(chorus)

I have been ready at your hand,
To grant whatever you would crave,
I have both wagered life and land,
Your love and good-will for to have.

(chorus)

If you intend thus to disdain,
It does the more enrapture me,
And even so, I still remain
A lover in captivity.

(chorus)

My men were clothed all in green,
And they did ever wait on thee;
All this was gallant to be seen,
And yet thou wouldst not love me.

(chorus)

Thou couldst desire no earthly thing,
but still thou hadst it readily.
Thy music still to play and sing;
And yet thou wouldst not love me.

(chorus)

Well, I will pray to God on high,
that thou my constancy mayst see,
And that yet once before I die,
Thou wilt vouchsafe to love me.

(chorus)

Ah, Greensleeves, now farewell, adieu,
To God I pray to prosper thee,
For I am still thy lover true,
Come once again and love me.

Chorus:
Greensleeves was all my joy
Greensleeves was my delight,
Greensleeves was my heart of gold,
And who, but my lady greensleeves

Greensleeves

2 - Counting

Tweaking Your Twinkle... with rhythm

The exercises on the following pages are designed to give a student some experience with counting as well as an introduction to reading rhythm.

The tune is Twinkle Twinkle Little Star. There are a bunch of different rhythmic variations shown for this melody and they use different combinations of half, quarter notes, and eighth notes.

First, you'll probably want to read through them without trying to play them. Don't even worry about the tune, at first. This is about rhythm. The phrases shown under the notes in the first two measures of variations 1-9 will help you hear the rhythm that the quarter and eighth notes indicate. I borrowed the idea and some of the phrases from the Suzuki Method of learning to read music. Instead of looking at each note individually, learn to see a measure as a short phrase, just as you see a series of letters as a single word.

This is the first variation on the Twinkle theme... all eighth notes. "Wish-I-had-a-mo-tor-cy-cle" is eight syllables, one for each eighth note in the measure.

Twinkle – 8th Note Variations in Common Time

Start slowly, say 60 bpm. Set the metronome at 120 bpm, so each click is an eighth note. Tap your finger on the quarter notes (every other click), 1-2-3-4, say "**Wish**-I-**had**-a-**mo**-tor-**cy**-cle." When you feel the rhythm, say **DA**-da-**DA**-da-**DA**-da-**DA**-da. Do the same drill for the rest of the variations. When you can say it, you can learn to play it.

Exercises 10 through 12 turn Twinkle into a waltz, and exercise 11 shows Twinkle in 6-8. Exercise 14 goes back to 4-4 time, but uses triplets so Twinkle becomes a blues shuffle.

These few rhythmic variations I've shown on the following pages are similar to the approach taken by Ted Reed in his classic book, *Progressive Steps to Syncopation for the Modern Drummer*. This book shows hundreds of rhythmic patterns using combinations of quarter, eighth, and 16th notes. A lot of these patterns make killer strumming patterns for playing rhythm guitar, mandolin, banjo, etc. It costs about $8 and it's a pretty painless way to really accelerate beginning reading skills. Well done, useful, and inexpensive, *Progressive Steps to Syncopation for the Modern Drummer* is worth owning and studying.

These exercises can also be viewed as an introduction to improvisation.

There are lots of ways to alter a theme. You can change the notes, you can change the rhythm, take the dynamics up and down (dynamics = volume and/or intensity... sort of). There are far more improvisational options and approaches than can be sensibly addressed here.

The "improvisations" I've shown here use all of the original notes in the same order, but apply different rhythms. These variations are pretty simple, symmetrical, repetitive, and predictable, but that doesn't change the fact that they are "improvised" melody lines. It's one way to tweak Twinkle, and the idea can be applied to other songs.

Twinkle is a French folk tune from the 18th century and when Wolfgang Amadeus Mozart was 17 years old, he used his melody as a starting point for his playful and ever expanding "Variations." I found a version on iTunes by John Novacek, "12 Variations on Ah! Vois Dira-Je, Maman" and it's a dollar well spent. I highly recommend that you find a version and listen to it. I've seen Wolfgang credited with composing the melody, as well as his father, Leopold. Others think that it probably existed as a folk tune before Leopold was born. For certain is the fact that Wolfgang twisted it pretty hard. Leopold had young Wolfgang out on the road doing paying gigs before he was five. Evidently, he was one seriously scary, young piano picker. I wonder what instruments he'd be playing if he was 17 today?

Mozart titled his poem "Ah! Vois Dira-Je, Maman," and a rough translation of the lyric he wrote is:

Ah, let me tell you mother, the cause of my torment.
Papa wants me to reason like a grown-up.
I say that candy has greater value than reason.

Sounds like young Wolfgang was like lots of adolescent humans and having some trouble relating with his Papa. Imagine that. I'm with Wolfie on this one.

It's such a simple tune and one we dismiss as a "nursery rhyme," but the questions it asks is a good one.

Consider for a moment two stars. First, our favorite "little star" cleverly named The Sun. It is roughly a million miles across, about *93 million miles* away and from that distance it's powerful enough to thoroughly toast your skin... in just a couple of hours. Imagine driving at 100 miles an hour, 24 hours a day, no coffee breaks or nothin'... if you leave right now it will take more than 100 years to get to the sun. That's a big fire.

A distance of 93 million miles from our little planet to the sun means the diameter of the circle we trace around the sun is well over 180 million miles. You'd have to drive the Caddy for 200 plus years at 100 miles an hour to go across our orbit. (200+yearsX3.1415 would get you around the circle.)

Next, consider Betelgeuse (BET'L juice), the star that marks Orion's red "shoulder," upper left. Betelgeuse would not fit inside earth's orbit. If it suddenly replaced The Sun, we would be inside it.

Goodness Gracious, Great Balls of Fire! This little star is the single largest object that you can see with your naked eye. (Cool book alert: *Secrets of the Night Sky, The Most Amazing Things in the Universe You Can See With the Naked Eye*, by Bob Berman. If you've ever wanted to know more than you do about the night sky, this book is full of interesting stuff, well written by a guy who knows. A fellow guitarist, too. I think.)

Here's the theme. Lyrically, I figure it's at least as interesting as most of the "love gone wrong" songs I'm acquainted with. Mozart proved it can be great music. The tabs show an easy way to play this French folk tune while you wonder what Betelgeuse means. You can play all the variations in this exercise using this position, as well as most of the tunes after Twinkle that are shown as counting exercises.

Twinkle – 8th Note Variations in Common Time

2 - Counting

Twinkle – 8th Note Variations in Common Time

Twinkle – 8th Note Variations in Common Time

2 - Counting

Twinkle – Variations in 3-4 Time

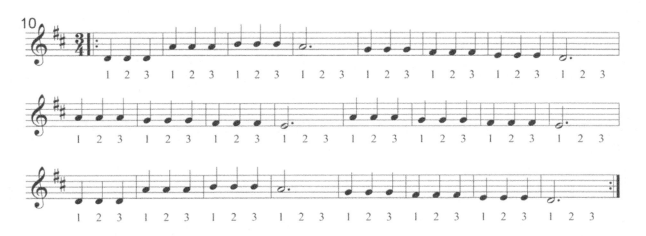

10

| 1 2 3 | 1 2 3 | 1 2 3 | 1 2 3 | 1 2 3 | 1 2 3 | 1 2 3 | 1 2 3 |

| 1 2 3 | 1 2 3 | 1 2 3 | 1 2 3 | 1 2 3 | 1 2 3 | 1 2 3 | 1 2 3 |

| 1 2 3 | 1 2 3 | 1 2 3 | 1 2 3 | 1 2 3 | 1 2 3 | 1 2 3 | 1 2 3 |

11

Twin kle twin kle lit tle star   how I won der what you are
1 2 3   1 2 3   1 2 3   1 2 3   1 2 3   1 2 3   1 2 3   1 2 3

Up a bove the world so high   like a dia mond in the sky
1 2 3   1 2 3   1 2 3   1 2 3   1 2 3   1 2 3   1 2 3   1 2 3

Twin kle twin kle lit tle star   how I won der what you are
1 2 3   1 2 3   1 2 3   1 2 3   1 2 3   1 2 3   1 2 3   1 2 3

12

| 1 & 2 & 3 & | 1 & 2 & 3 & | 1 & 2 & 3 & | 1 & 2 & 3 & | 1 & 2 & 3 & | 1 & 2 & 3 & | 1 & 2 & 3 & | 1 & 2 & 3 & |

| 1 & 2 & 3 & | 1 & 2 & 3 & | 1 & 2 & 3 & | 1 & 2 & 3 & | 1 & 2 & 3 & | 1 & 2 & 3 & | 1 & 2 & 3 & | 1 & 2 & 3 & |

| 1 & 2 & 3 & | 1 & 2 & 3 & | 1 & 2 & 3 & | 1 & 2 & 3 & | 1 & 2 & 3 & | 1 & 2 & 3 & | 1 & 2 & 3 & | 1 & 2 & 3 & |

Twinkle – Variation in 6-8 Time

Twinkle – Variation with Triplets in 4-4 Time

2 - Counting

Counting

1. What is being measured when counting? _____

2. Notes and rests are used to describe these bits of time. They are called *WHOLE* notes and rests, _____ notes and rests, _____ notes and rests, _____ notes and rests, _____ notes and rests.

3. All of the notes are named by their relationship to a _____ note.

4. Rests indicate the absence of music. **True   False**

5. A half rest measures a slightly shorter span of time than a half note. **True   False**

6. Often a measure of music is referred to as a _____ of music.

7. A 12-bar phrase is _____ measure of music.

8. One whole note occupies as much time as _____ half notes, _____ quarter notes, _____ eighth notes, _____ 16th notes, _____, 32nd notes, and _____ 64th notes.

9. Identify the following notes and rests.

10. A person doing the "count in" to the beginning of a song is similar to a person at a race who says "On your mark… get set… GO!" **True   False**

11. These symbols are called _____

12. They represent the circumference of Jupiter. **True   False**

13. The top number tells how many _____ are in each measure.

14. The bottom number tells what kind of _____ is used to measure one _____.

15. is pronounced **two-four** time, and it means there are _ beats in each measure and a _____ note is _____ _____.

16. 𝄞 **3/4** is pronounced _____-_____ time, and it means there are _____ beats in each measure and a _____ note is _____ _____.

17. 𝄞 **4/4** is pronounced _____-_____ time, and it means there are _____ beats in each measure and a _____ note is _____ _____.

18. 𝄞 **C** is pronounced _____-_____ time, and it means there are _____ beats in each measure and a _____ note is _____ _____.

19. 𝄞 **7/4** is pronounced _____-_____ time, and it means there are _____ beats in each measure and a _____ note is _____ _____.

20 𝄞 **3/8** is pronounced _____-_____ time, and it means there are _____ beats in each measure and a _____ note is _____ _____.

21. 𝄞 **6/8** is pronounced _____-_____ time, and it means there are _____ beats in each measure and a _____ note is _____ _____.

22. 𝄞 **9/8** is pronounced _____-_____ time, and it means there are _____ beats in each measure and a _____ note is _____ _____.

23. 𝄞 **12/8** is pronounced _____-_____ time, and it means there are _____ beats in each measure and a _____ note is _____ _____.

24. Very often, when the top number in a time signature is divisible by 3, you are required to do that division in order to decide how many beats are felt in a measure. **True   False**

25. Duke Sharp lied when he said that basic arithmetic skills are not required to understand "musical mathematics." **True   False**

26. What this means is that a song that has a time signature 𝄞 **6/8** will often feel like there are two beats, each with three pulses. **True   False**

27. A song that has a time signature 𝄞 **9/8** will often feel like there are three beats, each with three pulses. **True   False**

28. A song that has a time signature will often feel like there are four beats, each with three pulses.
   True   False

29. All measures of music are played at the same tempo.   **True   False**

30. "Tempo" is a word that has just about the same meaning as "speed."   **True   False**

31. The tempo of a piece of music is indicated by the time signature.   **True   False**

32. These symbols are called _____ _____.

   ♩= 60   𝅗𝅥= 25   ♪=100   ♪=120   ♩= 50   𝅗𝅥= 40   ♪=160   𝅗𝅥= 30   ♩= 80

33. It tells how many beats are beats in each measure.   **True   False**

34. ♩ = 60 means there are _____ beats in _____ _____, and that a _____ note is _____ beat.

35. 𝅗𝅥 = 25 means there are _____ beats in _____ _____, and that a _____ note is _____ beat.

36. ♪ = 100 means there are _____ beats in _____ _____, and that a _____ note is _____ beat.

37. ♩ = 50 means there are _____ beats in _____ _____, and that a _____ note is _____ beat.

38. 𝅗𝅥 = 40 means there are _____ beats in _____ _____, and that a _____ note is _____ beat.

39. Which of the three metronome settings in each of the following lines indicates the quickest tempo? (A, B, C, or NONE)

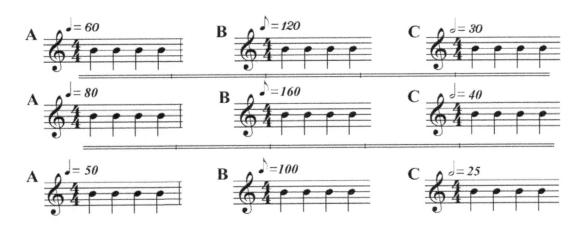

40. Largo is approximately _____ to _____ bpm on a metronome.

41. Adagio is approximately _____ to _____ bpm on a metronome.

42. Andante is approximately _____ to _____ bpm on a metronome.

43. Moderato is approximately _____ to _____ bpm on a metronome.

44. Allegro is approximately _____ to _____ bpm on a metronome.

45. Presto is approximately _____ to _____ bpm on a metronome.

46. Prestissimo is approximately _____ to _____ bpm on a metronome.

47. The first sound played by an instrument is always played on beat #1.   **True   False**

48. The first sound made by a vocalist is always on beat #1.   **True   False**

49. The first measure in the following example is known as a _____.

All My Lovin
John Lennon and Paul McCartney

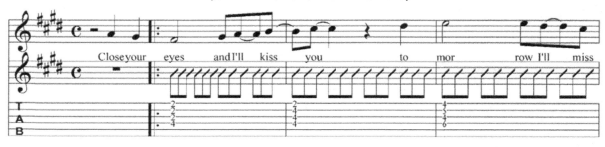

50. The notes in a pickup measure occur (before – during – after) the count in.

51. Those notes are called "pickup notes."   **True   False**

52. Pickup notes are only found in a pickup measure.   **True   False**

53. The notes in the second measure are called _____ _____.

All I've Got To Do
Lennon and McCartney

Intervals: Part One | Chapter 3

Often, when people use the word "interval," it is in reference to time, as in "an interval of five minutes" or something similar.

Musical intervals are different. In the language of music, the word is used to help describe and define a difference we hear between different tones.

It's quite easy to *see* and understand musical intervals, either on a keyboard or guitar or on a staff of written music. Learning to *hear* and recognize intervals by their sound takes a bit longer. It is definitely in your best interest to develop both skills.

A clear understanding of a musical interval is necessary.

Any reasonable person might ask "Why is it necessary?" Especially since what you want to do is play your instrument and not get bogged down with a bunch of arcane definitions.

Well, this is one way to explain it. Imagine that you wanted to learn to paint. You get some brushes, paints, a canvas, and an easel, and off you go. You set up your easel overlooking a lush valley with a river meandering through it with mountains in the background and a crystal blue sky, and you start splashing colors on the canvas. An hour or two later, there will probably be **something** on your canvas that **resembles** the scene you were viewing.

Not hard to imagine, is it?

The reason you would be able to do that and probably create something recognizable (more or less) on your first attempt is because you bring a lot of knowledge with you. Basic stuff that you take for granted.

The sky is always above the mountains, the water runs downhill, the grass is green. You know what blue is, and you instantly recognize a lot of different shades of blue. You won't paint the sky green and the grass blue by mistake. The same is true for all the other primary colors and many of the variations. Red, blue, yellow, black, brown, purple, orange… there are no mysteries there for you. You probably know that if you mix blue with yellow, you'll get green and you can alter that shade of green by mixing more yellow or blue. So you can paint something that just about everybody will look at and say, "That's a valley and a river and some mountains."

In the language of music, notes (tones), intervals, and counting are the basics. These are words and symbols we use to describe, identify, and locate sounds on all instruments.

The notes in music can be thought of as something similar to the primary colors in painting. Counting helps define the size and shape of the canvas. Intervals describe how we combine and use those notes to create different textures and patterns.

As you remember, counting measures the length of a song. Counting tells us how long a note lasts and how much space is between the notes. Counting lets us measure the length of a song, one note at a time.

Intervals work in another dimension, vertical distances. Counting measures length, intervals measure height.

One note by itself is not an interval. More than one note, and you've got an interval.

When notes are played in sequence one after the other (or in this case, written), it's a "melodic" interval.

Melodic interval

When notes are played simultaneously, it's called a "harmonic" interval. In written music, vertical alignment always indicates events that are supposed to occur same-ol'-timeously.

Harmonic interval

Either way, intervals just quantify the vertical distance between the notes. Counting measures length and intervals measure height. The two are totally separate ideas, independent of each other.

Fretted instruments offer an easy way to see intervals. On the neck of any fretted instrument an interval is simply the physical distance between two notes, similar to the distance between the marks on a ruler.

Play a note, any note on any string. Then play a different note on that same string. We can then determine the interval between those two notes by counting the number of frets that separate those two notes.

On a ruler, there are 12 inches, all identical. This group of 12 units defines a single larger unit called a "foot." By coincidence, 12 notes all separated by identical distances (intervals) define a musical unit called an octave.

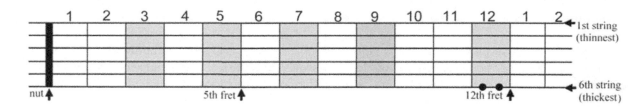

Defining and understanding intervals is based on something as simple as having the ability to count to 12. A quick course in remedial arithmetic may be in order at this time.

A fretted instrument also presents a couple of problems for the beginner learning to identify intervals. One is the fact that the frets all look pretty much the same. There are no obvious distinctive features that show a visual pattern that can be helpful in recognizing and understanding intervals. I'm using a guitar neck for the illustration, but it's essentially the same on the other fretted instruments.

In addition, the intervals occur going across the width of the neck as well as up and down the length of it. At first it can be a little like 3D chess. Complicated.

So, for many of the illustrations, a keyboard is best because its physical layout makes it easier to visualize and illustrate many of the concepts and it shows all of the same measurements. In addition, everything is color-coded. There is a single line of notes to consider, not six.

3 - Intervals: Part One

Almost everyone is familiar with the appearance of a piano keyboard. White keys and black keys arranged in a pattern that repeats from one end of the keyboard to the other. The notes are **always** in the same alphabetical sequence.

These letter names (naturals) identify the white keys and those are the only ones we need at this point.

Everything illustrated on a keyboard works exactly the same way on a guitar, mandolin, or banjo as it does on a keyboard. The fretboard on most string instruments is dark colored, often black. If you were to take nearly any fretted instrument and paint the frets white that are the naturals on any string (A, B, C, D, E, F and G), the resulting black and white pattern would be identical to the black and white pattern on a keyboard. Each string can be thought of as an individual keyboard. Find **E-F-G-A-B-C-D-E-F** anywhere on the keyboard and compare the sequence and pattern to the same notes shown on the fretboard.

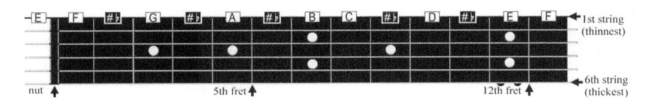

For this first look at intervals, we don't need to use the black notes. Soon, when we measure and define these intervals precisely, they will be counted, but just for now we'll ignore them.

There are only seven intervals that especially concern us at this point. They're named a "**second**," a "**third**," a "**fourth**," a "**fifth**," a "**sixth**," a "**seventh**," and an "**octave**." 2nd, 3rd, 4th, 4th, 5th, 7th, and octave.

It's just a matter of counting the natural note names to define the interval. Count to three and you've got a 3rd. Count to five and you've got a 5th. There's no such thing as a 1st because an interval describes distance. Just as you really can't go **from** one inch **to** one inch on a ruler, from middle C to middle C is no distance… therefore, no interval.

There are music theorists who would quite correctly insist that from middle C to middle C technically is an interval called a unison. Fortunately, they are not here, so we don't have to discuss it.

For those unbending and meticulous music theorists who feel this should be examined in detail, I'll quote one of my favorite musical experts, Dave Barry, who on several occasions has said "Neener, neener, neener."

One other thing… I'll be talking about moving "**up**" and "**down**" the keyboard and the neck of the guitar and this has nothing to do with gravity. I'm referring to the relative pitch of the notes. On a piano to go "**up**" means to go from left to right, and to go "**down**" means to go from right to left. If you go **up**, you get a higher note; if you go **down**, you get a lower note.

On all fretted instruments, to go **up the neck to a higher note**, you'll move your hand **toward your body**. To go **down the neck to a lower note**, you'll move your hand **away from your body**.

If you move to a **higher string**, you will move to a string that is **closer to the floor**. If you move to a **lower string**, you'll move to a string that is **closer to your chin**. Seems down-side-up, I know, but that's the way it is. Get used to it.

We'll start with the largest "basic" interval, an octave.

When you go from any note to the very next note of the same name, that's called an "**octave**."

Look at the keyboard below. Start with any white key. Like E for instance. Count all the white keys in sequence until you get to the same letter you started with. **Count 1,2,3,4,5,6,7,8. Say E,F,G,A,B,C,D,E.** An octave always includes all seven of the letter names with the one on each end being the same.

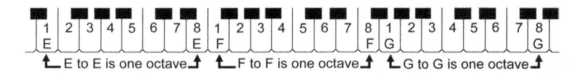

Here is an example of the eight natural in an octave played on a single string. Moving 12 frets on a single string on just about any fretted instrument produces an octave.

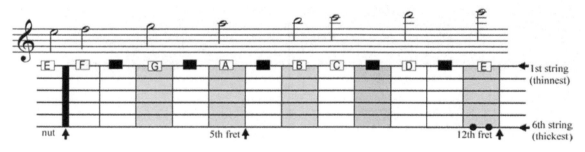

Remember "Over the Rainbow" from the Wizard of Oz? The first two notes when Judy Garland sang "Some – where" is an octave. The first two notes in "Take Me Out to the Ballgame" are an octave apart.

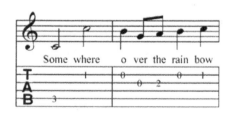

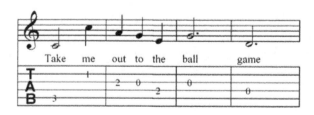

Something that is possible on fretted instruments as well as keyboards is the ability to play two notes simultaneously. This can't be done on a trumpet, for instance. Playing two notes at the same time on string instruments is sometimes called a "double-stop."

The next illustration shows double-stop octaves being played on the 6th and 4th strings, skipping over the 5th string. It's useful to learn to recognize the visual appearance of intervals on the page as well as on the neck of your instrument. Try playing this on your guitar using your thumb and a finger on your picking hand to "pinch" both strings at the same time.

When shown on the staff, an octave almost always has one note that appears on a line, and the other note is on a space. It you count the lines and spaces on the staff (including both end-notes) you'll count eight. Surprise, surprise, surprise! Humor me, count the examples I've shown.

Same drill, this time on the 5th and 3rd strings. Notice that your fingers keep the same relative position on the fretboard as they had on the previous example.

I see this octave as kind of a medium-angle diagonal line, pointing up the neck, skipping one fret and one string. I tend to use my first finger and my ring finger, or my middle finger and pinky on my fret hand for these "octave double-stops."

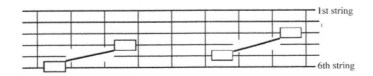

Just keep moving across the neck to the 4th and 2nd strings. Notice the "angle" changes, this time with two frets between the notes. I use my first finger and pinky for this one.

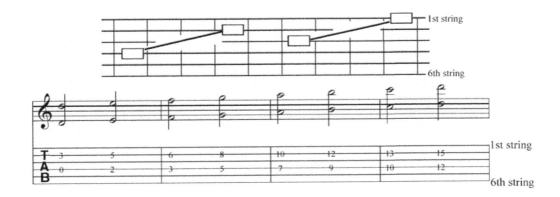

Here are the octaves on the 1st and 3rd string. These span two frets, as shown on the previous page.

Just because I show these examples using only the "natural" notes… the white keys on a keyboard… you're not limited to the notes on those frets.

The preceding examples show octaves that are played by using every other string: 6th and 4th strings together, 5th and 3rd strings together, 4th and 2nd strings together, and the 3rd and 1st strings together. You can also play double-stop octaves by skipping two strings and using the 6th and 3rd strings together, the 5th and 2nd string together, and the 4th and 1st together.

Spend some time getting accustomed to playing octave double-stops. Not only is it a cool sound, the fingering position becomes very useful for playing chords, scales and other things. Ten hours invested into becoming acquainted with this technique is well worth your time. As mentioned in "**Note Names**," octaves are also useful in tuning stringed instruments.

OK… that's about it for octaves. Make sure you get it before you continue. Play some octaves and look at them on the staff. Close your eyes while you play and listen to the sound. Learn to connect the sound that you hear with the shape of your hand and the dots on the page.

Moving right along…

On any keyboard, begin with any white key; **count it as 1**. Then take the white key nearest to it (either direction) **count it as 2**. You've just measured the distance between those two notes as an interval of a **2nd**. It doesn't matter whether you go up or down, the process is the same.

Remember, use the white keys only… skip the black ones as if they don't exist. In fact, how about if I just hide them for now…

So, on our keyboard if you play any white key, and then the white key nearest to it, up or down, you've played an interval referred to as a 2nd. I'll start with an E since it matches a guitar string.

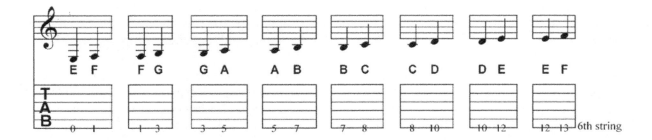

Notice how the notes move up the staff. From a line to a space is a 2nd, from a space to a line is a 2nd, etc.

From **D** up to the next **E** is a 2nd and from **E** up to **F** is a 2nd. From **F** up to **G** is a 2nd and from **G** up to **A** is a 2nd. From **A** up to **B** is a 2nd, and from **B** up to **C** is a 2nd. Turn around and count down the other way and it's the same… from **C** down to **B** is a 2nd, from **B** down to **A** is a 2nd, from **A** down to **G** is a 2nd, etc.

All of the intervals are found and named in the same simple, straightforward manner.

Begin with any white key and count it as 1, count the one next to it as 2, count the next note as 3, count the one next to it as 4, and the interval between the two notes on the ends is a 4th. 1,2,3,4,5 and you have a 5th. 1,2,3,4,5,6 is a 6th. 1,2,3,4,5,6,7 is a 7th.

Just like octaves, all the intervals can be played on one string or on adjacent strings.

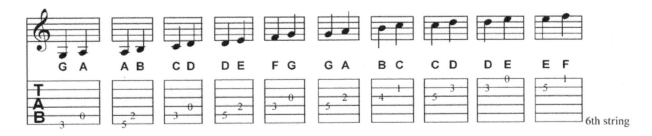

Next is 3rds.

There are different varieties of 2nds and 3rds, and I haven't presented quite enough information at this point to offer a sensible explanation of why they are different. Coming soon to theaters near you, in "**Intervals: Part Three.**" Going up, the interval between **C** and **E** is a 3rd. Going down, the interval between **E** and **C** is a 3rd. The interval between **A** and **C** (up) or **C** and **A** (down) is a 3rd. Between **E** and **G** (up) is 3rd. **G** and **E** (down) is a 3rd.

On the next page you can see how 3rds are spaced on the staff; 2nds are most often shown as being on an adjacent line and space; and 3rds can usually be recognized at a glance because they frequently appear on the staff as space to space with one line in between, or line to line with one space in between.

And, as always, learn to recognize the "shapes" and "designs" and "patterns" that your fingers make moving on the fretboard when playing these intervals.

Thirds, 4ths, 5ths, and octaves are important and useful intervals. Spend some time playing these intervals as they are shown on the next few pages. Memorize this stuff. Know what they look like and what they sound like.

Seeing intervals is easy. Learn to *hear* these intervals and know their names. It's not real hard, but it does take practice. Hum the tones when you play them. Close your eyes while you play them and listen. Trying it once or twice is *not* practice. As always, play each of these examples several thousand times before moving on.

Well, maybe you don't have to play it that many times before you continue. Do it a few times now, and make this little drill a part of your practice for a while. This is a sound you'll hear a lot, so learn to recognize it and learn to play it. The first three examples below are illustrated as harmonic intervals. The last one shows the same 3rds as melodic intervals. These can be lots of fun after you mess with them for a while.

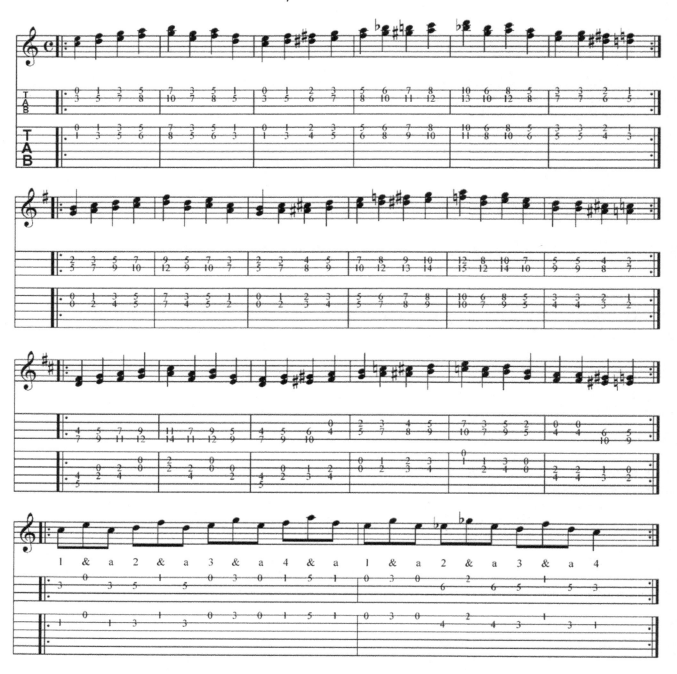

3 - Intervals: Part One

Reflections

"Approach your guitar intelligently, and if there are limits, don't deny them.
Work within your restrictions.
Some things you can do better than others, some things you can't do as well.
So accentuate the positive."
Chet Atkins

Asked why they like rock music, one high school student said
"I like rock music because you don't have to pay attention in order to get it."

Bach opens a vista to the universe.
After experiencing him, people feel there is meaning to life after all.
Helmut Walcha

"Bear in mind, if you are going to accomplish anything,
that your success does not depend upon the brilliancy and the impetuosity with which you take hold,
but upon the ever lasting and sanctified bulldoggedness
with which you hang on after you have taken hold."
Dr. A. B. Meldrum

"Begin with the end in mind."
Dr. Stephen Covey

"Beethoven can write music, thank God. He can do nothing else."
Ludwig van Beethoven

"Be true to it. Every music has it's own soul."
Ray Charles

"Beyond a wholesome discipline, be gentle with yourself.
You are a child of the universe, no less than the trees or the stars; you have a right to be here."
From Disiderata

"Big shots are only little shots who keep shooting."
Christopher Morley

"But the moment you turn a corner and you see another straight stretch ahead,
there comes some further challenge to your ambition."
Oliver Wendell Holmes

"Classical music is one of the best things that ever happened to mankind.
If you get introduced to it in the right way, it becomes your friend for life."
Yo-Yo-Ma

"Consider the postage stamp:
Its usefulness consists in the ability to stick to one thing till it gets there."
Josh Billings

This is NOT the intro to "Brown Eyed Girl"

Brown Eyed Girl by Mr. Van Morrison… it was a big hit when it first came out in 1967, and people still love it. It's one of those rare tunes that crosses the age barriers, too. Jim Averitt and I were playing a little function at Gallatin Gateway Elementary School in 2004, and a couple of kids in the 4th grade requested it so they could get up and sing it with us. They knew every word and every riff.

So, I made a few changes to avoid infringing on the copyright. This little song of mine titled "For My Pal Hal," uses exactly the same notes in the same order, but this is in 6/8 time. See page 84 for another take on this riff.

It's transposed to five different keys. You don't need to know what "key" or "transpose" means to play these. We'll get to that in "**The Key**." Maybe you know the chords, maybe not. If not, you will soon. They're here when you're ready.

3 - Intervals: Part One

There are six strings on the guitar and they are separated by a little more than ¼ inch.

Since you've just played the 3rds, you noticed that there is also a musical interval between each pair of adjacent strings.

As you know, the string names starting with the 6th string, (the thickest one) are EADGBE.

Here are the same six notes as they appear/sound on a keyboard.

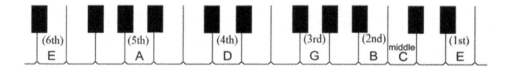

The 6th string is E, the 5th string is A.

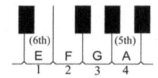

E **up** to A is a 4th, E, F, G, A. Count 1,2,3,4. The interval between the two strings is a 4th.

Can you hum a few notes of the "Wedding March?" You know, the part that goes "Here comes the bride." The interval between "**here**" and "**comes**" is a 4th. The "Bridal Chorus" is from "Loehengrin" (1841) by Richard Wagner. Mark Twain playfully insisted "Wagner's music is really a lot better than it sounds." The first notes of Auld Lang Syne have the same sound.

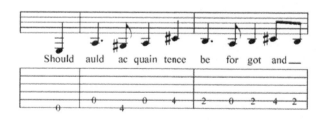

Associating a familiar tune with a specific interval and humming or singing these intervals while you play them is probably the quickest way to get them locked into your musical memory. A up to D (5th string to the 4th string) is a 4th. "Here comes the bride"… same sound.

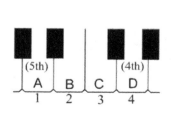

D up to G (4th string to the 3rd string) is a 4th. "Here comes the bride."

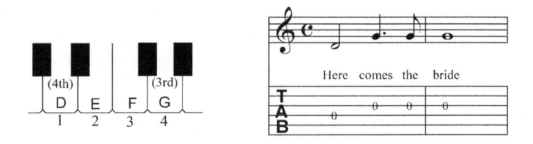

Here's a switch. From G to B (3rd string to the 2nd string) is a 3rd. There's a tune many people know that can illustrate a 3rd. "**Are** you **sleep**—ing, **are** you **sleep**—ing, Brother John, Brother John?" The interval between "Are" and "**Sleep**" is a 3rd. "**Sleep**" down to "—**ing**" is the same 3rd. The opening notes of Beethoven's Fifth Symphony are a 3rd. Ba ba ba baam.

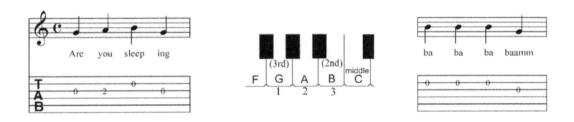

Finally, B to E (2nd string to the 1st string) is a 4th again.

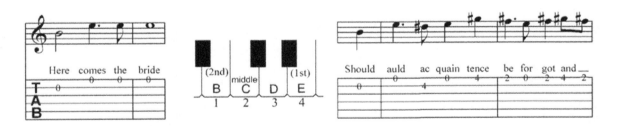

It's useful to remember that the interval between most of the open strings on a guitar is a 4th. This will come up again in subsequent chapters and is a piece of information you'll use a lot.

The single exception is the interval between the G string and the B string, which is a 3rd.

In the last few years, guitars with seven strings have become popular. The additional string is thicker than the traditional 6th string and is tuned to B, a 4th lower than the 6th string E.

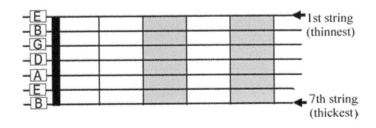

Parallel Fourths

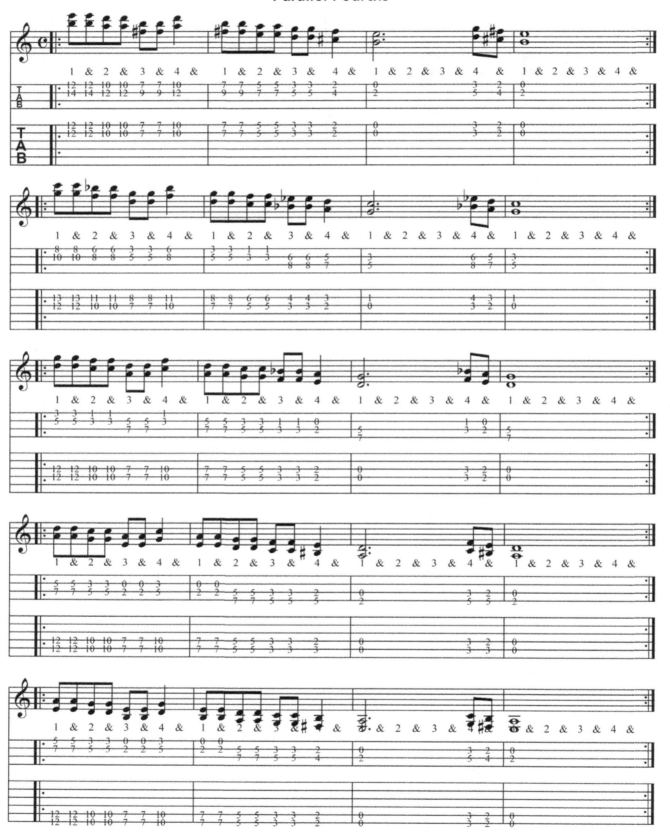

3 - Intervals: Part One

Reflections

"Country music is three chords and the truth."
Harlan Howard

*"Decide what you want, decide what you are willing to exchange for it.
Establish your priorities and go to work."*
H. L. Hungt

*"Destiny is not a matter of chance, it is a matter of choice.
It is not a thing to be waited for, it is a thing to be achieved."*
William Jennings Bryan

"Difficult things take a long time, impossible things a little longer.
Unknown

"Difficulties increase the nearer we approach the goal."
Johann Wolfgang Von Goethe

"Discipline is remembering what you want."
David Campbell

*"Do not be desirous of having things done quickly.
Do not look at small advantages.
Desire to have things done quickly prevents their being done thoroughly.
Looking at small advantages prevents great affairs from being accomplished."*
Confucius

"Do not let what you can't do interfere with what you can do."
John Wooden

*"Don't be afraid to give your best to what seemingly are small jobs.
Every time you conquer one it makes you that much stronger.
If you do the little jobs well, the big ones will tend to take care of themselves."*
Dale Carnegie

"Don't be discouraged. It's often the last key in the bunch that opens the lock."
Unknown

*"Don't let the fear of the time it will take to accomplish something
stand in the way of your doing it.
The time will pass anyway.
We might just as well put that passing time to the best possible use."*
Earl Nightingale

"Dreams are extremely important. You can't do it unless you imagine it."
George Lucas

Next is 5^{ths}.

Major and minor chords contain a total of three notes and two of them are separated by a 5th. When you play the exercises for 5^{ths} you're playing 2/3 of the notes in these chords. (Chords... coming soon.)

Remember that most of the strings on a guitar are separated by a 4th? Well, mandolins and violins are tuned in 5^{ths}.

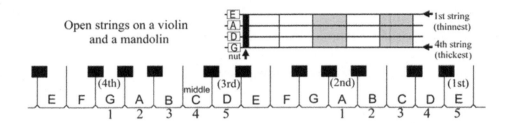

Violas and mandolas are also tuned in 5^{ths}. The lowest note on these two instruments is a C, followed by G, D and A.

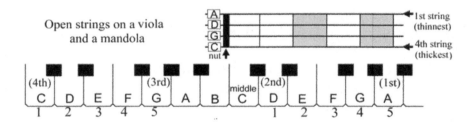

Cellos and mandocellos are also tuned in 5^{ths} with a C for the lowest note, but an octave lower than mandolas and violas.

You may have heard of "power chords." Gotta wonder... who named this? A power chord is frequently played using three notes... two of them an octave apart, and a note in between that is a 5th above the lowest note. If you play the exercise shown on the next page, you will learn five different ways to play all 12 power chords. I'll define "chord" and tell you how to name them in "**Major and Minor Chords**," but I thought you should know that you can learn to play a lot of chords right now. 12 x 5 = 60. As yourself, "Is this worth an hour of practice?"

The 5th is an important interval. Practice it. Learn to hear it, as a melodic interval and a harmonic interval. Play it and sing it, too.

As always, take the songbook you're working with and label every interval you're able to identify. Look for harmonic intervals and melodic intervals. Look for 2^{nds}, 3^{rds}, 4^{ths}, 5^{ths}, 6^{ths}, 7^{ths}, and octaves. If you run across intervals larger than an octave, plan on taking a second look at those after you've read the chapter on "**Beyond Major and Minor Chords**."

Intervals are the same on any instrument. On a guitar, on a piano, or a trumpet... clarinet, harp, banjo, or oboe... whatever... they're the same. The notes are produced by a different mechanism, so a bassoon makes a different noise than a viola, but the notes themselves and the intervals are the same on all instruments.

Asian and Indian musicians divide an octave differently than we do here in the West, so this doesn't always apply to instruments from other culture; but for the majority of the instruments, we're likely to come in contact with it's true.

Fifths, Another Name for Power Chords

The rhythm here is a little bit tricky to read. Use the counting drill where you tap two fingers… left-right-left-right, etc., on the 8th notes. Go slow, tap your fingers and say BOP BOP BOP or something at the right time. Think Deep Purple, "Smoke On The Water." The first BOP in the second measure happens on the & of 1. Two tied 8th notes are played as a single quarter note.

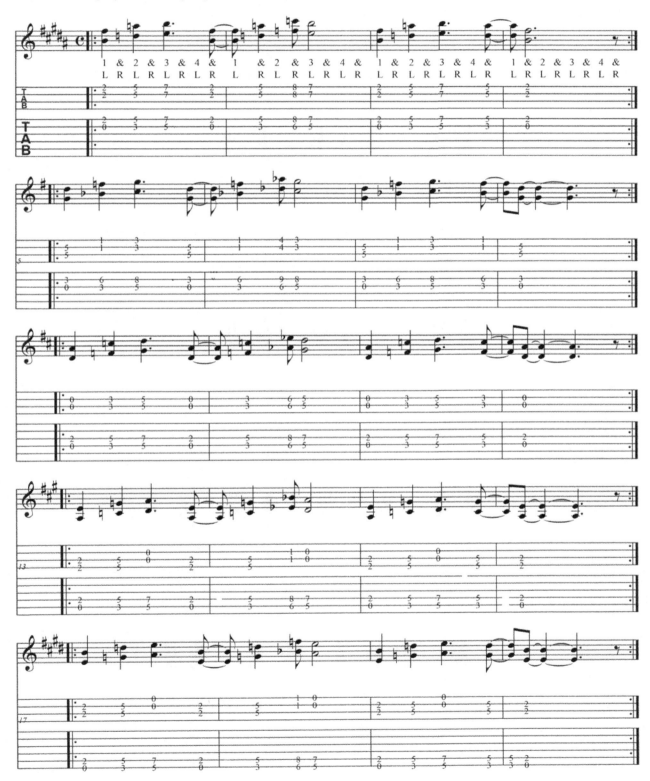

Inverting Intervals

In a playing context, this is a fairly advanced concept with regard to how it is used.

But it is an idea that is quite easy to comprehend and this happens to be an appropriate place to introduce the concept.

What I'll do is show the mechanics of it without trying to explain too much about how it is used.

It's like knowing two different trails that both lead to the same destination and one is shorter.

For example, if for some reason you need to know the name of the note that is a 7th below C, what you have to do is think backward through the alphabet, starting with C. Try it.

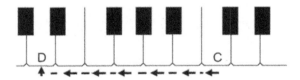

It's not exceptionally difficult. Passing backward from A to G is the trickiest part for a lot of people.

Easy as that may be, it is loads easier to go up a 2nd. You still get the same note name and there's no drawkcab ← tebahpla ← ot ← kniht ← tuoba ←.

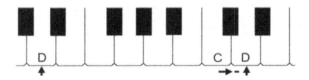

Anyway, the magic number is nine. Up a 2nd gets you to the same note name that going down a 7th does. 2+7=9.

Up a 3rd or down a 6th. 6+3=9.

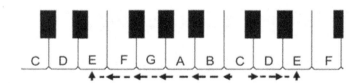

Down a 4th or up a 5th. 4+5=9.

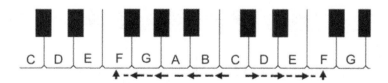

Be aware of this concept of inverting intervals. When you're playing it can be a useful tool for finding your way around the neck.

Reflections

"Drugs have nothing to do with the creation of music.
In fact, drugs are dumb and self-indulgent.
Kind of like sucking your thumb."
Courtney Love

"Egos and personalities scream… while the soul whispers."
Elmore Leonard

"Even if you're on the right track, you'll get run over if you just sit there."
Will Rogers

"Everybody has a different kind of talent
and a different timetable as to when they develop."
Itzhak Perlman

"Every kind of music is good, except the boring kind."
Gioacchino Rossini, composer of The Barber of Seville, William Tell, Cinderella

"Everyone is trying to accomplish something big,
not realizing that life is made up of little things."
Frank Clark

"Everyone was using tiny brushes and doing watercolors,
while Jimi Hendrix was painting galactic scenes in Cinemascope.
We are working in a field of mystical resonance, sound and vibration…
that's what makes people cry, laugh and feel their hair stand up"
Carlos Santana

"Everyone who got where he is has had to begin where he was."
Robert Louis Stevenson

"Every worthwhile accomplishment, big or little, has its stages
of drudgery and triumph; a beginning, a struggle and a victory."
Ghandi

"Fall seven times, stand up eight."
Japanese Proverb

"Finish each day and be done with it. You have done what you could.
Some blunders and absurdities no doubt crept in; forget them as soon as you can.
Tomorrow is a new day; begin it well and serenely
and with too high a spirit to be encumbered with your old nonsense."
Ralph Waldo Emerson

"First say to yourself what you would be; and then do what you have to do."
Epictetus

This isn't the intro to Brown Eyed Girl either... but it's closer

As I mentioned, I've been playing Brown Eyed Girl for years. What I didn't know until recently is that I've been playing it wrong. Maybe nobody else noticed either. This is how I learned it and it's sound is very similar to the riff on the original recording, which was played using 3rds. My incorrect version is a good example of inverting intervals, because I learned to play it as a 6th. I also changed the last two bars completely for this example. Lots of the notes are played on the & of the beats, or syncopated. It can be tricky at first. Go slow, tap the 8th notes, da daa daa da daa. Say it first, then play it. I think the riff was played by Eric Gale or Al Giorgioni. According to Mr. Morrison, he has never received ANY royalties for this tune, due to a shady contract he signed without legal assistance, which left him responsible for all recording costs and gave all rights to Bang Records, then owned by Bert Berns.

3 - Intervals: Part One

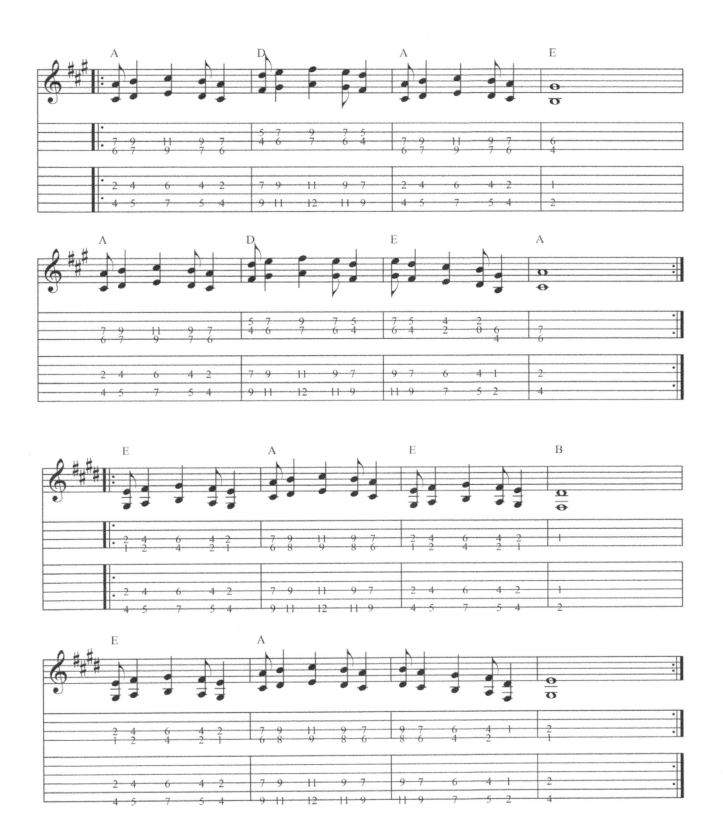

3 - Intervals: Part One

The Blues Turnaround

Here's another useful phrase that uses 6th. It's probably most commonly encountered in blues tunes, but it shows up in lots of other styles, too. It's versatile… you'll hear it used as an intro, ending, and in the middle. We'll get to definitions for "chords" and "keys" soon. You don't need them to play these things.

Lots of songs have a verse/chorus type of structure and the chords will often be a little different between the two sections. Usually the last chord in the verse sort of leads to the first chord in the chorus, and the last chord in the chorus leads to the first chord in the verse. Circular. Blues tunes are frequently written in a 12-bar form that just repeats. Lyrically, the verse and chorus will be different but the chords are the same. A turnaround happens at the end of a 12-bar phrase and it leads your ear back to the first chord in the first measure. Notice that this one starts on the second beat. Rest-&-a-2-&-a-3-&-a-4-&-a- whole note.

I searched around a bit and the word "turnaround" doesn't seem to have an exact definition, even though it's used a lot. "A one or two-bar phrase at the end of a verse or chorus" combines three different definitions that I found.

Again, I showed it in different keys so you can try it using different combinations of strings. The last one at the bottom right isn't descending 6th, but it's a variation that is common. Notice that the first two notes are separated by a 4th. The top note doesn't move, the bottom note descends in half-steps, and by the end, it's opened up to a 6th. These all resolve to the chord indicated by the key, so it's more of an ending.

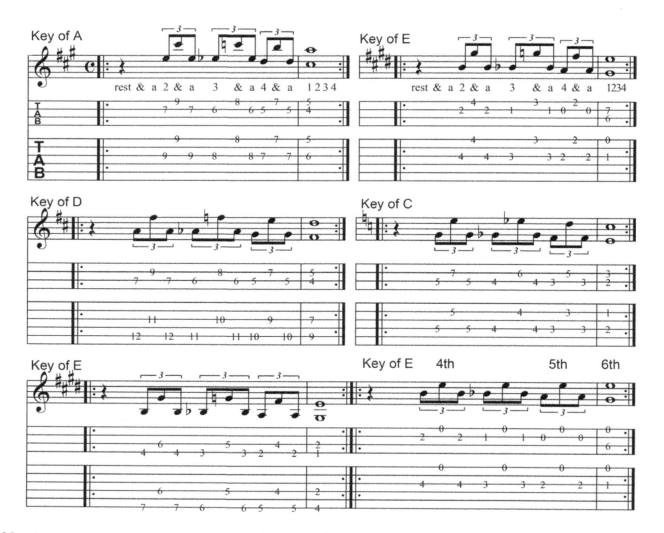

3 - Intervals: Part One

Twinkling Around with Intervals

When two notes are played at the same time, we hear what is called harmony. In these examples, the highest notes make the melody of our favorite tune, "Twinkle Twinkle Little Star." The lower note is a harmony note. The first example, "Twinkling Seconds" does not sound especially pleasant to western ears. Harmonies that sound like "wrong notes" are called "dissonance." Some like it, some don't. Well, actually, most people don't. At any rate, it isn't "wrong" unless you were trying to do something else. The other examples use 3rds, 4ths, 5ths, 6ths and octaves, and will sound much sweeter than the 2nds.

Twinkling Seconds

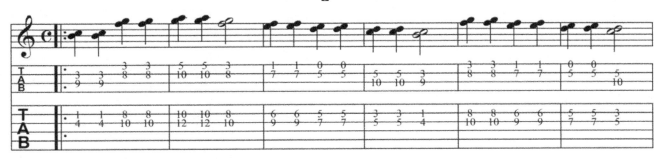

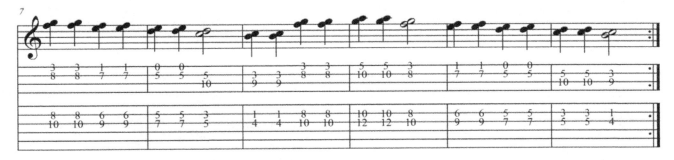

Twinkling Thirds and Fourths

Twinkling Fifths and Sixths

Twinkling Octaves

3 - Intervals: Part One

3^{rds} and 4^{ths} ... Key of A

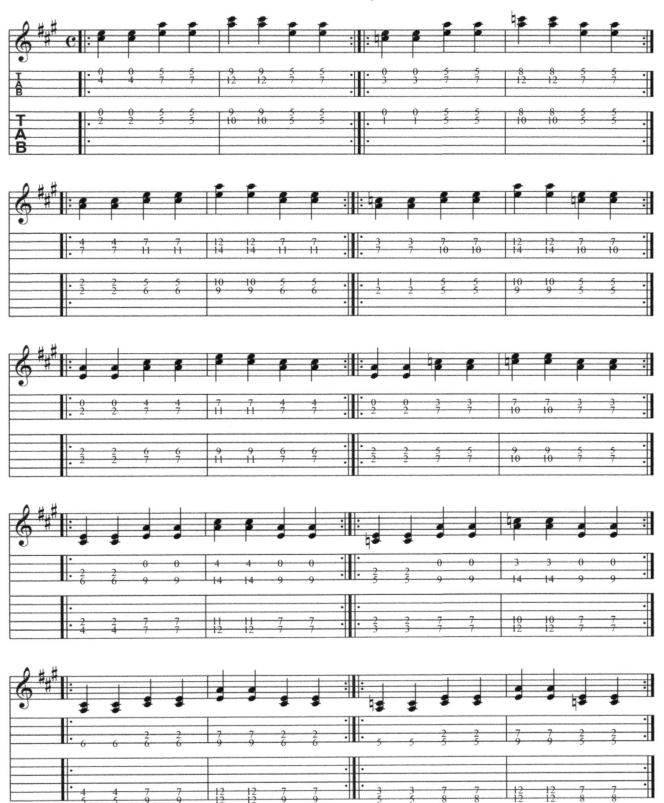

3^{rds} and 4^{ths} ... Key of B

3 - Intervals: Part One

3^{rds} and 4^{ths} ... Key of C

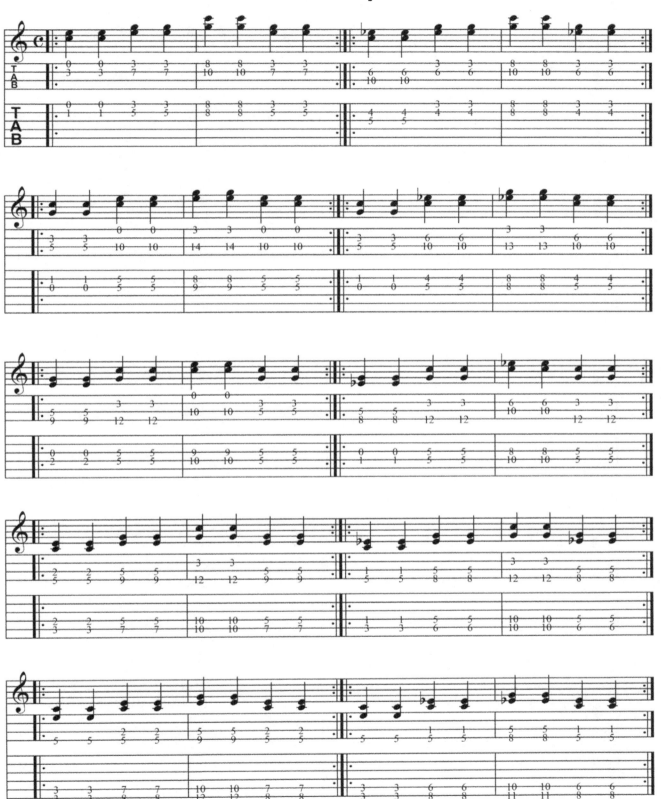

3^{rds} and 4^{ths} ... Key of D

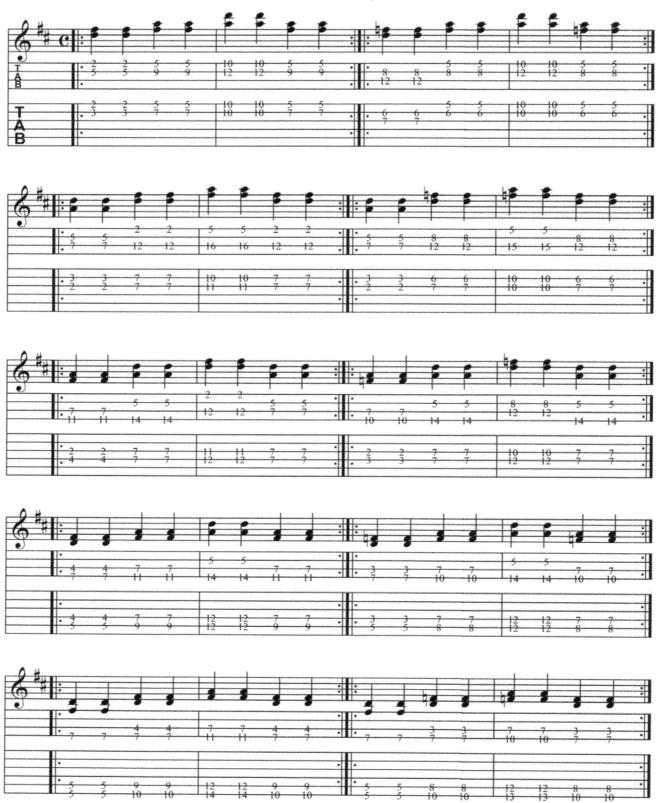

3 - Intervals: Part One

3ʳᵈˢ and 4ᵗʰˢ … Key of E

3^{rds} and 4^{ths} ... Key of F

3 - Intervals: Part One

3^{rds} and 4^{ths} ... Key of G

Intervals: Part One

1. Notes are heard as being "higher" or "lower." Gravity plays an important role in the "elevation" of notes.
   True   False

2. Intervals on saxophones and other wind instruments are different than intervals on pianos and guitars and other stringed instruments.   **True   False**

3. If you play a note on a piano, then play a note that is higher, the second note will be to the _____ of the first note.

4. If you play a note on a piano, then play a note that is lower, the second note will be to the _____ of the first note.

5. On a fretted instrument, the notes become _____ as you move your hand close to your body.

6. On a fretted instrument, the notes become _____ as you move your hand further away from your body.

7. On guitars, mandolins, electric basses, the highest string is the one _____ the floor in a normal playing position.

8. On guitars, mandolins, electric basses, the lowest string is the one _____ your chin in a normal playing position.

9. When notes are played simultaneously, the interval is called a _____
   _____

10. Identify the following intervals:

   2nd 5th 7th ___ ___ ___ ___ ___ ___ ___ ___ ___ ___ ___ ___ ___ ___

11. When the notes are played in sequence one after the other the interval is known as a
    _____ _____

12. Identify the following intervals:

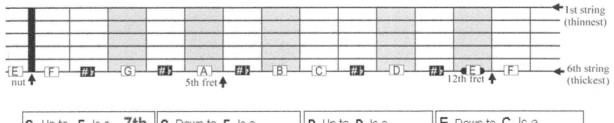

G Up to F Is a **7th**	G Down to F Is a	D Up to D Is a	E Down to C Is a
D Up to B Is a **6th**	D Down to B Is a	C Up to C Is a	B Down to E Is a
A Up to C Is a **3rd**	A Down to C Is a	G Up to A Is a	F Down to D Is a
E Up to F Is a **2nd**	E Down to F Is a	D Up to G Is a	A Down to F Is a
B Up to G Is a	B Down to G Is a	E Up to G Is a	G Down to B Is a
F Up to A Is a	F Down to A Is a	B Up to F Is a	F Down to B Is a
C Up to E Is a	C Down to E Is a	C Up to B Is a	A Down to E Is a
G Up to D Is a	G Down to D Is a	F Up to G Is a	D Down to F Is a
E Up to E Is a **oct**	E Down to E Is a	A Up to D Is a	C Down to G Is a
D Up to A Is a	D Down to A Is a	G Up to E Is a	E Down to B Is a
F Up to E Is a	F Down to E Is a	B Up to D Is a	B Down to A Is a
A Up to B Is a	A Down to B Is a	C Up to A Is a	G Down to C Is a

Reflections

*"From the metaphysical point of view there is nothing that can touch the formless
except the art of music which in itself is formless."*
Hazrat Inayat Hkan

"Go for the moon. If you don't get it, you'll still be heading for a star."
Willis Reed

"Goals allow you to control the direction of change in your favor."
Brian Tracy

"Great art is as irrational as great music. It is mad with its own loveliness."
George Jean Nathan

*"Great music is that which penetrates the ear with facility and leaves the memory
with difficulty. Magical music never leaves the memory."*
Sir Thomas Beecham,
created the London Philharmonic & Royal Philharmonic orchestras

"Great things are not done by impulse, but by a series of small things brought together."
Vincent Van Gogh

"Happy are those who dream dreams and are willing to pay the price to make them come true."
Unknown

*"Having an exciting destination is like setting a needle in your compass.
From then on, the compass knows only one point… its ideal.
It will faithfully guide you there through the darkest nights and fiercest storms."*
Daniel Boone

"He conquers who endures."
Persius

"He was a Titan, wrestling with the Gods."
Richard Wagner, commenting on the music of Ludwig van Beethoven.

"High achievement always takes place in a framework of high expectation."
Jack Kinder

"How monotonous the sounds of the forest would be if the music came only from the Top Ten birds."
Dan Bennett

"I am always doing things I can't do. That's how I learn to do them."
Pablo Picasso

"I am not discouraged, because every wrong attempt discarded is another step forward."
Thomas Alva Edison

Intervals: Part Two | Chapter 4

OK… now it's time to include the black notes, otherwise known as sharps and flats.

This symbol **#** is pronounced "sharp."

This symbol ♭ is pronounced "flat."

On a keyboard it's easy to see them. The seven white notes are called naturals (A,B,C,D,E,F and G), and the five black ones are called sharps and flats. That's a total of 12 different tones. That's all there are. You won't be discovering any new ones until you become acquainted with Ravi Shankar or other Asian and Indian musicians.

For example, the Persian scale begins with the same octave we've been discussing and divides it into 43 different tones. We cut our musical pie into 12 tones, theirs if cut into 43. Same pie. Those are some thin slices.

The Persian Piano has red, yellow, blue, and orange keys as well as black and white keys and weighs close to three tons. The keyboard is 17-1/2 feet long. You have to wear roller skates to play it.

Only kidding, there's no Persian Piano, but the 43-tone octave is real. There is another scale used in Asia that begins with the same octave and divides it into only seven tones.

A piano is "color coded" and that makes it easy to see the naturals and easy to talk about them. So for now, just to have a visual reference (our "keyboard"), we'll continue to call them "black" notes and "white" notes.

There's really no such thing as "black" notes and "white" notes except on a keyboard. All the other instruments use exactly the same 12 notes only without the convenient colors. The sounds are the same, the names are the same, just no colors. Too bad… it's really kind of handy.

"Inches" describe a distance between two points on a ruler. Basic distances on a ruler are called inches, and there are 12 inches in one foot. And every rule or tape measure is the same… an inch is the same no matter where you get your ruler.

No matter where you begin on the ruler, 12 inches is a foot. From zero to 12 is a foot, and from one to 13 is a foot and from two to 14 is a foot, three to 15, etc.

Intervals describe a distance between two notes the same way that inches describe a distance on a ruler.

In music, the smallest interval (distance) is called a **half step**. And to continue to use the ruler analogy, there just happens to be 12 half steps in an octave.

A half step is the same musical distance on every instrument just as a half inch is the same on any measuring device.

Look at the keyboard and notice the numbers just above the keys. They don't mean anything, it's just an illustration to count the half steps in an octave. After it gets to 12, it starts over again.

In this instance, the #1 corresponds to E, 2 corresponds to F, 4 is G, 6 is A, etc. I could have started numbering at any note, black or white, and it would not make any difference.

On a guitar, a mandolin, a banjo, a bass, etc, moving from any fret to the next fret on the same string is always a half step. In addition, sequential half steps can be played on adjacent strings just like the other intervals. It's a bit of a stretch, perhaps, depending on the size of your hand, but it's there. It's still (1) half step from the C on the 6th string to the C# on the 5th string, even though it looks farther. Appearances can be deceptive.

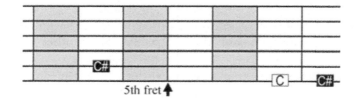

"**A**" is a note. "**B**" is a note. "**C**" is a note. "**D**" is a note.

(pronounced "sharp") is *not* a note. ♭ (pronounced "flat") is *not* a note.

Those symbols can be thought of as arrows pointing in a direction… up or down.

On a keyboard, up (#) is to the right and down (♭) is to the left.

On a string, toward your body is up (#), away from your body is down (♭).

Up goes higher (#) in pitch, and down goes lower (♭) in pitch.

If someone says, "That note is a little sharp," it means "Careful with that axe, Eugene, you're likely to cut yourself."

No. Saying a note is a little bit sharp means that it's a little too high. Loosen the string.

If someone says, "It's a bit flat" it means that it's too low. Tighten it up.

When a # (sharp) is attached to a note on paper, it indicates that you go higher in pitch **by an interval of (1) half step**. When a ♭ (flat) is attached to a note it indicates that you go lower **by an interval of (1) half step**. # is up. ♭ is down. # is higher. ♭ is lower.

Alone, sharps and flats don't name notes. To help name a note they must be used in conjunction with a **Natural**.

A	B	C	D	E	F	G
A#	B#	C#	D#	E#	F#	G#
A♭	B♭	C♭	D♭	E♭	F♭	G♭

4 - Intervals: Part Two

Look at the keyboard illustration below. The white key all the way to the left is "**C natural.**" The next white key is "**D natural.**" And… there is a black note in between **C** and **D.**

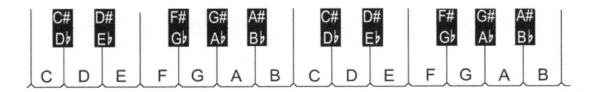

All the black notes have two names. When a note has two names, it is said to be "enharmonic." Maybe Chrysti the Wordsmith knows why. I don't. (**www.wordsmithradio.org**) Chrysti is an accused accomplice in a cool local band called "The Awesome Polka Babes." In any single piece of music the enharmonic notes will always be called one or the other. **A#** or **B♭**… **C#** or **D♭**… **D#** or **E♭**… **F#** or **G♭**… **G#** or **A♭**. Well, maybe not always, but 98% of the time, for sure.

You'll also notice that when sharps and flats are drawn on the staff, the symbol precedes the note, but it is spoken the other way around. Sorry, I can't offer any explanation for that, either.

Tablature indicates C# with the number 4 written on the 5th string. There are no # or ♭ symbols needed on tablature.

We talk about the enharmonic notes as being "between" the naturals. It's easy to see on a fretboard.

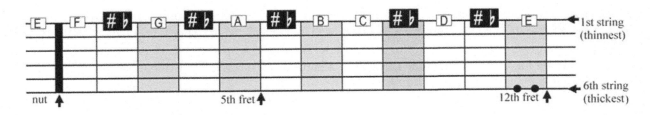

You can call the black one in between F and G "**F#,**" because it's a single half step above F natural, or you can call it "**G♭**" because it's a half step below G natural.

There are rules that determine whether "flat or sharp" is the correct name, but until you understand a bit about scale structure and keys, the explanation won't make much sense, so we'll wait.

Meanwhile, back at the farm... there's a black key in between G and A. It can be called **G#** because it's (1) half step above G, or it can be called **A♭** because it's (1) half step below the A. There's a black key in between A and B. It can be called **A#** because it's (1) half step above A, or it can be called **B♭** because it's (1) half step below the B. There's a black key in between C and D. It can be called **C#** because it's (1) half step above C, or it can be called **D♭** because it's (1) half step below the D. There's a black key in between D and E. It can be called **D#** because it's (1) half step above D, or it can be called **E♭** because it's (1) half step below the E. If this is a new idea for you, I suggest you read this paragraph aloud a couple of times.

Go back to the fretboard illustration on *page 3*. You'll notice that there are two places where there are two "white" notes right next to each other with no black note in between. Between **E** and **F** and between **B** and **C** there are no black notes. From B to C is a half step, and from E to F is a half step.

There are occasions when it is correct to refer to these white keys as **B#, C♭, E# or F♭**, and it has absolutely nothing to do with what color the key happens to be.

Sharp # and Flat ♭ indicate direction, not color!!

OK! That is all the note names there are... seven "naturals," **A B C D E F G**, and 10 "enharmonics" (five ♭ flats and five # sharps).

There are occasions that double flats ♭♭ or double sharps ## are required to satisfy certain "rules of theory." There is no way to explain those rules at this point, (we'll get to that in "**The Key**") but you should be aware that you might encounter ♭♭ or ##, and it's not a misprint. Usually, when a double sharp is needed, the symbol "**x**" is used instead of **##**. Two sharps means go up two half steps. Two flats means go down two half steps. If you look at it on a piano keyboard C**x** = D and G♭♭ = F.

Sharps and flats are also sometimes referred to as "accidentals." (You could check with Chrysti for a definition of accidental, or go to this fine online music dictionary; *OxfordReference.com*)

There is one other "accidental." It's called a "natural" and it looks like this... ♮.

A natural tells you to move a note by (1) half step, just like sharp and flat. This one is difficult to fully explain at this point, but this is the right place for the attempt. A truly correct explanation of how a "natural" functions requires some comprehension on the part of the explainee of what a "musical key" is, and we're not anywhere near that yet. An incomplete explanation that works (at this level) is that a natural means "go from a black note to a white note." A natural cancels a flat or a sharp. A natural can either raise a flatted note by (1) half step, or lower a sharpened note by (1) half step. It is used for the same reasons that you would use a sharp or a flat, and when shown on the staff it precedes the note it is supposed to change, just like sharps and flats. That much is true, it's just incomplete. I'm afraid I'm going to have to let it go at that, because I can't assume you have the vocabulary required for a full explanation. This is how a natural works and plays in a natural environment.

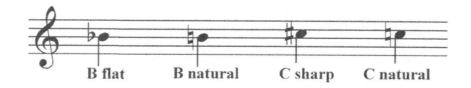

4 - Intervals: Part Two

That's it! No one will ever be able to surprise you with a brand new set of notes. It's a whole lot less complicated than the alphabet.

A half step is the smallest interval in our system.

Everything can be measured and described using half steps. However, it's also convenient to have a larger interval to work with. So, two half steps can be combined to make a single "whole step."

Important Note: We're using the words "half" and "whole" again. Half steps and whole steps (measuring vertical distances) have absolutely no connection to half notes and whole notes, which are measuring time. These are totally different ideas.

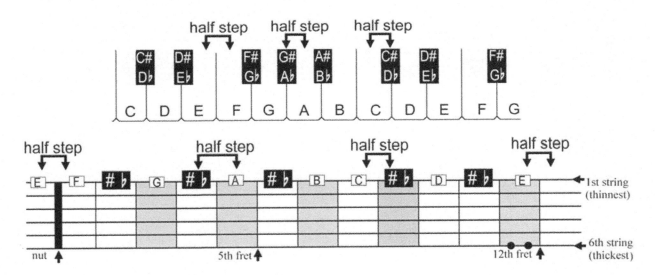

B to C is a half step. From C to C# is another half step. So, if we combine the two half steps, from B to C# is one "whole" step. Let's continue up the keyboard (or guitar, mandolin, banjo, bass neck... remember they're really about the same, they just look different).

From E up to F is a half step. From F to F# is another half step. So from E to F# is one whole step.

From B♭ to B is a half step. From B to C is a half step. So, from B♭ to C is one whole step.

From D to D# is a half step. From D# to E is a half step. So, from D to E is a whole step.

From F # to G is a half step. From G to G# is a half step. So, from F# to G# is a whole step.

These examples have shown whole steps occurring in all possible color combinations: from a white key to a black key; from a black key to another black key; from a black key to a white key; and from a white key to a white key.

Any combination is OK… two half steps always make a whole step, as in "Take a whole step away from the car!"

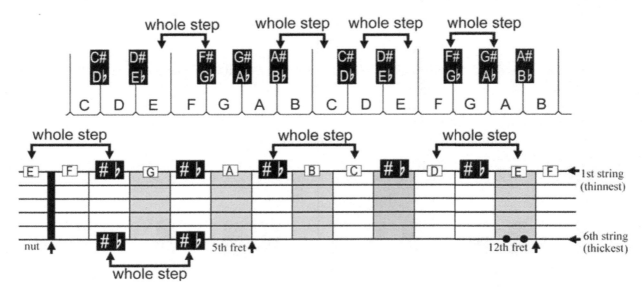

You may sometimes see the word "tone" used in place of the word "step." This is common in British and European publications. Half tone and whole tone. When used in the context of intervals, an American half step is the same as an English/Australian half tone and an English/Australian whole tone is the same as an American whole step. Different words describing the same idea, and it might confuse you if you encounter it in another book.

There are two places you'll encounter these sharp and flat symbols on a sheet of music. There is something called a "key signature" that appears at the left end of each line of music. You don't need to understand keys or key signatures for this explanation.

Notice that the key signature for G has a # located on the line that indicates the note F. That means that every F you encounter will be played as F#. High ones, low ones, and every other one. You don't have to put a # beside every F in the piece, that's what the key signature means. The key of F has a B♭ in the key signature, so every B is B♭. The key of A uses three sharps, C#, F# and G#, and you play those three notes as sharps each and every time you encounter one.

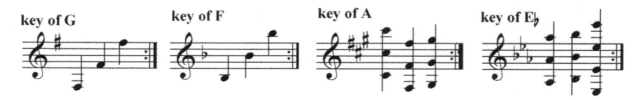

You'll also find them scattered here and there throughout a piece of music. When that happens, it's only a temporary thing. This is when they're referred to as an "accidental." It's not accident, the composer did it on purpose, but it's not exactly the note implied by the key signature, and it goes away at the beginning of the next measure.

Notice there are four B notes in the first measure. The first one has a ♭ symbol and the others don't. But if you look at the tab, you'll see that they're all played the same. An accidental stays in effect until the end of the measure. I want to hear that B♭ in the second measure, too, so I have to write it in again… the accidental went away at the bar line. In the third measure, I don't want to tweak that note and it automatically reverts to what is indicated in the key signature. I wrote the last accidental G# on purpose, but it sounds like an accident.

4 - Intervals: Part Two

Lar ry had a lit tle lamb   lit tle lamb   lit tle lamb   Lar ry had a lit tle lamb whose   fleas were all named Moe

If you want to change a note for part of a measure, you can use the natural symbol. There are sharps, flats, and naturals shown as accidentals in this example. If this was arranged for six Telecasters and played at sufficient volume levels, it could sound like an accident involving a cat and a blender.

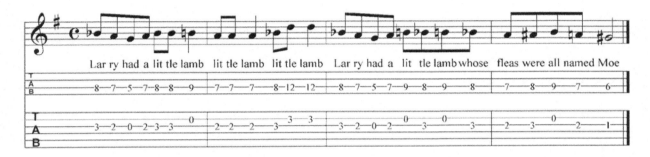

Lar ry had a lit tle lamb   lit tle lamb   lit tle lamb   Lar ry had a lit tle lamb whose   fleas were all named Moe

If the key signature indicates that a particular note will be sharped or flatted, but you want to change it, you would use the natural symbol.

In the key of A, you'll always play a C# unless directed otherwise by an accidental. The first measure starts with an accidental on the C#, and it continues through the end of the measure. The natural symbol lowers the C# to C natural. In the second measure it reverts back to C# because the bar erased the accidental. You don't have to put a # symbol there, the key signature told you that. In the third measure, it changes back and forth, so you have to show each one.

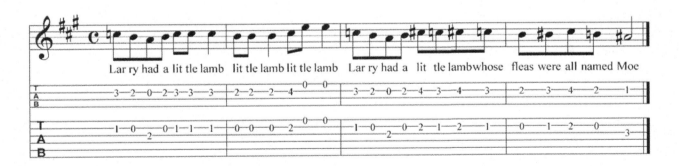

Lar ry had a lit tle lamb   lit tle lamb lit tle lamb   Lar ry had a lit tle lamb whose   fleas were all named Moe

I've noticed that beginning players often seem to attach a lot of importance to playing sharps and flats. I've heard students attempt to ask all sorts of questions about sharps and flats and their significance. These questions usually seem to involve some sort of apprehension about the physical aspect of playing them.

These inquisitive students don't have quite enough vocabulary to enunciate their concerns, so I've never been exactly certain what they are asking, but it's become obvious that plenty of people think there is something intrinsically different about sharps and flats.

There isn't any real difference. They're the same as all the others. If all 12 tones had letter names, A-B-C-D-E-F-G-H-I-J-K and L, and the staff had more lines and spaces there would be no need for sharps and flats. The structure of this system of written music requires them, but they're basically the same as the naturals.

A single five-line staff with only two ledger lines is enough to represent two full octaves when using seven different letter names in conjunction with sharps and flats.

Twelve different letter names and two or three additional lines on the staff would be unreadable and would show on octave. Five lines and four spaces is visually friendly.

I'm not certain, but it seems that sharps and flats must have been invented to maintain this system of only five lines in a staff. Sharps and flats can seem unnecessarily confusing at times, but I think they're part of a rather elegant solution to a tricky problem in ergonomics. How do we write all this stuff on as few pages a possible in a form that regular people can read?

When you look at a keyboard, you'll notice that the black and white keys are different sizes and shapes. The black keys are taller than the white keys. There is a slight physical adjustment required to play them.

On a fretted instrument, there is no such physical difference. C# is exactly as tall as C or D.

Sharps and flats are part of this system and you do need to know about them, but I can't sensibly tell you why at this point. They will begin to matter in "**Scales**" and "**The Key**," but for now this will have to do.

There's one last important point I need to make.

The lyrics to this song do not have anything to do with my friend, Larry Campbell. Absolutely no connection. None. Honest. Would I lie?

As far as I know, Larry doesn't even have a sheep anymore. I'm confident that Larry doesn't name all fleas. (You might want to ask Pinky about *his* sheep!) You can see Larry (and Curly) on the cover of my CD, *Pickin' After Midnight.* Larry's the one who's cooking the lamb chops on the campfire.

Reflections

*"I been doing the same things as in my younger days, when I was coming up, and
now here I am, an old man, up there in the charts. And I say, well, what happened?
Have they just thought up the real John Lee Hooker, is that it?
And I think, well, I won't tell nobody else!
I can't help but wonder what happened. "*
John Lee Hooker

*"I cannot give you the formula for success, but I can give you the formula for
failure, which is: Try to please everybody."*
Herbert Bayard Swope

"I don't know anything about music. In my line you don't have to."
Elvis Presley

"I don't write music for sissy ears."
Charles Ives, eminent composer whose music is deemed excessively dissonant by traditionalists.

"I got rhythm, I got music, I got my man, who could ask for anything more?"
Ira Gershwin

*"I know canned music makes chickens lay more eggs
and makes factory workers produce more.
But how much more can they get out of you on an elevator?"*
Victor Borge

"I may not be there yet, but I'm closer than I was yesterday."
Unknown

"I think of music as a menu. I can't eat the same thing every day."
Carlos Santana

*"If a man does not keep pace with his companions,
perhaps it is because he hears a different drummer.
Let him keep step to the music he hears, however measured and far away."*
Henry David Thoreau

*"If a man is not good, what has he to do with the rules of propriety?
If he is not good, what has he to do with music?"*
Confucius

*"If I have ever made any valuable discoveries,
it has been owing more to patient attention than to any other talent."*
Isaac Newton

"If music be the food of love, play on."
William Shakespeare

Intervals: Part Two

1. This symbol # is spelled and pronounced _____.

2. This symbol ♭ is spelled and pronounced _____.

3. The smallest musical interval is called a _____ _____.

4. There are _____ half steps in an octave.

5. Half steps are the same on all instruments.   **True**   **False**

6. When a # (sharp) is attached to a note, it indicates that you go _____ in pitch by an interval of _____ _____ _____.

7. When a ♭ (flat) is attached to a note, it indicates that you go _____ in pitch by an interval of _____ _____ _____.

8. When a note has two names, it is said to be _____. (no, not schizophrenic)

9. The black note in between A and B can be called _____, because it's (1) half step _____ A, or it can be called _____ because it's (1) half step below the B.

10. The black note in between C and D can be called _____, because it's (1) half step _____ C, or it can be called _____ because it's (1) half step below the D.

11. The black note in between D and E can be called _____, because it's (1) half step _____ D, or it can be called _____ because it's (1) half step below the E.

12. The black note in between F and G can be called _____, because it's (1) half step _____ F, or it can be called _____ because it's (1) half step below the G.

13. The black note in between G and A can be called _____, because it's a single half step _____ G natural, or you can call it _____ because it's a half step A natural.

14. Although the symbols **#** and ♭ usually associated with the black keys, there are times when white keys will be called **B#, C♭, E#, or F♭.**   **True**   **False**

15. Two half steps can be combined to make a single _____.

16. Half steps and whole steps are identical to half notes and whole notes.   **True**   **False**

Use the keyboard or guitar neck at the bottom of the next page to name the following intervals:

17. B up to C is a _____ _____.

18. From C up to C# is a _____ _____.

19. From B up to C# is one _____ _____.

20. From D up to D# is a _____ _____.

21. From D# up to E is a _____ _____.

22. From D up to E is a _____ _____.

23. From B♭ down to A is a _____ _____.

24. From A down to A♭ is a _____ _____.

25. From G♭ down to F is a _____ _____.

26. From F down to E is a _____ _____.

27. From G♭ down to E is one _____ _____.

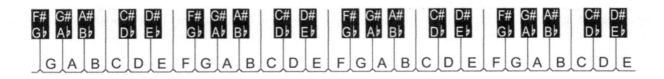

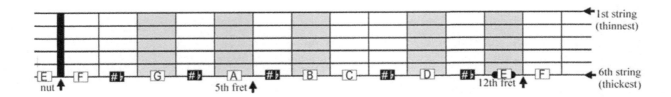

Intervals: Part Three Chapter 5

By now, I'm sure you've noticed that all the 2^{nds} and 3^{rds} are not identical with regard to the number of keys or frets spanned. You probably remember back in "**Intervals: Part One**" where I mentioned that there are different types of 2^{nds} and 3^{rds}.

The interval from B to C is only a single "half step," no black keys. The interval between C and D is larger. Because there is a black key between C and D, this "2nd" is made of two "half steps." And, if you look at the 3^{rds} described while ignoring the black notes, you'll see that again, some have more "half steps" in the interval than others.

So we need to refine or "fine tune" our definition of the intervals. It's kind of like learning to distinguish between colors that are similar: turquoise blue, navy blue, and sky blue. Same basic color, we're just adding a descriptive word to be a bit more specific.

There are two types of intervals and all of the intervals begin as one or the other, so the names you've already learned remain the same… a 2nd, a 3rd, a 4th, a 5th, a 6th, a 7th, and an octave. Now we'll add descriptive words to those intervals.

> #1. There are "**perfect**" intervals: 4^{ths}, 5^{ths}, and octaves are perfect intervals.
> #2. There are "**major**" intervals: 2^{nds}, 3^{rds}, 6^{ths}, and 7^{ths} are major intervals.

Perfect intervals and major intervals can be altered in two ways.

1. Perfect and major intervals are altered by decreasing the span of the intervals (1) half step. The word most often used to indicate a smaller interval is "minor." "Flat" or "flatted" is also used to indicate a smaller interval. The word "diminished" is very similar to the word "flat" with regard to how it affects an interval. To "flat a note" means "lower the note (1) half step." To "diminish an interval" means "decrease by (1) half step."

For instance, **C** to **E** is a major 3rd. Decrease the interval by (1) half step and it is known as a minor 3rd or a flatted 3rd.

2. Perfect and major intervals can also be altered by expanding the interval by (1) half step. The word used to describe expansion is "augment." "Augmented" is very similar to the word "sharp" with regard to how it affects an interval. To "sharp a note" means "raise the note (1) half step." To "augment an interval" means "expand the interval by (1) half step."

Let's start with octaves. An octave is a "perfect" interval.

An octave doesn't change. There's rarely a "descriptive" word attached to the word "octave" so there's nothing new to remember. The theory police will want to talk about a diminished octave, and there actually is such a thing, but almost nobody cares.

In my world, an octave spans 12 half steps and always has the same note name on each end. Start on a white key or start on a black key, it doesn't matter.

One whole step is a major 2nd. Decrease the interval by (1) half step and it is known as a minor 2nd. But in realty, you'll almost never hear anyone refer to a "2^{nds}". A 2nd is most often called either a "half step" or a "whole step."

Soon you will encounter an augmented 2nd, which means you'll expand the major 2nd by (1) half step… for a total of three half steps.

3^{rds} are next. 3^{rds} begin as major 3^{rds}. Every major 3rd spans four half steps. C to E is a major 3rd. G to B is a major 3rd. F to A is a major 3rd. Four half steps = major 3rd.

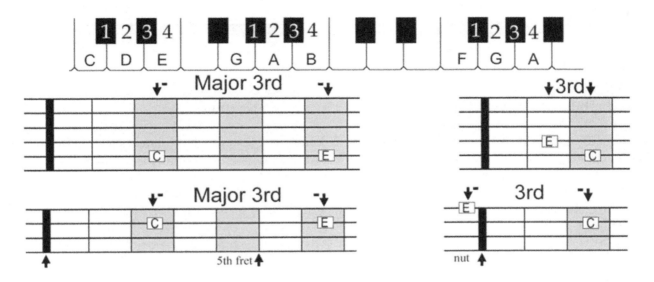

If you flat the higher note in a major 3rd, and leave the lower note in place, the size of the interval has been made smaller, from four half steps to three half steps. It is now called a minor 3rd or a flat 3rd.

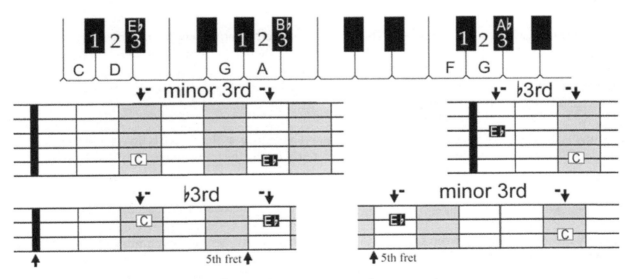

From C to E♭ is a minor 3rd. From G to B♭ is a flat 3rd. From F to A♭ is a flat 3rd.

Like almost everything else we've looked at, this is simple stuff. It's a little confusing at times because of all the numbers. But it's not especially difficult, taken one idea at a time. If you can count to four, you can identify 3^{rds}. They are usually referred to as major 3^{rds} and minor 3^{rds}.

This sequence of major and minor 3rds probably has a familiar sound. Spend some time familiarizing yourself with this example, as it's one of the most important structural components in popular music.

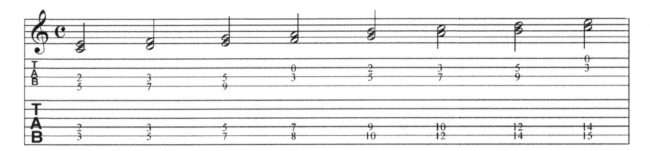

The illustration is drawn on the A and D strings, but you can (and **should**) play it everywhere. Go back to the examples in "**Intervals: Part One**" if you don't remember 3rds on the other strings.

I don't want to confuse the issue at this point with "rare and unusual" variations, but I should mention that there is also an interval called a "diminished 3rds," and it is different than a minor 3rd. An example would be B# to D. It's a detail that is not terrifically important right now, and we haven't talked about things like why "**B#**" could suddenly be the name of the white key we've learned to know and love as "**C**". We'll get to that soon enough. Just so you know there is a thing such as a diminished 3rd. This will probably be the only place you'll ever encounter the critter.

Here's where we are so far:

> One (1) half step is a half step (or a minor 2nd, but you won't hear that too often).
> Two half steps make a whole step (or a major 2nd, but you won't hear that too often).
> Three half steps make (usually) a minor 3rd, sometimes an augmented 2nd and sometimes a diminished 3rd.
> Four half steps make a major 3rd.

Next is five half steps, which is a "perfect" 4th. What makes it perfect? I don't know. Most of these "rules" were laid down by a bunch of monks back around the 15th century and there's no telling what these guys were thinking. I mean, for starters, it seems like they could have used 12 letters for 12 notes and dispensed with all this "Sharps and Flats, Natural and Accidental" stuff, but they didn't. Had I been consulted, I'm sure I could have made other useful suggestions… but noooo!

In any event, five half steps is a perfect 4th. It is usually just referred to as a "4th." There is no such thing as an "augmented major 3rd" which could also describe five half step. And, by the same token, there's no such thing as a "flatted or diminished 4th, which would be four half steps… a major 3rd.

There is an augmented 4th. An example is from **F** up to **B**, which is an augmented 4th… six half steps.

This is exactly the middle note between **C** and **C**. From C to F# is six half step, and continuing up the keyboard, from F# to C is six half steps.

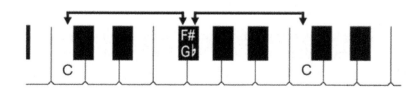

Six half steps is usually called a "flatted 5th" or a "tritone." Augmented 4th describes the same number of half steps, but flatted 5th is the phrase used most often.

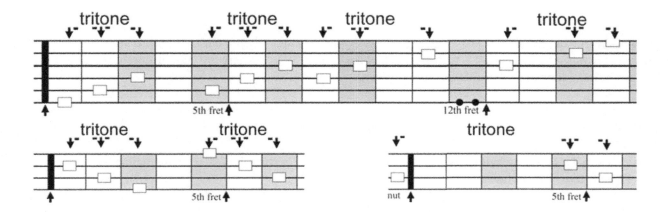

Seven half steps is a "perfect 5th."

Eight half steps is usually called an "augmented 5th" or a "sharp 5th" (#5th).

Nine half steps is a major 6th. Major 6th is really the only 6th you hear much about. Although a "diminished or minor 6th" is an accurate description of eight half steps, people usually say #5th or augmented 5th. Ten half steps could be an augmented 6th, but is usually referred to as a "flatted 7th."

Ten half steps is a flatted 7th. This interval is nearly always referred to as a flatted 7th, not a minor 7th, because there is a chord called a minor 7th. There is also an interval called a diminished 7th, and that interval is discussed in the chapter on diminished chords.

Eleven half steps is a "major 7th."

Finally, 12 half steps completes an octave. Start on any note, count 12 half steps, and you will arrive at a note that has the same letter name as where you began.

Go back to the songs in your workbook that you used for labeling the intervals from "**Intervals: Part One**" and refine your answers. Major 3^{rds} or minor 3^{rds}, etc.

Inverting Intervals

Now that all of the notes are included (flats, sharps, and naturals) and you have a fair understanding of major and minor intervals, it's time to return briefly to inverting the intervals.

When we first touched on the idea of inverting intervals, it was using only the naturals within an octave. The magic number was nine... up a 2nd is the same as down a 7th and 7+2=9. There are eight different tones in an octave, not nine, but one of the tones is counted twice.

Since we know 2nds, 3rds, 4ths, 5ths, 6ths and 7ths come in different sizes, we have to take that fact into consideration when inverting intervals.

C up to A is a major 6th. Nine half steps. C down to A is a minor 3rd. Three half steps. Nine half steps + three half steps = 12 half steps. One octave.

A major 3rd + a major 6th will **not** fit in an octave. There are four half steps in a major 3rd and nine half steps in a major 6th. Add the half steps in these two intervals (four half steps + nine half steps = 13 half steps) and it's beyond the 12 half steps span of an octave. A minor 3rd + a minor 6th = 11 half steps, one short of an octave.

So, it's not quite enough to say that a 3rd inverts to a 6th. To be correct on your Theory 101 exam, you'll have to include the words **major** and **minor** and **perfect** in the descriptions of the intervals.

A **major** 3rd + a **minor** 6th. A **minor** 2nd + a **major** 7th. A **perfect** 5th + a **perfect** 4th.

When you're talking with the band, that's probably not necessary, but it's a detail that you want to know about.

Take 10 minutes and use this keyboard to examine a few of them.

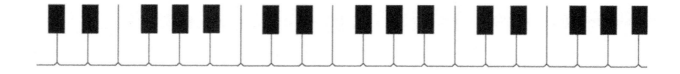

Reflections

"If music could be translated into human speech, it would no longer need to exist."
Ned Rorem

*"If one dream should fall and break into a thousand pieces,
never be afraid to pick one of those pieces up and begin again."*
Flavia Weedn

"If we are facing in the right direction, all we have to do is keep on walking."
Buddhist Saying

"If you can walk you can dance. If you can talk you can sing."
Zimbabwe Proverb

"If you don't know where you are going, you might wind up someplace else."
Yogi Berra

*"If you focus on results, you will never change.
If you focus on change, you will get results."*
Jack Dixon

"Imagination is the highest kite one can fly."
Lauren Bacall

"In music one must think with the heart and feel with the brain."
George Szell

"In music the passions enjoy themselves."
Friedrich Nietzsche

*"In reading the lives of great men, I found that the first victory they won
was over themselves… self-discipline with all of them came first."*
Harry S. Truman

In rejecting the Beatles, 1962: "We don't like their sound, and guitar music is on the way out."
Decca Recording Company

*"It had never occurred to me before that music and thinking are so much alike.
In fact you could say music is another way of thinking, or maybe thinking is another kind of music."*
Ursula Le Guin

*"It is one of the strange ironies of this strange life that those who work the hardest,
who subject themselves to the strictest discipline, who give up certain pleasurable things
in order to achieve a goal, are the happiest.
When you see 20 or 30 runners line up for a distance race in some meet, don't pity them,
don't feel sorry for them. Better envy them instead."*
Brutus Hamilton

Just a minor change to "Brown Eyed Girl"... now she's "My Brown Eyed Gorilla"

Now that you know a little bit about major and minor, I thought you might enjoy learning another way to play "Brown Eyed Girl"... incorrectly. There are loads of wrong ways to play "Brown Eyed Girl," and it's remarkable just how easy and fun it is to twist something like this! Doing it the wrong way intentionally is one way to think about improvisation. "My Brown Eyed Gorilla" is how "Brown Eyed Girl" might sound if it was played in a minor key. I included a bass note for the guitarists. Notice the bass notes are all open strings except the B in measures 4 & 8. I inverted the interval there for the guitars, so it's pretty easy to play with your thumb and two fingers. The mando tab stays in 3rds.

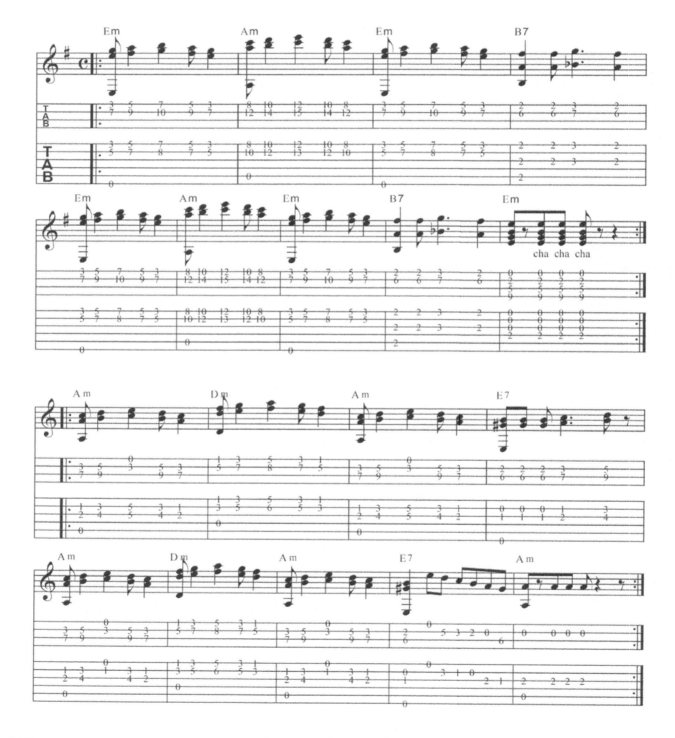

Invert My Brown Eyed Gorilla. Don't It Make Her Brown Eyes Blue?

Bertha D. Blues

Here is a series of three intervals that make up a significant percentage of blues and "classic Rock & Roll." There are people who have made entire careers and lots of loot mostly doing slight variations on what you see on this page. This is the essence of EVERYTHING Chuck Berry recorded. You might as well learn it, too.

These last four measures show another turnaround. It's shown here as harmonic intervals, but you can do it like the ones shown in "**Intervals: Part One**", too.

Now make it swing (we'll get to a definition of swing soon). Apply this triplet feel to the example. Say, then play it.

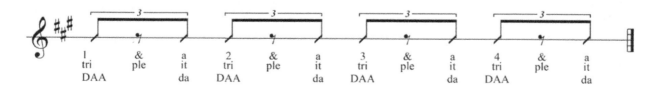

Melodic Intervals... Key of A

Melodic Intervals... Key of B

5 - Intervals: Part Three

Melodic Intervals... Key of C

Melodic Intervals... Key of D

5 - Intervals: Part Three

Melodic Intervals... Key of E

Melodic Intervals... Key of F

Melodic Intervals... Key of G

Intervals: Part Three

1. There are _____ basic types of intervals and all the intervals begin as one or the other.

2. There are _____ intervals.

3. There are _____ intervals.

4. These basic intervals can be altered in _____ ways.

5. One way perfect and major intervals are altered is by _____ the span of the intervals by (1) half step. The word used to indicate a _____ interval is "minor."

6. The words _____ and _____ are also used to indicate a smaller interval.

7. The word _____ is very similar to the word "flat" with regard to how it affects an interval.

8. To "flat a note" means "_____ the note (1) half step."

9. To "diminish an interval" means "_____ by (1) half step."

10. Perfect and major intervals can also be altered by _____ the interval by (1) half step.

11. The word used to describe expansion is "_____."

12. The word "augmented" is very similar to the word "_____" with regard to how it affects an interval.

13. To "sharp a note" means "_____ the note (1) half step."

14. To "augment an interval" means "_____ by (1) half step."

15. The number of half steps is what determines the name of any interval.   **True   False**

16. C up to _____ is a major 3rd.

17. _____ up to B is a major 3rd.

18. F up to A is a _____ _____.

19. From F down to _____ is a minor 3rd.

20. From _____ down to E is a minor 3rd.

21. _____ half step is a half step.

22. _____ half steps is a whole step.

23. _____ half steps is a minor 3rd.

24. _____ half steps is a major 3rd.

25. _____ half steps is a perfect 4th.

26. _____ half steps is a flatted 5th.

27. _____ half steps is a perfect 5th.

28. _____ half steps is a tritone, or #5th.

29. _____ half steps is a major 6th.

30. _____ half steps is a flatted 7th.

31. _____ half steps is a major 7th.

32. Twelve half steps are an _____.

33. Six half steps is the center point in an _____, and is frequently referred to as a _____.

34. When inverting intervals, be aware that one of the intervals will be _____ and the other one will be _____.

It winds from Chicago to LA. Over 2,000 miles along the way. Get your kicks on Route 66. Explain.

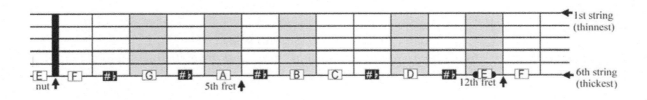

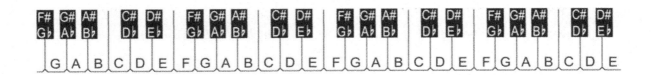

Reflections

"It is only by introducing the young to great literature, drama and music,
and to the excitement of great science that we open to them the possibilities
that lie within the human spirit...enable them to see visions and dream dreams."
Eric Anderson

"It may be that those who do most, dream most."
Stephen Butler Leacock

"It's not that I'm so smart, it's just that I stay with problems longer."
Albert Einstein

"It's not the work that's hard, it's the discipline."
Unknown

"It seems to me that those songs that have been any good,
I have nothing much to do with the writing of them.
The words have just crawled down my sleeve and come out on the page."
Joan Baez

"It takes a lot of devotion and work, or maybe I should say play,
because if you love it, that's what it amounts to.
I haven't found any shortcuts, and I've been looking for a long time."
Chet Atkins

"It's easy to play any musical instrument.
All you have to do is touch the right key at the right time...and the instrument will play itself."
J.S. Bach

"I've always felt rock and roll was very, very wholesome music."
Aretha Franklin

"I worry that the person who thought up Muzak may be thinking up something else."
Lily Tomlin

"I would advise you to keep your overhead down; avoid a major drug habit;
play everyday, and take it in front of other people.
They need to hear it, and you need them to hear it."
James Taylor

"Keep away from people who try to belittle your ambitions.
Small people always do that, but the really great make you feel that you, too, can become great."
Mark Twain

"Keep on going, and the chances are good that you will stumble on something when you are least expecting it.
I never heard of anyone ever stumbling on something while sitting down."
Charles F. Kettering

Scales

'A musical scale has no resemblance to what covers most fish and you can't weigh anything with one. The origin of the word as used in music is "scala" and refers to a ladder, which was probably used to "climba the walla."

Just as a ladder is a series of steps, a scale is a series of tones.

Intervals are used to measure the length of the steps between the notes in every scale.

As intervals can be considered the "pieces and parts" used to construct scales, scale tones are the "fundamental elements" of other musical structures, such as chords and melodies.

There are lots of different scales (styles of ladders). There are chromatic scales, major scales, minor scales, diminished scales, whole tone scales, and more.

The good news is that for the most part, at first we're only concerned with one of those scales.

More good news is that when you come to understand how this one scale is built and defined, all of the rest will be much easier to understand as you encounter them.

And to make it even easier, you're probably already familiar with the sound of this scale. It goes **DO RE MI FA SO LA TI DO**. Did you sort of hear the tones in your head as you read that? Can you hum it? Most of the time it's referred to as a Major Scale. It can also be called the Ionian Mode. (Modes, coming soon.)

Solfege (**DO RE MI FA SO LA TI DO**) is a system of referring to scale tones that substitutes these syllables for the individual letter names. Since all major scales use the same sequence of intervals, they all sound very similar, so it is useful to be able to use this kind of "code" instead of having to always remember the specific letter name for each tone. There are some exercises in this chapter.

The term "major scale" is kind of a general description; the way "guitar" is a general description. If somebody says they have a guitar, you know it's not a banjo, but you don't know whether it's a Martin or a Gibson or a Kopp, a Fender or a Gretsch. (Kopp Guitars, extraordinary instruments, handmade in Bozeman, Montana by master luthier Kevin Kopp. (www.kevinkopp.com). See www.dukesharp.com for a short instructional rafting video featuring my good friend, Kevin, running Hermit Rapids on the Colorado River in the Grand Canyon. I'm the passenger. This is NOT my favorite way to do Hermit. Kevin's also a kayaker, so he thinks being upside down in a boat on a river is OK.)

The term "major scale" identifies a series of tones that most western listeners and musicians recognize, but it doesn't really identify exactly *which* notes are used. Then, by adding a note name, as in "**G** major scale," the precise location of **DO** on your instrument is specified.

Any note can be **DO**. To find a "C major scale," play a C on any instrument, call it **DO**. Hum **DO RE MI FA SO LA TI DO** and that is the C major scale. For a **G** major scale, play a **G** on any instrument, call it **DO**, hum **DO RE MI FA SO LA TI DO**, and that is the **G** major scale.

If you could play the keys in this illustration and you first played the **C** farthest to the left, and then played every white key in sequence until you reach the **C** that is farthest to the right, you would have played a **C** major scale over two octaves.

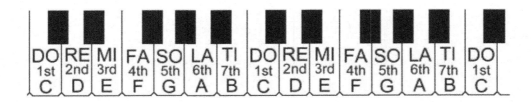

If we visualize each individual scale type (major scale, minor scale, diminished scale, etc.) as a ladder, (a series of steps) it's as if al the ladders are the same height, **one octave**.

There is a major scale that begins on each piano key, black and white. All major scales contain exactly the same number of notes and the notes are always separated by the same sequence of intervals. Each minor scale contains exactly the same number of notes and the notes are always separated by the same sequence of intervals. All diminished scales contain exactly the same number of notes and the notes are always separated by the same sequence of intervals.

Stand up all major *scalas* next to each other and the rungs of all the ladders will match up exactly. One ladder might be pink and one might be blue, but they are the same shape and size. The space between the steps, or the intervals between the notes are identical, no matter which note = **DO**.

There are a few rules (five altogether) that determine exactly which notes are used and the size of the interval between the steps (notes) of the major scale. This series of intervals creates the sound associated with the major scale.

Here are the first four rules for identifying the **major scale** on any instrument.

> **Rule #1** There are seven different notes. **Always!!** All major scales consist of seven different notes. It is usually played as a series of eight consecutive tones, but the first tone and the last tone have the same letter name. Each of these tones is called a "degree" and they are numbered: 1st degree, 2nd degree, 3rd degree, 4th degree, 5th degree, 6th degree, and 7th degree.

> **Rule #2** Between the 1st and 7th degrees there can be no repetition of a letter name. The notes on both "ends" of a scale are the same, but the octave note is also the beginning of the next series. There really isn't an "end." Theoretically, these things reach well beyond the dark side of the moon. "To infinity and beyond." Between the octave notes no letter name can be repeated.

> **Rule #3** You can't repeat a letter and you can't leave any out, either. Use all seven note names with no omission of any letter names.

> **Rule #4** is the notes always occur in alphabetical order. **Always!**
> F G A B C D E F G A B C D E F G A B C D E F G A B C D E F A etc.

The C major scale begins with **C**, and consists of **C D E F G A B & C**

The G major scale begins with **G**, and consists of **G A B C D E F# & G**

The D major scale begins with **D**, and consists of **D E F# G A B C# & D**

The F major scale begins with **F**, and consists of **F G A B♭ C D E & F**

Use of #'s and ♭'s is necessary to maintain the correct interval between the notes of the scale while using all seven note names.

Notice the F# in the G major scale. If that note was written and played as G♭, you would hear the correct tone and it would sound just like the major scale. But in order to maintain a consistent written system, in identifying scales we have to use all seven letters with no repetition, so it's F with a # **not** a G with a ♭. The sound is the same and it really doesn't matter what you call it in your own thoughts, but to use the letter G twice violates Rule #2.

It's often useful to think of the tones as their numerical position in the scale and also as their "solfege" (do, re, mi, etc.) equivalent. The 1st degree of the scale, also known as the DO, has one other name that is used to identify it. The first note of a scale is known as the **Tonic**. The tonic = DO = the 1st scale degree.

1st	2nd	3rd	4th	5th	6th	7th	1st
DO	RE	MI	FA	SO	LA	TI	DO
TONIC	*	*	*	*	*	*	TONIC

C major scale   **C** is the tonic. The tonic is also DO and the 1st scale degree.
A major scale   **A** is the tonic. The tonic is also DO and the 1st scale degree.
E♭ major scale   **E♭** is the tonic. The tonic is also DO and the 1st scale degree.
B♭ major scale   **B♭** is the tonic. The tonic is also DO and the 1st scale degree.

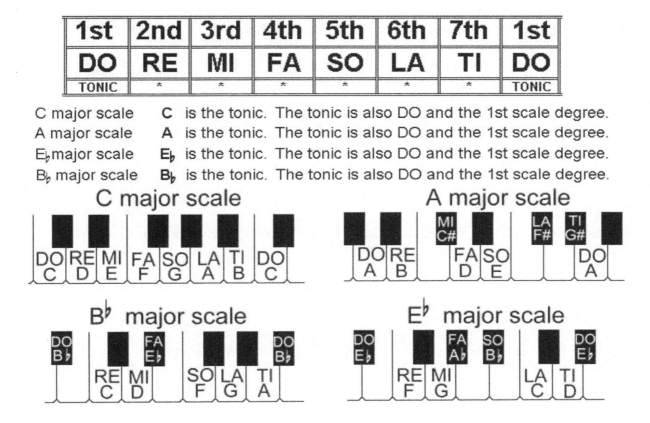

Take a good look at these next two scales. Compare the keys used and their names. Some odd things happen to the note names in the C# scale with regard to black and white keys.

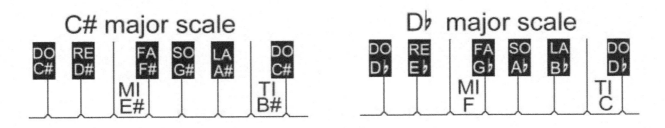

Until now, only black keys had the words sharp and flat attached to them. In the C# major scale, the white keys we're accustomed to named C and E have to be called B# and E# in order to comply with Rules 1 and 2.

While we're on the subject of several names for a single item, there is yet another set of names that are used for these same tones in the major scale. These are the ones that the instructor at the university will probably want to use. You've seen the **tonic** and **octave** a bit already, so you're familiar with 25% of them. These two are used much more frequently than the other six.

All eight names are: **tonic** (DO), **supertonic** (RE), **mediant** (MI), **subdominant**(FA), **dominant** (SO), **submediant** (LA) **leading tone** (TI), and **octave** (DO). I did take one semester of Theory 101, and that is the only place I've ever had occasion to use 75% of those names. I had to go look them up a minute ago. Now you've seen them and have an idea what they are. Maybe it will be more useful to you than it has been for me.

A brief recap of major scales:

> **Rule #1** There are always seven different note names.
> **Rule #2** No letter name can be repeated until the 8th degree is reached.
> **Rule #3** No letter name can be omitted.
> **Rule #4** The notes always occur in alphabetical order. Those rules are the ones that have to do with the written descriptions of the major scale.

Rule #5 This rule is played on an instrument. The notes in a major scale are found by using the following series of seven intervals. On any instrument, clarinet, banjo, flute, guitar, piano… all of them work according to this rule.

First choose a note, any note. Then, going up the keyboard (that's to the right)… Move one **W**hole step, **W**hole step, **H**alf step, **W**hole step, **W**hole step, **W**hole step, **H**alf step.

So, Rule #5 in 13 words—a **W**hole, **W**hole, and a **H**alf, a **W**hole, **Whole,** **W**hole, and a **H**alf.

For guitar fingering, there are four basic patterns I'll illustrate, and I've numbered them 1 through 4. I've encountered two different ways of identifying these movable scale forms in various publications. Numbering them like this seems the least confusing to me. These form numbers don't indicate any degree of relative importance, it's just a reference. Nor do they apply to other instruments. These forms are specific to guitar. I included mandolin tabs for all of the scales, but I've never seen scale patterns for any other instruments referred to as "forms" like they are for guitar. I don't know why. Maybe because I haven't looked.

Here is what is known as a "C major scale." C is the first note and the following notes occur in the sequence of intervals described by Rule #5.

Major Scale – Form #1

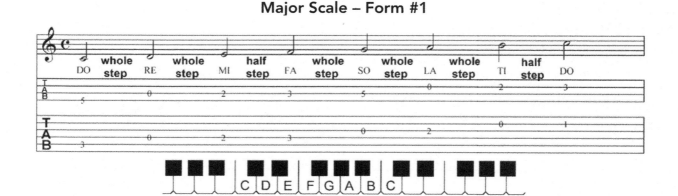

Learn these forms well. Try these now. Be aware of the tonic and where it repeats at octaves. Be aware of which finger is used to play the tonics, the 3rds, and the 5ths (DO, MI and SO). It wouldn't hurt to go back to the examples in "**Intervals: Part One**" of octaves, 3rds, 4ths, and 5ths for a moment.

Mastering these forms is a way to begin playing "lead guitar," a way to start experimenting with notes that will get you into the ballpark, right away, without having to search up and down the neck. These forms provide a bunch of relevant possibilities in a relatively condensed space, only four or five frets.

When you're playing a solo, the scale and form should be completely invisible to the listener. Practice them until you can "play with them" the way a pro basketball player can "play with" a basketball. Those guys can spin it on a finger, pass behind the back and between your feet… running at full speed while looking the other direction. The great ones play with a basketball like it's an extension of their body. That's the kind of familiarity with the neck you can develop by learning these forms. Mastery of the scales is not the goal. The goal is to be able to move and respond by reflex instead of conscious thought. You want to anticipate, not react. This is a good way to get there.

This example of form #2 is shown beginning with C again and uses the same sequence of whole and half steps, but this time there are no "open strings." The notes are all the same, some of them are just in different places on the fretboard.

Major Scale – Form #2

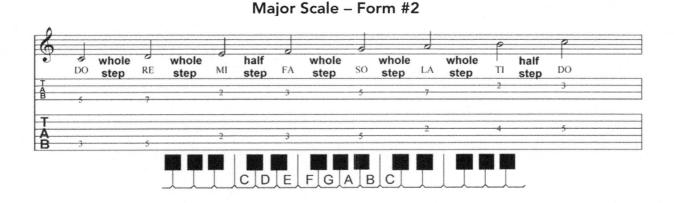

OK… are you ready for a little magic trick? Move this same form up one whole step and it's now a D major scale. In this form, your middle finger is playing the tonic on the 5th string and your pinky lands on the 3rd string tonic plus RE on the 5th string, your first finger will play MI and LA, ring finger gets TI.

Major Scale – Form #2

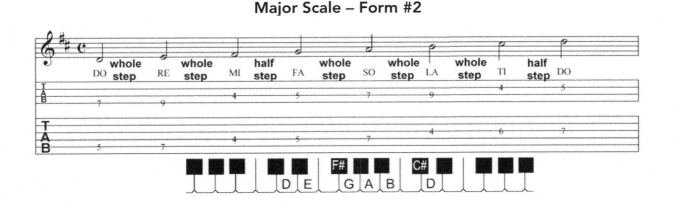

Due to the fact that there are no "open strings" used in this scale form, you can move the form up and down the neck and still have a major scale. Use the same fingers; play the same pattern on the same strings with a different starting point and it's a "new" scale. It is still a major scale, but it has a different first name. Begin with your second finger playing DO on the 4th fret and end with your pinky on the 6th fret and it's now a C# major scale because the first role is C#.

I'll show four ways to play a major scale on a guitar. Since there are 12 different possibilities for a tonic note for each of these forms, in a way you will know 48 different scales. 12 x 4 = 48.

Learning these four forms is an important step in mastering your instrument and it isn't especially difficult. It just takes time. The exercises are easy… what's tough is the self-discipline required to do them every day. If you invest a few hundred hours over the next couple of years into becoming really familiar with these forms, you'll get a big return on your investment.

This concept of "learn one form and then play it everywhere" applies to every scale or chord or exercise that uses no open strings. In most cases, when you learn one, you have actually learned 12.

Even the first one we looked at is movable, if you begin with your pinky instead of the ring finger. This is the same pattern, one half step higher. Take a look at how many black keys the piano player uses in a C# major scale. There are some unusual note names, too.

Major Scale – Form #1

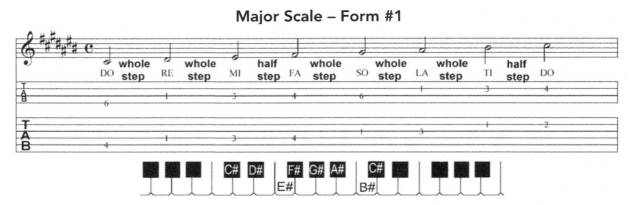

Your index finger is now playing the scale degrees that were open strings in the first example, RE, SO and TI. Third finger plays MI and LA, first finger plays TI and your pinky plays the low tonic and FA. This scale can be hard to reach at first if you try it beginning with your pinky on a C#, fourth fret as shown. It's much easier to use the same pattern, but begin with your pinky on the 10th fret, G. Practice it up on the neck for a while and gradually move it down the neck as your fingers become accustomed to the stretch.

This form spans two octaves. It starts on the 6th string and continues to the 1st string. Your pinky will be playing all the notes on the 8th and 9th frets. Your first finger will be taking care of notes on the 5th fret. Notice the big stretch on the D string between LA and TI (3rd and 4th fingers) in the lower octave.

Major Scale – Form #3

6 - Scales

Since it's another "movable form" you may want to first practice this one as high on the neck as you can because the frets are closer together and the stretch is easier.

And this is #4. Like #3, the tonic is on the 6th string.

Major Scale – Form #4

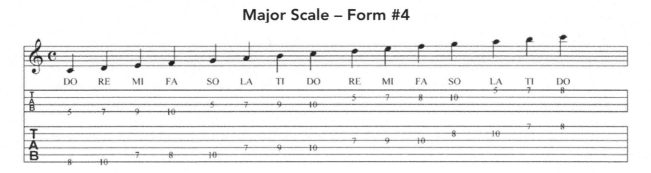

In your song workbook go to the songs that you used for identifying intervals. Look over the melodic intervals for any series of three or more notes that are separated by 2nds. Since most scales consist of seven different notes, three notes in a row comprise nearly 50% of a scale. It is very common to find "scale fragments" consisting of three, four or five more notes as parts of melodies (the notes a singer sings... more on melodies later).

In this Beatles tune, "Nowhere Man," there are three consecutive descending scale tones in the second measure, in the fourth measure, and in the sixth measure.

If we dissect the next melody, "Don't Get Around Much Anymore" by Duke Ellington, you can see lots of scale fragments. The pickup measure is MI-RE-DO, SO-FA-MI. The third measure is the same. This phrase would use all eight tones except Mr. Ellington skipped over TI and LA between DO and SO. The fourth measure has five descending scale tones in a row, SO, FA, MI, RE and DO, then it jumps up one octave. The first four notes in measure six can be seen as a portion of a chromatic scale and the last four notes in this phrase can be recognized as part of the "major blues scale."

You may know the Christmas carol, "Joy to the World." The first eight notes are a descending major scale. The intro to a tune by the Grateful Dead, "Friend of the Devil" is also based on a descending major scale. The major scale is ubiquitous (existing or being everywhere at the same time; constantly encountered) and the more familiar you become with it, the easier it will be to play by ear. Look for it in every song; it's probably in there somewhere.

The exercises at the end of this chapter called "**Intro to Major & Minor Scales**" are exercises that only use five scale tones within a single octave. They are really quite useful for a few reasons. One reason is that smaller bits of scales are much more commonly used in actual songs than the full eight-note scale. It's easier to begin "improvising" using an abbreviated set of notes, too. In addition, three of the five notes create all of the basic chords (next chapter). It is definitely worth your time to become very, very familiar with these exercises. Fifteen to 20 minutes a day is *not* excessive. Playing smooth and steady 8th notes at about 75 bpm is a good initial target. Developing the ability to play smooth five-note scales at 75 bpm should be a priority for just about everybody.

Sing along with these exercises. You want to develop the ability to recognize DO-RE-MI-FA-SO any time you hear it. Scale practice is possibly the best ear training exercise that there is. I haven't found a better one. Singing along speeds up the process of totally absorbing the sound of this sequence. You don't have to sing like Aaron Neville, the goal is to make a solid connection between the sound the instrument makes and the sounds in your head. **The major scale is the consistent reference point that is used for figuring songs out by ear… in all styles of music.**

Reflections

"Music is a thing of the soul...
a rose lipped shell that murmured of the eternal sea...
a strange bird singing the songs of another shore."
Josiah Gilbert Holland

"Music is the art of thinking with sounds."
Jules Combarieu

"Music is the fourth great material want of our natures.
First food, then raiment, then shelter, then music."
Christian Bovee

"Music is the only language in which you cannot say a mean or sarcastic thing."
John Erksine

"Music is the shorthand of emotion."
Henry Wadsworth Longfellow

"Music makes one feel so romantic... at least it always gets on one's nerves...
which is about the same thing."
Oscar Wilde

"Music melts all the separate parts of our bodies together."
Anais Nin

"Music that gentlier on the spirit lies,
Than tired eyelids upon tired eyes."
Alfred, Lord Tennyson

"Music washes away from the soul the dust of everyday life."
Bertold (Red) Auerbach

"Music was my refuge.
I could crawl into the space between the notes and curl my back to loneliness."
Maya Angelou

"Music... the one incorporeal entrance into the higher world of knowledge
which comprehends mankind but which mankind cannot comprehend."
Ludwig van Beethoven

"My dear fellow, my whole life is moved by the principle
that the one thing which is more important than peace is music.
It is because I believe that, that I am poor."
Robertson Davies

Modes

There are seven common modes and "mode" is very nearly synonymous with the word "scale."

Just as "major scale" can be thought of as an abbreviation for "whole step, whole step, half step, whole step, whole step, whole step, half step," "Ionian mode" refers to precisely the same series of intervals.

Conveniently enough, the white keys are enough to illustrate all seven modes, too. Each mode is just a sequence of half steps and whole steps.

There is a ton of information I'm going to skip here. A complete discussion of modes would probably require another volume, as well as another writer since I really don't know a lot about them.

At the same time, "mode" is a concept that's easy to grasp at this point. I'll show you what modes are and one way to play each of them, provide a few examples, and if you want to study them further, you will have a basic knowledge of their structure.

The easiest place to begin is with the Ionian mode because "Ionian mode" is just another way to say "major scale." Both terms describe exactly the same sequence of intervals. Whole, whole, half, whole, whole, whole, half.

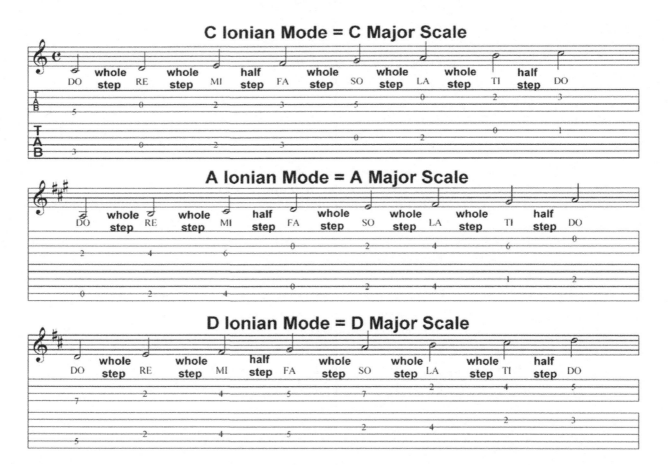

Three of the modes have a major 3rd between the tonic and the 3rd degree and have a "major" quality to their sound. They are the Ionian mode, the Lydian mode, and the Mixolydian mode.

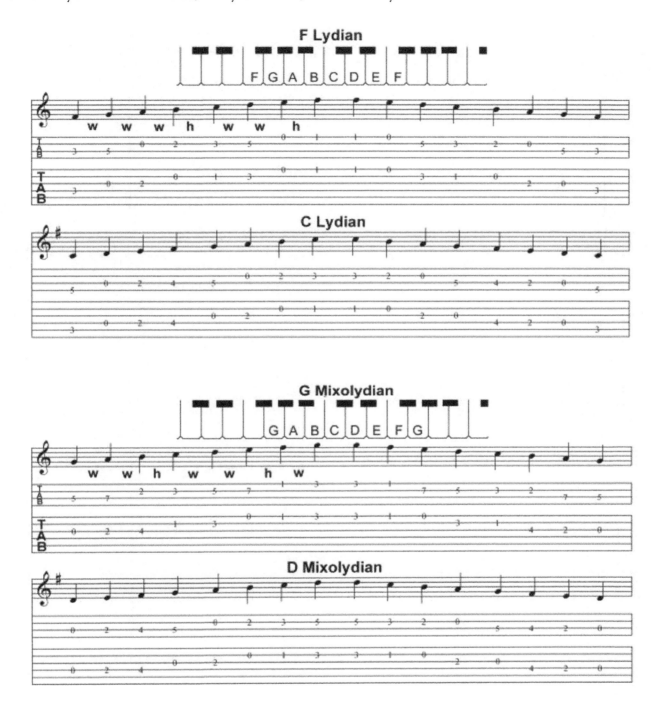

And as usual, all of these forms I've shown for modes fall into the "Twelve for the price of one" category. Pretty nifty.

One difference between the major family of modes and the minor family is that the minor modes have a minor 3rd between the tonic and the 3rd. Another difference is that two of the major sounding modes have a half step between the 7th and octave (TI and DO). In the minor modes, this interval is a whole step. This combination of a ♭3rd and a ♭7th in the minor modes is beginning to lean toward what we think of as "blues."

The Road to Lisdoonvarna

6 - Scales

The Aolian mode is one of the minor modes. The Aolian mode is also referred to as the "natural minor scale," in the same way that the Ionian mode is more commonly known as the "major scale."

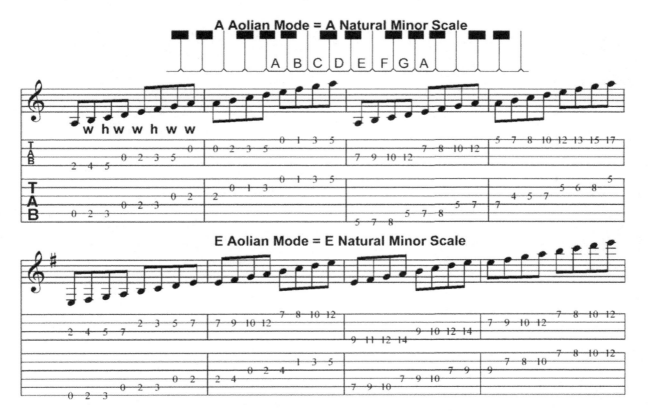

Aolian is also considered to be the "relative minor" of the Ionian mode. The Aolian mode can be a useful tool for memorizing the names of the notes on the fretboard. If you play it as shown here, starting with the note A, you can say the note names out loud as you play them. There are no sharps or flats in A Aolian, so it's just a matter of saying the alphabet, A through G. As you know, there are several places to find A.

Begin with the open A string as the first note of the mode. Then start with the A that is on the second fret of the G string. Next, play it as shown above. You get the idea. I am not usually interested in those brutal, overnight memorization projects, but I will do an exercise like playing this mode three or four times each time I pick up the guitar. Look at the neck while you play the mode and say the alphabet out loud. That's how I learned the neck. It only took a few weeks and I learned a mode, too, all at the same time. All of the modes are illustrated here using only naturals, so you can do the same drill with any of them, if you like. If you know where the naturals are, the accidentals fall into place without having to memorize them.

There is a book called the *Fiddlers Fakebook* by David Brody, Oak Publications, that has several hundred fiddle tunes in it. It's really quite cool.

They're nearly all written with mostly quarter notes and 8th notes, so it's not especially intimidating. One of the interesting things Mr. Brody did in the book was to identify all of the tunes according to which mode is used. It provides an excellent way to become familiar with some of these modes. Since it's all in standard notation, if you can read just a little, the songs are available to all instruments. This book is worth your time and money.

The tunes on the next pages are examples of modal songs. In "**Counting**," I showed an example of *Greensleeves* (A Aolian). I should admit that I altered a few notes in *Greensleeves* because I can. I tend to prefer the sound of harmonic minor over natural minor. The notes I changed are all marked with accidentals, # (sharps). If you want to play it as it was originally written, just flat those notes.

The Battle of Aughrim

6 - Scales

Scalloway Lasses

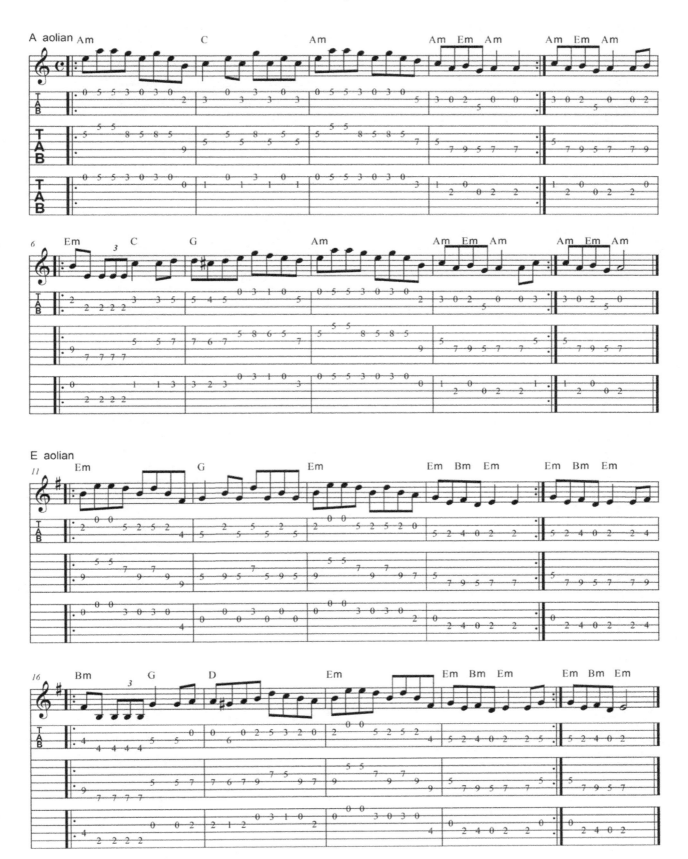

The Swallow Tail Jig
Irish Jig E Aolian
Two Grass Crew recorded a version of this tune, and you can hear a clip at www.TwoGrassCrew.com or buy it at iTunes.

6 - Scales

Three more "minor" modes

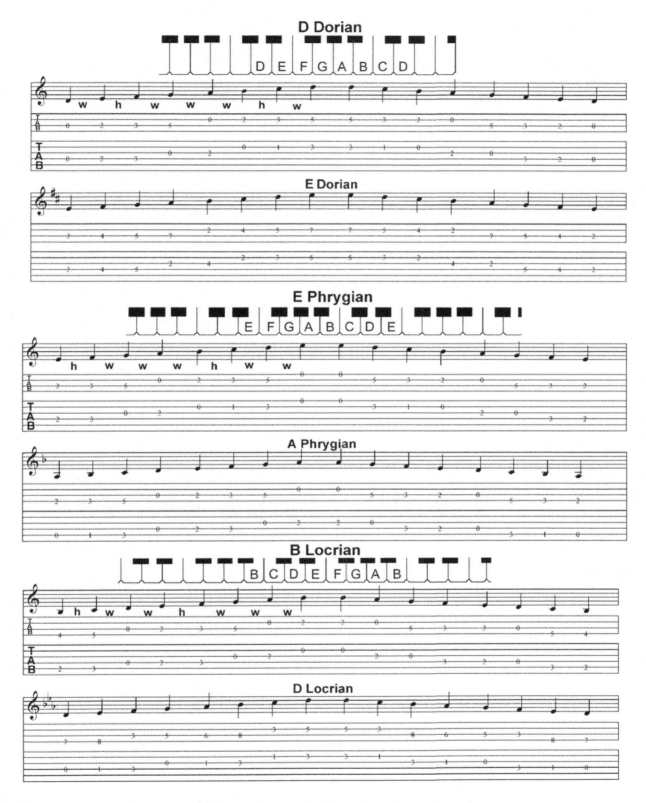

The Ionian mode usually is thought of as the first mode in a series of seven. In order:

Ionian – Dorian – Phrygian – Lydian – Mixolydian – Aolian – Locrian

More Scales

All of the scales and modes we've looked at so far use only half steps and whole steps to separate the tones and have seven different notes.

There are scales that have more than seven degrees and scales that have fewer than seven. There are also scales that use intervals larger than one whole step.

The chromatic scale doesn't skip any notes. Start anywhere and play every note in succession, only half steps. The chromatic scale has 12 different tones. Guitarists look at the tab and notice that there are four notes on each string. This makes it a pretty convenient exercise for those of us who have four fingers on our fret hand.

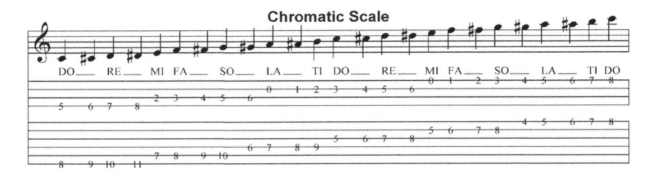

It's easy to remember the sequence of intervals for a diminished scale: H-W-H-W-H-W-H-W. Start with a half step, then a whole, half, whole, half, whole, half, whole, and that sequence adds up to eight different tones before you reach the octave. An octave makes a nine-note pattern. On a guitar, that can lay out as three notes per string. You can also "reverse" the order: start with a whole step, then a half, whole, half, whole, half, whole, half.

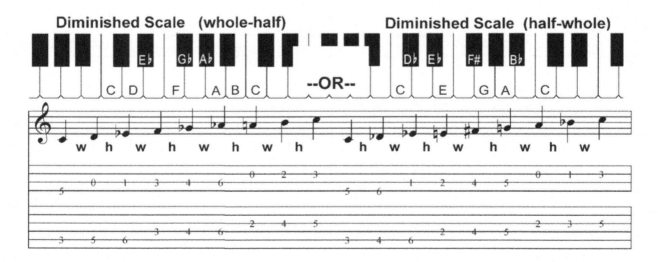

A whole tone scale is a series of whole steps, and that sequence uses six different tones.

Whole Tone Scale

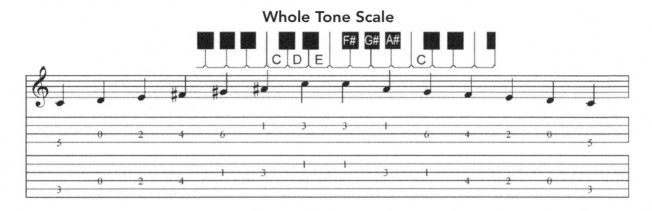

A "pentatonic scale" is a five-tone scale. **Penta**=five **tonic**=tone. Any five-note scale is a pentatonic scale. One of the most common is called the major pentatonic scale. It can be best described as derived from the major scale.

Start with a major scale and skip two of the notes. DO, RE, MI, SO, LA are the tones in the major pentatonic scale. Tonic, 2nd, 3rd, 5th, and 6th degrees.

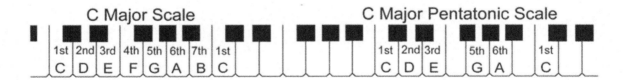

A classic example of this scale that's familiar to lots of people is the intro riff to "My Girl." What a great song! It was written by Smokey Robinson, made famous by the Temptations, and was a number one hit in March of 1965.

Pentatonic Study based on "My Girl" Intro

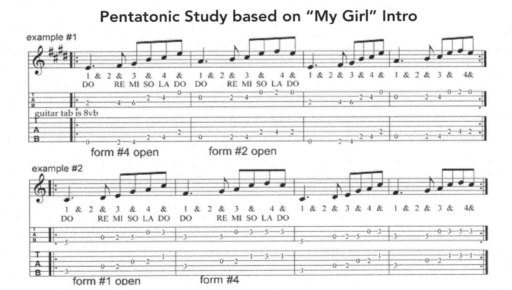

Take a few minutes to practice this riff. It's easy in the open positions as shown here. If you know the tune it should come pretty quickly. You have to listen to stuff to learn to play by ear. Ask yourself, "Is this classic tune worth an educational investment of 99 entire American pennies?" Then go purchase your very own copy. This tune is worth a dollar to just about anybody.

Sing along with the riff, as well as the song about 37 times. The next illustrations show the major pentatonic scale in closed forms, so you can learn how to play it anywhere. It's a dandy way to burn the major pentatonic scales into your head as well as your hands.

I put forms #1 and #3 on the page together so you can get a look at how similar the shapes on the fretboard are to each other. As usual, it's the 3rd between the G and B strings that breaks the visual symmetry.

Look at the first example of "My Girl." The first note in the first measure is E, and you play the scale up to the octave. The second measure does the same thing, except it starts on A. These are shown in the open versions of Forms #3 (E) and #2 (A). Tonics are separated by a 4th.

Look at the second example. The first note in the first measure is C, and you play the scale up to the octave. The second measure does the same thing, except it starts on F. The first measures is the open versions of Form #1 (C) and the F is the second octave in Form #3. Tonics are separated by a 4th.

Practice the closed forms in pairs like they're shown here, with the tonics a 4th apart. When you've learned the fingering pattern, make it sound like the intro to "My Girl."

Major Pentatonic Scale – One Octave – Form #1 – Tonic is on the 5th string

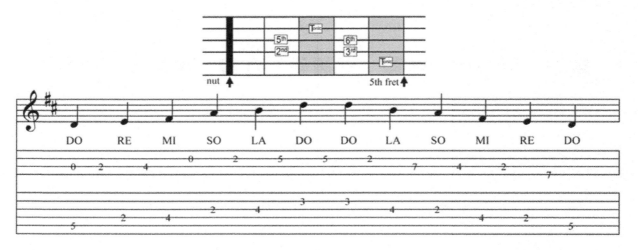

Major Pentatonic Scale – One Octave – Form #3 – Tonic is on the 6th string

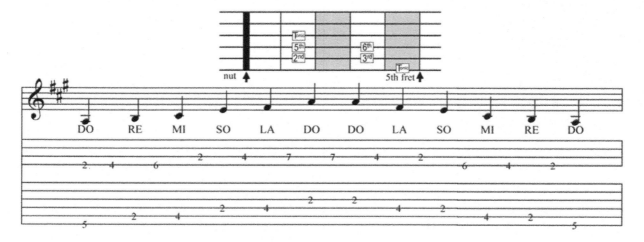

These two forms are identical for their lower octave. The shape changes when we get to the B string, but one shape gets an octave of both of these. Most song melodies stay within an octave and lots of songs have melodies that are made from just these five notes. When you get into "blues" tunes, you might listen to 95 tunes before you hear someone sing or play anything other than these five notes.

Major Pentatonic Scale – One Octave – Form #2 – Tonic is on the 5th string

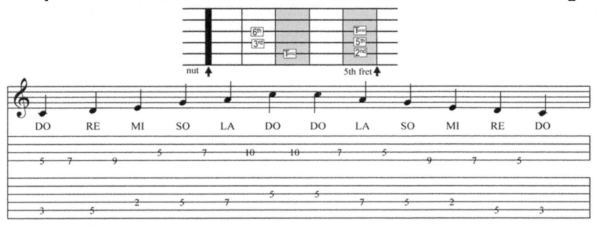

Major Pentatonic Scale – One Octave – Form #4 – Tonic is on the 6th string

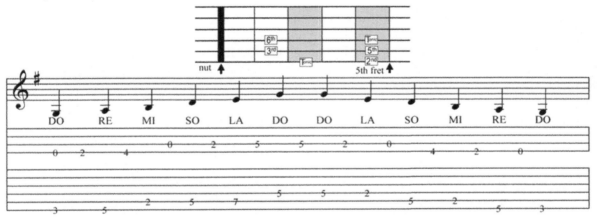

Form #5 is the odd one, it doesn't match with any others.

Major Pentatonic Scale – One Octave – Form #5 – Tonic is on the 4th string

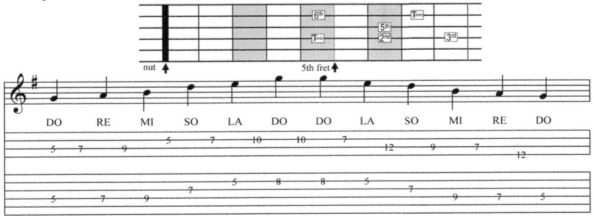

Try this tune, "Amazing Grace." It's at least as familiar as "My Girl" and it's 16 bars long, 100% major pentatonic. Sing the tune a few times with the regular lyrics. Then try replacing them with the solfege syllables. Then play it. Establish the sound in your head before you play.

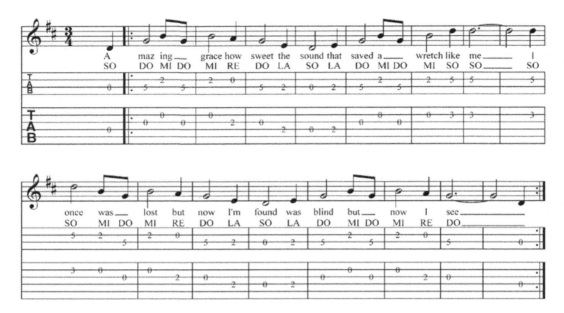

Victor Wooten often incorporates "Amazing Grace" into a bass solo and is without a doubt my favorite non-traditional version of this song. Take a minute to check it out on YouTube. Mr. Wooten's brothers are all accomplished musicians and his guitarist brother, Regi, taught Victor to play. Regi is known as "teacha" around Nashville and they are only two of the many inspirational instructors at Victor Wooten's Bass/Nature Camp. (www.victorwooten.com) Attend if you can.

Here are the major pentatonic scale forms extended to include all six strings.

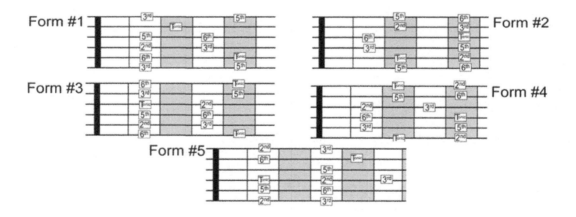

Not only do all five forms all include all six strings, they "overlap" or join like puzzle pieces and continue up the neck, until you run out of instrument. The highest frets in Form #1 are the lowest frets in Form #2. The highest frets in Form #2 are the lowest frets in Form #3. Form #3 becomes #4, #4 becomes #5, and #5 joins #1. Just bend the neck of your guitar around backwards in a circle till the 12th fret joins the nut.

No! Wait! Don't do that! But it's OK to think that. Form #1 is always found sandwiched between Forms #5 and #2, just like the note A is always between G and B. It's all circular... but the circles happen in straight lines. Unusual circles. Makes it tough to visualize, sometimes.

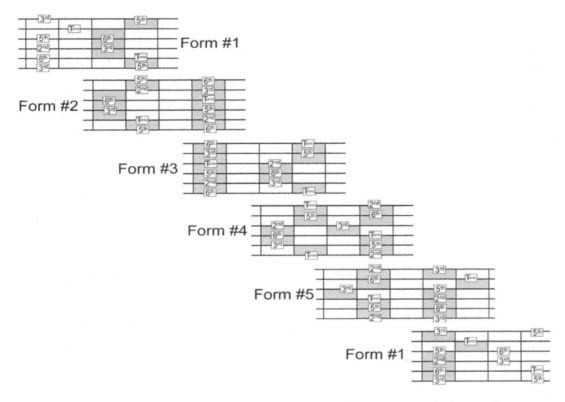

Form #1

Form #2

Form #3

Form #4

Form #5

Form #1

And remember that since these pentatonic scale forms are derived from major scale forms, the same sort of "overlap" exists for the major scales as well.

People sometimes refer to these pentatonic forms as "blues boxes," and it's pretty easy to see why. Play the four notes that are on just about any two adjacent strings and it makes a little box design. Find other boxes and play with them. Thinking of these things as geometric designs or shapes can be helpful for memorization.

Next, let's take a look at the minor pentatonic forms.

There's a piece of really good news I have for you about learning the minor pentatonic forms. You already know them. Sort of. Then it gets a little messy.

Remember the term "relative minor" and how the major scale and the natural minor scale are considered "relatives?" The C major pentatonic scale uses exactly the same five notes that the A minor pentatonic scale uses. The same five tones. Start with C as the tonic and you'll hear a scale that sounds major, due to the major 3rd between the tonic and the 3rd. If you play the same five notes but play A as the tonic, you hear a minor scale.

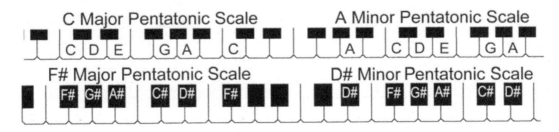

The A minor pentatonic scale uses the same notes as the C major pentatonic. F# major and D# minor use the same tones. That means you can play essentially the same fingering form, but you look for the tonic in a different place.

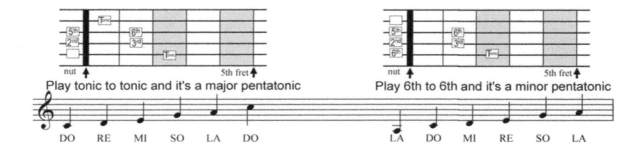

Play tonic to tonic and it's a major pentatonic

DO RE MI SO LA DO

Play 6th to 6th and it's a minor pentatonic

LA DO MI RE SO LA

Now, if we take the minor pentatonic scale and add two notes to it, it becomes what is referred to as the "blues" scale. By the way, "blues scale" did not originate as a term in classical theory and "blues scales" are not rigidly defined the way "minor scales" are defined. "Blues scale" is street jargon and is interpreted somewhat loosely.

Minor Blues Scale

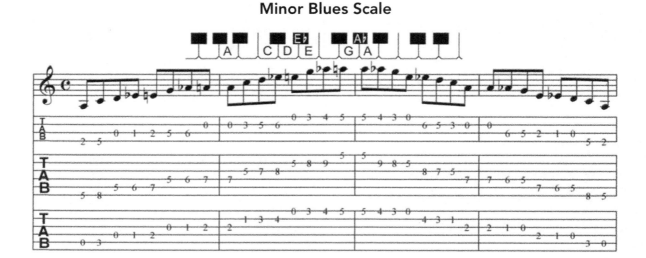

The same sort of alteration/addition can be made to the major pentatonic scale, too. You might hear this called the "country blues scale." A flatted 3rd and 6th are usually thought of as being more in the family of "minor" tones… but "blues scale" is street jargon, etc.

Major Blues Scale

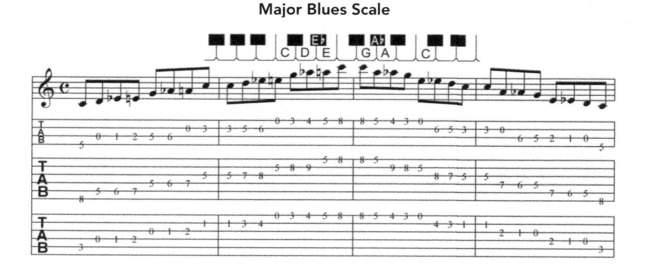

Next… minor scales.

Most western listeners hear songs that use primarily the major scale as a bright and happy sound. In comparison, tunes built around minor scales are usually thought of as sadder and darker.

There are three commonly used minor scales. They're called the "natural minor scale," the "harmonic minor scale," and the "melodic minor scale." Each consists of seven degrees plus the octave, just like the modes. There are two things that all minor scales have in common.

> 1) The interval between the tonic and the 3rd degree is a minor 3rd.
> 2) The interval between the tonic and the 5th degree is a perfect 5th.

The Aolian mode is known as the "natural minor scale." It is also sometimes called the "pure" minor scale or the "relative" minor scale.

The "relative minor" scale is the natural mode that begins on the 6th degree of the major scale. Aolian (natural, pure minor) is the darker side of the happy Ionian mode.

The sequence of intervals in the "pure and natural minor scale. The harmonic minor scale seems to be the one that is used the most and is the basis for the most songs that are written in a "minor key." The harmonic minor scale has a half step from the 7th degree to the octave, but a natural minor scale has a whole step between the 7th degree and the octave.

Harmonic Minor Scale

Here's a little experiment you can do to help hear how this small change affects the sound of a scale.

Play, or even better, sing a major scale three or four times, slowly. Then do it once more and STOP BEFORE you play the octave note. DO-RE-MI-FA-SO-LA-TI-DO… DO-RE-MI-FA-SO-LA-TI-DO… DO-RE-MI-FA-SO-LAT-TI----*----*----------*----------!!!!!!!!!!!!

Kind of leaves you hanging, doesn't it? Now, try the same thing with the harmonic minor scale.

I bet you really want to hear that last, satisfying tonic note. I bet you already played it.

TI is known as a "leading tone," meaning it "leads" your ear to a point and you anticipate something following it.

That half step between the diatonic 7th degree and the tonic "pulls your ear to the tonic" harder than the flatted 7th whole step does. That pull gets intensified in the harmonic minor scale, partly because of the unusual interval that happens right before it, between the 6th and 7th degrees.

Back to intervals for a moment. Do you remember that a major 6th is nine half steps above the tonic? That's the distance between the tonic and the 6th degree of the major scale.

In the natural and harmonic minor scales the distance between the tonic and the 6th degree is only eight half steps, or a flatted 6th.

In the harmonic minor scale, that flatted 6th creates a space of three half steps (in this case known as an augmented 2nd) between the 6th and 7th degrees.

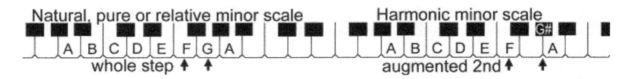

A flatted 3rd and a flatted 6th in a scale or chord create a very "minor" sound. The major 7th that is in this otherwise heavily minor scale, in addition to an interval of an augmented 2nd, is what gives the harmonic minor scale that cool, exotic sound.

Onward, into the fog… the melodic minor scale is next.

This one is unique because it is one set of intervals as it ascends and a different set of intervals as it descends.

As it ascends, if we compare it to the major scale, the only difference is that the 3rd is flatted.

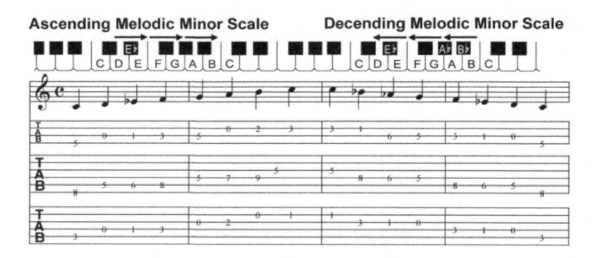

Going back down it is the same as the natural minor scale with a flatted 3rd and flat 7th. Why? I'm sure I don't know.

There is also a "jazz minor scale." It's the same as the ascending melodic minor scale, with no alterations. Same notes, up and down.

Since I've mentioned modes and jazz scales, and I've used examples in "**Reading the Road Map**" that refer to songs from *The New Real Book* (Sher Music), there is one last scale I felt like I needed to define, because you will find chords in that book (and others) that are derived from this scale. It's called an "altered" scale. A lot of the time you'll see "altered" abbreviated to "alt." Unfortunately, I know absolutely nothing useful to tell you, except the fact that it exists in the world of jazz players.

So I asked Craig Hall about it and this is what he has to say about altered scales:

"Altered Scales: The mixolydian mode has always been an important scale for jazz players. Jazz theorists who were looking back on what Charlie Parker (and others) played found that bebop players very often played notes over dominant 7 chords that were foreign to the mixolydian scale. These "unusual" notes were implied by the chord symbol. The players had found a group of notes which all had quite a bit of tension against the dominant 7 chord.

The bebop cats loved those notes (1, ♭2, #2, 3, ♭5, #5, ♭7) and shied away from tamer notes (2, 4, 6). The effect was to make dominant 7th chords lean ever more strongly toward the chord it was heading for anyway. The use of these notes was so persistent in the recordings of these bop players that theorists invented a scale name to facilitate talking about it. They used the term "altered scale" because several of the notes are altered notes compared to the mixolydian scale. At some point, someone noticed that the "altered" scale is the 7th mode of the ascending melodic minor scale.

Almost all the modes derived from the melodic minor scale have become important in jazz, and are an essential part of the modern jazz player's repertoire. Se Mark Levine's theory books for in depth treatments of these scales."

Thank you, Craig. (Craig *really* does know about this stuff, or else he is extraordinarily adept at making things up.)

The "Altered" Scale

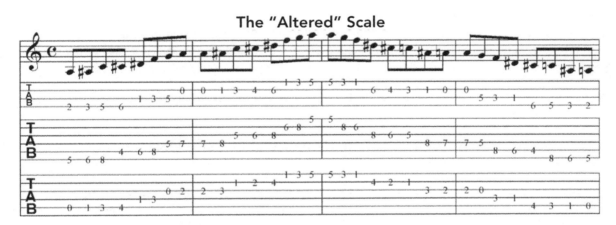

OK. Here are all these scales. Now what? ***Practice Playing Them. Every Day.***

But it's not really about becoming good at scales. That seems to be about as useful as being good at push-ups. "Whoa, dude! Lookit him go!" Push-ups are an activity that might be mildly interesting to observe for several consecutive seconds, but substantially less interesting for actual participation.

I don't care what you do about push-ups, but you should practice scales… a lot.

Several years ago, I watched about 25 lesson videos. There were lessons from everybody from Chet Atkins to Steve Vai. I bet 15 of these great players and teachers made a point to recommend lots of scale practice.

It finally occurred to me that if there *was* a better way, undoubtedly one of these guys would have figured it out and said, "Don't do scales, do this other thing." Instead, most of them said, "Practice scales. Every day."

So, as an experiment, I decided to try it for two months. A minimum of 30 minutes a day, every day, no excuses, and no exceptions.

Years later, I can say that I have yet to find an exercise that packs so much benefit into such a small space. If I find something better, I'll do that. Meanwhile, a daily minimum of 30 minutes of scales and variations on scales using a metronome (or drum machine or rhythm track) is part of my life.

If you practice scales, you will become good at scales. I bet most professional athletes are good at push-ups, sit-ups, and all sorts of exercises. The great ones probably do a series of fundamental exercises every day, as a regular part of their training. I bet none of them cares a lot about sit-ups.

I am convinced that Mr. Vai *knows* all about scales. And he still practices scales and variations on scales.

The hours that experienced players devote to practicing scales are not about *learning* a scale any more than a workout is about learning to lift a weight or do a sit-up. You can learn where the notes in any scale are found on any instrument in about 20 minutes.

Scale exercises are a platform for developing musical techniques and physical skills. Scale exercises are about ear training. Scale exercises are about coordination and dexterity with both hands. Scale practice is about strength and flexibility and agility. It's about developing the physical skills required to execute a musical idea. Scale practice is about eliminating the mechanical obstacles to playing musically.

Many people seem to think that scale practice is just for people who want to be great "lead players."

Wrong.

In the next chapter you'll learn that all the chords are derived from the major scale and all chords are named using the scale degrees. Not only will scale exercises make it easier to hear, understand, and finger all the chords, you'll learn in the next couple of chapters they make it easier to learn and play a variety of interesting strumming patterns.

When you're not primarily concerned with the mechanical aspects of playing a rhythm part, learning a bunch of songs is really pretty easy.

Daily practice of scale exercises will radically speed up the process of developing the physical ability to turn the musical ideas that are inside your head into sounds on an instrument.

Eddie Van Halen once said, "You can have a musical idea inside your head, but if you can't execute it, what's the use? You have got to have the technical side down. If you do (have the technical side down), you'll be playing and all of a sudden you'll have an idea in your head and your fingers will just go with it."

If you will incorporate 15 to 30 minutes of fundamental scale practice into your daily musical workout, every few months you'll notice that you are a little quicker, smarter, stronger, and more agile and accurate with both hands. In other words, you're a better player.

Mastery of the basics is the only way a person really masters any skill or craft. As you've seen, the major scale is the foundation for many scales, all the modes, loads of the vocabulary, and nearly all Western music. Just learning that single scale very well is enough to radically improve your playing.

If you dig around, you'll find that lots of virtuoso teachers and players will recommend daily scale practice. It isn't because there's any shortage of schtuff to practice. The **ONLY** that they recommend it is *because it works*.

There's no other reason to do it… except… when you start to get good at it… believe it or not… it's fun!

Scales are easy. The real challenge lies in that generally unpopular area referred to as "personal discipline." Ya gotta wanna.

Introduction to Major & Minor Scales

These exercises use only the first five notes of the scales. They're easier to learn this way and in some ways more useful than the full eight-note scale. In the next chapter, you'll learn about major and minor chords, and these abbreviated scales contain all of the important parts of the chords (tonic, 3rd, and 5th degrees make a chord). Once you have five notes under control, it's easy to add more.

It's important and useful to be aware that there are lots of different types of scales.

But, as a practical matter, there are only five that are of real interest to most players. The major scale, natural minor, harmonic minor, major pentatonic, and minor pentatonic are the big five. Next would be the blues variations of the pentatonics.

These few exercises will allow you to become very familiar, very quickly, with major and minor, which comprise about 40% of the hot list, in addition to being the foundation of all the rest. That's a lot, so there's no good reason to rush through this stuff. If you'll invest about 25 hours of good workout time on these, the others come pretty quickly. Fifteen minutes a day for four months is about 25 hours.

These alone are 100% adequate for most people. If your goal is to be a good, solid rhythm guitarist in a few styles, to strum the tunes you write while somebody else does the fancy stuff, look no further. Major and minor scales will get you there. It's the shortest road, in my opinion.

Guitarists, in these exercises that use open strings, match the fret shown on the tab to the same finger on your fret hand. Your index finger is 1, middle finger is 2, ring finger is 3, and pinky is 4. When the tab shows a note on the first fret, use your first finger. When it shows a note on the 4th fret, use your pinky. I play right-handed, so my left hand is the one fingering the notes.

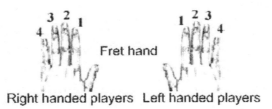

At first, it's easiest to reach the notes on the first and second strings, so start here and gradually work your way across the neck. Go slowly, and **hum the notes as you play them**. Use solfege syllables or come up with a few words.

Introduction to Major & Minor Scales

One of the most frustrating things for lots of beginning students is the nearly unavoidable conclusions that their fingertips do not seem to be directly connected to their brain. The brain makes what would appear to be a simple request, like "Will the tip of the first finger please go over and gently press on the first string right there beside the first fret?" and the tip of the finger suddenly feels and acts like it's being controlled by a committee of spastic aliens on the moon. "Just whose fingers ARE these, ANYWAY!!??" It's normal. It's been known to provide occasional moments of amusement for someone sitting in the teacher's chair in a lesson. Sometimes it resembles nothing so much as an attempt to push two magnets together that have the same poles facing each other. It will go anywhere but where it's being aimed. Simple repetitive exercises are the quickest way to establish the missing link. What you're after in the beginning is to just get your fingers to do what you're asked them to do. It helps to be polite when you ask, of course, but it helps more to practice. Notice that all of these use only two strings and that nearly all have three of the five notes on a single string. For beginners, it's often a good thing to begin by just playing those three notes, up and down for a few hours. You don't get any bonus points for trying the hard stuff first. Your fingers have no previous experience with this sort of action. Do easy things till you get it going and gradually complicate the issue.

Introduction to Major & Minor Scales

A major and minor are Form #4. E major and minor are Form #5. The pickup notes and bass runs that are so common and so necessary to play good rhythm guitar are often three and four-note scale runs that have their roots on the open 5th and 6th strings. When you can play these as quarter notes, apply the one-bar rhythm pattern at the bottom of the page.

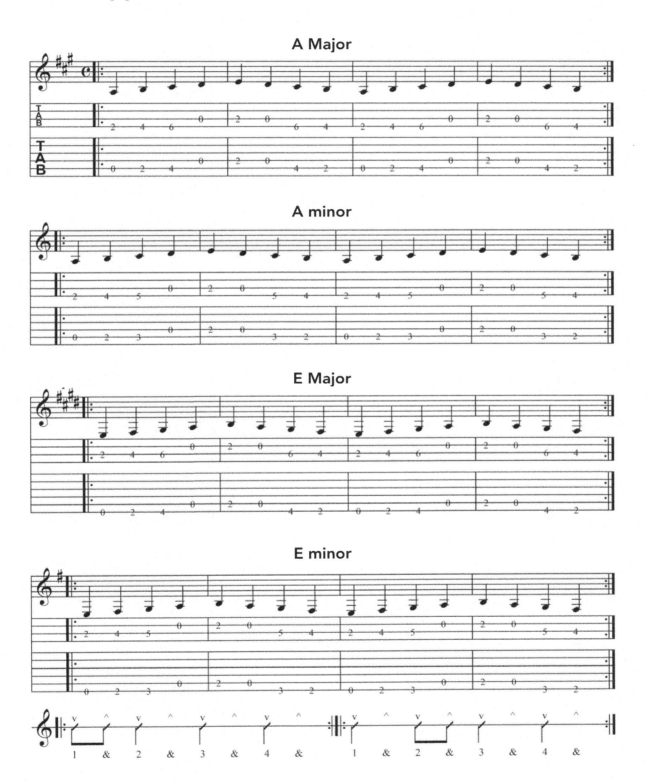

Introduction to Major & Minor Scales

G major and minor are Form #3. C major and minor are Form #1. Again, bass runs and pickup notes. If you skip the 2nd and 4th degrees and play on the tonic 3rd and 5th degrees, you're playing an "arpeggiated triad" and getting a head start on the next chapter, "**Major and Minor Chords**" where you'll find out about triads and chords. An arpeggio is kind of like a scale, kind of like a chord.

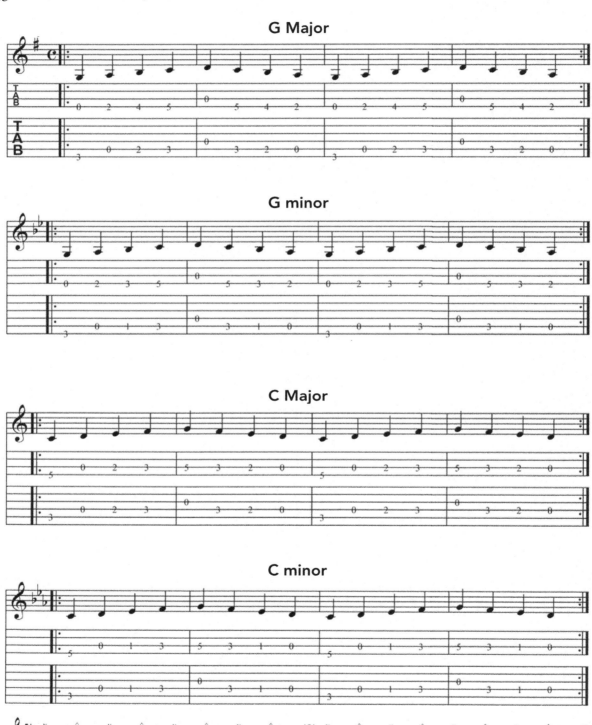

G Major

G minor

C Major

C minor

Introduction to Major & Minor Scales

In the beginning there was extreme difficulty with the dreaded F chord. For just about everyone. It's not just you. It's hard. Spend some time with this five-note F scale and you'll get a good start on the monster. In the next chapter, you'll learn about triads, which is a three-note chord that these abbreviated scales contain. Notice the asterisks above the notes in the guitar tab. Those three are a 100% complete, usable F chord. Same tones are a chord on a mando, but you can't play all three simultaneously. Chord tones played individually = arpeggio.

Introduction to Movable Forms

These exercises are the ones that begin to build your familiarity with the entire neck. Notice that these three forms are identical fingering for the five-note segment of the scale shown. Makes learning them a breeze. Learn (1) five-note shape for three forms. When you have it down, it's easy to extend each one to an octave. The 1st, 3rd, and 5th tones of nearly all scales… major, minor, diminished, whole-tone, you name it… create chords. The asterisks in these examples show the 1st, 3rd, and 5th tones. Keep it in mind and be aware you're learning chords as well as scales when you play these drills. Details soon. Use your pinky on the 8th fret. When you have a form memorized, go back to the Twinkle variations in "**Counting**" and apply those one-bar rhythms to these exercises. Then they start to sound like music.

Introduction to Movable Forms

Again, all but one of these five-note extracts use identical fingering. Use your middle finger on the 8th fret. Form #3 E♭ Major is the one that's different, due to the 3rd between the G and B strings. Use your first finger on the 8th fret.

Introduction to Movable Forms

Here are a few more minor scales. Once again, the fingering is identical for four of them and I put the one that makes the adjustment for the G-B string interval at the bottom. First finger on the 8th fret. The rhythm pattern is triplets this time. **down**-up-down **up**-down-up is how you should pick consecutive sets of triplets. It's tricky.

Reflections

*"Like music and art, love of nature is a common language
that can transcend political or social boundaries."*
Jimmy Carter

*"Look at a stone cutter hammering away at his rock,
perhaps a hundred times without as much as a crack showing in it.
Yet at the hundred-and-first blow it will split in two,
and I know it was not the last blow that did it, but all that had gone before."*
Jacob A. Riis

"Look at the stars sometimes. They are only notes... they are music."
Pat Conroy

*"Medicine, to produce health, has to examine disease;
and music, to create harmony, must investigate discord."*
Plutarch

*"Most people never run far enough on their first wind
to find out they've got a second."*
William James

"Music causes us to think eloquently."
Ralph Waldo Emerson

*"Music creates order out of chaos:
for rhythm imposes unanimity upon the divergent,
melody imposes continuity upon the disjointed,
and harmony imposes compatibility upon the incongruous."*
Yehudi Menuhin

*"Music expresses that which can not be said
and on which it is impossible to be silent."*
Victor Hugo

*"Music first and last should sound well, should allure and enchant the ear.
Never mind the inner significance."*
Sir Thomas Beecham

*"Music hath charms to soothe the savage breast, to soften rocks,
or bend a knotted oak, by magic numbers and persuasive sound."*
William Congreve

*"Music is a higher revelation than all wisdom and philosophy.
Music is the electrical soil in which the spirit lives, thinks and invents."*
Ludwig van Beethoven

Movable Forms for Guitar

The numbers indicate which finger should be used on the fretboard. I've only shown fingering for complete octaves, but the frets marked with an asterisk * are scale tones. For example, in Form #1, the three asterisks on the 1st and 6th strings indicate the 3rd, 4th, and 5th scale degrees. The lowest note indicated by a finger number is the tonic. The minor pentatonics begin on the 6th degree. The major scale is the Dorian mode, but each of these forms will also generate the other six modes by beginning and ending with a different degree. Be sure to notice that the fingering for Forms #1 and #3 are nearly the same for one octave, and that Forms #2 and #4 are identical.

Take a quick look through the advanced chord diagrams and notice how many of those chords span four frets. (**"Beyond Major and Minor Chords"**) They are all derived from these scale forms and working out on these scales while using the correct fingering is the quickest way to develop the strength and flexibility required to hold those chords. If you pay attention to the scale degrees now, it will be a big help with understanding the names and structure on those chords, too.

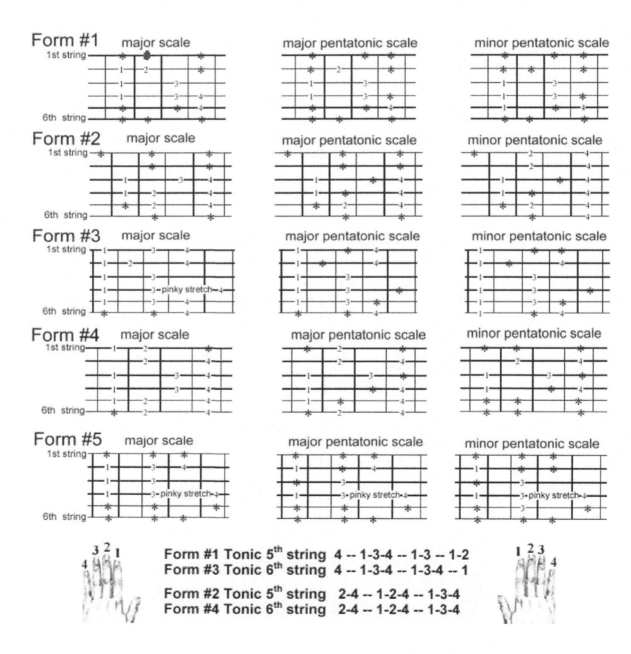

Form #1 Tonic 5th string   4 -- 1-3-4 -- 1-3 -- 1-2
Form #3 Tonic 6th string   4 -- 1-3-4 -- 1-3-4 -- 1

Form #2 Tonic 5th string   2-4 -- 1-2-4 -- 1-3-4
Form #4 Tonic 6th string   2-4 -- 1-2-4 -- 1-3-4

Movable Forms for Mandolin, Mandola, Violin, Viola, Cello and Tenor (11) Banjos

Maybe you noticed that there are never more than three notes to be played on any single string in the forms shown for guitar. That's mainly due to the size of the instrument. Five frets is a long stretch on a guitar. Mandolins and violins are much smaller and it's generally pretty easy for most adult humans to reach seven frets. These one-octave movable scales I've shown span six frets.

You'll recall that strings on all of these instruments are separated by the same interval… a perfect 5th. Since the relationship is the same between any two adjacent strings, it allows you to transfer anything that works on the first and second strings to the second and third strings, as well as the third and fourth strings. Compare the fret numbers in the tabs for the major and pentatonic scales shown.

Look at the fingering diagram for the major scale. Notice that the pattern of whole steps and half steps is identical on both strings. This four-note pattern (W-W-H) is sometimes called a "tetrachord." It's possible to describe a major scale as "two tetrachords separated by one whole step." You'll remember that the interval between the 4th (FA) and 5th (SO) degrees of a major scale is one whole step. I've seen a couple of books that used this structure as the primary way of describing the major scale. It never made any sense to me until I noticed this pattern fingering a major scale on instruments tuned in 5ths. Tetrachords as major scales aren't visually obvious on other instruments or other forms, but they're in every one of them.

It produces a visual pattern that's easy to remember. The little numbers above the notes are suggested fingerings. Even if you don't have a mandolin, mandola, violin, etc., memorize a couple of these patterns and when you do encounter one, you'll be able to play something… instantly!

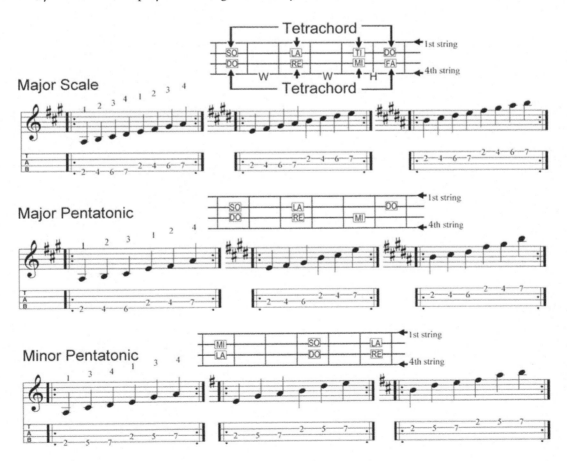

Just one more set of easy movable forms for the whole family of string instruments that are tuned in 5ths. There are a bunch of them. If you learn how to operate one of them, you have a big jump on all the rest.

Always be aware that the different instruments live and work in the same structure. I remember a student asking if a sax uses these same scales. I always assume that if one person asks a question, there are 50 others who don't know either, but they didn't want to ask. The answer is YES! The mechanical apparatus is different, but the music is the same. I've overheard more than a few conversations between students who are studying different instruments and many don't seem to be aware that their knowledge and skills are not limited to their current choice of instrument.

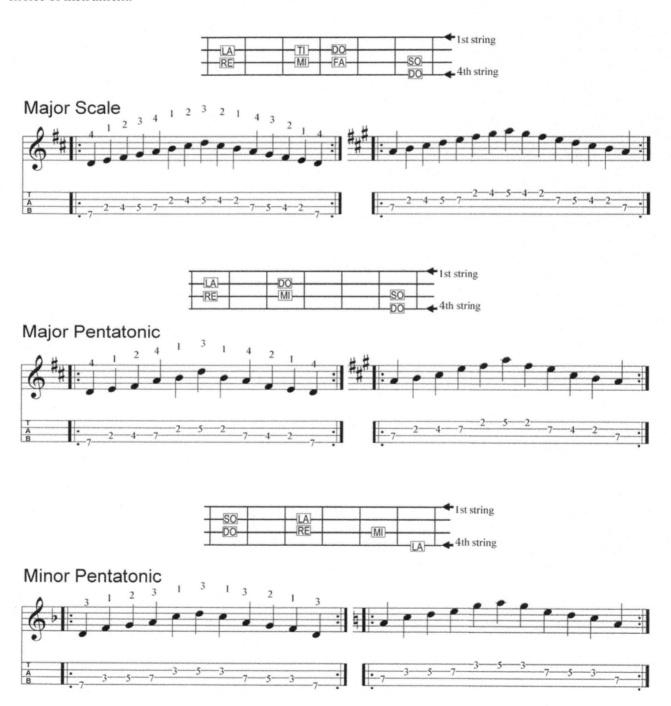

Combining movable forms

When you see someone playing a solo and their fret hand is moving up and down the neck, one end to the other, it's reasonable to assume that they're using different forms than the ones I've shown. Nope. Same scales, same forms, they're just sliding from one form to the next. These scales span two octaves.

A way to use a metronome and basic scale forms to develop speed and accuracy... with both hands

This outlines a way to use basic scales and a metronome to develop speed and accuracy with both hands, all over the neck. I used only five notes for this illustration, (DO, RE, MI, FA, SO) which is what the **Intro to Major and Minor Scales** on the next few pages use. The scale shown on this page is the first five notes of an A natural minor scale (Aolian mode). You can apply this process to all scales.

I've shown a metronome setting of 75 bpm, but if that is too quick at first, then back it down to 60 bpm or whatever is comfortable for you. Your goal should be "smooth and even," so play these at a tempo that is slow enough that you can play it perfectly. You definitely do not want to "practice mistakes" which is what you will do if you try to go too fast. "Speed is a product of familiarity" is something that I saw in an interview with a famous rock shredder... I think it was Eddie Van Halen, but I'm not sure. Whoever said it first is not too important, but the concept is sound.

Read through it first.

At first, I suggest that you set the metronome to 150 bpm when you want to practice at 75 bpm. That way the metronome is marking the eight notes. If you want to practice at 60 bpm, set the metronome at 120.

People usually find that the down stroke is easiest, to begin with. "Alternate picking" means that you pick in both directions... down, up, down, up down up, etc.

The symbol that indicates picking a string with a down stroke is **V**. It's placed above the staff and it looks like a little arrow pointing down.

The symbol in most commercial publications that indicates picking a string with an upstroke is ⊔. Although it resembles the letter "U," it's nearly always square, so I'm pretty sure it's not an abbreviation of "up." I haven't the slightest clue why it is not a little arrow pointing up. Seems unnecessarily cryptic, compared with the down stroke symbol, but that's the way it is.

There doesn't seem to be 100% agreement among publishers of music books and you may see publications that have these symbols reversed.

My computer doesn't have a key that makes this ⊔ thing, so instead, I used this little arrow ∧ which conveniently enough points up, to indicate the upstrokes.

Begin by playing this line using all down strokes. The metronome is ticking away at 150 bpm, indicating 8th notes, so you should play a note on every other click.

Consider that in order to make two consecutive down strokes, you have no choice but to bring the pick back up past the string without touching it. So, even though you are only playing quarter notes, your pick is moving at a speed that will produce 8th notes. All you have to do is hit the string on the way back up. It's easier said than done at first, so be patient with yourself. Your goal is smooth and even sounding notes.

Even if you can play this faster than what I've suggested, wait until you've played all the way to the end of this little drill before you crank up your metronome. You'll get up to bullet speed soon enough. **Never practice mistakes!** Go slow and get it right.

6 - Scales

Practice for a few minutes playing each note four times… down, up, down, up… smooth and steady.

Now, you'll double the speed of the hand that's on the fretboard… instead of picking each note four times, you'll play each note twice.

I bet you're beginning to see the pattern. When you're able to play it glassy smooth, play the notes twice as fast with the fret hand again.

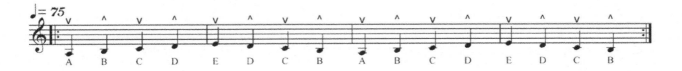

Now, you're going to go back to playing each note four times, but they'll be 8th notes, all played with down strokes.

Next, alternate picking. Smooth and steady. No mistakes with either hand.

Keep in mind that while there are only a few steps to this process, it's likely to take more than a couple of hours of focused practice before you're ready to move to the next step. Double the speed you're playing, one hand at a time.

Next…

Want to go faster? Of course you do! Repeat the same steps. Don't change the metronome. Your pick hand goes back to only down strokes. Play four 16th notes with your pick before you change notes… two times for each metronome click. Smooth and even. DO NOT PRACTICE MISTAKES!

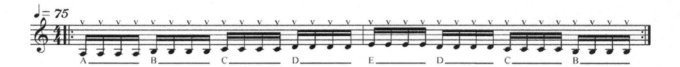

I'm sure that you know what's next, but I'll show you anyway…

Got the pick moving like it's supposed to? Double the speed of the other one…

Have I mentioned that the most important thing is to be sure you're playing very smoothly before you move to the next step? And I wouldn't want to neglect to remind you to "NEVER PRACTICE MISTAKES!" I mean, really… can you think of any idea that's dumber than practicing mistakes? Go slow, get it right, a whole bunch of times in a row. It's faster that way.

The term "Legato" means to play in a smooth, graceful, connected style. "Staccato" means a style of playing in a detached, separated, distinct manner. Practice both ways. Either style, you want the notes to be uniform… in tone and duration. Later you can start to color the phrases.

Here you are, playing at four times the speed you were a couple of months ago.

When this has been perfected, it's time to bump up the metronome a few notches. You may be tempted to set it at 100 bpm, but you'll probably find that when you get up to the 16th notes, it's pretty tough to keep up. Incremental increases… 75 to 85 to 95, etc., is really more effective than just trying to force yourself to race. Remember how many different places you can find the same five notes. Do the same drill in different places on the neck.

Playing while the metronome counts 8th notes is a good way to get introduced to a metronome and develop some smooth, steady speed skills.

It's equally important to learn to play 16th notes dead in time while the metronome counts quarter notes, half notes, and even whole notes. It can be a bit harder this way. Get good at this and drummers and bass players will love you.

A metronome is not especially expensive and is one of the most useful practice tools that you can learn to use. Almost nobody is willing to learn to practice with one. The ones who do learn tend to be pretty good players. Maybe that's just an amazing coincidence. Maybe not. They practice.

Unless you just take right to it, you can plan on at least 10 or 12 hours of remarkably un-fun practice time. It's really quite difficult at first for nearly everyone. It was hard for me. I suggest that you learn to do it anyway. It is absolutely worth the time and trouble. Blinking lights are OK, I suppose, but be sure to get one that makes a nice, loud click and try to wear it out. My Sabine cost about $30, and I use it a lot.

In addition to a metronome, you can get a drum machine. I have a steam-powered Alesis SR-16 that I've been using forever, and it's a blast to practice with. The new machines are much more versatile and pretty easy to use. Without checking, I think they're available in the $100-$150 range, and you'll need some sort of amplifier, too. Home stereo gear is not usually recommended for stuff like this. In addition to practicing in time, you'll learn loads about what rock-solid grooves sound like because there are a bunch of them built in. Plug it in, turn it on, and hit "PLAY." ROCK-N-ROLL!! RIGHT NOW!! A good investment, if you have some extra cash. And FUN!

I do *not* recommend that you use a drum machine *instead* of a metronome as a practice tool. Drum machines can be a lot of fun and you can learn things about drums that you can't get from a metronome, but for general practice a metronome is a better tool. Get one and learn to use it!

Using Solfege

Here are some familiar tunes that are nearly 100% diatonic. As soon as you're able to play one of the major scale forms pretty well, you should try these songs. After all, that's what scales are for… playing songs.

I assume that most people reading this book do not read music fluently. So, you're likely to think that the key signatures shown on the following exercises are pretty intimidating.

The reason I used all of these keys is so you'll recognize that the solfege can be used to "read" the notes, and virtually ignore the jumble of sharps and flats. In this exercise **sharps and flats do not matter**. In this context, solfege is about the relationship between the tones, not the names of the notes on the staff. It doesn't matter which note you call DO. Sing these wherever it's easiest for you. At first, *don't even think* about playing these, just sing the tunes. Ignore the notes on the staff, just sing the lyrics while you try to think DO-RE-MI. After you do that a few times, sing DO-RE-MI instead of lyrics.

There are a couple of things I should mention about solfege.

One is that the correct syllable for the 5th degree of the major scale is "SOL" and throughout this book I used "SO." The reason I did that was in many of the illustrations, lack of physical space was an issue. I wanted to make any lettering as large as possible for easy reading, so I dumped one letter. Rather than use SO on illustrations and SOL for text references, I stayed with my "incorrect" version. I trust that it won't cause any confusion.

A couple of these tunes are not 100% diatonic and solfege does accommodate the chromatic scale by the use of variations to the original seven syllables.

Because I used a couple of these other syllables in the examples, I thought I should probably let you know that I'm not just making them up, the way I did SO.

There is a set of syllables to indicate sharps and a different set to indicate flats.

These are the syllables for **sharps**.   DO **Di**   RE **Ri**   MI   FA **Fi**   SO **Si**   LA **Li**   TI   DO

These are the syllables for **flats**.   DO   TI **Té**   LA **Lé**   SO **Sé**   FA   MI **Mé**   RE **Ra**   DO

Here are two different ways of using solfege to describe the natural minor scale, or the Aolian mode. Aolian begins on the 6th degree (LA) of the major scale. This is the one I used for the examples.

LA TI DO RE MI FA SO LA

This is the other way to use solfege for natural minor. Notice the flat 3rd (**Mé**) and flat 7th (**Té**)

DO RE Mé FA SO Lé Té DO

Most college level music programs offer classes in "Sight Singing" and solfege is used. If you understand this system well, it can be a good tool to make reading music easier. It's worth investing some time to understand solfege.

I've included enough familiar examples for you to see how the system works. Before you try it with the solfege syllables, just hum through the tune you want to start with. Don't worry about the solfege syllables at first, just get the tune in your head. Use the words you already know. After you go through it a few times, replace the lyrics with the solfege syllables. The last step is to play them, slowly and correctly, using the scale form you're best at.

When you have a handle on it, I suggest that you take your trusty songbook and label the melody notes ("**Melody and Harmony**") in your favorite songs with solfege syllables and learn to sing them using the syllables instead of the lyrics. This is a skill that will be an important part of the exercises in the last chapter, "**Putting It All Together**."

Twinkle Twinkle Little Star

Twin	kle	twin	kle	lit	tle	star	how	I	won	der	what	you	are
DO	DO	SO	SO	LA	LA	SO	FA	FA	MI	MI	RE	RE	DO

Up	a	bove	the	world	so	high	like	a	dia	mond	in	the	sky
SO	SO	FA	FA	MI	MI	RE	SO	SO	FA	FA	MI	MI	RE

Twin	kle	twin	kle	lit	tle	star	how	I	won	der	what	you	are
DO	DO	SO	SO	LA	LA	SO	FA	FA	MI	MI	RE	RE	DO

Mary Had a Little Lamb

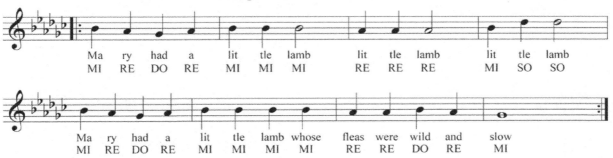

Ma	ry	had	a	lit	tle	lamb	lit	tle	lamb	lit	tle	lamb
MI	RE	DO	RE	MI	MI	MI	RE	RE	RE	MI	SO	SO

Ma	ry	had	a	lit	tle	lamb	whose	fleas	were	wild	and	slow
MI	RE	DO	RE	MI	MI	MI	MI	RE	RE	DO	RE	MI

Auld Lang Syne

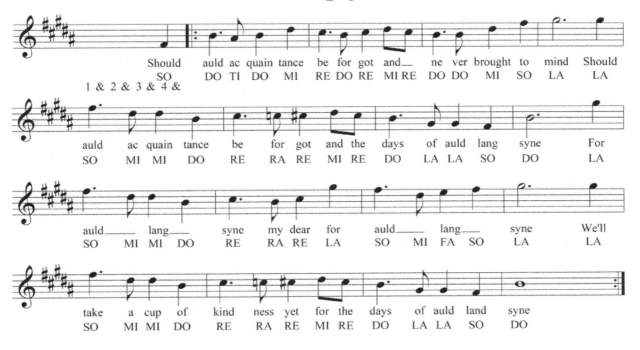

	Should	auld	ac	quain	tance	be	for	got	and	ne	ver	brought	to	mind	Should
	SO	DO	TI	DO	MI	RE	DO	RE	MI RE	DO	DO	MI	SO	LA	LA

1 & 2 & 3 & 4 &

auld	ac	quain	tance	be	for	got	and	the	days	of	auld	lang	syne	For
SO	MI	MI	DO	RE	RA	RE	MI	RE	DO	LA	LA	SO	DO	LA

auld	lang	syne	my	dear	for	auld	lang	syne	We'll
SO	MI	MI	DO	RE	RA	RE	LA	SO	MI	FA	SO	LA	LA

take	a	cup	of	kind	ness	yet	for	the	days	of	auld	land	syne
SO	MI	MI	DO	RE	RA	RE	MI	RE	DO	LA	LA	SO	DO

Deck the Halls

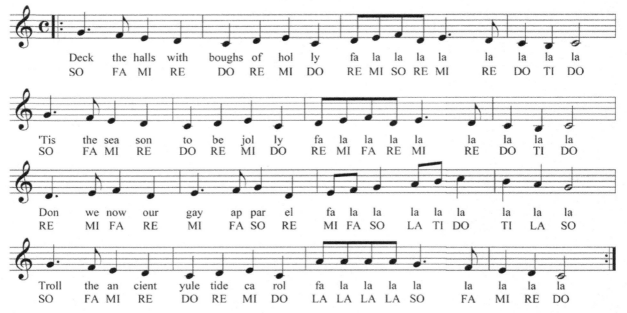

Are You Sleeping

Oh Tannenbaum

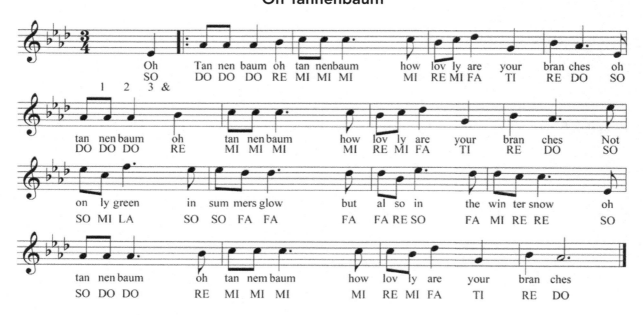

6 - Scales

Oh Susannah
Stephen Foster

Silent Night
Joseph Mohr

Greensleeves

Traditional tune, Lyrics by Henry Tudor

We Three Kings of Orient Are

Rev. J. H. Hopkins

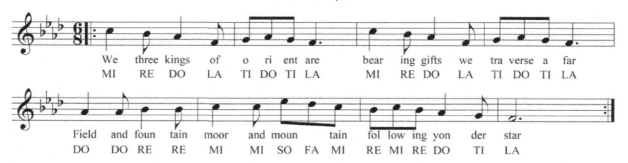

Introduction to Scale Variations

These next pages introduce a few ways to practice scales in a way that is much more applicable to actual songs and lead patterns than simply running straight up and down the scale from end to end.

I used Form #1 in the open position on guitar for these examples, but by now I'm sure you understand that they can be applied to all forms. In addition, the patterns shown will work for any scale that has seven tones in an octave.

Before you try to play them, look at the shapes made by each group of 8th notes for each exercise. I've labeled the scale for you, and each group of 8ths begins with the next scale degree. The examples of 3rd span a 3rd, 4ths span a 4th, and 5ths span a 5th.

The example "3rds and 5ths" introduces a structure called an arpeggio. It's a cross between a scale and a chord.

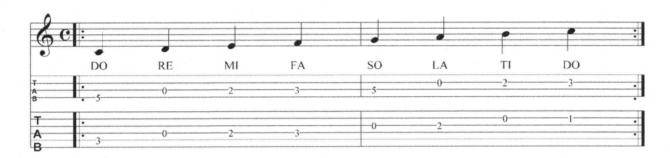

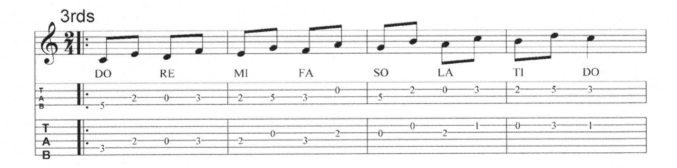

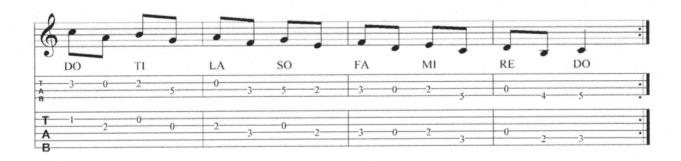

3rds

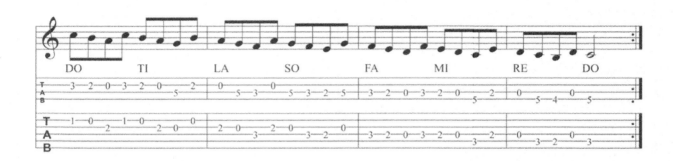

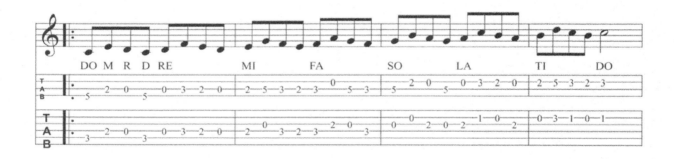

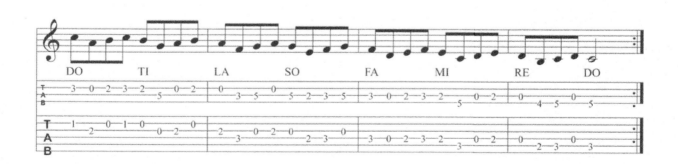

182   6 - Scales

4ths

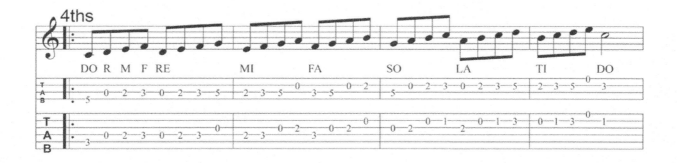

DO R M F RE   MI   FA   SO   LA   TI   DO

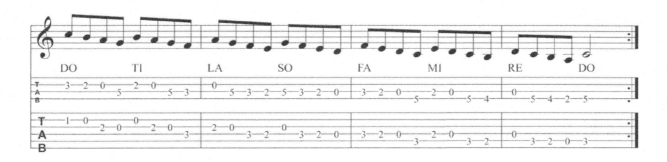

DO   TI   LA   SO   FA   MI   RE   DO

3rds and 5ths

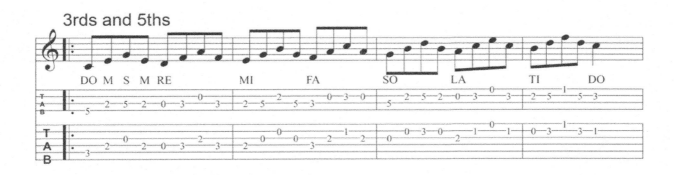

DO M S M RE   MI   FA   SO   LA   TI   DO

DO   TI   LA   SO   FA   MI   RE   DO

Linking Open Position Scale Forms

A series of chords is known as a chord progression and the most common progression is called a one-four-five progression. I'll cover all of that in detail soon.

The first line is a five-note scale for two measures. The 3rd measure and most of the 4th contain an arpeggio that spans one octave. It's the "one chord" in the progression. Line two does about the same thing, and it's the "four chord." Line three is the "five chord" and line four comes back to the "one chord." The tonic note for each form is the first note on each line.

Linking Open Position Scale Forms

Whenever possible, I've included mandolin tabs as well as guitar tabs. This particular exercise has notes that are well below the range of a mandolin, so the notes as written can't be played on a mando. But a mandola gets down there, so these tabs would technically be for a mandola. The tabs still work for mandolin and all the other four-stringers that are tuned in 5ths, but the names of the notes on the staff will change depending on which instrument you're playing.

Linking Closed Position Scale Forms

We're back in mandolin range here. Closed forms here, no open strings, so you can push it all over the neck.

6 - Scales

Linking Closed Position Scale Forms

Each of the lines in these "Linking Forms" examples outlines a chord in a 1-4-5 progression, the most common progression in pop music. Even if you are clueless about chords and progressions at this point, it's useful to observe that the tonic note for all three chords as shown on this page is on the same fret. On this page the three tonic notes are E, A, and B. Look at the same three notes but rearrange them... B, E, and A. The interval from B up to E is a 4th and the interval from E up to A is a 4th. A series of tonic notes (or root notes, next chapter) in a progression having a relationship that is structured by the interval of a 4th is one that occurs over and over and over in every genre of "popular" music... rock, country, classical, blues, jazz... all of them. A guitar is tuned in 4ths. Of course, you recall that if you invert a 4th it becomes a 5th... just about the same animal. The four-stringers are (usually) tuned in 5ths. This is either an amazing coincidence... or perhaps... the instruments are engineered with the music in mind. These relationships do sort of pose a musical version of "the chicken or the egg" question. Are the instruments designed to fit the music or is it the other way around? Be sure to call Pinky and share your innermost feelings on the subject.

Major and Minor Scale Study based on "Lonesome Fiddle Blues"
Millie and Vassar Clements

Anyone who is into bluegrass fiddle has probably heard of Vassar Clements. My favorite version of this tune was recorded by Old And In The Way. Vassar played fiddle and the rest of the lineup was Jerry Garcia (banjo), David Grisman (mandolin), John Kahn (bass), and Peter Rowan (guitar).

The first half of this tune alternates between five-note major and minor scales (mostly) so it first right in with those exercises I know you've been working on. It's an instrumental and the "run pony" stuff is there to help you with the rhythmic phrasing. There's also a "B" section to the tune, not shown.

Lonesome Fiddle Blues
Vassar and Millie Clements

Here it is again in a different key.

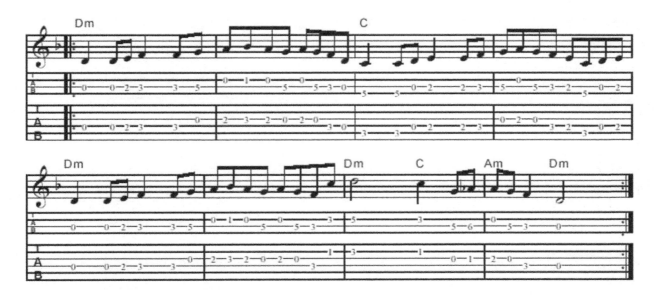

One more time, this time in a closed movable form.

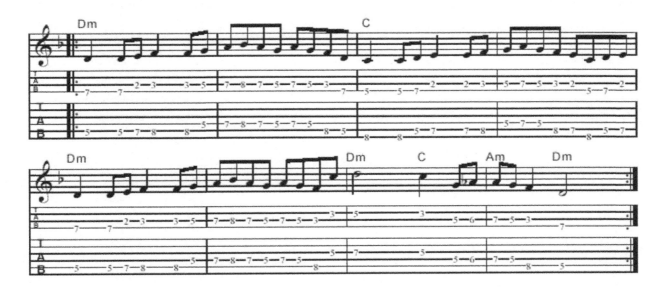

Hall of the Mountain King
Edvard Greig

Here's a familiar melody that lots of people like. Apparently, Edvard Greig didn't like it much. He thought it was too much like "pop" music. Like "Lonesome Fiddle Blues" it alternates between major and minor scales and this section stays within a fiv e-note range.

Hall of the Mountain King
Edvard Greig

Pop music or not, this one is still fun to fool around with. It's a good reminder of the fact that you don't need a jillion notes to create memorable music.

Sailor's Hornpipe

Here's another tune that will give you a good major scale workout. Again, the whole thing lays within a form so you can play either line of tab without having to move your hand up or down the neck… except in measure #12 of the closed form tab where you have to slide Form #1 up a whole step for a few notes (… * …).

Sailor's Hornpipe

If you'll take the time to learn this one and "Blackberry Blossom" in all the positions I've supplied here, it will take you a long way down the road to being able to play lots of bluegrass tunes and lots of Celtic music. In this book, it's more about the forms than the tunes. Get these forms nailed down and literally hundreds of tunes will be way easier.

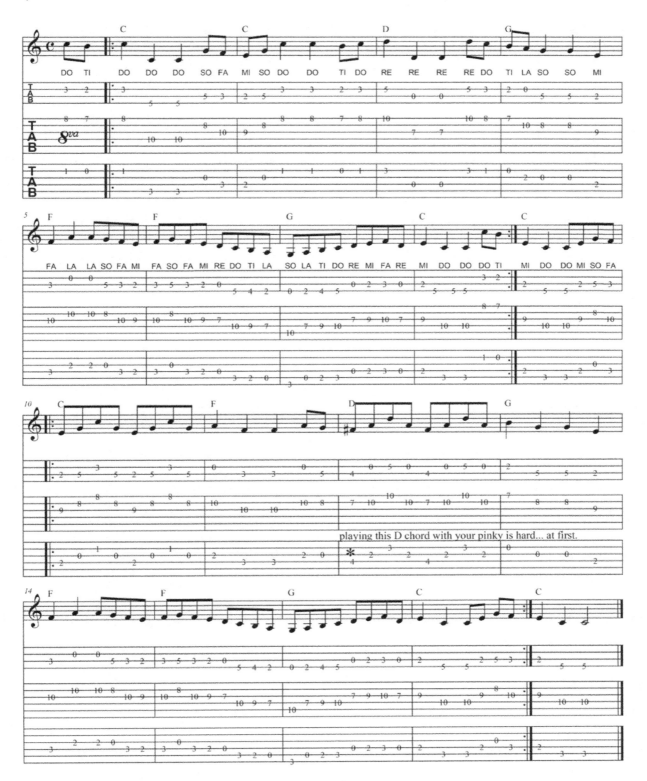

playing this D chord with your pinky is hard... at first.

Blackberry Blossom

"Blackberry Blossom" is a classic tune that's been recorded by lots of artists. Doc Watson's version is my favorite, followed closely by Tony Rice. It's also a great way to hear the major scale into the context of a tune. Notice the solfege going right straight down the scale in the first half of the song.

6 - Scales

Blackberry Blossom

Here it is again, open and closed forms. Most people learn this tune only in the open position, but it's really pretty easy in the closed forms. It lays within a span of four frets, except one note in the fourth measure.

Combining Major Pentatonic Scale Forms

These four bar examples are divided in half. Each half uses exactly the same notes, but you'll switch between the forms.

Form #3 Pinky plays the tonic   Form #4 Middle finger plays the tonic

Form #1 Pinky plays the tonic   Form #2 Middle finger plays the tonic

Form #4 Pinky plays the tonic   Form #5 Middle finger plays the tonic

Form #2 Pinky or third finger plays the tonic   Form #3 First finger plays the tonic

Familiar Riffs Based on the Major Pentatonic Scale

Although these riffs can be analyzed as having their foundations in the scales mentioned, I'd be willing to bet that none of them were written by thinking, "I think I'll invent a riff using the _____ scale! (Fill in the blank with any scale.) When I start my scale exercises, usually I'll begin by running the scale end to end a few times and then I begin to tweak it. I'll do arpeggios, patterns using 3rds and 4ths and basically anything that comes to mind. Loosely structured stream of consciousness, I guess you might call it. I'll usually play patterns that fit nicely into two or four-bar phrases. Every now and then something appears and I'll think, "That was cool… wonder what I can do with that!?" There's no way for me to know for sure, but I suspect that lots of things originate in a similar fashion. Notice that they don't usually extend beyond an octave. The originals didn't use "straight-8th" rhythm pattern as shown here. I did that for a pick-hand exercise. The mando tab provides a good clue to the rhythmic phrasing that was played on the original recordings.

Major Pentatonic Study based on "Ramblin Man" by the Allman Brothers

Major Pentatonic Study based on "Jessica" by the Allman Brothers

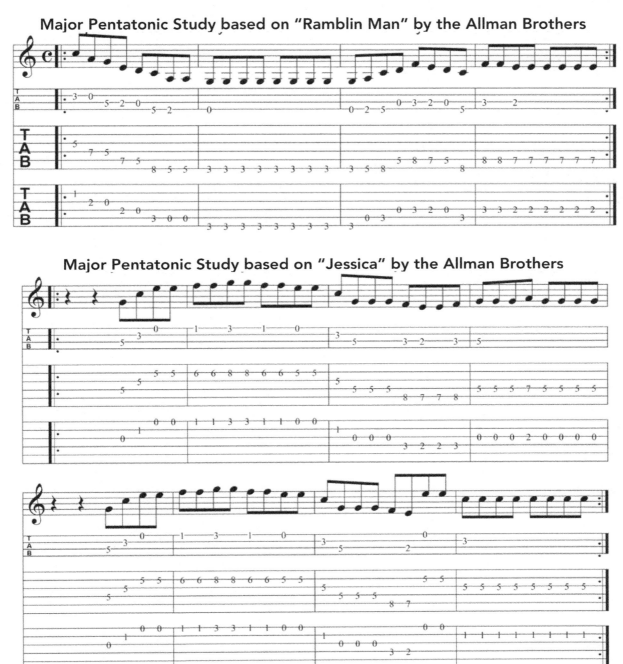

Major Blues Scale Riff

This is a familiar sounding little thing, but it's not exactly like any tune that I know of. It's fun to play and you'll hear lots of variations of it. This is laid out as standard 12-bar phrase, and uses a 1-4-5 progression. You'll learn about those details soon. Play it down low with your left hand on a piano and it's boogie blues. I beamed these 8th notes to show single beats, usually they would be learned into two-beat groups.

6 - Scales

Here's more of the same, in different places. To get your bearings, play the major scale a few times in the form I've shown below the tabs. The bottom guitar tab shows Form #1 starting with your pinky on the 5th fret. That generates a D major scale, which matches the first chord shown. It's not a coincidence. We'll get to that soon. For now, warm up on the major scale for a couple of minutes before you tackle these, it will be easier at first.

Three Familiar Intro Riffs Based on the Major Blues Scale

6 - Scales

Minor Blues Scale Riff

This is a lot like the Major Blues Scale Riff, but it's a few bars longer. You may notice that the notation doesn't always match the octave shown in the tabs in this section. I'm just squeezing more variations onto a page whenever possible.

Minor Blues Scale Riff

Here we go again, same riff in a few different locations. Playing everything you know in several different forms in different places on the neck is a REELY REELY GOOD habit to develop. You learn more than you might imagine that way. I didn't duplicate all of these examples because there is any shortage of tunes or riffs. If you learn these in a few spots, it will be easier to learn a thousand others.

Combining Minor Pentatonic Forms

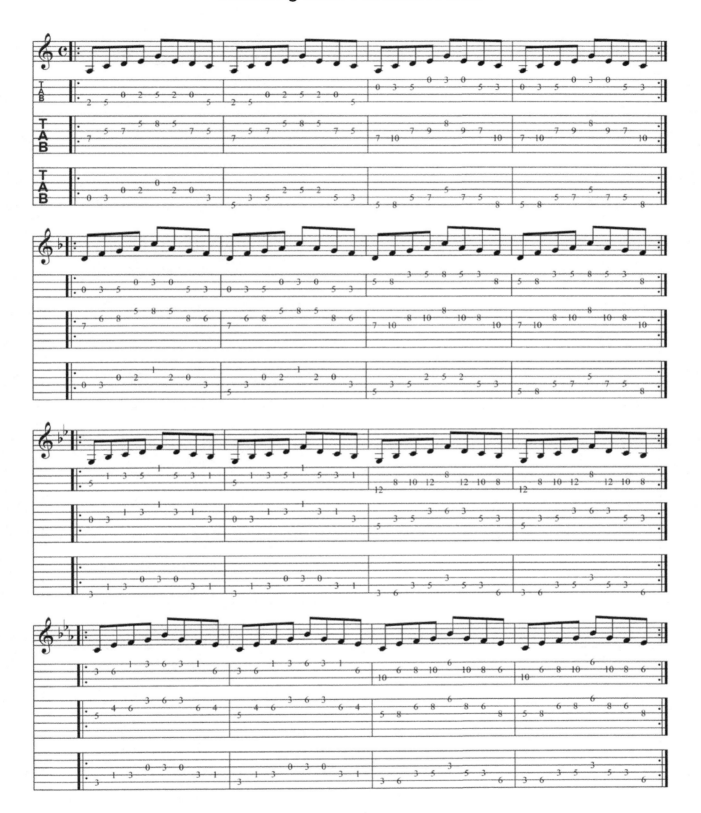

Familiar Intro Riffs Based on Minor Pentatonic and Minor Blues Scales

Minor Pentatonic / Minor Blues Study Based on Black Dog by Led Zeppelin

Minor Pentatonic / Minor Blues Study Based on Heartbreaker by Led Zeppelin

Minor Pentatonic / Minor Blues Study Based on Sunshine Of Your Love by Cream

Minor Pentatonic / Minor Blues Study Based on Iron Man by Black Sabbath

Familiar Intro Riffs Based on Minor Pentatonic and Minor Blues Scales

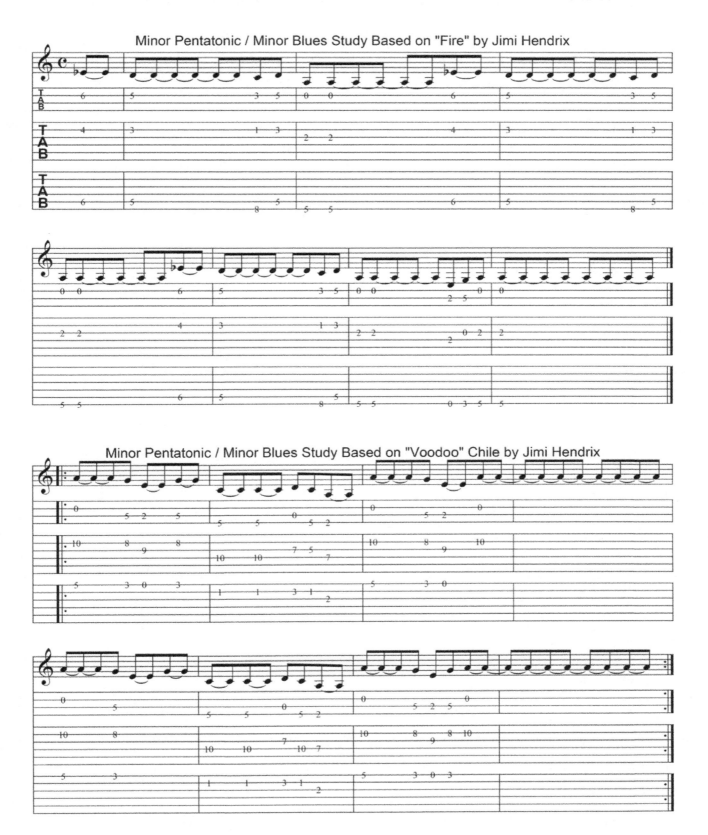

Scales

1. Just as a ladder is a series of steps, a scale is a _____ _____ _____.

2. _____ are used to measure the length of the steps between the notes in scales.

3. Each of these tones in a scale is called a _____ and they are numbered _____ through _____ .

4. The notes in a major scale always occur in _____ _____.

5. All _____ note names must be used in every major scale with _____ repetitions and _____ omissions.

6. The sequence of intervals in a major scale is _____ step, _____ step, _____ step, _____ step, _____ step, _____ step, _____ step.

7. The tonic of a G major scale is _____.

8. The tonic of a D major scale is _____.

9. The tonic of a A♭ major scale is _____.

10. The tonic of a an F # major scale is _____.

11. _____ is a system of referring to scale tones that eliminates the need to use the individual letter names replacing them with the syllables ___ ___ ___ ___ ___ ___ ___ .

12. Only certain notes can be referred to as DO.   **True   False**

13. There are _____ common modes and "mode" is very nearly synonymous with the word _____.

14. _____ mode is another way of saying major scale.

15. _____ mode is another way of saying natural minor scale.

16. A _____ scale uses all 12 notes.

17. The interval between the degrees of a chromatic scale is __ _____ _____ .

18. A whole tone scale is a series of _____ _____ and there are _____ different tones.

19. A pentatonic scale uses _____ tones.

20. The tones in a major pentatonic scale are the _____, _____ , _____, _____, and _____ degrees of the major scale.

21. The tones in a minor pentatonic scale are the _____, _____ , _____, _____, and _____ degrees of the major scale.

22. The C major pentatonic scale and the A minor pentatonic scale use exactly the same notes.   **True   False**

23. The minor pentatonic scale becomes the minor blues scale with the addition of _____ notes.

24. The major pentatonic scale becomes the country blues scale with the addition of _____ notes.

25. There are _____ commonly used minor scales.

26. They are called the _____ minor, the _____ minor, and the _____ minor.

Major & Minor Chords Chapter 7

The simplest definition of a chord is this: three or more notes played at the same time.

There are some two-note combinations that can be called chords and some three-note combinations that would be real tough to name as a chord, but when discussing major and minor chords we can work with the simple definition… three or more notes played at the same time.

A "triad" is also a three-note structure. The word "triad" means "three notes" and is not quite exactly synonymous with "chord," but real close.

Each of the three notes in a chord has a name that describes its scale degree or function in the chord.

The first tone is known as the "**root**" of the chord. The **root** of a chord is similar to the tonic of a scale. The **root** is the note that names the chord. For instance, a C chord has a C note as its root, a G chord has a G note as its root, a D# chord has a D# note as its root, an E♭ chord has an E♭ as its root, etc.

The next two notes are named the 3rd and the 5th.

Each of those numbers refers to the interval between the note and the root of the chord. From the root up to the 3rd is a 3rd, and the interval from the root up to the 5th is a 5th.

Here are some major and minor chords (triads). Each has three notes, one root, one 3rd and one 5th.

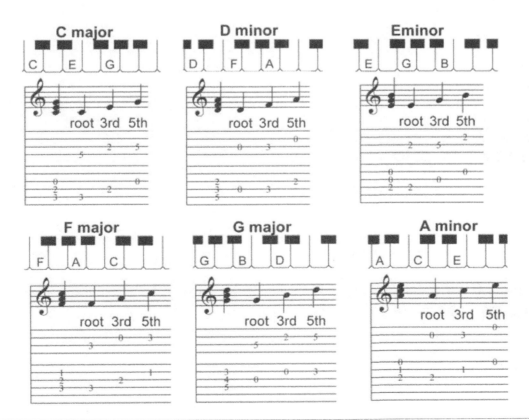

If someone asked, "What is the quality of the chord?" the correct answer is **not** "Oh, it's a good one." In the language of music, the word "quality" refers to whether a chord is major or minor (or a couple of other qualities we'll meet later). Soon we'll be adding notes to these triads to make bigger chords, but they will still retain their major or minor quality.

Major

All "**Major Chords**" contain three different notes… a **root**, a **3rd**, and a **5th**.

The interval between the root and the next note up is a major 3rd.

Start with any note. This will be the root of the chord. Count up four half steps, which is a major 3rd. That's the second note. The 3rd. The 3rd is the second note in a chord. I know it seems odd, but that's the way it is. The names come from the interval between the root and the tone. The second note is a 3rd above the root, so it's the 3rd of the chord.

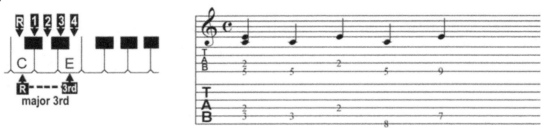

The interval between the 3rd and the 5th is a minor 3rd.

The top note in a major chord is seven half steps above the root, which you remember is a perfect 5th.

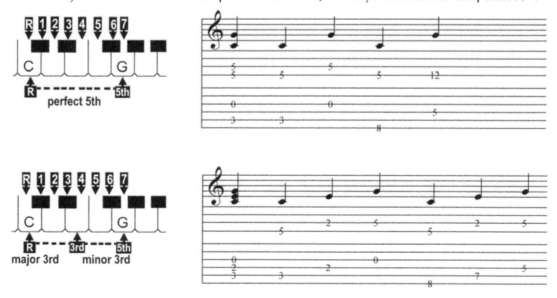

Minor

Next on the hit parade will be minor chords.

All "**Minor Chords**" contain three different notes… a **root**, a **3rd**, and a **5th**.

The interval between the root and the 3rd is a minor 3rd.

Start with a root, count up three half steps and that's the second note.

C major chords and C minor chords (and all the other) share two notes: the root and the 5th. The 5th is a perfect 5th above the root in a minor chord, just like a major chord.

Recap: There are two types of chords… chords that have a major quality and chords that have a minor quality. Both consist of three different notes… known as **Root, 3rd, and 5th**. The three notes span an interval of a perfect 5th.

When referring to major chords, all you have to say (or write) is the letter name. If you say, "It's a G chord" that means "It's a G major chord." If you say, "It's an E chord" that means "It's an E major chord." If you say, "It's an F# chord" that means "It's an F# major chord. You don't have to say or write the word major… it's implied and understood.

This indicates one measure of a G major chord, followed by one measure of a C major chord, followed by another G major chord, followed by a D major chord.

All other chords, beginning with the minor chords, have "adjectives" attached to the "letter name."

You have to say "minor." When written, there are a couple of different ways it's shown. The most common way to indicate minor is to add a lower case m after the letter name.

Am = A minor and **Gm** = G minor. Another very common symbol used to indicate minor is the "minus" symbol. **A-** = A minor. **G-** = G minor. **C#-** = C sharp minor. **Eb-** = E flat minor.

This is how to use intervals to construct a chord anywhere on the neck. Here's a major 3rd and a minor 3rd played separately. The major 3rd is on the 4th and 5th strings and the minor 3rd is on the 3rd and 4th strings.

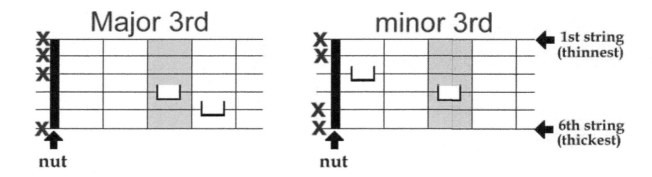

If you combine the two intervals the resulting three-note shape is a major chord. Voila! Just like magic, stack up two intervals, it's a C# chord. The root is on the 4th fret of the 5th string... the note is C#. The root names the chord.

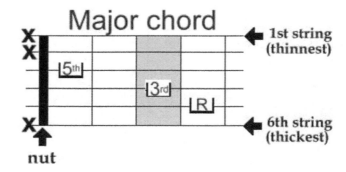

Keep in mind that we're only using the strings that have R, 3 or 5 shown on them. Mute the other three strings, or just don't pick them... indicated by an X on the string.

Move that entire shape up one half step and the root then falls on D note. Now it's a D chord.

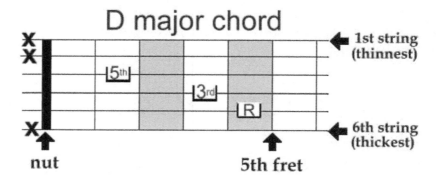

Move it down until the root is on the 3rd fret of the 5th string and now it's a C chord. The 5th falls on the open G string.

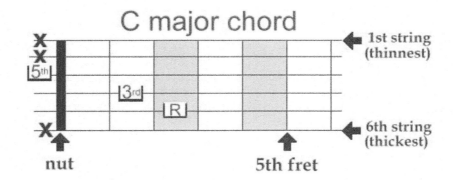

C major chord

1st string (thinnest)

6th string (thickest)

nut   5th fret

Now move it over so the root is on the 6th string, 3rd fret. It is now a G chord because the root note is on a G. The 5th is on the open D string.

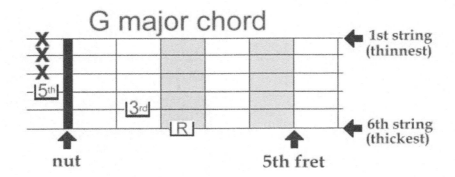

G major chord

1st string (thinnest)

6th string (thickest)

nut   5th fret

Here's a bonus… by moving it up and down the fretboard this one shape will voice a total of 12 major chords.

And how many different major chords are known to exist?

In all of music there are 12 major chords.

Does the same process of learning one shape and moving it around get all the minor chords, too?

O yes o yes o yes.

Since the only difference between a C major and a C minor is the 3rd, you can just take the shape that produces a major chord and alter the 3rd, as shown on the next page. And, of course, the same alteration is possible in all 11 of the other major chords, too, no matter where they might be played on the neck.

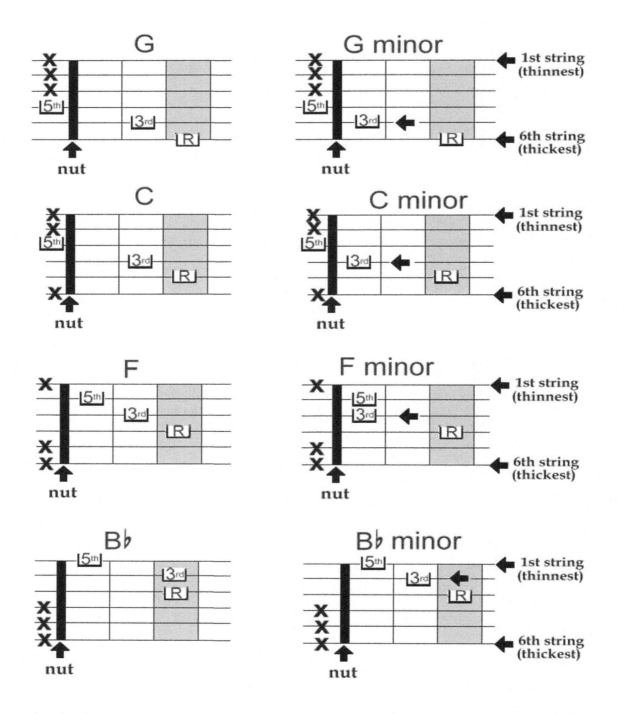

Notice that the shape changes when the triad uses the 2nd, 3rd, and 4th strings and the 3rd, 2nd, and 1st strings. Remember, the intervals between the strings are not always the same. The interval between most of the strings is a perfect 4th… five half steps.

Except between G and B… the 2nd and 3rd strings. From G to B is a major 3rd, only four half steps. As a result, on a guitar the three-note shape that works on strings six, five, and four; and strings five, four, and three, has to be adjusted when we get over to strings four, three, and two. We still get the same sequence of intervals, and the sound quality is the same, it just looks different on the fretboard.

Now, if you have already learned to play some chords on a guitar, you probably learned the G chord as shown below, strumming all six strings. The chords I've been showing have only three notes. What's up with that?

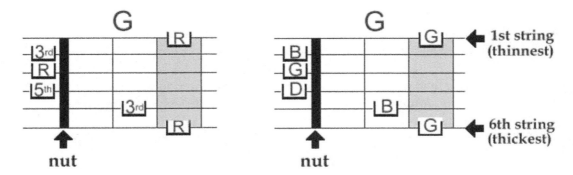

When you strum an open G chord on a guitar, the six individual notes are **G B D G B G. R-3-5-R-3-R**. There are three root notes, two 3rds , and one 5th.

Here are the same six notes on a keyboard.

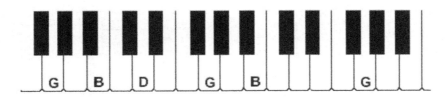

On a keyboard, with 10 fingers, you can play 10 notes at once, 11 if you use your nose. A basic G chord might be: **G D G B D B G B D. It is still a G chord**. Arrange them in any sequence you like. Whether the first note is D, B, or G, it doesn't matter.

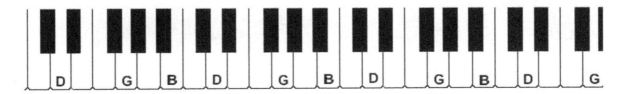

This is a variation on a G chord that I use a lot. I substitute a D on the 2nd string for the open B. Still a G chord? Yes. **R-3-5-R-5-R**. Another common variation is to mute the A string and play it as a five-note chord… 6th string G, mute the 5th string, 4th string D, 3rd string G, 2nd string (D or B) and 1st string G.

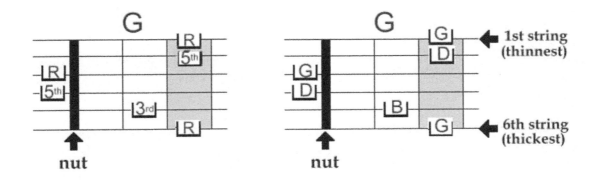

You can duplicate any or all of the three notes and rearrange them in any order, and it is still the same chord you started with.

CEGCEG… R-3-5-R-3-5… is a C major chord that contains two roots (C & C), two 3rds (E & E) and two 5ths (G & G). Or mix them up. The notes EGCECG make a C major chord with the 3rd in the bass… 3-5-R-3-R-5. GECCEG is a C major chord with a 5th in the bass… 5-3-R-R-3-5.

Important point: **You don't have to play all six strings to make a chord.** Three notes, three strings are always enough to make a complete major or minor chord and a lot of times you can get by with only two.

Don't let a chord diagram with lots of notes on it intimidate you. Grab two or three of those notes and that will usually suffice. Later, you can add the others if you want to.

If you play these illustrations one note at a time, you'll find that the only difference between these forms and the pentatonic scale forms you learned earlier is that these are simplified: they're missing two of the tones. (When you play a chord one note at a time, it's called an arpeggio.)

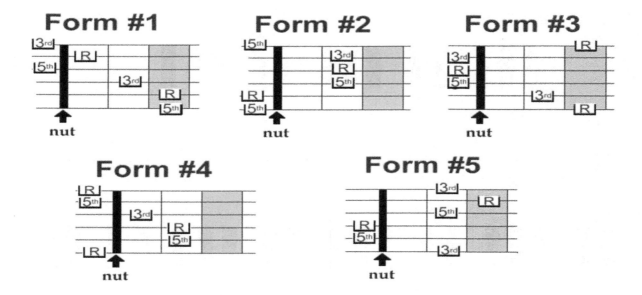

If you already know some basic guitar chords, I trust you noticed that each form shown above is one of the first chords that you learned. "First position" or "open position" means that the chords are played using as many open strings as possible.

These five major chords (C, A, G, E, D) are the only major chords that can be played using all six strings and have at least two open strings. They are the foundation of **all the chords** that are played on a guitar. These same five "shapes" or "forms" are just moved to different places on the fretboard just like we do with scales.

When they are played using no open strings, they are known as barre chords. Most people try to learn Form #4 as the first barre chord and Form #2 next. Frequently, that satisfies a person's desire to play barre chords, because it's really hard at first.

In one of Doc Watson's lesson videos, someone asked him about barre chords. If you don't know who Doc Watson was, just understand that he was without a doubt one of the finest pickers to ever inhabit this planet. When asked about barre chords, Doc said, "I never really learned how to do those… it's pretty hard." I didn't quite fall out of my chair.

The triads I showed are derived from these barre chords. We'll take a closer look at triads soon. They are much easier to play than barre chords and they help build strength so you can eventually play full barre chords… if you want to. Doc Watson has proved that it isn't required.

Sometimes you will see these forms referred to using a chord name instead of a number.

Because Form #1 creates a C major chord when played using as many open strings as possible, it is sometimes called "the C form" when played as a barre chord.

Because Form #2 creates an A major chord when played using as many open strings as possible, it is sometimes called "the A form" when played as a barre chord.

Because Form #3 creates a G major chord when played using as many open strings as possible, it is sometimes called "the G form" when played as a barre chord.

Because Form #4 creates an E major chord when played using as many open strings as possible, it is sometimes called "the E form" when played as a barre chord.

Because Form #5 creates a D major chord when played using as many open strings as possible, it is sometimes called "the D form" when played as a barre chord.

If you look at them in sequence, there's a mnemonic to help remember them… C-A-G-E-D.

For the most part, particularly when trying to describe the forms, it's way too confusing to use the letter names. Whatever works for you is OK with me. The important thing is to learn them.

In a very real sense, these five forms are the foundations for every chord that can be played on a guitar.

It is absolutely worth your time to memorize these five forms. That is to say, you should know exactly where to find every root, 3rd, and 5th in all five forms. That knowledge is a powerful tool that you will use as long as you play.

Go through your songbook and notice how many of the chords shown are either major or minor chords. Chances are good that well over half of the chords will be one or the other.

Does that mean that if you know these five forms you can fake your way through 50% of the chord changes in just about all of the "pop tunes" ever written?

Well… yeah… sort of. For sure, it's a good place to start.

Chord Inversions

"Inverting a chord" means to change the sequence of the tones. A triad has three possible inversions. Each inversion has a name. R-3-5 is "root position," 3-5-R is the "first inversion," and 5-R-3 is the second inversion.

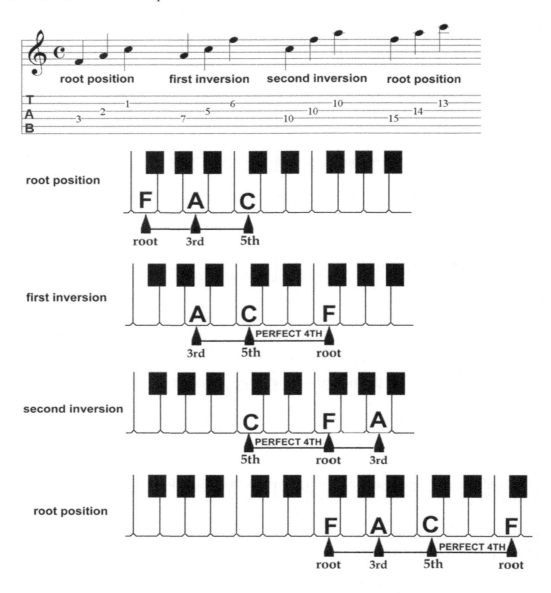

Did you notice the new interval? It's not really new, of course. You just don't see it till you reach the octave. This is a good time to recall "inverting intervals," too.

Often the 5th nearest the root is a 4th below instead of a 5th above. If you understand that... congratulations! It's pure gibberish to most people, but it's really useful for musicians because root to 5th is one of the most important relationships in music.

Each of these triads is an "extract" from the forms shown earlier and is often an excellent substitute for the full six-string barre chord... with a lot less pain involved. Doc uses these a lot.

As you play through these illustrations, keep in mind that each inversion is a 100% complete major chord. This first illustration shows four different C major chords. Each inversion will produce all 12 major chords. So... this single illustration can be used to play 36 different major chords. To get an additional bunch of chords from this simple illustration, just flatten the 3rds and all of these major chords become minor chords.

Take a look at the triads on the staff. Root position looks the same no matter where you find it. The first inversion always looks the same and so does the second inversion. You can learn to identify little structures like these at a glance.

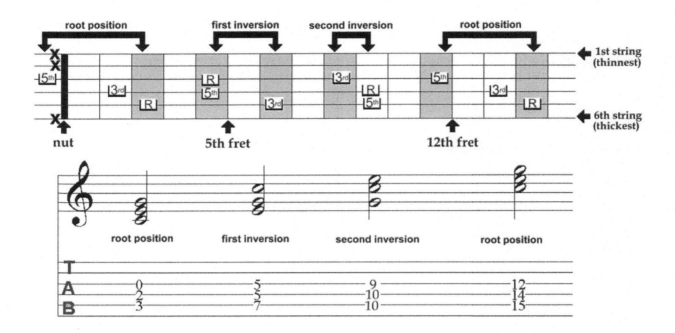

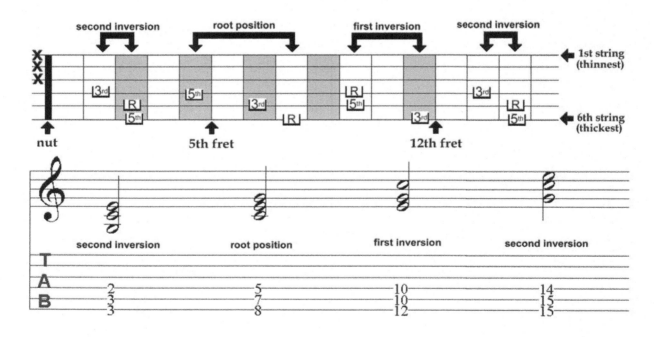

Keep in mind that you are not limited to the combinations I've shown. The triads are shown using adjacent strings, but you can skip strings, use combinations of two, three, four, five, or six strings… whatever you like. These triads not only produce dozens of major and minor chords, but also serve as a foundation on which we can build other chords that consist of more than three notes. We'll do that in the next chapter. Take some time with these and it will be time well invested.

Barre chords and triad inversions

An important part of learning to play guitar is recognizing the "shapes" or patterns that your fingers form when you play chords.

When I'm learning a new chord, sometimes it helps me to think of them as geometric shapes... connect the dots. Straight lines, diagonal lines, trapezoids, squares, and triangles.

I'll give you an introductory idea of how triads work on these three strings, but you should learn them on the others, too.

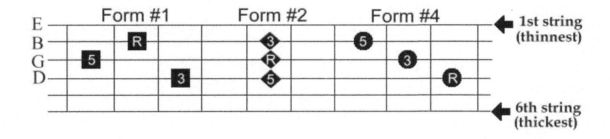

The first triad (shown by squares) can be seen as a triangle or a tent or an upside down V or whatever works for you... (careful about what you choose... this is actually a psychological test and the results will be made available to music police all over the known universe).

The next triad (shown by diamonds) is a straight line and is derived from Form #2. Go back to page 214 for a moment and you'll see that when using the 2nd, 3rd, and 4th strings, Forms #2 and #3 use the same three notes. I'm not skipping Form #3, it's just redundant for this illustration.

The last triad in the line can be seen as a diagonal line shown by three black dots and is derived from Form #4.

Play any of these triads on the strings as shown, anywhere on the guitar, and it is a major chord.

I chose to use these three strings to illustrate this idea for a couple of reasons. One is that they're easy to reach on a guitar, even for people with smaller hands. In addition, a five-string banjo also has D, G, and B strings, just like a guitar; so, this section will also give you a good start on playing a banjo. Guitarists, you can lower your first string E a whole step to D, ignore your 5th and 6th strings, and you have a facsimile of a banjo.

5 String Banjo

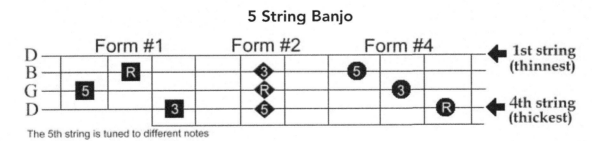

The 5th string is tuned to different notes

As the root note is the note that will name each chord, that one is the most important.

Here, you'll play only three notes from each form, a root, a 3rd, and a 5th, the ones that are on the D, G, and B strings.

This three-note chunk of Form #4 has the root as the lowest note, followed by the 3rd and the 5th. On these three strings, this generates a "root position" triad.

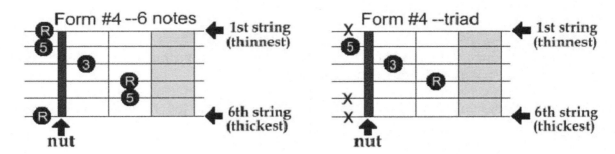

I use the triads that occur using the 2nd, 3rd, and 4th strings a lot, but that doesn't mean that you can't use other combinations of strings. For example, notice that in Form #4 there are two other ways to play a root, 3rd, and 5th combination using adjacent strings. Strings one, two, and three will get you to a major triad, as well as strings three, four, and five.

Now for Form #1. Start with all six strings, then extract and play three notes, a root, a 3rd, and a 5th. On these three strings, this generates a "first inversion" triad.

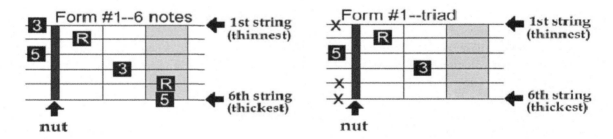

This triad is the first inversion because the 3rd is the lowest note, followed by the 5th in the middle, with the root on top.

In Form #1, there are three other ways to play a major triad using adjacent strings. There is a second inversion triad using strings one, two, and three, as well as on strings four, five, and six. You'll also find a root position triad on strings three, four, and five.

Form #2. Start with all six strings, then extract and play three notes, a root, a 3rd, and a 5th. This is the second inversion... the 5th is on the bottom, 3rd on top with the root in the middle. This is a "second inversion" triad on these three strings.

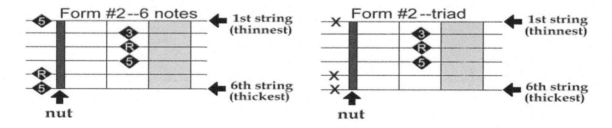

These forms are all "movable." Wherever you move the form, you will still get a major chord. These triads are just abbreviated versions of barre chords that are easier to play.

Depending on the situation, triads are often a better option than a six-note chord. If you're playing with a full band or even just one other guitar, using fewer notes can frequently be adequate accompaniment without getting in the way of the other instrument(s). Often when playing music, especially in a band or a group setting, a good thought to keep near the surface is this: **"Less is more."**

Here is a triad from Form #4 used to play several different major chords.

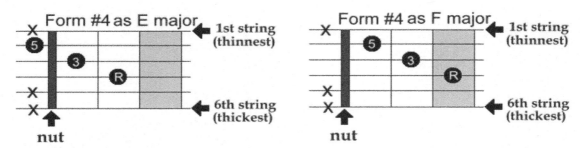

The root note is E, so the chord is E.   The root note is F, so the chord is F.

Here is Form #2 in a few different places.

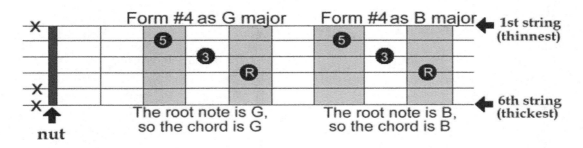

Here is Form #1.

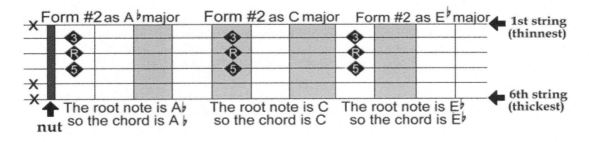

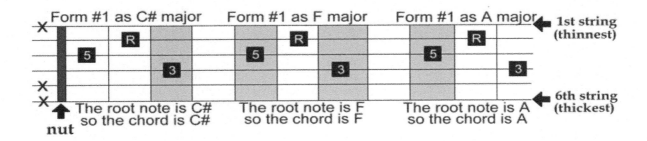

The first step in learning to play advanced chords is understanding the alteration of the 3rd. In the next chapter we'll do the same sort of thing with the other tones, as well. Be sure to memorize the location of the root, 3rd, and 5th for each of these inversions. It's relatively easy at this point since we're only looking at three strings. Then you'll have a foundation to work with that is easy to alter and extend. This knowledge will be useful for as long as you play.

One of my musical heroes is Mark Knopfler. He's a great producer, writer, and player. One of his signature guitar riffs is to use triads and play them as arpeggios at bullet speed. Check out one of his first radio hits, "The Sultans of Swing." Gotta love it!

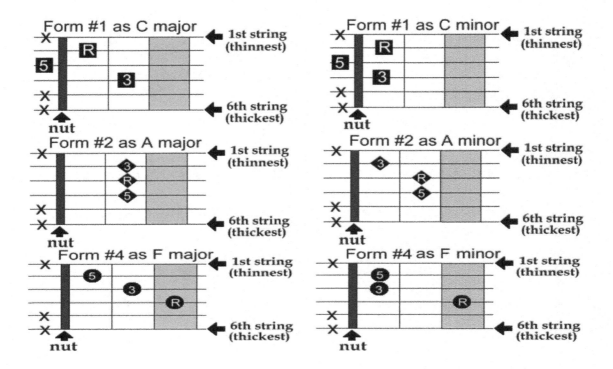

You will have some practice spelling chords at the end of this chapter. It's a useful skill and not very hard. There are only 12 chords. Two hours of focused study will take you a long way on this one. Don't skip through this little exercise; make sure you do it. Use the keyboard or the guitar illustration. After you understand it, look through your songbook and notice the melody note (see "**Melody and Harmony**") that is vertically aligned with the chord and word. In nearly every instance (nearly eight out of 10 by my count), that note will be the root, 3rd or 5th of the chord being played.

In this example taken from "Nowhere Man" by the Beatles, the first melody note is B, which is the 5th of an E chord. Last note in the same measure is E, the root of the E chord. The first note in the second measure is D, which is the 3rd of a B chord and the last note in the second measure is the root of the B chord. First note in the third measure is a A, the root of an A chord and the other note C# is the 3rd of A. Last measure walks down the scale from SO to MI, the 5th and 3rd.

Nearly every note begin sung is the root, 3rd or 5th of the chord being played. Look at other songbooks, this is something you can expect. This is an extremely important fact to remember whenever you're trying to figure out the chords for any song. If you can sing the tune, and you've been practicing singing along with your five-note scale exercises, it's not too hard to guess the chord, because the choices are limited, especially if you know what key the tune is in (coming soon). If the chords weren't supplied, you would have to guess. In this case, the B note in the first measure could be the root of a B chord (major or minor), the 3rd of a G, the flatted 3rd of an Ab minor, or the 5th of an E chord. When you practice your scales, notice the chords that are created by every other tone. Sing the scales and sing the triads. This is something that we'll come back to in the last chapter, "**Putting It All Together,**" so start practicing now.

For those of you who have been playing guitar for a while and know some songs, I'd recommend you try playing everything you know using these triads, instead of the open position chords. You'll find new things and it will open the door to playing some lead lines. Have fun.

Intro to Triad Inversions

I recommend learning these inversions two at a time. A good place to start is at about 60 bpm, so set your metronome to count 8th notes at 120 bpm. Take it one line at a time until you can do it perfectly for about a minute. Do the major inversions, then do the minor inversions, then start to mix them up. When you have them under control, bump up the metronome to maybe 140.

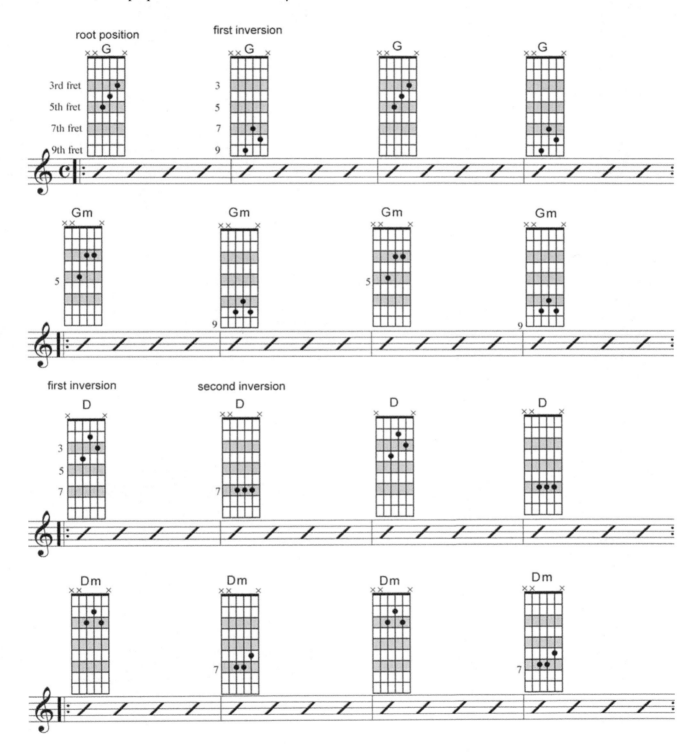

Intro to Triad Inversions

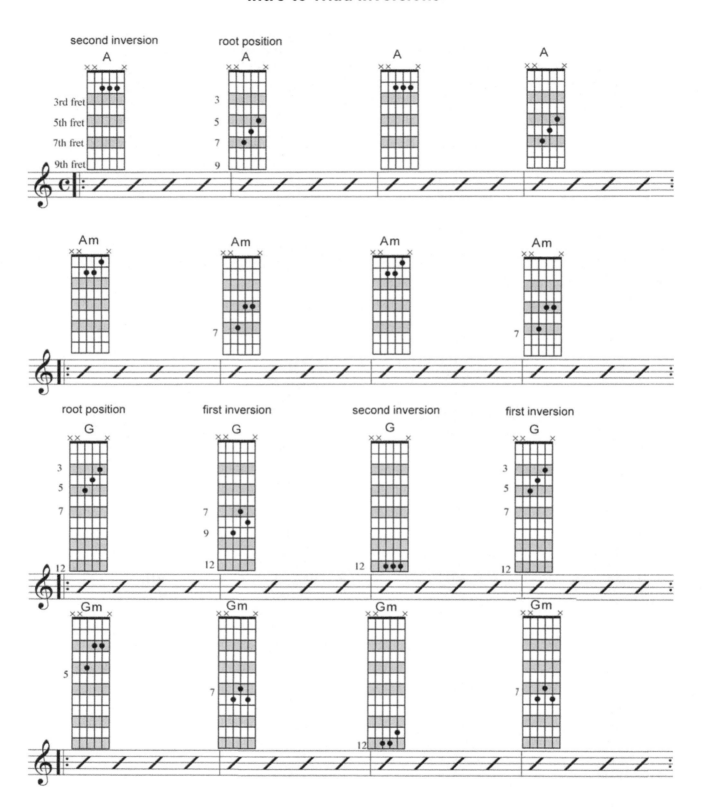

7 - Major & Minor Chords

Diatonic Inversions for Instruments Tuned in 5ths

I didn't isolate the triads for these inversions. Notice that in these forms the 1st and 4th strings always show the same tone. So if you play strings 1-2-3, you get a triad, and if you play strings 2-3-4, you get a different inversion.

As always, flatting the 3^{rds} will turn these major forms into minor chords. The first G chord shown here has two 3^{rds} and they both have to move.

There are a few different ways to finger major and minor chords on these instruments and I've shown the ones that are easiest to grab.

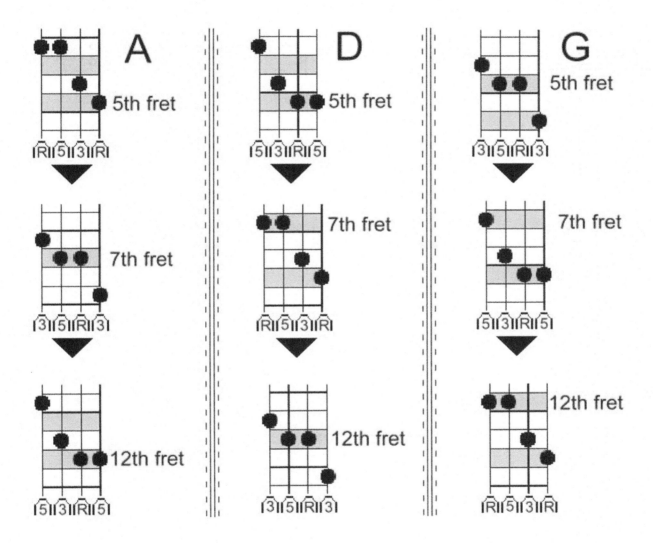

Three-chord triad drill

This exercise links three chords into a common progression. Before you play, notice the spacing on the staff between the notes in each chord. All of the root position triads look alike, first inversion all the same and the second inversion has a unique appearance. You might as well learn what they look like, too.

I designed this with guitar in mind and it works for the mando team, too, but some of the chords span seven frets. I've tried to keep beginners in mind most of the time when showing chords, and some of these are easy. A stretch of seven frets is normal on mandolins and mandolas, but some shown here will be impossible for most to reach on anything much larger than a mandola.

7 - Major & Minor Chords

Three-chord triad drill

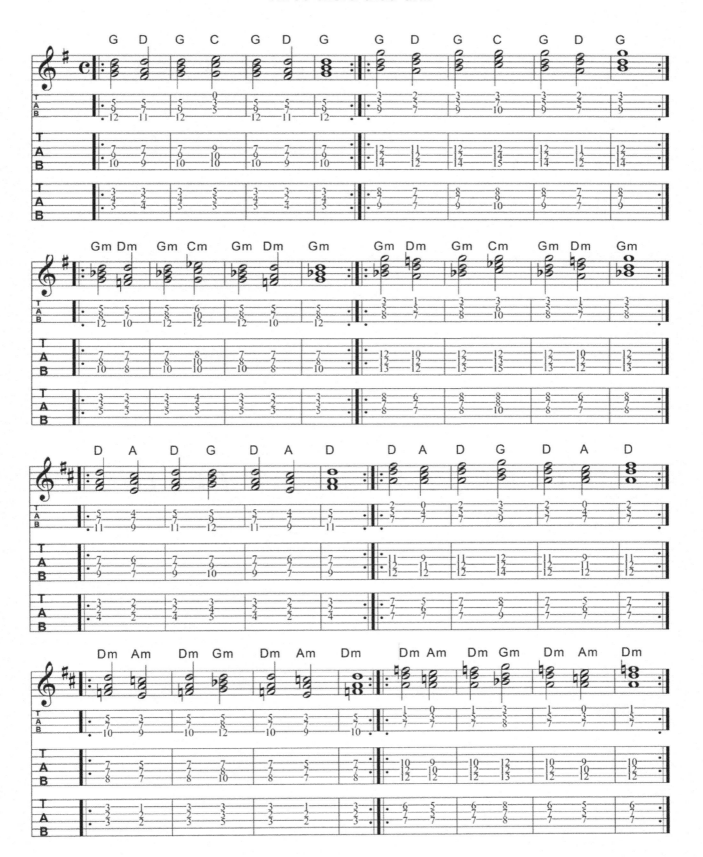

Twinkling Triads

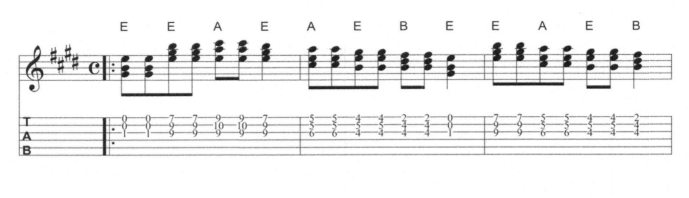

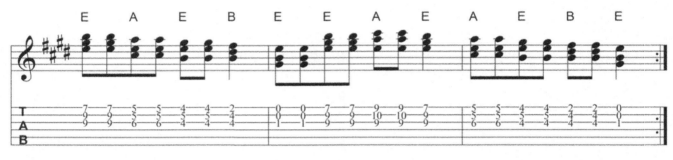

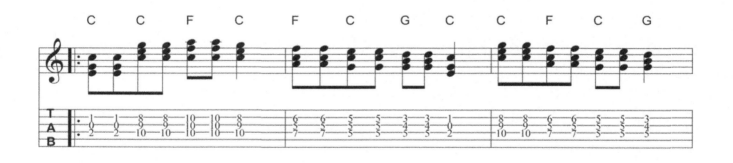

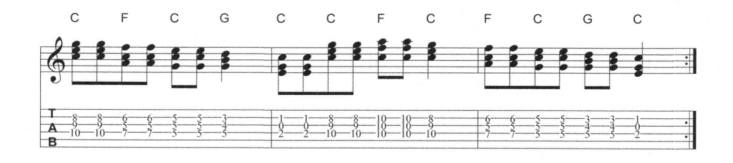

7 - Major & Minor Chords

Twinkling Triads

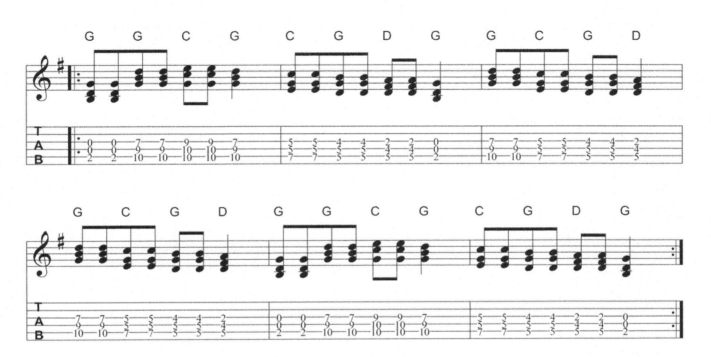

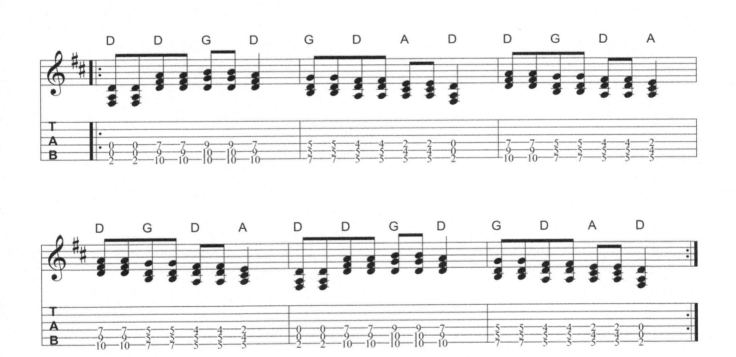

Major and Minor Triad Study Based on "Hotel California"

"Hotel California" was written by Felder/Henley/Frey. These triads will sound a lot like that tune. There are a couple of strumming patterns at the bottom of the page for you to use when you're comfortable making the changes on the fretboard.

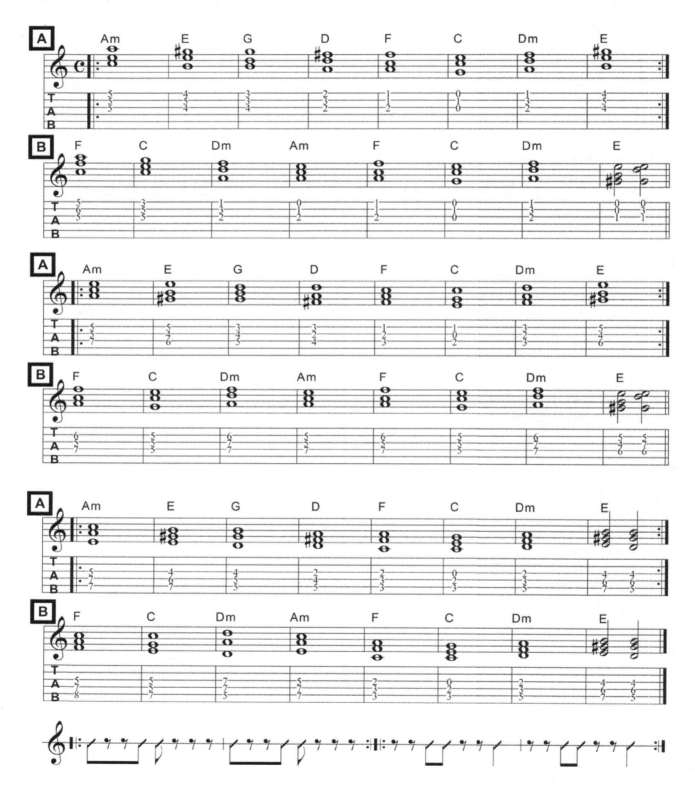

Into to open position chords – The Two Chord Drill

If you are new to guitar, this is a good way to get started on the chords in the open position. Each of these lines has two chords that share at least one note, and/or have similar shapes. The idea is to change smoothly from one chord to the next with the least amount of hand/finger movement. 75 bpm is a good tempo to being learning these changes. Set your metronome at 150 bpm so it's counting 8th notes, and practice each line 47,000 times. At first, don't worry about strumming anything. Start the metronome, grab a chord, and alternate between two chords a dozen times before you add the other hand. Then start to strum the chords on the first beat. While the metronome is ticking off the next three beat, you're moving your fingers to be in position to strum the next chord on the first beat. See strumming pattern #1 at the bottom of the page. When you can do that smoothly, use pattern #2. Same drill, use the rests to get in position so you ALWAYS play the next chord on the first beat. Go slowly, don't practice mistakes. More about strumming patterns soon.

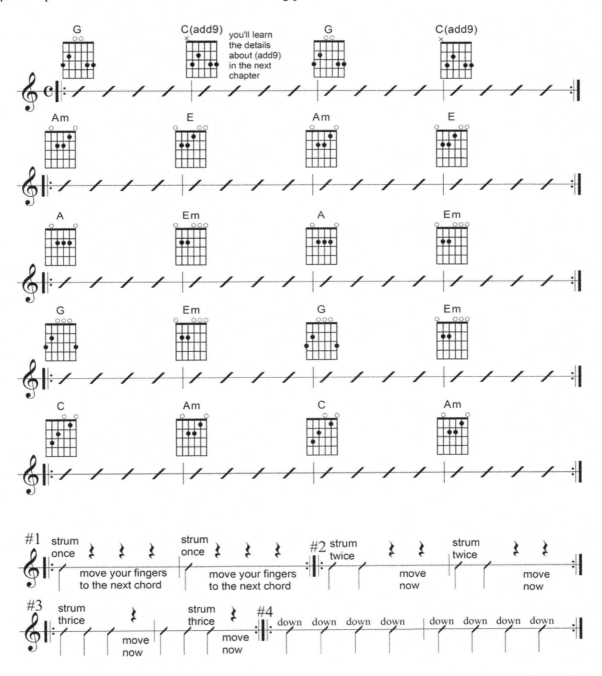

Intro to open position chords – The Two Chord Drill

I like this two-chord approach to learning chords. Learn several "pairs" of chords and soon it's no problem to string the pairs together. Do the ones that are easiest for you at first and do them a lot. Practice the strumming hand on the easy ones. Ignore the hard ones for a while. As your strength and coordination improve, add the tougher ones. I've seen stubborn people get all hung up on an F chord and fight with it for weeks. Three weeks later, they STILL can't play it and they can't play anything else either. Take some time to get into shape. "Don't allow the things you can't do prevent you from doing the things you can." Develop your motor skills on the easiest things and after a while there won't be any hard chords. Well, not too many. There are four more strumming patterns. Say it, then play it.

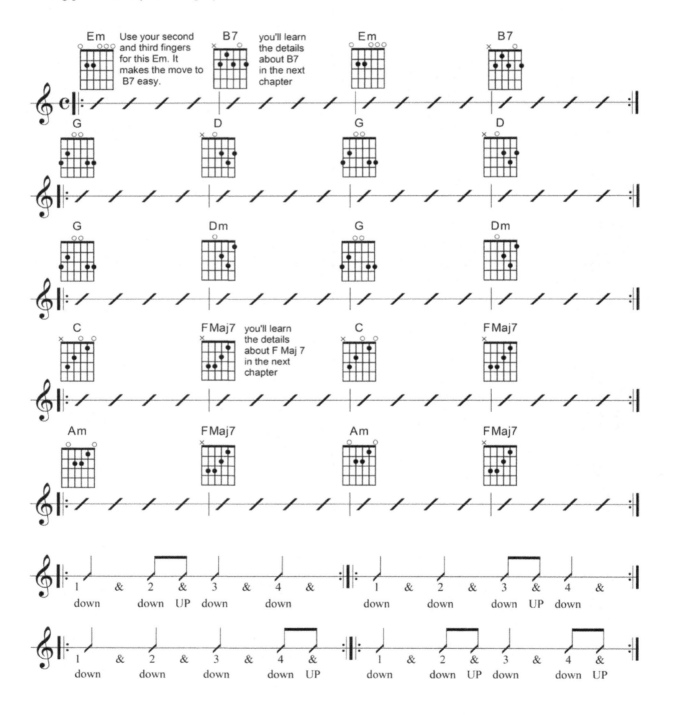

Intro to open position chords – The Two Chord Drill

The next two pages show chords that haven't been identified quite yet... I'll do that in the next chapter. Except for the F6, they're all open position chords and they are the first step beyond basic Major and Minor chords. Play the ones you can, and as your hand becomes stronger you'll be able to play all of them. These are all "dominant 7" chords and they have a unique voice. Compare the sound of A7 on this page with the A Maj 7 on the next page.

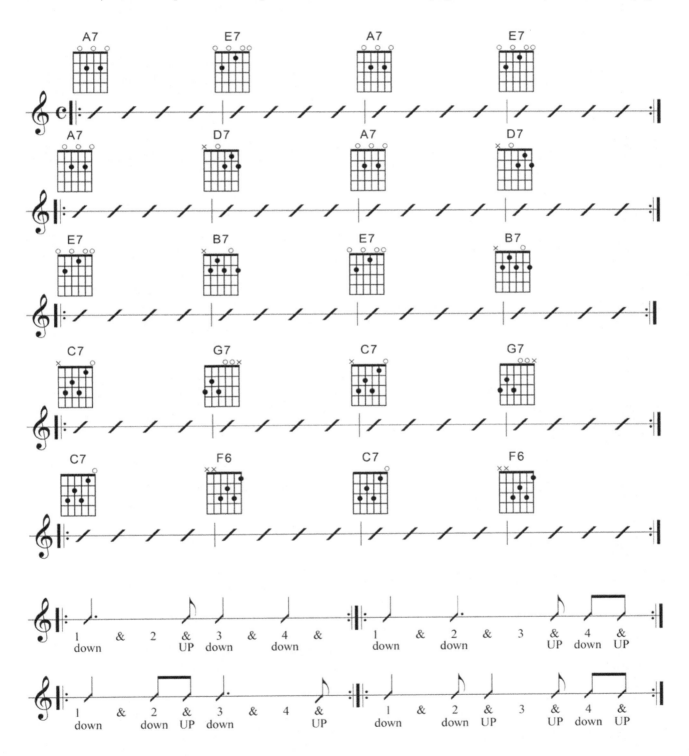

Intro to open position chords – The Two Chord Drill

Major chords, minor chords, and 7th chords are by far the most common chords that are used in pop music. Whether you like blues, rock, bluegrass, folk, or country, you'll find these are everywhere. Major 7 and minor 7 chords are probably the next most often encountered. Learn to recognize the different sound associated with each type. Major chords have a unique voice as do the others. Learn to hear them. It is a skill that can be acquired and while you're learning to play them, make sure you're associating a name with the sound that you're making. Play them, hear them, name them.

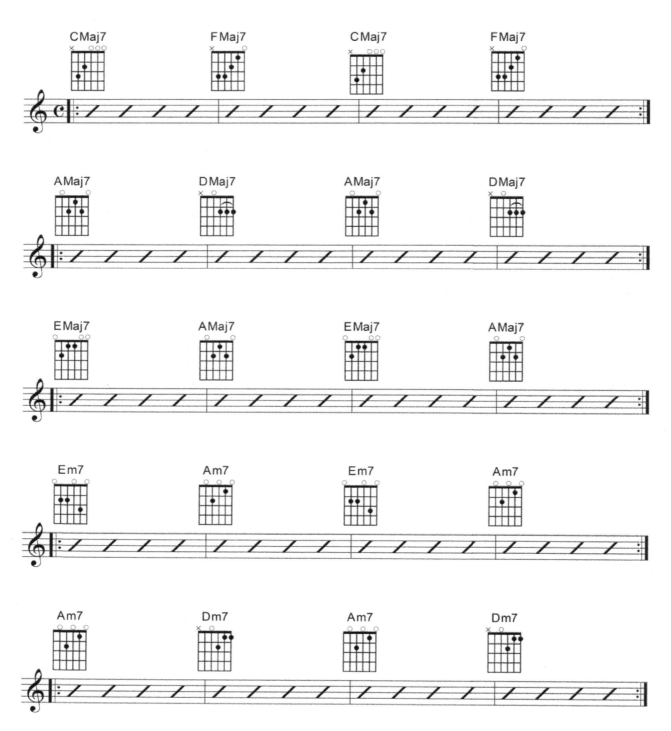

7 - Major & Minor Chords

Chords for Instruments Tuned in 5ths

Here are some open chords for the mandolin, mandola, and tenor banjo players. Nearly all of them use at least one open string. These are all pretty easy to grab on a mandolin, even those that don't have any open strings. We haven't talked about the "dominant 7" chords yet, that's next chapter, but that doesn't mean you can't start playing them now.

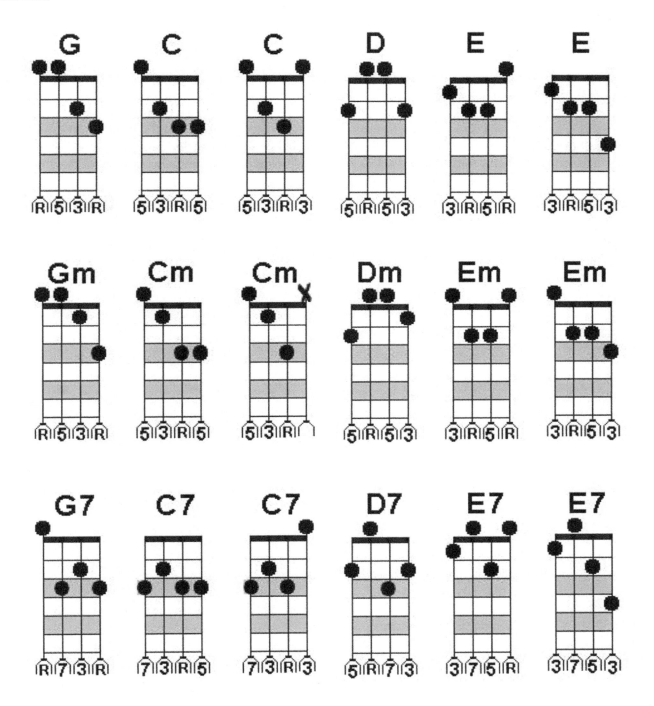

Strumming Patterns

Now that all of you beginning players have some chords to strum, we need to discuss this business of "strumming patterns."

If you're looking at nearly any songbook, including those that say something like "easy chords for guitar," and you're listening to recordings of the tunes, you'll probably notice that there is nothing on the page that even remotely bears the slightest resemblance to what the guitarist is playing. Learning to "read" music fluently will not give you the ability to see on the page the "rhythm guitarist's" line that you can hear on the recording.

Don't worry. It isn't because you're too dense to decipher the information in a "beginner" songbook. The information is not there, even though that is what is implied by the book title.

There are chord symbols that correspond to the beats where chord changes occur, a line of melody notes and the lyrics, but that's about it, even in "beginner" books. I included tabs for the melody and many books do, too. I didn't include chord diagrams, some books do. The songs in a book will have something that manifests this...

First, the notes shown on the staff have essentially nothing at all to do with strumming the chords. I've been asked dozens of times how to strum the notes that are shown on a page that looks a lot like this. It's a very common question. And if one person asked, 10 others wondered the same thing, I figure.

Those notes are the ones that the vocalist is singing. Notice that they match up with the words. Things that line up vertically in a staff system occur simultaneously.

This tells me that I'm supposed to do something with an A minor chord in the first measure, and then maybe stop during the second measure.

Well, actually, you're supposed to continue wanking on the A minor until you come to a different chord symbol. I'll usually write the chord symbol on the first beat of each measure anyway, unless there are a bunch of measures in a row that don't change. I'd fill in an Am on the first beat of measure seven, too.

7 - Major & Minor Chords

"Strum pattern 1" is probably on a page near the front of the book with about a dozen other strum patterns, somewhere a long way from the page you're looking at.

The "strumming patterns" at the front of the book will look something like this… (notice the pick direction symbols… they are opposite of what I showed in "**Scales**").

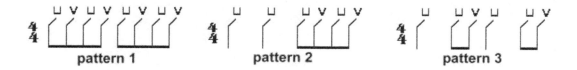

Somehow, a beginner is supposed to make sense of this and play something musical. It doesn't really seem fair. I'll try to help you out a bit.

Let's start by taking a look at the strumming patterns. The time signature shouldn't be a mystery to you by now. We're looking at three one-measure patterns in 4/4 time.

Back in "**Note Names**" there is an illustration of rhythmic notation, shown on a staff with a single line. These "nearly notes" in the strumming patterns represent the time values of quarter notes and 8th notes. No staff is required to represent these simple rhythms.

Pattern 1 shows four beats in a single measure, using all 8th notes.

The first Twinkle variation shown in "Counting" corresponds to pattern 1. Say "wish-I-had-a-mo-tor-cy-cle-wish-I-had-a-mo-tor-cy-cle-wish-I-had-a-mo-tor-cy-cle" and that is the rhythm indicated by this series of 8th notes. Pattern 2 sounds like Twinkle, third variation… "Hot Rod Motorcycle." Pattern 3 is Twinkle, fourth variation… "Run po-ny run po-ny."

From the available clues on example #1, it's reasonable to surmise that in the first measure of "You Are My Moonshine" you should grab a C chord and merrily strum up and down.

Yuck. You may be thinking, "If kitty poop was audible, this is what it would sound like!"

So, you try pattern 2.

Then, quite sensibly, you ignore the strumming patterns, because #2 is not an improvement.

Example #2 of "You Are My Moonshine" is a little closer to what "strumming pattern 1" is supposed to indicate.

For a simple "strumming pattern," a guitarist in a folk or bluegrass band often plays a single bass note, usually the root of whatever chord is indicated on the 5th or 6th string on the first beat of the measure. Then she'll strum the other notes in the chord on the higher strings on the "and of one" (which is the 8th note between the first and second beats). On the second beat will be another bass note, often the 5th of the chord, then strums the chord no the "and of two." Root, strum, 5th, strum, root, strum, 5th, strum, root, strum, 5th, strum, etc. This is still a pattern using a "straight 8th" rhythm", known as an "alternating bass" pattern, and it is a bit more refined than simply whacking all six strings down, up, down, up, down, ad nauseum.

Those little "runs" that you hear the "rhythm" guitar playing in between the chord strums leading to the next chord in sequence are usually three and four-note "scale fragments."

example #2

7 - Major & Minor Chords

Look at the three 8ᵗʰ notes in the pick-up measure and the first note after the beginning repeat sign in the example #1. Those are the 5ᵗʰ, tonic, 2ⁿᵈ, and 3ʳᵈ of A minor.

There is no indication on the sheet of music that you're really supposed to be doing any bass runs, but you hear them all the time.

Here's a pattern from The Beatles Book, 100 Easy Songs (Hal-Leonard). For "Nowhere Man" page 106, the recommendation is to use strumming pattern 6, which looks like this:

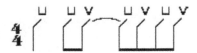

The Beatles Complete Scores also has "Nowhere Man," but this book has accurate transcriptions of what was actually played on the recording. The rhythm guitar part was often a four-bar pattern that looks more like this:

Even if you are not yet able to read rhythm, it's obvious that the strumming pattern suggested in The Beatles Book, 100 Easy Songs is not identical to the recording as shown in The Beatles Complete Scores. Measures 2 and 4 use "strumming pattern 6," while the first, third, and fifth measures use two different patterns, neither of which is in the list of strumming patterns supplied at the front of the book.

In order to play "rhythm guitar," you need to combine some skills. One skill is to learn the chord shapes on the fretboard. For most people, that is the easiest, but for some reason, that is the area that most players seem to obsess about. Learning a dozen open position chords usually doesn't require more than 15 or 20 hours of focused practice.

Another skill is strumming or picking the strings so the chords and scales you're fingering on the fretboard actually make a sound. If you don't strike the string with something, they don't make much noise. Most people tend to neglect the hand that is actually causing the strings to vibrate and in my experience, that is the hand that the majority of people have the most difficulty with. Maybe that's why they don't want to practice it. It's kind of hard, at first.

Most people can count in time with just a little bit of practice and tap their hands in time with music, or tap a foot, etc. Turning the ability to recognize and feel basic rhythms into the ability to produce a "musical strumming pattern" requires considerably more hours of practice than learning 15 chords. Yet most people devote most of their practice time to learning some chords and then wonder why it doesn't sound musical.

In the vast majority of situations, you're expected to invent a rhythm guitar line. It doesn't have to be complicated and it should be fairly repetitive. That is the most useful aspect of the single measure strumming patterns provided in commercial songbooks. Repetitive. Repetitive. Repetitive.

The main thing is to be consistent with timing and to play something that "supports" the vocalist or soloist. If there are bass and drums playing, too, you'll often try to match and complement a rhythm that they are playing. There are lots of times that I focus on just the snare drum and try to lock in with that one instrument. That doesn't mean that I'm strumming only on the snare hits, it means the snare is my main reference point.

The third skill is to develop sufficient coordination with your strumming hand to play "strumming patterns" that incorporate single notes with chords that use fewer than six notes.

This is where those scale exercises from the previous chapter come in. One of the extremely important benefits of scale exercises is pick control. This is the ability to choose a specific target and hit it with your pick. A single string is narrow and it takes practice to be able to hit just the A string, for instance, while missing the E and D strings.

Scale exercises are often perceived as an exercise only for those who want to be "lead" guitarists. Wrong.

It has been my experience that the shortest line toward this goal of being a good rhythm player is to practice two exercises separately, scales and strumming, and over the course of 100 hours or so they will begin to merge. Of course, that is only the physical part of the process. You also should listen to all of the instruments that contribute to the groove. Listening closely to what you're trying to learn is practice time, too.

To practice strumming, I recommend using the Ted Reed book or something similar. For most people, mimicking a rhythmic pattern is much easier than reading one from a page. "Counting" shows a few examples of rhythmic patterns that are illustrated with some short phrases that help translate the dots on the staff into a rhythmic pattern.

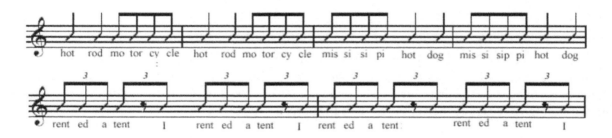

When you look at any rhythmic pattern, try to find a way to first "speak" the rhythm. Can you guess what the most coordinated muscle in your body is? The one you use the most... your tongue.

Turn the metronome on or tap your finger or your foot or whatever, and get a steady pulse going. Then say "hot rod motorcycle" about 92 times (or whatever it takes to hear and feel the rhythm).

When you have a rhythm going, change it to daa daa da da da da, daa daa da da da da. "Mississippi Hot Dog" becomes da da da da daa daa, da da da da daa daa.

When you can hear a rhythm, then you can mimic it with your hand. It's really tough for most people to take something directly off of the page straight to their pick. Your mouth is more coordinated. Do the easy thing first, listen to it, then reproduce it.

Since the focus of this exercise is to develop dexterity in the hand you strum with, initially you don't even want the other hand to be part of your awareness. Mute the strings with your fret hand. Or put a handkerchief between the strings and the fretboard. Initially, the goal is to hear no notes... you're trying to make your lovely old Martin sound like a percussion instrument.

In fact, it seems to me that since we are whacking the strings with an object (a finger or a pick), just like a drummer smacks the snare with a drumstick or slaps a conga with her hand, a guitar is a percussion instrument.

Turn on your metronome and work through the exercises.

Listen to drummers and percussionists. Listen to the bass lines. Listen to the rhythm guitarist. Listen to the mandolin. Mimic the rhythms these players are creating. Learn to "speak" the rhythms before you try to apply them to your instrument.

Ideally, your strumming hand should be as coordinated and dexterous as any percussionists' hands.

As an "accompaniment" instrument, the guitar has the unique ability to simultaneously carry three separate musical lines: bass, percussion, and chords. When reading about it, it may seem like an impossible task, but in reality it isn't nearly as difficult as it sounds.

Consider for a moment the number of different tasks that you unconsciously and simultaneously perform in the act of rising from a chair and walking across a room. Motor skills in healthy humans are nearly perfect. Except in the very young or old, we rarely stumble. We can learn skills like riding a bike or skipping a rope or driving a car in a fairly short period of time.

The same is true with regard to strumming rhythm patterns on a guitar. All that is required is practice. So… practice.

People tend to invest lots more of their practice time into learning to finger chords than they put into learning to control the pick hand. But it seems to me that the hand that is causing the strings to vibrate is the one that's usually driving the bus.

We've all seen people dancing and grooving to drum solos. See if anybody even taps a toe while you just switch between chords without strumming something.

I supplied a bunch of single measure rhythm patterns for you to practice with.

Step #1. Put your guitar down and limber up your lips, toes, and fingers.

Start slowly. If you have a metronome, set it at 120 bpm so it's marking 8th notes for 60 bpm. Count out loud: "One and two and three and four and" and tap each quarter note in the first example. Go to the second measure and tap the 8th notes.

The third measure is where the variations begin. Learn to say it before you try to play it. Keep tapping quarter notes with your foot or something. Measure three might be da-da DOM DOM DOM, and measure four would be DOM da-da DOM DOM or something.

You recall how the rhythm guitar in "Nowhere Man" is a four-bar phrase. Start linking these into two measure patterns as soon as you can. Everything here is common time so they're like Lego, they all hook up. You can play number 33 on the first page followed with number six on the third page, if you want to. *Progressive Steps to Syncopation for the Modern Drummer* by Ted Reed, has lots more.

I didn't include songs to practice in this chapter, but there are some in "**Progressions**." There is a website at **www.folkguitar.us** that has chord charts for several hundred folk songs and fiddle tunes.

The "chart format" that they're shown in is explained in "**Reading the Road Map**." Find a few songs you're familiar with and practice your chords and strumming.

Swing

Swing has to do with a sensation of forward momentum, a rhythmic musical drive that makes you want to dance, or, in technical terms… "Makes ya wanna shake yer bootie."

Initially, swing is usually discussed and described in terms of the length of 8th notes.

If you divide each beat exactly in half, it's called playing "straight-8th" notes. In classical music, an 8th note in 4/4 time is always meant to sustain exactly one half of a beat, and all the other note values are intended to be precise and identical. Notice the vertical alignment of the notes on the three lines below. Straight-8ths . The majority of rock, folk, and bluegrass tune are played with a straight-8th feel.

In swing 8th notes, the first 8th note is a little longer than the second 8th noted. The easiest way to think about this is to say that the beat is divided into three parts, and swing 8th notes are the first and third parts of the beat.

That is not really a swing rhythm. The duration or length of the first note in a pair of swing 8ths is a variable thing. Different musicians interpret swing in different ways. Also, the ratio will vary with the tempo of the music. At slower tempos, an exaggerated swing will usually groove, and at fast tempos straighter 8ths usually feel better. Swing 8ths fall somewhere between all the others, as shown below. It's a feel thing, not a precisely defined object. Jazz and blues tunes tend to have more of a swing feel than rock and folk. A shuffle, common in blues and jazz, is usually played as a solid triplet feel. It can swing, for sure, but it's a slightly different feel. Check out Mike Gillan (drums) and Craig Hall (bass) on the title track from my CD Yucca Pie. These fellows can swing very hard, yes, indeed.

Regardless of how exaggerated or subtle the difference in duration between the two 8th notes may be, the second "half" of each beat is usually accented. In addition, beats two and four are usually stressed a little more than one and three. The amount of accent is open to individual interpretation.

Not only does swing involve messing with the duration of 8th notes within a beat, but it can also involve messing with the beats themselves.

Sometimes you want to play "in front of" or "on top of" the beat, meaning that instead of playing each note exactly when it is drawn on the page, you anticipate slightly and play everything a tiny fraction of a beat early, pushing the beat, which generates a sense of forward momentum. You can also play behind the beat, meaning that everything is delayed slightly, which is a more relaxed groove.

Another subtle aspect of swing is that everyone in a band probably isn't swinging with the exact same feel. For example, the bassist may be playing with a triplet feel (shuffle), while the drummer can be playing closer to a dotted 8th and a 16th, and the keyboard might be playing nearly straight-8ths. In addition, the rhythm section may be playing on the front of the beat, with the guitar playing on the back of the beat.

It's usually not as if everyone sits down together on a break, talks about it and says, "You go here and I'll go there." It's more likely that everyone just feels it a little bit differently. This creates an audible but nearly invisible sort of tension that can be really cool. Magic. Grooves deep enough to lose a pick-up truck in. Can't really talk about it sensibly, but when it's happening and it's good, you can almost touch it.

Everything still counts 1 & 2 & 3 & 4 &. The tempo remains consistent, and the metronome would be nailing the beginning of each beat dead-on. The band sort of falls in somewhat loosely around it. If you're pushing or lying back by the value of "almost-a-16th" you're just playing out of time, so "somewhat loosely" means you're still supposed to be right close to the mark, just not exactly on it.

A jazz tune that is supposed to be played with a swing feel is counted and written just exactly like a bluegrass tune that is a straight-8th feel.

How do you know what to do?

When it's supposed to swing, the word "swing" will be written somewhere, usually above the first measure. There is also a symbol, as shown below, that means the same thing.

Lots of the 8th-note grooves I've shown on the next pages can be played as swing-8th rhythms. Play them both ways and you can also make them shuffle grooves by thinking triplets.

It Don't Mean A Thing If It Ain't Got That Swing

Maybe you've heard that tune, maybe not, but the groove is what makes you move. Get serious about these next few pages. This is an introduction to what you use to make G, C, and D be bluegrass or reggae or funk or folk or rock or blues or ska or whatever. There are way more basic grooves than basic chords. If you know 15 chords and one rhythm pattern, you'll be the most boring player around. If you know three chords and can spank them out in about a dozen different movin' grooves, you can have people dancing all night long. There's a lot of music on these "rhythm pattern" pages. I hope you're here often.

7 - Major & Minor Chords

It Don't Mean A Thing If It Ain't Got That Swing

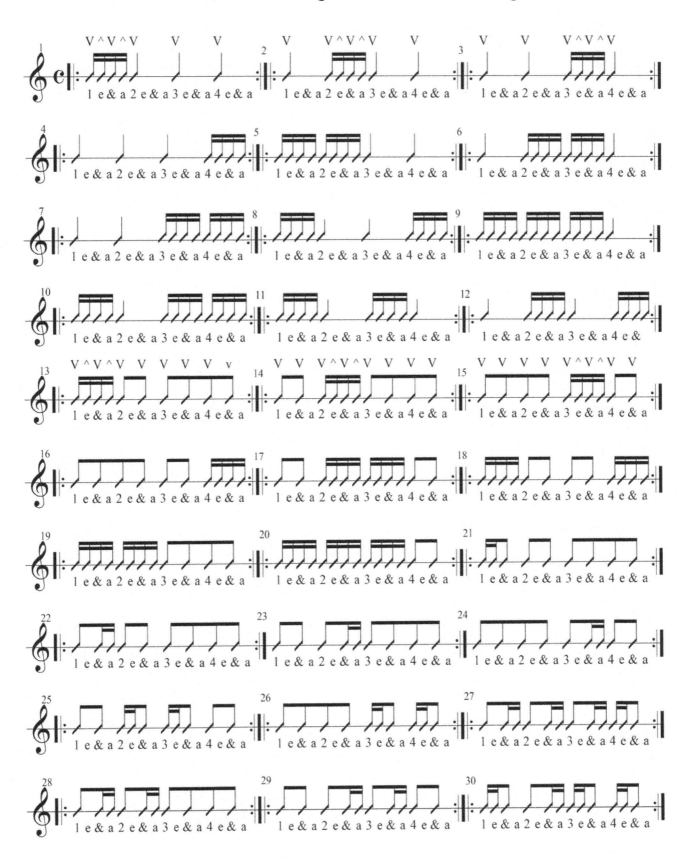

It Don't Mean A Thing If It Ain't Got That Swing

You pretty much have to sort out pick direction on your own when you're playing triplets. When you play these slowly, you can use all downstrokes and it will give you a real solid swing thing for blues. The faster you go, the tougher it is to do consecutive downstrokes on the last beat of a triplet figure and the next beat.

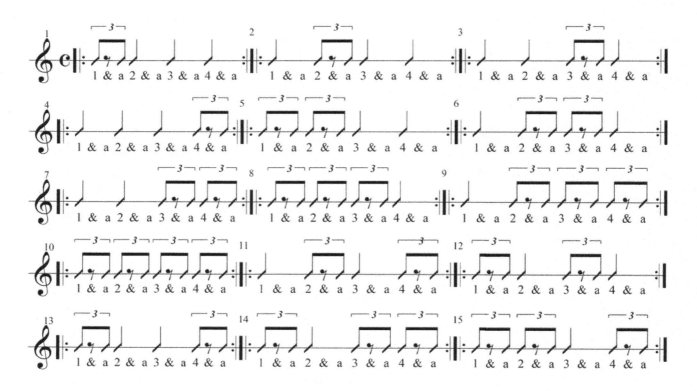

These are some of the same patterns, they're just strung together more or less at random. Play through them. Apply the "more or less at random" idea to the other pages, too. Then start alternating between a measure that uses triplets followed by a measure of 8ths and quarters, back to a measure of triplets, etc.

It Don't Mean A Thing If It Ain't Got That Swing
Syncopation

A syncopation or syncopated rhythm is any rhythm that puts an emphasis on a beat, or a subdivision of a beat, that is not usually emphasized. Essentially, syncopation is about rhythmic surprise. You can create that surprise by choosing to accent different beats, as in 1-2-3 and 4, or parts of the beats, as in 1-e-&-a.

In most styles of music in the Western world, accents generally fall on the beats. The most common rhythmic structure has four beats to a measure. In most styles of Western music, the first beat of the measure is the strongest and the third beat is next. So the simplest form of syncopation is to accent the second and fourth beats instead. In jazz, blues, and rock, beats two and four often feel strong than one and three. When two and four are accented especially heavily, it is sometimes called a "backbeat" rhythm. The "swing" rhythm in big band jazz and the "back beat" of many types of rock are types of syncopation. You hear the kick drum playing beats one and three, a little laid back, with the snare smacking the back beat on two and four.

Since all four beats are usually heard as relatively strong pulses, the next place to find "unexpected" accents is between the beats, or on the "AND" of the beats. Ska is a style that accents all four "ANDS" so heavily that you almost don't hear 1-2-3-4.

The intro for "Brown Eyed Girl" is syncopated. It's not that the accents fall between the beats, but the melody does.

Syncopations can happen in the melody, the bass line, the rhythm section, in the accompaniment. Any spot in the rhythm can be given emphasis. To practice hearing syncopations, listen to some ragtime or jazz. Tap your finger or your foot on the beats and then notice how often important musical "events" are happening "in between" your taps.

Many of the following patterns have syncopations. I moved the "&" counter a little higher so you can see them easier. When you're doing the basic down-up-down-up sort of strumming motion, the syncopated beats are on the upstroke. Say it first, then play it.

Reflections

*"My mother drew a distinction between achievement and success.
She said that achievement is the knowledge that you have studied
and worked hard and done the best that is in you. Success is being praised by others.
That is nice but not as important or satisfying.
Always aim for achievement and forget about success."*
Helen Hayes

"Never mistake activity for achievement. "
John Wooden

*"Never regard your study as a duty,
but as the enviable opportunity to learn to know the liberating influence of beauty
in the realm of the spirit for your own personal joy
and to the profit of the community to which your later work belongs."*
Albert Einstein

"No dream comes true until you wake up and go to work."
Unknown

*"Nobody trips over mountains.
It is the small pebble that causes you to stumble.
Pass all the pebbles in your path and you will find you have crossed the mountain."*
Unknown

*"Nothing can stop the man with the right mental attitude from achieving his goal;
nothing on earth can help the man with the wrong mental attitude."*
Thomas Jefferson

"Nothing is too high for a man to reach, but he must climb with care and confidence."
Hans Christian Andersen

*"Nothing of importance is ever achieved without discipline.
I feel myself sometimes not wholly in sympathy with some modern educational theorists,
because I think that they underestimate the part that discipline plays.
But the discipline you have in your life should be one determined
by your own desires and your own needs,
not put upon you by society or authority."*
Bertrand Russell

*"Obstacles are those frightful things you see
when you take your eyes off your goals."*
Unknown

*"Obstacles don't have to stop you. If you run into a wall, don't give up.
Figure out how to climb it, go through it, or work around it."*
Michael Jordan

Arpeggios

Arpeggio (ar-PEJ-ee-o). "The notes of a chord played in succession rather than simultaneously." "In the manner of the harp" or "like a harp" are English approximations of the Italian word "arpeggio." It's part scale, part chord.

The "Moonlight Sonata" is one of Beethoven's best known and well loved pieces. On a Steinway Grand it's dark, moody, and moving. I've heard it as a cell phone's ring tone, too. A little something gets lost in the translation. The section you hear on a cell phone is entirely based on arpeggiated triads.

"In the Mood" by Joseph Garland has been recorded by about 80 different artists. That's a lot. The hook melody line that so many people remember is based on arpeggiated triads.

Mark Knopfler's guitar solo on "Sultans of Swing" consistently finds its way into various respected "Top 10 Greatest Guitar Solos" type of lists. Anyone who heard Dire Straits live knows that band and that solo could make you jump up and down and holler. The most famous passage in the solo is based on arpeggiated triads.

"Hotel California" has another one of those incredible guitar solos that deserves recognition as a truly great one. I've seen this one voted as "The Greatest Guitar Solo Of All Time" or some such, more than once. Right. But it's a great tune and a "killer git-tar thang" by anybody's standards. I love it. Joe Walsh had just joined The Eagles and is playing part of this solo with Don Felder. The famous line at the end that goes into the twin guitar part is based on arpeggiated triads.

Bluegrass banjo players spend half of their lives playing arpeggios. Bass players in many genres of music spend much of their time playing roots and 5ths . They don't play too many chords, but they do use lots of arpeggios getting from DO to SO. Listen to the string section in nearly any piece of classical music and you'll hear plenty of arpeggios. Lots of Eddie Van Halen's signature "tapping" riffs are blistering fast arpeggios.

Many electric keyboards have a built-in device called an "arpeggiator." When you turn it on, any group of notes you press on the keyboard are automatically played as an "arpeggio"… in sequence from the lowest note to the highest. It doesn't care if you play a conventional chord or a random group of notes. The reason arpeggiators are a standard feature in so many good keyboards is because playing chords as arpeggios is such a common technique in all styles.

"Moonlight Sonata," "Hotel California," and "Sultans of Swing" all have extended sections of arpeggios and playing these examples is a good way to be introduced to them. But just as you're more likely to encounter "scale fragments" than complete scales in songs, short phrases that use arpeggio are much more common in pop music than these long phrases that I included here.

As always, take your songbook and look through your favorite songs. Notice how many times you find three and four-note arpeggios like these: the first phrase of "The Star Spangled Banner" is an arpeggio… SO-MI-DO-MI-SO-DO. The first phrase in "Michael, Row Your Boat Ashore" is an arpeggio… DO-MI-SO-MI-SO-LA-SO. "Jingle All The Way" = MI-SO-DO-RE-MI.

For centuries, some of the most memorable bits of music… played on pianos, banjos, bass, and screaming guitars… have used arpeggiated triads as an extremely important feature in the music.

There are two ways to use chords. You can play several notes at a time or you can play the notes individually. Learning to recognize "arpeggios" as "chords" is an important aspect of playing by ear. Learning to play them makes it pretty easy to play selected chunks of these two great guitar solos, and tons of other stuff.

When you know what a scale is and you know what a chord is, an arpeggio doesn't require much explanation. Don't interpret this lack of text as an indication of their relative significance. I used a bunch of pages for the arpeggio examples and exercises because arpeggios are really important. They're also a blast to play with. Have fun.

Arpeggios Open Forms

Form #1

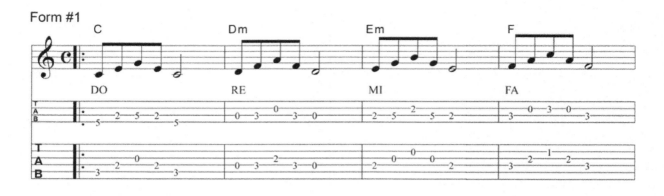

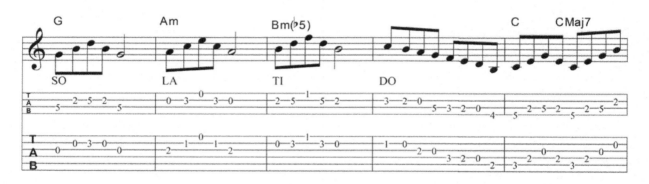

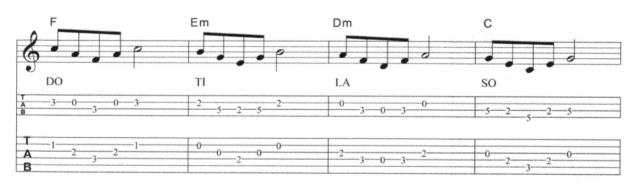

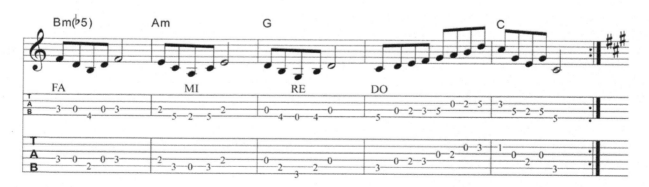

7 - Major & Minor Chords

Arpeggios Open Forms

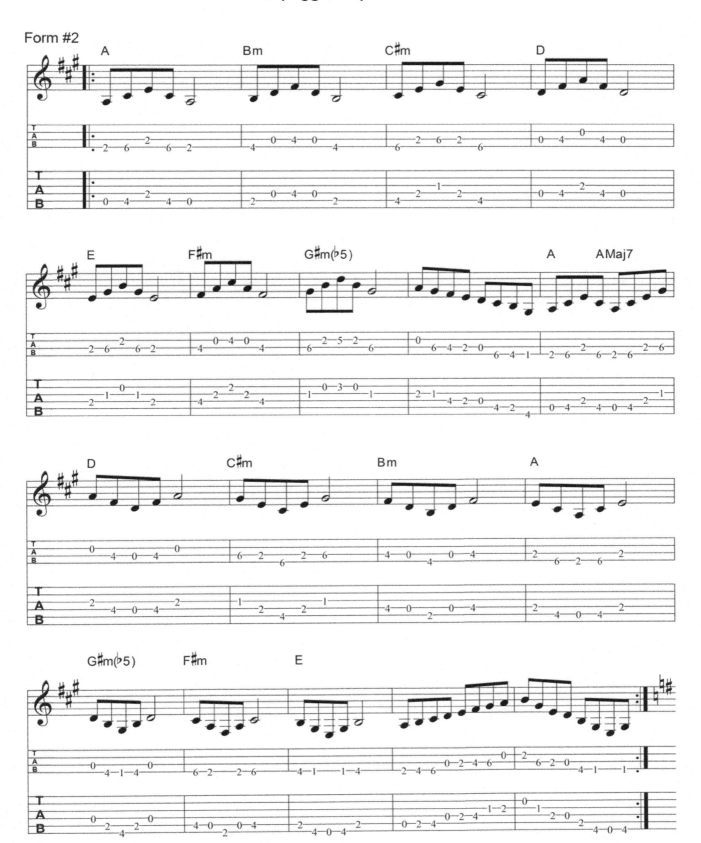

Arpeggios Open Forms

Form #3

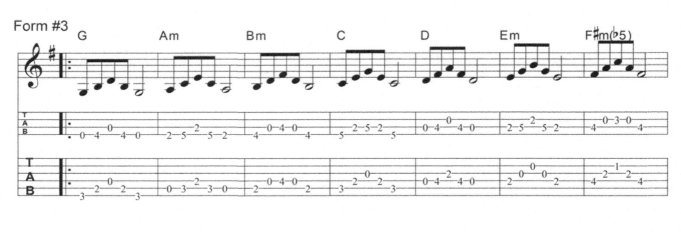

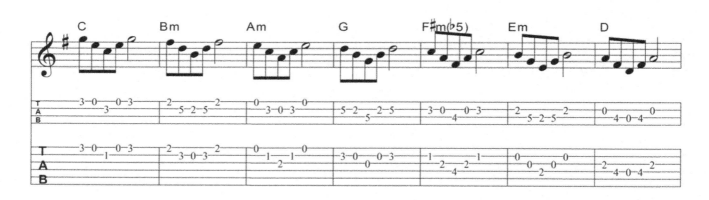

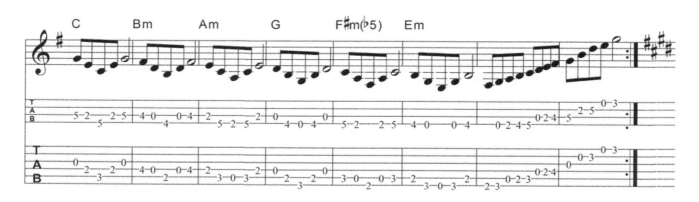

7 - Major & Minor Chords

Arpeggios Open Forms

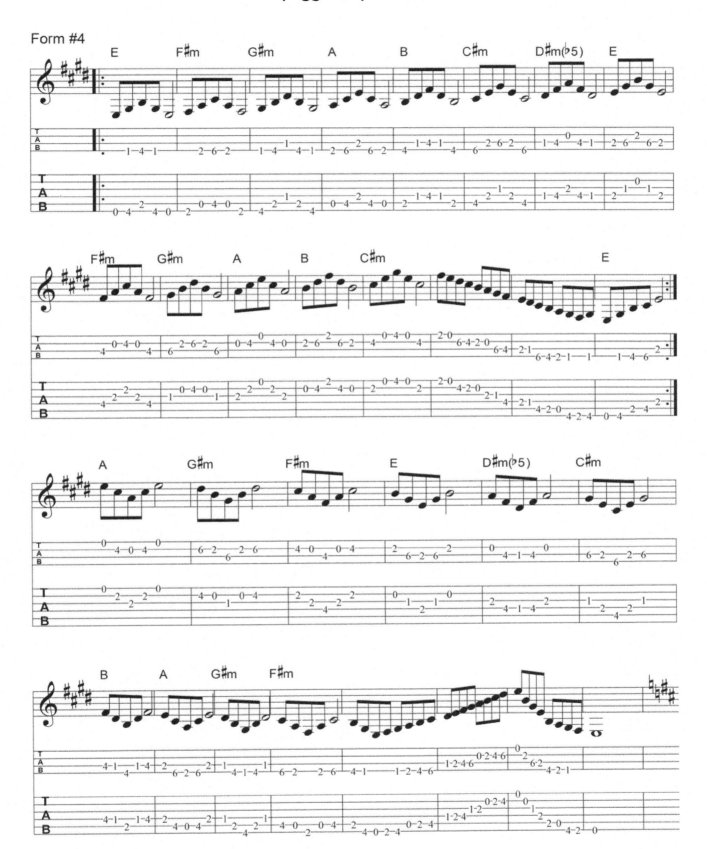

Arpeggios Open Forms

Form #5

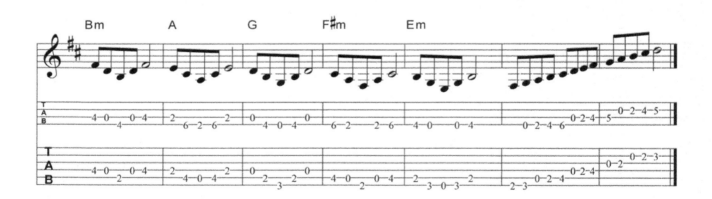

7 - Major & Minor Chords

Arpeggios Closed Forms

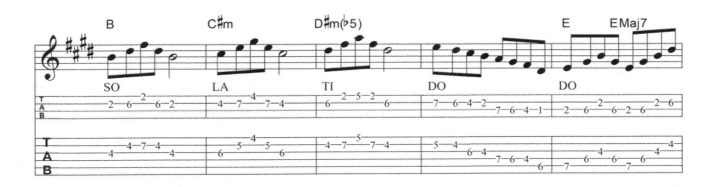

Arpeggios Closed Forms

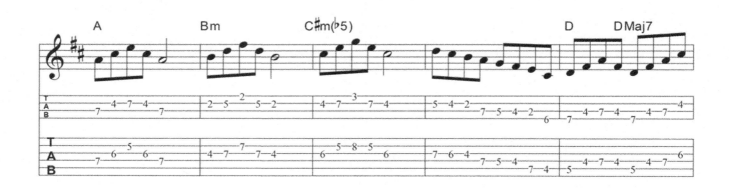

7 - Major & Minor Chords

Arpeggios Closed Forms

Form #3

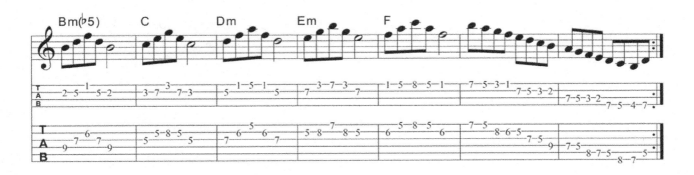

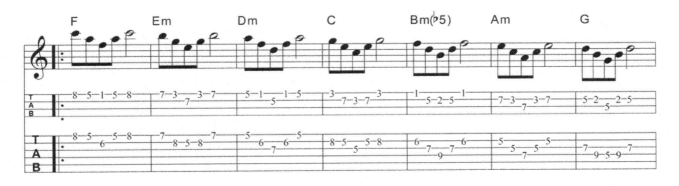

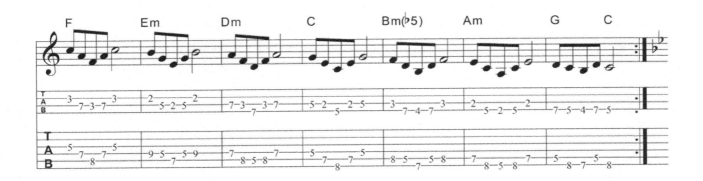

Arpeggios Closed Forms

Form #4

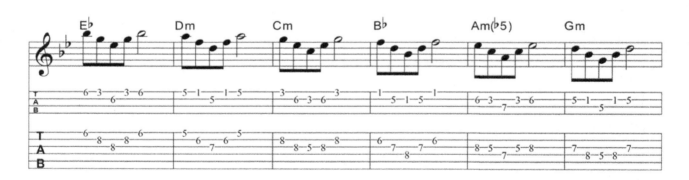

7 - Major & Minor Chords

Arpeggio Study Based on "In The Mood"

"In The Mood" was written by Joseph Garland

There are millions of songs, but few have been recorded by as many different artists as "In The Mood." It was a signature song of Glen Miller's big band and later Benny Goodman's. If you have never listened to big band era music, you're missing something really great. It was a musical renaissance like what happened to Rock and Roll in the '60s and '70s. These people were PLAYERS. No flashy light shows, no smoke machines, no amplifiers or effects pedals, big teams of musicians playing together and they could very thoroughly ROCK THE BLOCK in a very sweaty way. And the DANCERS! Swingin with the big bands must have been FUN.

Each of these measures will hold eight 8th notes. There are three notes in a triad. Three consecutive 8th note triads is nine notes and the ninth one spills over into the next measure. I beamed the 8th notes incorrectly in the first measure so the triads aren't disguised as a four-note structure. I dumped them entirely in measures three and four. Measures 5-12 look the way you will usually see a series of 8th note triads, beamed into two beats. That's a common way to see a series of three-note arpeggios. You'll see it again in the "Hotel California" guitar solo. Since it turned up in 50 percent of the classic examples I found, it seemed like I should point it out. Visually, it looks like a four-note thing, but the chord/arpeggio is a triad.

Arpeggio Study Based on "Sultans of Swing"
"Sultans of Swing" was written by Mark Knopfler

Not only is Mr. Knopfler a great player, he's earned loads of respect as a producer, too. He's probably best known as the main vocalist and lead guitarist in Dire Straits, but he's also made solo albums and played in other bands. Notting Hillbillies is one of my favorites. You'll find him playing on recordings by other artists, including Bob Dylan, Eric Clapton, and Chet Atkins. He's produced albums for Tina Turner and Randy Newman that I'm sure of, and probably others. In addition, he has scored the music to several films… "Local Hero," "The Princess Bride," "Cal," "Last Exit to Brooklyn," and "Wag the Dog." On Alchemy (and when I saw Dire Straits at Red Rocks, lucky me), he played this riff an octave higher than shown here… faster than a speeding locomotive.

Arpeggio Study Based on "Sultans of Swing"
Mark Knopfler

This illustrates one way to use arpeggios as an improvisational device. Suppose "Sultans of Swing" is on your set list and you've got the solo. Maybe you want to play something that acknowledges the signature riff that Mr. Knopfler played in his solo, but you don't want to play exactly the same line.

Here, I created a minor image of the arpeggios. The chords are the same chords, I just turned them down-side-up. I placed the staff with the mirror image above the original and an octave lower because it creates such a clear visual representation of the idea.

In the original and the mirror image, each triplet figure begins on the same note, but each uses a different inversion. The mirror image in measure one is 3-5-R, or the first inversion. The original is the second inversion 5-R-3.

You can also "reverse" the arpeggio in the original. Play the same inversion, but instead of starting with the third and descending to the fifth, you could begin with the fifth and ascend to the third. Then you could do the same thing to the mirror image and you would have two, new twin lines. How about beginning with a root position triad?

Analyze it, imitate it, then tweak it and twist it any way you can.

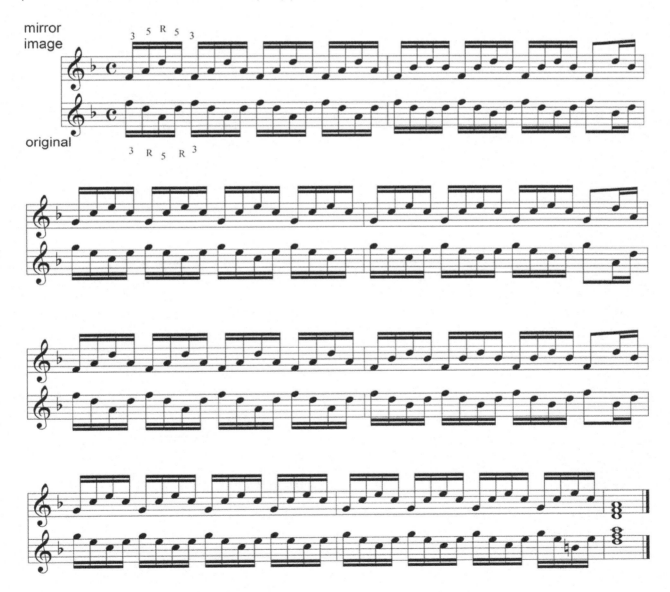

Arpeggio Study Based on "Hotel California"
"Hotel California" was written by Don Henley, Glen Frey, Don Felder

This is similar to the twin guitar solo in "Hotel California." Don Felder gets credit for the intro guitar riff for this song (not shown). I'm guessing he played the part I've shown as "Guitar 1" and Joe Walsh did the second line I've shown as "Guitar 2." The Eagles did this in B minor, an octave higher than I showed it. I wanted to use as many of the triads I showed a few pages ago and when they play it high on the neck, they use two strings and do pull-offs and hammer-ons. I also wanted it to be in an open position for beginners so I transposed it to A minor. You'll learn how to do that in "The Key." Think of this as a series of triads instead of hundreds of individual notes and it's almost like erasing two-thirds of the dots on the page. The beams make it look like groups of four, but it's all triads. Both tabs give you the same notes. Play it both ways and you'll find places to switch between them. This is a great way to learn chords all over the neck. If you don't already have this tune in your music collection, you should. You can get it for 99 cents at iTunes. It's worth more than that.

7 - Major & Minor Chords

Arpeggio Study Based on "Hotel California"

We won't discuss harmony in any detail for a while yet, but this second guitar part is a harmony line. This is the same kind of thing Duane Allman and Dicky Betts used to do in the Allman Brothers Band and the same thing you'll hear twin fiddles doing.

If you have those triad inversions working for you, they're a great way to get a bunch of twin guitar parts going. Find another guitar player to play this with. One can strum the chords while the other plays the tab shown. Then switch. Then try the twin solo. One plays the Guitar 1 tab on the previous page, while the other plays Guitar 2 on this page. Do it for a while and then trade lines. When you're both playing closed forms, it's easy to move it up to B minor, or any other key.

The chord progression in this song is nearly identical to the changes in a song by Ian Anderson (Jethro Tull) from their 1969 album, Stand Up. Notice that the intervals between the chord roots are mostly fourths and fifths. Bach liked the same sort of motion. This is standard stuff. Everybody uses phrases that move the way the chords in this song move.

Harmonized Arpeggio Study Based on "Hotel California"

You don't always need two guitars to play an "arpeggiated twin guitar line." It's fun to fool with this, so I included it. Remember the example of thirds and sixths from the "Brown Eyed Girl" intro? This is shown in 3rds… you can do this line as sixths, too.

Arpeggio Study Based on "Hotel California"

Here it is for all you four-stringers.

Arpeggio Study Based on "Hotel California"

7 - Major & Minor Chords

Arpeggio Study Based on "The Moonlight Sonata"
"Quasi una Fantasia" or "Almost a Fantasy" Piano Sonata #14 in C# minor Opus 27 #2
Ludwig von Beethoven

The name "Moonlight Sonata" didn't come about until 10 years after Beethoven's death in 1826. In 1836, a German music critic, Ludwig Rellstab, wrote that the music reminded him of moonlight on Lake Lucerne in central Switzerland. Since then, "Moonlight Sonata" has been the title. Mr. Beethoven composed the piece in Hungary during the summer of 1801, and it was published in 1802. Some believe that it was inspired by Beethoven's passion for the Countess Giulietta Gucciardi because he dedicated the sonata to her. Others think it was related to the darker emotions Beethoven experienced when he took funeral watch at the side of a friend who died young. To me, it sounds more like a solemn funeral hymn than a romantic moonlit night. The popular name obviously has no connection to Beethoven's title, Almost a Fantasy. I don't know if his hearing had begun to fail when he wrote the Piano Sonata #13 in C# minor Opus 27 #2. The topic is arpeggios and the right-hand piano part is a great way to practice them because it's such a cool piece of music. I transposed it to A minor because I wanted to play it on a guitar in an open position and this worked best for me. I've only shown the first of four movements. There are lots of left-hand bass notes for the piano that don't exist on a guitar, so I just left them all out. There's a melody line that I left out. The chords will suggest a bass note. Beethoven didn't write this using chord names like I've shown, so none of them are "correct." You'll find lots of the triads that were shown earlier. There are some chords that I haven't defined yet... coming soon. Mostly, it's not too tough, but there are places where beginners will have trouble making the stretches. Play the easy parts for now and skip the hard parts. Mess around with it for a couple of weeks and move along. Try it again in six months. I made two different tabs and you'll find places where it's convenient to switch from one to the other. The recordings I've heard are played at around 50 bpm. A measure will be almost five seconds long. Scan through this and notice that there are usually no more than two chords in each measure. It's slow, so even at full speed you have a couple of seconds to make the moves.

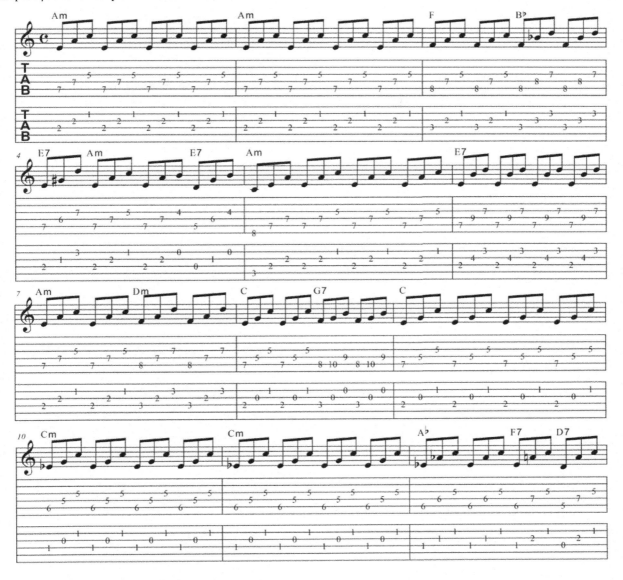

Arpeggio Study Based on "The Moonlight Sonata" (pg 2)

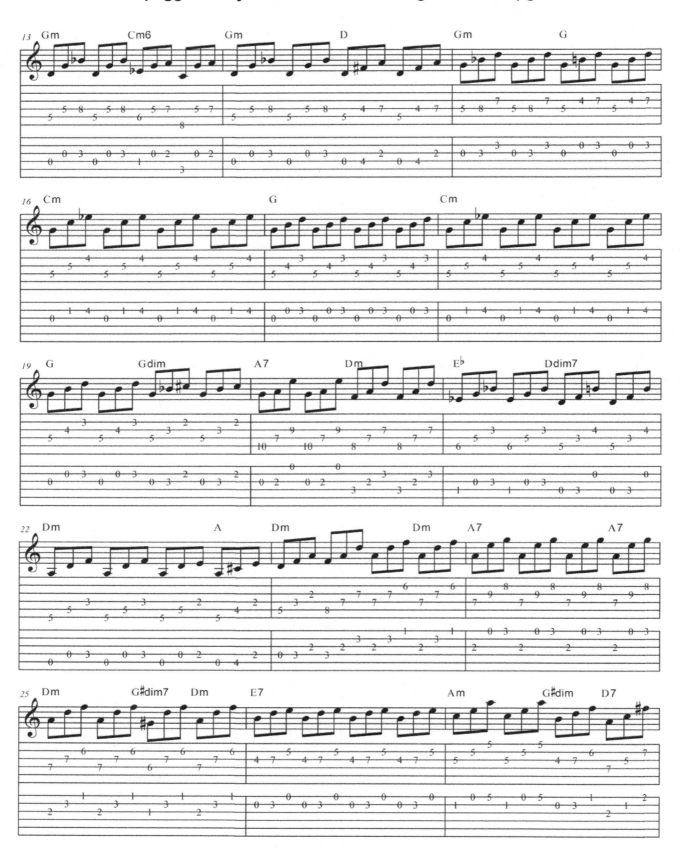

7 - Major & Minor Chords

Arpeggio Study Based on "The Moonlight Sonata" (pg 3)

Arpeggio Study Based on "The Moonlight Sonata" (pg 4)

7 - Major & Minor Chords

Arpeggio Study Based on "The Moonlight Sonata" (pg 5)

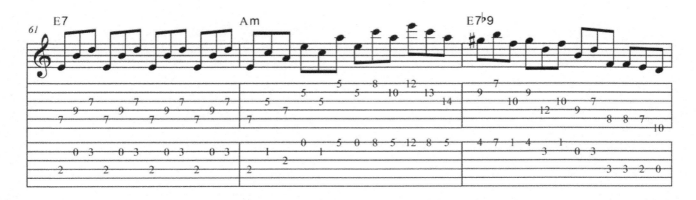

Arpeggio Study Based on "The Moonlight Sonata"

Bela Fleck, one of the great banjo players of all time, recorded this tune with Edgar Meyer (bass) and Gary Hoffman (cello) for a Grammy winning CD titled "Perpetual Motion". None of the songs are played on the instruments for which they were written. It's amusing to imagine Ludwig von Beethoven playing a banjo. I highly recommend that you find a copy of this recording. If you're one of those people who think that banjos, accordions and the like are dumb, soulless instruments then you need to listen to Mr. Fleck play "The Moonlight Sonata". Talk about MOODY. The bass just growls, and you'll hear the cello carry melody line, not shown here. This is the key they recorded this in, and it's slow, so you can play along using this transcription. I don't suppose that this is exactly the way that Mr. Fleck plays it. I tabbed the banjo part so it's easy to see the triads. There are a few places that the notes go below the range of a banjo and mandolin... I moved them up an octave and put an asterisk * in the tab. Guitarists, you should play along with the recording too. You can use the chords from the guitar transcription in A minor if you put a capo on the third fret. Lower your high E string a whole step to D and you can play this banjo tab. It's also a good reading exercise. Put away your instrument. Start the recording and follow along. Tap the beats, the first note of each triplet figure. It's five minutes long. Invest an hour into listening to a piece of amazing music. Imagine Beethoven and the Countess sailing in a boat on Lake Lucerne sipping fine wine... with Ludwig strummin' on the old banjo. The title on the Bela Fleck CD is "Piano Sonata #14 in C# minor Opus 27 #2". Ninety-nine cents.

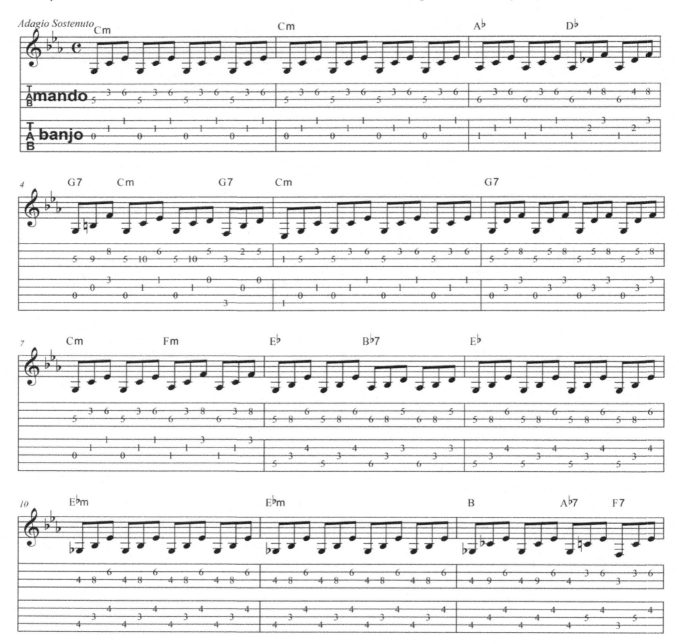

7 - Major & Minor Chords

Arpeggio Study Based on "The Moonlight Sonata" (pg 2)

Arpeggio Study Based on "The Moonlight Sonata" (pg 3)

7 - Major & Minor Chords

Arpeggio Study Based on "The Moonlight Sonata" (pg 4)

Arpeggio Study Based on "The Moonlight Sonata" (pg 5)

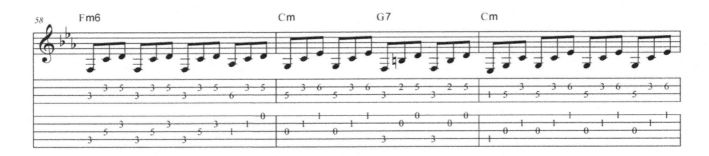

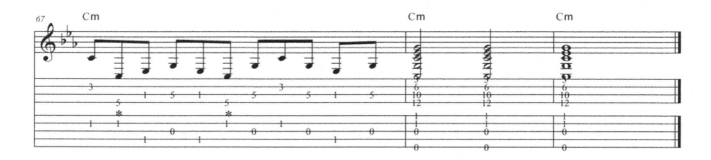

Major and Minor Chords

1. The simplest definition of a chord is this: _____.

2. The word _____ is very similar to the word "chord."

3. Each of the three notes in a chord has a name that describes its _____ and _____ in the chord.

4. The first tone is known as the _____ of the chord.

5. The root note is the note that names the chord. True   False

6. The next two notes are named the _____ and the _____.

7. Each of those numbers refers to the _____ between it and the _____ of the chord.

8. There are two _____ of chords _____ chords and _____ chords.

9. The interval between the root and the 3rd of every major chord is a _____ _____.

10. The interval between the root and the 5th of every major chord is a _____ _____.

11. The interval between the root and the 3rd of every minor chord is a _____ _____.

12. The interval between the root and the 5th of every minor chord is a _____ _____.

13. When referring to major chords, all you have to say (or write) is the letter name.
    True   False

14. There are three common ways to indicate a minor chord. G _____ , G _____ , and
    G _____.

15. The difference between a major chord and a minor chord is the interval between the root and
    the _____ .

16. "Inverting a chord" means to _____ _____ _____ of the tones.

17. There are _____ inversions for major and minor chords.

18. R-3-5 is known as the _____ position.

19. 3-5-R is known as the _____ _____.

20. 5-R-3 is known as the _____ _____.

21. When playing guitar chords, you are required to play all six strings at all times.
    True   False

22. Spell C major _____ _____ _____. Spell C minor _____ _____ _____.

23. Spell D major _____ _____ _____. Spell D minor _____ _____ _____.

24. Spell F# major _____ _____ _____. Spell F# minor _____ _____ _____.

25. Spell G# major _____ _____ _____. Spell G# minor _____ _____ _____.

26. Spell E♭ major _____ _____ _____. Spell E♭ minor _____ _____ _____.

27. Spell B♭ major _____ _____ _____. Spell B♭ minor _____ _____ _____.

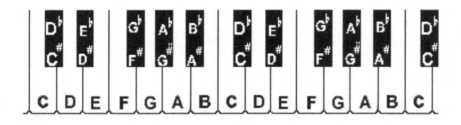

28.-37. Name the chords shown and identify root, 3rd, and 5th in each one.

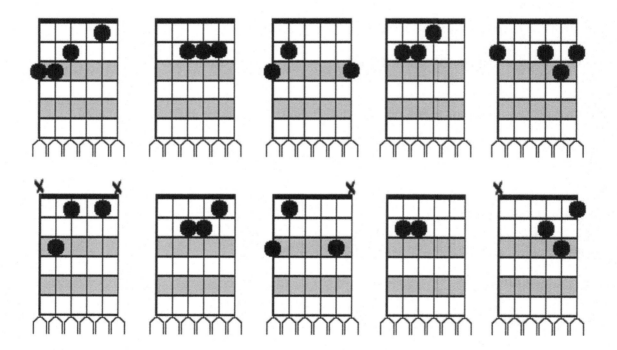

Beyond Major & Minor Chords | Chapter 8

To briefly recap major and minor chord structure, we can say that they share these two characteristics:

    1. Both consist of three notes, known as the root, the 3rd, and the 5th.

    2. They both span seven half steps, from the root up to the 5th.

Now we'll expand on this base. What we're going to do is **extend** the basic three-note chords by **adding notes to the initial triad**. By the time we're done, you'll see some chords that have more than seven different notes.

Then we'll **alter** some of the notes that are in the chords. Every tone in a chord can be altered. Theoretically, a chord can have 12 different notes. At that point, we run out of notes. As far as I can tell, that is the only reason it stops at 12.

For these examples and explanations, we won't alter the root. That's the consistent reference point we'll use in identifying any additional notes we may choose, or any alterations made to the basic chord.

When a chord is written with only a note name (A, B, Db, Eb, F#, G#, etc.) it is a major chord.

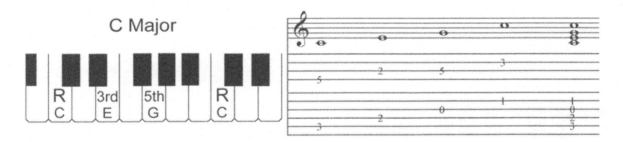

So… we start with a **C**. Just "**C**," nothing more, means we're talking about a C major chord. The numbers used to locate or define the tones included in all chords (3rd, 5th, 7th, 9th, etc.) are derived from two slightly different sources.

One source is intervals. The number is the same as the size of the interval separating a note from the root of the chord. The other source is the major scale. Each of the numbers is a degree of the scale.

Both are essentially accurate and will get you there. Neither is precisely correct in 100% of the chords.

For most of these explanations, I find it easiest to use scale degrees.

Later in this chapter, we'll have to make one adjustment to the size of a scale, as we know it, and that will be to expand the scale from one octave to the two octaves. The largest interval available within a single octave is a 7th and we'll need 9ths, 11ths, and 13ths.

C6, C7, Cmaj7, Cadd9, C11, and C13 are examples of extended chords. When we **extend** major chords, we simply add notes to the original triad.

We always begin with a triad and then extend the chord to make a four-note chord.

All "**6**" chords, E6, G#6, B♭6, A6, any of them and all of them, are built using the root, 3rd, 5th, and 6th tones of a major scale.

To indicate that you're adding the 6th scale degree to the basic triad, you just attach the number of the additional scale degree to the letter name of the chord.

This is a **C6**. Pronounced "C six." Spelled **C-E-G-A**. Root, 3rd, 5th, and 6th. You won't be able to play the chord on a guitar shown at the far right on these two examples and a few others… use an arpeggio to hear the tones.

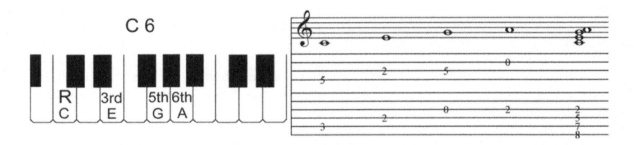

That is how you extend a chord. It is that simple. Welcome to the world of "jazz chords."

Now we'll **alter** a note in that chord… flat the 3rd… to change a C6 chord into a **C-6**.

Pronounced "C minor six." Root, ♭3rd, 5th, 6th = **C minor 6, Cm6 or C-6.**

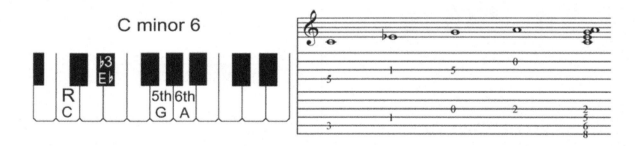

A chord symbol is read just like you would read a sentence… from left to right, one symbol at a time. Each additional word, symbol, or number after the initial letter name indicates specific instructions: alterations, additions, and extensions to the initial major triad.

First you name the chord, **C**.

Then, you move through the notes in the chord in order and mention any changes and/or additions to the major triad. If you tweak the triad in any way, it needs to be explained in the chord symbol.
The first note in a chord is the root. The root won't change.

After the root is the 3rd. Since we altered the 3rd by flatting it, we have to include the word "minor." Minor can be written three ways: **C minor, Cm, and C-.**

After the 3rd, the next note in the chord is the 5th. We're not touching it, so no mention is made. Next case.

We added the 6th tone. Reading from left to right, the chord is a **C minor 6**, which is the same as **Cm6**, or **C-6**. It is just a C chord with a flat 3rd and an additional 6th.

The additional tone is the 6th degree of the scale and is the 6th above the root. However, when pronouncing chord names, usually the "th" is dropped from the number. Say C minor *six* instead of C minor sixth. C minor *seven* instead of C minor seventh. C minor *nine* instead of C minor ninth.

Second example. Using the scale degrees, we'll extend the major chord and add the 7th tone. Remember that all the intervals are either "perfect" or "major." This chord is called **C Major 7**. Root, 3rd, 5th, and 7th. **C-E-G-B.**

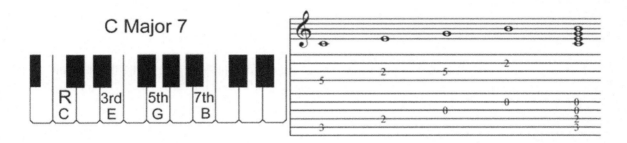

Major 7 means that we extend the chord by adding the 7th tone of the major scale. The new tone is a major 7th away from the root. The chord diagram will usually say "Major 7" or "Maj7," although sometimes a small triangle △ is used to replace the word "major." Upper case letter "M" can also be used, as in CM7, but it's the least common.

CMaj7, C Major 7 and **C △ 7** all mean the same thing… add the 7th degree of the scale to the major triad. All are pronounced "C major seven."

Now, let's alter the major 7 chord. Since we're not altering the root notes in these examples, the first note we can change is the 3rd.

What's this new chord called? We'll run the same drill as before. First you name the chord, **C.**

Then, beginning with the root note, you move through the notes in the chord one by one, and mention any changes.

We won't touch the root. After the root, the next note is the 3rd. Since we're flatting the 3rd, we have to say so. **Cm** or **C-.**

After the 3rd is the 5th. The 5th is not being changed in any way, so no mention is made. Then we added the diatonic 7th tone to the minor triad, so it is a minor major 7 chord.

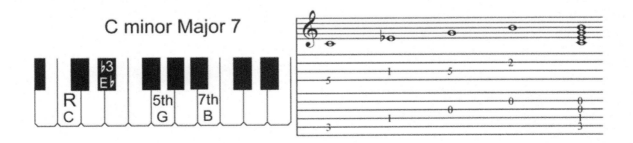

C minor Major 7, or Cm Maj7 or C-△7. Root, ♭3rd, 5th, 7th . Use of both **Major** and **minor** in the same chord name can be a bit confusing, so if this seems about as clear as mud right now, it's OK. Think of it like this:

When you have a C chord, then alter the 3rd (flat it), a C major chord becomes a C minor chord. Root, ♭3rd, 5th.

When you begin with a C6 chord, then alter the 3rd (flat it), a C6 chord becomes a **C minor 6.** Root, ♭3rd, 5th, **6th.**

When you have a CMaj7 chord and flat the 3rd, the CMaj7 chord becomes a **C minor Major 7.** That's a **C minor chord with a Major 7** added to it.

There are two distinct species of 7 chords.

Species #1. The **_Major 7_** chords add the **_7th scale tone_** to the basic triad. The 7th degree of the major scale is a major 7th above the root. Root, 3rd, 5th, 7th. When you say or write D Major 7, B ♭Maj7, G# △7, it means Root, 3rd, 5th, and diatonic 7th.

Species #2. **_Dominant 7_** means that we've **_altered the 7th tone._** Use a flatted 7th instead of the diatonic 7th. Root, 3rd, 5th, ♭7th. If you say or write C7, A7, D♭7, F#7, or whatever, it is implied and understood that you mean dominant 7 using a Root, 3rd, 5th, and ♭7th. **Just adding the number 7 to the chord name indicates dominant 7 chords.** G7, D7 A♭7 and C#7 mean dominant 7. You don't have to say the word "dominant" when referring to dominant 7 chords, the way you have to say "major 7." I don't know why.

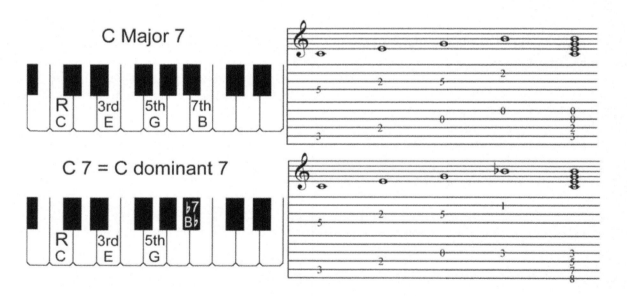

C7 is pronounced "C seven" and means "**C dominant 7**"… which is a C major triad with a flatted 7th added to it. **Root, 3rd, 5th, ♭7th.**

Then, you can simply flat the 3rd of a C7 to make a C minor 7. Cm7. C-7. **Root, ♭3rd, 5th, ♭7th.**

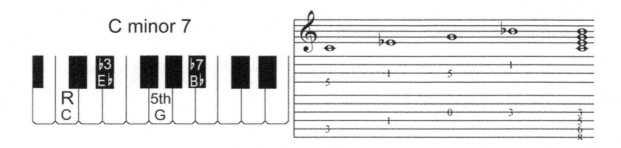

Regarding the use of the word "dominant"… in the section on scales I listed a set of names for the tones of the major scale. "Dominant" is the word that classical theorists use to indicate the 5th degree of the major scale. If we use 3rd to construct a diatonic four-note chord beginning with the 5th (dominant) degree, that chord is a dominant 7 chord. I'm willing to guess there's a connection, but I can't prove it.

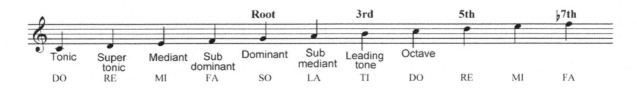

When referring to any chord using the diatonic 7th, you must use the word "**Major**". When referring to any chord using the flatted 7th, you just add the number 7 after the letter name of the chord. C seven.

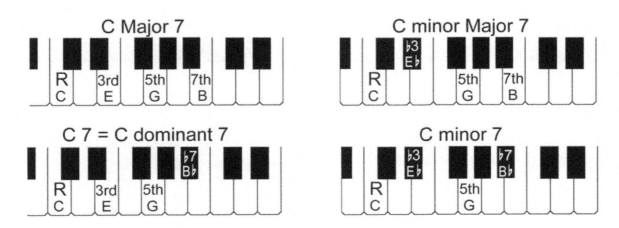

So far, we've added the 6th and 7th tones to the initial root, 3rd, and 5th.

A minute ago we did "minor Major 7." If you reverse the words and say, "Major minor 7" it doesn't make sense. It sort of describes a dominant 7 chord (a Major 3rd and a ♭7th) but not really. You 'll never see any "Major minor 7" chords because there is no such animal.

We can also include the 4th degree in a chord. Frequently, the symbol used to indicate including the 4th is "**sus**" as in **Csus**. **Sus** is an abbreviation often used for **suspended 4th**. The number **4** is not always used when referring to this chord. If you see **sus** attached to a chord letter name it usually means **sus4** or **suspended 4th**. I'm not sure what "suspended" has to do with it… sounds more like something to do with high school to me, but there it is, big as life and twice as natural… **sus4**. I didn't invent this stuff.

Looking at the notes on the keyboard you can see that the 3rd, 4th, and 5th are in a pretty tight group. Since the 3rd, 4th, and 5th are all so close together if you play all three at the same time, it's likely to sound cluttered, muddy. In a **sus4** chord, the 3rd is frequently left out. Root, 4th, and 5th. Lots of jazz players I know really like that "cluttered sound" so don't get the idea you're required to dump the 3rd.

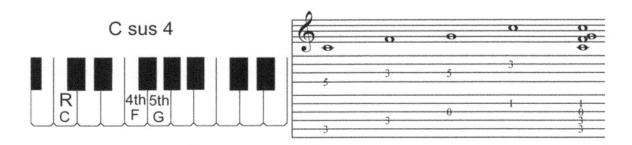

Occasionally, you'll see **sus2**. Guess what? It means you add the 2nd, keep the 3rd, if you want to.

There is also a two-note chord that is named with a number… it's the root, plus the 5th… **C5**. It's sometimes called a "power chord." **C5, A5, G#5**, etc., indicates a chord that uses only the root and the 5th. We usually think of chords as a three-note structure, so technically this is more of an interval than a chord, but everybody calls it a "power chord." It's real common and very useful. If you're playing with several other instruments, it's often a good idea to play chords with fewer notes. The 3rd has a very strong voice. When you're backing up a soloist, leaving the 3rd out of your chords will allow more harmonic options for the soloist and power chords do that.

Sus4 chords, 6 chords, both varieties of 7 chords and their minor cousins all extend the major triad by using notes that are within the first octave.

Now we'll extend the chords beyond the octave.

There are two ways that we extend chords into the second octave. The first way is to just **add the tones to the basic triad**. Just like the 6 and 7 chords do. Start with a triad and **add** notes.

The root appears on the 1st and 8th scale degrees, but it isn't numbered the way the rest of them are. In chord structure, it's always the root. The other tones have number and the numbers continue past the root.

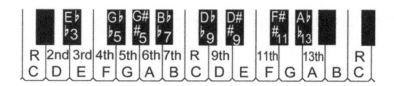

The first degree above the octave is the 9th. It's a 9th above the lowest root. To name/number the new tones, you just keep counting up the scale degrees past the root, and pretend that the octave note is the 8th tone. It's not especially difficult to imagine, since it *is* the 8th tone.

When you want to extend a chord past the octave, you use the word "**add**." The "add" chords are four-note chords.

C add 9 means start with a C chord, and add the 9th. Really nice, I think.

Now try adding the same tone to the chord, but do it in the first octave instead, right between the root and the 3rd. Same four tones but a very different sound.

I can still hear the major chord, and I can hear the added 9th, but to me, it's blurry and indistinct, the result of too many notes being played too closely together.

It also might sound indistinct to me because my amp goes to 11 and I like to stand near the drummer. In a rock band that can be the equivalent of hanging out near an artillery range.

To me an **add 11** chord always sounds a little dissonant, maybe because the 3rd and 4th have only a half step separating them. That sort of dissonance doesn't appeal to everybody, but those wacky jazz players will spend evenings and weekends learning to clump notes together. Go figure.

But… if I flat the 3rd, and then add the 11th, to make a **Cm add 11,** I really like it. To my ear, it helps to have a little more space between the notes so they have room to breathe.

Add 13 sounds just about exactly like a **6** chord… you won't see an **add 13** too often.

A chord symbol is just a recipe that is read from left to right. Start with a major triad and then change it according to the directions in the chord symbol.

Another way to extend into the next octave is to add tones to the "7 chords." Start with a four-note chord as a foundation and add notes to it.

As you recall, there are two types of 7 chords… dominant 7 and major 7. First, let's have a look at extending the dominant 7 chords.

When there is just a number (or numbers) attached to a letter name, such as C9, F#11, B9, E♭13#9, it means you're adding notes to a dominant 7 chord. These chords begin as a four-note chord (Root, 3rd, 5th, ♭7th) and the extensions are tacked on to that chord.

C9 is Root, 3rd, 5th, ♭7th, and 9th. Five notes.

At this point, there is an obvious pattern. Chords are constructed using every other scale degree. Each new note is a 3rd higher than the previous one.

This is known as "stacking 3rds" . Lock this phrase and concept in your head.

C11 is Root, 3rd, 5th, ♭7th, 9th, and 11th. Six notes. **C13** is Root, 3rd, 5th, ♭7th, 9th, 11th, and 13th. Seven notes.

Another way to extend chords is to add tones to a major 7 chord.

When we add tones to a major 7 chord, everything works exactly the same as extending dominant 7 chords; the only difference is that the abbreviation "**Maj**" replaces the number **7** in the chord name.

CMaj9 is C – E – G – B – D.	Root, 3rd, 5th, 7th, and 9th.	Five notes.
CMaj11 is C – E – G – B – D – F.	Root, 3rd, 5th, 7th, 9th, and 11th.	Six notes.
CMaj13 is C – E – G – B – D – F – A.	Root, 3rd, 5th, 7th, 9th, 11th, and 13th.	Seven notes.

When you play "**add**9, **add**11, **add**13" chords you just add one note to the triad to make a four-note chord. It doesn't matter if the chord has a major quality or a minor quality. Add the scale degree specified by the number.

When you play "9, 11, and 13" chords, you begin with a four-note chord, a *dominant 7 chord,* and you add tones from that point. Also, you can keep all the extensions as you add new ones. When there is a just a number attached to a chord name (except 6), it means you are starting with a dominant 7 chord. Root, 3rd, 5th, ♭7th, plus extensions. **C9, D11, G13**.

When you play "major9, major11, and major13" chords, you begin with a four-note chord, a *major 7 chord* and add tones to that foundation.

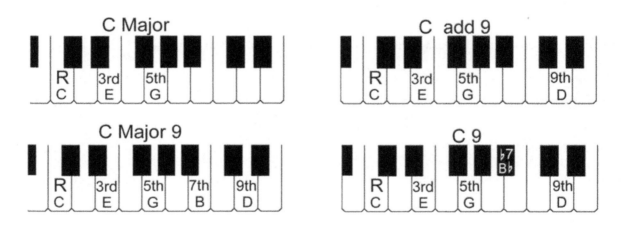

There is still one alteration we can make to a chord. Until now, we've simply been stacking thirds to construct chords. We can also include altered scale tones in chords that are already extended beyond the initial triad, and the new tones won't necessarily fall into the same pattern of 3rds.

A very common sound that helps create a bit of "musical tension" is known as a "7, #9" chord. Pronounced, "seven sharp nine." Remember to play this in different places on the neck—it's 12 chords in one. The root is on the 5th string, don't play the 1st and 6th strings.

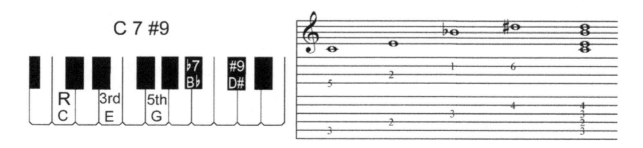

8 - Beyond Major & Minor Chords

C7#9 (read one at a time, left to right) is a C major triad extended to include a flatted 7th, and then adds an altered 9th... altered by raising it one (1) half step. The C7#9 shown here begins with Form #1, raises the root on the second string three half steps to the #9th and omits the 5th on the third string by raising it to the flatted 7th.

C – 6 ♭9 #5 is a C chord with a flatted 3rd to make it minor, add the 6th degree, add the 9th degree, and lower it one (1) half step, find the 5th, and raise it one (1) half step.

Now, for me, that process is too complicated to use in a playing situation. I simply can't think through all of those different steps and get a chord assembled on my guitar before the gig is over and everybody else is wrapping wires.

Fortunately, this explanation isn't about how to build a chord on the fly. This is about understanding what all of those letters, numbers, abbreviations, and symbols mean.

There is another kind of symbol you'll see in nearly every songbook. A "slash" chord. **D / F#**, or **A / G**, and **C / G** are a few examples.

This symbol reads just like all the others, from left to right. The first letter tells which chord you are to play. Nothing new so far.

The second letter, to the right of the slash, specifies a single note. It means that note is to be used as the lowest note in the chord.

D / F# means play a D chord and include an F# note on the lowest string played. D over F# in the bass.

A / G means play an A chord and include a G note on the lowest string played. A over G in the bass.

So, to translate the slash symbol into words, I guess the slash means something like "with the following bass note." **D / F#**... D with the following bass note F#, or maybe D over F# in the bass.

Since you spent all that time spelling chords after the previous chapter, you probably noticed that the low note specified in the examples might or might not be part of the chord that's named on the left side of the slash mark.

For example, a D major chord is spelled D, F#, A... so **D / F#** specifies an inversion that has a low 3rd in the chord.

But G is not part of an A major chord. A major is spelled A, C#, E. **A / G** means you should add a G note (a flatted 7th) to the A major chord, but use it as a bass note. It has a very different flavor than if you add the same G note on top or in the middle of the chord. Try it.

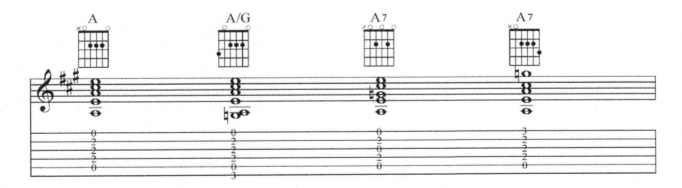

This next phrase may sound familiar. Often, slash chords are used this way… to create a walking bass line that leads to the next chord. Anytime you see a series of slash chords, it's sensible to check and see if this is the case. It might not turn out that way, of course, but it occurs frequently enough that it's worth considering. In this case, it's a descending bass line.

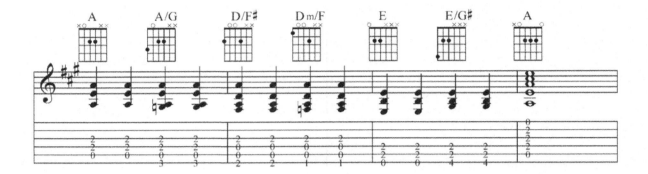

The slash is also sometimes used to substitute for the word "**add**." For example, C6/9 means play a C6 chord and add the 9th (no 7th). **C6 add 9** means the same thing that **C 6/9** does.

The notes in a C Maj13 are C-E-G-B-D-F-A. That's seven notes. Every note in the scale, in fact. Take a look through any jazz guitar book and you'll see plenty of "13" chords.

But a guitar has only six strings and you can't play two notes simultaneously on a single string.

So… this begs the question, "How do you play a seven-note chord on an instrument that can only voice a maximum of six notes at a time?"

There is a simple solution to this puzzler.

You leave some out.

In fact, when somebody is using lots of those "big jazz chords" on a guitar, banjo, or mandolin, they are usually playing abbreviated versions of the chords.

A keyboard player might use all seven notes of a 13 chord, and then duplicate three of them. Ten fingers, ten notes. A guitar is sometimes restricted to playing certain notes in the chord. A mandolin, having only four strings, is certainly not playing seven different notes simultaneously. The 3rd and 7th are usually included, along with the extensions, but the root and 5th can often be omitted without losing the sound of the chord. And using root and 5th, plus extensions (no 3rd) is common.

When you see those big extended chords on a chart, you kind of feel obligated to try and play the whole thing. Even if you do mange to get all the notes indicated by a chord symbol, a lot of the time it still won't sound quite right.

Often the arranger is trying to indicate all of the harmonies played by all of the instruments on the original recording that was probably done by a six or seven piece band. Chances are good that you won't be able to exactly reproduce the same sound on a single guitar.

Usually, you can "reduce" a big five, six, or seven-note chord to the basic triad or a four-note 7 chord and still hear close to what you need, especially if there's another instrument or two covering some of them.

For example, Major 9 (five tones), Major 11 (six tones), and Major 13 (seven tones) can frequently be reduced to four-note Major 7 chords and still sound right, or at least close enough. The 9, 11, and 13 chords can be reduced to four-note dominant 7 chords and often work just fine.

The chord examples on the next few pages are illustrated using extensions and alterations to an A major triad to let you hear some of the chords we've been building.

Take note of the fact that when you play an A chord in the open position, three of the strings are open and you fret three of the notes. One of the open strings is the root, A. The 5th of an A chord is E, and is found on the two other open strings.

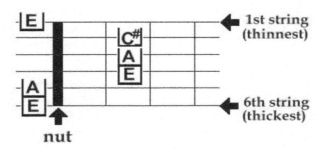

You can strum all six strings while you play these inversions of an A chord, but it's a little easier to hear these alterations if you don't play the 6th string. When you alter the notes in any of the inversions shown on the D, G, and B strings, you will have the open low A as the root, so you can hear the alterations in the proper context. I trust you noticed these are the same inversions found earlier in Major and Minor chords.

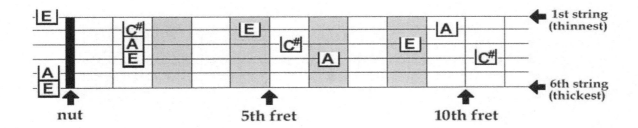

Lowering a root of the major triad creates these extended chords. If you **play the 5ᵗʰ string open, plus the three notes on the diagram**, you'll get a good idea of the sound of all of these chords. Even beginners with small hands can usually reach the notes located on the 2ⁿᵈ, 3ʳᵈ, and 4ᵗʰ strings.

The shaded frets on these diagrams correspond to the marker dots on a guitar neck at the 3ʳᵈ, 5ᵗʰ, 7ᵗʰ, 9ᵗʰ, and 12ᵗʰ frets.

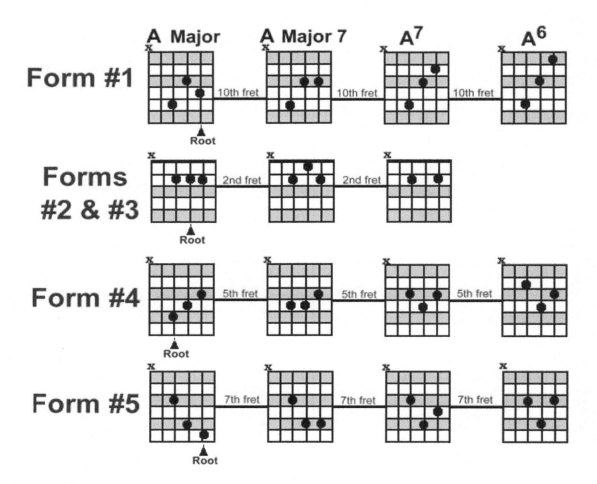

Consider for a moment that this half-page diagram shows four different ways to play an A chord, four different ways to play an A major 7 chord, four different ways to play an A7 chord, and three different ways to play an A6 chord. That adds up to 15 "different" chords. Of course, these will work with 11 other root notes, too. 12x15=180 different chords and these combinations shown here are limited to four strings with the root on a single string. Flat the 3ʳᵈˢ and you've just learned 360 chords. Exponential growth.

When you see a book that says, "*45 hillion-jillion chords*," or something like that, what you'll find inside is every combination and inversion that is conceivable using all six strings and 12 different root notes. It certainly *doesn't* mean that there are that many *different* chords. Books like these can be useful, but they unintentionally intimidate players by making lots of people think that there are thousands of different chords instead of a few dozen. How would you know?

It's hard to say exactly how many different chords exist… major, minor, sus2, sus4, 6, 7, major 7, minor 7, etc. I found a list with just under 90 chords. I've trimmed it down to 75 chords. If you understand inversions, know about a dozen of them real well and are familiar with another dozen, your chord vocabulary will far exceed that of most players.

8 - Beyond Major & Minor Chords

Altering the 3rd of the major triad creates these chords. Flatten the 3rd to get a minor chord and raise it to get a suspended 4th.

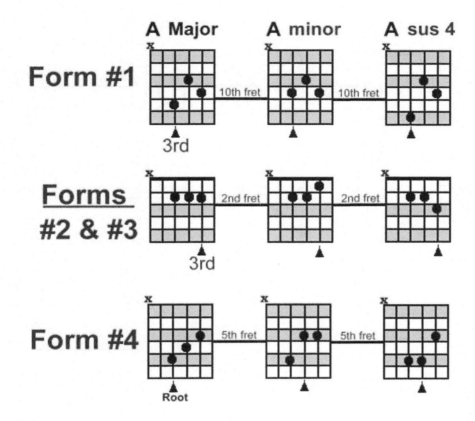

As always, go to the songbook you're using and look for these extended and altered chords. If it has tablature that shows what the guitarist was actually playing, notice whether every note in the chords indicated by the diagram is what was played.

When my beginning students have been playing major and minor chords and scales for three or four weeks, I'll have them close their eyes while I play some basic triads to see if they can identify the quality by ear. Hardly anyone misses more than a few out of 20. These are often people who are still having a bit of trouble humming along with scales, kind of embarrassed to sing because they miss the notes. They still are able to discern a subtle change of one note in a triad well over half the time.

Soon, they can also distinguish major 7 and dominant 7 with ease. This is an acquirable skill.

All of these chords have unique voices. As you learn them, be sure to close your eyes and listen to them as you name them. An important part of playing by ear is to learn to associate the sounds you hear with their names.

Raising the 5th creates these chords.

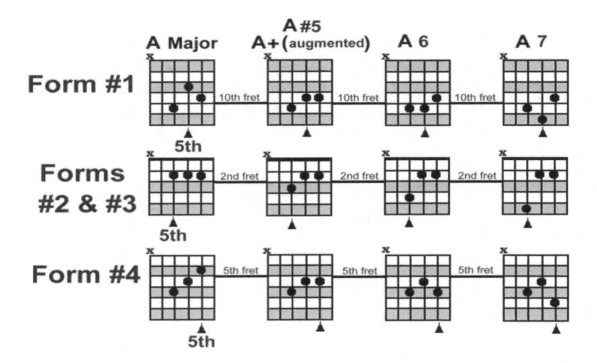

Here's a fairly comprehensive list of chords. If you learn the 16 chords that are underlined, your chord vocabulary will be adequate for playing nearly anything.

Forms #1 and #2 have the lowest root on the 5th string and Forms #3 and #4 have the lowest root on the 6th string. You should learn at least two forms of each of the chords… one with a 6th string root and one with a root on the 5th string.

Major, **5**, **aug**, aug-add9, maj♭5, sus2, sus2/4, sus2#11, **sus4**, sus4/6, sus4/6/9, **6**, 6add11, 6/9, add9#11, add 11, add#11, **maj7**, maj7#5, maj7#11, maj9, maj9#11, maj13.

Minor, m-aug-add9, m-♭5, m-sus2, m-sus2/4, m-sus2#11, m-sus4, m-sus4/6, m-sus4/6/9, **m6**, m6add11, m6/9, m-add11.

7, 7sus4, **9**, 9sus4, 11, **13**, 13sus4, 7♭5, 7♭5♭9, 7♭5#9, 7#5, 7#5H9, 7#5#9, 7♭9, 7#9, 7#11, 9H5, 9#5, 9#11, 11♭5, 11#5, 11#5♭9, 11♭9, 13♭5, 13♭5♭9, 13H9, 13#9.

m7, **m7♭5**, m7♭9, m7♭13, **minor-major7**, major-minor9, m9, m11♭5, m9#11, m13, **dim7**, half dim.

Remember the word "enharmonic?" It's the idea that a single note can have two different names. For example, F# and G♭ are the same tone. In these chords with altered tones, remember that a #11 is the same note as a ♭5 and a #5 gets the same note as a ♭13. Technically, a C7#11 is different than a C7♭5, especially for a keyboard player, but on a guitar, banjo, or mandolin, in nearly all situations no one would recognize a difference.

There is a classic book that is both inexpensive and useful when learning extended and altered chords. *Mickey Baker's Complete Course in Jazz Guitar* (Lewis Publishing) is well worth the current $7.95 retail price. It's a real live bargain at twice the price if you'll go through it. The first page of chords and the exercises that go with them are enough to keep nearly anybody busy for a while.

Forty-five Hillion-Jillion Chords... almost

This takes you through lots of the extended chords and they're arranged in a I-IV-V progression (pronounced one-four-five progression) in the key of A. The details about keys and progressions are coming soon, and you don't need them to play this. You'll probably need to use your thumb and three fingers to do this one. Your thumb plays the bass note and each finger plays a string. It's pretty easy.

First, take a look through the drill and notice that all of the bass notes are on open strings. That leaves a triad and you'll alter that triad one note at a time. The triads for the A and E are on strings 2-3 and 4. I put the triads for the D changes on strings 1-2 and 3, so you can use the open D strong for your bass.

Some of these are tough to reach on a mandolin and I left the bass notes off the mando tab so you're just messing with triads.

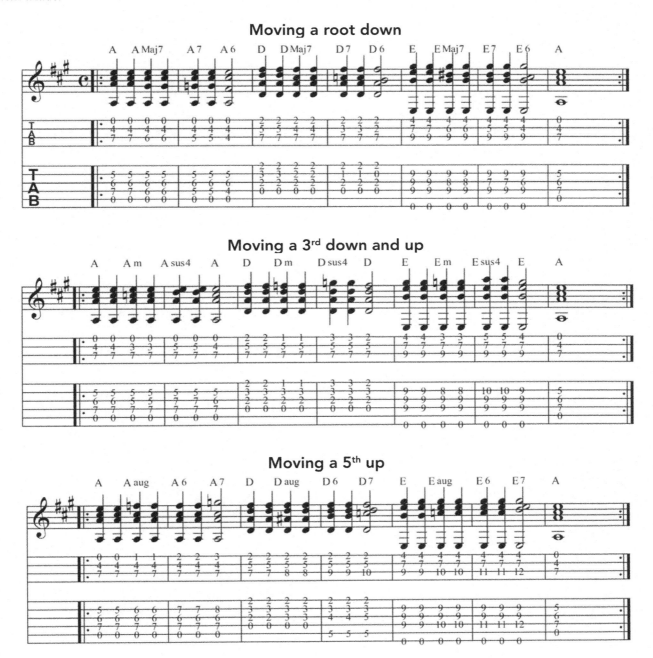

Extended Arpeggios

Both of these exercises begin with a chord and then by moving a single note (sometimes two) create a new chord. Most of the motion in #1 is on the 4th string, and the first five measures are similar to the intro to "Stairway to Heaven" by Led Zeppelin. In #2, most of the action is on the 2nd string. As always, tabs for the 2nd, 3rd, and 4th strings work for both guitars and banjos, but the banjoliers will have to ignore the 1st string, re-tune it, or make a two-fret adjustment on the tab.

8 - Beyond Major & Minor Chords

Altering Dominant 7 Chords

Altering the 5th and 9th tones of chords based on dominant 7 chords is very common. This shows a couple of useful variations on that theme. These chords don't lay out well for mandolin or banjo, but if you understand the principle of what's happening here, you can apply it to those instruments as well. Begin with a chord, alter a note in the chord, and then identify the new tone in the chord symbol. D minor seven flat five is a bit of a mouthful, but it's not especially hard to comprehend if you say it slowly.

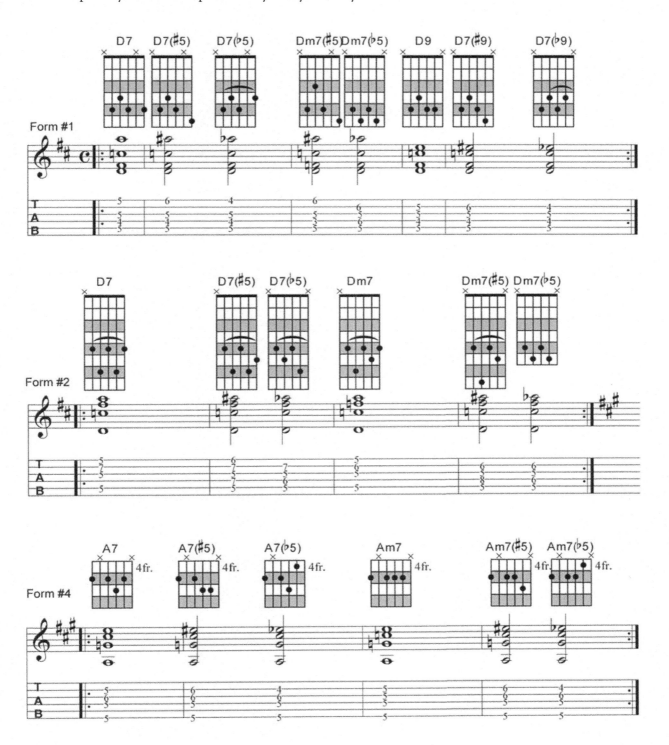

Stacking 3rds

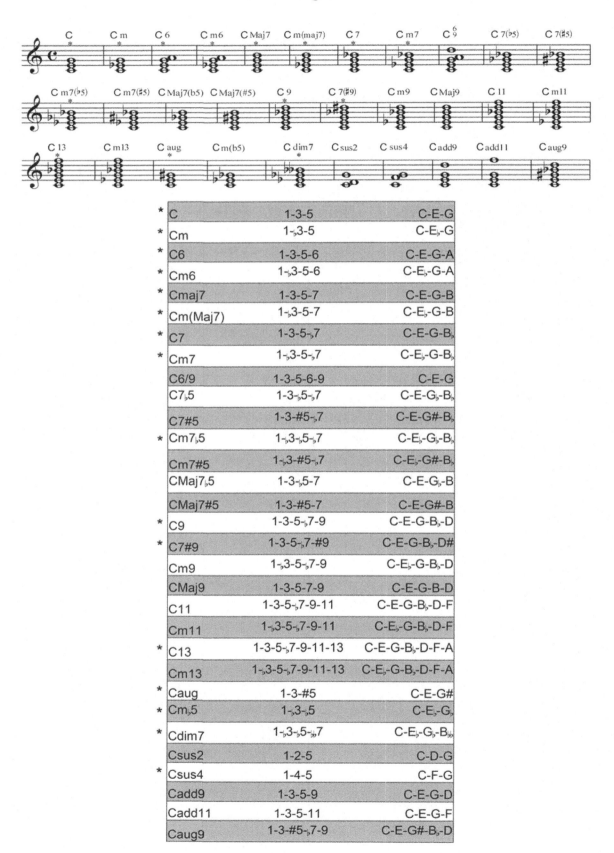

*	C	1-3-5	C-E-G
*	Cm	1-♭3-5	C-E♭-G
*	C6	1-3-5-6	C-E-G-A
*	Cm6	1-♭3-5-6	C-E♭-G-A
*	Cmaj7	1-3-5-7	C-E-G-B
*	Cm(Maj7)	1-♭3-5-7	C-E♭-G-B
*	C7	1-3-5-♭7	C-E-G-B♭
*	Cm7	1-♭3-5-♭7	C-E♭-G-B♭
	C6/9	1-3-5-6-9	C-E-G
	C7♭5	1-3-♭5-♭7	C-E-G♭-B♭
	C7#5	1-3-#5-♭7	C-E-G#-B♭
*	Cm7♭5	1-♭3-♭5-♭7	C-E♭-G♭-B♭
	Cm7#5	1-♭3-#5-♭7	C-E♭-G#-B♭
	CMaj7♭5	1-3-♭5-7	C-E-G♭-B
	CMaj7#5	1-3-#5-7	C-E-G#-B
*	C9	1-3-5-♭7-9	C-E-G-B♭-D
*	C7#9	1-3-5-♭7-#9	C-E-G-B♭-D#
	Cm9	1-♭3-5-♭7-9	C-E♭-G-B♭-D
	CMaj9	1-3-5-7-9	C-E-G-B-D
	C11	1-3-5-♭7-9-11	C-E-G-B♭-D-F
	Cm11	1-♭3-5-♭7-9-11	C-E♭-G-B♭-D-F
*	C13	1-3-5-♭7-9-11-13	C-E-G-B♭-D-F-A
	Cm13	1-♭3-5-♭7-9-11-13	C-E♭-G-B♭-D-F-A
*	Caug	1-3-#5	C-E-G#
*	Cm♭5	1-♭3-♭5	C-E♭-G♭
*	Cdim7	1-♭3-♭5-♭♭7	C-E♭-G♭-B♭♭
	Csus2	1-2-5	C-D-G
*	Csus4	1-4-5	C-F-G
	Cadd9	1-3-5-9	C-E-G-D
	Cadd11	1-3-5-11	C-E-G-F
	Caug9	1-3-#5-♭7-9	C-E-G#-B♭-D

8 - Beyond Major & Minor Chords

major

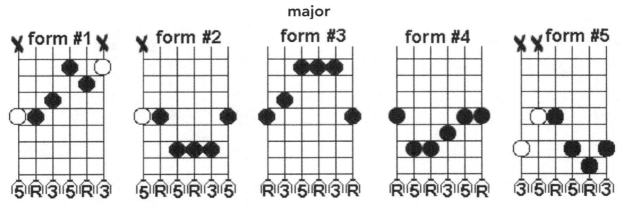

Root, 3rd and 5th are supplied in the major chord diagrams for all five forms. I suggest that you fill in the blanks as you learn the chords.

minor

dominant 7

minor 7

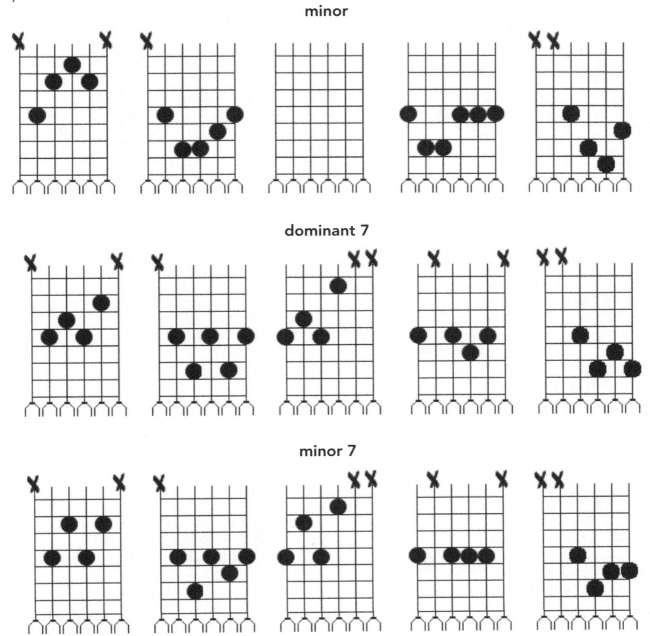

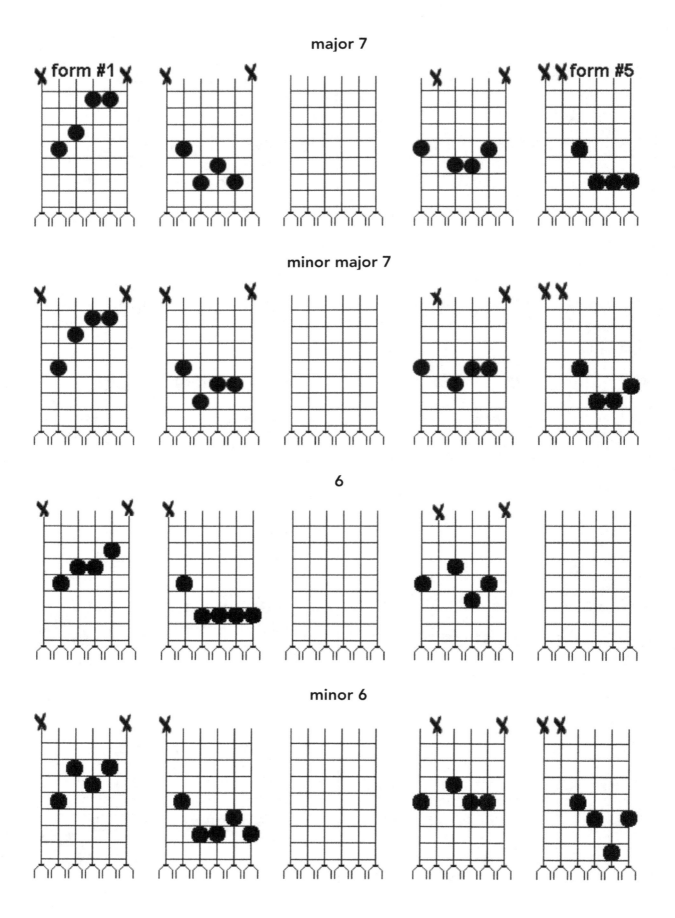

8 - Beyond Major & Minor Chords

sus 4

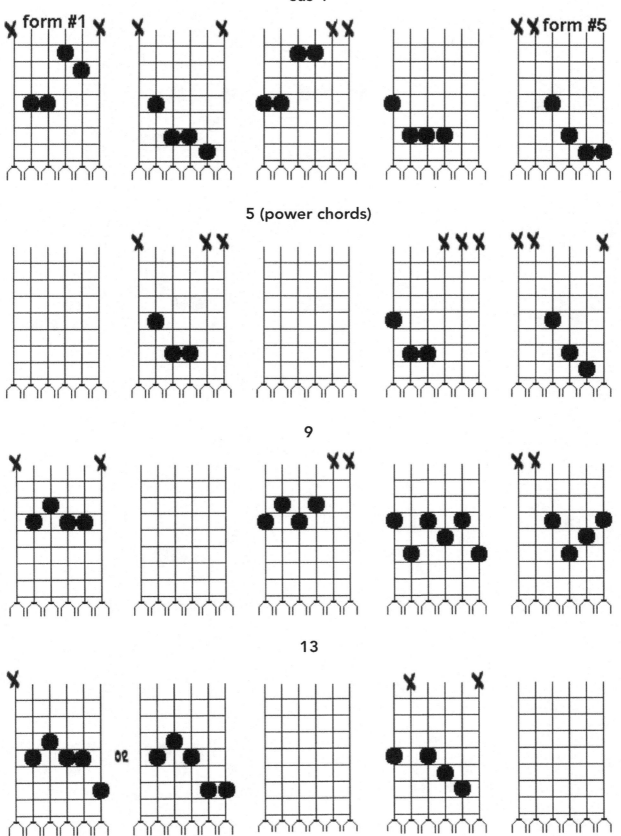

5 (power chords)

9

13

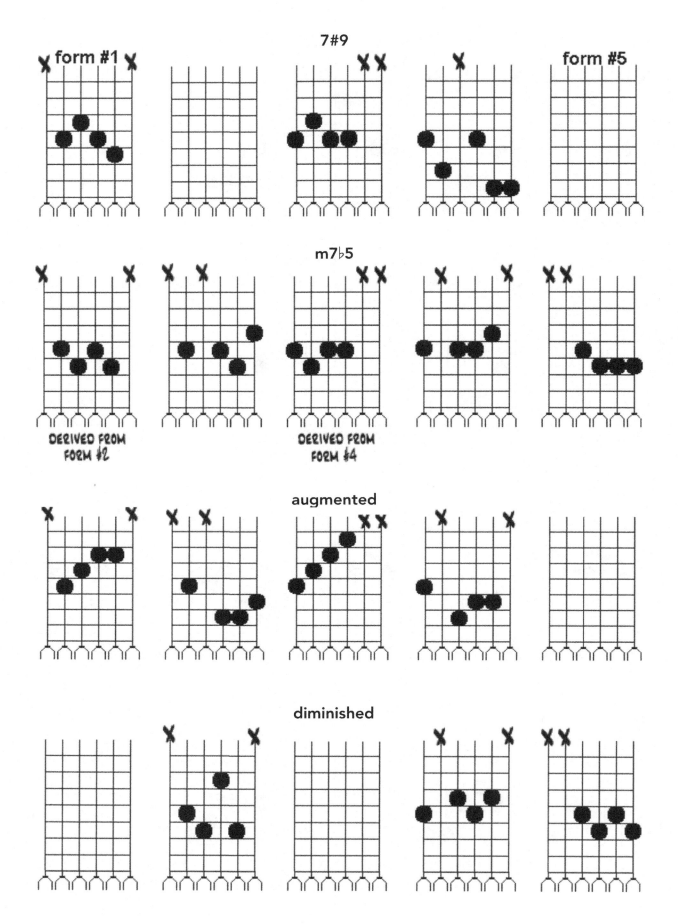

8 - Beyond Major & Minor Chords

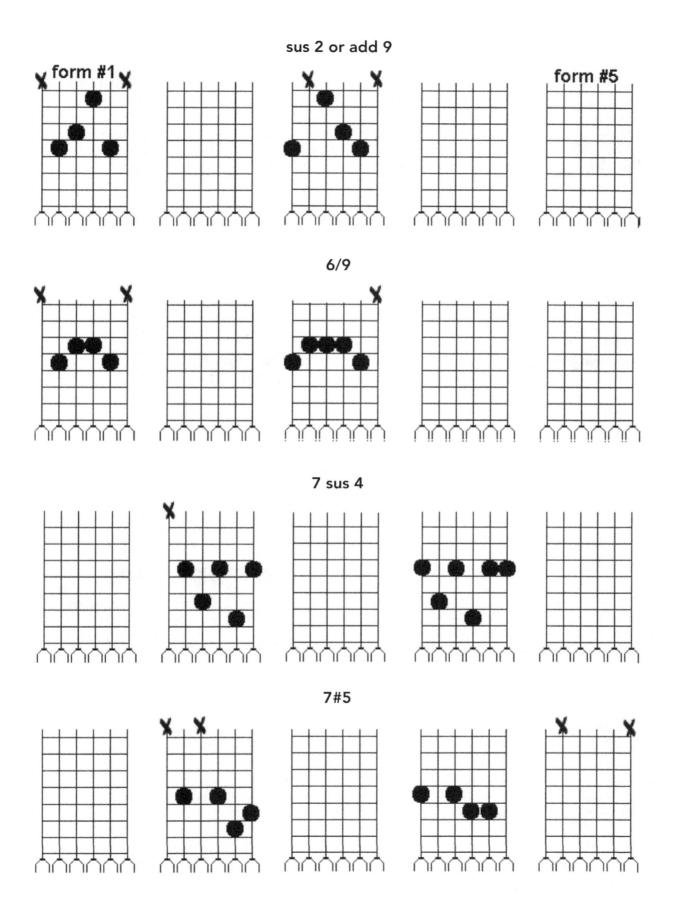

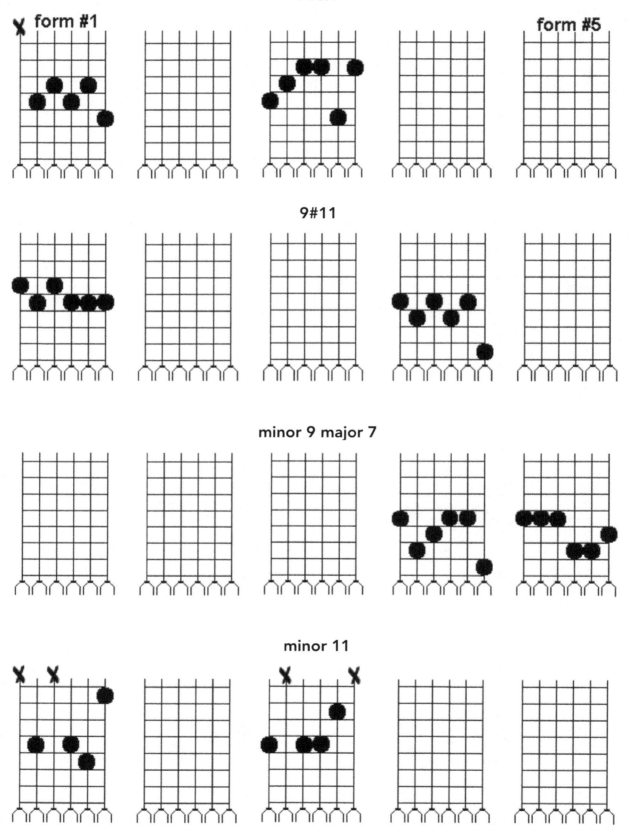

302   8 - Beyond Major & Minor Chords

Here are some chords that you can name yourself. If you assume the lowest note shown is the root of the chord, you can figure out the "real" names. Shay Larson told me that George Harrison called chords like these "naughty chords." My good friend, Mike Parsons, calls them "L chords." Says they sound "L" to him. Use them at random at a bluegrass jam and you can suddenly be the center of attention. Someone will probably offer to help you tune your guitar. Play three or four of these chords followed up by a nice big G major chord and you can hear the musical version of a technique called "tension and release." I've learned to really like the "dissonance" that happens in these chords, but it does seem to be an acquired taste. Try them, you might like them.

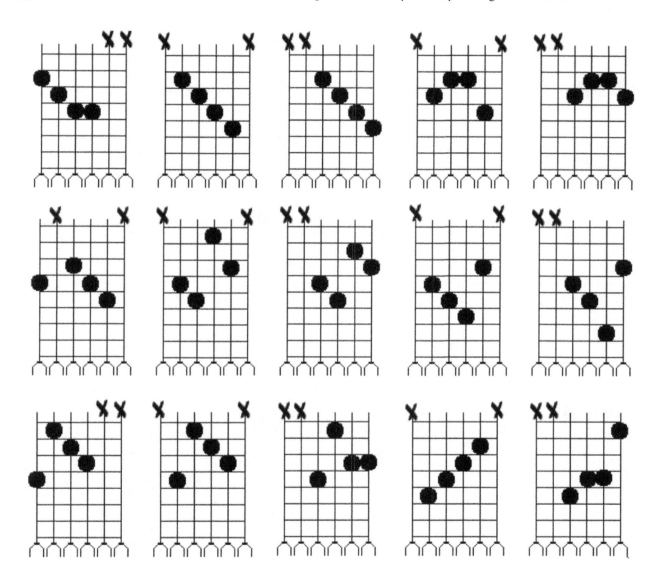

Altered and Extended Chords for Instruments Tuned in 5ths

major

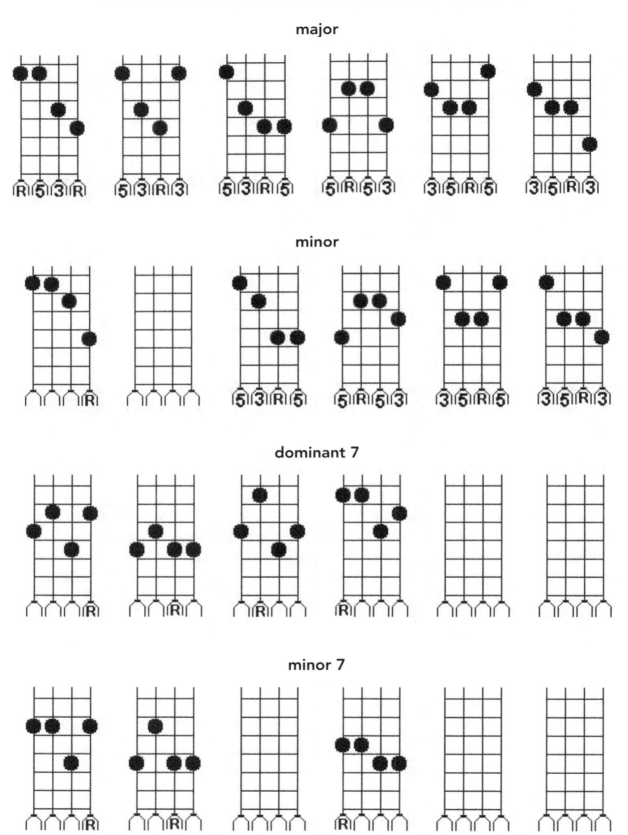

minor

dominant 7

minor 7

8 - Beyond Major & Minor Chords

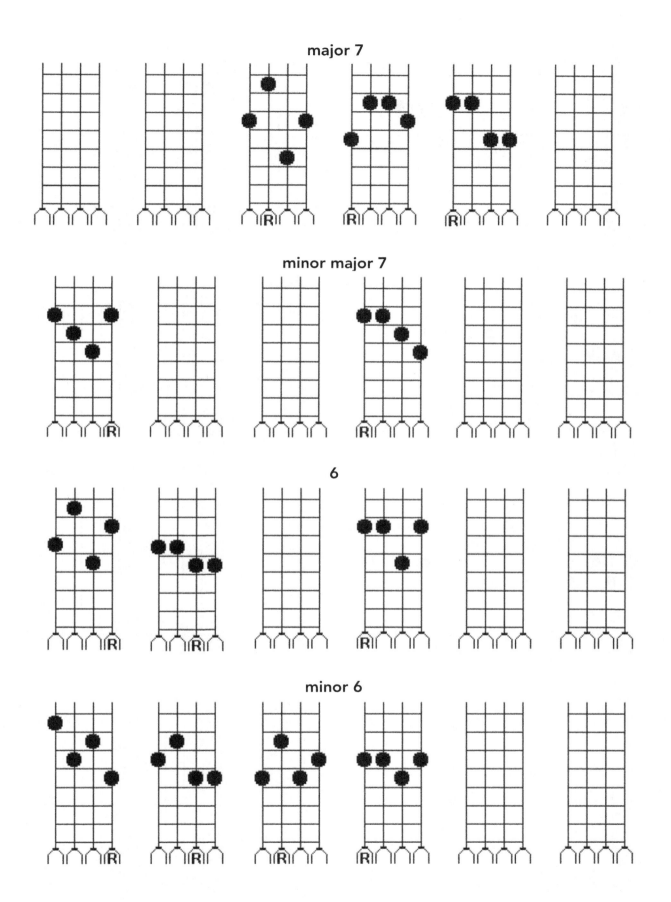

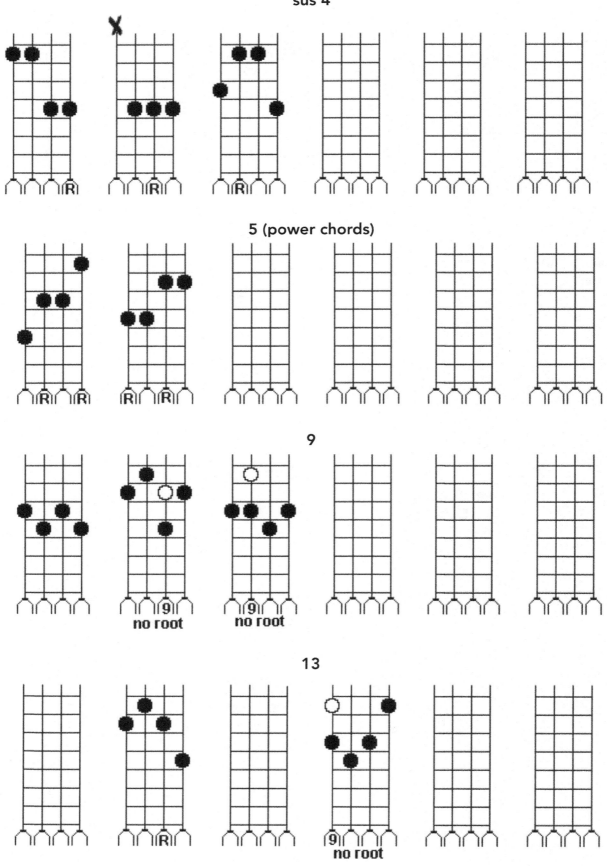

8 - Beyond Major & Minor Chords

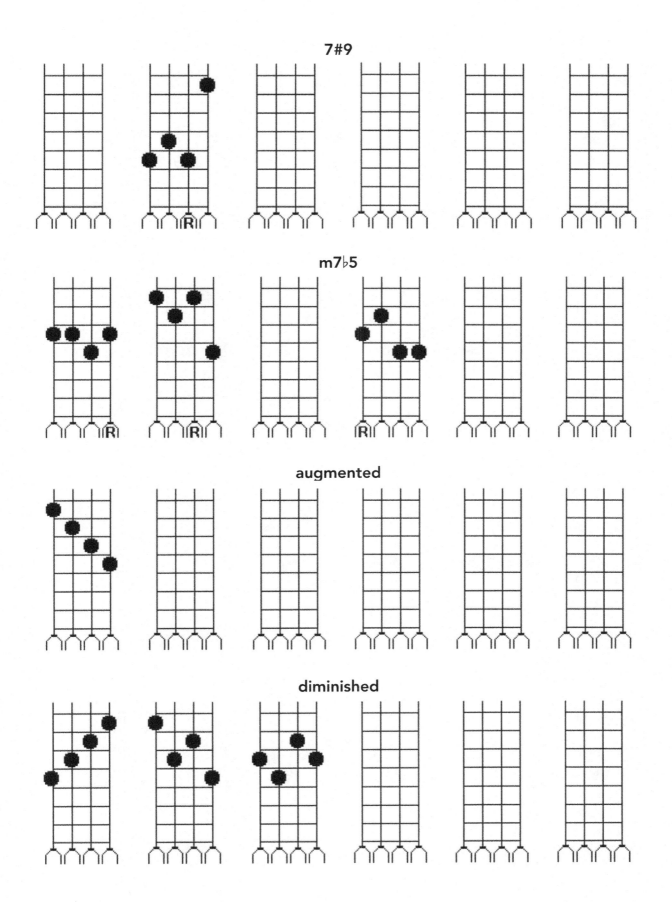

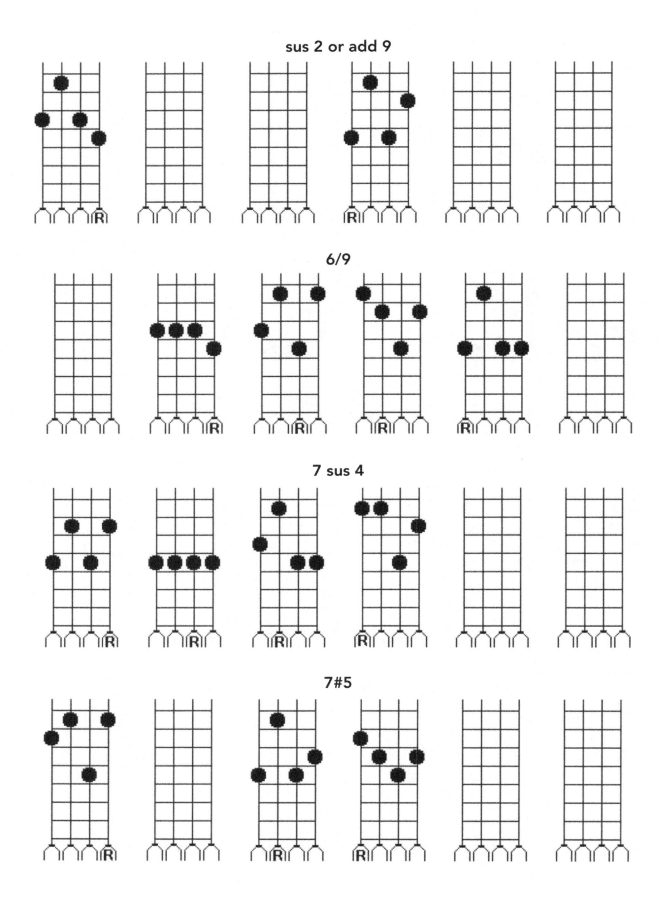

8 - Beyond Major & Minor Chords

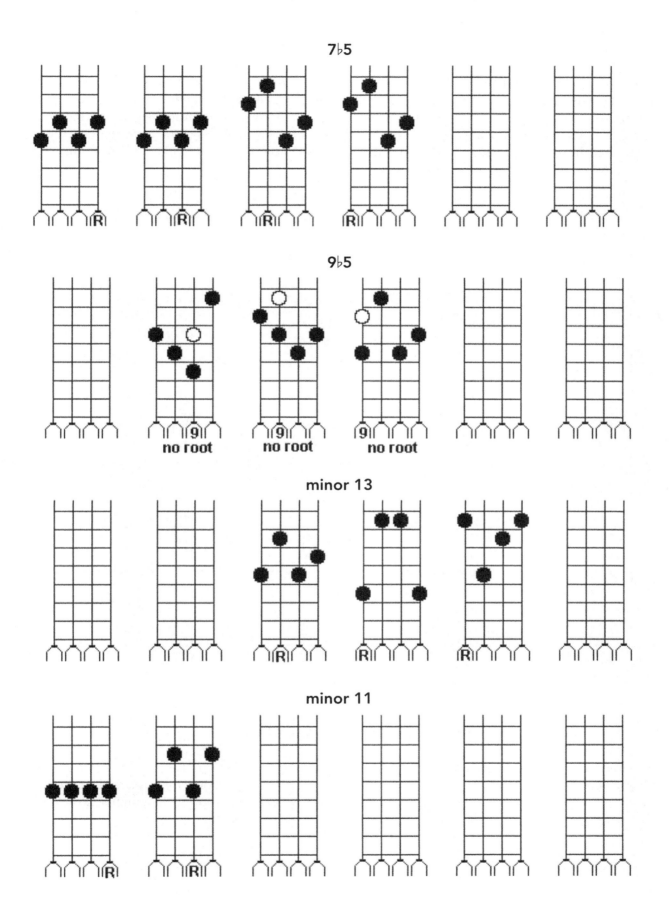

The Two-Chord Drill

Invest some cash and some listening/practice time into big band recordings that have fellows like Django Reinhardt, Freddie Green, and Charlie Christian playing guitar. You'll hear these guys banging out a style of accompaniment ("comping" chords) that's called "four to the bar"… one whack per beat. They were trying to keep a volume level that could be heard with a bunch of raging horn players blasting away and a high-energy drummer, using heavy strings, a heavy pick, and with relatively high action to get the guitar as loud as possible.

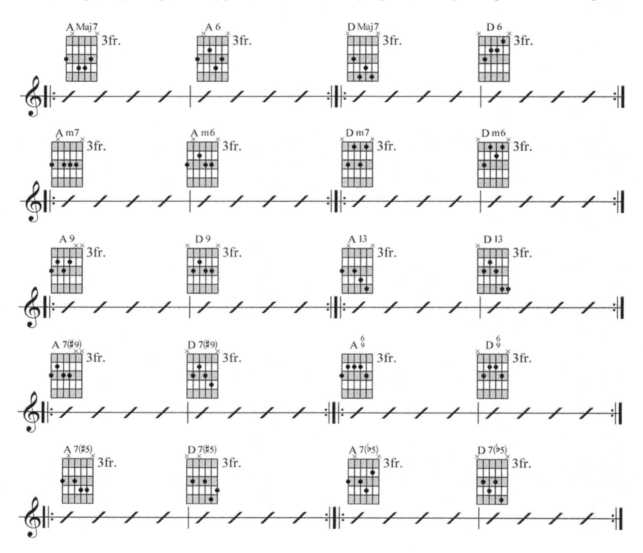

The Charleston Beat, Layed Back

Here's a groove I learned from a Joe Pass book, *Chord Encounters for Guitar, Book 1.*" He called it *The Charleston Beat, Layed Back.*" Mr. Pass said, "This is good for settling down the rhythm section if there is a tendency to rush. Nine out of 10 times, this will get things into a groove." It's also great for grooving these simple two-chord exercises. Do it very slow, very slinky, and very layed back. I bet you'll write a song.

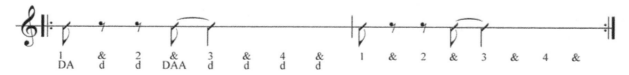

8 - Beyond Major & Minor Chords

Here are three 8-bar phrases that use some of these chords

As usual, the chords that show the lowest note on the 6th string are derived from Form #3 and #4 and the chords that show the lowest note on the 5th string are derived from Form #1 or #2.

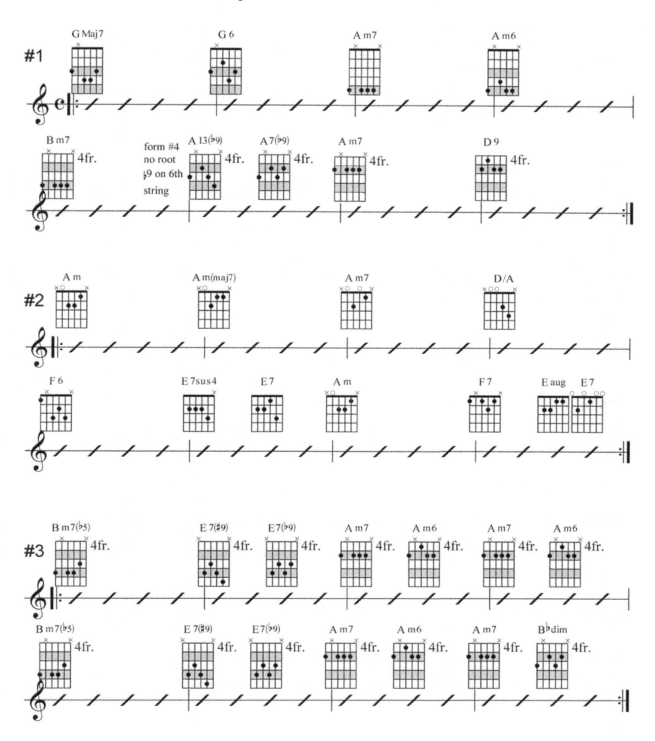

Beyond Major and Minor Chords

1. Major and minor chords can be _____ by _____ notes to the initial _____.

2. Every tone in an extended chord can be _____.

3. Theoretically, a chord can have _____ different notes.

4. To indicate that scale tones are being added to the basic triad, you attach the _____ of the tone you're adding to the _____ name of the chord.

5. The number refers to the _____ between the scale tone being added to the chord and the _____ of the chord.

6. A chord symbol is read from _____ to _____, one symbol at a time.

7. Each additional word, symbol, or number after the initial letter name indicates specific instructions: alterations, additions, and extensions to the initial three-note major triad indicated by the letter.
    True   False

8. All **6** chords use the tonic, _____, _____ and _____ tones of a major scale.

9. In a C-6 chord, the letter C represents the notes _____, _____, and _____. The (-) symbol is pronounced _____ and means that the _____ is to be _____. The number 6 means that the _____ tone of the ____ major scale has been added.

10. All **major 7** chords use the tonic, _____, _____, and _____ tones of a major scale.

11. C _____ _____, C _____ _____ and C _____ are all abbreviations for a chord that is spelled C-E-G-B.

12. If the 3rd of a C major 7 chord is flatted, it is called a C _____ _____ 7 chord.

13. All **dominant 7** chords use the tonic, _____, _____, and _____ tones of a major scale.

14. A dominant 7 chord is indicated by adding the number _____ to the letter name of the chord as in C _____.

15. If you say or write C7, A7, Db7, F#7, it is implied and understood that the tones are the root, _____, _____, and ___ _____.

16. When you say or write D major 7, Bbmaj7, G# △, etc., it means the tones are the root, _____, ____, and _____ _____.

17. **Sus** is an abbreviation often used for _____ _____.

18. **C5, A5, G#5,** are two-note chords that use only the _____ and the _____ and are frequently called _____ _____.

19. One way to extend chords into the second octave is to just _____ tones to the basic triad.

20. When a chord is extended past the octave, and there is no _____ tone, diatonic or flatted, you use the word "**add**."

21. The "add chords" are _____ note chords.

22. **C add 9** means start with a _____ chord and add the _____ tone.

23. **E add 11** means start with an _____ chord and add the _____ tone.

24. **G add 13** means start with a _____ chord and add the _____ tone.

25. **Cm add 9** means begin with a _____ chord, flat the _, and add the 9th.

26. Another way to **extend** into the next octave is to **add the tones to the** "7 chords."   **True   False**

27. This time you start with a _____-note chord and add notes to it.

28. **C add 9** is root, ____, _____, _____, and _____, for a total of _____ notes.

29. **C9** is root, _, _____, _____, and _____, for a total of _____ notes.

30. **C11** is root, _____, _____, _____, _____, and _____, for a total of _____ notes.

31. **C13** is root, _____, _____, _____, _____, _____, and _____, for a total of _____ notes.

32. If the abbreviation _____ is in the chord name, then it means you're adding tones to the major 7 chord.

33. **Cmaj9** is root, _____, _____, _____, and _____, for a total of _____ notes.

34. **Cmaj11** is root, ____, _____, _____, _____, and _____, for a total of _____ notes.

35. **Cmaj13** is root,____, _____, _____, _____, _____, and _____, for a total of _____ notes.

36. How do you play a seven-note chord on an instrument that can only voice a maximum of six notes at a time?
    _____

37. **D / F#** means _____ over _____ in the bass.

38. **A / G** means _____ over _____ in the bass.

39. **Em / G** means _____ over _____ in the bass.

40. **C 6/9** means play a _____ chord and add the _____.

Chapter 9

Augmented, Diminished and (alt.) Chords

There are still two triad qualities that remain to be defined. As you recall "major" is a quality and "minor is a quality. The two triads that remain are called augmented and diminished.

Augmented triads are easy to understand as the major and minor triads, but they do have some unique characteristics that keep them in their own category. Diminished is just a bit more complicated and confusing, but not terribly difficult.

Augmented first, because it lives in, or at least near, the family of major chords.

Like all the other chords, augmented chords are built by "stacking 3rds". Begin with a root note, add a second note a 3rd above the root, and then add another note a 3rd higher.

Unlike the major and minor triads, both intervals in an augmented triad are the same... two major 3rds. Two major 3rds combined is root, 3rd, and # *5th*.

Augmented =more=up=bigger. An augmented chord is just a little bit "bigger" than a major chord. All major and minor triads span an interval of seven half steps (a perfect 5th). An augmented triad spans eight half steps.

The abbreviation "aug" is used to indicate an augmented chord. The "plus sign"... "+"... is the symbol used to indicate an augmented triad.

The chord symbols "**Caug**" or "**C+**" are pronounced C augmented. **F#+** and **F#aug** are pronounced F sharp augmented.

Pick a note, any note. Stack a major 3rd on it (four half steps), then another one, and that is an augmented chord.

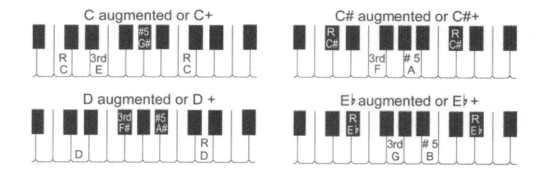

There are no inversions of augmented chords.

If you stack three major 3rds, the fourth note will be an octave higher than the first note. It's perfectly symmetrical, no matter where you start in the chord.

So, when you play what should be the first inversion, instead of being an inversion, it becomes a new augmented chord and the lowest note is the new root.

This is what happens when you attempt to make inversions from an augmented triad. The three notes in a C augmented are C, E, and G#. Each becomes the root of a new chord and the other two notes become 3rds and 5ths.

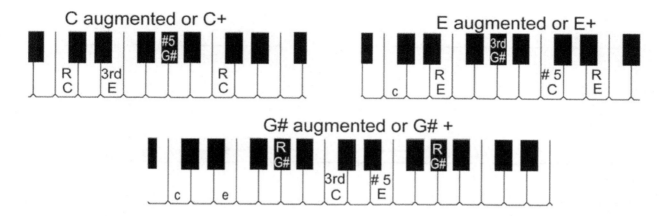

An augmented chord can be named by any of the three notes in the chord. So, a single fingering shape on the guitar is three entirely different chords all at once and they are all exactly the same. Got that? Truly weird.

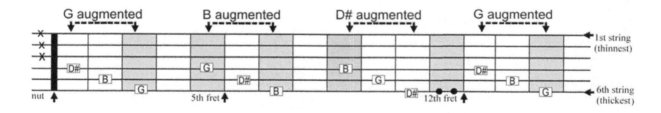

Play the first triad shown above: G, B, and D#. Listen to the sound. G, B, and D# is a G+ chord.

Then slide all three notes up a major 3rd so the lowest note is B, with D# and G as the other two notes. Listen closely and compare the sound to the first triad. The quality of the sound remains the same, but this time these three notes form a B+ chord.

Now, slide all three notes up another major 3rd so the lowest note is D#, with G and B as the rest of the triad. The quality of the sound remains the same, but this time these three notes from a D#+ chord.

Each of these triads contains the same three notes, and can be named by any of the three notes, but it minimizes confusion to use the lowest note played as the name of the chord.

As always, these triads can be played in many different places on the neck. Notice the note names are the same on each fretboard in all four chords, but the chord names are different.

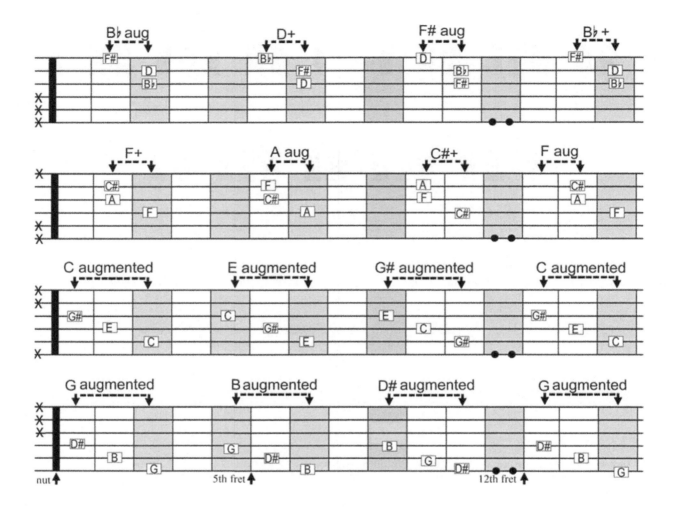

Augmented chords played alone sound kind of odd. "Odd-mented or augmented chords" as Mr. Larry Barnwell (a.k.a. Alphonso Major, accused conspirator in the rockabilly band "Chicken Lips") refers to them. The raised 5th creates a kind of musical tension... a sense that something else needs to be played... kind of like waiting for the other shoe to hit the floor. Resolution is required.

Because the major scale is the consistent reference point used for the numerical descriptions of chords, it's easiest to describe an augmented chord by using the major scale as the reference point... root, 3rd, and #5th.

You will also occasionally encounter augmented 7th chords, augmented 9th chords, etc. These extensions mean exactly what they meant in the previous chapter. You add the scale tone that the number specifies. Simple.

Diminished

Diminished is next, and it is in the minor family.

Stacking two diatonic 3^{rds} above the 7th degree of the major scale generates a diminished triad. In the key of C, the notes are B, D, and F. TI, RE, and FA.

Like the major, minor, and augmented triads, making a diminished triad is once again just a matter of stacking 3^{rds}, but in this case it is minor 3^{rds}.

The quality of this triad is ambiguous in its sound. It certainly doesn't sound "resolved," and you definitely want to play another chord after it, but it doesn't lead as strongly to the **I** chord like an augmented or a dominant 7 does. (You'll find out about the **I** chord in the chapter "**The Key.**" For now, **I** is a Roman numeral and pronounced "the one chord" and is the primary chord in any key.)

As you recall, major chords, minor chords, and augmented chords are frequently played as triads. Diminished chords nearly always consist of four tones.

There are two distinct varieties of four-note diminished chords.

The first one we'll look at is called a diminished 7. There are three ways to indicate this chord on paper. When someone says, "C diminished" what is usually meant is C diminished 7. The symbol for diminished is a little circle "○" or a little circle with a 7... "○7"... either one. "C○7" and "C○" both mean C diminished 7. Usually what is spoken is "C diminished."

Here are the notes in a C diminished 7. C, E♭, G♭ and A.

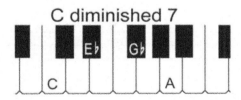

This is where diminished chords start to fuzz out around the edges. Up to this point, all chord extensions or alterations made to triads referred either to the scale degree being added to the triad or the interval between the root of the chord and any additional notes. Consider the tones in a diminished 7 as they relate to the degrees of the major scale. Root, ♭3, ♭5, and 6th degrees, right?

It's true that the fourth note in the diminished 7 chord lands on the 6th degree of the major scale. That fourth note is also a 6th above the root of the chord. But... because that fourth note is a 3rd above the 5th of the chord it's called a 7th and not a 6th. Well, yes... but... no... I mean... I think... I thought... uh... This is a crystal clear example of music theory at its murkiest. Try it again, slowly.

Whatever name you attach to that fourth note of a diminished 7 chord, "diminished 7" is one of the correct chord names.

Diminished chords are symmetrical in the same way that augmented chords are and inverting a diminished chord is an exercise in futility. Every time you get to the next inversion, it vanishes and a new chord takes its place. A diminished 7 can be named by each of the four notes in the chord.

These have their root (name) on the 4th string, the lowest note in the chord.

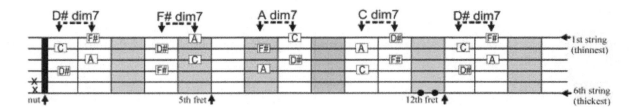

Here is a sequence of chords with the root on the 5th string. Take a look at the diagonal line that runs through C, F#, and C that are on the 5th and 4th strings (or D#, A, D#). The interval is a flatted 5th. The "flat 5," also known as a "tritone," is a big deal in jazz harmony. I'm not going to go into it, because I'm nearly clueless on this particular subject; but if you are interested in jazz, be aware that this is a "naturally occurring interval" in a diminished chord.

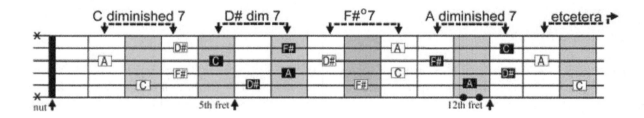

Here are two more diminished 7 shapes with the root on the 6th string.

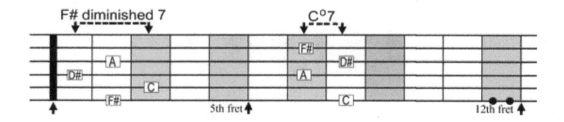

The other type of four-note diminished chord is called a "half diminished" chord. Its structure is identical to the diminished 7 chord for the first three tones. The fourth tone breaks the pattern of using only minor 3rds. A circle with a slash... Ø... is the symbol that represents half diminished. C Ø and C Ø7 are pronounced C half diminished.

Now, if you're like me and you thought it was a bit of a stretch to call the fourth tone in a diminished 7 a "7th," you're gonna love this: because in the "half diminished" chord, the fourth tone actually *does* land on the flatted 7th degree of a major scale. Is this obvious fact sufficient reason to call this animal the diminished 7 chord? Nope. Why not? I don't know. Remember that bandstand theory grew up in bars, and sometimes I suspect that just maybe possibly everybody wasn't 100% sober at all times.

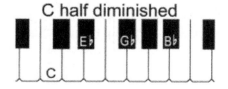

To me, that name is more than just a little bit misleading. Similar to the way that the name "The Patriot Act" is misleading, except there's no premeditated and malicious intent to confuse and manipulate with regard to the chord names. I think it might be better to think of it as a "nearly diminished" chord. How about diminished? "Demolished chords" is what Sandy Dodge, pedal steel player in www.twang calls them. (Real country music wherever there's a plug-in: Buck Buchannan, Sandy Dodge, Russ Olsen, John Regan, and Jim Lewis. (www. twang.org)

What's more, the tones in a half diminished already have a different name that is 100% consistent with the system of using major scale degrees to identify chord tones. C minor 7♭5 produces the same series and leaves out all of the confusion. Just remember, "half diminished" is a synonym for "m7♭5." The name "half diminished" may have originated in the Department of Redundancy Department."

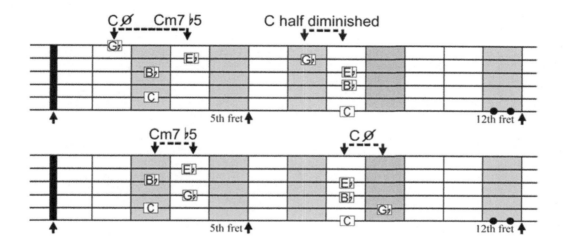

There's still one more little weirdness to deal with when naming triads.

You'll remember that major triads, minor triads, and augmented triads are frequently used as triads. Saying **C major** indicates a major triad, **C minor** is a minor triad and **C augmented** refers to an augmented triad.

Well, diminished triads are different than all of the others. Somehow, everyone has neglected to give diminished triads a name that includes the word "diminished." I suspect that the same fellow who decided to relocate middle C for guitarists' written music might have had something to do with naming diminished chords. He certainly did not eschew obfuscation. (I saw "eschew obfuscation" on a bumper sticker and had to look up both words.) (www.m-w.com).

A diminished triad is usually described as "minor ♭5" chord. That name is consistent with the rules we're accustomed to for naming chords and it works just fine.

Now, after all that, I need to let you know there is a way to make the root, 3rd, 5th, and 7th tones of the diminished chords agree with the scale degrees. All you have to do is stop using the major scale, and instead, assign numbers to the tones in the diminished scale (page 148). When that's the reference, R-3-5-7 match up just the way they should. It's like using the whole tone scale (page 149) to arrive at a diatonic augmented chord.

It didn't occur to me until SEVERAL YEARS after I had written this chapter to try using a different scale to find the numbers. I felt I had no choice but to revise the chapter, and I did it. Then after reading both versions, I decided to inset the "correct" explanation for the numbers here, mainly because I'm so accustomed to using the major scale for my reference point.

Remember the list of 75 different chords on page 292? Well, structurally, about 97% of them agree with the major scale. It's way easier for me to use the major scale to understand diminished and augmented chords than try to remember and apply the details about the whole tone scale, which has six tones in an octave, and the diminished scale which has eight degrees. If swapping scales works for you, it's OK with me.

Demented chords, according to Alphonso. It's tough to disagree when discussing the nomenclature.

Reflections

"One may go a long way after one is tired."
French Proverb

*"One of the commonest mistakes and one of the costliest is thinking that success
is due to some genius, some magic, something or other which we do not possess.
Success is generally due to holding on, and failure is often due to letting go.
You decide to learn a language, study music, take a course of reading,
train yourself physically. Will it be success or failure?
It depends upon how much pluck and perseverance that word "decide" contains.
The decision that nothing can overrule,
the grip that nothing can detach will bring success.*
Maltbie Davenport Babcock

"Only sick music makes money today."
Freidrich Nietzsche (1844-1900)

"Our greatest glory is not in never failing, but in rising up every time we fail."
Ralph Waldo Emerson

"People with goals succeed because they know where they're going."
Earl Nightingale

"Perseverance is not a long race; it is many short races one after another."
Walter Elliott

"Problems are not stop signs, they are guidelines."
Robert Schuller

"Remember, you can earn more money, but when time is spent, it is gone forever."
Zig Ziglar

*"Success is not measured by what you accomplish
but by the opposition you have encountered,
and the courage with which you have maintained the struggle
against overwhelming odds."*
Orison Swett Marden

"Success seems to be largely a matter of hanging on after others have let go."
William Feather

*"The difference between perseverance and obstinacy
is that one comes from a strong will,
and the other from a strong won't."*
Henry Ward Beecher

Augmented and Diminished Chords

9 - Augmented, Diminished and (alt.) Chords

Augmented and Diminished Chords for Instruments Tuned in 5ths

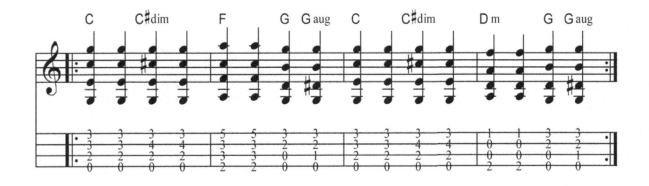

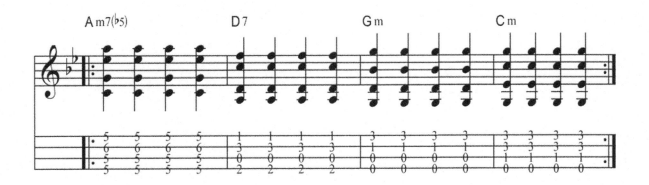

Augmented and Diminished Chord Study Based on "Ain't Misbehavin' "

Harry Brooks, Andy Razaf, & Fats Waller

Here's a great tune that has a lot of augmented and diminished action. There are loads of cool versions of this one. My favorites include Fats Waller, who was an amazing pianist and composer, and Leon Redbone's version. It seems that many people have heard the name Leon Redbone, but don't know that he's a fine, fine fingerstyle guitarist. If you haven't listened to these two fellows play, you should make the effort. It's worth your time and a couple of dollars.

9 - Augmented, Diminished and (alt.) Chords

Augmented and Diminished Chord Study Based on "Ain't Misbehavin' "

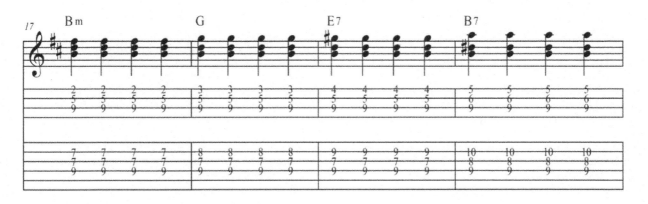

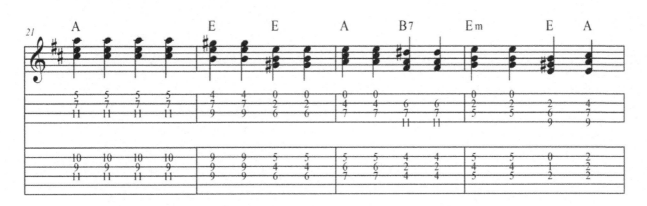

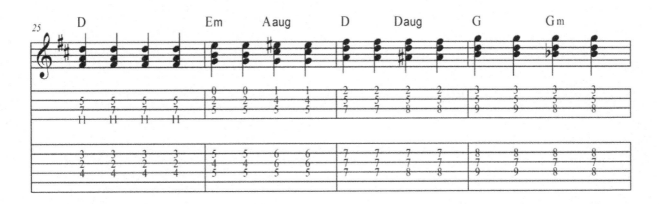

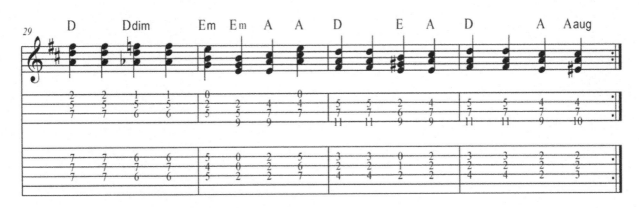

9 - Augmented, Diminished and (alt.) Chords

Augmented, Diminished, and Chord Study based on "Bewitched"
Lorenz Hart & Richard Rodgers

Bewitched, Bothered, and Bewildered is the way many people name this tune, but it's just "Bewitched." It was first performed in a 1940 Broadway stage show called "Pal Joey," and sung by Vivienne Segal. It's been recorded by some of my favorite vocalists, including Ella Fitzgerald and Linda Ronstadt. There are several instrumental versions that are worth checking out, too. One I especially like is from some sessions featuring Stan Getz, Oscar Peterson, Herb Ellis, and Ray Brown, titled "Stan Getz and The Oscar Peterson Trio." "Bewitched" is part of a medley so it's kind of short, but Getz and company sure make it work for me. Most people do it as a ballad, but Benny Goodman's band recorded a version that swings right along, with Helen Forest doing the vocals. This song was popular before most of the current residents of Planet Earth arrived and there's a good chance you haven't heard it. Find a couple of renditions and listen to them.

Don't be intimidated by the key signature. Except in a couple of places, all of the chords are triads. The key of A flat allows most of the chords to be played on the 2nd, 3rd, and 4th strings without needing many notes above the 12th fret, which helps beginners and those with smaller hands to reach these chords. Notice the note on the 14th fret on the guitar tab in measure four. That's difficult on a classical guitar because the body and neck join at the 12th fret and there's no cutaway, but it's not too tough for most other guitars.

Mandolins, as usual, there are a few spans of seven frets, and even a couple that span eight… see the A dim in measure one. You'll probably have to use arpeggios for those, or find a different way to play the ones you can't reach.

9 - Augmented, Diminished and (alt.) Chords

Augmented, Diminished, and Chord Study Based on "Bewitched"

This arrangement is **NOT** intended to show the way a jazz guitarist would play this tune. The triads are all on strings 2, 3, and 4, so the banjoliers can play it, too. The chords are fine, and you'll notice they usually lead nicely from one to the next, but a guitarist comping chords in a band setting would probably be using all six strings, staying closer to the middle of the neck. This arrangement is about letting you hear some of these complex chords in the context of a song.

As you know, nearly all of these chords would consist of more than three notes if played on a keyboard, and as I mentioned on page 288, we guitarists often play abbreviated versions of chords. You'll notice some triads shown will have two different chord names for a single triad. Notice the tab in measure 18, for the B flat m7, and compare it with the A flat triad in measure 23. This is not an error or misprint. Consider the word "Right." It can mean "correct" and it can also mean "the opposite of left." You understand which definition to apply according to the way it's used. Similarly, how we hear a given triad is determined by the root note of the chord.

Have a friend play the bass notes as you play the triads. If the bass plays a B flat when you play the B flat m7 triad shown, that's the chord you'll hear. If the bass plays a D flat when you play the same triad, you'll hear a D flat major chord.

(alt.) Chords

The peculiarities of diminished chords should have you ready for a look at one last oddball chord.

Back in "**Scales**," I described a scale known as the "altered scale." Occasionally, particularly in jazz books, you'll encounter a chord symbol that looks something like this: **C7(alt.)**. This means that you can/should include some notes from the altered scale in your chord.

By now, you're well aware that a C major scale uses only the white keys on a piano. The C altered scale skips most of those. It kinda looks like you're after every available "wrong note" compared to a major scale.

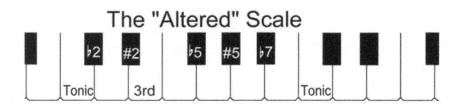

Suppose you want to play a C7 (alt.). If you begin with the tonic and use the standard template of stacking 3^{rds} , you will have a **m7♭5**. Perfectly OK.

But **(alt.)** chords aren't really that specific about insisting on using certain tones. Most of the other chord names indicate particular tones. Not so when you see the **(alt.)** symbol. You get to choose the tones you want to include. C7(alt.) could contain C – D♭ – G# and B♭, if that's what you like.

Since the previous chapter was largely a discussion of "extensions and alterations" to foundational triads, and **(alt.)** is an abbreviation for "**altered**," the name **(alt.)** chord can be a little confusing. This is not really an alteration, it's a chord that comes from a different scale. **(alt.)** is usually parentheses, as shown.

This can create some really cool sounding chords. Try them in jazz tunes and Latin stuff.

And, as I've mentioned, the root is not always required in a chord. If you were to sit down at a piano, close your eyes and play the piano with your elbows, you could say, "Oh, I'm just improvising some variations on the C7 (alt.) chord" and it would be true. Sort of. There are WRONG notes during alt chords, just like any other chords, so if you hit D, F, G, or B, your elbow is playing a wrong note. (And, you probably remember that the black keys alone generate an F# major pentatonic scale as well as a D# minor pentatonic scale… another example of musical multiple personalities.)

It also provides another way to explain in technical terms any high-profile wankers you might hit in a solo.

For example: You seriously flubbed the entire solo in "You Are My Sunshine." The bass player is looking at you like you've just sprouted a third eyeball.

"I just love using that (alt.) scale with polyrhythms, makes these same old tunes so fresh!" you might say, pre-emptively, before he has a chance to ask if you've recently had a brain transplant, or something equally supportive.

Different authors will sometimes have a different explanation for the scale from which (alt.) chords are derived. You'll recall I said that the term "altered scale" is used because several of the notes are altered notes compared to the Mixolydian scale. Also, the "altered" scale is the seventh mode of the ascending melodic minor scale (1, 2, ♭3, 4, 5, 6, 7)."

Jamey Aebersold books call it the "diminished whole tone" scale, because the first four notes look like a diminished scale and the last three are a whole tone scale. (**www.aebersold.com**).

The term "altered scale" was invented by guys who, 20 years after Charlie Parker died, looked back to the recordings of early jazz players to try to figure out what made them sound so "beeboppy." What they decided is that the heightened tension over dominant 7th chords, by avoiding 9, 11, and 13, and playing instead ♭9, #9, #11, and ♭13, is one of the things that gives bebop its wave-like flow… a continual tension (altered chords and lines) and release… well-behaved lines over tonic chords. (**www.cmgww.com/music/parker**)

All the modes of the altered scale are now in common use among jazz fanatics. A book called *The Developing Improviser: The Melodic Minor Scale*, which is volume 4 of a series of play-along books by Ramon Ricker at Eastman School of Music deals with it all and if you're one of those jazz fanatics, is REALLY REALLY fun to work on. (**www.esm.rochester.edu/faculty/ricker_ramon/**)

It you want to hear what players sound like after studying all the modes of the altered scale, you can check out pianist Billy Childs (**www.billychilds.com**), saxophonist Michael Brecker (**www.michaelbrecker.com**) or guitarist Pat Martino (**www.patmartino.com**) to name a few.

And, if you want to, check out Craig Hall, (**www.dalyjazz.com/craighall.html**) the fellow who has supplied all of the information in this discussion of (alt.) chords and scales. He's also a featured guitarist and bassist on one of my CDs: "Yucca Pie." (**www.dukesharp.com**)

A Google search will tell you that Craig Hall is *"The best dormitory in Chico. Off campus housing for Chico State and Butte College students."*

When he's not masquerading as a dormitory, he's an incredible jazz musician.

Augmented, Diminished, and (alt.) Chord Study Based on "Angel Eyes"

Matt Dennis, Earl Brent

This is a great blues progression, but it is not easy. It was introduced in a 1953 movie called "Jennifer" and was performed by Matt Dennis singing Mr. Brent's lyrics. This song is harmonically complex with augmented chords, half diminished chords, (alt.) chords, and 13 chords, and it's fun.

Like "Bewitched," (pg. 327) nearly all of these chords are 'incomplete' as a triad. If at all possible, after you've practiced the triads a bit, have someone play the bass notes (the root of the chord) on a piano, a bass, or another guitar, while you play the triads.

Again, like "Bewitched," this arrangement is not really the way a guitarist would play this. These three strings are fairly easy for beginners to reach, and it transfer directly to a banjo, too, so there are some compromises in the arrangement that accommodate more pickers.

For the mando family, you'll notice few of the triads span seven frets... see the Gm in measure 17.

Augmented, Diminished, and (alt.) Chord Study Based on "Angel Eyes"

It's been recorded by several of the great ones from that era, including Frank Sinatra and Ella Fitzgerald. A more recent take on it that I like is by k.d. lang. I tend to prefer instrumental versions of songs when I can find them, and as usual, Oscar Peterson's recording is on my list of favorites. It was written as a slow ballad and nearly everyone does it that way, but I found a rendition by the Ahmad Jamal Trio that has a bit more drive to it than the others I'm familiar with.

A few examples of (alt.) chords

Here are some (alt.) forms in some four-bar progressions. This will let you get an idea of what they sound like. They're laid out for guitar and some are next to impossible to reach on a mandolin, so think arpeggios and remember how unspecific (alt.) chords are about your choice of notes. There are a few places here where the chord diagram doesn't exactly match the tab… it's a way to show a couple of different options.

Augmented, Diminished, and (alt.) Chords

1. Augmented chords are in the family of _____ chords.

2. Augmented chords contain _____ notes.

3. All augmented chords span _____ half steps.

4. Unlike the major and minor chords, there is only _____ kind of interval in the augmented chord.

5. The interval separating the notes in an augmented chord is a _____.

6. _____ is the most common symbol used to indicate an augmented triad.

7. C+ is pronounced _____ _____.

8. An augmented chord can be named by any of the notes in the chord.   **True   False**

9. There are _____ inversions of an augmented chord.

10. C-E-G# is a _____ _____ chord.

11. E-G#-C is a _____ _____ chord.

12. G#-C-E is a _____ _____ chord.

13. An augmented chord can be derived from a major scale by sharping the _____-degree.

14. It can also be found as a naturally occurring chord in the _____ _____ scale.

15. Diminished can be thought of as being a cousin in the _____ family of chords.

16. All diminished triads span _____ half steps.

17. Unlike the major and minor chords, there is only _____ kind of interval in the diminished triad.

18. The interval separating the notes in a diminished triad is a _____ .

19. Diminished chords nearly always contain _____ notes.

20. There are _____ types of four-note diminished chords.

21. A diminished 7 chord consists of _____ different notes.

22. The fourth note is a _____ _____ above the 5th.

23. The symbol for C diminished 7 is _____.

24. C○ is pronounced _____ _____ _____.

25. The other four-note diminished chord is called a _____ _____.
26. CØ and C Ø7 are both pronounced _____ _____.

27. The structure of a half diminished chord is identical to the diminished 7 chord, for the first _____ tones.

28. In the "half diminished" chord, the fourth tone can be found on the _____ degree of a major scale.

29. C half diminished consists of the same four notes as a _____ .

30. A diminished triad is usually described as _____ chord.

31. (alt.) chords are constructed using the "altered" scale.   **True   False**

The Key

Chapter 10

A key can be accurately described as a group of chords that sound good together.

Of course, there's quite a bit more to it than that, but that's a good place for people who play chord instruments to begin understanding keys. A key is a group of chords that sound good together.

A group? How many is a group?

In each of the keys we'll be considering, there are a total of seven chords.

This explanation of keys is focused on the "major keys." There are also "minor keys," and "modes" which can be thought of as "keys," but we'll just look closely at the major keys. All the others follow the same sort of formula and after you get a grip on the concept of major keys, the others tend to fall into place.

All major keys function in exactly the same way. The relationships between the chords are identical in each key, so we need to examine only one. It's like scales. Understand one and the others are easy.

Arpeggios blur the line between scales and chords and they begin to seem like three views of a single animal to me. Major scales and major keys are also so similar to each other in the context of this book that much of the knowledge you have of scales will help with understanding keys. The arpeggio exercise from "Major and Minor Chords" you've been practicing diligently transfers directly to this discussion of keys. Everything is connected to everything else.

When someone says, "It's in the key of C," right away you'll probably guess that C is likely to be one of the chords and probably even an important one. You might also guess that the C major scale has a role in this business. Good guesses.

C is the first triad in the key of C. There are six more triads that "occur naturally." "Occur naturally" means that only the seven notes from the C major scale are used to form the triads. These triads are said to be "diatonic," which means, "They use only scale tones." Another way to say it is that these chords can be stacked by using only DO, RE, MI, FA, SO, LA, and TI.

There are seven different tones in a major scale and seven different diatonic chords in a key.

This is not just an amazing coincidence. Each of those seven tones is the root of a triad.

There are **three major** triads, **three minor** triads, and **one diminished** triad **in every major key.**

Each of these "naturally occurring chords" uses tones from the scale. Since we're going to use only the scale tones, you don't need to count half steps to figure out major and minor 3^{rds}. Just stack the 3^{rds} using every other note and the major and minor part will take care of itself. This should be familiar, it's the same as the arpeggio exercises from "**Major and Minor Chords.**"

1st + 3rd + 5th is a chord.   2nd + 4th + 6th is a chord.   3rd + 5th + 7th is a chord.
4th + 6th + 1st is a chord.   5th + 7th + 2nd is a chord.   6th + 1st + 3rd is a chord.
7th + 2nd + 4th is a chord.

Frequently, Roman numerals are used for numbering chords to achieve a visual distinction between chord numbers and the other numbers that are used in musical "shorthand."

The 1st scale degree is the root of the first chord in any key and it's called the "I" chord (pronounced "the one chord").

The **1st degree** in the C major scale is the note "C". The first chord in the key of C major is a **C** chord.

The I chord in the key of C

The **2nd degree** is D, and is the root of the ii chord. The two chord in the key of C is **D minor**. Lower case Roman numerals can be used for minor chords, but the lower case letter "i" is commonly used, because the dot makes it easier to distinguish a minor chord from a major chord. It is still pronounced "the two chord."

The ii chord in the key of C

The **3rd degree** is E, and is the root of the iii chord. The three chord in the key of C is **E minor**.

The iii chord in the key of C

The **4th degree** is F and is the root of the **IV** chord. The four chord in the key of C is **F major.**

The IV chord in the key of C

The **5th degree** is G and is the root of the **V** chord. The five chord in the key of C is **G major.**

The V chord in the key of C

The **6th degree** is A and is the root of the vi chord. The six chord in the key of C is **A minor.**

The vi chord in the key of C

That leaves one chord, the vii chord. If you count the intervals in this triad, you'll see that it has two minor 3rds, which makes it a diminished triad.

The vii chord in the key of C

These seven triads "C, Dm, Em, F, G, Am, Bdim" comprise what musicians think of as "the key of C."

Nothing to it. *There are seven diatonic triads in all "major" keys. Each one is stacked on a scale degree. These are the "naturally occurring" chords. The I, IV and V triads are major. The ii, iii and vi triads are minor, and vii is diminished.*

What I meant when I said that the chords in a key "sound good together," is that you can play these naturally occurring chords in any sequence imaginable and it will sound quite musical.

Try these four-bar examples. Each line is an example of a "progression" in C. The next chapter, "**Progressions**," will provide lots more information regarding progressions. For the moment, progression = series.

Repeat each line a few times before going to the next one. Play them backward. Skip from line to line. Then make up some of your own. I kept these progressions real simple, four beats per chord, but that's certainly not necessary.

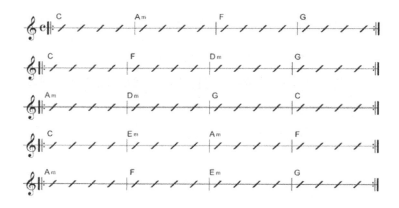

It isn't as if this system of naming or identifying chords in a key establishes "rules" as to which chords you're "allowed" to use. (Some classical theorists will disagree… that's OK with me.) Just because a tune is written in a particular key, it doesn't mean that there won't be some non-diatonic chords. That is to say, there can be non-diatonic minors substituted for diatonic majors, non-diatonic majors substituted for diatonic minors and other variations.

For example, even though the diatonic **ii, iii,** and **vi** are minor chords, it's very common to use D major, E major, and A major when in the key of C.

When D, E and A are played as major chords in the key of C, they are still thought of and referred to as the **II, III,** and **VI** chords, you just make note of the fact that this time they are major and not minor.

Suppose you want to use an E♭ major chord in the key of C, just because you feel like it. There is no E♭ in the C major scale, so that would make it a chord that is "non-diatonic" in the key of C.

It's perfectly OK to use the chord. It's encouraged. Go for it. The numbers are only a way to identify chords, not limit your choices.

Since E minor is the **iii** chord, and E♭ is one half step lower than E, you just call E♭ major a "♭**III** chord" in the key of C.

You want to use E♭ minor 9? Dandy… it's a "♭ **iii** ⁹ **chord**." You want to use A major in the verse and A minor in the chorus? Fine… it's the "**VI chord**" in the verse and the "**vi chord**" in the chorus.

There is also a system called "the Nashville number system." It is nearly identical to the system of Roman numerals, except Arabic numerals are used… 1, 2, 3, 4, 5, 6, and 7. For minor, use the lowercase letter "m." 2m is the two minor. 3m7 is the three minor seven.

We pretty much have to use the Arabic numerals (1, 2, 3, etc.) for intervals (3rd, 4th, 5th, etc.) and for chord numbers (A6, B7, C9, etc.), so I used the Roman numerals throughout the text when referring to chord names to minimize confusion. On most of the songs, I used the Nashville numbers.

If any note in a piece of music feels more like a "resting point" than other notes, then the music is said to be "tonal" and is in "a key." Most music is in this category. In fact, it's so difficult to avoid "being in a key" that learning to avoid it took a few decades of some serious attention by some good composers early last century, Schoenberg leading the way.

"Key" is a reference point… it's a baseline… it's a place to begin. It provides good solid clues to help you anticipate which notes and chords are most likely to occur in a piece of music.

Basic knowledge of keys instantly shrinks the probable number of chord root notes in any piece of music to six. In addition, you have clues about the qualities of the chords. It's easier to "guess correctly," and when you do guess right, even if it takes six tries, that's playing by ear.

Transposing and Modulation

You may be wondering, "What is with all these numbers?!" After all, A-B-C is really not any more difficult than **I, II, III**. Maybe easier, in fact, since about the only place you might see Roman numerals is on an old clock or on the library or something.

This is where we begin to put all those chord numbers to use. There are lots of numbers here, because I'll also be mentioning intervals. Go slowly.

Transpose and modulate are two different words that mean "to change keys."

Modulate means to change from one key to another while you're still playing the tune… without stopping.

One way to modulate from one key to another is to make a chord "substitution" in the measure just before you want to change keys. The chord (or chords) that are used to modulate smoothly from one key to another have a way of leading your ear to the I chord in the new key. They will usually be present in both keys, but not necessarily of the same quality. This first example is like that.

Suppose you're playing "Auld Lang Syne" in the key of C and suddenly you're inspired to modulate to the key of D.

Here's one way to do it. When you get the **I** chord in the last measure, instead of holding that chord for four full beats, you can insert a **VI** chord for the last two beats of the measure.

In the key of C, the naturally occurring **vi** chord is minor. For this standard modulation we want the **VI** chord… an A major chord. (naturally occurring = diatonic = only scale tones)

Now think about the chords in the key of D. The **V** chord in the key of D is an A major chord. That chord will be the connection or link to the new key.

It's like a magic trick… "Ladies and gentlemen, before your very ears… behold… minor six will be transformed into MAJOR FIVE!!"

This modulation works for *any* song that ends with the **I** chord.

Conveniently enough, *most* songs end with the **I** chord. If you do the same modulation 12 times, you'll be back in the key of C.

The Circle of Seconds, I call it. Works in every key, every time. Anything that has 100% success rate is a rarity worth observing.

Before you play this, look through it. The first section is in C, and then it modulates up one whole step twice, each time using the **VI** of the first key, which becomes the **V** of the new key. Notice how the new key signature is tagged on to the end of the line. It's a great, big "DETOUR" sign.

Somehow our ears have been conditioned to want to hear a **I** chord follow a **V** chord and that's what happens with this move. But when the **vi** of C is played as **VI** of C, to my ear it continues to sound like the **VI** of C until a split second after I play the new **I**, and then it's almost like aural hindsight… anticipating backwards. Can't really do that, I guess. Maybe if the universe reverses the expansion and collapses in on itself time will run in a different direction.

Another common modulation is to move the key up a 4th. Here's another appearance of a recurring theme in pop music: Chord roots separated by 4ths. This time it's the root note of the **I** chord… of two consecutive keys… that are separated by a 4th.

The last chord in "Auld Lang Syne" is a **I** chord. When you're in the key of C, you will substitute a **I** dominant 7... C7... for the last two beats of the last measure. When you play the **I** of the new key, your ear will be ready to believe that the **I** is following a **V** chord. If you play this modulation 12 times in a row, you wind up back in C. I think I'll call it "The Circle of Fourths." The last chord in each key is a "one-seven" chord, not a "seventeen" chord.

How do you know which chords to use in the new key?

Simple. You "transpose" the chords.

Transposing is the thought process or pencil and paper part of modulating.

You can memorize the seven diatonic chords for 15 different keys if you want to. Won't hurt you a bit, I'm sure.

I don't intend to do that.

It's true that I do know the names of the **I, IV,** and **V** chords in all keys. Well... I can figure them out for every major key in under 30 seconds, which is nearly always quick enough in my world. But in a playing situation, instead of memorizing all the keys, I have learned to play a bunch of progressions (next chapter) using a few forms so I don't always have to think about all of the letter names.

For the times that I do have to write out a modulation, I just use the transposing chart that you'll find near the end of this chapter, page 415.

A fair question right about now is "Why bother?" If all keys work exactly the same way, and the relationships are the same, why go to the trouble of transmogrification or ovulation or whatever it's called?

Well, there are a few reasons.

On a guitar, mandolin, and banjo, a person usually learns the open position chords first instead of barre chords because open position chords are much easier to play. In addition, open strings ring like bells. When you press your finger on a string to make a fretted note the sound quality changes. Open strings sound great on guitars, mandolins, banjos, and just about any string instrument.

Suppose you find a simple three-chord tune that you would like to play that's written in F#, but you're having a bit of trouble with F#, B, and C# (**I, IV**, and **V**). You can transpose it to G (for instance) and F#, B, and C# become G, C, and D. Now there are lots of open strings and zero barre chords. It's ringy and chimey. Chimey? Ringy and dingy? Easier to play.

So, now you're playing the song in G and life is good... except... you can't sing the song because it's too low.

Here's another reason to transpose. Bump it up one whole step to A and now the **I, IV**, and **V** chords will be A, D, and E. Higher? How about C? ... C, F, and G.

Soon, we'll take a look at "transposing instruments," a heading that includes lots of brass and woodwinds. When guitars and horns play together, for sure there's a whole lotta transposing going on.

"Layla," by Eric Clapton and Jim Gordon, has an intro in D minor, but the song "modulates" to E major for the verse. "What do you do when you get lonely..." Then when it gets to the chorus "Layla, you've got me on my knees..." it goes back to D minor. Probably for no reason other than it sounds cool. "And I Love Her" by the Beatles modulates up one (1) half step for the last verse. My guess is that it was just a little bit of ear candy somebody came up with in the studio, something to give the listener a fresh noise at the end of the tune. Changing keys for the last verse is much more common than jumping back and forth between keys like "Layla" does.

Any song can be played in any key. You can switch around in the middle of the song if you like. Suit yourself. No rules. Most of us have a vocal range that is fairly limited, so sometimes we transpose songs to get the melody in a range that we can reach. We also transpose so the chords are in keys that are physically easier to play.

That's why we transpose. This is how to do it, using the numbers. Here's "Auld Lang Syne" again, shown in the key of F#. I bet I've played this tune 500 times and before this project, I'd also bet I had never done it in F#. So we'll transpose it from the key of F# to the key of G where it is played more often. This is what we'll start with.

The first step is to number the chords. To do that, you first find the note names of the major scale that corresponds to the key the song is in, then give each one a number. Remember, initially, the **I, IV,** and **V** chords are major; **ii, iii,** and **vi** chords are minor; the **vii** chord is diminished.

DO	RE	MI	FA	SO	LA	TI	DO
I	ii	iii	IV	V	vi	vii	I
F#	G#	A#	B	C#	D#	E#	F#

Next, write the numbers in above/below/beside/near the appropriate chord.

Next, find the scale for the new key and number the scale degrees.

DO	RE	MI	FA	SO	LA	TI	DO
I	ii	iii	IV	V	vi	vii	I
G	A	B	C	D	E	F#	G

Now, just replace the old chords with the corresponding new ones.

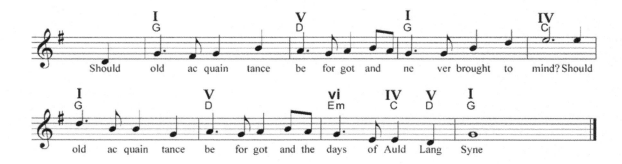

You transpose the chords using chord numbers. I, ii, iii, IV, V, vi and vii… numbers that are derived from the scale degrees. The scale degree names the root of the chord.

You can play any song in any key. Songs are frequently written in a key that suits the songwriter's vocal range, or because those are the only chords the songwriter could play on the guitar. If a guy knows G, C, and D, but can't play an F, then he's probably going to write in the key of G and avoid the key of C. People don't usually write "popular" songs for guitar in keys like F# because it's a little tough to play there on a guitar… it's not because there's anything especially different or wrong with the key of F#.

People say that Hank Williams, Sr., only knew six chords. He's recognized as one of the greatest songwriters of all time in his genre. If you can't play all the barre chords and all the fancy jazz chords, but you still have a lot of fun with it… who cares? It's not a contest. You can play most songs with a real small chord vocabulary and write a lot, too.

Key Signature

It you have a recording you're listening to and trying to figure out how to play some of the songs on it, it's a matter of trial and error to figure out the key for each tune.

Standard notation uses what is called a "key signature."

All the way to the left of the first line of music is a group of sharps or flats that will tell you which key the tune is in. What it is telling you is the name of the major scale that the tune is based in and which chords you are most likely to encounter. There's a lot of information in that small space.

At first glance it may appear to be a random jumble of odd-looking symbols, but it's actually quite simple to understand and it's always consistent.

There are two groups of keys… sharp keys and flat keys.

There is a different key signature for each of the sharp keys and a different key signature for each of the flat keys. There are no new names introduced here, we just keep on using the same old alphabet: A, B, C, D, E, F, and G.

There are seven sharp keys, seven flat keys, plus one that has no sharps or flats, our old friend, the key of C, for a total of 15 keys.

I hope you're thinking something like "Wait a minute! There are only 12 different notes! How can there be 15 different keys?"

That's a good question and it seems to me that the answer is tied up with that rule for major scales that says you have to use all the names. As you'll see, some of the keys "overlap." Remember the word "enharmonic?" Some of the flat keys use exactly the same tones as some of the sharp keys and it seems rather cumbersome to me. I'm sure there are good reasons for the redundancies. I just don't happen to know what they are.

There are five black keys on a keyboard. Four of the key signatures show more than six sharps and flats. This isn't about colors, it's about the rules for spelling scales.

At any rate, let's start with C as shown in the treble clef. In the space between the clef and the first note is where the key signature lives. In this case, although it looks like there's no one home, what this means is that you're in the key of C.

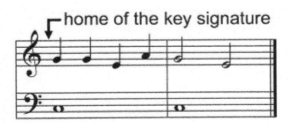

If you see a piece of music and there are no sharps or flats between the clef sign and the first note, it means the piece is in the key of C (of A minor… details coming soon).

The key of C has no sharps or flats. All of the other keys have some.

In every topic we've covered so far, one thing that has been consistent is the alphabetical sequence of the notes… A, B, C, D, E, F, and G.

That is not the case here. When keys are arranged according to the number of accidentals used, they appear in a sequence of perfect 5ths, not alphabetically. Here you begin with C.

Here is what is known as the "sharp" keys in order.
Key of C has zero accidentals. Going up from C in perfect 5ths names all seven "sharp keys."

1. Key of G has one sharp.
2. Key of D has two sharps.
3. Key of A has three sharps.
4. Key of E has four sharps.
5. Key of B has five sharps.
6. Key of F sharp has six sharps.
7. Key of C sharp has seven sharps.

Here are the flat keys. Going down from C in 5ths names all seven "flat keys."
Key of C has zero accidentals.

1. Key of F has one flat.
2. Key of B flat has two flats.
3. Key of E flat has three flats.
4. Key of A flat has four flats.
5. Key of D flat has five flats.
6. Key of G flat has six flats.
7. Key of C flat has seven flats.

Somehow, C has become the center point for keys. Seems like a bad idea to me, but it is what it is. If it shows up on my ballot, I'm voting against it.

For the foreseeable future, we'll begin at C, **not A**, and move a perfect 5th (up or down) and add an accidental each time.

To play a major scale beginning with G, you have to play one sharp. A single sharp symbol between the clef symbol and the first note means you're in the key of G. It means a G major scale is the foundation for this key.

Key of G Major

SO   SO   MI   LA   SO   MI

Every time you run across an F (indicated by the arrows) high or low, bass or treble clef, you play F sharp. You don't have to put a # beside every F as it occurs on the staff because the key signature has already told you that.

You'll recall that when we first examined the structure of scales you learned to build scales by using a certain sequence of whole steps and half steps. A major scale is W-W-H-W-W-W-H. The key signature automatically generates the same series of intervals. I can't decide if the keys are based on the scales or if the scales are created by the keys. It's one of those "Which came first, the chicken or the egg?" sort of questions for me.

In any event, the name of the key signature will tell you which scale is the foundation for the song.

I think the reason key signatures were developed was to save on the ink used. Kidding, sort of. The vast majority of music is diatonic. That is to say that the vast majority of notes in any given piece of music will be naturally occurring scale tones from whatever key the tune happens to be in. DO, RE, MI, FA, SO, LA, and TI. Western instruments are designed so that a major scale can be played with relative ease. This is not a coincidence, it's 100% intentional. It does seem to pose another one of those "which one came first?" puzzles. Were the instruments designed to fit the music or is the music dictated by the physical properties of the instruments?

In the key of C, there are no sharps or flats in the key signature. This tune can be played on just the white keys of the piano. Notice the solfege equivalents for these tones.

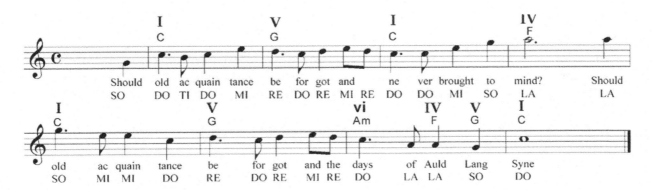

But, suppose that you wanted to write it in the key of B. The key of B uses five sharps. A#, C#, D#, F#, and G#.

Without a key signature, every time one of those notes is used, a # symbol has to be inserted. It is still DO-RE-MI, etc. 100% diatonic, but now there are a bunch of additional squiggles on the page.

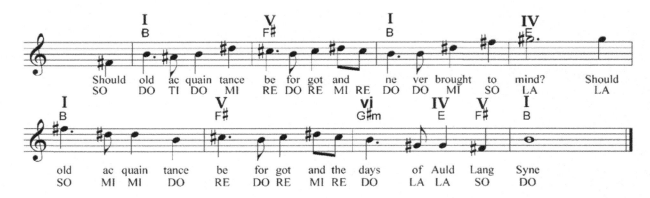

Here it is in B again, but this time using a key signature. All the extra squiggles are safely contained in their own area where they won't interfere with reading the notes.

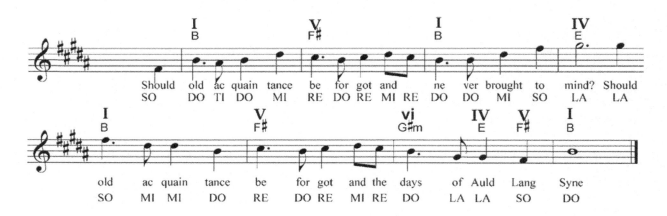

One way to put this bit of information to use is when you look at any piece of music, you can glance through it and know that until you see an accidental that is beside an individual note (either a # or a ♭ or a ♮), it's all major scale tones. This idea is covered in more detail in "**Melody and Harmony**."

A perfect 5th above G is D. Two sharps are needed to make a major scale that starts on D and there are two sharps in the key signature for D major.

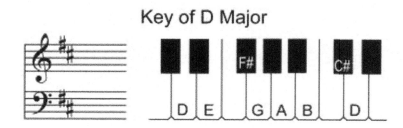

This sequence… C to G to D… is the beginning of what is known as the "Circle of 5ths". We'll get to that soon.

There is a detail I should mention before we go further. It's actually lots more important than a detail, but it doesn't require a lot of explanation.

Each key signature represents two keys or scales. One is a major key and a major scale of the same name. The other is a minor key. It's the key that is built on the natural minor scale (Aolian mode), and *not* the harmonic minor scale. The name of the minor key represented by a key signature… is a minor 3rd lower… than the major key represented by the same key signature. Read that again, aloud, a couple of times.

Take a look at the transposing charts in this chapter, starting on page 367. Take a few minutes to compare the chords found in the key of C major with the chords in A minor, page 368. Compare the chords in G major with the chords in E minor. Compare F major and D minor. Compare A major and F# minor. Compare the notes in the C major scale with the notes in the A natural minor scale. Compare the notes in G major scale with the notes in the E natural minor scale. When considering any major chord and the minor chord whose root is a 3rd lower, the minor chord is called the "relative minor." These relatives share a single key signature.

So, how do you know whether a song is in a major or minor key?

Usually, the chord that is being played when the first words are sung is the I chord. If it's a major chord, then you're probably looking at a tune in a major key. Usually. Not always, but often enough that it is a relatively safe bet. The other place that you're likely to find the I chord is the last chord in the song. Usually. Not always, but certainly more than 75%. I'd guess over 95%.

You sort of have to guess. If there is some doubt and you need to know, look at the first and last chords and that will usually tell you.

Get out your songbook and the transposing chart and write the name of the key next to the key signature. Look all the way through the song to see if there are any key changes indicated. Label the chords with the Roman numerals or the Nashville number system.

Now that you have a basic understanding of keys, scales, and clefs, it's possible to explain some aspects of instruments you'll probably encounter that are referred to as "transposing" instruments. There are a lot of them. Most brass and woodwinds are transposing instruments.

For historical reasons (some might say hysterical) the players in an orchestra do not all use music that is written in the same key signature, even though they are all playing the same piece at the same time.

This gets a little crooked through here. Take it slow and plan on coming back a couple of times.

Pianos, violins, flutes, and some others are "non-transposing" instruments.

The pitch that a note has when played on all of these non-transposing instruments is called "concert pitch." This is one of the things that musicians all over the planet recognize and agree on. We're talking physics here. 261 Hz* = concert middle C, and that is what we hear when pianos, flutes, and violins play middle C as written on the page. 440 Hz is concert A and it's the first A above middle C.

When a B♭ clarinetist plays the middle C written on his sheet of music, the clarinet produces a tone measured at 233 Hz. The piano key that matches 233 Hz is B♭, one whole step below concert middle C. The E♭ alto sac plays middle C on her page and gets a note that is measured at 155 Hz. That note matches the E♭ found one 6th (nine half steps) below the piano's middle C.

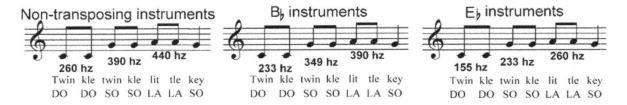

Looking at the example above, it's reasonable to assume that all three instruments would be producing identical notes. With matching key signatures and clefs, they should be the same.

Instead, if you heard a piano, clarinet, and sax simultaneously playing the first note as shown above, it would sound like the root, 5th, and 6th of a an E♭6 chord with the sax playing the low root and the piano playing the 6th. If all three continued playing, each successive "note" would sound like another 6 chord. Interesting, no doubt, possibly the origin of complex jazz harmonies, but that's not what those fellows were trying to achieve.

To persuade the transposing instruments to agree which silent dot on the page corresponds to the audible sound we measure at 261 Hz, the dots on the staff are shifted… transposed… by a different interval for each family of instruments. Concert pitch is the constant and the interval refers to a distance above or below the concert middle C.

Since B♭ is one whole step lower than C, the B♭ clarinet player needs the music to be written one whole step higher than C (the key of D, two sharps) so the DO it plays matches the DO the piano is playing. Since E♭ is nine half steps (a 6th) lower than C, the E♭ alto clarinet player needs it to be written nine half steps higher than C (the key of A, three sharps) so the DO it plays matches the DO the piano is playing. Now they will all play the "Twinkle" melody in unison, even though this example looks kind of like the way the previous example sounds.

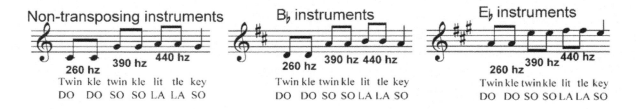

There is a family of B♭ players who think of 233 Hz as C. There is a family of E♭ players who refer to 155 Hz as C. There are about 40 others with their own definition of C. Everyone involved is 100% aware that none of those pitches match the 261 Hz tone the piano player calls C, which happens to be the one that is universally recognized as "concert C."

Why… please tell me why… would any relatively sane group of people agree to such a demented and convoluted scheme? There's no profit motive that I can see. This is twisted.

Some of the bedlam arises for good reasons. For instance, several instruments have ranges that lie mostly above the treble clef staff or below the bass clef staff.

It would be a real pain to write those notes "honestly" because if they did not transpose an octave, an overabundance of ledger lines would make reading cumbersome. Visually, it would be cluttered, not to mention the additional physical space required on a page to leave room between staffs on blank sheets. I bet *that* was fun. These people wanted as much usable information on a page as possible. It's relatively easy to move the dots an octave or two so most of them fit on or near the normal staff.

There are other reasons that have to do with the development of the various instruments. These people were the cutting edge of the music scene. They were experimenting with all aspects of music, and they were building new instruments, too. Since they couldn't alter the sounds electronically, they had to alter the sizes, shapes, and materials of the tubes, reeds, boxes, valves, tubs, and strings that were producing the sounds.

On woodwind instruments, such as the clarinet, there is one major scale that is played (more or less) by simply lifting each finger sequentially from the bottom to the top. Whether you're holding a B♭ clarinet, of a C, D, or E♭ clarinet, you'll get a major scale out of any of them by lifting each finger sequentially from the bottom to the top. You have to move some air, of course, but that's a different topic. The saxophones have the same fingering pattern as clarinets, and they produce a major scale in the same way. The lowest note produced when you've plugged up all the leaks is the note that gives the instrument its name. When you pick an open string on a guitar, it makes the lowest tone that string can produce, and that note names the string. Same idea. D string… D clarinet.

Each of the different clarinets, saxes, trumpets, etc., is a different size. As a general thing, bigger tubes, thicker strings, and bigger boxes create deeper pitches. In the Baroque ear, when Mr. Johann Sebastian Bach was writing an unbelievably enormous quantity of amazing music and fathering a similar quantity of standard children, a professional clarinet player would come to the gig with several different sized clarinets, each for playing in a specific key. Two keys actually… the major "home key" and its relative minor.

Apparently, the clarinet that had the richest, most pleasing voice was the size that produced a B♭ scale. No one really knows how, but at some point the B♭ clarinet became the standard, preferred to the C, D, and E♭ clarinet. If they had preferred the sound of the C sized clarinet, sax, trumpet, etc., we wouldn't be having this discussion. Many of the other families of instruments, including the mandolin family and the violin family, have similar histories and the ones that have become established as the "standards" are the ones that made the nicest noises.

All 12 chromatic tones can be produced by all of these transposing instruments, just like a single guitar string does, so they aren't actually limited to only playing certain keys, but each has a "home key" (scale) and it's often easiest to use an instrument whose home key matches the key the piece is written in.

To enable the trumpeter to use the same fingerings regardless of which size trumpet he was playing, the composer needed to decide which trumpet would be played on each piece (dictated by what key the piece was in) and he would write the trumpet's music in a key that enabled the trumpeter to use "home key" fingering as much as possible. Unless he was annoyed with the trumpeter.

This meant the clarinets, trumpets, and others would be reading music written in the key of "C" or "D" while others were not playing in that key at all. But it all sounded fine even though they were all thinking of different keys.

Clear as mud? To quote David Crosby, "Just beneath the surface of the mud… there's more mud. Surprise!"

On a keyboard, the C major scale is played by pressing the white keys sequentially, beginning with C. On paper, that scale shows zero sharps and zero flats. Middle C is on the first ledger line below the staff using the treble clef and to show a span of two full octaves requires only two ledger lines above the staff. For reading and writing this is convenient. It's an agreeable situation for those who read for organs, pianos, and accordions. Evidently, it seemed like such a good idea that they decided that woodwinds and brass should also be written with their respective home keys shown with the same two octave range nearly centered on the staff. It really does make some sense.

This is a beautiful thing for the player who has four different clarinets and a couple of saxes. Her entire stack of music works for the whole instrument collection without the inconvenience of having to learn a bunch of new scale fingerings. No worries, as long as she's playing at home by herself.

However, confusion often reigns when the horn players show up to pick with the guitar players. Suppose you're hanging out jammin' one evening and a couple shows up with a B♭ clarinet and an E♭ alto sax. You're playing a standard 12-bar blues thing in A.

Since both horn players have a different A, and neither agrees with your A, how would you tell them which key (scale) they should use?

The truth is that most horn players understand this business of transposing and you probably won't have to help them with it.

Also true is that most guitar players are close to being 100% clueless about how to do this.

Guess what? It's really not difficult. If you can count to 12 and know the names of the notes, with a little practice you should be able to handle it.

You can do it the way I did earlier and count the steps. B♭ is one whole step below C, so when the guitar is playing in C, the B♭ clarinet is thinking one whole step above C, which is D, and they match at 260 Hz. DO = DO. If the guitar is playing in A, the B♭ clarinet is thinking one whole step higher… B… and you're locked in. When the guitar plays B♭, the B♭ clarinet thinks C.

That's pretty simple. It gets trickier as the size of the interval increases.

Fortunately, there's an illustration that will let you make the calculation without even having to count to 12. This only goes to seven, so I can leave my shoe on for this one.

It's a little invention of mine I like to call the "Circle of 5^{ths}."

OK… so I didn't invent it, or the other circles either. Music does that without my assistance.

The letters outside the circle name the key and major scale. The numbers inside tell you how many accidentals are in the corresponding key signature and major scale. C with zero accidentals is top dead center. When you move around the circle to the right, it names the seven sharp keys according to how many sharps there are. Start with C, not A, and go around the circle to the left and you have the seven flat keys.

They intersect and cross at the bottom. Remember enharmonics? The keys of G♭ and F# sound the same and look the same when played on an instrument, but they are spelled differently. The same is true for the keys of C# and D♭, and for B and C♭. The horns usually prefer thinking in flat keys, so they'll probably choose D♭, instead of C#.

Here's how you use this diagram to converse sensibly about transposing keys with the horn section.

Look at the Circle of 5^{ths}. The key of E♭ is three clicks around the circle to the left of C. To make her written middle C (155 Hz) sound like the guitar's middle C (260 Hz), she'll need to be thinking about the scale that is three clicks to the right of C, which is the key of A.

If the guitarist is playing in A, you could amaze your friends by glancing at this handy-dandy diagram and saying, "We're in A, so the E♭ sax will be in G♭ (three clicks to the right from A) and the B♭ clarinet will be in B (two clicks to the right from A).

If you're in E, the E♭ instruments use the key that is three clicks to the right of E… D♭. The B♭ team uses the key that is two clicks to the right of E… G♭.

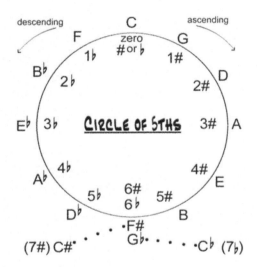

Here's one way to use this transposing instrument info as one of your tools for figuring out recorded music by ear. One of the things you always have to sort out is "What key is this song in?" Guitar players tend to think in terms of the keys of C-A-G-E and D. They are sort of like the "home keys" for us. The brass and woodwinds are happier in the flat keys. So, if there is a horn section, or any orchestrated backup in the song, you're working out and you're searching for the key. Try B♭, E♭, A♭ and D♭. B-E-A-D, plus G, all flat keys. It won't always get you there, but often enough that it's worth remembering.

Composers also have to recognize that some instruments are transposed a whole octave PLUS some goofy interval. A baritone sax transposes a full octave, plus a 6th and a tenor sax transposes a full octave, plus a whole step. There are instruments that are transposed from "concert pitch" by one and two perfect octaves. There is a piccolo that is transposed a minor 9th, and one that transposes a minor 7th. There are clarinets transposed a whole step above C and a whole step below. There are some that sound a minor 3rd, a perfect 4th, and a perfect 5th below what is written.

It's difficult to imagine, but when you watch a conductor who is reading a score, he is actually thinking in several keys AT ONCE, because his score shows all those instruments in their respective keys. No wonder he has trouble with complete sentences in radio interviews and can't remember which continent he's standing on.

It sometimes seems that we could dispense with all the letter names, keys, and transposing and the like, and just say that everything is in the key of DO. After all, that's what a lot of those transposing gyrations are about, trying to get everyone to agree how to name which tone = DO. Solfege doesn't seem too much more complicated than having a couple of dozen different definitions of 260 Hz.

I know that I often think about music that way. For the most part, I can think about tunes as DO-RE-MI-FA-SO-LA and TI. Chords are I, ii, iii, IV, V, vi, and vii. In all keys on all instruments. On the surface, as an explanation, it seems to simplistic to be valid, yet with sufficient background knowledge it is in fact a very accurate, versatile, and useful system. No batteries required, either.

Sometimes publishers will print three versions of the same book. One will be the C version, which is the one that most people reading this book will want. The other two, the B♭ version and the E♭ version are for the horn players. Guitars, mandolins, and pianos can still use them, but you have to transpose everything. The B♭ version would require that everything be transposed up a whole step, and the E♭ version would have to be transposed down a minor 3rd.

In "**Note Names**" are illustrations of the notes found on a mandolin and a mandola. Notice that the interval between the strings of both instruments is a 5th.

If you play a line of mandolin tablature, but you're holding a mandola instead of a mandolin, and play the tablature, not the notation, the tune would sound right; but it will be a different key. This is shown as mandolin tab and the notes shown are what would sound if played on a mandolin. If you play the same tab on a mandola, it will still be "Twinkle," but it would be in the key of F instead of C. To play them in unison on the two instruments, one will have to be transposed. The mandola is a transposing instrument like the guitar is. Both sound an octave lower than written.

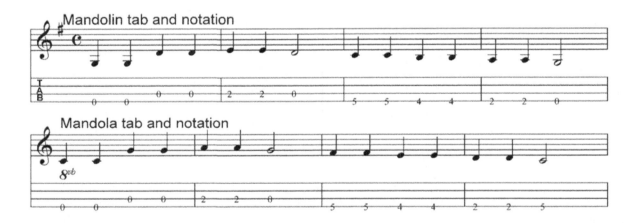

It's easy to see the similarity between a mandolin and a mandola and to see how these two are similar to a violin and a viola. All four instruments have four strings and are roughly the same size. A mandolin is tuned to the same four tones as a violin: G, D, A, and E. A viola and a mandola also share the same four notes: C, G, D, and A.

If you can play a mandolin, you can automatically play a mandola and tenor banjo because the fingerings are the same.

The same sort of relationship exists within the wind instruments. An E♭ clarinet has the same valves in the same locations as the valves on a B♭ clarinet. The fingering pattern that produces a major scale on the E♭ clarinet will also give you a major scale on the B♭ clarinet, but it will be in a different key… B♭. If you can play a clarinet, the fingerings on that instrument will work for saxophones.

All of the families of musical instruments operate within the same basic "theoretical structure." All are designed to accommodate the major scale. All use the same 12 notes on the same five-line staff using the same scales… with certain written adjustments to compensate for the physical properties inherent in different families of instruments.

Most of the ideas in this book can be applied to all instruments, the only thing you have to do is develop the coordination required to produce the sound. As soon as you can play a major scale on any instrument, you are on your way to being able to play it… "by ear."

Harmonicas (often referred to as a harp) are instruments with built-in home keys. People playing guitars often encounter harmonica players and it can be a magical combination. It's also possible to play both instruments at the same time, by using a rack to hold the harmonica in place, leaving both hands free to play the guitar (or banjo, mandolin, etc.).

The two most common types of harmonicas are the chromatic harmonica and the diatonic harmonica. The chromatic harmonica plays all 12 tones, or a chromatic scale. The diatonic harmonica produces a major scale. Most blues, rock, and folk players use diatonic harmonicas.

I'll give you a look at the note layout on a 10-hole diatonic harmonica and you'll get a basic idea of how these little instruments work in the context of keys, chords, and scales.

There are holes on the edge of the harp. Each hole produces two notes, one when you blow through the hole and a different one when you "draw" the air back through the harp… they're known as "blow notes" and "draw notes."

On a C harp, the 10 "blow" notes are C-E-G-C-E-G-C-E-G-C. As you can see, this is simply root, 3rd, and 5th of the I chord in the key of C.

Notice that it spans three full octaves. In comparison, from the low E string on a guitar's sixth string to the high E note on the first string, 12th fret, is three octaves. A harp has a wide range of notes for an instrument that fits in your pocket.

All diatonic harps use the same root, 3rd, and 5th layout. On an "A harp" the blow notes are A-C#-E and on a "G harp" the blow notes are G-B-D.

The other four diatonic notes are "draw notes." Remember the definition of diatonic: uses only scale tones. The blow notes give us the 1st, 3rd, and 5th degrees of the major scale, so some of the draw notes should be the 2nd (D), the 4th (F), the 6th (A), and the 7th (B) degrees.

Starting with the first hole, the draw notes on a C harp are D-G-B-D-F-A-B-D-F-A.

These notes produce a chord also, but the root is not found in the first hole. The draw notes produce a G9 chord. The lowest draw note is the 5th and the second draw note is the root. Those are followed by the 3rd, 5th, 7th, 9th, 3rd, 5th, 7th, and 9th. For playing most folk tunes and "campfire" songs, you want a harp that is the same key that the guitarist is playing in. If somebody is playing a guitar and singing "Happy Birthday To You" or "Oh Susannah" in the key of C, you want a C harp. If they are playing in F, you want an F harp. A harmonica player is like the trumpet player from the 1700s, and comes to the gig with several harps.

The blow notes on a diatonic harmonica give you the **I** chord and the draw notes produce the **V** chord (plus some extensions), as well as two of the notes in the **IV** chord. In the next chapter you'll learn more about something called "a **I, IV, V** progression"… for now, I'll just say that those three major chords comprise the bulk of "folk music."

But according to Scotty Boehler, the legendary harp player in the legendary Groovemeisters, Fossils, and The Shuffle Bums, if you want to play stuff that is more like "blues," you use a harp that is in a different key than the key the guitar player is using. This is why.

Go slowly through this, it can be kind of confusing. If you're up to speed in the area of spelling chords, this is simple; it is not even remotely similar to the complicated key shuffling antics of the transposing instruments, just in case you wondered.

Imagine that you're going to play a blues standard like "Kansas City" in the key of G. In the next chapter you'll learn that a basic blues progression typically uses three chords, **I, IV,** and **V** (with some alterations and extensions to the chords). Look at the transposing chart and you'll see in the key of G, the **I, IV,** and **V** chords are G, C, and D.

On a C harp, the 10 blow notes are C-E-G-C-E-G-C-E-G-C, and the draw notes are D-G-B-D-F-A-B-D-F-A. Like the horns, harps are named by the lowest note they produce.

In "**Scales**" you learned that flatting the 3rd and 7th tones of a major scale are the alterations that we call "blues." So… that's what you want this diatonic harmonica to do.

A blues harp player cleverly uses the draw notes for the **I** chord. The chord you get when using the draw notes of a C harp is a G9, with the root on the second hole. Suddenly, you have some "bluesy" sounding notes to play for the **I** chord. We're a third of the way there already.

The dominant 7 chord is nearly always appropriate to use on the **V** chord in blues tunes. In the key of G, the **V** chord is D. Starting at the fourth hole, the draw notes are D-F-A, which translate to the root, ♭3rd and 5th of D minor. The ♭7th in a D7 chord is the note C, which is available as a blow note in four convenient locations. Now we have a bluesy sounding **V** chord. Two out of three.

In the key of G, the **IV** chord is C. To play blues, the ♭3rd and ♭7th are important sounds on the **IV** chord, but at first glance, neither E♭ or B♭ seem to exist on a diatonic C harp.

Well, one of the qualities that make a harmonica so cool is the ability to "bend" the draw notes down to lower pitches. You're not limited to the seven diatonic tones in a major scale. When note is bent on a harp, the new note can be a half step lower than the original note. There are players who can accurately bend notes as far as a step and a half and hit the ones in between too… and there are basketball players who can regularly hit three-point shots. Takes practice.

Notice that the third draw note is a B note, the diatonic 7th of a C major scale. When you bend the third draw note down one (1) half step, you get a B♭, which is the ♭7th in a C7 chord. B♭ is also the flat 3rd of G, the **I** chord. Bingo. Now you have blues notes to play on a diatonic harp, for all three chords of a basic blues progression. It's tough to produce an E♭ note on a C harp, for a ♭3rd on the **IV** chord, but you can live without it.

You may be wondering… ***"How can anyone play anything while thinking about all that stuff?!"***

Nobody does, as far as I know. Just playin' the blues. That's just an explanation of why it works.

This technique of using a C harp to play "blues in G" is called "cross harp" or "second position."

To play "cross harp" use a harmonica that is a 5th lower than the key the guitar plays in. One click to the left. When the guitarist is playing blues in A, the harmonica player wants a D harp. When the guitarist is playing blues in E, the harmonica player wants an A harp. Of course, I'm confident you remember that business of inverting intervals. Up a 5th gets you to the same note name as down a 4th.

I'm an advocate of learning to play more than one instrument. Even though the notes are the same on all instruments, differences in the sounds, the layout of the notes, and the mechanical aspects of producing the notes allows/forces you to think differently.

An instrument like a harmonica is relatively inexpensive and quite portable. As of this writing, you can anticipate spending somewhere in the range of $18 to $25 for a decent harp. If you're considering spending a few years in prison, you might want to take some with you.

Three of my favorite harp players (besides Scott) are Norton Buffalo *(www.norton-buffalo.com)*, Charlie McCoy (**www.charliemccoy.com***)*, and Toots Thielemans (**www.tootsthielemans.com**). They're all amazing and can be found on lots of recordings.

Tin whistles and recorders are also good choices for an inexpensive second instrument. They are (usually) based on a major scale in different keys and can be surprisingly versatile.

Think back to the modes for a moment. All of the modes can be played using only white keys of a piano. Ionian is DO to DO, Dorian is RE to RE, Phrygian is MI to MI, Lydian is FA to FA, Mixolydian is SO to SO, Aolian is LA to LA, and Locrian is TI to TI.

A tin whistle, which has a range of only two octaves of a major scale, can produce a full octave plus a few notes, for all seven modes, by simply using a different hole for your tonic. After you finish the chapter on "**Melody**" and understand the relationship between the major scale and most melodies, these "simple" instruments may seem more interesting to you. I hope so, anyway.

An advantage of learning an instrument that is small enough to play in the front seat of your car is that you don't have to subject your friends and family to the squeaks or squawks that you'll inevitably produce for the first 15 or 20 hours. Go sit in a parking lot in another neighborhood, blast away, and let the passersby think what they will. Your housemates will appreciate your thoughtfulness, even if they have no clue what you're up to.

Capos

A capo (pronounced kay-po) is a little clamp that attaches to the neck of an instrument and it presses the strings down behind a fret.

This makes the fretboard shorter and the effect is that you have a new set of "open string" names.

All the fingerings stay the same. You play the same chord forms, because the intervals between the strings don't change, but the name of the chord you play is different because the root of the chord is on a different fret. This is similar to the clarinetist who has a few different sized clarinets for different keys. On a guitar, banjo, and others, we adjust the length of the strings with a capo. A clarinetist picks up a different sized instrument and gets the same kind of result.

Here are the names of some notes in four places on a guitar neck, in standard tuning.

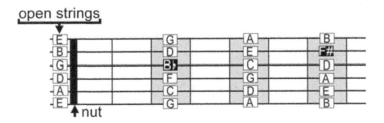

If you put a cap on the third fret (maybe 1/8 inch or so behind it, exactly parallel to the fret) the names of the "open strings" are all changed. But notice that the notes on the rest of the fretboard remain the same. This is obvious when you see it, but it's a common question.

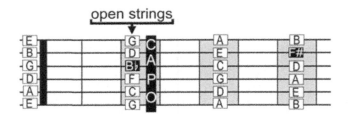

What the following illustration shows is playing Form #1 in three different places using a cap. The fingering remains the same and the number of "open strings" stays the same, but the name of the chord is different each time. It's like a mechanical barre chord aid. You play the chord, it makes the barre. "Capo 1" means the capo goes just behind the first fret, "capo 2" means it goes just behind the second fret, etc.

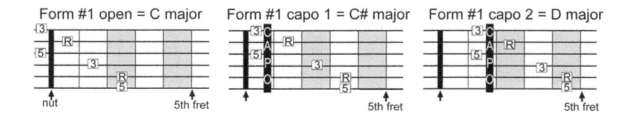

There are lots of reasons to use a capo.

Let's say that you only know three chords: G, C, and D, and you really like the song, "Auld Lang Syne." Those three chords are enough to play the song, but the low notes are just too low for you to sing.

Put the capo on the second fret, play the same forms, and now you're in the key of A. Your fingers are still playing what you're accustomed to calling G, C, and D, but the notes under your fingers have changed. If you put the capo on the third fret and play the chords you call C, F, and G, you'll be playing E♭, A♭ and B♭ and the horn section will love it.

I - IV - V Key of G Major

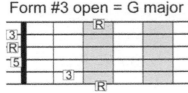

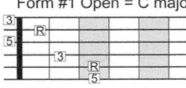

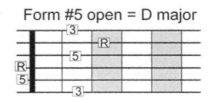

I - IV - V Key of A Major

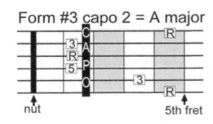

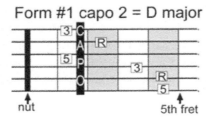

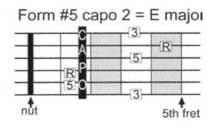

It can be more than just a little bit confusing to talk about. For instance, if you are not using a capo and your friend has a capo on the second fret and you want to hear an A chord (concert pitch), you'll probably have to say, "Play a G." It can easily turn into something like that Abbott and Costello routine, "Who's on first?!" (Listen here: (**www.phoenix5.org/humor/WhoOnFirst.html**). It's about five minutes long and funny. Buy it here: **abbottandcostellocollectibles.com**).

Most of us are accustomed to calling "Form #3 in the open position" a G chord, no matter where we put the capo. So if I'm playing G, C, and D with my capo on the second fret, even though the actual "concert pitch" names of my chord roots would be A, D, and E, I'm usually still thinking G, C, and D. If I put the capo on the fourth fret, the chords produced by the fingering patterns I've learned to call G, C, and D are matching up with what the piano player knows as B, E, and F#. Must have taken a wrong turn somewhere because suddenly we seem to be on the same confusing planet that the transposing instruments live on.

All six instruments shown below are playing what the piano player would correctly identify as a C major chord (or arpeggio… one horn can't do chords).

Not one of them thinks they're playing a C.

First guitar on the left thinks he's playing A, middle guitar is thinking G, and the one on the right thinks she's got an E, because that's what those shapes make in the open position. The horns all identify their triad by the first note they play on the staff. The clarinet is certain he's playing E, the sax says it's A♭, and the flute is playing F. They're all ignoring the piano player.

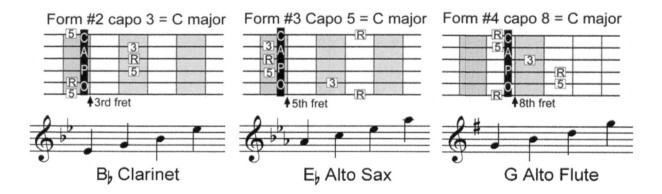

Trying to pin down what key a song is in can be like trying to attach Jell-O to a wall with a staple gun. It might be easier to bonk "Jumpin' Jack Flash" with a Fender Twin from 50 paces.

Solfege is your special friend. DO-RE-MI-FA-SO-LA-TI. I-ii-iii-IV-V-vi-vii. It's the translator between all the instruments and all the keys. In solfege, all keys share the same names for the tones and the chord numbers match up nicely. It doesn't matter where the dots appear on your neighbors' music, or what name is associated with a shape on the fretboard. What matters is the relationships. So long as the distance between DO and SO is consistent, then it doesn't matter which line or space is assigned to DO. It makes me wonder why we even bother with all the other stuff.

Limited chord vocabularies or vocal ranges are not the only reasons to use a capo.

The neck of a guitar is tapered slightly, getting wider as you go up the neck. My fingers are kind of fat, and there are times that I like to gain that tiny bit of width so I'm not as likely to mute a string accidentally.

When there are two guitars playing together, it can be really cool if one person puts a capo on so that you are each playing different forms of the same chords, both guitars using as many "open" strings as possible.

For example, if you and a friend are playing "Auld Lang Syne" in C using Form #1 for C, Form #4 for F, and Form #3 for G in the open position, the other can put the capo on the fifth fret and use Form #3 as a C chord, Form #1 for F, and Form #5 for G.

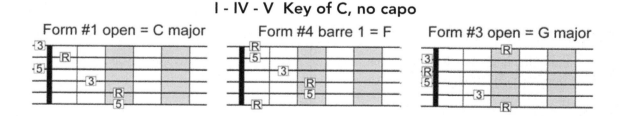

I - IV - V Key of C, capo 5th fret

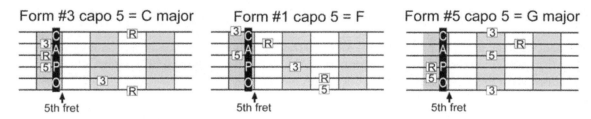

Form #3 capo 5 = C major   Form #1 capo 5 = F   Form #5 capo 5 = G major

5th fret   5th fret   5th fret

Listen to "Here Comes the Sun" by the Beatles. The song was recorded in the key of A, but in order to play the signature guitar line, you have to use Form #5 for the **I** chord, which in the open position is a D chord. So George Harrison put a capo on the seventh fret, used Form #5, and that's how they got that sound.

Something to be aware of when using a capo is that the capo is stretching the strings down a little bit and will pull the guitar just a little bit out of tune… just a hair sharp. So always check your tuning when putting it on or removing it. This isn't a big issue if you're playing alone, but if you're playing with other people you're better off to check.

There are "partial capos" that are notched and only change certain strings, so they actually change the intervals between the strings and all these forms we've been using go right out the window. A capo is not especially expensive, a really useful tool, and kind of fun. It's definitely worth investing a few dollars and hours and learning to use one. Get one and goof around with it, and if you have any questions, call Pinky.

Speaking of changing the intervals between the strings, maybe you've heard of "open tunings."

"Standard tuning" on a guitar is E-A-D-G-B-E. The term "standard tuning" implies that there must be "un-standard tunings" as well.

There are loads of them and some of them are called "open tunings" because when you strum all six strings open, you get a chord, usually a major chord. Now the guitar has a "home key."

This is how you change from standard guitar tuning into an open tuning. We'll start with what is called "open E tuning." What you'll do is tune the strings so they make a Form #4 chord.

First, spell the chord you want to make. The notes in an E major chord are E (root), G# (3rd), and B (5th). Take a look at the open strings in standard tuning and you see two of those notes. The first, second, and sixth string are E, B, and E. If you leave the sixth string as E, lighten the fifth string A up one whole step to B, raise the fourth string D up one whole step to E, and then raise the third string G one (1) half step to G#… you have an open E tuning. You get exactly the same notes when you play an E chord the usual way… Form #4 in the open position. This one is real popular for playing blues slide stuff. One reason blues players like it is because it's easy to find the flatted 3rds and 7ths for the **I** chord. They're in a straight line across the neck on the third fret.

Form #4 Standard Tuning   ### Form #4 Open Tuning

A slide player's pick hand does what it usually does, but she'll slip a tube over a finger on her fret hand. Most use their ring finger or pinky. It's kind of like a movable fret. You don't push the strings down to the frets with your slide. It barely touches the strings, with just exactly enough pressure to get a clear note without rattling.

Whether it's made of steel, glass, or porcelain, the slide is straight. When you cover all six strings with the slide and slide it up the neck, it makes a Form #4 major chord. Your basic barre chord with no pain. The **I** chord is open, the **IV** chord is on the 5th fret, and the **V** chord is on the 7th.

And guess where you find the bluesy sounding flatted 3rds and 7ths for the **IV** and **V** chords? Three frets higher. Flatted 7ths are available two frets below the roots.

Notice the "blues box" that appears when you look at the four "blue" notes on any two adjacent strings, excluding the third string. The same sort of blues box pattern exists in all open tunings. A flatted 3rd will *always* be found three frets above a root and a flatted 7th will *always* be three frets higher than a 5th. *ALWAYS*. Guitars. Banjos. Mandolins. Mandolas. Bass. Ukuleles. In any tuning. Well… not on a dulcimer.

Playing normally, without a slide, you have a nice wide target on the fretboard. As long as your finger lands somewhere in between two frets, the highest fret will make the note. If the instrument is in tune, your note will be in tune.

When you play with a slide, the target shrinks way down and becomes a little smaller than the fret wire. There is only one correct spot on a guitar's high E string to get 440 Hz A, and it's a very small spot.

All of the other spots are ***wrong***. So sorry, but to play slide in tune, close just isn't good enough. "Close doesn't tally," say the archers. It's similar to playing a violin or its cousins. There's some room for error, but not a lot. You gotta get it right.

When you're playing without a slide the frets automatically chop the string off at the right point. A slide player has to place the lowest round edge of the slide directly above the highest point on a fret.

In addition, to make a six-note chord sound like a musical chord instead of an injured cat, the slide has to be *exactly* aligned with the frets. It isn't easy at first, but that's true of many things. After a few hours of weird noises, you'll start getting it right sometimes. It's hard. Practice makes better.

Some of my favorite slide players are Duane Allman, Ry Cooder, Jerry Garcia, Lowell George, David Gilmour, David Lindley, Jim Lewis (local Bozeman player), Bonnie Raitt and Derek Trucks. Bonnie Raitt is better known as a songwriter and vocalist, but this woman plays slide with the best of them. I've never listened much to the older Delta players who invented this style and heavily influenced my bottleneck-slide playing heroes.

Open A is also used a lot for bluesy sounding slide stuff. Robert Johnson used this one a lot. (**www.deltahaze. com/dhcrj.html**). An A major chord is spelled A-C#-E. Again, three strings in standard tuning are already there. You just have to raise three string one whole step. Raise the second string from B to C#, the third string from G up to A, and the fourth string from D up to E, and that's open A. E-A-E-A-C#-E. The "blue notes" are on the third fret.

Form #4 Open Tuning

Form #2 Open Tuning

A G major chord is spelled G-B-D. The second, third, and fourth strings don't need to be changed to make an open G tuning. Instead, this time you lower the first, fifth, and sixth strings a whole step each and it's open G. D-G-D-G-B-D. Guess where the flat 3rds and flat 7ths live?

At this point, it's useful to forget about the note names and think of these tunings as roots, 3rds, and 5ths. It's really not so much about the chord names… A tuning or E tuning or whatever… as it is about the sound produced by a particular arrangement of the chord tones.

Another open G is R-3-5-R-3-5. Hum DO-MI-SO-DO-MI-SO. This one is used a lot by bluegrass Dobro players. The open E described earlier is R-5-R-3-5-R. DO-SO-DO-MI-SO-DO. You will get the same sound if the first and sixth strings are both D, or if they are both F#, as long as the tones are R-5-R-3-5-R.

The open A is 5-R-5-R-3-5. The first open G shown above is the same… 5-R-5-R-3-5.

Lower the 3rd (or 3rds if there are two) in any of these and they become minor open tunings.

Then there are other common tunings that just get a different sound. Drop D means that you start with standard tuning then lower the sixth string to a D note. This gets a great bass note for a D chord and makes playing in the key of D interesting. Big bottom. Talk about mudflaps…

You can get the same sequence of intervals by doing a "partial capo" on the second fret… the capo presses strings one through five and raises them a whole step, but stops before it touches the sixth string. That leaves the sixth string as E. The capo'd strings are: the fifth string, which is now "open" B; the fourth string will be E; the third string will be A; the second string will be C#; and the first string "open" will be F#. Play what looks like a D, leave the sixth string open. Now you have a Form #5 "open" E chord that looks like a D chord and sounds very different than the Form #4 E we're used to.

E Major Standard Tuning Partial Capo

There's D-A-D-G-A-D. Lower the first, second, and sixth strings by a whole step.

Jimi Hendrix and Stevie Ray Vaughn (among many others) liked to tune to E♭. This means that you lower all six strings from standard tuning one (1) half step to E♭ A♭ D♭ G♭ B♭ E♭. Kind of like a capo in reverse. All the "regular" chord forms still work the way you're used to, but it sounds a bit bigger, fuller. And, because the tension on the strings is less, you can use a heavier gauge of strings and that thickens up the tone even more. What looks like an E chord on a guitar is now E♭ to the piano player, what used to be a G chord is now G♭, etc.

In all of these tunings, you're still working with the same 12 notes, they're just in different places on the neck. Once you locate DO, you still flat the 3rd (MI) to get a minor chord and raise it to get a sus4 (FA). Lower a root by a half step and it's a major 7 (TI), drop it another half step it's a dominant 7 (ta).

And just because you have tuned to an open A, it doesn't mean that you can only play in that particular key. Remember that a blues harp player uses a C harp to play in G and all of the transposing instruments with their "home keys" that still play in other keys.

Even standard tuning can be seen as a chord. If you strum all six strings open in standard tuning, you can say it is an Em11 chord. E-A-D-G-B-E are the notes. E is the root, A is the 11th, D is the $\flat$7th, G is the $\flat$3rd, and B is the 5th.

You hear steel players talking about C6 and E9 tunings and such. These instruments usually have upwards of eight string and pedal steels usually have two separate necks. They tune them to bigger chords. Same principle. You can tune your instrument to any chord you want to.

There are certain advantages to playing an open tuned guitar in its "home key," but there are certain advantages when you don't, too.

You can barre the seventh fret in any open tuning, call it the **I** chord, and then strumming the open strings would be the **IV** chord, and the second fret barred would be the **V**, for example.

Just ask Mr. Jim Averitt**. Jim works on the Flying D Ranch here in Gallatin Gateway, Montana, and in his spare time writes lots of music. He's a great songwriter and guitarist and often uses an open tuning and then doesn't use that chord as the **I** chord. It's a neat effect.

Jim is one of those people who is living proof that you don't need to know *any* of the information in this book to write, record, and play lots of great music. When I met Jim, he had already recorded a couple of CDs, he'd been on tour with several "big name" players, and played bar gigs for years with a few real good bands. He didn't know the names of most of the chords he was playing and couldn't tell you what key he was playing in.

Alternate tunings can be great fun and if you're in a rut, can help inspire some new ideas because suddenly the same old guitar is almost like a totally different instrument.

***By the way but off the topic, Jim has been kind enough to let me record a few of his tunes and one of my favorites is "Justin's Theme," which we did for my CD, "Yucca Pie." I like it a lot, or we wouldn't have taken the time to record it, of course, but besides being such a cool tune, it also features some other friends who are exceptional jazz musicians. Mike Gillan on drums, Craig Hall on bass, and Bob Nell on piano. They don't get to record together very often, so it's a treat to hear them work their magic on Jim's tune… as well as a few of mine.* **www.dukesharp.com**.

Reflections

*"The difference between the impossible and the possible
lies in a person's determination."*
Tommy Lasorda

*"The drops of rain make a hole in the stone
not by violence, but by oft falling."*
Lucretius

*"The first requisite of success is the ability to apply your physical
and mental energies to one problem without growing weary."*
Thomas Edison

"The gem cannot be polished without friction, nor man perfected without trials."
Chinese proverb

*"The goal you set must be challenging.
At the same time, it should be realistic and attainable, not impossible to reach.
It should be challenging enough to make you stretch, but not so far that you break."*
Rick Hansen

*"The great end of education is to discipline rather than to furnish the mind;
Train it to the use of its own powers, rather than fill it with the accumulation of others."*
Tyron Edwards

*"The greater the difficulty the more glory in surmounting it.
Skillful pilots gain their reputation from storms and tempests."*
Epictetus

"The greatest oak was once a little nut who held its ground."
Unknown

*"The man that hath no music in himself,
nor is not moved with concord of sweet sounds,
is fit for treasons, stratagems and spoils;
The motions of his spirit are dull as night,
and his affections dark as Erebus:.
Let no such man be trusted.
Mark the music."*
William Shakespeare

*"The man who can drive himself further once the effort gets painful
is the man who will win."*
Roger Bannister

If it is a transposing instrument, the note written as C sounds as the note of the instrument's transposition. On an E♭ alto saxophone that note sounds as a concert E♭, on an A clarinet that note sounds as a concert A. The bassoon is an exception, it is not a transposing instrument, yet its "home" scale is F.

Brass instruments, when played with no valves engaged (or, for trombones, with the slide all the way in) will produce a series of notes which form the overtone series based on some fundamental pitch, e.g., the B♭ trumpet, when played with no valves being pressed can play the overtones based on B♭. Usually, that pitch is the note which indicates the transposition of that brass instrument. Trombones are an exception, they do not transpose; instead reading at concert pitch, although tenor and bass trombones are pitched in B♭, alto trombone in E♭.

It is interesting to note that, with the exception of the bass trombone, all of the instruments in United Kingdom brass band music (including cornet, flugelhorn, tenor horn, euphonium, baritone horn, tenor trombone, and even the bass tuba) are notated in treble clef as transposing instruments in either B♭ or E♭.

In conductors' scores, most often the music for transposing instruments is written in transposed form, just as in the players' parts; but a few publishers, especially of modern music, provide conductors with music which is all at concert pitch. The argument for the latter practice is that it makes the pitch relationships of the entire sound easier for the conductor to read. The advantage of traditional practice is that it facilitates spoken communication in rehearsal since conductor and player are looking at the same notation.

Instruments in C (15ms) – sounds two octaves above what is written
    Glockenspiel

Instruments in D♭ (high) – sounds a minor 9th above what is written
    D♭ Piccolo

Instruments in C (8va) – sounds an octave above what is written
    Piccolo
    Celeste
    Soprano (descant), sopranino, bass, great bass recorder
    Tin whistle
    Xylophone

Instruments in B♭ (high) – sounds a minor 7th above what is written
    Piccolo trumpet (may also be tuned to A)

Instruments in A♭ (high) – sounds a minor 6th above what is written
    A♭ Piccolo clarinet

Instruments in E♭ (high) – sounds a minor 3rd above what is written
    E♭ Soprano clarinet
    Sopranino saxophone

Instruments in D (high) – sounds a major 2nd above what is written
    D Soprano clarinet
    D Trumpet (may also be tuned to E♭)

* A selection of Instruments in C (unison) – sounds as written; these are non-transposing instruments
    Piano
    Vibraphone
    Flute
    Oboe
    Bassoon
    Alto trombone
    Tenor trombone when written in tenor or bass clef
    Bass trombone
    Euphonium or baritone horn when written in bass clef
    Tuba
    Violin
    Mandolin
    Viola
    Mandola
    Cello
    Mandocello

Instruments in B♭ – sounds a major 2nd below what is written
- B♭ Soprano clarinet
- Soprano saxophone
- Trumpet
- Cornet
- Flugelhorn

Instruments in A – sounds a minor 3rd below what is written
- Oboe d'armore
- A Soprano clarinet
- A Trumpet

Instruments in G – sounds a perfect 4th below what is written
- Alto flute
- So-called Turkish clarinet

Instruments in F – sounds a perfect 5th below what is written
- English horn
- Horn
- Basset horn

Instruments in E♭ – sounds a major 6th below what is written
- Alto clarinet
- Alto saxophone
- Tenor horn

Instruments in C (8vb) – sounds an octave below what is written
- Guitar
- Banjo
- Bass flute
- Double bass
- Bass guitar
- Contrabassoon

Instruments in B♭ (low) – sounds an octave and a major 2nd below what is written
- B♭ Bass clarinet
- Tenor saxophone
- Euphonium when written in treble clef (British brass band music)
- Baritone when written in treble clef (British brass band music)

Instruments in A (low) – sounds an octave and a minor 3rd below what is written
- A Bass clarinet (obsolete)

Instruments in E♭ (low) – sounds an octave and a major 6th below what is written
- E♭ Contra-alto clarinet
- Baritone saxophone
- E♭ Tuba when written in treble clef (British brass band music)

Instruments in B♭ (super low) – sounds two octaves and a major 2nd below what is written
- B♭ Tuba when written in treble clef (British brass band music)
- B♭ Contrabass clarinet
- Bass saxophone

Timpani

In the 17th and early 18th century, timpani were often treated as transposing instruments as they were almost always tuned to the tonic (DO) and dominant (SO) notes of the key the piece was written in. These were notated as C and G, and the actual tuning was indicated at the top of the score (for example, Timpani in A-D). This notation style was not universal: Bach, Mozart, and Schubert (in his early works) used it, but their respective contemporaries Handel, Haydn, and Beethoven wrote for the timpani at concert pitch.

These pages taken from en.wikipedia.org/wiki/Transposing_instrument and reprinted by permission.
Kennan, Kent Wheeler. *The Technique of Orchestration,* Second Edition. Englewood Cliffs, New Jersey: Prentice-Hall, Inc., 1970, 1952; ISBN 0-13-900316-9
Del Mar, Norman (1981). *The Anatomy of the Orchestra.* Univ. of California Press.

Transposing Exercise
These four-bar progressions are in the key of C. Transpose them to A, G, E, and D.

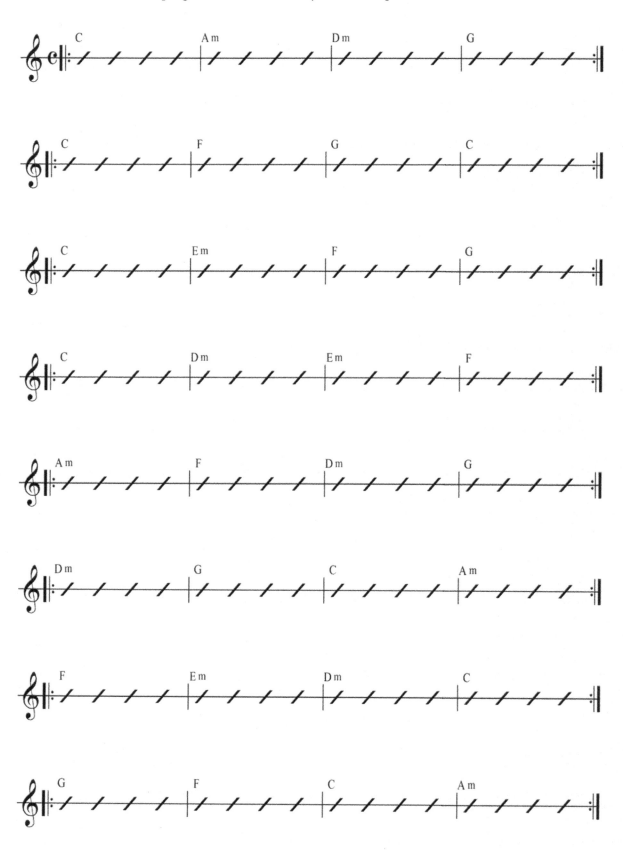

10 - The Key

Transposing Chart for Major Keys

The sequence of intervals that generates the Ionian mode is W-W-H-W-W-W-H

Sharp Keys	I chord	ii chord	iii chord	IV chord	V chord	vi chord	vii chord
C 0 #	C Major DO	D minor RE	E minor MI	F Major FA	G Major SO	A minor LA	B m♭5 TI
G 1 #	G Major	A minor	B minor	C Major	D Major	E minor	F# m♭5
D 2 #	D Major	E minor	F# minor	G Major	A Major	B minor	C# m♭5
A 3 #	A Major	B minor	C# minor	D Major	E Major	F# minor	G# m♭5
E 4 #	E Major	F# minor	G# minor	A Major	B Major	C# minor	B m♭5
B 5 #	B Major	C# minor	D# minor	E Major	F# Major	G# minor	A# m♭5
F# 6 #	F# Major	G# minor	A# minor	B Major	C# Major	D# minor	E m♭5
C# 7 #	C# Major	D# minor	E# minor	F# Major	G# Major	A# minor	B #m♭5

Flat Keys	I chord	II chord	iii chord	IV chord	V chord	vi chord	vii chord
C 0 ♭	C Major	D minor	E minor	F Major	G Major	A minor	B m♭5
F 1 ♭	F Major	G minor	A minor	B♭ major	C Major	D minor	E m♭5
B♭ 2 ♭	B♭ Major	C minor	D minor	E♭ Major	F Major	G minor	A m♭5
E♭ 3 ♭	E♭ Major	F minor	G minor	A♭ Major	B♭ Major	C minor	D m♭5
A♭ 4 ♭	A♭ Major	B♭ minor	C minor	D♭ Major	E♭ Major	F minor	G m♭5
D♭ 5 ♭	D♭ Major	E♭ minor	F minor	G♭ Major	A♭ Major	B♭ minor	C m♭5
G♭ 6 ♭	G♭ Major	A♭ minor	B♭ minor	C♭ Major	D♭ Major	E♭ minor	F m♭5
C♭ 7 ♭	C♭ Major	D♭ minor	E♭ minor	F♭ Major	G♭ Major	E♭ minor	B♭ m♭5

Transposing Chart for Natural Minor Keys

The sequence of intervals that generates the Aolian mode is W-H-W-W-H-W-W

Sharp Keys	i chord	ii chord	III chord	iv chord	v chord	VI chord	VII chord
A- 0	A minor	B m♭5	C Major	D minor	E minor	F Major	G Major
	LA	TI	DO	RE	MI	FA	SO
E- 1#	E minor	F# m♭5	G Major	A minor	B minor	C Major	D Major
B- 2#	B minor	C# m♭5	D Major	E minor	F# minor	G Major	A Major
F#- 3#	F# minor	G# m♭5	A Major	B minor	C# minor	D Major	E Major
C#- 4#	C# minor	D# m♭5	E Major	F# minor	G# minor	A Major	B Major
G#- 5#	G# minor	A# m♭5	B Major	C# minor	D# minor	E Major	F#Major
D#- 6#	D# minor	E# m♭5	F#Major	G# minor	A# minor	B Major	C# Major
A#- 7#	A# minor	B# m♭5	C# Major	D# minor	E# minor	F#Major	G# Major

Flat Keys	i chord	ii chord	III chord	iv chord	v chord	VI chord	VII chord
Am 0	A minor	B m♭5	C Major	D minor	E minor	F Major	G Major
Dm 1♭	D minor	E m♭5	F Major	G minor	A minor	B♭ Major	C Major
Gm 2♭	G minor	A m♭5	B♭ Major	C minor	D minor	E♭ Major	F Major
Cm 3♭	C minor	D m♭5	E♭ Major	F minor	G minor	A♭ Major	B Major
Fm 4♭	F minor	G m♭5	A♭ Major	B♭ minor	C minor	D♭ Major	E♭ Major
B♭m 5♭	B♭ minor	C m♭5	D♭ Major	E♭ minor	F minor	G♭ Major	A♭ Major
E♭m 6♭	E♭ minor	F m♭5	G♭ Major	A♭ minor	B♭ minor	C♭ Major	D♭ Major

Transposing Chart for Harmonic Minor Keys

The sequence of intervals that generates the harmonic minor scale is W-H-W-W-H (W+H)-H
Notice that there are some "double sharps." We have to use all seven letter names.

	i chord	ii chord	III chord	iv chord	V chord	VI chord	VII chord
A- / 0	A minor	B m♭5	C +	D minor	E	F Major	G# m♭5
E- / 1#	E minor	F# m♭5	G +	A minor	B	C Major	D# m♭5
B- / 2#	B minor	C# m♭5	D +	E minor	F#	G Major	A# m♭5
F#- / 3#	F# minor	G# m♭5	A +	B minor	C#	D Major	E# m♭5
C#- / 4#	C# minor	D# m♭5	E +	F# minor	G#	A Major	B# m♭5
G#- / 5#	G# minor	A# m♭5	B +	C# minor	D#	E Major	F## m♭5
D#- / 6#	D# minor	E# m♭5	F# +	G# minor	A#	B Major	C## m♭5
A#- / 7#	A# minor	B# m♭5	C# +	D# minor	E#	F#Major	G## m♭5

	i chord	ii chord	III chord	iv chord	v chord	VI chord	VII chord
Am / 0	A minor	B m♭5	C +	D minor	E	F Major	G# m♭5
Dm / 1♭	D minor	E m♭5	F +	G minor	A	B♭ Major	C# m♭5
Gm / 2♭	G minor	A m♭5	B♭ +	C minor	D	E♭ Major	F# m♭5
Cm / 3♭	C minor	D m♭5	E♭ +	F minor	G	A♭ Major	B m♭5
Fm / 4♭	F minor	G m♭5	A♭	B♭ minor	C	D♭ Major	E m♭5
B♭m / 5♭	B♭ minor	C m♭5	D♭	E♭ minor	F	G♭ Major	A m♭5
E♭m / 6♭	E♭ minor	F m♭5	G♭	A♭ minor	B♭	C♭ Major	D m♭5
A♭m / 7♭	A♭ minor	B♭ m♭5	C♭	D♭ minor	E♭	F♭ Major	G m♭5

Transposing to the Dark Side

Here are some of our old favorites with a different color. I transposed these to a relative minor key. I like harmonic minor a little more than natural minor. In harmonic minor, the V is a major triad. That's usually a good clue for whether a song is in a natural minor or harmonic minor key.

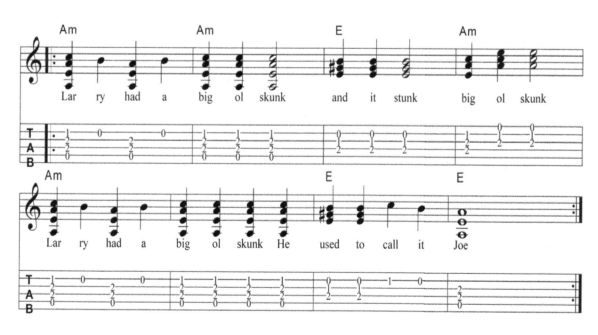

Bingle Jells

Oleg Sighin'

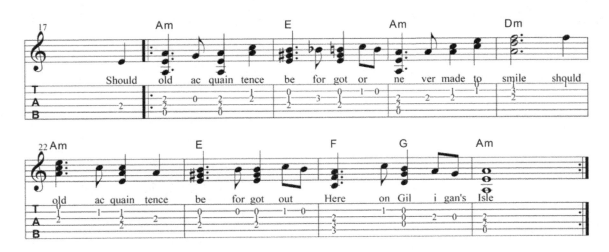

Silent Night... sort of

10 - The Key

Friends who actually know something about modes have told me that people usually don't think of these last five modes in the same way that we use Ionian and Aolian, i.e. "keys." However, if you want to play "After the Battle of Aughrim" from "**Scales**" in F Dorian or G# Dorian instead of D Dorian, this will work. I didn't fill in all of the chord names for these five remaining modes on the following pages. I thought that you would like to use your knowledge of scales to fill them in on your own.

Transposing Chart for Dorian Mode

The sequence of intervals that generates the Dorian mode is W-H-W-W-W-H-W

Sharp Keys	i chord	ii chord	III chord	IV chord	V chord	vi chord	VII chord
D	D minor	E minor	F Major	G Major	A minor	B m♭5	C Major
	RE	MI	FA	SO	LA	TI	DO
A	minor	minor	Major	Major	minor	m♭5	Major
E	minor	minor	Major	Major	minor	m♭5	Major
B	minor	minor	Major	Major	minor	m♭5	Major
F#	minor	minor	Major	Major	minor	m♭5	Major
C#	minor	minor	Major	Major	minor	m♭5	Major
G#	minor	minor	Major	Major	minor	m♭5	Major
D#	minor	minor	Major	Major	minor	m♭5	Major

Flat Keys	i chord	ii chord	III chord	IV chord	V chord	vi chord	VII chord
D	D minor	E minor	F Major	G Major	A minor	B m♭5	C Major
G	minor	minor	Major	Major	minor	m♭5	Major
C	minor	minor	Major	Major	minor	m♭5	Major
F	minor	minor	Major	Major	minor	m♭5	Major
B♭	minor	minor	Major	Major	minor	m♭5	Major
E♭	minor	minor	Major	Major	minor	m♭5	Major
A♭	minor	minor	Major	Major	minor	m♭5	Major
D♭	minor	minor	Major	Major	minor	m♭5	Major

Transposing Chart for Phrygian Mode
The sequence of intervals that generates the Phrygian mode is H-W-W-W-H-W-W

Sharp Keys	i chord	II chord	III chord	iv chord	v chord	VI chord	vii chord
E	E minor	F Major	G Major	A minor	Bm♭5	C Major	D minor
	MI	FA	SO	LA	TI	DO	RE
B	minor	Major	Major	minor	m♭5	Major	minor
F#	minor	Major	Major	minor	m♭5	Major	minor
C#	minor	Major	Major	minor	m♭5	Major	minor
G#	minor	Major	Major	minor	m♭5	Major	minor
D#	minor	Major	Major	minor	m♭5	Major	minor
A#	minor	Major	Major	minor	m♭5	Major	minor
E#	minor	Major	Major	minor	m♭5	Major	minor

Flat Keys	i chord	II chord	III chord	iv chord	v chord	VI chord	vii chord
E	E minor	F Major	G Major	A minor	Bm♭5	C Major	D minor
A	minor	Major	Major	minor	m♭5	Major	minor
D	minor	Major	Major	minor	m♭5	Major	minor
G	minor	Major	Major	minor	m♭5	Major	minor
C	minor	Major	Major	minor	m♭5	Major	minor
F	minor	Major	Major	minor	m♭5	Major	minor
B♭	minor	Major	Major	minor	m♭5	Major	minor
E♭	minor	Major	Major	minor	m♭5	Major	minor

Transposing Chart for Lydian Mode

The sequence of intervals that generates the Lydian mode is W-W-W-H-W-W-H

Sharp Keys	I chord	II chord	iii chord	iv chord	V chord	vi chord	vii chord
F	F Major	G Major	A minor	B m♭5	C Major	D minor	E minor
	FA	SO	LA	TI	DO	RE	MI
C	Major	Major	minor	m♭5	Major	minor	minor
G	Major	Major	minor	m♭5	Major	minor	minor
D	Major	Major	minor	m♭5	Major	minor	minor
A	Major	Major	minor	m♭5	Major	minor	minor
E	Major	Major	minor	m♭5	Major	minor	minor
B	Major	Major	minor	m♭5	Major	minor	minor
F#	Major	Major	minor	m♭5	Major	minor	minor

Flat Keys	I chord	II chord	iii chord	iv chord	V chord	vi chord	vii chord
F	F Major	G Major	A minor	B m♭5	C Major	D minor	E minor
B♭	Major	Major	minor	m♭5	Major	minor	minor
E♭	Major	Major	minor	m♭5	Major	minor	minor
A♭	Major	Major	minor	m♭5	Major	minor	minor
D♭	Major	Major	minor	m♭5	Major	minor	minor
G♭	Major	Major	minor	m♭5	Major	minor	minor
C♭	Major	Major	minor	m♭5	Major	minor	minor
F♭	Major	Major	minor	m♭5	Major	minor	minor

Transposing Chart for Mixolydian Mode

The sequence of intervals that generates the Mixolydian mode is W-W-H-W-W-H-W

Sharp Keys	I chord	ii chord	iii chord	IV chord	v chord	vi chord	VII chord
G	G Major	A minor	B m♭5	C Major	D minor	E minor	F Major
	SO	LA	TI	DO	RE	MI	FA
D	Major	minor	m♭5	Major	minor	minor	Major
A	Major	minor	m♭5	Major	minor	minor	Major
E	Major	minor	m♭5	Major	minor	minor	Major
B	Major	minor	m♭5	Major	minor	minor	Major
F#	Major	minor	m♭5	Major	minor	minor	Major
C#	Major	minor	m♭5	Major	minor	minor	Major
G#	Major	minor	m♭5	Major	minor	minor	Major

Flat Keys	I chord	ii chord	iii chord	IV chord	v chord	vi chord	VII chord
G	G Major	A minor	B m♭5	C Major	D minor	E minor	F Major
C	Major	minor	m♭5	Major	minor	minor	Major
F	Major	minor	m♭5	Major	minor	minor	Major
B♭	Major	minor	m♭5	Major	minor	minor	Major
E♭	Major	minor	m♭5	Major	minor	minor	Major
A♭	Major	minor	m♭5	Major	minor	minor	Major
D♭	Major	minor	m♭5	Major	minor	minor	Major
G♭	Major	minor	m♭5	Major	minor	minor	Major

Transposing Chart for Locrian Mode
The sequence of intervals that generates the Locrian mode is H-W-W-H-W-W-W

Sharp Keys

	i chord	II chord	iii chord	iv chord	V chord	VI chord	vii chord
B	Bm♭5	C Major	D minor	E minor	F major	G Major	A Minor
	TI	DO	RE	MI	FA	SO	LA
F#	m♭5	Major	minor	minor	Major	Major	minor
C#	m♭5	Major	minor	minor	Major	Major	minor
G#	m♭5	Major	minor	minor	Major	Major	minor
D#	m♭5	Major	minor	minor	Major	Major	minor
A#	m♭5	Major	minor	minor	Major	Major	minor
E#	m♭5	Major	minor	minor	Major	Major	minor
B#	m♭5	Major	minor	minor	Major	Major	minor

Flat Keys

	i chord	II chord	iii chord	iv chord	V chord	VI chord	vii chord
B	Bm♭5	C Major	D minor	E minor	F major	G Major	A Minor
E	m♭5	Major	minor	minor	Major	Major	minor
A	m♭5	Major	minor	minor	Major	Major	minor
D	m♭5	Major	minor	minor	Major	Major	minor
G	m♭5	Major	minor	minor	Major	Major	minor
C	m♭5	Major	minor	minor	Major	Major	minor
F	m♭5	Major	minor	minor	Major	Major	minor
B♭	m♭5	Major	minor	minor	Major	Major	minor

The Key

1. A _____ can be accurately described as a group of _____ that sound good together.

2. There are a total of _____ naturally occurring chords in every major key.

3. "Occur naturally" means that only the _____ _____ are used to form the chords.

4. These chords are said to be _____ which means "only scale tones."

5. Each of the _____ tones of a _____ scale is the root of a triad.

6. There are _____ major chords and _____ minor chords in every major key.

7. The chord sequence for all major keys is: major-_____-_____-_____-_____-
_____-_____.

8. The 1st tone in the C major scale is the note _____. The first chord in the key of C major is
a _____.

9. Frequently, _____ _____ are used for numbering chords.

10. The 1st scale tone is the _____ of the first chord in any key and its Roman numeral equivalent is the
"_____" chord (pronounced "the one chord").

11. "The Nashville Number System" uses Arabic numbers instead of Roman numerals to substitute for
chord names. **True   False**

12. In solfege, the three tones that make the 1 chord are _____ _____ _____.

13. The 2m chord in the key of C is ____ _____. The three solfege tones are _____ _____ _____.

14. The _____ chord in the key of C is E minor. The three solfege tones are ____ _____
___.

15. The **IV** chord in the key of C is _____. The three solfege tones are _____ _____
___.

16. The **V** chord in the key of C is _____. The three solfege tones are _____ _____
___.

17. The 6m chord in the key of C is _____. The three solfege tones are _____ _____
___.

18. The **vii** chord in the key of C is _____. The three solfege tones are _____ _____
___.

19. In solfege, the three tones that make the VII chord are _____ _____ _____.

20. In the key of C, 2m-5-1 indicates the chords _____ _____ _____.

21. In the key of C, 1-4-5 indicates the chords _____ _____ _____.

22. In the key of C, 1-3m-6m-5 indicates the chords _____ _____ _____.

23. _____ and _____ are two different words that both basically mean "to change keys."

24. _____ means to change from one key to another while you're still playing the tune.

25. _____ is the thought process, or pencil and paper part of modulating.

26. Any song can be played in any key.   **True   False**

27. The collection of sharps and flats at the beginning of a staff system is called a _____ _____.

28. Each key signature indicates _____ different keys.

29. One is a _____ key and the other is a _____ key.

30. The name of the minor key represented by a key signature is a minor 3rd _____ than the major key represented by the same key signature.

31. – 37.   Identify the keys as shown below.

38. The name of the key signature will tell you which scale is the foundation for the song.   **True   False**

39. All the players in an orchestra use music that is written in the same key signature.   **True   False**

40. There are _____ instruments and there are non-transposing instruments.

41. Pianos, violins, flutes, and some others are "non-transposing" instruments. The pitch that a note has when played on all of these non-transposing instruments is called _____ _____.

42. Duke Sharp invented the Circle of Fifths.   **True   False**

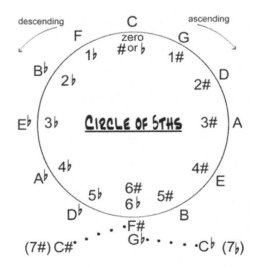

43. If a guitar is playing a tune in the key of C, what key would an E♭ instrument use? _____

44. If a guitar is playing a tune in the key of G, what key would an E♭ instrument use? _____

45. If a guitar is playing a tune in the key of D, what key would an E♭ instrument use? _____

46. If a guitar is playing a tune in the key of A, what key would an E♭ instrument use _____

47. If a guitar is playing a tune in the key of E, what key would an E♭ instrument use _____

48. If a guitar is playing a tune in the key of C, what key would an B♭ instrument use _____

49. If a guitar is playing a tune in the key of G, what key would an B♭ instrument use _____

50. If a guitar is playing a tune in the key of D, what key would an B♭ instrument use? _____

51. If a guitar is playing a tune in the key of A, what key would an B♭ instrument use _____

52. If a guitar is playing a tune in the key of E, what key would an B♭ instrument use _____

53. All of the families of musical instruments operate within the same basic "theoretical structure."
True   False

54. All are designed to accommodate the major scale.   **True   False**

55. All use the same 12 notes on the same five-line staff using the same scale with certain written adjustments to compensate for the physical properties inherent in different families of instruments.   **True   False**

56. If a guitarist knows only three chords, G, C, and D, he can use a capo to transpose those chords to any key.
True   False

57. _____ is the translator between all the instruments and all the keys.

Chord Progressions

You hear the tires rolling and then stopping. The engine is turned off and the car doors open and close. You hear two of your friends talking to each other and their footsteps coming to your door, and then a knock on your door, and ringing the doorbell, too, talking all the while.

Now… here's a little listening game. Imagine being presented with a recorded version of that sequence of events, six months later. This is the trick: you're supposed to figure out what it is that you're hearing on the recording, without being given any clues at all regarding what it might be. It could be a recording of the zoo at feeding time for all you know.

The first time you listen to it you might not know exactly what it is, but hearing your friends' voices would provide some reference points. Rewind, play it again. By the fourth time through the recording, you could probably snap your fingers at the same time the car door shuts and when the knuckles hit the door, and before listening 10 times you would probably have the whole puzzle solved.

In a way, that sort of memory is at the heart of playing by ear. That is, hearing, recognizing, and identifying familiar sounds.

The other part, reproducing the sounds, is to a certain extent just a matter of coordination and muscle memory. A person who can "play piano by ear" for instance, can do the same thing with any instrument, once sufficient coordination has been developed. The coordination simply provides a way for the sounds in your head to be expressed on an instrument.

In *Webster's Dictionary*, a musical progression is described as "the manner in which chords or melodic tones follow one another, a succession of chords or tones."

Another definition refers to a mathematical progression: "a succession of quantities in which there is a constant relation between each member and the one succeeding it."

Yet another definition of progression is: "a passing successively from one member of a series to the next, succession; sequence."

A comprehensive online dictionary I use (**dictionary.onmusic.org**), created by Richard Cole, Virginia Tech Department of Music, and Ed Schwartz, Virginia Tech New Media Center, defines a progression as "a series of two or more chords that are played in succession." (July 2021 - onmusic.org not available - use OxfordReference.com)

I think a good working definition of a chord progression combines bits of all of these examples… a chord progression is "a sequence or series of chords in which there is a relationship between each chord and the one succeeding it."

It's important to notice that there is no restriction placed on the number of different chords in a chord progression. There are lots of songs that use only two chords, hammering away at the same two pegs from beginning to end. There are also progressions that churn through a dozen or more changes before repeating a sequence. There are no rules in pop music.

Also, there are no specific instructions that describe exactly what the "relationship between each chord or melodic tone" will be, only that there is some relation. Which is another way of saying there are no rules. Play any group of chords in any sequence you like and it's OK. It's a legitimate "progression" even if you're the only person on earth who can discern the relationships… and you might be fibbing. It's still OK.

Classical theorists reading this will probably want to discuss the differences between "progressions" and "retrogressions." OK. I'll tell you everything I know. There is such a thing as a "retrogression," and it is significantly different than "progression" in the way it is spelled. Hopefully, that clears up any questions you may have regarding retrogressions.

Retrogressing back to progressions.

Practically speaking, in a performance or a band, if spontaneous and rhythmically random chord improvisation comprises the bulk of your repertoire, as a general thing you will probably cause serious anxiety when playing with the other children and not often draw large, appreciative audiences.

So, what we're going to consider here are chord progressions as they relate to "popular" songs. Songs you might play with friends at parties or out Christmas caroling or picnics, or songs you hear on the radio or your CD collection or online and might play at a bar gig or wedding.

Here in the western hemisphere of our little planet, we tend to use and re-use certain sequences of chords in all genres of our music… from jazz to reggae to bluegrass to classical to folk to blues to metal.

NO matter what your musical preferences are, or which continent you live on, the same 12 notes are used, keys are identified by the same scale/chord sequences and progressions are constructed using the same basic chords. Wolfgang Amadeus Mozart, Wes Montgomery, Bob Marley, Ozzie Osborne, and Hank Williams all used the same 12 notes. So will you… that's all there are.

A progression that uses only two chords has the fewest moving parts, so that seems like a good place to begin. How about we use the key of C for a change. Surprise!! As you know, the first six chords in the key of C are C major (**I**), D minor (**ii**), E minor (**iii**), F major (**IV**), G major (**V**), and A minor (**vi**).

When spelling a C chord (C-E-G) and an A minor chord (A-C-E), you'll notice that the two chords both use the notes C and E. Is this a "relationship?" Yes. The **I** chord and the **vi** chord share that same relationship in all major keys. Remember "relative minor?"

Play C for four beats, then A minor for four beats, and repeat ad nauseum. That would be referred to as a "**I vi**" progression in the key of C.

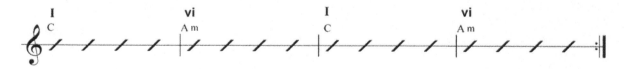

C major (C-E-G) and G major (G-B-D) share the G note. Play C for four beats, then G for four beats, repeat a few times, and that is a "**I V**" progression in the key of C.

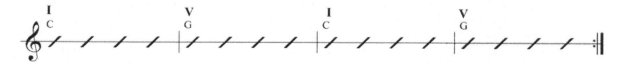

A **I V**[7] is an example of a common two-chord progression. "Tulsa Time" (recorded by Eric Clapton), "Jambalaya" (Hank Williams, Sr.), "Take Me Back to Tulsa" (Bob Wills), "Chugalug" (Roger Miller) use only the **I** and **V** (or **V**[7]). "You Can't Always Get What You Want" by the Rolling Stones is about 98% **I** and **IV**. There are certainly hundreds, probably thousands, of tunes that use only two chords.

D minor (D-F-A) and F major (F-A-C) share the notes F and A. In the key of C, those two chords played in sequence could be referred to as a "**ii IV**" progression.

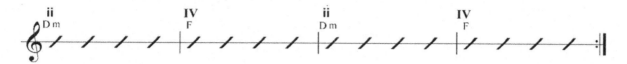

I IV V is the chord progression that comprises the majority of blues, rock, country, and bluegrass songs. There are literally thousands of songs that use only these three chords.

In a playing situation, if somebody said to you, "This song is easy, it's just a '**I IV V**' in C"… it doesn't necessarily mean that the progression is going to be only C, F, and G in that order with an equal number of beats on each chord. The progression might be "**I-IV-V**" or "**IV-V-I**" or "**V-I-IV-I**" or some other combination. "**I IV V**" in C just means that C, F, and G are the three chords that are used most in that song. "This Land Is Your Land" is a **I IV V** that starts on **IV**.

This could be referred to as a "**I IV V**" in C.

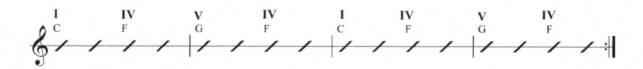

So could this.

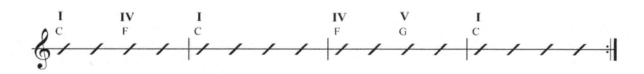

"**I IV V**" is probably the single most common three-chord combination. Thousands upon thousands of songs, from the first chord to the last, use only these three chords. Sometimes the song will be in a major key, sometimes a minor key, in many different time signatures, and with different grooves. You can play a whole lotta music with just the **I IV V**.

A point to be aware of is the interval between the root of the **I** chord up to the root of the **IV** chord, and the interval between the root of the **I** chord down to the root of the **V** chord.

Remember inverting intervals?

From the root of the **I** up to the root of the **IV** is a 4th. Between the root of the **I** chord and the root of the **V** is a 5th. Right? Until you invert the interval and go **down** from the root to the **V**. Then the root of the **V** chord is also found a 4th away from the root of the **I** chord.

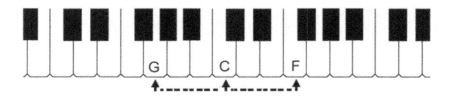

Now let's go the other way. From root of the **I** up to the root of the **V** is a 5th. Between the root of the **I** chord and the root of the **IV** is a 4th, until you invert the interval and go down to the root of the **IV**. Then it is a 5th.

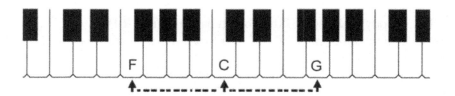

On a piano the root of the **I** chord can be seen as being exactly in the middle between the roots of the **IV** chord and the **V** chord. Visually it's balanced, symmetrical.

Most of the strings on a guitar are separated by a 4th.

What that means to guitarists is that you can move the root of a chord from the fifth string to the fourth string and then to the sixth string while staying on the same fret and play a **I-IV-V** in any key and it doesn't really require intense concentration.

Here's an example of using simple power chords in the key of D.

This example showed the root on the fifth fret and the result is a **I-IV-V** in the key of D. And, the root of the **I** is on the A string, right in between the **IV** chord and the **V** chord.

Notice that the root for all three chords is found on the fifth fret. The fifth fret on the fifth string is a D, so this is in the key of D.

Move up one (1) half step to the sixth fret and you have a **I-IV-V** in D#. Move down to the fourth fret, it's a **I-IV-V** in Db. Up to the seventh fret and it's a **I-IV-V** in E. Down to the third fret and it's a **I-IV-V** in G. This illustration shows a very simple chord: root, 5th, and root. But it works the same way with all of the chords that are more complex, too.

Remember, the **I-IV-V is the single most common three-chord progression in pop music.** Blues, bluegrass, folk, and rock are all heavy users of the **I-IV-V** progression. The chords will usually be a bit more complex than I've illustrated, but this is the nucleus of it, right here.

Here's another bonus. When you locate **I-IV-V** in any key if you know the major scale, you have solid reference points for finding the rest of the chords.

I is always a half step above vii, and a whole step below ii—in all keys.
IV is always a half step above iii and a whole step below **V**—in all keys.
V is always a whole step above **IV** and a whole step below vi—in all keys.

Without any research at all to back me up, I'm going to guess out loud right here in public that the second most common three-chord sequence would be "**ii-V-I**." I'm not aware of as many songs that use only **ii-V-I**, but there are a lot that use **ii-V-I** for much of the tune. **ii-V-I** is especially important in jazz, but you'll find it everywhere.

And guess what? Between **ii** and **V** is a 4th, and between **I** and **V** is a 4th.

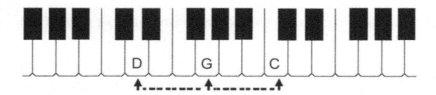

Get your songbook and observe how often the roots of sequential chords are separated by 4^{ths}. I'll discuss it later in this chapter on the page called "What else can you do with two-five-one?" it happens a lot and it's sometimes real convenient that a guitar happens to be tuned mostly in 4^{ths}. Somehow, I don't think that's just a happy accident. Somebody, a long time ago, figured out something important and useful. I wouldn't be surprised if it was an ancestor of Craig Hall.

Mandolins, violins, mandolas, violas, and cellos are tuned in 5^{ths}, so it works the same way, only "upside down," sort of.

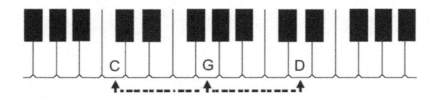

This eight-bar phrase in the key of C starts with **ii-V-I**, then goes to **IV-V-I**, then to **vi-ii-V-I**.

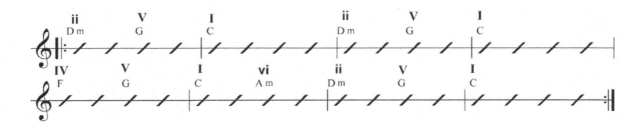

I play in an acoustic duo called Two Grass Crew with a really fine musician, Mike Parsons, who mostly plays mandolin and fiddle. He can play anything, actually, but in this outfit it's mando and fiddle. We've taken the liberty of rearranging a couple of Bach's pieces to suit our own purposes.

We like to play them using chords, which is not the way they were written. When you look at the roots of the chords that are implied by the two lines that Mr. Bach wrote, you'll see this motion of 4ths through both tunes. I included the chords we use (and a tabbed melody line) for both songs in this chapter. These tunes are fun to play using the triads in this chapter, as well as open position chords.

So, think back to chord structure for a moment. Recall the tones used by the ii chord (re, fa, and la) compared to the tones used in the **IV** chord (fa, la, and do). Nearly the same triad. We western humans seem to like the sound of **I-IV-V** and **ii-V-I**. I can't explain why, but it certainly is true. If you plan on writing a pop hit, this is not a bad place to start.

Although there are thousands of tunes that use only two or three chords from top to bottom, thousands more will combine two or three short progression that last for a couple of measures into longer phrases that may fill eight, 12, or 16 bars.

Understanding that an enormous percentage of songs use simple progressions as a "structural base" is an extremely useful tool for "playing by ear." When you take the time to familiarize yourself with a handful of common progressions, you will start to hear them in your favorite songs.

You won't necessarily be able to identify the "key," but you can learn to recognize "**I-IV-V**" and "**ii-V-I**" and "**I-vi-ii V**" and "**I-III-IV**", etc. These are identifiable sounds. Just like a meadowlark and a robin and a chickadee all have voices that are similar to each other, yet distinct and unique, progressions have characteristics that are audible and identifiable. I have many friends and acquaintances who can identify progressions correctly and with relative ease, and none is a "musical genius."

This is an acquirable skill. It just requires practice. So… practice. The exercises in this chapter are intended to facilitate the process.

It seems to me that the first step is to recognize that these patterns exist, and then find some of them in the music you enjoy, and then practice playing them and listening for them.

My ear probably functions internally just the same as your ear does, but my memory has been taught to recognize sounds and my hands are "trained" to find those sounds. It's not magic, it's not a "gift." It's largely a result of hours of sitting by my stereo with an instrument and working.

So… I hope that "How can I practice hearing progressions?" is on your list of questions now.

I can recommend a few things. There is no such thing as "the most important" or best way to train your "ear." The main thing to remember is that you are training your mind, and repetition, repetition, repetition is the key.

One way is to play them… in different places on the guitar. I've supplied a few common progressions at the end of this chapter so you can start playing them right away.

Start with the first position, or "open" chords. Play **I IV V** in G. **G, C, and D. Fifty times. A hundred times. It takes a while.**

Play **I-IV-V** in A.	**A, D, and E.**	**Fifty times.**	**A hundred times.**	**It takes a while.**
Play **I-IV-V** in C.	**C, F, and G.**	**Fifty times.**	**A hundred times.**	**It takes a while.**
Play **I-IV-V** in D.	**D, G, and A.**	**Fifty times.**	**A hundred times.**	**It takes a while.**
Play **I-IV-V** in E.	**E, A, and B.**	**Fifty times.**	**A hundred times.**	**It takes a while.**

The easiest way that I know of to do this is to use simple triads on the B, G, and D strings as shown on pages 424-427. You don't need a six-note barre chord in order to hear the progressions.

Mix them up. I-IV-I-V or IV-I-V-I or V-IV-I, or whatever. Make some up. Play it for a while in one position, and then move to a different fret and play there for a while. REPETITION. REPETITION. REPETITION.

If you will take the time to examine the progressions in 50 of your favorite songs, you'll learn a lot more than if I burn 50 pages trying to explain it.

Here's what you should do. Get the songbook you're working with and the transposing chart and number all of the chords in one song. Then go back and look for the I chord. Notice which chord precedes I and which chord follows I. Go all the way through each song and look at groups of three and four chords that begin or end with the I chord. If you are working with *The New Real Book* (Sher Music), it would probably be excessive to analyze all 400 songs, but it would be a good thing to examine at least 15 or 20 of them. Many songwriters seem to have favorite progressions, so it's helpful to check out more than one artist. "Analyze and imitate, it's the only school that is necessary."

A "normal" workweek is 40 hours. It you'll invest this much time analyzing the progressions in your favorite tunes over the course of a couple of months, the return will be big.

Play through the progressions on the following pages. I showed a few possibilities, but there are lots of other combinations.

The chart a few pages back shows nine different progressions in C and you can use the open position chords to hear the progressions.

After you get familiar with playing these progressions as shown, there are loads of variations that you can experiment with.

You can alter the 3rd in all of them, any that are shown as major chords can be played as minor chords; any that are shown as minor chords can be played as major chords.

A common substitute is to replace any chord with the diatonic triad that is a 3rd away. That means you could substitute **ii** or **vi** for the **IV**. In the key of C, that would be substituting D minor or A minor for F.

Try replacing the **I** chord with the **iii** or **vi**. In the key of C that would be replacing C major with A minor or E minor.

Definitely try playing the progressions using all the extended and altered chords from the chapter "**Beyond Major and Minor Chords**."

Learning to use these numbers for chords and solfege for notes in a way eliminates all the individual keys, at least in the process of thinking about songs and figuring them out. In western music, it's almost as if there is only one key… the key of DO.

This isn't true, of course, but it's not exactly incorrect either, when considered in this context. It's an extremely useful concept because it can help simplify the process of figuring songs out by ear.

In this context, when trying to find the roots of the chords in a new tune, there are only six probable root notes… DO, RE, MI, FA, SO, and LA… with an occasional mystery chord. For beginners (and me, too) the key of G works well on a guitar because **I-ii IV-V** and **vi** are all easy chords. Bm (the iii chord) is a bit harder, but it's not used as often. The key of C works well, too, but most beginners have trouble with the F chord, and **IV** is more commonly used than the **iii** chord. I can usually sort out the progression pretty quickly and then it's just a matter of transposing the key to accommodate the singer.

Initially, I'm not terrifically concerned about the chord extensions and alterations, that comes later, but I want to get the chord qualities (major or minor) right. When I can hack my way through it slowly, that's what I do... play it a bunch of times slowly in this simplified form. When you play through it 20 times, you'll find all the root notes, but you start thinking, "That chord doesn't sound quite right... maybe it should be a minor instead. Or maybe it's a major 7."

Often, I'll use the triad progressions you're about to learn for this part of the process, because when you can play them well, it's easy to try a bunch of keys.

Recall the trumpet player from the Baroque era and his collection of trumpets. He read in the key of C, knew a single fingering pattern, and applied it to all of the different sized horns.

What about the present day harmonica player who has a different harp for each key? Like the trumpet player, a harp player can know a single pattern of blow and draw notes and by using different harmonicas, play really well in all keys.

Remember how capos work? You can learn a few open position chords on a guitar (G, Am, C, D, and Em, for instance) and those few chords are enough to play a **I-IV-V** progression, a **ii-V-I** progression, and a **I-iv-ii-V** in the key of G. By using a capo, you can play those same progressions in all keys, using the same fingering.

I play piano a little bit, and I do OK with the key of C, but I'm certainly no keyboard player. I usually play guitar in live band situations, but I have been hired to play keys a couple of times (in last minute desperation) and they did not play all the tunes in the key of C. However, modern keyboards often have an electronic capo built in. Push the right buttons and it automatically transposes the keyboard so I can continue to play in C while the rest of the band is playing in A or F# or B♭ or whatever.

Whether you find it easier to use Roman numerals or the Nashville number system is a matter of personal preference. You should definitely learn to understand this system, because it is the quickest way to analyze a chord progression. If you can analyze it, you can imitate it, and then you can alter it, to make up your own progressions.

Experiment. A lot.

Think about it... 20 hours of focused practice on the **I-IV-V** and then 20 hours getting real familiar with the **ii-V-I** (see "Doin' the Two-Five-One" in this chapter) is only 40 hours. It's not a lot if you intend to play music for the next 100 years or so, considering the fact that these two three-chord progressions are by far the most commonly encountered progressions in pop music. If you will spend the time required to recognize the sound of these progressions, you will be a long way down the trail of learning to "play by ear."

The triads shown on the next pages can be a regular part of your daily "scales and variations" workout. Notice that the root notes as shown make most of a major scale. I left the seventh triad out because a **V7** is used a lot more often than the diminished triad. You'll figure it out. Have fun.

Something I've made no attempt to explain is how to do this and be musical about it. That's a big part of the magic and mystery, how two people can play essentially the same notes, and convey two entirely different stories. Feel, groove, dynamics, and phrasing are all concepts that contribute to making progressions and scales into musical expression and creativity.

Part of the process of "analyze and imitate" is recognizing the techniques your favorite players use to communicate. It's not just the notes. Phrasing and feel are often more important than the choice of notes. Acoustic or electric, clean or distorted, heavy or gentle, loud or soft, there are thousands of combinations of techniques employed to adapt these progressions to every style of music.

Reflections

*"The marvelous richness of human experience would lose something of rewarding joy
if there were no limitations to overcome. The hilltop hour would not be half so wonderful
if there were no dark valleys to traverse."*
Helen Keller

*"The meaning of song goes deep.
Who in logical words can explain the effect music has on us?
A kind of inarticulate, unfathomable speech,
which leads us to the edge of the infinite, and lets us for a moment gaze into that!"*
Thomas Carlyle

"The most stupendous miracle in all music."
Richard Wagner, commenting on the music of Johann Sebastian Bach

"The music plays the band."
Bob Weir

"The only way around is through."
Robert Frost

*"The price of success is hard work, dedication to the job at hand,
and the determination that whether we win or lose,
we have applied the best of ourselves to the task at hand."*
Vince Lombardi

"The race is not always to the swift, but to those who keep on running."
Unknown

"The road to success is dotted with many tempting parking places."
Unknown

"The secret of success is constancy of purpose."
Benjamin Disraeli

*"The things we fear most in organizations, fluctuations, disturbances, imbalances,
are the primary sources of creativity."*
Margaret J. Wheatley

*"There is always music amongst the trees in the garden,
but our hearts must be very quiet to hear it. "*
M. Aumonier

"The shorter way to do many things is to do only one thing at a time."
Wolfgang Amadeus Mozart

*"The spirit, the will to win, and the will to excel are the things that endure.
These qualities are so much more important than the events that occur."*
Vince Lombardi

Some four-bar progressions

Here are a few phrases for you to practice. I supplied chord names for five keys, so you can strum through them right away without having to do a bunch of pencil work. But if you want to really learn this stuff, you **need to do the pencil work**. I suggest that you make some charts and write these out in several keys.

Remember the discussion of Strumming Patterns when I mentioned that you're expected to make up your own part? Well, that's what you should do here. At first, play them as shown, with two strums on each chord. If you're just learning the chords and it's tough to change chords that quickly, strum four times before you change, or eight times… or 98 times.

Then start to experiment with different strumming patterns. One way to alter this pattern of two beats on each chord is to strum each chord three times. Suddenly you have a whole bunch of waltzes. Want to get real wild? Experiment with different time signatures. Strum the first chord in each measure three times, the second chord twice, and now you're playing in 5/4 time. Four strums on the first chord and three on the second chord, and you're playing in 7/4.

Then, alter the qualities of the chords… turn the major chords into minor chords and the minor chords into major chords. Experiment with extensions and alterations. You can mix up the different lines. Play line 1 followed by line 6, then maybe line 3, then line 9… whatever. Play them backwards. Skip from the first measure of line 1 to the second measure of line 2 to the third measure of line 3, etc.

When you play something that you think sounds cool, write it out and name it. No one can "copyright" a chord progression, so these progressions and all of the rest of them in this book… and EVERY OTHER BOOK… are fair game to use as a foundation for your own songs. Go for it. It's fun. Remember what Raymond Chandler said, "Analyze and imitate. No other school is necessary." Analyze the progressions in your favorite artists' songs and imitate them. Play the same chords with a different feel, sing a different tune, make up some different words, and voila!… you're a songwriter… you might wind up on the cover of the *Rolling Stone*.

ALERT!! In the previous paragraph I wrote, "No one can copyright a chord progression" and suggested that you go ahead and do it. Then, several months later I was forced to research some copyright infringement cases and found one instance of a judgment in a copyright infringement case which ruled that it IS possible to own a progression. The estate of Duke Ellington successfully sued the estate of Billy Strayhorn over royalties paid for the song "Satin Doll." The court found that a harmonic progression alone could support a claim of copyright interest in a derivative musical work. So, in spite of the fact that there are thousands of compositions that use identical progressions, it is remotely possible that you could wind up in VERY DEEP DOO DOO if you copy and use pre-existing progressions. (I am not about to show the chords to "Satin Doll" here!) I promise, I won't sue you if you use the progressions I've shown here. But there is a saying among the copyright lawyers in England… "Hits Cause Writs." If you manage to create something that is commercially successful, you become a target for an infringement lawsuit. George Harrison (The Beatles) was sued for his song "My Sweet Lord" which is very similar to the song "He's So Fine" by Ronald Mack (recorded by The Chiffons). Harrison said that he did not knowingly use the melody of the Chiffon's song. The decision was unique in that the court acknowledged that Harrison might have *unconsciously* copied the tune. The court stated: "His subconscious knew it already had worked in a song that his conscious mind did not remember… under the law that is infringement of copyright, and is no less so even though subconsciously accomplished."

There is a famous (and somewhat cynical) line that I have seen attributed to Picasso, Van Gogh, and T.S. Eliot… "Good artists borrow, great artists steal." Another is, "If you use one author's work, that's plagiarism. If you use 10 authors' work, that's research." Albert Einstein said, "The secret to creativity is knowing how to hide your sources."

"Analyze and imitate" is a valid approach to developing your own style. Using existing progressions as a foundation for your own songs is absolutely OK, I believe. Be creative… write a new melody, change the time signature, do something different… and make it "your own."

Eight Four-bar Progressions

I	ii	iii	IV	V	vi	vii
C	Dm	Em	F	G	Am	Bdim

I	ii	iii	IV	V	vi	vii
A	Bm	C#m	D	E	F#m	G#dim

I	ii	iii	IV	V	vi	vii
G	Am	Bm	C	D	Em	F#m

I	ii	iii	IV	V	vi	vii
E	F#m	G#m	A	B	C#m	F#dim

I	ii	iii	IV	V	vi	vii
D	Em	F#m	G	A	Bm	C#dim

Four Eight-bar Progressions

Here are four eight-bar progressions that you'll find in many styles. If you're playing a banjo in the key of G, then these will sound bluegrassy. Crank up the distorted electric guitar, use "power chords" and they should sound like rock songs. If you play with a swing feel and use lots of six chords (C6, G6/9, etc.), it will sound like country swing. Use the keys of A and E with a hard shuffle and they will sound like blues. There are major keys and minor keys shown below.

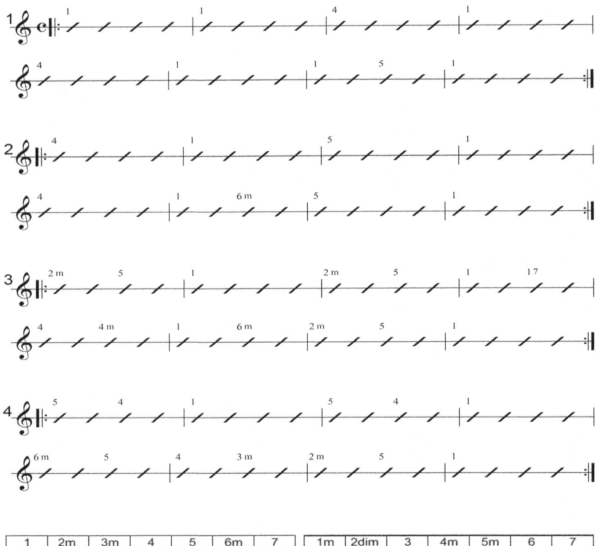

1	2m	3m	4	5	6m	7
C	Dm	Em	F	G	Am	Bdim
A	Bm	C#m	D	E	F#m	G#dim
G	Am	Bm	C	D	Em	F#m
E	F#m	G#m	A	B	C#m	F#dim

1m	2dim	3	4m	5m	6	7
Am	Bdim	C	Dm	Em	F	G
Em	F#dim	G	Am	Bm	C	D
Dm	Edim	F	Gm	Am	B	C

Using Triads in Progressions

Have you ever seen a guitarist who is playing what seems to be a really complex chord progression, but somehow barely moves the hand that's fretting all the chords? This is an introduction to how that works.

Any five-fret section of a guitar neck spans two full octaves, plus a major 3rd. That is enough notes to play any chord without having to shift your hand up or down the neck.

I limited this illustration to three strings: D, G, and B, but it works no matter how many strings you use. Using triads is a good approach to take when you're playing with another guitarist who is using mostly open chords, or any kind of band situation. Often when there are a couple of other instruments, it's a good thing to play fewer notes. Sometimes I like to pretend that I'm a three or four-piece horn section because more notes can get in the way of the other players. The extended triads I showed in "**Beyond Major and Minor Chords**" are fair game here, I'm just using simple triads for the explanation.

Notice that the difference between the **I** chord and the **vi** chord is a single note. Same is true for the **I** and **iii** chords, the **IV** and **vi**, as well as the **ii** and **IV**. Notice that changing from **I** to **ii** is just a matter of sliding the **I** chord up one whole step and flatting the 3rd. Same drill to get from **iii** to **IV**.

The shading on these fretboards is there to show how triads in a given key all fit in a small space on the neck. The bar that joins the fretboards just marks the middle. Notice that at least five out of six triads can be played within a span of four frets. The root is indicated by a circle. When Form #5 is played on these three strings, there is no 3rd, which makes it a power chord. I still think that's a silly name for a chord.

6 Diatonic Triads Using Form #1 as the I Chord

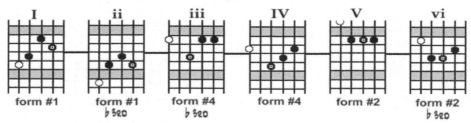

6 Diatonic Triads Using Form #2 as the I Chord

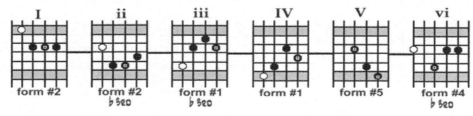

6 Diatonic Triads Using Form #4 as the I Chord

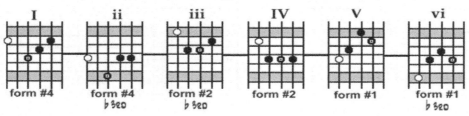

Common Progressions Using Form #1 as the I Chord

Progressions Using 3 Chords

Progressions Using 4 Chords

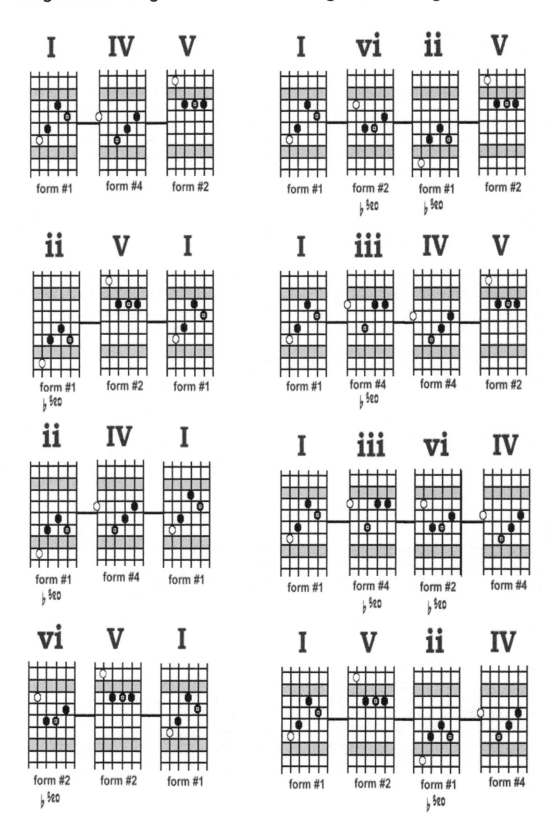

11 - Chord Progressions

Common Progressions Using Form #2 as the I Chord

Progressions Using 3 Chords

Progressions Using 4 Chords

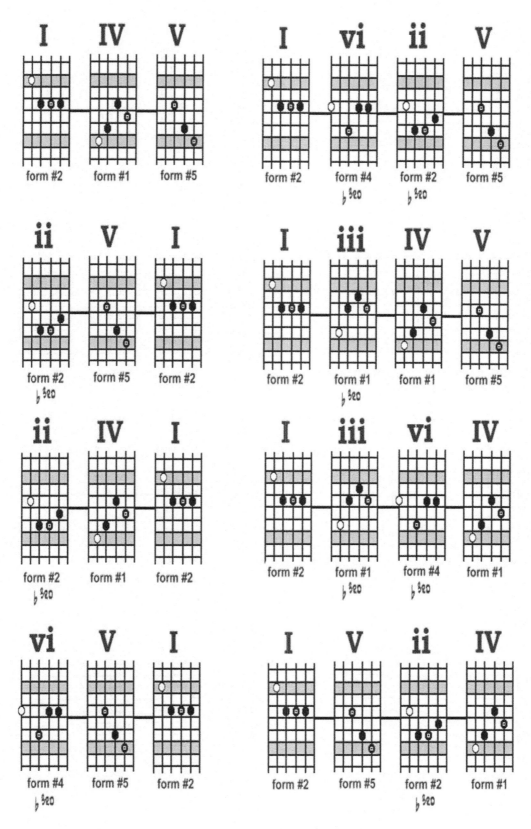

Common Progressions Using Form #4 as the I Chord

Progressions Using 3 Chords   ## Progressions Using 4 Chords

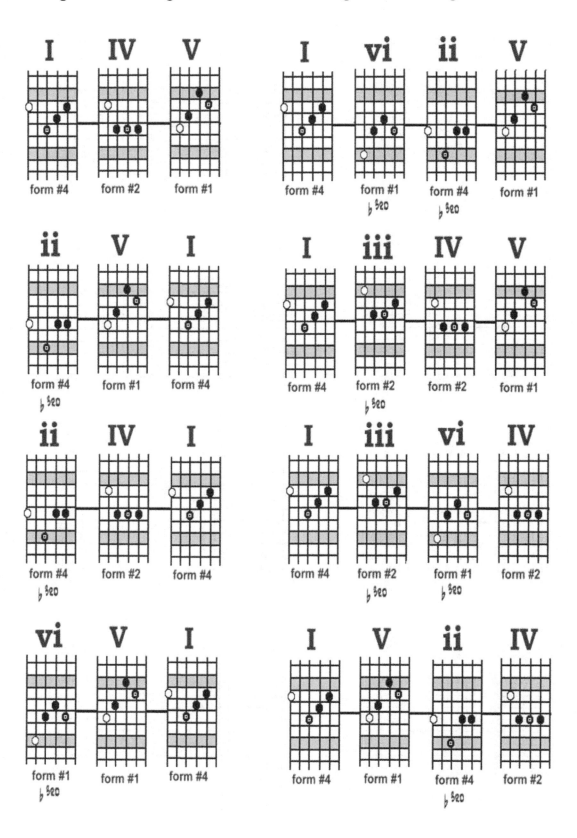

More of the Same… On Different Strings

I use the triads shown on the second, third, and fourth strings a lot, but there is no reason to limit yourself to those three strings. Here are the same progressions using triads on other strings. Eventually, you want to be able to "mix and match" using all of these triads. You might play part of a song, the first verse for example, using the triads on the second, third, and fourth strings. Then play the next part (chorus) using triads on strings three, four, and five. When you play the second verse comes around, you could go back to strings two, three, and four, but this time maybe use a different form for the **I** chord, so you would be playing the same chords, but in a different place on the neck.

The notes on the staff are an excellent visual reminder of how little motion is required to play these progressions. If you have a keyboard, play these progressions on it, too.

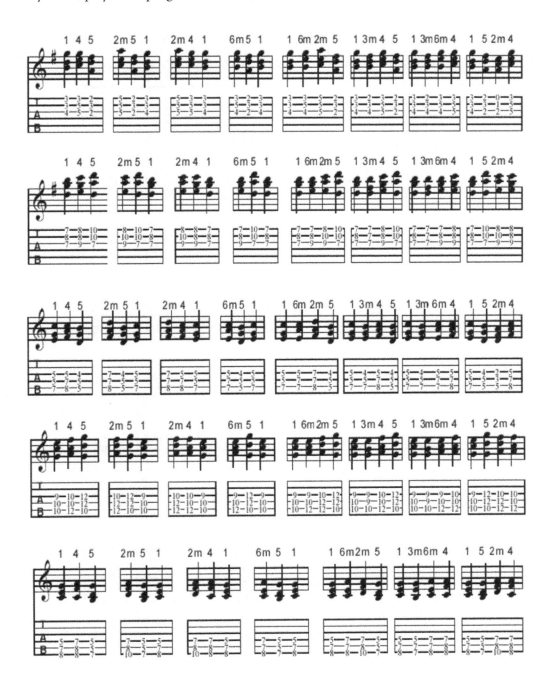

This series will work for mandolin, mandola, and tenor banjo. On these instruments you often look for the roots of chords on the first and second strings. The **I** chord on this page has the root on the first string.

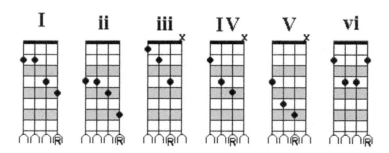

Progressions Using 3 Chords   ## Progressions Using 4 Chords

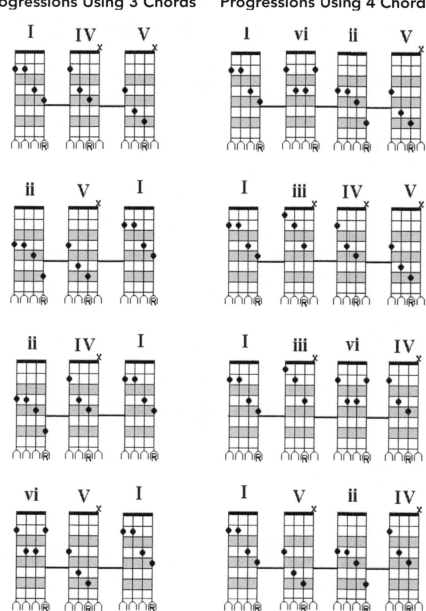

11 - Chord Progressions

The root of the **I** chord is on the second string in these progressions.

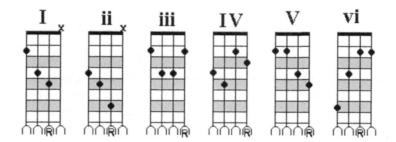

Progressions Using 3 Chords

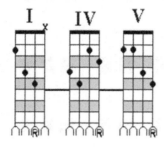

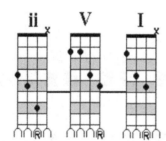

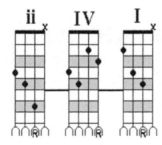

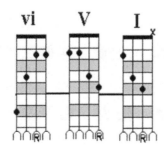

Progressions Using 4 Chords

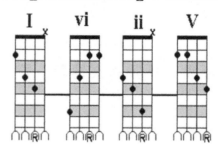

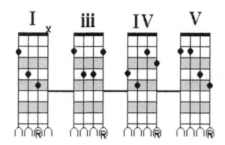

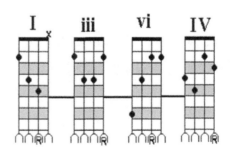

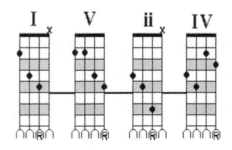

Simple Progressions Using Triads on a Keyboard

This is a look at one way that the triad progressions we're examining lay out on a keyboard. These are the same as if a guitar was playing Form #4 as the **I** chord, with DO on the 10th fret of the fourth string. You don't need to be an accomplished pianist to be able to make this stuff work on a keyboard. You'll want to play a left-hand bass note with each chord.

It's very useful to be able to visualize a keyboard. I can think about music using that visual image and the key of C to figure things out when I'm nowhere near an instrument. If you think driving while talking on a cell phone is dangerous, try driving while thinking about chord stuff. Never mind. It's a bad idea. Gets way too exciting sometimes. Have you ever driven on a sidewalk?

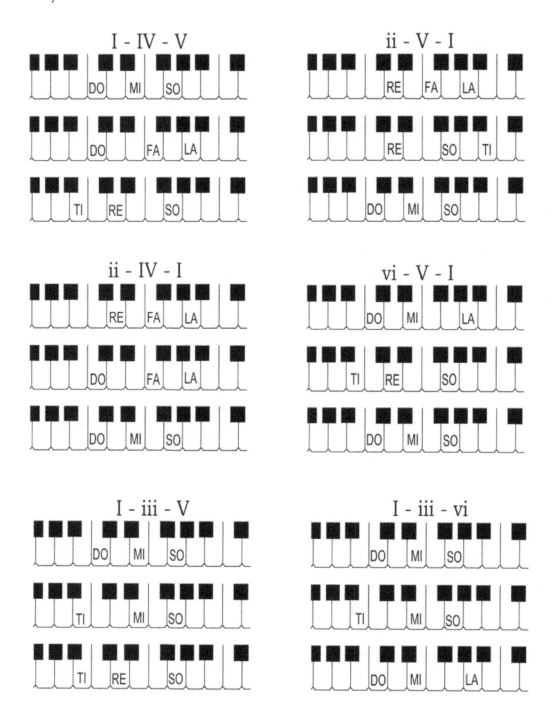

Reflections

"We will either find a way, or make one."
Hannibal

"What a poor appearance the tales of poets make
when stripped of the colors which music puts upon them,
and recited in simple prose."
Plato

"What this power is I cannot say. All I know is that it exists.
It becomes available only when a man is in that state of mind in which he knows
exactly what he wants and is fully determined not to quit until he finds it."
Alexander Graham Bell

"What you get by achieving your goals is not as important
as what you become by achieving your goals."
Zig Ziglar

"When God created Man,
he gave him Music as a language different from all other languages.
And early man sang his glory in the wilderness;
and drew the hearts of kings and moved them from their thrones."
Kalil Gibran

"When I don't like a piece of music, I make a point of listening to it more closely."
Florent Schmitt

"When I hear music I fear no danger, I am invulnerable, I see no foe.
I am related to the earliest times and to the latest."
Henry David Thoreau

"When people hear good music,
it makes them homesick for something they never had, and never will have."
Ed Howe

"When the world says, "Give up," Hope whispers, "Try it one more time."
Attributed, **Alex and Jerry Sharp, Hopi Glenn**

"When we rejoice in great music and art,
it is but the flexing of instincts learned in the previous life."
Neal Maxwell

"When you come to the end of your rope, tie a knot and hang on."
Franklin D. Roosevelt

"When your heart is in your dreams, no request is too extreme."
Jiminy Cricket

Doin' the Two-Five-One

Here's a 16-bar phrase that you can use to get accustomed to a two-five-one progression. Use any of the chords on the next page, all I show here are the chord roots and quality. This is common in a live situation. You'll get a chart with minimal information shown and you frequently get to choose which extensions are appropriate according to what you like best.

Don't forget to try it in a bunch of different keys. There's a little bit of room between the staffs so you can write changes for a couple of keys, but at some point you'll probably want to write out some new charts (see page 482).

In addition to **ii-V-I**, you'll notice a few other chords. Measure 10 has a **iv** chord, measure 11 has a **iii** chord, followed by **VI** and **II**. There is a **I-vi-ii-V** turnaround in bars 15 and 16. You'll have to make some adjustments. For example, in the key of G, the **vi** chord is an E minor, so just use any of the D minor forms, but move the root up one whole step.

Speaking of roots, you'll notice there are several instances when the voicing that is shown has no root in it. The letter R shows where it is. You'll notice that it isn't necessary to play a root and still get a cool sound. I recommend that once again you fill in the blanks at the bottom of the chord diagram so you know which tones you're playing.

Once again, my thanks to Craig Hall for his help with this exercise. The way these three-chord groups move from one chord to the next is an excellent example of voice leading. When you look at the diagrams, notice how little motion is required between the chords.

If the four-note chords on the next page are a bit beyond your skills, practice playing the changes using the diatonic triads as shown on the diagram at the bottom of this page. You'll get there, just keep practicing.

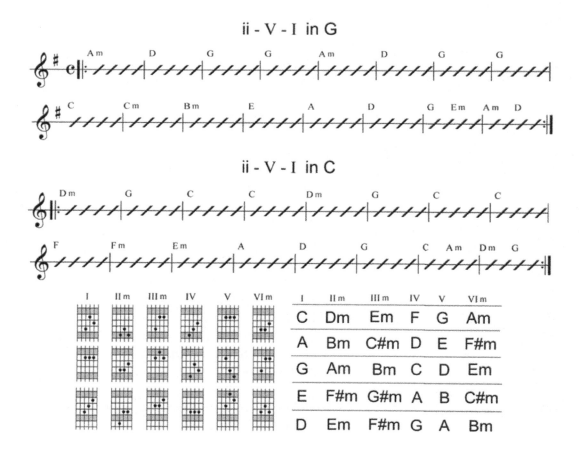

ii V I in G

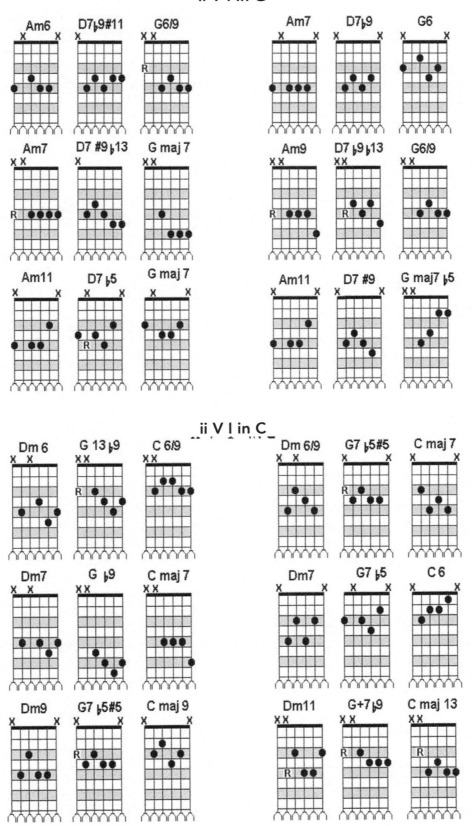

ii V I in C

What else can you do with two-five-one?

You'll remember that I've mentioned the importance of the interval of a 4th in regard to progressions. Notice that these three root notes (D-G-C) will generate a ii-V-I progression in the key of C, and that they are separated by an interval of a 4th.

Look at the key of G as shown below in the transposing chart. Those same three root notes (D-S-C) can be seen as I-VI and V. If you play the ii-V-I progressions as shown on the previous pages, but make the quality of all three of the chords major, the same pattern produces I-IV-V in the key of G. Magic.

The I-IV-V and the ii-V-I are probably the two most common three-chord progressions in pop music, followed closely by vi-ii-V. Have a look at the key of F. Make the G and D both minor chords and the C a major chord and now it's vi-ii-V in the key of F.

Look at the key of B♭. Play all three as some sort of minor chord and you have ii-iii-vi in B♭. Look at E♭. The diatonic vii chord is rarely used as central figure in a chord progression, but there is certainly no rule that says you can't use it.

There are many structures in music that serve "double-duty" when you make certain small adjustments. The ii-V-I is an important progression and so are the I-V and V progression and the vi-ii-V. In some aspects, they are very similar to each other.

It is absolutely worth your time to analyze the chord progressions that are used by your favorite artists. Nearly everyone makes use of 4ths between the root notes of the chords. Be aware of the concept of inverting intervals while you're doing it. Up a 4th and down a 5th from C (for example) generates an F note.

The exercise on the previous pages is labeled "Doin' the Two-Five-One" but as you can see, with some effort and brain sweat, this motion of 4ths generates much more than a single progression. Try to wear these pages out, you will learn more about "pop" music than you might imagine. In fact, 7-3-6-2-5-1 can be viewed as a single progression. Check out the tune "Blues for Alice," by Charlie Parker. Parts of this progression, like 6-2-5 and in fact, 2-5, and even just 5-1, are all, then, part of that same progression. (Thanks again, Craig Hall.)

"Autumn Leaves" (Joseph Kosma) is another well-known tune that cycles through a series of 4ths. It's commonly played in the key of G (natural) minor. The verse starts with the iv chord, plays four beats on each chord, and the only non-diatonic chord is the V chord, played with a major quality instead of minor.

That old favorite, "Michael, Row Your Boat Ashore," is 1/// 1/// 4//// 1/// 3m/ 6m/ 2m/// 5/// 1///.

Since there are no "rules" as to which chord extensions and alterations are "correct," you can use most of them in a live situation as long as you don't interfere with what else is going on, such as another chord player (keys, guitar, banjo, etc.), a soloist who has his own idea of how he wants the harmony treated, or a big band arrangement with specific horn lines, etc. Not all situations are open to unbridled alteration. Any 7#9 will sound really weird in "You Are My Sunshine," for example, even if you are using it on the V chord.

I've shown you the tip of the iceberg here, and that's about it. This is another one of those topics that a serious player could spend years digging through and never each the end of it.

I chord	ii chord	iii chord	IV chord	V chord	vi chord	vii chord
C Major	D minor	E minor	F Major	G Major	A minor	B m♭5
G Major	A minor	B minor	C Major	D Major	E minor	F# m♭5
F Major	G minor	A minor	B major	C Major	D minor	E m♭5
B♭ Major	C minor	D minor	E♭ Major	F Major	G minor	A m♭5
E♭ Major	F minor	G minor	A♭ Major	B♭ Major	C minor	D m♭5

Eleven Variations on a 12-bar Blues

An enormous percentage of pop music is framed in a 12-bar format. The phrase "12-bar blues" is a reference to that structure. I saw a diagram several years ago that Tuck Andress made showing a few variations of a basic blues progression. I thought it was a good idea, so I borrowed it and expanded on it a bit. (Tuck Andress is a really great, relatively unknown player. (**www.tuckandpatti.com**). If you like Christmas carols on guitar, search for Tuck Andress on iTunes. He has recorded wonderful versions of a lot of the carols I used for examples in this book, as well as one of my favorite versions of "Over The Rainbow.") A real live bargain at 99 cents each.

I didn't know loads of variations at the time, but Craig Hall did, so I asked him if he could supply all the changes. Craig is a remarkable fellow. In addition to being an outstanding musician and a walking encyclopedia of musical information, he has odd habits like climbing around on giant-sized rocks. Mount Shasta, for example. There are no stories about Craig leaping tall buildings at a single bound, but there is a tale about him changing clothes in a public phone booth during a little celebration after wrapping up a recording session with Michael Myers down in Boise. Someone had disguised a couple of quarts of vodka as Kamikazes, and we thought it was safe for human consumption. I think he frightened the person who was in there using the phone.

The following pages show Craig's variations. The top row of chords in the shaded band that is slightly separated from the others is a basic, blues progression in A.

Each line expands on that initial base. Just follow each numbered line and you'll get a great introduction to lots of blues changes. There are diagrams for all the chords you need on the facing page.

These are arranged as if each set of changes is a separate entity, but you can mix them up, too. Use variation #1 for four bars, then variation #2 for four, then #11 for four bars, if that's what you want to do.

This is in A. Number the chords and transpose all over the place. The chords Craig supplied are all movable, so you can use them for the transpositions, too. All of a sudden, this page has about a million ways to play the blues.

This could be called "Eleven Variations on Major Blues," with the I and IV as major chords. But if you flat the 3rd in I and IV, and use a m7♭5 on the V chord, it becomes "Eleven Variations on Minor Blues." Two million ways to play blues changes.

But that's probably not enough for you.

Try using 6 and 6/9 chords for I and IV. Now you're playing what sounds like "swing" or "country/jazz." If you reduce the chords to basic diatonic triads, it will be "advanced changes" for folk and bluegrass.

The chords diagrams I used are basically centered around form #4 as the I chord on the fifth fret, but there's no reason you can't start with A7 in the open position.

There's a lot here, and it will probably be kind of confusing at first.

I have two suggestions: 1. Go slowly. 2. Go slowly.

Get one line down, then add to it. There are guys who have been playing for years who don't know this stuff. I just learned it, and I've been playing guitar for close to 40 years. You'll learn a bunch of chords and (indirectly) about 1,000 songs.

Have fun.

Eleven Variations on a 12-bar Blues by Craig Hall

System 1

Bar 1	Bar 2	Bar 3	Bar 4	
A7	A7	A7	A7	
1. A7	D7	A7	Em7 · · A7	1
A7	D7 · D#dim	A7	Em7 · · Eb9	
3. A7	Bm7 · Cdim	C#m · · Fm7	Em7 · · Eb9	3
A7	D9	A7 · · Bm7	Bbdim7 · · C#m7	
5. A7 · Eb9	D9 · Ebdim7	A7 · · F9	Em7 · · Eb9	5
Ama7 · A#dim	Bm7 · Cdim	Ama7 · · Fm7	Em7 · · Eb7	
7. Ama7 · A#dim	Bm7 · Cdim	C#m7 · · D9	Ebdim · Em7 Eb9	7
A13	D9 · Bb13	A13	A7#5	
9. Ama7 Bm7 Cdim A7	D7 Em7 Ebdim7 D7	Ama7 Bm7 Cdim A7	D7 Ebdim Em7 Eb9	9
Ama7	G#m7b5 · C#7	F#m7 · · Fm7	Em7 · · Eb9	
11. Ama7	G#mb5 · G7	F#m7 · · Fm7	Em7 · · Eb9	11

∕ ∕ ∕ ∕ | ∕ ∕ ∕ ∕ | ∕ ∕ ∕ ∕ | ∕ ∕ ∕ ∕

System 2

Bar 1	Bar 2	Bar 3	Bar 4	
D7	D7	A7	A7	
1. D7	D7 · Ebdim	A7	A7	1
D9	Ebdim	A7	F#7	
3. D7	Ebdim7	A7 · · Fdim7	F#7 · · C7	3
D7	D#dim	A7 · · G7	F#7 · · Cm7	
5. D9	Dm7	C#m7	Cm7	5
D7	Dm7 · G7	C#m7 · · F#7	Cm7 · · F7	
7. D9	Dm7 · G7	Ama7 · · Bm7	C#m7 · · F#7	7
Am7	Am6	Ama7 Bbdim Bm7 Cdim	C#m7 G7 F#7 C7	
9. D9	G7 Am7 Bbdim G7	C#m7	F#7 G#m7 Gdim F#7	9
D7	G7	C#7	C7	
11. D9	Dm7	C#m7	C9	11

∕ ∕ ∕ ∕ | ∕ ∕ ∕ ∕ | ∕ ∕ ∕ ∕ | ∕ ∕ ∕ ∕

System 3

Bar 1	Bar 2	Bar 3	Bar 4	
E7	D7	A7	A7	
1. E7	D7	A7	Bm7 · · E7	1
Bm7	E7	A7 · · F#7	Bm7 · · E7	
3. Bm7	E7	A7 · · F#7	Bm7 · · E7	3
Bm7	E7	C#m7 · · F#7	Bm7 · · E7	
5. B9	Bb7	A7 · · C9	B7 · · Bb9	5
B7	E7	C#m7 · · Cm7	B9 · · Bb7	
7. Bm7 · C#m7	D7 · Ebdim	E7 · · F#m7	G7 · · E7	7
Bm7	Bb9	A6 · · C9	F9 · · Bb9	
9. B7	Bb7 Cm7 C#dim Bb7	A13 · · Bb13	B13 · · E7#9	9
B7	Bb7	A13 · · F#7	G7 · · G#7	
11. B9	Bb7	Bb7	Bb7	11

∕ ∕ ∕ ∕ | ∕ ∕ ∕ ∕ | ∕ ∕ ∕ ∕ | ∕ ∕ ∕ ∕

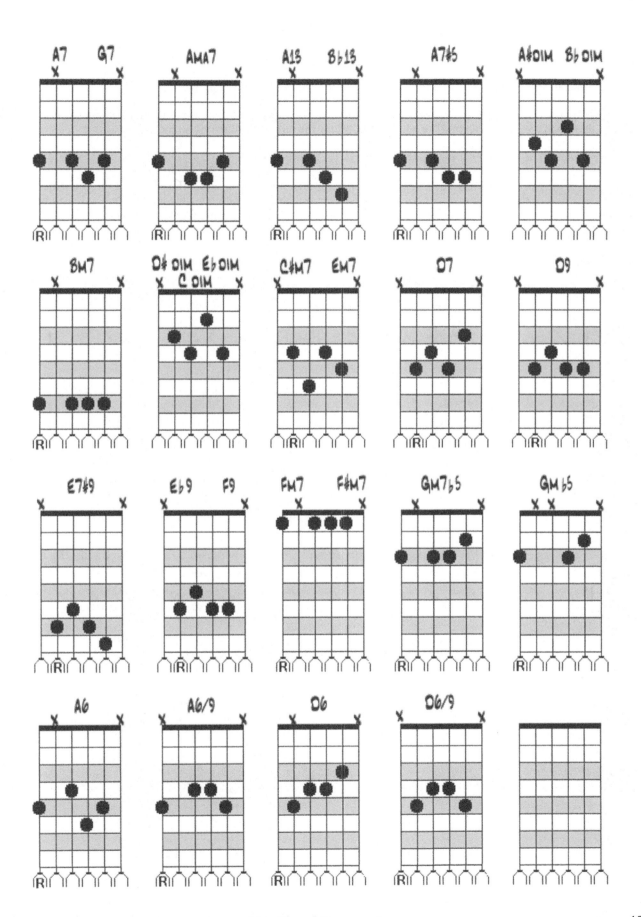

Half Step Substitution

Here is a way to add a lot of changes to a progression without having to learn a bunch of new chords.

This works especially well in jazz and swing tunes, but can be applied to lots of situations.

Passing chords are chords that lead from one chord to another. You're going to add a chord that will be a passing chord on the fourth beat of each measure. It will be like a little "lead in" for the target chord that is on the next beat.

The passing chords will be one (1) half step away from the target chord shown.

It doesn't matter if the passing chord is a half step higher or lower than the "target" chord, the effect is about the same. The chord on the first beat of the second measure is a D9. That means you could use either a D#9 or a D♭9 on the fourth beat of the first measure for your passing chord. Just use the same chord form that you're using for the target chord and slide to the target chord from the passing chord.

At fist, you may want to practice sliding to two target chords at a time, to get used to the move.

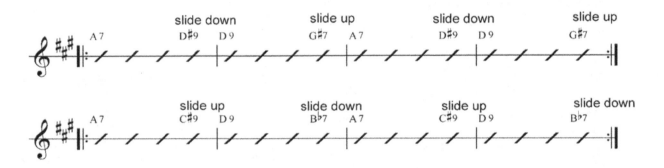

Could you start on the third beat of a measure a whole step away from the "target" chord? I don't know why not…

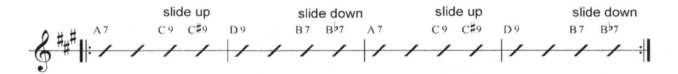

Half Step Substitutions in a 12-bar Blues

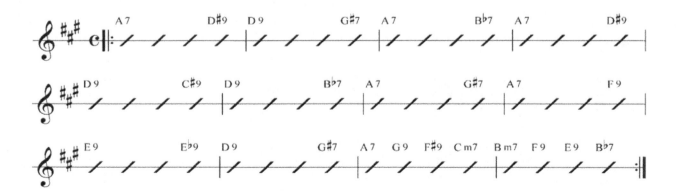

Half Step Substitutions in a 12-bar Blues

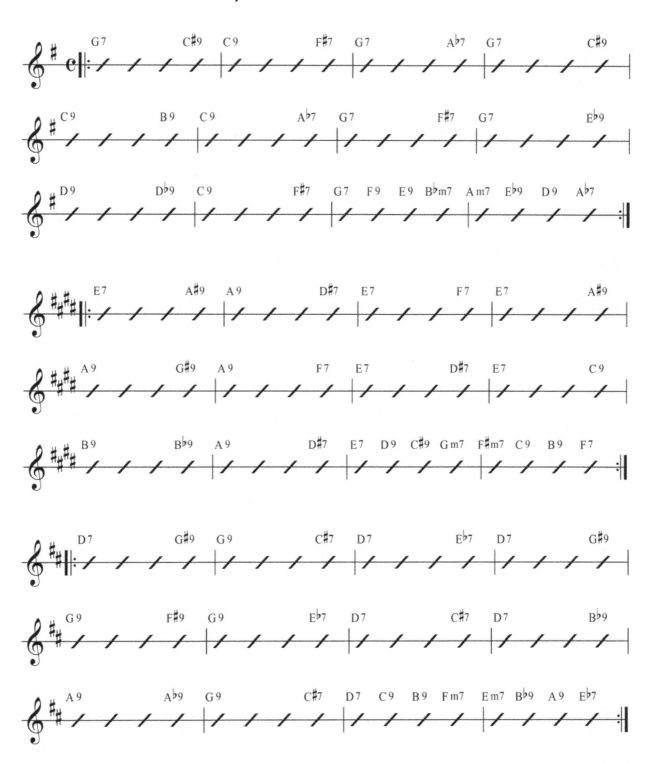

"Gavotte in A minor"
J. S. Bach

This piece and the next one, Bouree in E minor, both by J. S. Bach, are fun to play on today's fretted instruments. Notice how often the chord roots are separated by 4ths. A up to D, A down to E, etc. Of course, my usual disclaimer regarding the chords... Bach didn't write this using chords, it's counterpoint harmony. I included guitar transcriptions of both pieces in "**Melody and Harmony**." The chords I came up with are what I hear implied by the two lines that Mr. Bach wrote. Measure 16 and 24 have a few notes that go below the range of the five-string banjo, so I moved the tab up an octave and marked the sections with asterisks*.

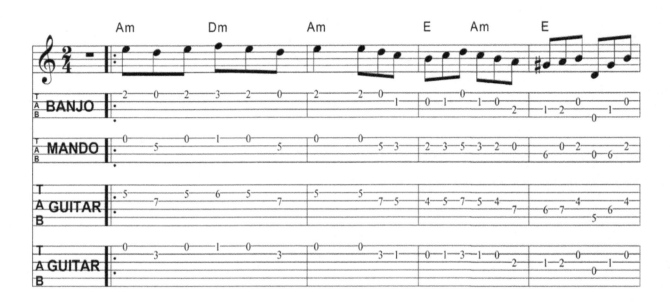

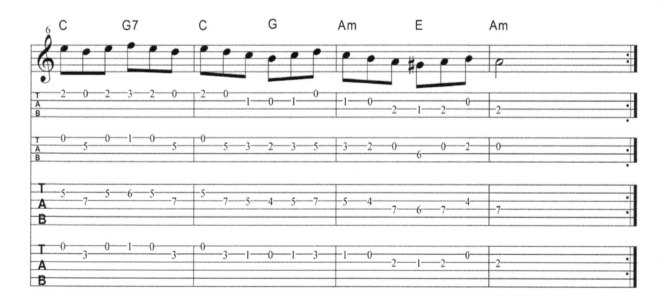

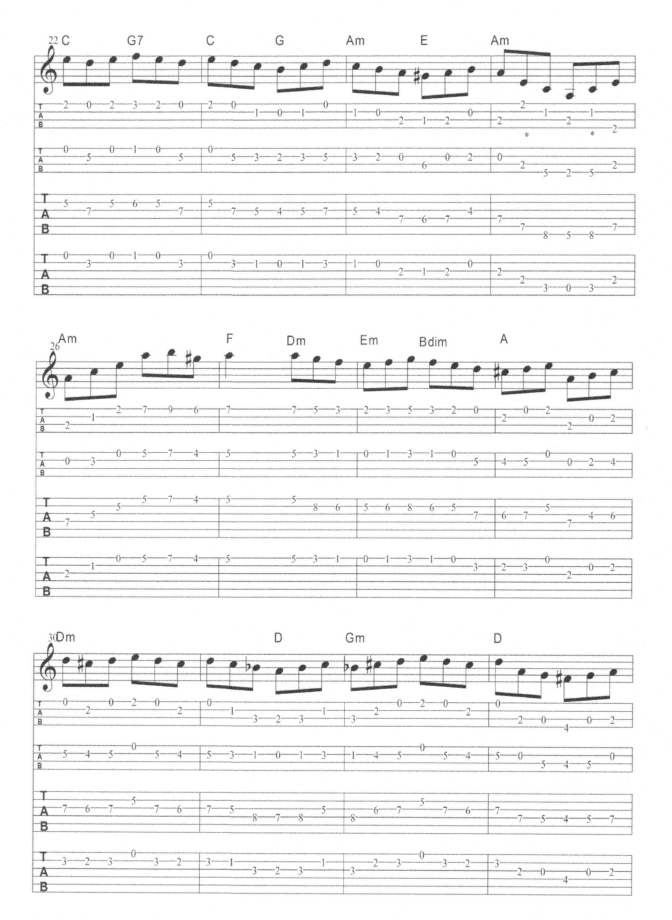

11 - Chord Progressions

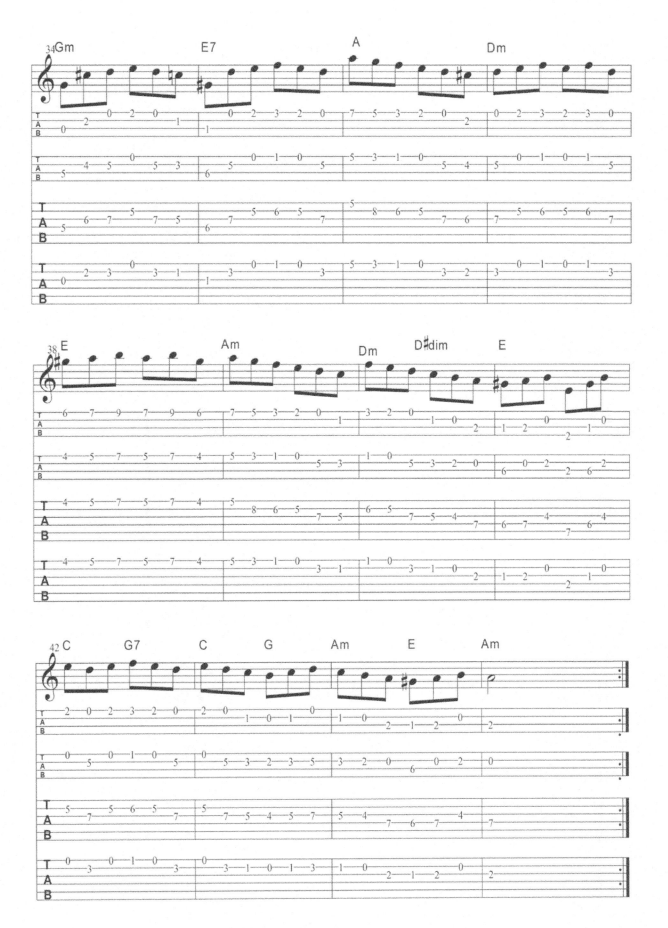

"Bouree in E minor"
J. S. Bach

Jethro Tull did a version of this and they did it with a seriously swinging blues feel with Ian Anderson playing the melody on a flute. It's cool as it can be. I've never heard anyone suggest that old Johann inverted the blues, but when you play this one with a swing feel it sure seems like he did. Everybody gets the blues sometimes.

11 - Chord Progressions

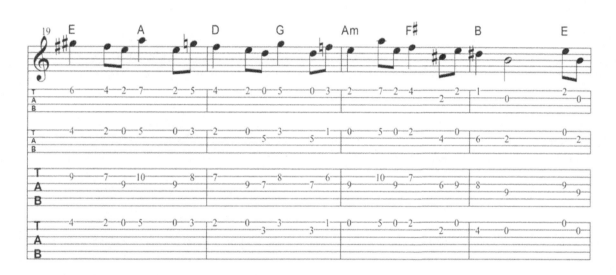

Progressions in Pop Music

Tens of thousands of blues, jazz, R&B, rock, folk, and bluegrass songs have been written on nearly identical chord progressions or "changes," as they're sometimes called. As you fool around with all these tunes, be aware that the progressions will turn up in other songs, too. When you can recognize progressions, you can instantly play songs that you've never heard before... because most songs use "standard" progressions.

Also be aware that you can use progressions like these as a foundation for your own songs. Twist a little here, tweak a little there, and it can be a brand new thing. Playing them in different keys is an important part of this exercise because even a simple I-IV-V can have a very different voice in a different key. That's one of the reasons that people can continue to write good music over simple changes.

I included the transposing chart and the fretboard diagrams on these pages so you can mess around with these things instantly and easily. After a while, you'll start to get a feel for which keys are best for you and then you should take the time to make your own charts. Chart them out in a couple of keys. There's a fairly detailed description of making charts in "**Reading The Road Map**" on page 482. It's a useful skill and you'll learn more than you might imagine just by making a bunch of charts.

Play them using triads, too, using the chord diagrams. For one thing, they give you a place to start fooling around with lead lines while your friend strums the progression using mostly open chords, or your buddy with the bass plays the roots. If your friend wants to play them with a capo on the first fret, the triads let you play all these songs in the flat/sharp keys, too.

Also keep in mind that these triads as shown apply to the five-string banjo as well as guitar. Consider for a moment that these simple chords will enable you to play all of these songs, in all keys, on two very different instruments. That's quite a lot of results for a little bit of effort, I think.

When you learn the progressions on a mandolin, all the fingerings transfer to the mandola, violin, viola, tenor banjo, and cello.

If you have access to a keyboard, definitely take the time to write out charts in the key of C and work out the progressions. Play the root of the chord with your left hand and a first inversion triad a couple of octaves higher with your right hand. After a while, you can start using other triad inversions to minimize the right hand motion and add the chord extensions, too. The relationships in these patterns are much easier for most people to see on a keyboard in the key of C than on stringed instruments and it is worth the extra effort. Lots of fuzzy musical concepts seem to clarify for people when they're able to see them presented on a keyboard.

There wasn't room on these pages to include strumming patterns, but you'll recall that there are a bunch of them in "**Major and Minor Chords**," page 244-247. When you get some of these chord changes going, copy a few of those rhythm patterns to your charts. When you start messing with the rhythm, often you'll either come up with your own versions of the tunes, or you'll start to hear them differently enough that they will morph into a completely different thing... and you're writing music. Analyze it, imitate it, then TWEAK IT!

There are sketches of 36 classic tunes on these few pages. All of them have been on set lists for different bands I've played in over the years. I've found all of them on iTunes for a mere 99 cents each.

Important note: The chord transcriptions in this chapter are the work of Duke Sharp and are for private study, research, or educational purposes, intended only to illustrate and compare the ways common chord progressions are used in popular music. All have been abbreviated, adjusted, and altered to remain in compliance with copyright laws and not infringe on the copyrights that are legally administered by other publishers. These representations of the chord progressions in copyrighted material are based upon recorded versions and live performances by different artists of the copyrighted material, usually a fusion of several recordings and live versions. As shown, they are Duke Sharp's interpretations of the chords used in those songs, and are not exact replications of any single printed, recorded, or live versions.

Progression Study based on "I Got Rhythm"
George Gershwin

A fact that composers have always depended upon is that chord progressions cannot be copyrighted as musical compositions. Thousands of different tunes have been written using identical chord sequences. For instance, Duke Ellington's "Cottontail," Charlie Parker's "Anthropology," and even "The Flintstones Theme," was written with basically the same changes that George Gershwin used for "I Got Rhythm." This one tune presents another one of those "tip of the musical iceberg" things, known in the jazz world as "The Rhythm Changes." For more information and links on this topic: (**en.wikipedia.org/wiki/Rhythm_changes**).

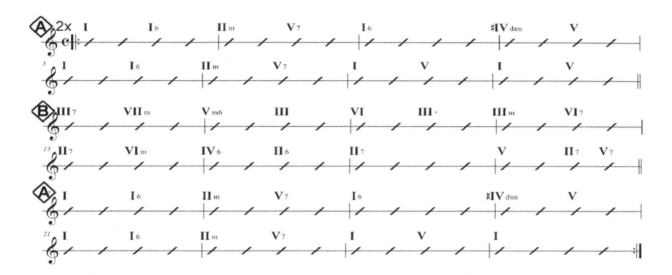

Progression Study based on "The Flintstones"
Hoyt Curtin, William Hanna, Joseph Barbera

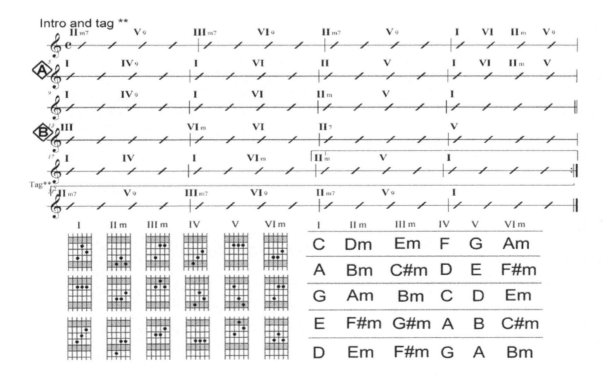

I to **III** is a memorable sound and all three of these tunes have that progression in the first two bars. Lennon and McCartney sandwiched a vii in, too. "Deal" isn't as well known, but it's one of my favorites.

Progression Study based on "Georgia On My Mind"
Hoagy Carmichael
Everyone needs to hear Mr. Ray Charles sing this song. 99 cents at iTunes.

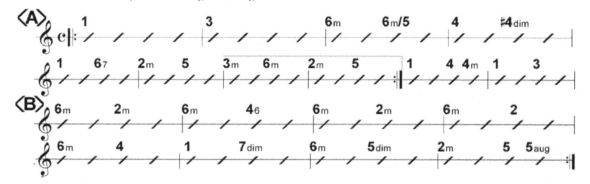

Progression Study based on "Yesterday"
John Lennon & Paul McCartney
Eric Clapton tells a story in his autobiography about hearing Paul McCartney singing the melody to this before the lyrics were written and he was singing "Scram-bled-eggs" in place of "Yes-ter-day."

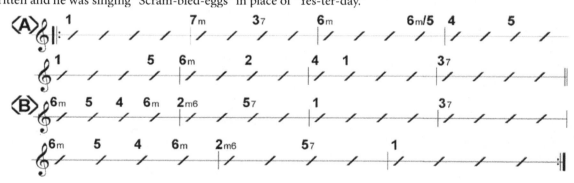

Progression Study based on "Deal"
Jerry Garcia & Robert Hunter
I can't really say that I have a "favorite" guitarist, there are just too many great ones and too many different styles, but any time I'm pressed for a name, I usually want to say Jerry Garcia. I've never heard anyone do what he was able to do. Whether it was the Grateful Dead, the JGB, or even David Grisman, when it was working, it was less about "guitar" or "songs" or "performing" or "a band" than it was about pure musical magic. Sometimes it was as if there was this tangible, but invisible thing loose on the planet. This is one of Jerry's classic tunes.

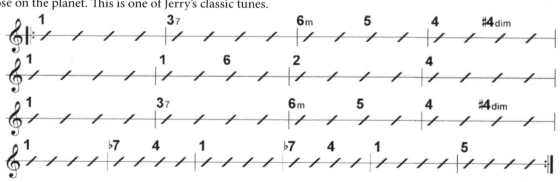

Progression Study based on "Desperado"
Glen Frey & Don Henley

IV to IV minor is a common sound and you'll notice it in this tune a few times. ii-V-I is a common theme here, in this case the II is major instead of minor. Sometimes you'll see the iii minor and the vi minor with II-V-I, and both are common sounds. I really like the way vi minor to II major works here. Notice the single measure of 2/4 at the end of Part A, the rest of the song is 4/4. Strumming this one in C or G on an acoustic guitar is really nice.

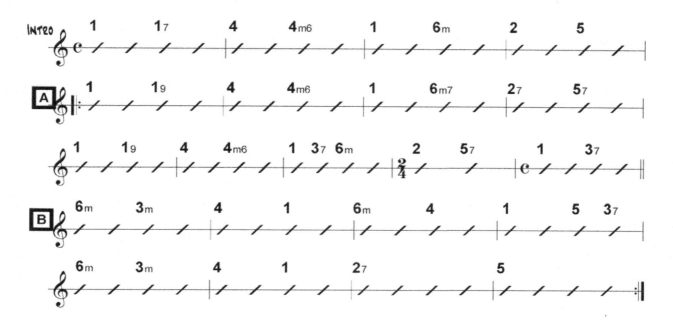

Progression Study based on "Nobody Knows You When You're Down and Out"
Jimmy Cox

This song has been recorded by lots of people, from Leadbelly to Rory Block, but Eric Clapton's version is the one I've heard most.

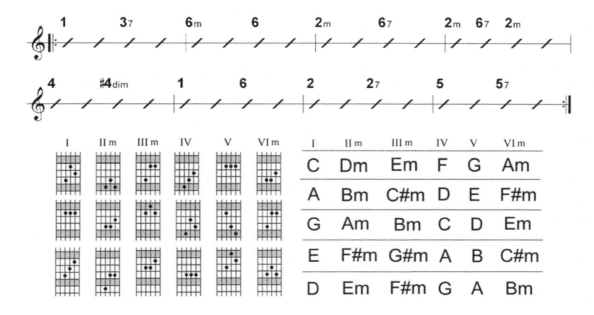

Progression Study based on "Don't Fence Me In"
Cole Porter

"Don't Fence Me In" and "Something in the Way She Moves" let you hear a very common type of progression that can fool you into a search for chord changes, but the only thing changing is the chord extension, not the root. One reason it's deceptive is that the note that is changing IS the root, but it's an octave above the bass.

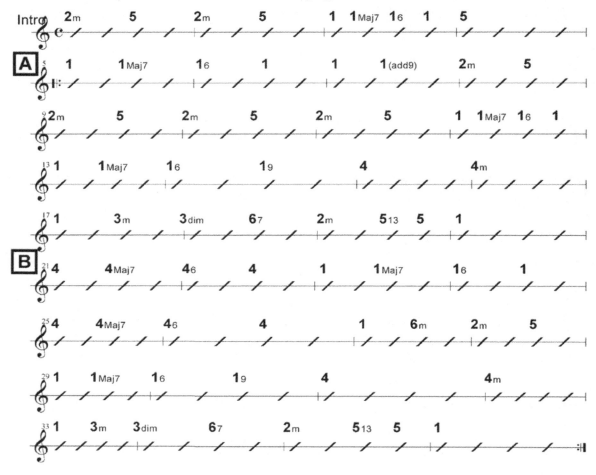

Progression Study based on "Something in the Way She Moves"
George Harrison

A beautiful tune, the song was written for his wife, Pattie Boyd, who inspired a lot of great music. "Layla" by Eric Clapton was also about her. When "Layla" was released, Eric reportedly told his good friend, George, that he was in love with Pattie, i.e., Mrs. George Harrison. Eventually, Mrs. Pattie Boyd Harrison became Mrs. Pattie Boyd Clapton.

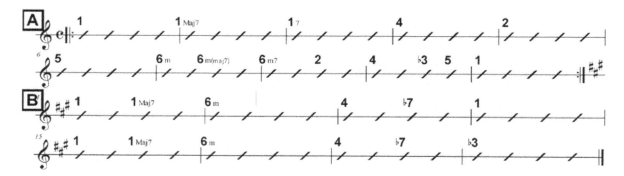

Progression Study based on "Crazy"
Willie Nelson

"Crazy" is by Willie Nelson. (**www.willienelson.com**) Mr. Nelson is known for the stories he tells in his songs, but I'm really a fan of the way he weaves melodies around standard changes. **I** to **IV** major is a distinct sound that you'll encounter a lot. "Crazy" has lots of **ii-V** in it, too.

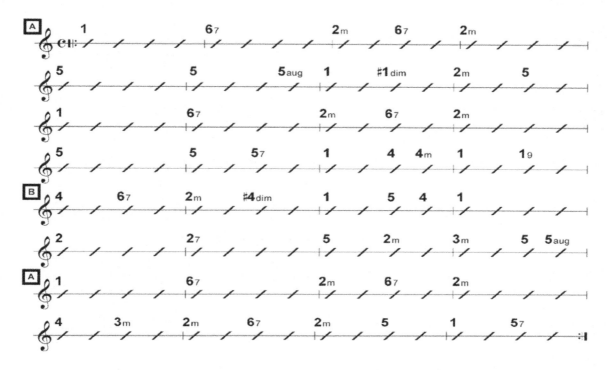

Progression Study based on "Keep on Truckin, Mama"

There have been dozens of verses for this song written over the years and it's a pretty standard progression. It's considered a "traditional" tune. You can make up your own verses if you want to. I learned it from listening to Jorma Kaukonen, one of my favorite fingerstyle guitarists, in the Hot Tuna days. This uses the non-diatonic **II** and **VI**.

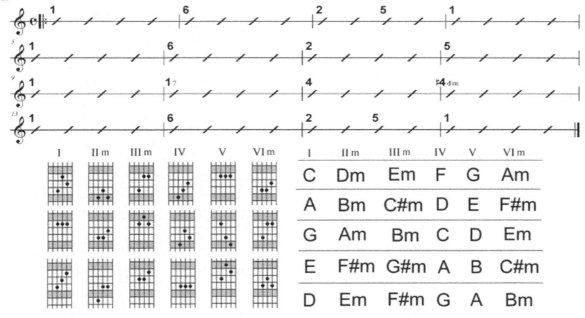

Progression Study based on "Wild Horses"
Mick Jagger & Keith Richard

Knowing which chord is the **I** chord is a bit of very useful information. Occasionally, you'll run across a song and you won't be sure which chord names the key, even if you have all of the chords correctly identified. This tune is a good example of a disguised **I** chord. In an overwhelming percentage of pop tunes, the chord that is being played when the first words are sung will be the **I** chord. In the tunes where the first chord doesn't name the key for you, the last one will. "Wild Horses" and "Little Wing" both disregard that conventional structure.

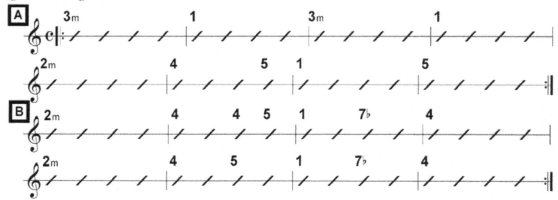

Progression Study based on "Little Wing"
Jimi Hendrix

Duane Allman and Eric Clapton recorded this tune as a tribute to Jimi Hendrix and it was released on "Layla and Other Assorted Love Songs." Hendrix never heard it because he died nine days after it was recorded. If you're alive and you like guitar solos, you should listen to it.

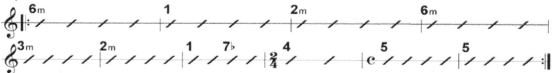

Progression Study based on "Sweet Georgia Brown"
Maceo Pinkard & Kenneth Casey

There are dozens of takes on this tune. Stéphane Grappelli, Django Reinhardt, Doc Watson, and David Grisman all recorded verses that I highly recommend for us string strummers. The piano pickers out there will probably want to hear Mr. Oscar Peterson rip it up. Try Benny Goodman's band. Truthfully, it won't hurt anyone to listen to all of them. Look at those names… and invest a few dollars. This one will fool you, too, starting on **vi**, but it does end on **I**.

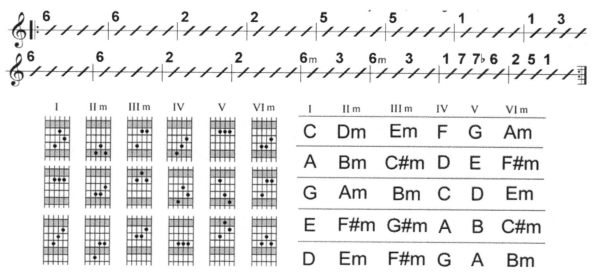

Progression Study based on "Sweet Baby James"

James Taylor

Here's one of my all-time favorite waltzes. The melody is as sweet as can be, the chords wind around through all the diatonic changes, and there are three parts instead of the "standard" A-B thing. Mr. Taylor has released over 20 albums, and in addition to his musical career, he has been active in environmental causes for a long time.

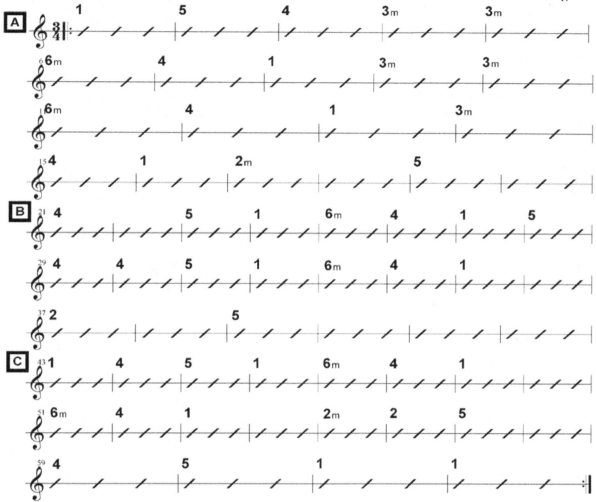

Progression Study based on "Tennessee Waltz"

Redd Stewart & Pee Wee King

Here's another classic waltz. Les Paul and Mary Ford recorded it in 1950. Mr. Paul was a pioneer in the development of solid-body, electric guitars, and invented loads of the things we find in modern recording studios.

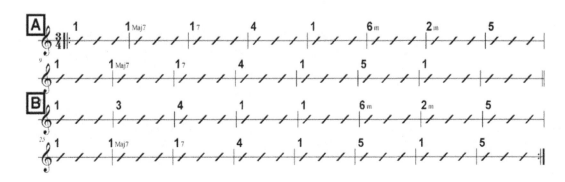

Just so you remember that a song doesn't need loads of chord changes like most of the songs I've shown, here are some real favorites that don't do much more than **I-IV-V**.

Progression Study based on "My Girl"
Smokey Robinson

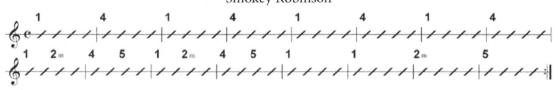

Progression Study based on "Brown Eyed Girl"
Van Morrison

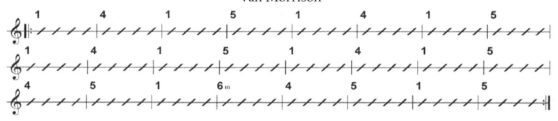

Progression Study based on "This Land Is Your Land"
Woody Guthrie

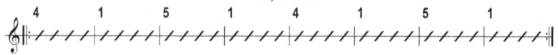

Progression Study based on "Louie Louie"
Richard Berry

This one is easiest in the key of A at first. The V minor is a cool twist on the progression.

Progression Study based on "Gloria"
Van Morrison

This is usually played in the key of E, which makes the ♭7 chord a D major. Easy. Get the sound in your head and then transpose to some other keys.

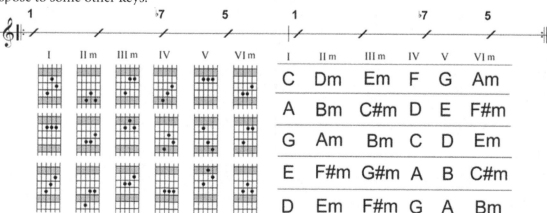

I	II m	III m	IV	V	VI m
C	Dm	Em	F	G	Am
A	Bm	C#m	D	E	F#m
G	Am	Bm	C	D	Em
E	F#m	G#m	A	B	C#m
D	Em	F#m	G	A	Bm

11 - Chord Progressions

Here a few variations of "minor blues." A 12-bar format using the 1-4 & 5 chords is what many people think of as blues, but blues isn't about certain chords being played in a certain sequence. These examples are in minor keys, but I used the numbers from the relative major key.

Progression Study based on "Saint James Infirmary Blues"
Cab Calloway

The Cotton Club in New York City was the premier jazz venue in the U.S., and Cab Calloway's band was the club's house band when Duke Ellington's band was touring.

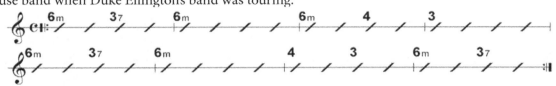

Progression Study based on "House of the Rising Sun"

The melody has roots in 17th century British folk songs. The Rising Sun has been a long-time symbol for brothels in British and American ballads. This song circulated widely among Southern musicians, black and white. Black bluesman Texas Alexander first recorded it in 1928. Alan Lomax transcribed a version in 1937 from the singing of a miner's daughter, Georgia Turner, in Middlesborough, Kentucky, adapting it to the form that was popularized by Josh White.

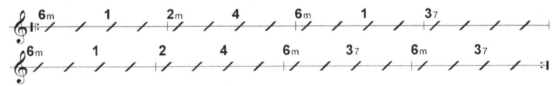

Progression Study based on "Hesitation Blues"
Billy Smythe, Scott Middleton & Art Gilham

The first and last chords will make you believe that it is in a harmonic minor key, but the chords in measures four through 11 seem to slide into the relative major key. I learned "Hesitation Blues" from the way Jorma Kaukonen played it with Hot Tuna in about 1971. I most recently heard him play in 2003, with Jack Casady on bass (of course) and Barry Mitterhoff playing mandolin. Don't ever miss an opportunity to hear these guys play. I've heard very good things from a few people who have gone to Jorma's "Fur Peace Ranch" in Ohio to study music with a bunch of pro teachers, sounds like a great time. (**www.furpeaceranch.com**)

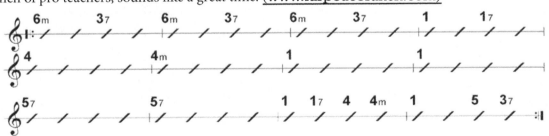

Progression Study based on "All Along the Watchtower"
Bob Dylan

Jimi Hendrix was the guy who introduced this tune to most of the world and his version is still my favorite take on it. It was also my introduction to the wah-wah pedal, and it was cool. It was on the set list when Bob Dylan toured with the Grateful Dead as his backup band and it's my favorite Dylan album. What a backup band! The album that was recorded on the tour is my favorite Dylan record.

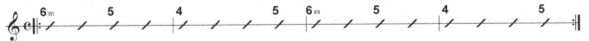

Progression Study based on "Blue Skies"
Irving Berlin

All three of these tunes use the same sort of motion in the first few bars. Mr. Berlin was fond of this progression, notice how similar it is to "Russian Lullaby" also penned by this incredible writer. When you analyze a bunch of songs by nearly any writer, you can't help but notice that most have a few favorite progressions that turn up regularly. It's a clue that as a songwriter you don't need to reinvent music every time you have a lyrical idea. The motion in these tunes is a lot like "Something" and "Don't Fence Me In," except those tunes are in major keys.

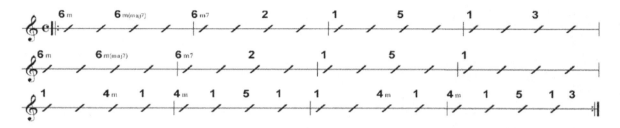

Progression Study based on "While My Guitar Gently Weeps"
George Harrison

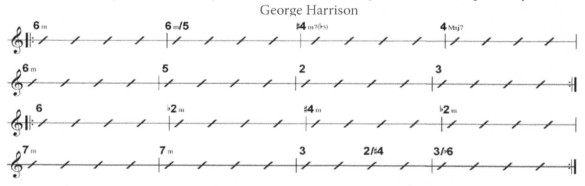

Progression Study based on "Russian Lullaby"
Irving Berlin

My favorite version of this is on Jerry Garcia's second solo album, "Compliments - Jerry Garcia." He also recorded it with David Grisman and that's cool, too.

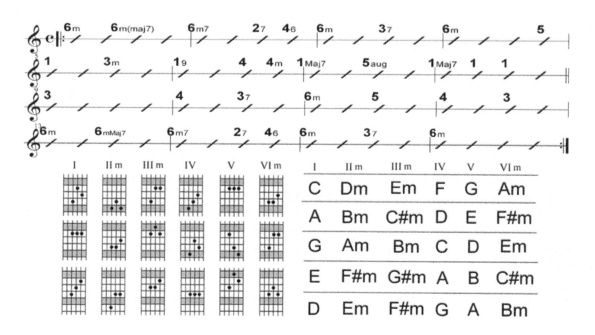

One of the things these three tunes have in common that I really like is that they sort of wander in and out of major and minor sounding phrases.

Progression Study based on "Shotgun Down the Avalanche"
Shawn Colvin
Shawn Colvin is one of my favorites. Writes cool tunes, great singer/player/performer. Get this one at iTunes, you'll probably want more.

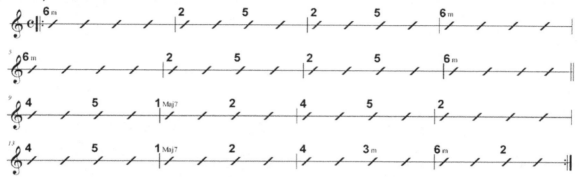

Progression Study based on "Ghost Riders In The Sky"
Stan Jones
There are those who consider this song to be the "greatest western song of all time." It's been recorded more than 50 times, with big band arrangements, country bands, and even a thrash/punk version I heard once. I like all the measures of 2/4, but not everyone does it this way.

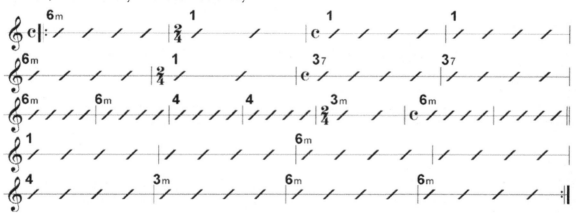

Progression Study based on "Scarborough Fair"
The fair at Scarborough was a huge event, lasting nearly two months. King Henry III granted a charter for the event in 1253 A.D., and it remained an important occasion for nearly 500 years. Evidently, the song was derived from a Scottish ballad, "The Elfin Knight," which has been traced back to about 1600-1650.

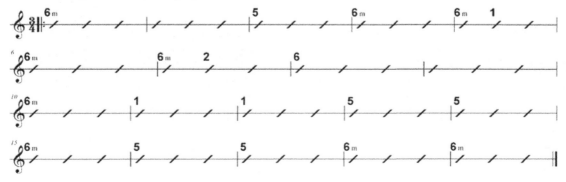

Progression Study based on "The Thrill Is Gone"

Rick Damell & Roy Hawkins

This is the tune that put Mr. B. B. King on the mainstream charts and became his "signature song." Nobody does it like The King, that's for sure. You might want to check out the version by David Grisman and Jerry Garcia for an acoustic take on this classic.

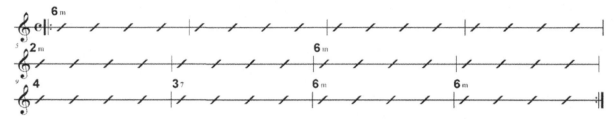

Progression Study based on "Black Magic Woman"

Peter Green

Carlos Santana made this popular in 1970, but Peter Green was one of the early members of Fleetwood Mac and they first recorded it in 1968. It's a great jam tune.

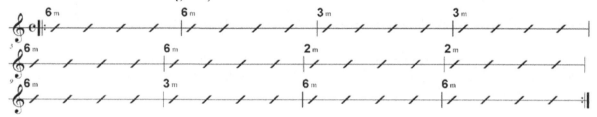

Progression Study based on "Last Dance With Mary Jane"

Tom Petty

I wish there was room for about 20 of this guy's songs. Somehow, he uses simple changes over and over and makes them sound different than everybody else. I've never had a chance to see him perform, but everyone I know who has been to a show hopes they have another opportunity. I'm going, if I get a chance.

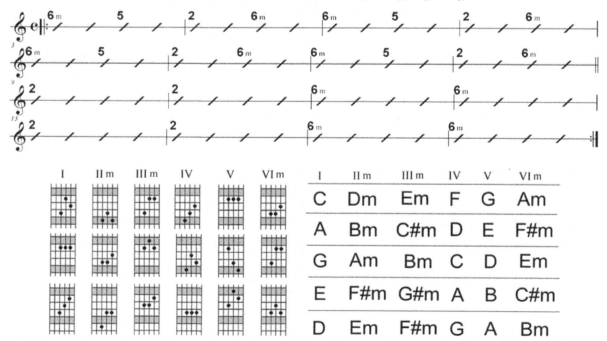

I	II m	III m	IV	V	VI m
C	Dm	Em	F	G	Am
A	Bm	C#m	D	E	F#m
G	Am	Bm	C	D	Em
E	F#m	G#m	A	B	C#m
D	Em	F#m	G	A	Bm

"New Coat of Paint"
Tom Waits

Here's another one of my favorite blues progressions. I like to do this in A minor because it makes for a cool descending bass run. Here's how A minor (6m) uses the open A string for its bass note, but when it goes to the 2 chord, D, I like to use F# for the bass. D/F#. The next two chords are F7 and E7, so the bass just continues down in half steps. Tom Waits is a great little-known songwriter with a distinctive style and lots of songs about odd characters in weird scenes. He's also an actor, has written music for films, and was nominated for an Acadamy Award. The Eagles covered one of his tunes, "Ol' 55" and Bruce Springsteen did "Jersey Girl."

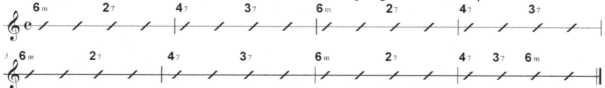

"Makin' Whoopee!"
Gus Kahn & Walter Donaldson

This song is from a musical called "Whoopee" and Eddie Cantor's was the first popular version of this tune in about 1928. My favorite is the one that Malcolm J. Rebennack, Jr., (better known as Dr. John) recorded with Rickie Lee Jones. I'm not the only one who likes this duet, they very much deserved the Grammy it won in 1989.

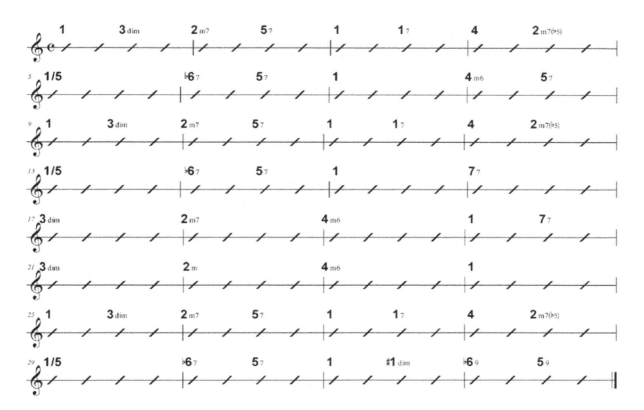

Reflections

"We will either find a way, or make one."
Hannibal

"What a poor appearance the tales of poets make
when stripped of the colors which music puts upon them,
and recited in simple prose."
Plato

"What this power is I cannot say. All I know is that it exists.
It becomes available only when a man is in that state of mind in which he knows
exactly what he wants and is fully determined not to quit until he finds it."
Alexander Graham Bell

"What you get by achieving your goals is not as important
as what you become by achieving your goals."
Zig Ziglar

"When God created Man,
he gave him Music as a language different from all other languages.
And early man sang his glory in the wilderness;
and drew the hearts of kings and moved them from their thrones."
Kalil Gibran

"When I don't like a piece of music, I make a point of listening to it more closely."
Florent Schmitt

"When I hear music I fear no danger, I am invulnerable, I see no foe.
I am related to the earliest times and to the latest."
Henry David Thoreau

"When people hear good music,
it makes them homesick for something they never had, and never will have."
Ed Howe

"When the world says, "Give up," Hope whispers, "Try it one more time."
Attributed, **Alex and Jerry Sharp, Hopi Glenn**

"When we rejoice in great music and art,
it is but the flexing of instincts learned in the previous life."
Neal Maxwell

"When you come to the end of your rope, tie a knot and hang on."
Franklin D. Roosevelt

"When your heart is in your dreams, no request is too extreme."
Jiminy Cricket

Melody, Harmony, Scales and Chords

Chapter 12

"Twinkle, twinkle, little star. How I wonder what you are."

"Jingle bells. Jingle bells. Jingle all the way."

"Some—where o---ver the rain—bow way up high."

"Take me out to the ballgame, take me out with the crowd."

These words trigger a nearly automatic response in western humans. I bet you sang all four lines.

That's what a melody is. In a song, the melody is the tune that the singer is singing. The notes, note the words.

I'm not about to attempt to explain how a composer creates a melody. I can't even say where the tunes I write come from, much less illustrate whatever incredible musical river Mozart might have been tapping into.

But, if you're trying to play some of your favorite songs by ear, I can suggest some useful clues regarding how to conduct a search for familiar melodies and the chords and harmonies that go along with them. As always, there are patterns when you know where to look for them.

If you're going fishing, where do you go to find fish? Obviously, the first requirement is a body of water because that's where the fish live. There used to be a lot of them. They rarely bother anyone.

If you're looking for a melody, the first place you go is to the major scale.

It occurred to me that nearly all melodies are mostly major scale tones and I had even briefly glanced through a couple of songbooks that supported that idea, but I hadn't ever really thoroughly checked it out until recently.

I was teaching at Music Villa in Bozeman, Montana (www.musicvilla.com 406-587-4761) while writing this book and there is always a wide selection of songbooks from all genres of music.

So I looked through 20 books. Red Hot Chili Peppers' *Californication; Motown Anthology;* Dave Matthews' Band *Under the Table and Dreaming; The Reggae Songbook;* Metallica's *And Justice For All; The Country Music Songbook Series, Volume 4;* Rolling Stones' *Tattoo You;* U2 *All That You Can't Leave Behind;* Cole Porter's *Love Songs;* Neil Young's *Harvest Moon;* Led Zeppelin's *The Best of Led Zeppelin, Volume 1;* Sheryl Crow's *The Globe Sessions;* Ani Di Franco's *The Best of Ani Di Franco for Guitar; The Willie Nelson Songbook;* Tori Amos' *MTV Unplugged;* Tracy Chapman; *The Eagles Complete, Volume 1;* and the *Grateful Dead Anthology.*

I think it's fair to say this is a wide enough variety of artists to constitute a cross-section of popular music. I intentionally stayed away from the jazz books because jazz is not usually considered "popular mainstream" and that is what we're examining here.

I used over 100 random tunes, a minimum of five songs from each book, and I counted each melody note in those songs. Well, not quite random. I used the first five songs in each book that were in major keys. Anyway... 100+ "random" pop tunes.

Then, I counted every accidental in the melody... that is every melody note that was anything other than **DO RE MI FA SO LA** or **TI**.

Over 90% of the melody notes were either DO RE MI FA SO LA or TI.

The majority of the remaining 10% of the notes were ♭3rds or ♭7ths... in other words, "blues" notes. Over 80% of the melody notes in all these tunes were five tones. DO, RE, MI, SO, and LA. Can you spell M-A-J-O-R P-E-N-T-A-T-O-N-I-C S-C-A-L-E?

I really didn't anticipate that the percentages would be as extreme as what I found. Eighty percent to over 90% is a lot.

It may be difficult to believe, but I did count them. You can take my word for it, or try it yourself. With *any* songbook. I can't say for sure, but I'd be willing to bet a bundle that the melodies in songs in minor keys are real similar to the structure I found in the major keys. If you come up with some real different results, I'm sure that Pinky would love to hear about it.

Now, just in case you're a player who just wants to be the equivalent of the "lead guitarist" with somebody else doing all the singing, you may think this is not especially relevant.

In fact, this idea is just as important to the soloist.

I did the same sort of exercise with a bunch of "classic rock," lead guitar solos, by people like Jimi Hendrix, Joe Walsh, Eric Clapton, Carlos Santana, Mark Knopfler, Jimmy Page, Jerry Garcia, and David Gilmour, and got just about the same results. I intentionally chose songs that had solos that I consider to be melodic and I didn't actually sit down and count all the notes, like I did with the vocal melodies... it's more of an estimate, but it's a good estimate.

Consider some classic guitar solos, things like Jimmy Page's "Stairway To Heaven," David Lindley's lap steel solo in "Mercury Blues," David Gilmour's ride in "The Wall," or Eric Clapton and Duane Allman's in "Layla." Often, you can pretty much sing along with the entire solo. Maybe you can't hit the high notes, but my point is that for the most part, great solos aren't predominantly about playing wild scale variations at warp 10. Melodic ideas, great phrasing, dynamics, and tone are elements that are usually more important than pure speed.

I didn't examine metal shredders and jazz players because they fall outside "mainstream pop," but this discussion is quite pertinent to playing melodic solos in just about any style.

If you look at the notes used by country, bluegrass, reggae, and folk lead players, you're right back in the range of 90% of the notes being major scale tones.

Singing along with scale exercises is an important step toward being able to incorporate vocal phrasing and melodic content into your solos. When your rides stop being more or less random notes from the "blues scale" and you start choosing the notes from the same scale to create a nicely phrased melodic idea... that's when your solos start to sound like solos.

Here is a tune you may be familiar with. On this page I counted 109 notes. What I was looking for was accidentals… # symbols, ♭ symbols, or ♮ symbols. In any piece of music, one of the main things accidentals indicate is that a note is something other than DO, RE, MI, FA, SO, LA, or TI. I transposed it to the key of C. All the way down in measure #22 is an F# that repeats four times. That's four accidentals out of 109 notes. Do the arithmetic, if you like. About 97% diatonic is what I get.

The lowest note is A in measure four and the highest note is D in the 23rd measure. The entire melody spans only 11 white keys—an interval of an 11th. Only slightly more than 1-1/2 octaves. (For guitarists, this might be a good time to briefly run through the major scale forms, #1 through #4, and relate the span of an octave and a half to those forms. For me, Form #1 works best for playing this particular tune.)

More statistics: DO, the tonic note of the key, occurs 22 times, which is nearly 20%. Only 20 of the 109 notes are either FA or TI, which means that over 80% are found in the major pentatonic scale of the **I** chord. Fifty-three of the notes, nearly half, are DO, MI, or SO, the root, 3rd, and 5th of the **I** chord. Eighty-one of the notes are found in the C major pentatonic scale. Eight-four of the notes are between the low tonic and the 6th degree.

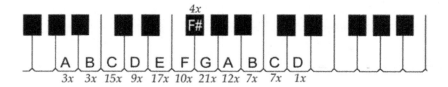

Whatever key any song is in, all the sharps and flats from the major scale are indicated by the key signature. The "accidentals" are notes that are not diatonic and are shown individually as they occur in the tune.

In other words, in any key, every note that doesn't have a #, or a ♭, or a ♮ symbol right next to it is either DO, RE, MI, FA, SO, LA, or TI.

Here are those same eight bars written in the key of E♭. There is still only one accidental.

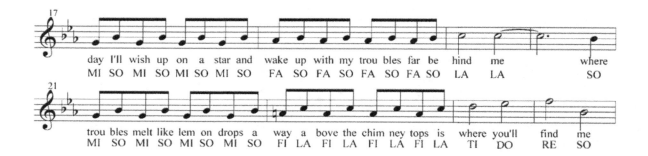

Measures two and 10 have SO, LA, TI, and DO in sequence.
Measures six and 14 have DO, RE, MI, and FA in sequence.
Measures seven and 15 have TI, DO, RE, and MI in sequence.

Out of 24 total measures, six measures (25%) contain four notes of a major scale, played in sequence.

I'm certain that there must be thousands of exceptions to this idea. "Most melodies can be found within the major scale."

There must be. But I went looking for them and didn't find very many. A remarkably small percentage of exceptions are what I found.

I recommend that you get a few songbooks by some of your favorite artists and do the same drill. Count the melody notes, count the accidentals, and then ask yourself, "How much time do you spend practicing major scales and pentatonic scales? That's where the melodies are. It's kind of encouraging to see that in essence, most tunes really aren't terrifically complicated. It's real useful to have a familiar and logical place to start when you're trying to learn a new song.

Mastery of the major scale and the diatonic chords generated by the major scale will take you a *long, long, long* way toward playing literally thousands of "pop tunes" by ear. (You might read that line aloud two or three times every time you sit down to practice.)

Now, let's take a look at some of the chords that can go along with that melody.

Take your time, look carefully and compare the melody line in the tablature with the dots that are in each chord diagram. For example, the tab shows the first melody note on the third fret of the 5th string, which is C on the staff, and that is also one of the frets indicated in the chord diagram. If you can spell chords and know the staff, it's even easier than looking at the dots on the diagrams to see the relationship between the chords and the individual melody notes.

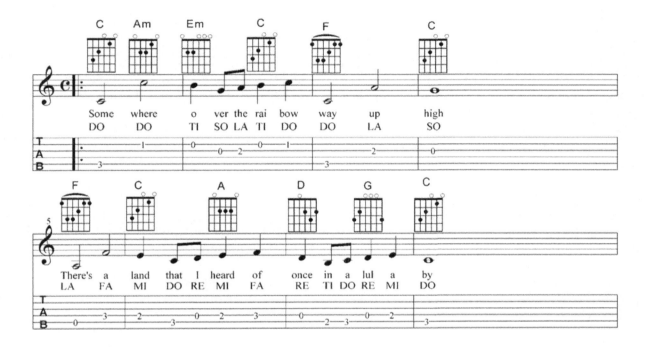

In the first measure, the two melody notes are C. First note C is the root of C major. Second note C is now appearing as the 3rd of A minor. Those two notes are an octave apart, the largest interval in this tune. The four notes: G, A, B, C that correspond with ver-the rain-bow are SO, LA, TI, and DO, half of a scale without variation. Three out of four are found in the C major pentatonic scale.

Second measure, G and B are the 3rd and 5th of E minor, B and C are the 7th and root of C major. Fifty percent are found in the C major pentatonic scale.

Third measure, C and A are the 5th and 3rd of F, the current chord. Also, C, A, and G are the root, 6th, and 5th of the I chord. One hundred percent are found in the C major pentatonic scale.

There are 23 melody notes in the first eight bars. There are three separate phrases in those eight bars (in the second, fifth, and sixth measures) that use four consecutive major scale tones… 12 notes. That's over 50% of the notes.

In nearly every instance, when you are playing the right chord, you are also playing the melody note somewhere in that chord. That is not to suggest that all melody notes will always appear as chord tones, they don't; but very often you can find the melody note within the chord in most songs. And many times when you see extended chords in a song, C6 or C Major 7 or whatever, the note indicated by the number will be the melody note. Not always, often.

These are not phenomena unique to this tune. It happens all the time, more often than not, in my experience.

Also observe the fact that out of the 12 chords shown in these eight measures, five of them are C. The **I** chord. This phrase begins with a **I** chord, it ends with a **I** chord, and nearly 50% of the chords played are the **I** chord.

Of the 12 chords, 10 are diatonic: **I, iii, IV, V, vi,** and the remaining two are **II** and **VI**. I couldn't decide how to count the total number of progressions in the tune, but **ii-V-I** happens a few times, and **I-VI-II-V-I** covers three measures out of eight, which is nearly 40% of an eight-bar phrase.

The reason that I have gone to the trouble of enumerating all of these statistics is because I am of the opinion that "figuring out songs by ear" is to a great extent a matter of being able to anticipate or predict what is likely to occur.

When you *know* that certain melodic sequences and chord combinations are used close to 90% of the time, "predicting" becomes quite a lot easier. There are not a lot of things I'm acquainted with that are quite as predictable as popular music. Cats chase mice, dogs like to chase pickup trucks, boys and girls like chasing each other, and pop music is diatonic. Not always. Usually.

That kind of knowledge combined with coordination can become a powerful tool for someone who directs a good bit of practice time toward those areas.

If you're going fishing, you start with water.

If you're looking for melodies, you check out the major scale. Want to practice something really useful that will enhance your ability to play songs by ear? Try a major scale, that's where the tunes are.

Obviously, it is ridiculous to suggest that melodies are no more than rearranged scales, but as individual components and phrases, each note can be identified as a scale tone and many phrases can be seen as scale fragments. Analyze and imitate.

Every word can be viewed as individual letters and there are 26 of them in our alphabet. Musical phrases can be seen as individual notes and most of them come from a pool of only seven choices, 12 at the outside. The alphabet is harder.

One thing you can do to begin to improve your ability to play tunes by ear is to go through all of the nursery rhymes, Christmas carols, campfire songs, etc., that you know and try to sound them out using the major scale. It really doesn't matter which scale form is used. The easiest way is to do it on a keyboard, key of C, highly recommended.

Focus on any major scale form until you can play 8th notes at around 60 to 75 bpm. "Auld Lang Syne, Jingle Bells, Home on the Range, Happy Birthday to You, You Are My Sunshine, Take Me Out To the Ballgame, On Top of Old Smokey, Joy To the World, Pop Goes the Weasel, Streets of Laredo, Away In a Manger, Hark the Herald Angels Sing," are all songs that you can find using the major scale. Practice on easy, familiar tunes. Working out on "Mary Had a Little Lamb" may seem a bit silly, but this is a useful step in learning to play melodic solos. It's not about learning the songs, you already know the song. It's about developing a skill. Don't forget what Mozart did with "Twinkle, Twinkle Little Star." Use simple, familiar melodies to develop the technique instead of beginning with the solo from "Stairway to Heaven." Once you develop the ability to sound out simple melodies that you can sing, fig uring out most of the notes in the "Stairway to Heaven" solo become fairly easy. If you can sing something, you can just about always fin d it on an instrument, particularly if you know where to look. Listen to the solos in pop tunes while you hum the vocal lines and you'll begin to notice that lots of players will base chunks of their solos on the vocal melody.

OK. Let's take a look at the other part of the tune.

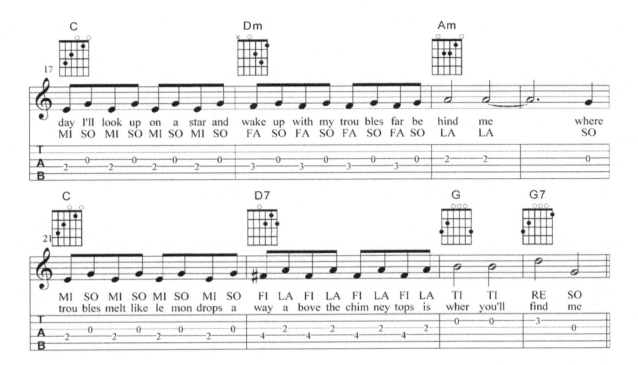

The first measure shown (#17) has E and G in the melody which are the 3rd and 5th of a C chord and are found in the C major pentatonic scale.

In the first half of measure 18, F and G are the 3rd and 4th of D minor chord, and then they become the 7th and root of a G7 when the chord changes.

Measures 19 and 20, A is the 6th of C and G is the 5th. Both notes are in the C major pentatonic scale.

Measure 21 is identical to measure 17.

Measure 22 contains the accidental. F# is the 3rd of a D major chord, which is the ii chord altered to become a II chord.

Measure 23 has the 5th and 7th of a D chord.

Measure 24 has the root and 5th of a G chord. Both notes are in the C major pentatonic scale. Although the I chord occurs in three out of eight possible spots, DO never makes an appearance.

For this example, I've shown the simplest chords that work nicely for this song. (This is not how it was written, or played in the movie, but if you look at a copy of the original score, you'll see the same relationships.) The entire melody of this phrase is contained in those chords, with the single exception of the G note played over the D minor chord in measure #18.

But, this tune is kind of a "pop jazz standard" and "jazz" usually means bigger chords.

"Bigger chords" brings us right up next to the word "harmony." We'll look at harmony when it is used as a second line, played or sung simultaneously with a melody. A melody is a series of single notes and in this context, so is harmony.

We've already observed that the melody note is usually contained within whatever chord is being played.

Well... guess what?!? Guess where the harmony notes are found!!

The harmony notes are found under the northeastern cornerstone of the wall surrounding the Grand Palace in Bangkok. Your mission, should you decide to accept it...

The harmony notes are also found within the same chord... and we're talking about triads here. A grand total of three notes to choose from. One of them is the melody note. In pop music, initially there are two probable harmony notes for any melody note *in any song by any artist*.

That fact should be repeated, for emphasis. Allow this to sink in. In pop music, there are two probable harmony notes for any melody note *in any song by any artist*.

This is why it is possible for a "fingerstyle" guitarist to play melodies at the same time she's playing harmonies and a bass line. All of the relevant notes, bass, melody, and harmony, are usually (nearly always) contained within the chord.

We start with a triad. One of those harmony notes will be the bass note, which is the lowest note played. It will usually be the root of the chord. One note of the triad is melody (which may be the root), one is the bass note, and the other note, either the 3rd or the 5th be default, is the "harmony" note.

Three-part harmony is not as complex as quantum physics.

Let's imagine that you're watching the "Wizard of Oz" and Judy Garland is singing "Over the Rainbow" in the key of C (she isn't).

The first note is C and the chord shown is C major. If you felt inspired to jump in and sing a harmony with Dorothy on that first C note, it would be a good plan for you to start with E or G, which are the 3rd and 5th of the C chord.

If you sing E, a third above the melody, then you are singing what is called "close harmony" as in "nearby harmony." If you choose to sing G, a 4th below the melody, that is also close harmony.

G a 5th above the melody and E a 6th below the melody are cool harmonies and absolutely OK and encouraged, but they are not "close" harmony... because there is a harmony note from the triad in between the C and G. Look back to the example on page 84 in **"Intervals Part One"**... which is *not* the intro to "Brown Eyed Girl." The melody is on the highest string (DO-RE-MI-RE-DO) and the harmony is a 6th below it with the 5th in between, but not played.

As a general rule, if you want to sing or play a harmony to any melody note, it's right on the edge of impossible to go wrong by using one (or two) of the other tones in the basic triad.

So… a sensible question at this point is: If we're using all three tones of a triad for melody, harmony, and bass, what is the difference between "harmony" and "chords?"

There isn't a difference in this context. Harmony is chords and chords are harmony. You "harmonize" a melody by adding chord tones.

Sometimes you'll want the harmony to be "close" to the melody note, sometimes you won't. Sometimes you'll use all three triad tones and sometimes you'll have enough voices to duplicate some of the triad tones.

When the three tones in the basic triad don't make the harmonized sound you're after, you can start bringing in other tones and extend the chord as far as you have voices. "Barbershop quartets" use four-part harmony. Swing era singers like the Andrews Sisters sing lots of 9^{ths} and 6^{ths}.

End of detour. We just got back to bigger chords… triads with "extra" notes.

Here is the same melody and the same progression (almost) with some additional chords and many of the chords extended just a bit. Often, the extensions will be the melody note.

These additional tones are simply more harmony notes layered above and below the melody. And for the most part, they are found somewhere in a series of 3rds above the root of the chord.

Now, let's take a look at how you might experiment with different harmonies in a tune.

This shows four different ways to harmonize the note C. Our ears are conditioned to hear the lowest note played as the root of the chord and these harmonies work as long as somebody is playing the root of the chord.

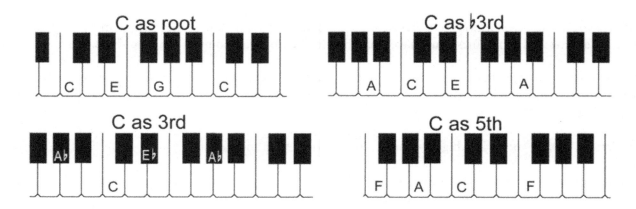

The bass note is crucial. Suppose you are playing an A minor chord in "Black Magic Woman," and the bass player is hanging on an A note. Everything is cool.

But if the bass player perversely decides to drop this A down a 3rd to F, your A minor triad (A, C, E) is instantly and unhappily transformed into the 3rd, 5th, and 7th of an F major 7 chord (F, A, C, E).

Now, if you, as a guitar, keyboard, banjo, clarinet player… add the same F note, an octave or two higher, while the bass player keeps hammering that low A note, the F note *you're* playing is heard as the 6th of an A minor, and it's still a Latin jazz rock thing.

It's important to note that this discussion of melody and harmony is set with a bass note on the root of each chord as it passes. According to Duke Brekhus, in pop music that is frequently the bass players' main job: PLAY THE ROOT! PLAY THE ROOT! PLAY THE ROOT SOME MORE!

This is a good place to mention a technique I (and plenty of others) use for "figuring a song out by ear." It has to do with listening and choosing an instrument to focus on to supply you with relevant clues. When I'm trying to sort out chords in a tune, the first instrument I listen for is the bass, because the bass is usually playing the root of the chord. When you look through the changes (progression) in any song, one thing you can nearly always depend on is that the bass will be playing the root of the chord, at the moment the chord changes. The next most likely note for the bass to play on the first beat of a chord change is probably the 5th followed by the 3rd. I hope you've noticed by now that chord changes occur most frequently on the first and third beats in the measure, so that is where you listen for the bass player to nail the root of the chord.

If you can find the root, it's a relatively easy process to determine the chord quality and the extensions being used as harmony tones.

I don't start with the guitar. There might be four of them on a recording and it can be tough to isolate one of them. There is (usually) only one bass, one kick, and one snare. These three instruments provide most of the clues you'll need to start the process of sorting out the chord changes if you don't have access to the written music or a chart of some sort.

The other player I want to listen for is the drummer. Very often the kick drum will be playing beats one and three, while the snare will be playing two and four. Find beat one, listen to the bass, and they will tell you where the chords change.

Here is my favorite example of what can happen when re-harmonizing a melody. We're accustomed to these 14 notes as "Twinkle, Twinkle Little Star." It's also the melody I learned for "The Alphabet Song."

Let's see how the harmony notes (the chords) relate to the melody. C major is spelled C-E-G. The first measure has two different notes, C and G. F major is F-A-C. In the second measure, the A note is the 3rd of an F chord. Third measure has an F note with an F chord, and an E, the 3rd of a C chord. G major is spelled G-B-D. The fourth measure has a D, the 5th of a G major chord and then winds up with a C.

Twinkle Theme

Now, check out "The Wonderful Whirled Twinkle." These are exactly the same notes, in the same order, right up through the beginning of measure nine. The feel (time signature) is different and it's re-harmonized. This might remind you of another tune that my pals at Hal Leonard would not allow me to show you. "It's a Wonderful World" was written by George Weiss, Bob Theile, and George Douglas. Think Satchmo (Louis Armstrong). Visualize whirled harmonies.

The Wonderful Whirled Twinkle

Let's look at the "new" chords. In measure one, C is still the root of C major. In measure two, G is now the 3rd of E minor. In measure three, A is the 3rd of F. In measure four, G is the 3rd of E minor. Skip to measure seven and the D note is the flatted 7th of an E7 chord. In measure eight, C is the 3rd of A minor. In measure eight, C is the 3rd of Ab major.

Dude! Cool Changes! And I said to myself, what a brilliant idea!

This process of substituting different chords is known as "re-harmonizing." Take a melody and play it the way you hear it. Rearrange the notes if you want to. Change the chords and the harmonies if you want to. Change the lyrics. Change the feel. It's OK. Check out Aretha Franklin's version of "Eleanor Rigby." They did all of those things. You can, too. You're not stuck with only one way to play a song. The odds are strong that whoever wrote the song is not in your living room ready to object to any changes you might feel like making. Twist it around any way you want to.

Evidently, neither Wolfgang Amadeus Mozart, nor Louis Armstrong, thought there was anything silly about sitting around and jamming on variations of "Twinkle, Twinkle Little Star." Mr. Armstrong even made a fair pile of loot doing it. Stevie Ray Vaughn and Buddy Guy did versions of "Mary Had a Little Lamb."

"Be true to it. Every music has its own soul," said Ray Charles. It's up to you to find it.

Usually, people use roots, 3^{rds}, and 5^{ths} for singing harmony notes. Seconds and 7^{ths} are more difficult to hear at first, but they also can work. You're more likely to use the 2nd as a "stepping stone" between the root and the 3rd. Same with the 6th and 7th. They'll often be used as "passing notes" (OxfordReference.com) in a harmony line that moves to the 3^{rds} and 5^{ths} while a melody line is stationary.

If you really understand chord structure and harmony, you can justify any "mistake" you might happen to make. "I *know* it's a gospel song. I did it on purpose, experimenting with different harmonies, playing flatted 9^{ths} and flatted 5^{ths} against the root."

With regard to improvised harmony lines, you really can't miss.
If you play two notes together and they're the same note, that's unison.
If you play two notes together and they sound good, that's harmony.
If you play two notes together and they sound terrible, that's jazz. (I'm kidding, I stole the joke.)

Experiment. All of these numbers and stuff are simply a means of identifying what you're doing, so you can do it again, if you like it and avoid it if you don't.

These diagrams on the following pages show harmonized major scales. This is a scale, so it is often a part of my daily scale workout. Same thing for the "harmonized harmonic minor scales" you'll encounter in a couple of pages. The "melody" notes are indicated with a dot on the chord diagram. The harmony notes are diatonic.

I expect you'll notice that these triads sound very similar to the arpeggios exercise in "**Major and Minor Chords**," and the triads in "**Progressions**." These triads move a harmonized scale up the neck and those triads go across the neck. I have no personal motivation for promoting these seven simple chords. I did not invent this stuff.

There is no sequence in western pop music that is more important. If you want to play by ear, learn this series of seven chords. Up, down, sideways, and backwards. Inside out and down side up. "Over, Under, Sideways, Down." This is the "Key to the Highway."

Wonderfully Whirled Twinklets

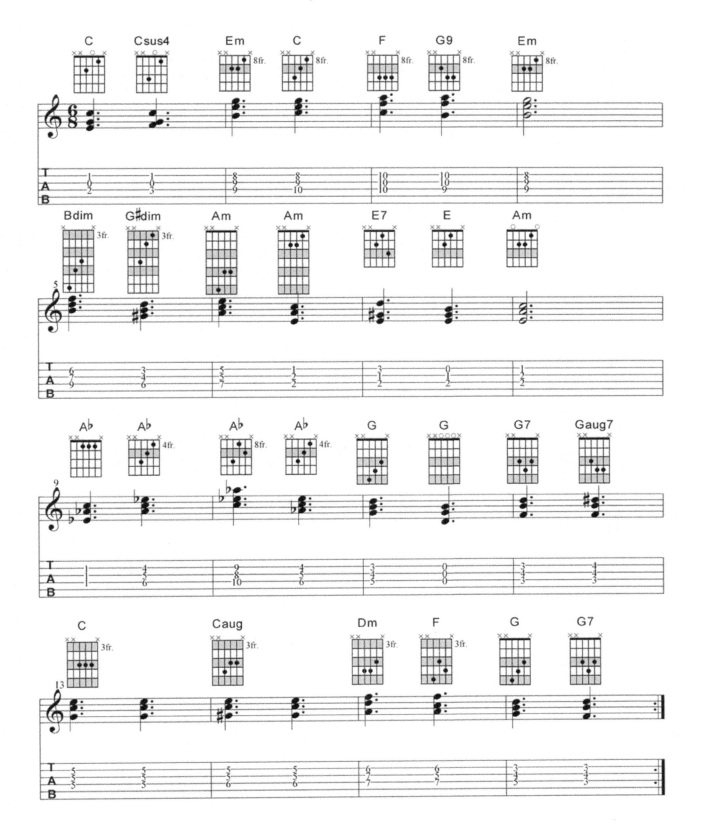

The Wonderfully Whirled Twinklet

12 - Melody, Harmony, Scales and Chords

Twinkle, Twinkle Little Star

This is a three-part harmony for guitar and banjo with the melody as the highest note. These chord inversions can be a long stretch on a mandolin, unreachable for most on a mandola. If you can't reach all three notes as a chord, do arpeggios instead. I just about always practice tunes using arpeggios instead of chords at some point, especially if it's laid out in triads the way this is. I included the fretboards on this page as a reminder of what the triad inversions look like. The next two pages use the same triads, so I left the fretboards off.

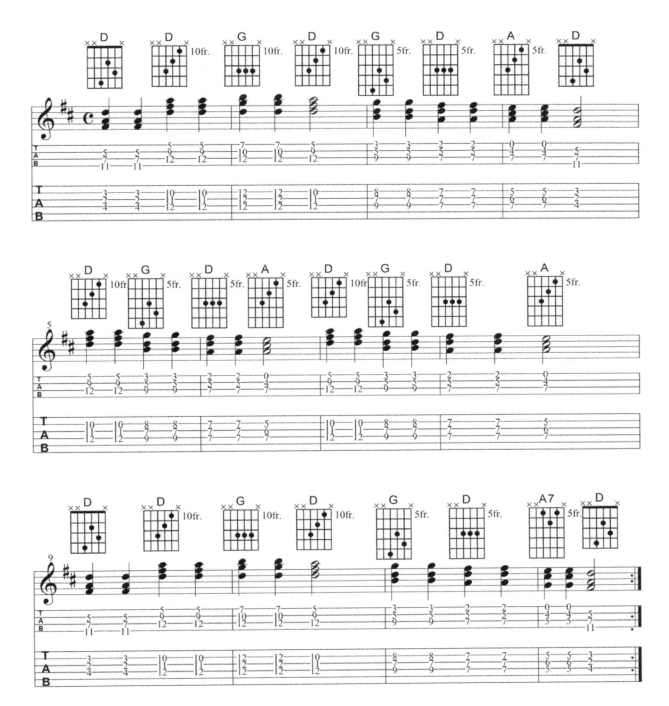

Twinkling Around With the Harmony

In three and four-part harmony, often you will find that the highest note is the melody. It's interesting to me how we seem to be conditioned to hear things that way. Here, I placed the melody in the center, on the guitar's third string. When you play this using triads as shown, the melody will not be as obvious due to its relationship with the harmony notes. The melody is the same, and the harmonies still just root, 3rd, and 5th. When you try this as arpeggios, play the melody note first. Take a look at the next example to see what I mean.

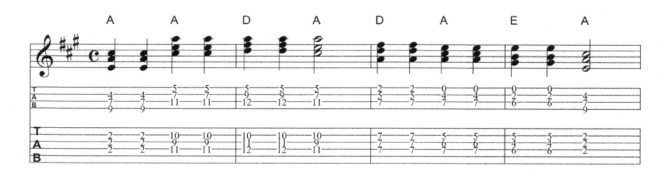

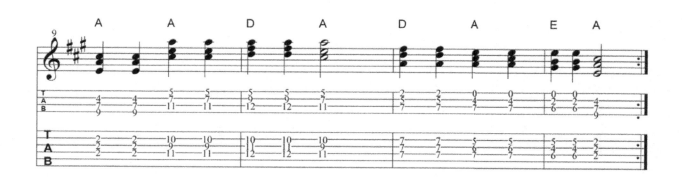

    12 - Melody, Harmony, Scales and Chords

Twinkle Yogurt, Melody at Bottom

This time the melody is on the bottom, where we're accustomed to hearing the bass. I included a good exercise for anyone who is learning to flatpick. Look at the pick direction arrows between the tabs. This is about playing triplets and the first three beamed eighth notes, your pick should go DOWN-UP-DOWN. The second group of eighth notes the pick should go UP-DOWN-UP, third group is DOWN-UP-DOWN, and the fourth group is UP-DOWN-UP. This is quite difficult at first, but it's about the best advanced pick control exercise I've come across. I learned this from Mike Parsons after he went to a seminar by Mr. Steve Kaufman (**www.flatpik.com**) at the Weber Mandolin Factory in Logan, Montana. (They're building great instruments… check them out at **www.webermandolins.com**). I think it's a good thing to pass along things that week to work and this drill is one that works. It's tough for sure, so go slowly and be patient. Mr. Kaufman travels quite a bit and although I've never had an opportunity to attend one of his seminars, my friends who have seen him agree that only does he play a bunch of instruments *really* well, he presents lots of good, usable stuff. You can find Steve Kaufman and a lot of other fine teachers and performers on **www.homespun.com**.

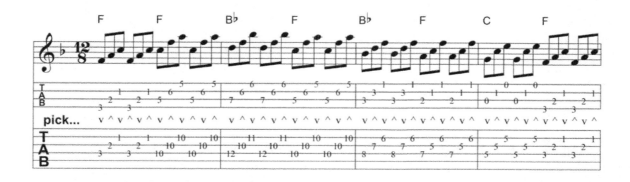

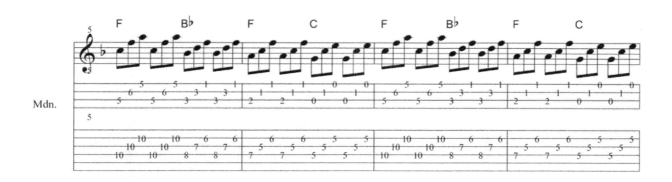

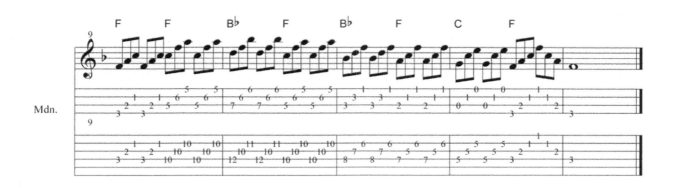

The Continuing Saga of the Diatonic Whirling Twinklet

Since I know you've been diligently practicing those triads on strings 2, 3, and 4, I thought I'd show yet another way to reharmonize this melody. The melody is the highest one and there is a different triad for each melody note. Some of the spans are tough to reach on a mandolin. Look it over first. Notice that there is only one note changed going from D to B minor and again from A to F# minor. That happens all the way through between sequential chords. Most players I know are more accustomed to reading tab and that's probably where you'll look first, but it is as easy to see in the notation, too.

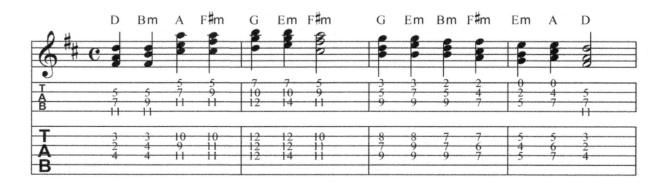

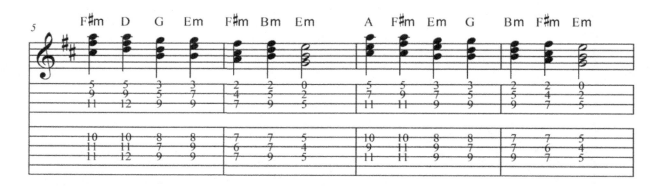

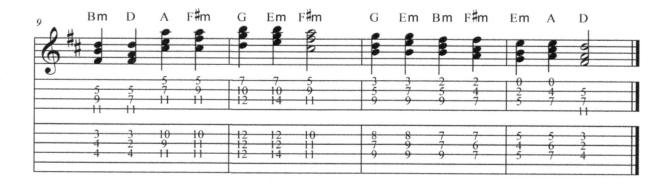

12 - Melody, Harmony, Scales and Chords

Twinkle minor seven flat five

Weiss, Thiele, and Douglas reharmonized Twinkle and made it beautiful. I reharmonized it for this example and it isn't beautiful. Interesting though. It's parallel harmony taken to an extreme. At first you'll probably hear the melody on the second string, but because all four notes are always maintaining the same intervals, you can play the melody on any string and think of the other three notes as harmony. This doesn't work as well on a mandolin, the spans are a bit long, but you'll get the idea, I think. No guitar tab, just slide the shape on the chord diagram up and down. Banjoliers get three notes. On guitar, these can also be heard as nine chords, first inversion, derived from Form #3. The first chord would be a G9, root low root would be the third fret, sixth string.

Silent Night
Joseph Mohr

Here's some mohr three-part close harmony for guitars and banjos. If you don't use the notes on the third string, then it's no longer "close" harmony.

12 - Melody, Harmony, Scales and Chords

Oh de Joy

This is a well-known theme from Ludwig van Beethoven's "Symphony #9 in D minor, opus 125, Chorale"…
usually known as "Ode to Joy." There isn't too much music I'm aware of that was written by deaf people. One
notable exception is Evelyn Glennie, who has written (at least) 53 concertos, 56 recital pieces, 18 concert pieces,
and two works for percussion ensemble. Beethoven wasn't completely deaf when he wrote this amazing piece
of music (the 9th Symphony). Apparently, at some point, he had the legs on his piano cut off so he could play
it while lying on the floor so he could feel the vibrations better. The melody is on top and I took a few liberties
with the harmonies. Please call Pinky if you object. This is lots of fun to play as arpeggiated triplets on a guitar
or banjo at 197 mph. Mandolin players… there are a lot of long stretches, a couple that span eight frets, you're
probably gonna have to use arpeggios.

Home On The Range
Brewster Higley and Dan Kelley

There's no way to know how Dan Kelley thought this melody should be harmonized. I like these chords. If you play it like you mean it, then it doesn't matter which chords you use. "Every music has a soul. Be true to it." The sentiments expressed by Mr. Higley have taken on a much greater significance for many of us in western Montana, with the relatively recent infestation of so-called "developers" anxious to wring every nickel out of "the last best place." We play this at nearly every Two Grass Crew gig and I've seen more than few old-timers singing along, not entirely dry-eyed. Us, too. Fortunately, it's still possible to get to Montana from Bozeman.

12 - Melody, Harmony, Scales and Chords

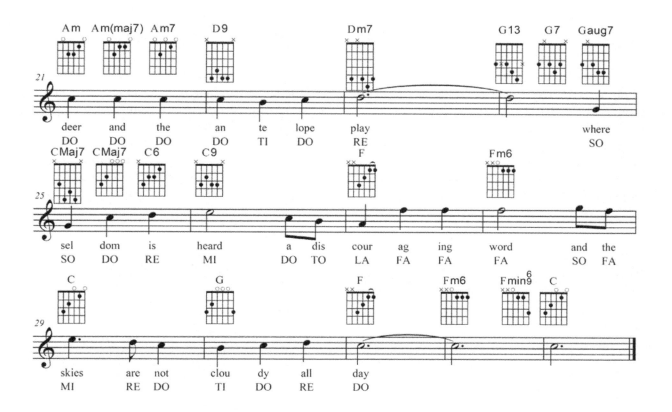

My Western Home
Dr. Brewster Higley

Oh give me a home
Where the buffalo roam
Where the deer and the antelope play
Where seldom is heard
A discouraging word
And the sky is not cloudy all day

Oh give me a land
Where the diamond bright sand
Throws its light on the glittering stream
Where glideth along
The graceful white swan
Like a maid in her heavenly dream

I love the wild flowers
in this bright land of ours
I love too, the wild curlew's scream
The bluffs and white rocks
The antelope flocks
That graze on the mountain so green

Oh give me the gale
Of the Solomon vale
Where the life stream so buoyantly flows
On the banks of the Beaver
Where seldom, if ever
Any poisonous herbage doth grow

How often at night
When the heavens were bright
By the light of the twinkling stars
Have I stood there amazed
And asked as I gazed
If their glory exceeds that of ours.

The air is so clear
The breeze is so pure
The zephyr so balmy and light
I would not exchange
My home here on the range
Forever in azure so bright

Oh Susannah
Stephen Foster

Here's another example of reharmonizing a simple melody. This was written with simple chords, I, IV, and V, but melodies are adaptable. This is similar to the version that Mr. James Taylor played on his album, "Sweet Baby James." I was way into bands like Deep Purple, Led Zep, and Jimi Hendrix when this came out and my friend, Dave Jones, bought this album. It had a big influence on my musical interests. Prior to this, I thought a guitar was supposed to be played loud and distorted, anything else was wimpy, and suddenly I realized acoustic instruments were every bit as cool. Since then, Mr. Taylor has been one of my favorite musician-songwriter-guitarists and two of his siblings—brother, Livingston and sister, Kate, are also thoroughly talented musicians and songwriters.

12 - Melody, Harmony, Scales and Chords

Harmonized Major Scale with Diatonic Triads

Harmonized Major Scale with Diatonic Triads

Many of the root position triads span seven frets on instruments tuned in 5ths, so they will be impossible for many people, but most of the others are playable. You'll also notice that some of the notes are below the range of a mandolin.

Harmonized major scale extended to include 7^{ths}

It isn't harmony until you play at least two notes at a time, but showing this as arpeggios and not as chords makes it possible to get the mandolin family here, too. Guitarists, this shows Forms #1-#4, open and closed.

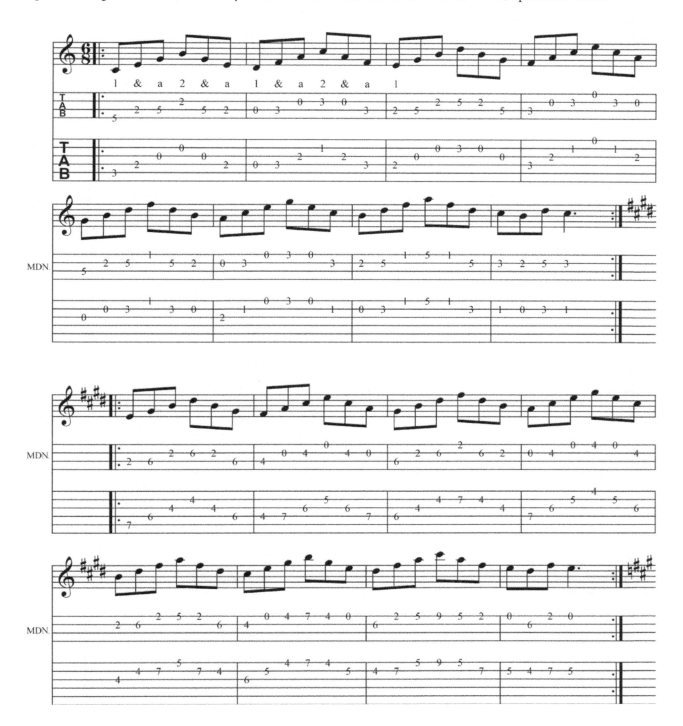

Harmonized major scale extended to include 7ths

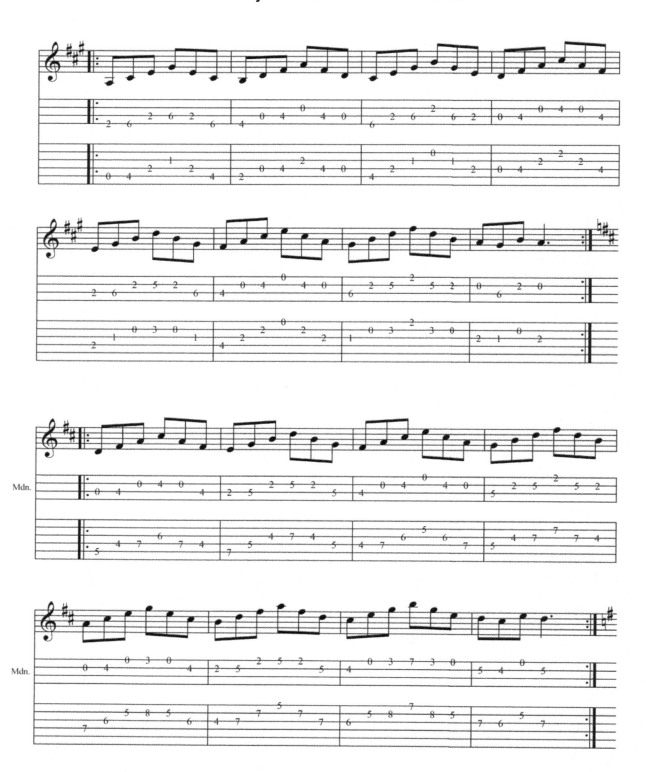

12 - Melody, Harmony, Scales and Chords

Harmonized major scale extended to include 7ths

Harmonized major scale extended to include 7ths

12 - Melody, Harmony, Scales and Chords

Harmonic Minor Scales... Harmonized

These are the diatonic triads generated by the harmonic minor scale. It sounds WAY different than the major scale, but there are no new notes. Minor, minor ♭5 (or dim), Augmented, minor, Major, Major and minor ♭5 is the sequence. I named the chords in the first line, but only provided the first chord for the others so you could have the enjoyment of labeling them. Notice that some of these begin with a root position triad and some start with the first or second inversion. The first chord names the scale.

Harmonic Minor Scales... Harmonized

12 - Melody, Harmony, Scales and Chords

Harmonic Minor Scales... Harmonized

"Bouree in E minor"
Johann Sebastian Bach

"Counterpoint" is a style of creating harmonies that is not based on chords. Instead two or more independent melody lines create the harmonies. J. S. Bach was one of the masters of this form and "Bouree in E minor" is an example. Nearly all orchestral music uses counterpoint, instead of chord based harmony, in part due to the fact that most orchestral instruments are capable of producing only one note at a time. So, the clarinets will be playing a melody and the oboe will be playing another melody, the violins will be playing a melody and the violas will be playing a melody. The sounds that are produced when they all play simultaneously are the very same chords that guitarists and pianists are accustomed to, but no one in an orchestra is thinking in terms of chords as we do. Four groups of instruments will make a sound that we can identify as a C major7 chord if the cellos play C, the bassoon plays E, the clarinets play G, and the violins play B. Texturally, it's very different than when all four notes are created by a single instrument, but you can still hear and identify chords. We start thinking "chords" when there are three or more notes played at the same time on a single instrument.

This piece is hard, but for anyone who's interested in fingerstyle it's worth the trouble. The little numbers that are beside the notes are suggested fingerings for your fret hand, but if you find ways to grab these notes that work better for you, that's fine. The chord diagrams I've shown include the two notes that make the original counterpoint lines. Although they really aren't "correct," it was helpful for me when I was learning this to be able to use familiar shapes to find the sounds instead of just two "unconnected" notes on a staff. You may find other chords that you like better… that's certainly OK with me.

Look through each melody line individually before you start to play it. The top melody line has a rhythmic pattern that repeats all the way through… two eighth notes followed by a quarter note sounds like "po-ny run, po-ny run." Notice that the low melody is nearly all quarter notes. Notice how the two lines tend to move in opposite directions… when the top line is going up, the bottom line is going down. It's often helpful to learn to play and sing each line before trying to combine them. If you do that, don't worry about the fingering numbers until you start to combine the two lines.

There are midi files at **www.GarageBandTheory.com** for this tune, but everyone should hear Leo Kottke play this piece. Another cool version was recorded by Jethro Tull. They did it with a swinging blues feel, with Ian Anderson playing the top melody line on a flute.

"Bouree in E minor"
J. S. Bach

Are you sure Bach did it this way? Well, I'd say probably. I get the impression that old Johann fooled around with every variation on a theme that he could think of and he could think of a lot of variations. It's easy, the harmony line sounds cool, and it's another illustration of the idea that you're allowed to twist a song any way you want to. The melody that Mr. Bach wrote is on top and I added a "parallel" harmony line a sixth below the melody.

Reading The Road Map | Chapter 13

Kitchens, bathrooms, and bedrooms are areas that are found in most homes. And, even though all bathrooms serve essentially the same functions in all houses, no two will be identical. And even though the rooms are all separate, distinct areas, there is some common theme that joins them into a single structure, with doors and hallways that allow you to wander from room to room.

The structure of a song is the skeleton that holds the different parts of the music together. It gives the song shape and each genre of music tends to follow a general structure. For example, most pop songs these days are structured on simple variations of a verse followed by a chorus, followed by another verse, followed by another chorus, and so on.

One way to visualize a song is as a series of "parts," like rooms in a house. The parts have a common theme and are linked together, but they are not identical to each other and each has a different "job to do."

Commonly used names for these song parts are:

Introduction (Intro)
It occurs only once. An intro can be several measures long, or just a couple of beats.

Verse
This is the "story" part of a song. Ordinarily the melody, chord progression, and the length are the same in all verses in any given son, but the lyrics change each time to develop whatever story is being told. Most songs you'll hear on the radio will have two or three verses.

> Dashing through the snow, in a one-horse open sleigh
> Over the fields we go, laughing all the way
> Bells on bobtails ring, making spirits bright
> What fun it is to ride and sing this sleighing song tonight…

…is the first verse to "Jingle Bells." It's 16 measures long, about average. Anywhere from eight to 32 bars could be considered kind of a "standard" range of how long a verse might be. There are no fixed rules. Some kitchens are big and some are small.

Chorus/Refrain
This is the part of the song that returns a few times, usually between the verses.

> Jingle bells, jingle bells, jingle all the way
> Oh what fun it is to ride in a one-horse open sleigh. Oh,
> Jingle bells, jingle bells, jingle all the way
> Oh what fun it is to ride in a one-horse open sleigh…

…is the chorus or refrain. The lyric, melody, and chord progression will (usually) be the same every time the chorus is played in the song. The melody in the chorus of "Jingle Bells" is different than the melody in the verse. That's the case in most songs. And since the melody in the chorus is different than the verse, the chord progression is probably fresh, too. In "Jingle Bells," the verse uses three chords. I, IV, and V. The chorus adds one new chord, the II. Again, anywhere between eight and 32 measures is common. In popular music, the chorus is often quite different than the verse melodically, rhythmically, and harmonically; may have a higher level of dynamics and activity; often with added instrumentation.

Solo/instrumental/ride
Not all songs have an "instrumental solo" section, but many do. In most cases, the progression will be identical to either a verse or a chorus. Everything is played about the same way that a verse or a chorus is played, except the "solo" instrumental will replace the vocalist.

Bridge
Most songs have an intro, verses, choruses, and some sort of ending, but a "bridge" is less common. Sometimes called an "interlude." It's often without lyrics, but not always. Sometimes it is the same as the Intro. Sometimes it's just another musical idea that seems to fit in a song, but not in as many places as a verse or chorus. A bridge is sometimes used to modulate to a different key, or to join two parts that don't "naturally" flow together. It can also be the "instrumental/solo" section. If somewhere in the middle of a song there's something that is musically and lyrically different from both verse and chorus, then that's the bridge.

Ending (tag, outro, extro)
Gotta have a way to get out of a song. Sometimes a tag will be very similar or identical to the intro. Sometimes in the last measure or two of a verse or chorus chords will be altered just a bit to create an ending. Sometimes the song will have an additional "ending part" tagged on to the last verse or chorus. Some songs just stop. Some songs end by fading out.

That's a good working list of song parts. Some songs will have several different parts and some songs have only one or two. Sometimes an intro will be 16 measures in length; sometimes a couple of whacks on a snare drum is the whole intro. A verse might be 24 bars or it might be four bars. Big bedrooms, little bedrooms. No rules.

Now that we have identified these parts, we'll join them together, one after another. One common outline for a song is: intro, verse, chorus, verse, chorus, solo over the verse, chorus, out (*). An intro, three verses, three choruses, and an ending. This "sequence of song parts" is referred to as the "form" of a song. The "form" is just an outline that tells in which order the different parts are to be played.

The part names "intro" and "ending" are clear as to their function in a song. The words "verse," "chorus," and "bridge," are a little bit vague. Plus, words like "chorus" and "verse" don't really work for labeling parts in tunes that have no lyrics, and there are loads of them. A different way of labeling and referring to different song parts that eliminates the need to define those words precisely is to simply label the parts A, B, D, D, and E, using as many different letters as needed. It's useful to differentiate these song part letters from chord names by drawing a box or something around them.

In the example shown two paragraphs above (*), if I substitute "A" for intro, "B" for verse, "C" for chorus and "D" for ending, the form would be shown as: A, B, C, B, C, solo over C, B, C, D. This system of using letters for labeling song parts works best for me, although it can be a little confusing at times because letters are already used for the names of the notes as well as chords.

The verse of "Jingle Bells" is 16 measures long and so is the chorus. One chorus, plus one verse, adds up to 32 measures. 3 verses + 3 choruses = 96 measures. Adding a four-bar intro and four bars for an ending yields a sum of 104 measures. Just using basic repeat signs allows the whole thing to fit on a single page.

An 8-/12 x 11 sheet of music paper will usually have eight to 12 staves on it. Song parts (verses, choruses, etc.) tend to be eight, 12, and 16 measures long, so it's common to divide each stave into four measures per line. Visually symmetrical = easier to follow. If I was to write all 104 measures of "Jingle Bells" from intro to ending, four measures per staff, 10 staves to a page, showing only the melody and chords, it would take 26 staves, which would fill two pages, plus part of a third page.

The melody and chords are the same in every verse, and even though you'll play it two times it's not necessary to write it out more than once. Same goes for the chorus. Write each one of them out one time, label the parts, and put a "legend" on the page and you have the whole thing on one side of a sheet of paper. See **example #1**. Easy. **Example #2** is identical except that I replaced the words "intro, verse, chorus, outro" with letters A, B, C, and D. The "legend" is what is referred to as the "form" and it just tells in which order you should play the labeled parts.

Example #1
# Jingle Bells
Form = Intro – verse, chorus (3x) outro

Example #2
# Jingle Bells
Form = A, B-C(3x), D

Example #3 shows what the first four measures of what "Jingle Bells" could look like in a score for an ensemble. It shows, note-for-note, what each instrument is supposed to play for an intro to Jingle Bells. If you were playing the oboe or viola or whatever, you would play four measures on this page, about 10 seconds worth of music, and turn the page for the next four measures. Play for 10 seconds, turn the page for the next four measures. Play for 10 seconds, turn the page for the next four measures, play for 10 seconds, etc.

Example #1 of Jingle Bells is 104 measures long. If I wrote a full score for "Jingle Bells" using 12 different instruments like example #3, 104 measures would fill nearly 30 pages. That's a lot of paper for about four minutes of music.

Just imagine what happens when instead of a four-minute arrangement for "Jingle Bells" the tune is something like Beethoven's Symphony #5 in C minor op. #67. It's just over 30 minutes of music with about a dozen other instruments in addition to the ones I've shown for "Jingle Bells." For something like that, the complete score starts weighing about the same as a half grown Labrador retriever.

A sheet of music can be thought of as a road map to help you go from point "A" to a safe arrival at point "B." You'll remember from the "Counting" chapter that there are words and symbols to set the "speed limit" and tell you when to slow down and when to speed up.

There are a handful of words and symbols that function just like other signs on the highway do. Some of these symbols and words tell you where to go in a song, sort of like a road sign that says "Next exit, 1 mile." Some musical symbols tell you to jump to a certain measure in a song. Playing a song that is spread out over more than one page can be inconvenient for a few reasons. One of those reasons is that when you're playing an instrument, your hands are busy and it's quite awkward to turn pages with your nose. That would be entertaining to watch, but inconvenient for the performer. Ideally, you want to have as much useful information on a single page as you can. "Useful information" is the central theme here.

Labeling song parts and using a legend to indicate the form is one way to minimize the number of pages required to represent a piece of music. Another way to do it is by using traditional symbols and words on and around the staff.

These symbols look kind of odd at first, but they're just like road signs that mostly give instructions for jumping to certain places on the page. There are only a few symbols that are used frequently. They are used in conjunction with a few words and phrases. As soon as those symbols, words, and phrases are translated into your native tongue, it's fairly simple to follow the directions.

If you drive, consider the "road sign" analogy for just a moment. You'll realize that there are a lot of signs on the road that you see and respond to, almost without thinking. Stop signs, signal lights, painted lines on the road, arrows painted on the road, yield, speed limit, school zone, street names, no left turn, right turn only, one way, flashing red lights in the rear view mirror, etc.

Most of those instructions can be shown two ways. One way is with simple pictures, diagrams, or symbols. And, of course, each of these pictures can be expressed in words. Nearly everybody who drives understands most of it. There are several Bozeman drivers who occasionally attempt to follow the instructions.

Jingle Bells
This shows a four measure intro for four vocalists and eight instruments

Some of the common road signs convey more complex instructions than you may have ever paused to consider. Even a simple stop sign has three different instructions attached to it. First, you're supposed to stop. Second is that you should stop at a certain place on the road (more or less). And third, you're supposed to go again, not shut off the engine and spend the rest of your life at that intersection. Stop is all it says. The instructions imparted by musical symbols are never more complex than a stop sign.

If you drive, chances are good that you are familiar with the translations of all of those signs I mentioned and more besides. You can probably do exactly what all of those instructions tell you to do while listening to the radio and talking on your cell phone and drinking a latte and never cause any major traffic disturbance. Unless you live in Bozeman. Then you feel entitled to run the red light in your enormous Exxon Valdez SUV 4x4 (with chrome brush guards) wearing a cowboy costume, looking oh so adventurous, outdoorsy, prosperous, and ridiculous talking on your cell phone and drinking a latte.

Following the directions on a sheet of music is much easier and less dangerous than driving, once your coordination has developed on your instrument to the same level of skill that most people have for driving a car, and you have a clear understanding of the musical symbols and signs. Consequences of a musical screw-up are rarely fatal. I've only been killed a couple of times. Depends on whom you happen to be working with, I imagine.

When you're reading through a piece of music and you see the beginning repeat sign, all you do is notice where it is and continue reading. Just keep cruising until you get to the ending repeat sign. Then, you jump back to the first one and go forward from that point again. This example is shown repeating only two measures, but usually a section to be repeated is eight or more measures. No matter how close together or how far apart they are, it works the same every time.

If that section is to be repeated more than once, above the ending repeat sign there will be something written to tell you how many times you should repeat that phrase.

It is also possible to show several adjoining sections that repeat.

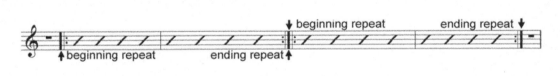

There is one more relatively common variety of a "repeat sign" and it's shown below… a diagonal slash with two dots. It's called a "measure repeat" and it means that you should repeat whatever was indicated in the previous measure. In the example below, you would play an Em9 using the rhythm pattern shown for two measures. In the third measure, the rhythm pattern changes and so does the chord. The measure repeat is drawn across the bar line and the number is a clue that this time you'll repeat the A9 pattern for two more measure. Those five measures are enclosed with repeat signs, so you'll play it again, Sam. The sixth measure has a rest in it so you don't play anything and you continue sitting quietly for a total of 23 measures. You won't encounter this "measure repeat" too often unless you're playing with an orchestra of some sort. This single line represents 33 bars of music.

Example #4, which began as "Don't Get Around Much Anymore," (Ellington, Strayhorn) identifies three different song parts with letters A, B, and C. I showed this in a "chord chart" format. The Real Book includes a normal five-line staff and the melody, but is otherwise very similar to this illustration. It says "medium swing" for a clue to a tempo, but the exact definition of "medium" can fluctuate according to how much coffee the drummer pounded before the set. The repeat signs show the section to be repeated, but there are no instructions with regard to how many times you go around. Your choice. There is a single measure at the bottom that shows some alternate chords and a rhythmic pattern and says it's OK to use it in certain spots. Notice that there is an eighth rest on the first beat. In this tune, that is referred to as a "kick" and the arranger doesn't want it during the solos.

This is enough useful information to be able to fake it and play a 30-minute version. You get to figure out an ending.

It's very common to play two verses in a pop tune before playing a chorus and that is one way that repeat signs are used. But there is a catch. Frequently, the second time through a verse or chorus, the music will be identical to the first pass, except for the final measure of the second time through. A slight change in the progression or melody can often help the tune flow smoothly to the next part.

Rather than write the whole thing out twice to accommodate that slight variation in only the last measure, there's something called a "second ending." It just means there is more than one ending to the section contained by the repeat signs.

Here's how this works. First, the instructions for how the repeat signs work don't change. The first time through, you pass the beginning repeat sign in measure #1 without slowing down. A few measures later, you pretty much ignore the little box that has the number 1 in it and you'll arrive at the ending repeat sign in measure #8. Jump back to the beginning repeat sign and play the phrase just like before. On this second pass through the section when you get to the end, you'll skip measure #8 that contains the ending repeat sign and the boxed in "1", and play measure #9 that has the boxed in "2" instead. That's the second ending. Since the end of that measure has a normal bar line, you just continue on to the next section. This second ending trick is about conserving paper and ink.

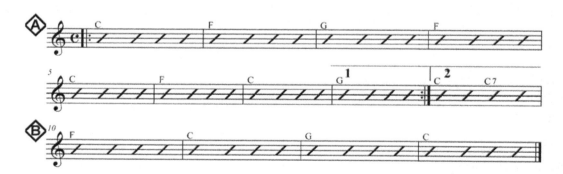

There aren't anymore variations on the repeat signs, although occasionally there is no "beginning" sign. In that case, you'll repeat from the very first notes on the page.

"**Da capo**" means "the beginning of the song." "**Da capo**" literally translated means "the top." The first notes on the page, the intro, the beginning, the edge. "Let's try it again from the edge" or "Take it from the top"... **Da capo**.

"**Al fine**" (pronounced al fee-nay) means "the end." Finish. Stop. It's all over now.

When you're supposed to play something from the beginning to the end with no "detours," those two words will be combined. "**Da capo al fine**" means go to the beginning and play it straight through to the end. **Da capo** is usually abbreviated to **D.C.**, so "**D.C. al fine**" is short for "**Da capo al fine**" and it means go to the beginning and play it through to the end.

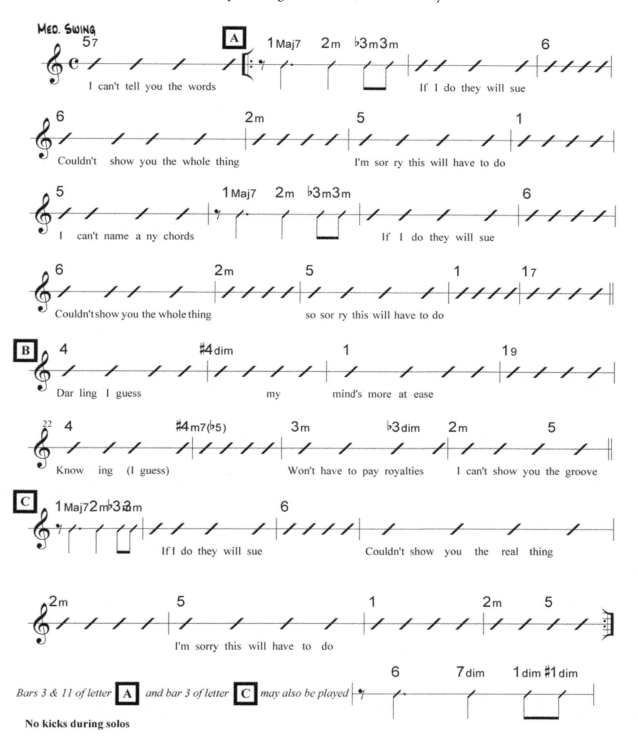

Example #4
Don't Get To Court Much Anymore
Duke Sharp - No rights reserved, show it to anyone

Our arrangement of "Jingle Bells" has three different parts. There is a four-bar intro, a verse, and a chorus. The verse and chorus repeat three times and then there's a tag, which is the same as the intro. I'm also going to insert a "bridge." This bridge will use the same progression as the intro and the "tag." The repeat signs and those two words (*Da capo* and *Al fine*) are sufficient trail markers to show a path through a fairly complicated structure: an intro, verse, chorus, verse, chorus, bridge, verse, chorus, and ending.

Here's how. Look at **Example #5.**

You start at the beginning. *Da capo*, the top of the page. There is no symbol at the beginning. This is our intro. Read from measure one through the beginning repeat sign in measure #5 all the way to the ending repeat sign in measure #36. There is a second ending indicated by the box containing the number "1". Jump back to the beginning repeat sign and play through to the second ending (skip measure #36 which is the first ending) where you find the instruction *D.C. al fine* in measure #37.

D.C. al fine means you go all the way back to the top of the page after you play measure #37 and play through (ignore) both repeat signs. You'll use the first ending at the repeat sign in measure #36, skip the second ending (measure #37), play the outro (measures #38 through #41), and stop where is says "*fine*"... the end.

There are two more common and useful symbols, the coda "*da coda*" ⊕ and the sign "*dal segno.*" 𝄋

Like a repeat sign, these road signs consist of more than one part, but this time there is also a word or phrase used with the symbol.

Each symbol is simply a marker that indicates a certain place to jump to on the page. A target. When you get to a measure that has a written phrase with the words "*al coda*" or "*dal segno, (D.S.)*" that is when you jump to the corresponding symbol. These might be thought of as the musical equivalent of a "detour" sign on the road.

The Italian words "*dal segno*" translate to "the sign" in English and are usually abbreviated to just two letters "*D.S.*"

The *dal segno* symbol is similar to the beginning repeat sign. When you encounter 𝄋, you just make a mental note of where it is on the page (the measure number can be helpful) and keep on reading. Then, when you encounter the abbreviation *D.S.*, it means go back to "the sign" 𝄋. You jump back to that spot in the tune and continue from that point. The letters *D.S.* say "jump now" and the 𝄋 says, "land here."

"*D.S. al Fine*" is a common instruction and what it means is that you go back to "the sign" 𝄋 and then continue to the end from that point.

Sometimes a song ends with a "special" phrase and that ending is referred to as a "Coda." I'm really not certain what the literal translation of "*da coda*" is. Here in Montana, we usually think of "North Da Coda" and "South Da Coda." John Wayne liked to talk about "Da Coda da West." I suspect that there is a different meaning in Italian. Probably something close to "ending" or "finale."

The *coda* ⊕ symbol works a lot like *dal segno* 𝄋 and it's a way to skip a section of a tune. A "coda" is a three-part symbol consisting of two symbols and the phrase al coda. These three pieces... ⊕ , *coda* and ⊕... are found in different locations on the page, but they are all part of a single "detour."

When you encounter the first symbol ⊕, you just make a mental note of where it is on the page and keep on playing. Again, it's similar to the beginning repeat sign. Then, when you see the words "D.C. al Coda" it means that you go back to the beginning of the song (*D.C. = Del Capo*) and play right up to the first ⊕. At that point, you skip directly to the second ⊕ and play until there is another detour sign or the song ends. Usually, it's the end of the song. You skip all the measures of music in between the two symbols.

When you see "***D.S. al Coda***," it means that you go back to "the sign" 𝄋 and play up to the first ⊕. At that point, you skip directly to the second ⊕ and play it to the end, following any new clues you might encounter after that point.

Example #5
Jingle Bells
Pierpont, James

Take a look at "I Love Lucy," **example #6**. In The Real Book (Sher Music), there are chords, lyrics, and a melody line, not to mention the cool arrangements. Chuck Sher, a reasonable man, said if I could get a print license, we could probably work out a deal so I could show his pages. Unfortunately, my request to purchase licenses was denied by the publisher that controls the print rights. So, this compromise sort of represents a version of a tune written by Elliot Daniel that Richie Cole recorded, a great alto sax player. Get The Real Book to learn all the secret information.

First, as always, just read through the whole page and take inventory of all the road signs and other clues. This example uses three sets of repeat signs, two first and second endings, a coda and a segno. There is a metronome setting and some new words.

The first clues you get are "Bright Samba," and a half note = 144. Can't really explain "bright samba"… it's a feel thing. Listen to some Tito Puente recordings and you'll get a much better idea of what a "bright samba" is than 16 pages of explanation can offer.

A half note = 144 for a metronome setting is a little confusing for me, so I switch it in my head to "a quarter note = 288" or, translated into words that I understand… 288 beats per minute. That's quick, she's about a mover, for sure.

There is a two-bar intro with repeat signs and the words "vamp till cue." A dictionary definition of vamp is "to improvise simple accompaniment or variation of a tune or phrase." That means you jam on those two measures till somebody (usually the soloist) gives you your "cue" to move on. Then you'll play measure three, which is the second ending for the two-bar intro.

What you're trying to accomplish here is to establish a "groove"… make it feel like something. "Simple accompaniment" is a good clue. If you're not the soloist, you probably want to play something harmonically simple, not a lot of riffs and runs. Lock in with the drums and bass for a solid rhythm thing and make a big, fat groove (**BFG**) for the soloist to play over.

There are three markers at measure four, **dal segno**, a repeat sign, and Part A. Remember that you'll come back to 𝄋 when you encounter the abbreviation **D.S.** Scan forward and you'll see first and second endings for Part A, and notice that both endings are eight bars. The ending repeat sign is in measure #19.

There is a ⊕ halfway through the second ending and remember that codas work in pairs. This is a the first one and you just notice and remember its location until you encounter the word **coda**.

Below the second ending it says, "Solo on Part A (both endings)." That means you'll play measure #4 through measure #19, skip back to measure #4 and this time you play measure #11, you skip the first ending (measures #12 through #19) and go to measure #20 and play the second ending. That completes one loop. Count it out and you get 32 measures. I'm not positive what "solo break-------" is about, but I think it means there is a rhythmic break in those measures when the one soloist is finished and the next one starts.

Then it says, "After solos, **DS al Coda**. It means that everybody who wants a ride (ride = solo) takes one, two, or 12 loops and after everybody has a turn, it's time to think about ending the thing.

Solos are done. Go to the 𝄋, take the repeat and play both endings, but in the middle of the second ending you'll skip from the end of measure #23 where the first ⊕ lives, directly to the second ⊕ at the beginning of measure #28, and continue from there. There's another set of repeat signs bracketing measures #32 and 33, with "vamp & solo till cue." After a while, Richie cues the band and you finish up with measures #34, 35, and 36. The crowd goes wild.

Notice that the first and second endings in Part A are way longer than the one-measure endings that I used for the previous examples.

If a band plays this tune and there's a flugelhorn, a banjo, an accordion, and a glockenspiel doing solos and everybody takes a ride a few times around on Part A, this could be a 20-minute epic and you can get all the important clues on one said of an 8-1/2 x 11 sheet of paper. I think that's pretty amazing. Useful, too.

Example #6
I Love Lucy
Elliot Daniel (as played by Richie Cole)

Here's an important point regarding the way repeat signs usually work when taking a "detour," either a 𝄋 or a ⊕. Classical players almost always ignore the repeats on the second time around unless specifically instructed to take them. "Specifically instructed" usually means the **D.S.** will also say "repeats good" or "take repeats" if you should take them on this pass. **D.S. repeats good** or **D.C. al Coda** take repeats means take the repeats. To be safe, if you're reading a chart for the first time at a rehearsal for "Jazz Band 101," you might just ask the bandleader, "Repeats good on the DS?" before the song starts.

Just as there can be more than one set of repeat signs in a single piece of music, 𝄋 and ⊕ can also be used more than once. If there are two sections to be indicated with "the sign," the first one will be shown with **D.S.** as usual. The second section will be marked with 𝄋𝄋 and the clue to jump there is **D.S.S.**

If there are multiple codas, the ⊕ at the target measures are labeled ⊕ *Coda 1*, ⊕ *Coda 2*, ⊕ *Coda 3*, etc., and the instructions to jump will be **D.S. al Coda 1**… **D.C. al Coda 2**… **D.S.S. al Coda 3**, or some variation.

There are a lot of fakebooks in all genres of music. A "fakebook" provides just enough clues about a song on one page, maybe two, to be able to fake it. Lyrics, melody, chords, and form. Some of them are really good and can be quite handy and good fun. A few hundred tunes packed into a small space. A clear representation of tunes/songs shown on a single page is a feature I look for when I'm buying a "fakebook." I usually avoid the books that have tabs for the guitar parts because once you find the correct inversion of the chords most of the single-note guitar parts will be right there anyway. One or two tabs, plus melody and chords, spreads a song out over too many pages for me.

What you see in fakebooks are very abbreviated versions of what you hear on a recording. There might be a dozen or more different instruments used on a recording. There are often two or more harmony vocalists, in addition to the lead vocal line. There might be two keyboards, three guitars, strings, horns, percussionists, drum kit, etc. Every note for every instrument is way more information than most people want.

A songbook (fakebook) will usually have the vocal melody written out, note-for-note, with the lyrics for the first verse under the melody notes. Chord changes are shown above the melody notes and the form may be indicated using letters (or part names). Traditional music symbols are often used in conjunction with a system of labeling parts. Sometimes there's a metronome setting to give you a suggestion for the tempo.

There is rarely much more detail than this. The bass part is not written out note-for-note, nor is the keyboard part, guitar part, percussion part, drum kit, etc.

The layout and arrangements of **Examples #4**, "Don't Get To Court Much Anymore" and #6, "I Love Lucy," are modeled on the The New Real Book from Sher Music. They use a combination of all of the systems shown… traditional musical symbols, metronome settings, and clues like "medium swing," words like intro, verse, chorus, etc., and letters to replace those words. I chose these tunes because they're familiar to lots of people and they very conveniently fit on a single page.

At a jam, rehearsal, or even a gig, if you're playing bass and somebody else is singing, you probably don't need to see the melody. The root notes of the chords and the form of the song are all you need. Same goes for guitar and any other "backup" instruments. Slashes indicating beats are often more useful than the melody line.

Example #7 shows "Jingle Bells" trimmed down to just this form. This minimalist variety of a piece of music is often called a "chart." It's the kind I've encountered and used most often. Sometimes a measure or two might have notation for a phrase that has to be played, but usually just chord names are shown.

Chord charts are frequently written at a jam or a lesson or between sets. It's just a very general road map without lots of details. Bass, guitar, keyboard, mandolin, and banjo can all use the same chord chart. The horn section will probably have to transpose theirs. If everyone is accustomed to reading the number system, you don't even need to transpose. They can be done on a napkin, if necessary. It's similar to giving the band driving directions for how to get from Bozeman, Montana to Pocatello, Idaho on the Interstate and saying only, "Go west on I-90 to Butte, then go south on I-15. Stop when you get to Pocatello." That will get you there, but it's up to you to fill in the details. If you're an experienced driver, that's probably sufficient information. Fakebooks, charts, and lead sheets are the way… enough information to get you there, and not much more.

Example #7
Jingle Bells

Reading and making charts are really useful skills. Neither is difficult, and I strongly suggest that you devote some time to learning the craft.

When you buy staff paper, it will usually be eight or 10 staves like the first line shown, below. I usually want four measures per line 1) I'll draw the center bar line first, every staff, straight down the middle of the page, and the end lines. 2) Next, divide those in half, so it's fairly symmetrical. 3) Next, I'll make slashes in maybe 24 measures. If the tune is in common time, each measure gets four slashes. Three-four time gets three slashes. Then fill in the chords so they line up vertically with the appropriate beat. If there is a pick-up measure, I divide the first measure in half. After a while, you won't need the slashes and you can use the staff for notation.

Using staff paper for charts is a good option, especially if there are places where you need to write a few notes for a certain book or phrase you don't want to forget. But if all you need are chords and you don't need any individual notes, a single line (percussion clef) will work just fine. You don't even need slashes to indicate beats, if you can keep the spacing of your chords proportional. I used 14 pt. Arial for this, and I can print 20 lines like this on a page with all four margins set at .7 inches. If you understand repeat signs and codas, 20 lines on a page (80 measures) is nearly always enough for a pop tune.

A single staff line with bar lines is enough to indicate chords as well as any specific rhythmic patterns that you may need to remember.

If you practice writing charts, it will be loads easier to read charts that someone else has written. It is definitely worth your time. Just copy them out of your songbook, or copy some from this chapter or "Progressions." Practice makes better.

Here is a way to show "Jingle Bells," on any old piece of paper. You've got an intro, an "A" part, and a "B" part. The beats are indicated by slashes and the chord changes occur on the first and third beats. Chord names or numbers, take your pick. For the ending, lots of eye contact and make sure everybody ends together on the same stage… I mean… ends on the same chord and beat.

form=intro AB 3x out		form=intro AB 3x out	
Intro	4/// - 1/// - 5/// - 1///	**Intro**	F/// - C/// - G/// - C///
A	1/// - 1/// - 1/// - 4///	**A**	C/// - C/// - C/// - F///
	4/// - 5/// - 5/// - 1///		F/// - G/// - G/// - C///
	1/// - 1/// - 1/// - 4///		C/// - C/// - C/// - F///
	4/// - 5/// - 5/// - 1/5/		F/// - G/// - G/// - C/G/
B	1/// - 1/// - 1/// - 1///	**B**	C/// - C/// - C/// - C///
	4/// - 1/// - 2/// - 5///		F/// - C/// - D/// - G///
	1/// - 1/// - 1/// - 1///		C/// - C/// - C/// - C///
	4/// - 1/// - 5/// - 1///		F/// - C/// - G/// - C///

It's possible to represent "Jingle Bells" on 30 pages of staff paper, or on half a napkin. It all depends on how much information you need to convey. If you are pretty familiar with a tune, the "napkin chart" can be perfectly adequate.

I don't know how many gigs I've picked up over the years in part because I can read charts. Lots. It isn't "reading music" in the way that orchestral players read, but I don't know what else to call it. When the tune starts, I'm listening real close to pick up the stuff that's not on the page, which is most of it. So I suppose that would be called "playing by ear." Before we kick off the tune, I'll scan the chords and since I can identify progressions, I'll recognize some of the progressions shown earlier. Scale practice has firmly embedded those sounds in my head and I know that scales will be involved in the melodies so I'll be listening for familiar runs. Using knowledge of scales and progression is playing by memory, I guess. When it's my turn for a solo, a combination of reading skills, listening, and memory give me a place to start. Using charts seems to be right in between what people think of as playing by ear and reading music. I listen to what's being played, paying close attention to the bass for chord changes and drums for groove, and I can sort of let my subconscious operate my hands because of all the time spent doing exercises. The clues are written down in case I can't hear/anticipate what's coming up.

Understanding just a few concepts, symbols, and words will allow you to access nearly every commercial songbook out there. Of course, there are more words and symbols that I've shown, but this is enough to get you started. As you encounter new ones, you'll add them to your vocabulary.

I suggest that you get a CD by one of your favorite artists and then order the matching "fakebook/songbook." Spend some time reading the music while you listen to the CD and follow along.

At first, choose songs that you already know pretty well. You want to be able to sing/hum along with the recording all the way from the beginning to the end.

For instance, suppose you choose a Beatles tune "Eleanor Rigby," from the album "Revolver." Open The Beatles Book, Easy Guitar, 100 Songs to page 41. Before you start the music playing, look the page over and notice all the symbols, repeat signs, codas, second endings, etc. Look for words like "Intro, Bridge, Verse, Chorus, coda, segno" and associated symbols and observe their locations on the page. Look at the chords and notice which beats the chords change on. Get familiar with what is on the page.

Then, put on the recording and just follow along with the lyrics. This should be easy since you already know the song. Do that a couple of times, or 20 times, and while you're listening, tap the beats. Repeat this until you can follow the lyrics on the page right along with the recording.

When you can follow the lyrics easily, look at the notes on the staff and follow the "road signs" instead of the lyrics, always tapping in time. Notice the chord changes and which beats they change on. If you know the chords that are shown, visualize playing those chords at the right time. Repeat the same song until reading the symbols, following the chord changes and following individual melody notes across the page is easy in that tune. Then, start the process again with a different song. This exercise is about reading a page of music, not playing written music. Leave the instrument in its case.

It doesn't take but a few hours to acquire the ability to fully understand repeats, codas, and segnos. At that point, the door to the enormous musical library that's out there is wide open.

The book that I use is The Beatles Book, Easy Guitar, 100 Songs published by Hal Leonard. I'm a very thoroughly dissatisfied Hal Leonard customer and I don't usually like to recommend Hal Leonard's products anymore, but that's a personal thing… they do publish lots of good books.

I've listed the tunes that I use in three groups of increasing complexity with regard to the number of segnos, codas, and other symbols. The tunes in Level 1 are the easiest to navigate. Within each level the tunes are just alphabetical and I think that "Her Majesty" is the easiest.

I use this book because of the musical variety available in a single publication. There is a lot that can be learned by examining Beatles' music. In addition, the music is familiar to lots of people and the CDs are easy to find.

Also, loads of artists have covered Beatles' tunes and it can be interesting to hear several different interpretations of a single song.

Level 1: Act Naturally, Come Together, Day Tripper, Eleanor Rigby, Her Majesty, Here There and Everywhere, Let It Be, The Fool on the Hill, While My Guitar Gently Weeps.

Level 2: And I Love Her, Girl, All My Lovin', Do You Want to Know a Secret, From Me to You, I'll Follow the Sun.

Level 3: Birthday, Hard Days Night, Love Me Do, Nowhere Man.

Reading music is a completely different skill than playing written music. It's been my experience that a novice player can learn to read a page of music at levels well beyond their ability to play. With practice, the playing skills will catch up to the reading skills. What a combo.

The next example "Mohair Man," is similar to a page from a Hal Leonard publication, "Nowhere Man" in The Beatles Complete Scores.

My goal was/is to use examples from popular music to illustrate the concepts and I did attempt to purchase a license so I could show you "Nowhere Man" by the Beatles. Unfortunately, my request was denied, so I twisted this illustration a bit. You can still see how they presented the tune in a commercial songbook without infringing on their copyright. It would have been better if they had just sold me the license.

That book has full transcriptions from the original recordings of every song the Beatles recorded. "Full transcriptions" means every note played by every instrument on 213 songs. It should probably come with a magnifying glass as standard equipment. For a person who wants to learn any Beatles tune, note for note, this is the book.

These pages are very similar to what a conductor in an orchestra uses, except that an orchestra typically uses a lot more instruments and different ones than a 60's pop-rock band.

First, notice that there are six different "instruments"... lead vocal, harmony vocals, an electric guitar, an acoustic guitar, a bass, and a drum kit. The "kit" is really a bunch of different instruments (kick, snare, hat, toms, etc.), but they're all shown on a single staff and usually thought of as a single instrument. There are five entire measures shown on this page.

The top staff is for the lead vocal. That's nearly always the case. The next staff is for the harmony vocalists. Two harmony lines are written on the same staff, which is labeled "chorus."

The next staff shows the electric guitar. Notice that it "lays out," doesn't come in till measure #15.

The next staff is for the acoustic guitar. There is a new word here, "tacet." It means "don't play for a while." "1 x tacet" means that the first time through you don't play, but when this melody line is sung again, jump right in.

Notice that there are no individual notes shown for this guitar part. Slashes with stems and flags for note values is called rhythmic notation. The slashes just mean you are supposed to "strum" the chord in this rhythm. Again, the tab is a bit different here, using the lines as a horizontal chord diagram. Dots show where your fingers go and the numbers below indicate which fret.

Bass is next. This is nearly standard tab with stems and flags, and notation in the bass clef.

The bottom staff shows the "kit." The lowest notes represent the kick drum (bottom space on the staff) and the highest notes are the high hat. The ones shown on the third space on the staff are for the snare drum. The note heads used for percussion instruments are not always oval or round like notation for other instruments; often they're more like little diamonds. Sometimes notation for cymbals uses an "x" for the note head with a stem and flags to show values. There is another new symbol here, the slash with a dot above and below that is in the middle of a measure. That just means, "Play what you played in the previous measure."

Mohair Man

The Needles

Next is the same tune, but in a different format and substantially reduced in the number of pages. It's another rendition of my song, "Mohair Man." It's useful to see how there can be great differences in how one song might be written in different publications and the reason I chose "Nowhere Man" is that I was able to find it in four entirely different formats. This page layout is nearly identical to the pages that show "Nowhere Man" in another Hal Leonard publication, The Beatles Book, Easy Guitar, 100 Songs, and similar to songbooks by lots of other publishers.

In spite of the abbreviation, we still find the lead vocal line written out, all the chords used are diagrammed, and the arrangement is clear. Since the bass player is usually hanging around the root of each chord, and 99% guaranteed to be playing the root on the first beat of each chord change, this also is enough information to get the bass player in the ballpark.

In addition, you'll remember from the discussion of harmony that the most likely harmony notes are contained in (or at least near) the chords shown.

I like this abbreviated format. There is lots of information in a small space. You'll find lots of commercial books that present the tunes in a layout like this.

I usually don't want tabs, mostly because it spreads a song out over too many pages. There are times it would be handy, especially because I read tab better than I read notation. But, if the chords are shown, any parts that might be tabbed will often be contained in (or near) those chords, and I'm willing to dig them out on my own.

It's rare that I want to play exactly what was played on a recording anyway, for a couple of reasons. One reason is that those lines won't really work in the usual jamming situation because you almost need to have the same instrumentation and arrangement as the recording for that tabbed part to "fit into."

The other reason is that I like making up my own part. If there is a "hook" that is such an integral part of the song that it has to be played, then I learn it. The intro for "Brown Eyed Girl" is an example. The guitar riff in "Day Tripper" is another. But more often than not, I just want the chords, melody, and words, and I'll make up my own arrangement. So far, no rock stars have showed up to complain about my lame versions of their favorite songs. I'll keep trying. It may be because they haven't heard me trashing their tunes.

The chord diagrams in publications like this are good for beginners and don't take up enough space to create a nuisance. Flipping pages when your hands are busy with an instrument and you're trying to follow along is a nuisance and tabs often cause that sort of problem.

You'll notice that it says "Strum Pattern: 6" and "Pick Pattern 4." Books often include eight or 10 examples of strumming patterns that will basically get you through a tune.

I've used my Beatles CDs to practice reading music. I put in a CD, turn to the matching song in the book, and read along while the tune is playing. I'm not even near a guitar. I'm simply reading the music, following the road signs, and looking at the melody and chords as they occur. Rewind, do it again. Rewind, do it again. Rewind, do it again. Rewind, do it again.

For me (and many of my students) this type of reading exercise has been very helpful for improving skills at playing written music.

First, choose a song that you know well. If you're familiar with the music before you start trying to read it, it doesn't take long before recognizing the symbols and skipping around according to their instructions becomes pretty easy. Then it's just a matter of playing the chords... sort of.

Mohair Man

The Needles

Strum pattern: 6   Pick pattern: 4

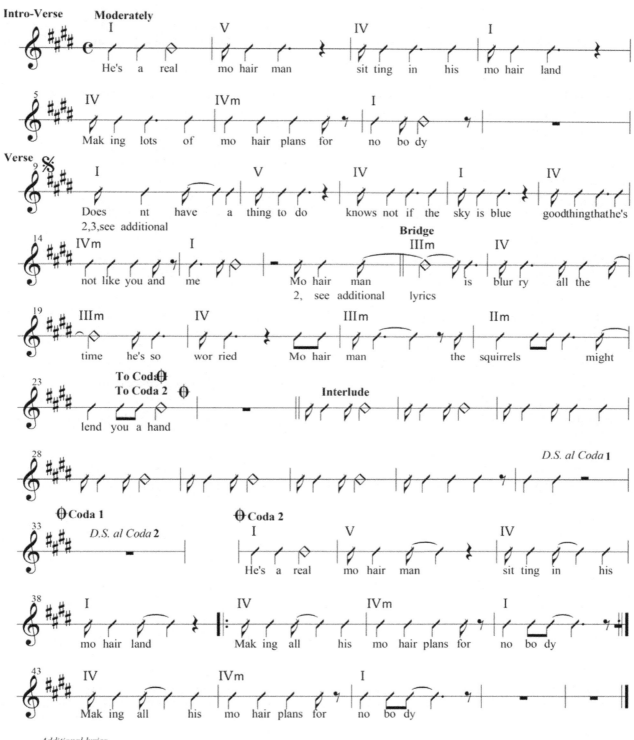

Additional lyrics
2. He's as rude as he can be
   etc.

Bridge 2. Mo hair man, he's worried
          etc.

3. Doesn't have a thing to do
   etc.

Next is a look at the way you will find tunes presented in The New Real Book. It's one of my favorite books. There are hundreds of tunes here and good arrangements. Mr. Chuck Sher was a helpful as he could be in my quest to show relevant examples. As usual, my attempt to purchase a license was unsuccessful, so again I had to compromise. As part of my "Suite for My Pal Hal," this is a song titled, "Odd, Them Leaves."

"Autumn Leaves" by Joseph Kosma and Johnny Mercer is a classic tune found on page 12 of The New Real Book. My song, "Odd, Them Leaves," is very similar, but I used a few different chords and I marked those differences with asterisks. I also wrote the melody, not shown here.

"B" section begins at measure 17, and the double bar lines at the end of measure 16. Double bar lines indicate a new section, just like the letters A and B or words like "intro, verse, chorus," etc. Double bar lines are a common symbol, but not as obvious as the other section markers.

Notice the first, third, sixth, seventh, and eighth lines. Above the usual chord symbols there is a second set of chords in parentheses. These are chords that will work, too. You get to choose which ones to play.

Also, notice at the bottom right corner where it says, "Melody is freely interpreted rhythmically." This is an important idea that applies to playing any music you find in fakebooks.

The page provides lots of clues to how to find your way through a tune. But it's really difficult, if not impossible, to indicate "phrasing" that a vocalist or soloist uses in an interpretation of a song.

Music is drawn very symmetrically on a page. All the eighth notes, quarter notes, chord symbols, etc., line up exactly in the proper location in each measure and it's all shown to be exactly in line with the beats and divisions of the beats.

In reality, it's almost never played that way by humans. Electronic music in various forms can be absolutely precise, but people (hopefully) don't play like machines. The beats pulse in a consistent fashion, but everyone "phrases" things differently. What's on the page is very dry and very straight and it's up to the performer to make it feel like music.

One way to illustrate how phrasing can make a difference in the way music is felt is to consider this sentence containing seven words. You can say the same words seven times in a row, but by emphasizing different words, it's possible to convey seven different meanings.

<u>**I**</u> didn't say he borrowed your charts.
I **didn't** say he borrowed your charts.
I didn't **say** he borrowed your charts.
I didn't say **he** borrowed your charts.
I didn't say he **borrowed** your charts.
I didn't say he borrowed **your** charts.
I didn't say he borrowed your **charts**.

This illustration shows emphasis on different parts of a spoken phrase. Musically, it's also very common for a performer to alter the duration of written notes (Melody is interpreted rhythmically freely) so notes can be longer or shorter, with different emphasis, according to the performer's interpretation. The pulse remains consistent, but maybe you want to "push" a little bit and play "on the front" of the beat. Or maybe you like it a little more laid back and tend to play "on the back" of the beat. It's your choice.

When using charts or fakebooks keep in mind that no matter how much information you find, or how "accurate" the information on the page might be, you'll still interpret in a way that is musical to you, the performer. Ink on a page is not music, it's a road map to help you find your way through unfamiliar territory. You have to do the driving.

Odd, Them Leaves

Consider the process of painting by numbers. There are little areas outlined, with numbers inside. There's a color key that shows different colors and each of those colors is associated with a specific number. When the colors indicated are tastefully and skilfully applied in the little numbered areas, the finished piece will accurately reflect the vision that a single artist conceived.

Those numbers and colors can be thought of as the equivalent to many of the words and symbols found on a sheet of music that are referred to as "expressions and articulations."

In most cases, an author is communicating directly with an audience of one. A playwright also uses words and is often delivering a message to an audience of one; however, in order for that message to be delivered to a roomful of individuals, a playwright usually requires several intermediaries… the actors and actresses, stagehands, set designers, and a director, among others.

As shown, simply changing the inflection on a single word in a sentence can substantially alter the way the sentence is perceived by the listener. A director coaches performers as to how the lines should be delivered according to his interpretation of the scene. These instructions can apply to the words spoken and also the physical postures that are part of communication, as well as the lighting, the other actors, and the props used in the set. All of these factors contribute to how an audience perceives a scene. Most of these directions will be presented verbally, not written as they are on a sheet of music.

Music is a rich, expressive language that transcends borders, nationalities, and the spoken word. There are composers and players who are somehow able to express the full range of human emotion and experience without a single word being spoken to the audience, just as some actors, painters, and sculptors, etc., can achieve language-free communication. And just as a playwright needs a team to communicate, a composer is speaking to an audience through a group of musicians.

Since individual members of a band or orchestra will interpret any given piece of music differently, composers have to write clues all over the place to help the musicians deliver the message that the composer intended.

Nearly all of my students have been Americans. Most Americans don't learn any language but English, and consequently, tend to view the words found on a sheet of music as complicated, mysterious, and confusing. In fact, they are typically very simple messages. Slowly, quickly, lovingly, forcefully, with emphasis, tenderly, gradually increase the tempo, gradually decrease the tempo, etc., are instructions that are commonly found on a sheet of music. There are words that suggest different physical approaches to creating the notes, such as "col legno" (with wood) telling the violins to use the wood of the bow and not the hair, and "col pugno" that means "strike the piano with a fist." It's a lot like painting by numbers. The composer says, "Do this here. Trust me, it will be a good thing."

It's easy to forget that moods and emotions are often the motivation behind many great pieces of music. Nearly everything on the page is intended to help tell the story, and is usually intended to be clearly and simply stated. In Italian. It seems to me that the majority of music we hear is linked with some sort of advertising and it is written, selected, and arranged for its tendency to stick in the memory, not for conveying any emotional message. There's lots of icky-gooey brain glue out there masquerading as music. Subtle nuance and inflection are not required.

It doesn't hurt anyone to become familiar with a second spoken language, but I also know that it is absolutely unnecessary for most of us to learn to instantly identify these hundreds of words and symbols. But at the same time, we do need to be aware of their existence, and more importantly, to remember why they exist and why they are used. It isn't because the composer had nothing else to do one day so he thought he'd write graffiti all over the music.

Composers and musicians employ subtle variables, colorations, textures, and shadings to communicate to those rare individuals out there who are actually listening. There is a space for one and two-word clues. Even when it isn't written down on a page, you want to play with all the emotion you're able to muster, because that's what makes the difference between music and notes in a row.

If you sing "Twinkle" like you really care, it might come out sounding like Satchmo singing, "It's A Wonderful World." It's not about the notes, it's about the feeling. That's what all those words and symbols are saying, "Play it like you mean it." Keep those adjectives in mind while you play your exercises and practice playing scales and everything else expressively and emotionally. That way, you're practicing music, not notes. There's a difference.

This is very similar to The New Real Book, too. It was transcribed from the version that George Benson did. Mr. Benson sang the lyrics and played the changes that Leon Russell wrote, not the silly stuff I had to use in order to avoid a legal battle with the corporation that controls the print rights. I also dumped the chords. There's not much new here, except at the bottom where it says, "Solo on vamp or on head ABA." The new word is "head." One common definition is "melody Jazz improvisation often involves a tune like 'This Masquerade.'" The first soloist (or vocalist) will usually play something very close to the written melody to establish and identify the song. That's referred to as "playing the head." In this case, since it says, "solo on head," it refers to the progression in parts A and B. The guitar solos over ABA, then the sax does ABA, then the keyboard does ABA, etc. When all the soloists are done, there are instructions at the bottom to lead you through an ending using codas and a segno. The New Real Book (and some other fakebooks) will supply lots of clues if you take a moment to read the page. I don't know how many people have recorded this tune, but George Benson's is my favorite. He's a great guitarist and he REALLY sings it.

This Masquerade
Leon Russell

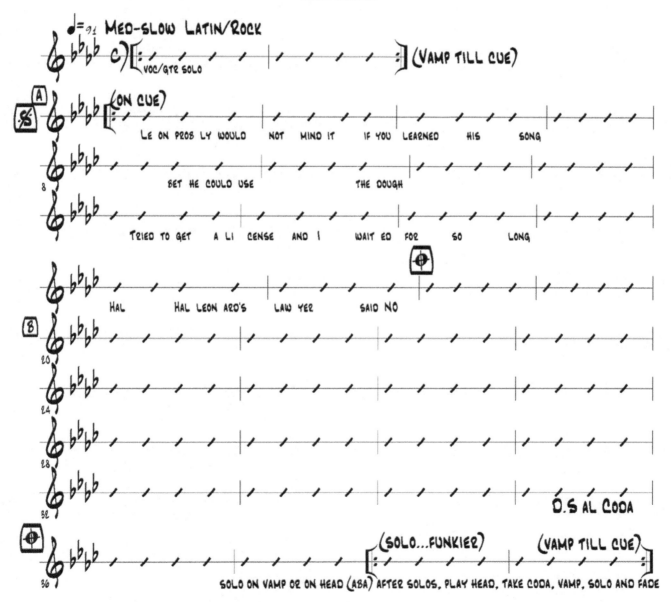

Here are a couple of examples of what I call "individual interpretation" in a tune called "Arkansas Traveler." These are similar to the transcriptions found in the Fiddlers Fakebook by David Brody, Oak Publications. This is another one of my favorite books and I think it's a great resource to have on your shelf. It's loaded with hundreds of good tunes in a good format. Like the tunes in The New Real Book, the tunes in the Fiddlers Fakebook only cost a few pennies each. Well worth it for a lifetime supply of music, in my opinion. Hear Mike Parsons blazing away on this one at Garage Band Theory.com > Author's Music.

This shows two different versions of the same tune. The first one is a "traditional" version. They're similar to each other, but not identical by a long shot. Which one is the "right one?" In my opinion, there's no such thing, but there are "purists" who would adamantly disagree with that opinion. That's OK with me. If you would like to express your opinion, please call my pal Hal. Operators are standing by.

There are fewer clues in this format than are typically found in The Real Book, but still plenty of information to play it at a jam or gig. Chords, melody, parts, and structure. The bass and harmonies are implied by the chords.

Arkansas Traveler 1

Arkansas Traveler 2

The 6-2-5-1 near the end of the A and B parts is the way we recorded this tune on Two Grass Crew – Gavotte in A Minor. Mike Parsons rips this one up on his fiddle. Go Mikey, go!

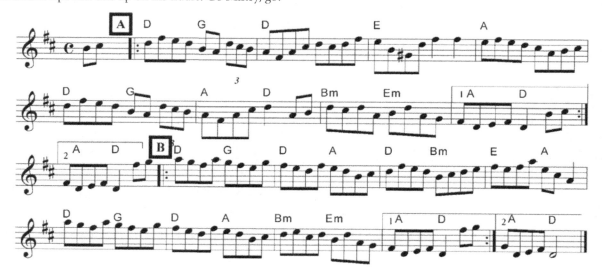

This next example is interesting. First item of interest to me is that it's a really cool tune and it's about 300 years old. Mr. Bach left the party at age 65 in the year 1750. This guy composed over 1,000 works. I don't recall hearing very much on the radio that seems likely to be of interest to anyone in 300 years.

These composers (Bach, Mozart, Beethoven, Haydn, etc) were the rock stars at the "cutting edge" of musical innovation. They didn't have electric instruments, but they were using state-of-the-art tools and experimenting with every combination they could.

They never heard a police siren or a chain saw. They never heard recorded music, and it was rare to hear any music at all. Those lucky people were never subjected to the "convenience" of cell phones and "personalized ring tones." Tuesday night bluegrass jams were uncommon. You couldn't just run down to Music Villa, 539 East Main Street, Bozeman, Montana (406-587-4761) and pick up a guitar, even if you had the money.

It is worth anyone's time to become familiar with some of the music created by people who were not influenced by all of the ugly noises that we are accustomed to and have been conditioned to consider "normal." Many were able to create and convey an enormous range of emotion and drama using a pencil and paper and orchestral instruments. No sex, no naughty words, no special effects, no outrageous behavior, just music. Making music is different than selling products. It seems that most of what is commonly called "music" is actually just a "product." The classical composers were trying to make a living with their art, so they were quite sensibly concerned with the commercial value of their works, but the market was quite different. Maybe Mozart, Bach, and Beethoven would be spewing the same sort of marketable noise that is so common today, too. Maybe. I hope not.

"Gavotte in A minor" is an arrangement of another of Mr. Bach's tunes. Like "Bouree in E Minor," "Gavotte in A Minor" is a dance tune from the period. It's kind of like saying "Polka in E Minor" or "Waltz in A Minor." I'm pretty sure neither a polka, nor a waltz, has much in common with a bouree or a gavotte, except that they are all dance steps.

There are a couple of new symbols on this page. First are the little numbers that are beside many of the notes. They tell which finger is to be used on the fretboard. 1 is your pointer finger and 4 is your pinky.

Classical guitar pieces can appear to be relatively simple at first glance because there are usually no chords and frequently there are only one or two notes being played at a time. But the correct fingering can be crucial to be able to play the piece smoothly. If I have to choose between two different written pages of the same piece and one supplies fingerings, that's the one I want. (I included chords.)

In the first line, the second and third measures have another number with a circle around it. These indicate which string should be used for a particular note. Remember, there are four middle C notes on a guitar and a note on the staff alone doesn't tell where you find it.

Finally, you'll notice at the end of the third line something that looks like "CII." The letter C means you're supposed to barre all six strings. My guess is that the C is an abbreviation of Capo, but that's only a guess. The Roman numeral II indicates the fret you're supposed to barre. CII means barre at the second fret. ½ C means "barre half the width of the neck."

Finally, you'll see the little italicized letters "m and I." Classical guitarists traditionally don't use a flatpick, they use their fingers and carefully maintained fingernails to make the strings vibrate. Those letters are suggestions for your picking hand.

Much classical and flamenco music is written in Spain and the letters P, I, M, A, and S are the first letters of Spanish words. P = pulgar = thumb. I = indice = index finger. M = medio = middle finger. A = anular = ring finger. The little finger is rarely used, but I've seen both the letters S and C used to indicate the pinky. I'm confident both letters stand for Spanish words, but I don't know what they are.

"Gavotte in A minor"
J. S. Bach

"Gavotte in A minor"

This next example is from Chicago Blues JamTrax for Guitar by Ralph Agresta. It's a CD/book that has full band rhythm tracks, but no lead instrument, so you can turn the CD up, crank your amp up to 11, and jam till the neighbors call the cops.

I think that playing along with accompaniment tracks like this is one of the best things available for practice… and it's not because it's a way to practice lead licks.

In order to "jam" with other people, a certain level of physical skill is required. It's also helpful if you're familiar with the tunes or can follow basic charts, but that isn't always necessary.

An extremely important skill, that is not often discussed, is the ability to divide your attention between to different things while continuing to breathe and not drooling on your shirt.

Obviously, it's necessary to pay attention to your own instrument and whatever you happen to be playing. At the same time, you also have to be able to focus on what everybody else is doing. This is what "playing music with other people" is all about, emphasis on WITH. In basketball, if your buddy is in the paint, going for the hoop, you want to be able to feed him a perfect pass. You have to be aware of what he's doing in order to pull it off.

It's not uncommon to see players who are so wrapped up in their own deal that they almost don't even notice when a song ends. Head down, jamming away, not listening, and oblivious to the rest of the planet. Not a desirable attribute in a musical teammate, no matter how cool the riffs are.

Practicing with JamTrax, or something like it, is an opportunity to listen closely to how a band works. You want to learn to listen to all of the instruments, individually and as a band, while you continue to play. This requires practice and awareness. These tracks are stripped down to essentials and every part is audible. No vocals, no solos, no fills. You can learn to hear what a rhythm section does. Put away your guitar and practice LISTENING. Soon you'll be able to HEAR.

When you repeat a three-minute rhythm track eleventy-hundred times, you'll begin to hear every nuance in every instrument. With JamTrax, you can listen to the bass and learn to play riffs that can complement that line. One of the most useful things that any player can do is learn to play bass lines, note for note. You can listen for the kick, snare, and hat, and find chunky rhythm riffs that contribute to the groove. Listen to how the bass and drum kit work together. Listen to the rhythm line the keyboard is using and try to cop the riff and play a harmony line.

This type of jam track will allow you to practice "splitting your awareness" so in a live jamming situation you can reduce the amount of time it takes to hear what is going on around you and find an appropriate part to play. If you want to play music with other players, the ability to listen and find a simple, tasty part is definitely a more useful skill than being able to play a bunch of flashy riffs. Playing music with a band is a team sport.

Back up tracks are also more interesting than a metronome, at first. It's enormously important to practice along with something that does, in fact, keep accurate time and most guitar players don't do this naturally. We tend to rush, rush, rush. Ask any drummer. It's fun to play fast and I like to do it, too, but when I'm practicing, I use a drum machine or a metronome or a track a lot of the time.

"Waiting on My Lady" is pretty typical. It's a 12-bar form and uses a standard I-IV-V progression in C. The little "bird's eye" symbol is a "fermata" and it means "hold whatever you're playing longer than the written value of the note"… it's an ending. The squiggly line means "strum kind of slow" and the "diamond" is about the same as a fermata.

The three patterns in this case are just descending scale forms. Use the C scale during the first four bars and change to F for measures 5 and 6. Back to C for bars 7 and 8, then G for one, F for one, and C for two bars. Do it seven more times, hit the repeat button, and do it again.

I can't say I'm 100% certain why there is a "pick-up note" for a scale, but there it is. It doesn't mean that it's wrong, just because I'm not accustomed to using the word in this context. As you recall, pick-up notes or pick-up measures are usually thought of as an incomplete measure before the first measure of a song. In these examples, the "pick-up note" is a 3rd above the tonic and the first beat of a complete measure. Pick-up notes usually lead to the first beat, and this use of "pick-up note" seems to mean "leading to the tonic."

Patterns 2 and 3 have a measure that is spanned by a dotted line with an 8 at the left end. That's an abbreviation of 8va that was described in "Note Names." You probably remember that it means play the notes in that measure an octave higher than written.

The riff samples work just like the scale patterns do, play the C pattern for the measures using C, etc.

Waiting on My Lady
From JamTrax

There are plenty of songbooks that will show tunes in a layout that is similar to this. All you get are chords and lyrics, which is enough if somebody in the room knows the melody. Your job, as the sing-along guitarist, is to "put your ears on" and pay close attention to the singer and get the right chord with the right word. This is also the way you'll see lyrics and chords on many Internet sites. Sometimes the chords are above the word where the chord changes, and sometimes it's just before the word.

G
Dashing through the snow

                 C
In a one horse open sleigh

Am   D
O'er the hills we go

D   G
Laughing all the way

G
Bells on bob tails ring

             C
Making spirits bright

Am   D
What fun it is to ride and sing

            G
A sleighing song tonight

(G) Dashing through the snow

In a one horse open (C) sleigh

(Am) O'er the hills we (D) go

Laughing all the (G) way

(G) Bells on bob tails ring

Making spirits (C) bright

(Am) What fun it is to (D) ride and sing

A sleighing song (G) tonight

Here's a chart for one of my tunes that I sketched on a break for the bass and keyboard players. There are no details here, just chord names, and a rough arrangement that requires listening and lots of eye contact. This kind of chart, and the one on the next page, is the kind I've encountered most often in a gig situation. Notice the mistake in the next to last measure in the solo section. Should be C# minor, not C minor. As I recall, neither Eddie T, nor Pinky, paid any attention to my blunder, just assumed it should be a C#m since it had been C#m for the whole tune.

Here are charts for two tunes. Tom Robison (an outstanding Scottish fiddler and teacher) hires me sometimes to play backup guitar for him. I'll get a stack of charts that look like this for the gig. Both tunes shown here have two parts. Play each part twice. AABB form. The repeat signs distinguish the parts. The vertical lines are measures and this shows that the chords change on the first beat of each measure. The "slash" chords in measures four, eight, and 12 of "Temperance Reel" aren't slash chords in this case… it means I should play E minor for the first two beats of the measure and a D chord for the last two beats. Tom didn't invent that, you'll see it other places, too. Same thing in measure 14 of "The Green Willis." No intros or endings shown. Pay attention, ears wide open, lots of eye contact, and plan on Tom cueing me for the endings. Fiddle players like to signal the end of a song by looking at you and raising one foot off the floor. It's easier than raising both feet. Nice big letters so it can be read at a glance. We do a bunch of tunes like this as little two and three-song medleys because they like to dance for about 10 minutes at a whack. For a dance, we play these a lot slower than a bluegrass outfit would, but to make "Temperance" last five minutes, we had to repeat the AABB sequence about 15 times, then slam straight into the next tune and do the same drill. Tom is one of those people who can improvise interesting solos over simple changes all night long… simply amazing.

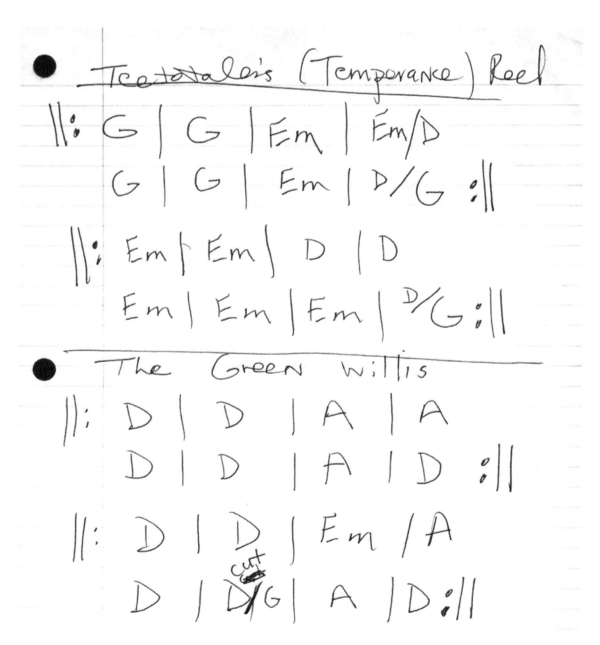

Is music the "universal language?" I don't know what they used on Mars before the water left the planet, but I do have an example of a chart I used in Thailand. In 2002, I went to Krabi in southern Thailand on the Andaman Sea to lock myself in an inexpensive room and work on this book. I met some local players and jammed with them a bunch of evenings by the pier at the Smoody Bar. I even got to do a short tour (four gigs) with a Thai folk band called Thai Lagoon. Wonderful people and good players. My hiking and picking buddy, Mai, made this chart for me.

Most of the songs were "traditional" Thai folk songs. In Thailand there are two "traditional" musical styles. One uses instruments like the "pi" and the "sa" and sounds like nothing you've ever heard (probably). The other uses guitars and fiddles, mandolins and accordions, bass and drums, and progressions that are familiar to Western ears. That's the Thai Lagoon band. There was a song we did every night (not shown here), a real pretty ballad that Sowl sang, and she is a dynamite vocalist. By the end of the song the second night, I was wondering why she kept missing the notes that came around a couple of times in every chorus of that ballad. This is a woman who does not miss notes, but she was singing a bunch of wrong notes, big time, and the same wrong notes, time after time. I couldn't understand the words, but I can hear pitch. I asked Mai about it and he told me the song was about the conflicts between ancient traditions and modern living and in parts of the song she was singing tones from the other, older tradition. That octave is divided into seven tones instead of the dozen we're used to. Imagine a piano with seven keys per octave, not 12. She was singing exactly the right note, and I was dead wrong, trying to hear "western" harmonies. What a singer!

Notice the chords and the part names. I speak very little Thai and can only read a few Thai words, but I was able to follow the phrasing and the chords. The chord names are the same everywhere, in Thailand, Brazil, or Tehachapi... A minor, E minor, G7 sus4, as well as things like intro and solo.

Carabao is a Thai band I like a lot that has received a bit of well-deserved international recognition. Carabao is a legend in the Kingdom, celebrated 25 years of music in 2007. The band rocks, and an important part of Carabao's popularity in Asia is the social and political commentary that is often delivered musically to their listeners, a genre known in Thailand as "pleng chee wit" or "songs for life." A few of my favorites can be found on YouTube. Search these song titles for a taste of some fine Thai music: "Kohn La Fahn," "Kon Thai Reu Plow," "Noom Bao Sao Parn," "Bua Loy," "Made in Thailand." (**www.carabao. net**).

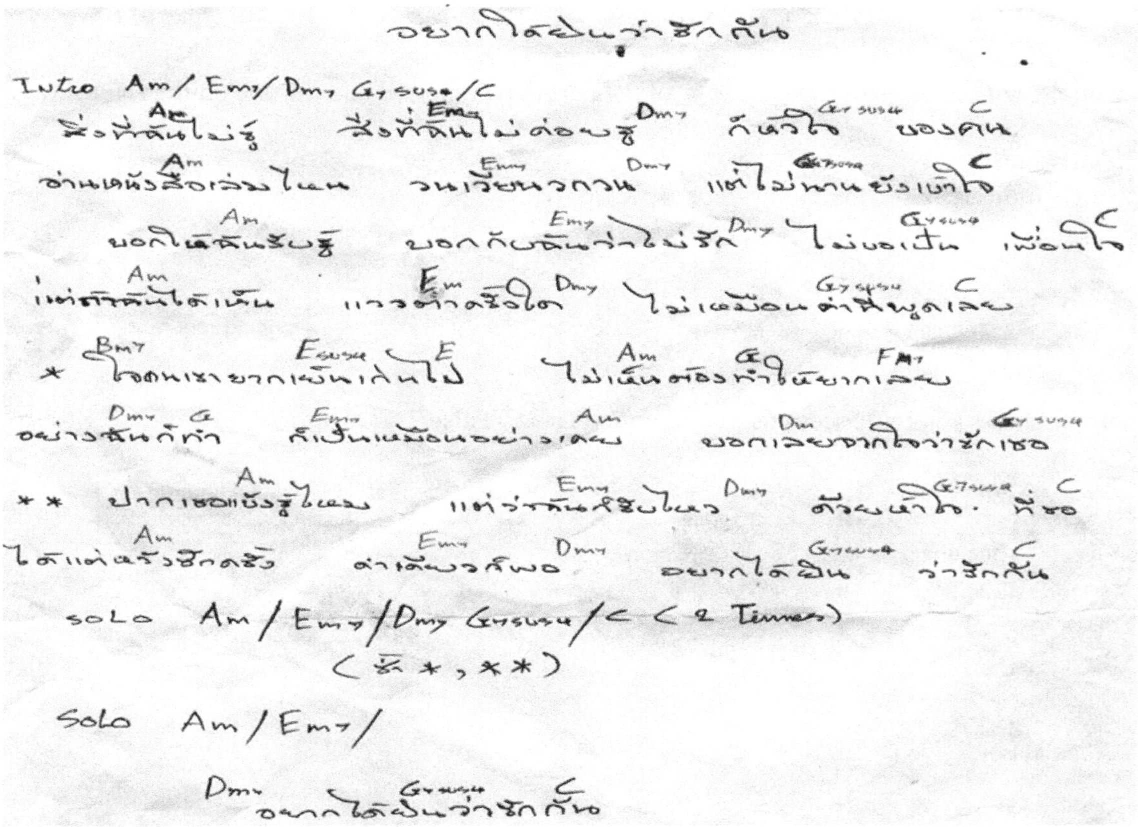

[Handwritten chart by Mai:]

Intro Am / Em7 / Dm7 G7sus4 / C

(verse lines with chords: Am / Em7 / Dm7 / G7sus4 C, repeated over Thai lyrics)

* Bm7 Esus4 E Am G Fm7
Dm7 G Em7 Am Dm G7sus4

** Am Em7 Dm7 G7sus4 · C
Am Em7 Dm7 G7sus4 C

Solo Am / Em7 / Dm7 G7sus4 / C (2 Times)
(* , **)

Solo Am / Em7 /

Dm7 G7sus4 C

Reading the Road Map

Commonly used names for song parts are:

1. _____ It occurs only once.

2. _____ This is the "story" part of a song.

3. _____ is the part of the song that returns.

4. During a (guitar or keyboard or sax or, etc.) solo in a pop song, everything is played just about the same way that a verse or chorus is played, except the "solo" instrument will replace the vocalist. **True   False**

5. A "sequence of song parts" is referred to as the _____ of a song. It is an outline that tells in which order the different parts are to be played.

6. A different way of labeling and referring to different song parts that eliminates the need to define those words precisely is to simply label the parts using as many different letters as needed. **True   False**

A⟨B⟩C△D

7. Here's one of the most common musical "road signs" called a _____.

8. The one on the left indicates the _____ of the part to be repeated and the one on the right shows the _____.

9. This example indicates a section that is to be repeated _____ .

beginning repeat ↑   3 times   ↑ ending repeat

10. This example shows adjoining sections that repeat. **True   False**

↓ beginning repeat   ending repeat ↓
↑ beginning repeat   ending repeat ↑

11. The last two measures show _____ and _____ endings.

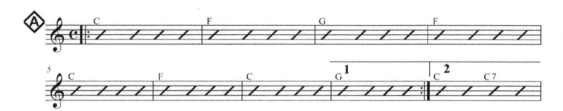

12. To read through this example, begin at measure # _____ and play to the end of measure
    # _____ .

13. Take the repeat and return to measure # _____ . Play through the end of measure # _____ .

14. Skip measure # _____ and play measure # _____ through measure _____ .

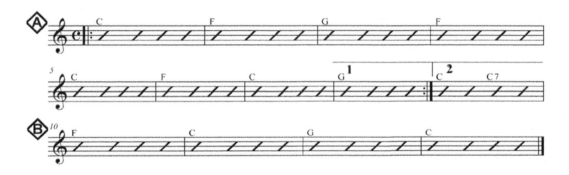

15. A diagonal slash with two dots is called a _____ _____ and it means that you should repeat
    whatever was indicated in the previous measure.

16. This example represents _____ bars of music.

17. _____ means "the beginning of the song" and is usually abbreviated to _____ .

18. _____ means "the end."

19. _____ means "go to the beginning and play it straight through to the end."

20. The symbol ⊕ is called a _____ .

21. The symbol 𝄌 is called _____ is usually abbreviated _____ .

22. Each symbol is a marker that indicates a certain place to jump to on the page.   **True   False**

23. When you encounter the abbreviation _____ it means go back to "the sign" 𝄌. You jump back to
    that spot in the tune and continue from that point.

24. _____ means you go back to "the sign" 𝄋 and then continue to the end from that point.

25. A "coda" uses _____ parts consisting of _____ ⊕ symbols and the phrase _____ . These three pieces are found in different locations on the page, but they are all part of a single "detour."

26. When you encounter the _____ symbol ⊕, you just make a mental note of where it is on the page and keep on playing. Then, when you see the words "D.C. al Coda" it means that you go back to the _____ of the song and play right up to the _____ ⊕. At that point, you skip directly to the ⊕ and play until there is another detour sign or the song ends.

27. You skip all the measures of music in between the two ⊕ symbols.   **True   False**

28. When you see _____, it means that you go back to "the sign" 𝄋 and play up to the first ⊕. At that point, you skip directly to the second ⊕ and play it to the end, following any new clues you might encounter after that point.

29. Just as there can be more than one set of repeat signs in a single piece of music, 𝄋 and ⊕ can also be used more than once.   **True   False**

30. If there are two sections to be indicated with "the sign," the first one will be shown with _____ as usual. The second section will be marked with 𝄋𝄋 , and the clue to jump there is _____.

31. If there are multiple codas, the ⊕ symbols at the target measures are labeled ⊕ _____ , ⊕ _____ , ⊕ _____ etc.

Putting It All Together | Chapter 14

At this point you have learned quite a lot about the pieces and parts of pop music. This is where we'll put it all together and figure out some songs "by ear."

Sing DO-RE-MI-FA-SO-FA-MI-RE-DO-RE-MI-FA-SO-FA-MI-RE a few times.

Then sing:　　Mary had a little lamb, little lamb, little lamb.
　　　　　　　Mary had a little lamb whose fleece was white as snow.

Here's the $64 question: Is the last note sung DO, RE, MI, FA, SO, LA or TI?

In pop tunes, the last note sung will be DO. At least 85 times out of 100. No kidding. Once again, I got out some songbooks and did the arithmetic. This is an important clue, my friends. In fact, for someone new to the business of figuring out songs by ear, the last note can be the best place to start. It will nearly always be DO.

　　Try "Hey Jude." Hey Jude, don't be afraid.
　　Take a sad song and make it better
　　Remember to let her into your heart
　　Then you can start to make it better.

　　　　Or　　　　　　　Somewhere over the rainbow, way up high
　　　　　　　　　　　　There's a land that I heard of once, in a lullaby.

　　　　Or　　　　　　　There's a lady who's sure all the glitters is gold
　　　　　　　　　　　　And she's buying the stairway to heaven.

This fact is related to a musical concept known as "resolution" which is defined as "the conclusive ending to a musical statement or phrase." Most pop songs "resolve" to the I chord, and most end with the root note of the chord.

If you can hum ANY tune, and you know where to find DO… AND you understand much of the previous 504 pages… you're about 90% of the way to finding the chords to songs by ear. This chart will be a handy reference for this exercise if you don't already have it memorized. This is worth memorizing. It's easy. When we're trying to work out the chords in a song, at first you just want the basic triads. Then you can extend and alter those chords to your heart's content.

chord number	root	3rd	5th
I	DO	MI	SO
ii	RE	FA	LA
iii	MI	SO	TI
IV	FA	LA	DO
V	SO	TI	RE
vi	LA	DO	MI
vii	TI	RE	FA

In order to do this exercise, good counting skills are necessary. In addition, you will need to understand solfege, as well as have the ability to hear and identify DO-RE-MI-FA-SO. It's ideal if you can hum it, because then you can learn to do this in your head. You should be able to play a major scale at about 90 bpm if you are going to make it work on an instrument. C major is easiest on a keyboard and also in the open position on a guitar. G major and D major work well for the banjo and on a mandolin. Try C and G with a mandola or tenor banjo.

If at all possible, sit at a piano or some kind of electronic keyboard while you're working through this because the relationships are easiest to see on a keyboard.

You'll want to know how to make a chord chart, and you need to understand chord structure and chord progressions. You'll need a good grip on song structure. A working knowledge of melody and harmony also contribute heavily to the process.

This is a good time to consider a phrase that many people have heard and quite logically think is probably part of this process. The phrase is "perfect pitch."

I do not have perfect pitch. What "perfect pitch" means is that a person has something like a tuning fork built into their consciousness. It's always on. They KNOW when a violin or a guitar or trombone is not perfectly in tune with concert A 440. I have heard that in extreme cases people with perfect pitch feel nauseous and have other nasty physical response when they have to listen to things that are out of tune. If things are not perfectly in tune, the person with perfect pitch can be an uncomfortable, unhappy listener.

Perfect pitch has absolutely nothing to do with figuring songs out by ear. You don't need it.

There is also something called "relative pitch." Relative pitch, being able to recognize the difference between "higher and lower," is a skill that is crucial to the process of figuring songs out by ear.

Right at the top of the previous page, I asked you to hum the first five notes of a major scale. DO-RE-MI-FA-SO. If you can sort of "hear" the scale in your imagination… that is what relative pitch is about. Begin with a tone and recognize the other tones as they relate to the first one.

The first tone doesn't have to have any relationship to concert A 440hz, 435hz, or whatever. The correct relationship between DO-RE-MI is what is important; the names of the notes are irrelevant.

If humming DO-RE-MI-FA-SO is tough for you, then practice singing along with the scales. The first five tones are enough notes to work with at first. It's an acquirable skill for most people. As always, several focused hours over the course of a few weeks will usually make a big difference.

You don't necessarily have to sing the scale correctly, perfectly in tune, in order to figure songs out by ear. It's what you hear inside your head that's important.

I have a good friend, Rich Robiscoe, who is an accomplished bass player, plays classical guitar, and has a degree in Music. He can play most instruments well enough to be a music teacher in a public school, which he has done. He's written at least one tune that was on the set list for the Hyalite Blues Band. He played on my first record and has been playing in local bands for over 20 years. He plays by ear and he can read, too. He gets calls to play bass in situations that involve reading charts, regular notation, studio gigs, and pick-up gigs where the band is doing standards and it's all "pay attention, play by ear." He owns a sound company, Semi Pro Audio, and frequently runs house and monitor mixes for different bands. He helped with some of the editing in this book. Rich is a good, versatile musician.

There are times when the sounds he produces when singing a major scale do not sound much like the major scale to the rest of us. Not even close, sometimes. It's surprising because he can play anything correctly, and hear tuning problems as readily as anyone else. It's obvious that he hears everything correctly, inside his head. He just can't always reproduce the tones with his voice. As a result of dedicated practice, he's learned to sing a couple of tune well enough to do onstage with The Hooligans, a cool, Bozeman band. They are blues tunes that have simple melody lines, but he's doing it. Practice makes better.

Anyway, I'm confident that Rich is not the only talented musician out there who hears just fine and understands the process, but somehow the voice just doesn't cooperate. Obviously, it isn't an advantage, but it doesn't mean you can't do this drill just because you don't sing perfectly in tune.

The process that I have been able to describe here on paper is very similar to the process I use to find chords and melodies for songs when I have no written clues. But it's maybe a little bit like trying to explain every step in the process of reading this sentence aloud. Anyone who is reading this book can probably read it aloud, but it's devilishly tricky to explain just how to do it. There are several processes occurring simultaneously and some are nearly impossible to put into words.

There are chess masters who are able to glance at a chess game in progress and instantly recognize the flow of the game, know what the best move is for either side and predict what is likely to occur. There are musicians who instantly recognize complex chord progressions, melodies and harmonies. I cannot explain the intuitive processes that are obviously occurring when people have such natural, unlearned abilities.

Figuring out songs by ear is not a process that lends itself to a verbal or written explanation, and that is partly why it appears to be a magical thing. Magic and intuition are inexplicable and both qualities are without a doubt part of music, but not this part.

Most of the skills and musical knowledge used for figuring out pop songs by ear can be described as a mechanical process that requires no genius, just patience, practice, and knowledge. The process is only "extraordinarily difficult to describe," not a result of "inexplicable natural abilities."

I've been playing music with friends and acquaintances for well over a quarter of a century. I've encountered lots of really great musicians, both professionals and hobbyists. The vast majority of these hundreds of musicians primarily play by ear. I can think of several who show skills that seem to be "magical, intuitive abilities" on a level with the hypothetical chess master mentioned above, but I bet as a percentage it's way under 5% of the players I've encountered who might be considered "musical geniuses."

All of us have improved whatever natural abilities we were born with by practicing. You can, too.

I'm not able to make an explanation of every aspect of this process that is as precise as an explanation of an "object" like an interval, a scale, or a chord; however, these pages do present a good way to approach the process and will allow you to gain lots of insight into how it works.

Nearly everyone can learn to recognize and identify sounds, and that is the central theme. If hearing and/or reproducing the sounds is difficult for you at first, remember that a keyboard provides a way to see and hear the relationships simultaneously, and it can be very helpful to approach this with obvious visual clues, in addition to the sounds.

There's a list of items we need to know about any song—length, number of parts, (intro, verse, etc.) time signature, feel, key signature, etc.

The easiest way to get started is to get a piece of staff paper and make a chart. After some practice, for simple tunes like the ones I use as examples, (and most pop tunes) you won't need the paper, but for now it's probably best to write the stuff down.

You have to be able to count the tune. Finding the first beat of the measure is crucial. You have to know about "pick-up measures" so you get the first beat in the right place.

Remember the other word for 4/4 time? It's common time. That's because it's the one you're most likely to encounter. Start off assuming it's in common time unless it's obviously 3/4 or 6/8.

Sing "Mary Had a Little Lamb." The last note will be DO. Mary had a little lamb, little lamb, little lamb, Mary had a little lamb whose fleece was white as DO-RE-MI-FA-SO-FA-MI-RE-DO-RE-MI-FA-SO-FA-MI-RE-DO Mary had a little lamb, little lamb, little lamb, Mary had a little lamb whose fleece was white as DO-RE-MI-FA-SO-FA-MI-RE-DO. Tap the beats in time while you hum the tune.

Take your chart and write out the words so they correspond to the beats.

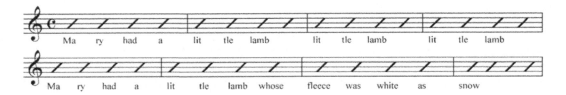

When that is sorted out, fill in the things that you either know for sure, or can at least make a reasonably confident guess. I call things that seem to happen over 90% of the time "for sure" and then adjust as necessary. Use a pencil, adjustments will be necessary.

I'm going to assume you've been doing your homework in the previous chapter and have analyzed enough songs by now to be able to make an "educated guess" as to what the first chord will be when the vocalist starts to sing the first verse.

I'm confident that the first and last chords played are likely to be the I chord, and they will probably be played on the first beat of those measures. So I write them in. You can also bet that the I chord will be used at least a third of the time, so we're expecting more instances of the I. The first beat of each measure is the first place that you anticipate finding chord changes, so I'll make a (mental) note that I have to come back and check the first beat in each measure.

Next, sing the scale a few times and then sing the melody a few times and find every place that DO occurs. That gives you a few points to use as a reference to find the other tones. Ma-ry had a little lamb, little lamb, little lamb, Mary had a little lamb whose fleece was white as DO-RE-MI-FA-SO-FA-MI-RE-DO-RE-MI-FA-SO-FA-MI-RE-DO-RE Mary had a little lamb, little lamb, little lamb, Mary had a little lamb whose fleece was white as DO-RE-MI-FA-SO-FA-MI-RE-DO-RE Mary had a little lamb… etc.

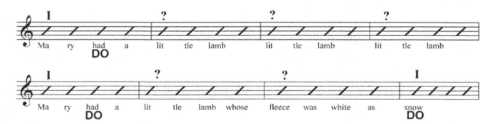

In this case, I found DO three times. Since it's in the first and last measures, that reinforces the guess regarding the I chord. This is the trial and error part of the show, so there are no guarantees, of course, but you're writing in pencil so you can "adjust as necessary."

Next, hum the tune and find every series that a note repeats. Then, sing DO-RE-MI-FA-SO and identify the tone. Write it down.

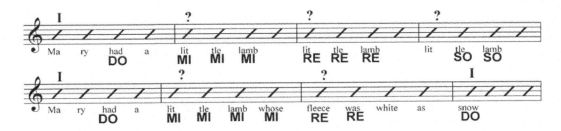

Now that you have DO sorted out, and all the repeated tones names, sing the scale and see if you can find any places where there area few consecutive scale tones. As you remember from the chapter on melody and harmony, this is a common occurrence, so you're on solid ground assuming some instances in every song. A series of scale tones is much more common in a melody than long intervallic leaps of 5ths, 6ths, 7ths and octaves.

It's reasonable to guess that the second and fourth notes in the first and fifth measures will be RE because DO is right next to them. You can try TI as well, for the same reason. It's also a good guess that the first note in measure four will be either MI or FA since both are between RE and SO.

After intervals of 2nds , (i.e. consecutive scale tones) you'll do well to look for 3rds, 4ths , and 5ths , which you know are the intervals between the notes in major and minor chords.

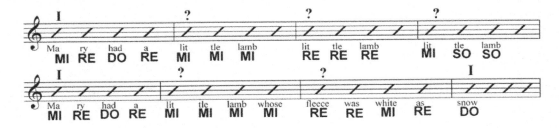

It's always a better-than-average bet that any melody note on the first beat of any measure is the root, 3rd, or 5th of whatever chord is being played. We assumed that the I chord would be used in the first measure, and the fact that DO and MI are the root and 3rd of the I chord reinforces that guess. DO and MI can also be the 3rd and 5th of the vi chord, but songs usually begin with the I, so we'll assume that's the case until proven otherwise.

The melody in measure five is identical to the melody in the first measure, so I'll assume the chord will be the same, too. Now, sing the tune while you strum the chords you've chosen for measure one, five, and eight, and check to see if the I chord seems OK. Works for me. It doesn't hurt to try the vi and IV chords just to be sure.

You can use your knowledge of chord structure and progressions to make a couple of guesses. In the second measure, the melody is one note repeated three times. MI can be the root of the iii chord, the 5th of the vi chord, or the 3rd of the I chord. The vi sounds pretty good, but this is a tune that overall has a major sound to it, so my money is on the I chord. Just because chords typically change on the first beat of a measure doesn't mean there's always going to be a new chord on that beat. The melody in measure six is almost identical to measure two, so I'm going to assume the chord will be the same, too.

The melody in the third measure is RE three times. RE is the root of ii and the 5th of V. Both are good candidates since we know that they are found in the two most common progressions (I-IV-V and ii-V-I). V is the first choice for the chord in measure three, with ii as a close contender. RE is also the 3rd of the vii chord (m♭5), a possibility, but not very likely. I'm writing down the V chord.

Measure four contains MI and SO, the 3rd and 5th of I. Those two scale degrees are also root and 3rd of the iii chord, but it's not among the first five chords that we've learned to anticipate (I, ii, IV, V and vi). I'm guessing the I chord lives here.

We already have written the I chord in measure five. I can't think of a reason to change it. Next. Since the melody in measure six is nearly identical to measure two, I'm betting that the chord will be the same, too.

Measure seven. There is another clue available from your knowledge of chord progressions you can use here. Since you've been analyzing progressions in songs by a few artists, you'll have noticed that it is very common for a V chord to precede I. We're already confident that measure eight is the I chord.

Combine that piece of knowledge with the fact three out of four melody notes in measure seven are the 5th of the V chord, and you can feel good about trying the V chord here. The only question is the third note (MI) in the measure.

Chords change most frequently on the first and third beats and this note is on the third beat. MI is not part of the diatonic V chord, so we probably need to check the other two possibilities, which are the root of iii or 5th of vi.

Personally, I like both of them. Harmonically interesting and certainly not dissonant, but it doesn't sound the way it did in my kindergarten class.

MI is also the 6th of the V chord, and that is the one that works best, to my ear. You can play the V6 chord if you like, but there is no need to do that. In this case, the note in question is a "passing tone" leading to the chord change at the beginning of the next measure.

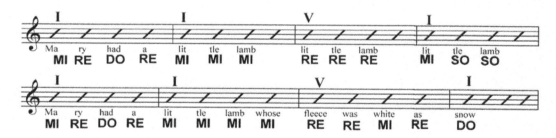

That is the chord structure for this tune. This process works for all tunes. The songs I included here are melodies that lots of people know. Try this for all of the tunes you're familiar with.

I've supplied several familiar tunes for you to practice on. Make some charts of your own and try it on every melody that you can sing. Even if it takes 47 hours for you to get the first one, that's OK. The idea is to accelerate the process. After you do it a couple of hundred times, it's much easier.

You can learn to do it at a dead run and get it right the first time, using no paper, with very few mistakes. Songs are predictable. Lots of major scale exercises and time invested in practicing progressions will make this a lot easier. Start with simple, familiar tunes. You don't get any bonus points for trying the hard stuff first. Practice makes better.

An interesting historical note about this rhyme… the words of "Mary Had a Little Lamb" were the first ever recorded. Thomas Edison recorded "Mary Had a Little Lamb" on tin foil (yes, tin foil) and played it back on his phonograph. Many of the rhymes I used at the end of this chapter have some significance in English history, but no specific historical connection can be traced to "Mary Had a Little Lamb." It was written by Sarah Hale, of Boston, in 1830.

Let's have a look at one that has a rhythmic signature that is a bit more complicated than "Mary Had a Little Lamb."

Finding the first beat is sometimes the trickiest part of the puzzle. You can always expect to find DO at the end (or MI), but there's no consistent landmark for finding the first beat that I can identify. What will cause you to miss the timing mark most often will be a pesky pick-up measure. It's natural to assume that the first word of a poem will correspond with the first beat of a song, but that is often not the case. If, for example, the first words occur on (3) eighth notes, as shown below, and you mistake that first note for the first beat of a measure, then you'll be off for the whole tune. "You Are My Sunshine" is a good example of a pick-up measure because so many people know the song; however, I can't show it to you.

This example has the same rhythmic pattern in the melody that "You Are My Sunshine" does, so look at it, and it might be helpful to hum the tune for "You Are My Sunshine." Notice the locations of the chord changes... the first beat of the measures. As you know, this is common.

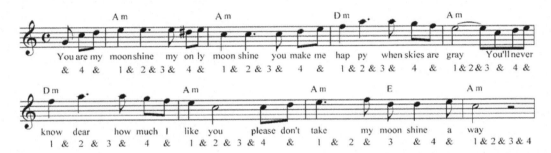

Here is the same thing, with no pick-up measure. Take a look at where the chords change.

You still have the same melody... the system of using DO, RE, and MI will still get you to the correct chords, but it is unusual for chords to change on the "and of 2." This is a clue that you've missed something with regard to the timing, and often, the problem will be a pick-up measure.

Lots of songs have pick-up notes and you need to be on the lookout for them. Unfortunately, I haven't been able to find any sort of clue that is as consistent for locating the first beat of a tune as there is for finding DO. This just takes practice and experience. A way to accelerate the process is to look at the music for lots of tunes you're familiar with while you listen to them and practice counting.

If you have a recording of the tune you want to learn, but no written clues, plan on listening to it several times before you take your instrument out of the case. How many is "several"? Maybe three times, maybe 29, maybe 218 times. Playing by ear requires listening and hearing. Practice makes better.

If there are bass and drums on the recording, you have plenty of available clues for locating the first beat as well as the chords.

The kick drum can nearly always be found on the first beat of a measure and often throughout the entire song on beats one and three, and nearly as often the snare will be banging away on the second and fourth beats. Kick-snare-kick snare-1-2-3-4- kick-snare-kick snare-1-2-3-4. The bass will usually be locked in with the kick drum.

Keep in mind that the first beat of a measure is the most common place for chords to change and the third beat the second most common, so you're listening for the bass and any chord instrument to land on any new chord at the same time the kick is playing.

Make a chart with slashes for the beats and work on one section at a time, either a verse or a chorus. Repeat that section until you have a good idea how many measures it is. Twelve, 16, and 32 measures are all pretty common, but there is no hard and fast rule. You just have to listen closely and pay attention.

When you have found the first beat, start the process that we went through in "Mary Had a Little Lamb."

Finding the first beat can be tricky. Say the poem aloud while you tap a finger to establish a rhythm and figure out which words coincide with the beats. One of those words will be on the first beat of a measure.

Finding DO is easier because it does frequently turn up in the same location in loads of songs. Not always the final note, but often enough to try looking there first.

I did come up with several pop tunes that don't end with the tonic note of the key. The Beatles have a well-deserved reputation for doing things a bit differently while still remaining solidly within "mainstream pop," so I looked through 100 of their tunes. I think they recorded about 175 songs. This site has lots of Beatles information and links. (en.wikipedia.org/wiki/The_Beatles)

"Baby, You're a Rich Man," "Bungalow Bill," "Dear Prudence," and "Norwegian Wood" end on SO. "Can't Buy Me Love," "Yesterday," "And I Love Her," "In My Life," "Penny Lane," and "Ticket to Ride," all end with MI. "We Can Work It Out" ends on a flat 7th. "Yellow Submarine" is in the key of G and it ends on the V chord (D), and the last note to be sung is the 5th of that V chord which is an A note. That makes the last note sung "LA." There are a couple of others where the last word is on the tonic and then slides to a 3rd or 7th.

I went through a couple of folk songbooks. One hundred percent of those tunes ended on DO. I looked at a couple of "country" and bluegrass songbooks—100% of those tunes ended on DO. I perused a couple of compiled "Greatest Hits" type of books, as in "songs of the 70's and songs of the 80's" and found about 90% end on DO, with the next most common tone to end a song being MI, followed by SO. I went through a couple of rock songbooks and found about 90% ended on DO.

I'll admit that after a while I was just skimming through pretty quickly and probably missed a few, but I'm certain that DO is by far the most common ending tone in a vocal line in pop music.

There must be thousands of tunes that don't end with DO. There must be. But, once again, I did try to find some and I couldn't find very many. Since "playing by ear" involves anticipating what is most likely to occur, this statistic should definitely be part of your process.

Imagine that you're out for a stroll and you find yourself humming "Oh Susannah" (or your favorite Dave Matthews tune… it works the same way), also imagine that you've been practicing singing the major scale and using solfege while you hum. Imagine that you understand how the solfege syllables can represent the root, 3rd, and 5th of the diatonic chords. Imagine that you remember that 90% of all melodies are diatonic and most songs use five chords… I-ii-IV-V and iv.

Suddenly, it occurs to you that the words "Well, I come from Alabama with" corresponds to "DO-RE-MI-SO-SO-LA-SO-MI-DO"… and bingo… SO-MI-DO… there is the root, 3rd, and 5th of the I chord!

Walk a little farther and you realize that the next line "a banjo on my knee" is "RE-MI-MI-RE-DO-RE" and it seems like there is a chord change that happens on the word "knee." You know that RE is the 5th of the V chord, and because of your knowledge of chord progressions you anticipate that V is a likely choice.

You keep singing and notice that the next line, "And I'm bound for Louisiana, my own true love for to see" is really similar to the first line. "DO-RE-MI-SO-SO LA-SO-MI, DO-RE-MI-MI-RE-RE-DO. The different in the two lines is the last two notes. The last note, RE, in the first line, indicates that it could be a V chord. For the second line, since you know that phrases often resolve to the I chord, that's a good guess.

Without even touching an instrument, you have a pretty good start on the chords for a song. Dash home, grab your guitar, mandolin, banjo, harmonica, or whatever, and try C for the I chord, and G for the V, and you realize that you're all over it! Amazing!

Is that how a person "figures out a song by ear?" It's real similar to the process I use, for sure. It's everything except the coordination required to lay the chords and melody. It's reasonable to assert that practice, knowledge, and memory play more important roles in that process than my ear.

Imagine you're looking at a song you've never heard in a fakebook in the music store. You've looked all the way through it and observed that it's mostly I-IV and V with an occasional ii and vi. Count the beats and hum the root note of the chords as they change. You don't care whether it's written in the key of G or C#. Solfege is king.

DO-DO-DO-DO / FA-FA-FA-FA / DO-DO-DO-DO / SO-SO-SO-SO
DO-DO-DO-DO / LA-LA-LA-LA / RE-RE-SO-SO / DO-DO-DO-DO

Most people can distinguish between major and minor chords after a couple of months of learning the beginning chords and that's the next step. Take each of those root notes and hum the appropriate triad. You've been practicing progressions, so you have a clue what the changes sound like. Decide which inversions to use and all the chord extensions and alterations later.

Look at the book and you note the fact that there are almost no accidentals anywhere in the melody line, which tells you that it's nearly all major scale tones. Analyze those accidentals… they're probably flat 3rds and 7ths . You've been practicing with the Ted Reed book, so you can recognize the rhythm of the melody line. Hum the scale to yourself a couple of times. The first note in the song will probably be DO, MI, or SO.

It is absolutely possible to read a page of unfamiliar music and get a pretty good idea of what it sounds like. Time invested in practicing scales and progressions helps immensely.

In addition to the traditional tunes you'll find on the following pages, I had about a dozen well-known "pop" tunes worked up to use as examples and exercises, but I was unable to obtain licenses for the songs.

So, you'll just have to take my word that this process works for the songs by your favorite artists, too. Better than taking my word, make some charts like the ones I've shown and use tunes that you know well. If you'll do this a bunch of times, using pencil and paper, before long you'll find that you can do it in your head. That is what "playing by ear" is all about.

There are a couple of things to keep in mind when working out rock and blues tunes. Frequently, melodies in both of these styles are derived mainly from the minor pentatonic scales. The minor pentatonic scale can be represented as 1 – ♭3 – 4 – 5 – ♭7. That can be represented in solfege two ways: DO-ME-FA-SO-TI will work, as will: LA-DO-RE-MI-SO.

The truth is, I don't often use either one when figuring out chords for a blues tune, because the chord structure is usually pretty simple. Not always, but usually. An enormous percentage of what I call "rock" is structurally pretty simple, too, and is often based around the I-IV-V progression, but I don't really know how to explain the process I use. I've been doing it so long that it's nearly automatic, without too much thought. It's a combination of trial and error, based on the assumption that it's likely to be variations and combinations of I-IV-V. The chords may be major or minor, but that three-chord progression comprises a substantial percentage of rock/blues tunes.

If you take a close look at the melodies in a bunch of rock and blues tunes, you can't help but notice that frequently they're only singing a few different notes. Using only notes from the minor pentatonic scale of the I chord for an entire vocal melody line is not at all uncommon. The melody line is not as useful for finding the chord changes in blues tunes as it is for "Over the Rainbow" or "Yesterday" or "Crazy."

When sorting out rock and blues tunes you can usually rely on the bass line to help find the chord changes. Remember that the bass player will nearly always be playing the root of the chord when the chord changes. That's what you want to listen for. I trust that you have been practicing the listening exercise I suggested… learning to distinguish between the different instruments so you can follow any of them through a tune.

If you can hear the bass line and can hum along with it, while you count, that will nearly always tell you where the chords are changing. The bass provides major landmarks and 99 times out of 100, the bass will be playing the root of the I chord (DO) at the end of the song.

When I'm anticipating chord changes in real time, like when I'm jamming with someone and they play a tune I've never heard, I rely less on the process I just described and more on a familiarity with song structure and progressions. I definitely listen closely to the melody, because it will usually be leading to the root, 3rd, or 5th of the next chord, but I'm also anticipating that the chord changes will occur in certain places. For instance, in a 12-bar phrase, I'm looking for changes on the first beat of the measure, in measures one, five, seven, and nine, maybe eleven and three, and that the changes will tend toward I-IV-V and I-vi-ii-V.

This business of "figuring songs out by ear" is not as straightforward as chord structure and scale structure are, so it's not easily reduced to an explanation in the context of a written page. You just have to do it a lot. The more songs that you learn to play, and the more that you listen to songs and analyze their structure, the easier it will become.

The best clue I can offer with regard to turning notes and chords into music and magic is this: Invest lots of time listening. Musically, it is arguably the best time investment you can make. Listen and analyze. A lot.

Practice playing progressions and listen for them in your favorite tunes. Practice scales (and sing along while you do) and listen for them in the music you enjoy. Go to the lyric/chord sites and find your favorite songs.

Learn to think about songs and visualize the notes and the chords even when you're away from an instrument… and a steering wheel.

Analyze everything you can. Imagine what you would learn, if over the course of a year, you were to analyze the melodies and chord progressions of 12 of your favorite artists. I'm not talking about learning to play every tune, I'm talking about understanding the structure of the tunes. A person with beginning physical skills can analyze anything that's on paper. People who are willing to regularly trade 30 minutes of television or Internet time for 30 minutes with a songbook and a pencil make real progress here.

When there are a bunch of people jamming together, you'll sometimes see players watching somebody else's hands and reacting to the changes. Those people usually make their chord changes a split second late. You'll see others who are listening more than watching. They're right in the groove. Learn to anticipate, not react.

These are skills that take time to develop, so be patient. Practice makes better.

There are 17 tunes on the next pages for you to practice with. This is a good way to practice making charts. The form I used to show the napkin chart of "Jingle Bells" will work just fine, but it's often helpful at first if you will use staff paper, draw the measures, and sketch in the beats as I showed in these examples.

I supplied "answers" for these examples, too. I took a few liberties in my choice of chords shown. For instance, I used vi-ii-V-I a bit more than you'll encounter in the books that also use "nursery rhymes" as examples.

Go ahead and harmonize the melodies any way you want to. It's allowed. It's encouraged. Don't write and tell me that you found "different" chords than the ones I used… that's half of the point of this book—to encourage you to find your own way.

Presumably, the songs I used for examples aren't on your hot-list of songs you just have to learn. Me, either. Sorry about that. Use them as exercises, but also remember the words of Ray Charles, "Every music has its soul. Be true to it." If you'll be open to it, it's probably there.

London Bridge Is Falling Down

The "London Bridge is Falling Down" nursery rhyme is based on one of the most famous landmarks in London. Its history can be traced to the Roman occupation of England in the 1st century and was made of wood and clay. Many disasters struck the bridges. Viking invaders destroyed the bridge somewhere around 1050 and it burned several times. The first stone bridge was designed was designed by Peter de Colechurch and construction began in 1176. It took 33 years to build and featured 20 arches. The flow of the Thames under the bridge was used to turn water wheels below the arches for grinding grain. By the 1300s, the bridge contained 140 shops, some of which were more than three stories high. In the 1820s, a new London Bridge was built north of the old bridge. The 1820s' London Bridge was moved, stone-by-stone to Lake Havasu, Arizona in the 1960s.

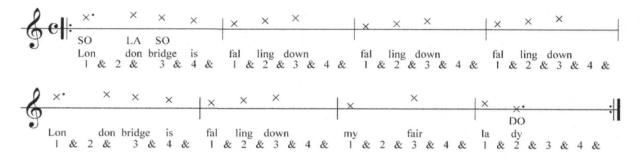

We Wish You A Merry Christmas

In medieval England "waits" were town watchmen whose job it was to patrol the dark streets. This post evolved into a kind of licensed musician. During the Christmas season they were allowed to go from door to door and serenade households in return for a gratuity, hence the lyric, "Bring us a figgy pudding." Their visits were not always welcome by those trying to sleep. The author and composer of "We Wish You A Merry Christmas" cannot be traced, but it is believed to date back to England in the 16th century. Over the years, the fashion for figgy pudding mentioned has faded. The recipe consisted of figs, together with butter, sugar, eggs, milk, rum, apple, lemon and orange peel, nuts, cinnamon, cloves, and ginger! (**www.carols.org.uk**)

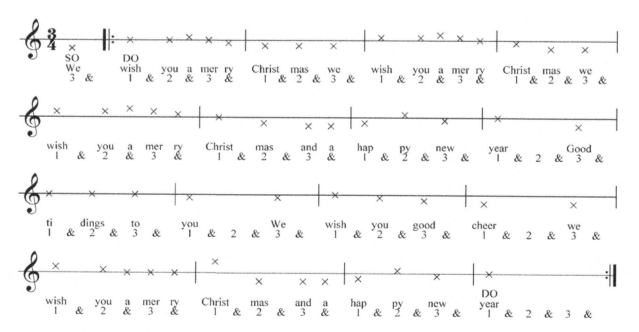

Home On The Range

Dr. Brewster M. Higley was a skillful physician with a love of music. He had written a poem when he was an early pioneer in Smith County, Kansas in 1871. The poem was called "Oh Give Me A Home." Dan Kelley, a member of the Harlan Brothers Orchestra, had been a bugler in the Union army during the Civil War. He was out walking one evening and as he walked, he hummed a tune while he thought of Dr. Higley's poem. As soon as he got home, he got a piece of paper and wrote out the melody. In 1934, William and Mary Goodwin of Tempe, Arizona, sued for infringement of copyright, asking $500,000 in damages. They claimed that Goodwin had written a song titled "My Arizona Home" and Mrs. Goodwin had composed the melody. Samuel Moanfeldt, an attorney, eventually contacted L. T. "Trube" Reese of Smith Center, who told him of the time he discovered the words on a piece of scrap paper in Dr. Higley's cabin back in 1873. He then found Clarence "Cal" Harlan, then 86 years old, and he asked Mr. Harlan to sing it. Nearly blind at the time, Mr. Harlan brought out his guitar and played and sang the song from memory. With that evidence and affidavits from numerous other people, Moanfeldt returned to New York City in 1936, with the proof that the song originated in Kansas. The song was adopted as the Kansas State Song on June 30, 1947.

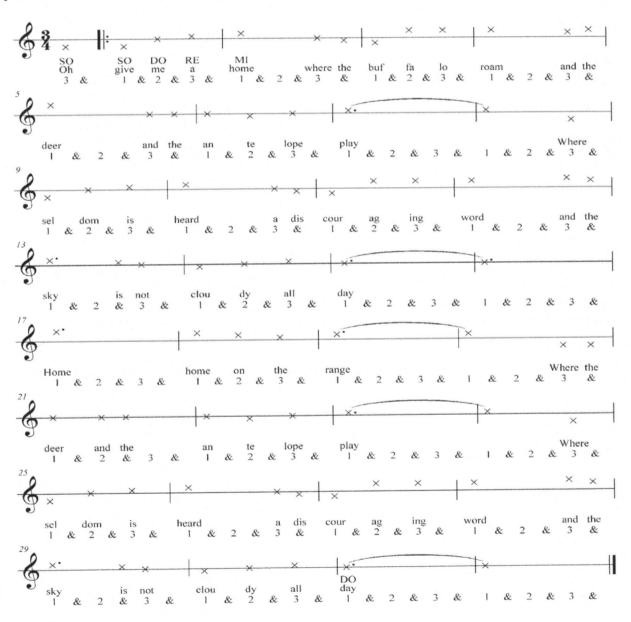

Take Me Out To The Ballgame

One day in 1908, while riding a New York City subway train near the Polo Grounds, Jack Norworth saw a sign that said, "Ballgame Today At the Polo Grounds." He had never been to a baseball game, but some "baseball related" lyrics popped into his head. Later, Albert Von Tilzer set the poem to music. Despite the fact that neither man had ever been to a baseball game when they wrote the song, "Take Me Out To The Ballgame" is the best-known baseball song on the planet and is one of the most widely sung songs in America.

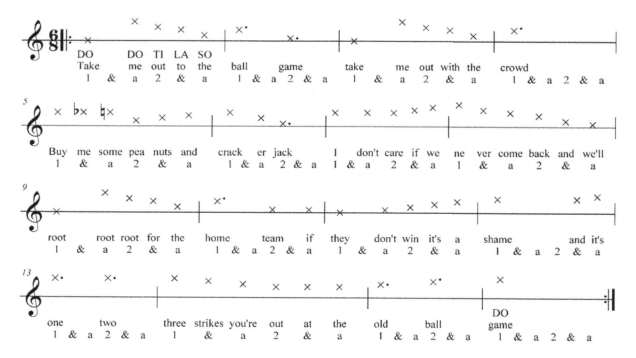

Red River Valley

Most everyone thinks that this classic originated in Texas. Well… maybe. It's a more than a little bit of a stretch to imagine a Texas cowboy singing "Do not hasten to bid me adieu." Research by Edith Fowke, a Canadian folklorist, indicates that the song probably came from the British troops who came to Manitoba, the Red River Valley of the North, who were there to put down the Metis Rebellion in the 1860s. (**www.plainsfolk.com**)

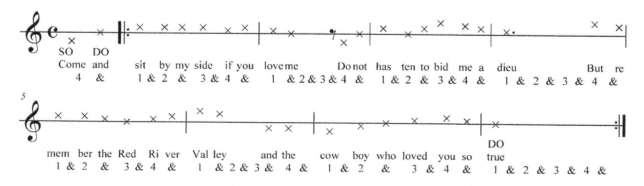

Three Blind Mice

Another rhyme from Jolly Old England. The "farmer's wife" would be Mary Tudor, the daughter of Henry Tudor (King Henry VIII). Queen Mary I was a staunch Catholic and her violent persecution of Protestants led to the nickname of "Bloody Mary." The line about a farmer's wife refers to the massive estates she and her husband, King Philip of Spain, possessed. The "three blind mice" were three Protestant noblemen who were convicted of plotting against the Queen. She did not have them dismembered and blinded as inferred in "Three Blind Mice," but she did have them burned at the stake! Another nursery rhyme which features "Bloody Mary" is "Mary, Mary, Quite Contrary, How Does Your Garden Grow?" (**www.rhymes.org.uk/mary_mary_quite_contrary. htm**)

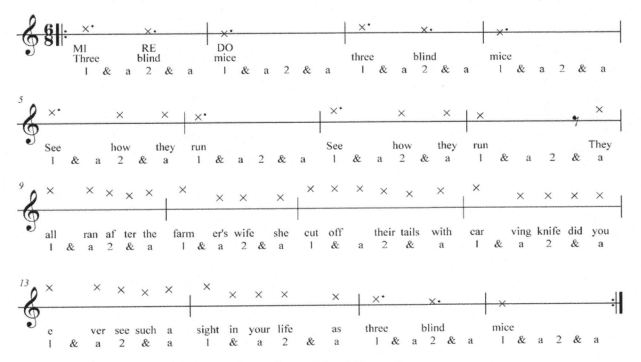

Pop Goes The Weasel

These words are derived from Cockney rhyming slang, which originated in London. Cockneys were a close community and had a suspicion of strangers and a dislike of the police. (They still do!) Cockneys developed a language of their own based roughly on a rhyming slang. It was difficult for strangers to understand as invariably the second noun would always be dropped. Apples and Pears (meaning stairs) would be abbreviated to just "apples." For instance, "Watch your step on the apples." To "pop" is the slang word for "pawn." Weasel is derived from "weasel and stoat" meaning coat. It was traditional for even poor people to own a suit, which they wore as their "Sunday Best." When times were hard, they would pawn their suit or coat on a Monday, and claim it back before Sunday. Hence, the term "Pop goes the weasel."

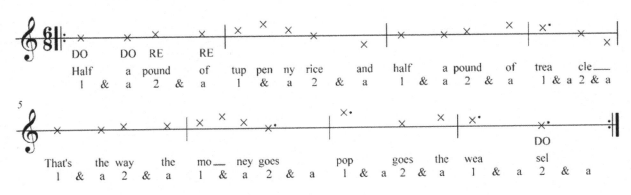

Silent Night

The German words for the original six stanzas of the carol we know as "Silent Night" were written by Joseph Mohr in 1816, when he was a young priest assigned to a pilgrimage church in Mariapfarr, Austria. His grandfather lived nearby and it is easy to imagine that he could have come up with the words while walking through the countryside on a visit to his elderly relative. The fact is, we have no idea if any particular event inspired Joseph Mohr to pen his poetic version of the birth of the Christ child. The world is fortunate, however, that he didn't leave it behind when he was transferred to Oberndorf the following year (1817). On December 24, 1818, Joseph Mohr journeyed to the home of musician-schoolteacher, Franz Gruber, who lives in an apartment over the schoolhouse in nearly Arnsdorf. He showed his friend the poem and asked him to add a melody and guitar accompaniment so that it could be sung at Midnight Mass. His reason for wanting the new carol is unknown. Some speculate that the organ would not work; others feels he merely wanted a new carol for Christmas and he loved guitar music. There are thousands upon thousands of Silent Night arrangements. Some are spectacular (the Mormon Tabernacle Choir comes to mind) and some are quite simple. You'll hear some people say, "We always sing the traditional melody," but the truth is, the melody most think is "traditional" is actually not the melody set down by Franz Gruber. The original 1818 manuscript has been missing for many years; however, we have the Joseph Mohr arrangement (ca. 1820) and several subsequent arrangements by Franz Gruber. The sections where we sing "All is calm, All is bright," and "Sleep in Heavenly peace," are different from what we learned in school and Joseph Mohr's arrangement (the earliest known manuscript available to us) has extra notes where we sing the words "Round" and "Holy" in the first verse. Adapted from an essay by Bill Egan, a staff writer for "Year 'Round Christmas Magazine."

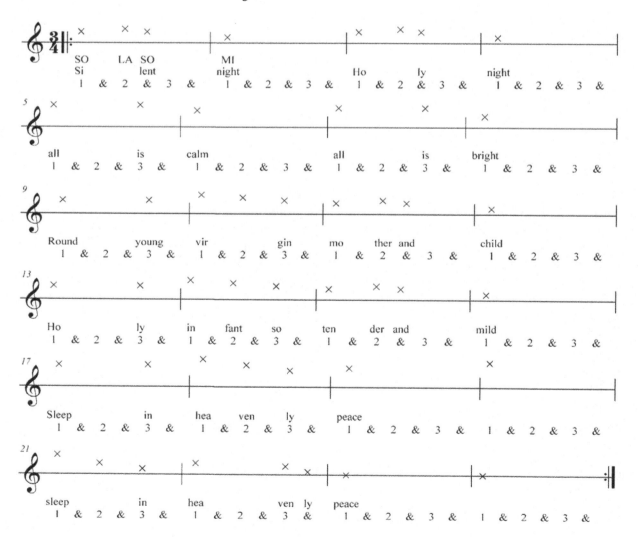

Oh Tannenbaum

First published in 1799, in Melodien zum Mildheimischen Liederbuch, it was probably based on a Westphalian folk song. There are many translations, almost none have any known attribution. This is the one that I encountered most, except I showed the German word "tannenbaum" instead of "Christmas tree."

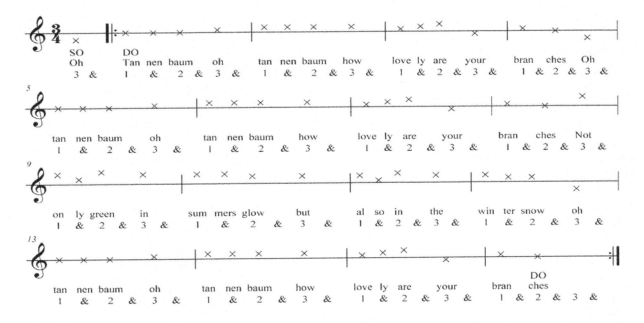

Auld Lang Syne

Robert Burns is the Scottish poet most often associated with the lyrics we sing. A reasonably accurate translation of the words "auld lang syne" is "times gone by." It's not an exact translation, but that's a good sense of what the phrase means. The song first appeared in print in 1796. The basic words date to at least 1711, though some scholars say it was known as early as 1677. "Auld Lang Syne" is one of the most familiar tunes in the world. Not only is the song sung by English speaking people on New Year's Eve, it is also used as a graduation song and a funeral song in Taiwan, symbolizing an end or a goodbye. In Japan, many stores play it to user customers out at the end of a business day. Before the composition of Aegukga, the lyrics of Korea's national anthem were sung to this tune. Before 1972, it was the melody for the anthem of The Maldives. The University of Virginia fight song (The Good Old Song) also uses the same melody.

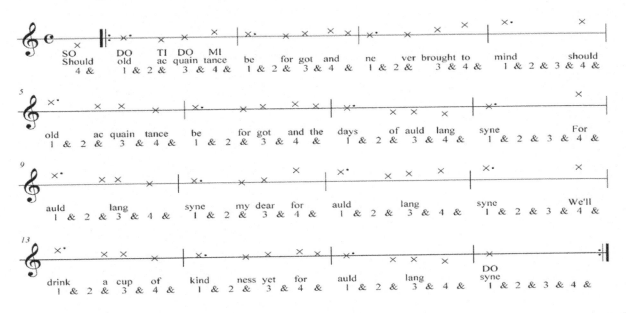

Oh Susannah
Stephen Foster

Stephen Foster was born on the outskirts of Pittsburgh on July 4, 1826. Foster tried to make a living as a professional songwriter and was definitely a pioneer in this respect, since this line of work did not yet exist in the modern sense. Due in part to the poor provisions for music copyright and composer royalties at the time, Foster saw very little of the profits which his works generated for sheet music printers. Publishers printed their own competing editions of Foster's tunes, paying Foster nothing. He wrote over 200 songs, but he earned a total of only $15,091.08 in royalties from his sheet music. Beginning in 1862, his musical fortunes began to decline and as they did, so did the quality of his new songs, at least in the perception of the contemporary public. This may well have been a result of his teaming with George Cooper, who took over the writing of lyrics for many of Foster's tunes. He died impoverished while living at the North American Hotel at 30 Bowery on the Lower East Side of Manhattan (possessing exactly 38 cents) at the age of 37. Many of his songs, such as "Oh! Susanna," "Camptown Races," and "Beautiful Dreamer," are still popular—nearly 200 years after their composition. (**en.wikipedia.org/wiki/Stephen_Foster**)

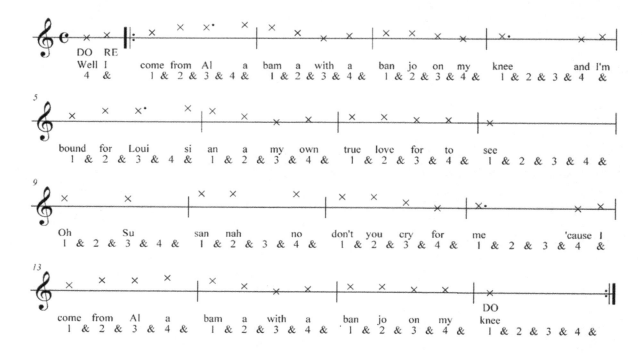

Row, Row, Row Your Boat

I couldn't find anything about this one, but I sure like bouncing around in a rubber raft on our western rivers, so I used the tune. We go down the stream, but often, not so gently. "Life is but a dream" is good, too.

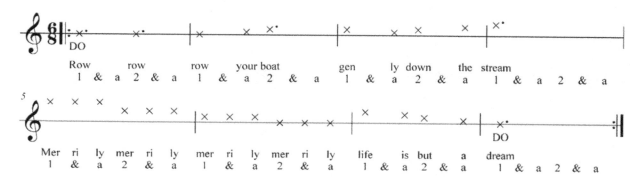

Jingle Bells
James Pierpont

Written in 1857 and republished in 1859, "Jingle Bells" was not written as a Christmas song. It's the 19th century equivalent of "Little Deuce Coupe" and originally titled "One Horse Open Sleigh." It memorializes the cutter drag races in Boston, Massachusetts where spiffed out sleighs would race between Medford and Malden Squares. Young James was a rogue; he abandoned his family several times, took up arms for the Confederacy (his father was a Boston Abolitionist minister), and after his first wife died, he abandoned his children to take another wife. Adapted from an article by Bob Bankard, Philly Burbs Special Sections.

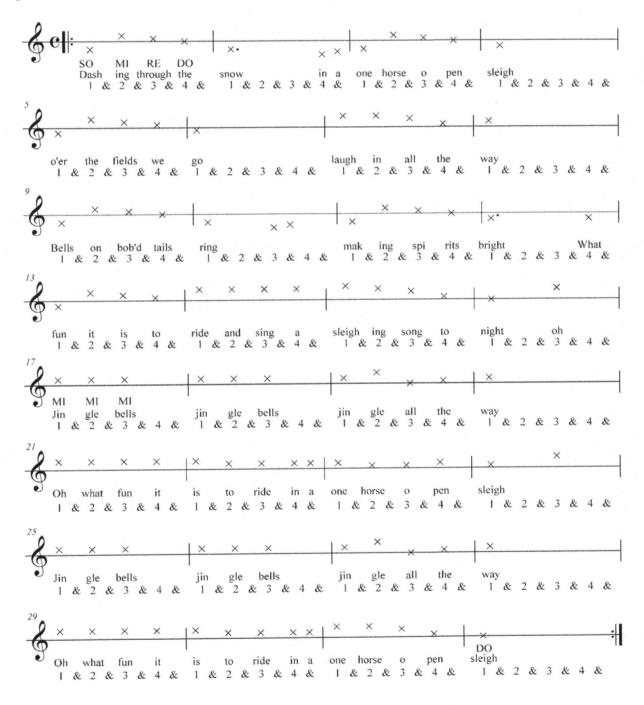

Rock-a-bye Baby

The story of the nursery rhyme relates to a family who lived in a tree-house which was formed within a massive yew tree. The yew tree concerned was believed to be nearly 2,000 years old. Kate and Luke Kenyon lived in what was locally called the "Betty Kenny Tree," a colloquialism for Kate Kenyon. The Kenyons had eight children. The yew tree still exists, but was severely fire damaged by vandals in the 1930s. Adapted from **www.rhymes.org.uk**. There is also a story regarding the origins of words to "Rock-a-bye Baby" in American history. The words and lyrics to the "Rock-a-bye Baby" rhyme are reputed to reflect the observations of a young pilgrim boy in America who had seen Native mothers suspend a birch bark cradle from the branches of a tree, enabling the wind to rock the cradle and the child to sleep. This rhyme is also known as "Hush-a-bye Baby" which is probably the correct title. The confusion probably occurred due to the popularity of the old Al Jolson classic song, "Rock-a-bye My Baby with a Dixie Melody." Look for arpeggios in this melody and they'll tell you the chords.

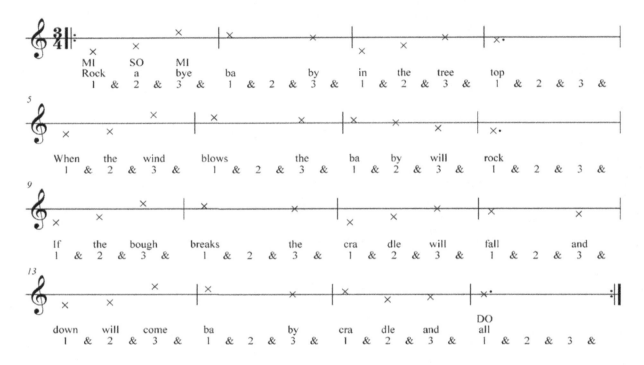

Are You Sleeping?

"Frère Jacques" is a well-known children's song in French. Translations of the song with the same tune are found in almost every country in Europe.

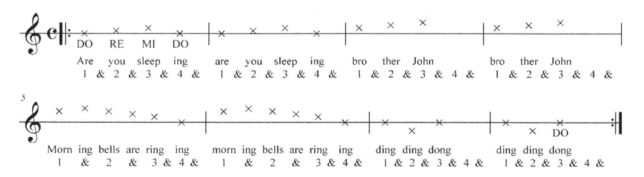

14 - Putting It All Together

Deck The Halls

If there's a carol which could be accurately categorized as totally uninhibited, it would be "Deck The Halls with Bows of Holly." Thoroughly and blatantly dedicated to frivolous merrymaking, with ideas like "gay apparel," "merry measure," "joyous," and "heedless," plus the whimsical "Fa la la la la, la la la la" refrain, "Deck The Halls" is the classical model of the jolly, secular carol. Reinforcing the light-hearted tone of the lyrics is the exquisitely vivacious, yet solid and substantial melody, which romps with free abandon throughout the decorated hall. Quoted from The Christmas Carol Reader, by William Studwell. As the only book that covers this elusive topic, The Christmas Carol Reader informs and entertains readers to over 200 songs of all types (sacred and secular), of all periods (Middle Ages through the 20th century), and from a number of countries and cultures.

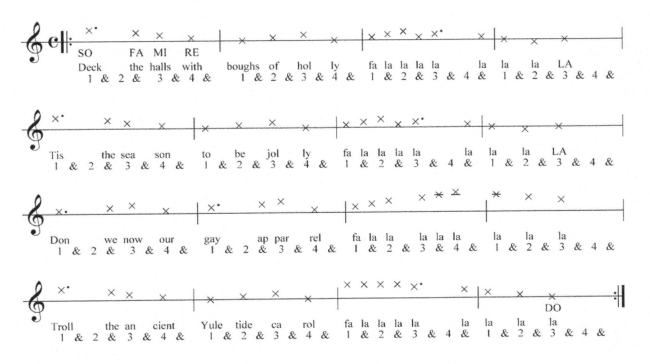

Yankee Doodle

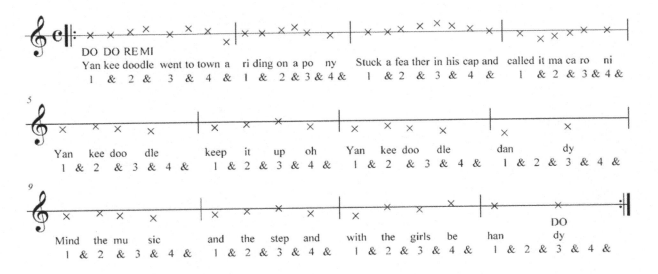

London Bridge Is Falling Down

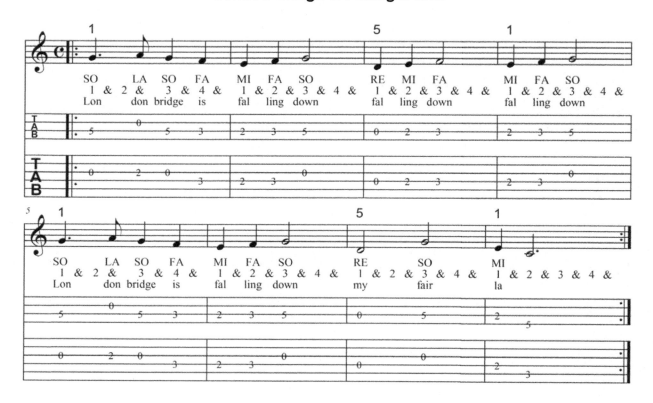

Are You Sleeping?

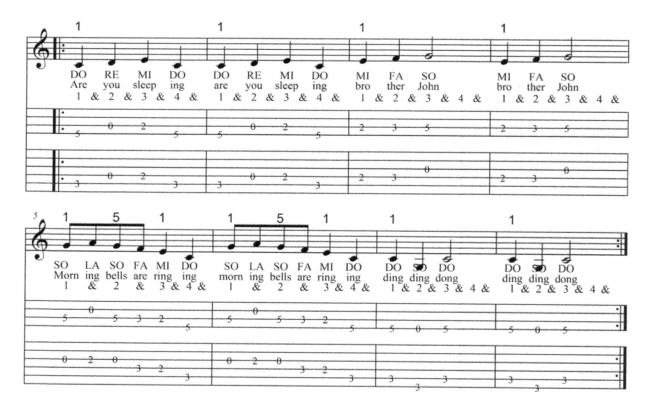

14 - Putting It All Together

Auld Lang Syne

Home On The Range

14 - Putting It All Together

Home On The Range (cont.)

Three Blind Mice

14 - Putting It All Together

Oh Tannenbaum

14 - Putting It All Together

531

Take Me Out To The Ballgame

14 - Putting It All Together

Red River Valley

Row, Row, Row Your Boat

Silent Night

14 - Putting It All Together

Silent Night (cont.)

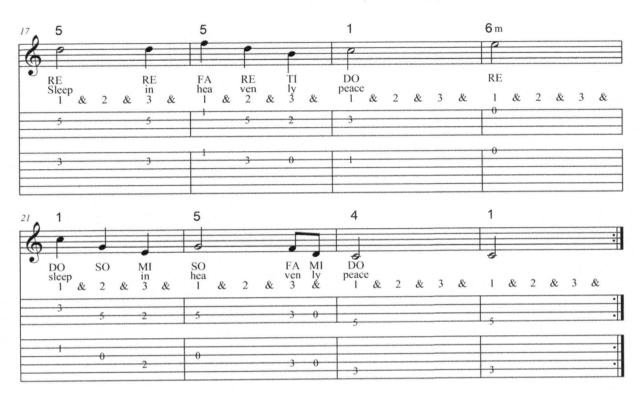

Pop Goes The Weasel

Jingle Bells

14 - Putting It All Together

Jingle Bells (cont.)

Oh Susannah

Rock-a-bye Baby

Deck The Halls

14 - Putting It All Together

We Wish You A Merry Christmas

Yankee Doodle

The origins of the words and music of "Yankee Doodle" are not known, exactly due to the fact that the song has many versions. The music and words go back to 15th century Holland, as a harvesting song that began, "Yanker dudel doodle down." In England, the tune was used for a nursery rhyme, "Lucy Locket." Later, the song poked fun of Puritan church leader, Oliver Cromwell, because "yankee" was a mispronunciation of the word "English" in the Dutch language and "doodle" refers to a dumb person. It was a British surgeon, Richard Schuckburgh, who wrote the words we know today that ridiculed the ragtag colorists fighting in the French and Indian War. Soon after, the British troops used the song to make fun of the American colonists during the Rebellion. Yet, it became the American colonists' rallying anthem for that war. At the time the Revolutionary War began, the colonists were proud to be called Yankees and "Yankee Doodle" became their most stirring anthem of defiance. Before the war, when the song "Yankee Doodle" first became popular, the word macaroni in the line that reads "stuck a feather in his hat and called it macaroni" didn't refer to the pasta. Instead, "Macaroni" was a fancy and overdressed ("dandy") style of Italian clothing widely imitated in England at the time. So, by just sticking a feather in his cap and calling himself a "Macaroni," Yankee Doodle was proudly proclaiming himself to be a country bumpkin (an awkward and unsophisticated person), because that was the way that many English regarded colonials at that time.

Reflections

"Where the willingness is great, the difficulties cannot be great."
Niccoló Machiavelli

"Where words fail, music speaks."
Hans Christian Andersen

"With ordinary talent and extraordinary perseverance, all things are attainable."
Thomas Foxwell Buxton

"Without music life would be a mistake."
Friedrich Nietzsche

"Without music, life is a journey through a desert."
Pat Conroy

*"Words make you think a thought.
Music makes you feel a feeling.
A song makes you feel a thought."*
E.Y. Harburg

*"Yesterday is but a vision, and tomorrow is only a dream.
But today well-lived makes every yesterday a dream of happiness,
and every tomorrow a dream of hope."*
Unknown

"You are the music while the music lasts."
T. S. Eliot

*"You can do what you have to do,
and sometimes you can do it even better than you think you can."*
Jimmy Carter

"You may be disappointed if you fail, but you are doomed if you don't try."
Beverly Sills
Chairman of the Board, Lincoln Center for the Performing Arts, opera singer

*"You must have long term goals
to keep you from being frustrated by short term failures."*
Charles C. Noble

"Your dreams come true when you act to turn them into realities."
Unknown

I WISH I KNEW WHO MADE THIS UP!
It came to me from Larry Barnwell in an e-mail.
If you get all the puns, you've been paying attention!

A C, an E-flat, and a G go into a bar.

The bartender says: "Sorry, but we don't serve minors."

So the E-flat leaves and the C and the G have an open fifth between them.

After a few drinks, the fifth is diminished: The G is out flat.

An F comes in and tries to augment the situation, but is not sharp enough.

A D comes into the bar and heads straight for the bathroom saying,
"Excuse me, I'll just be a second."

An A comes into the bar, but the bartender is not convinced
that this relative of C is not a minor.

Then the bartender notices a B-flat hiding at the end of the bar and exclaims:
"Get out now. You're the seventh minor I've found in this bar tonight."

The E-flat, not easily deflated, comes back to the bar the next night in a three-piece suit
with nicely shined shoes. The bartender (who used to have a nice corporate job
until his company downsized) says: "You're looking sharp tonight, come on in!
This could be a major development."

This proves to be the case, as the E-flat takes off the suit, and everything else,
and stands there au naturel.

Eventually, the C sobers up, and realizes in horror that he's under a rest.
The C is brought to trial, is found guilty of contributing to the diminution of a minor,
and is sentenced to 10 years of DS without Coda at an upscale correctional facility.

On appeal, however, the C is found innocent of any wrongdoing, even accidental,
and that all accusations to the contrary are bassless.

The bartender decides, however, that since he's only had tenor so patrons,
the sorpranout in the bathroom, and everything has become all too much treble,
he needs a rest and closes the bar.

Index

For this index, page numbers in **bold** indicate musical notation or tablature to be used for practice.

Answer Key

1 - Note Names

1. 7
2. A B C D E F G
3. hear, note
4. A
5. low
6. A
7. D
8. G
9. B
10. high
11. False
12. True
13. False
14. 12
15. Staff
16. 5, 4
17. Clef
18. Treble, Bass, C
19. C, Treble, Bass
20. expand
21. G, A, B, C, D D, C, B, A, G
    A, B, C, D, E E, D, C, B, A
    B, C, D, E, F F, E, D, C, B
22. 1, middle C
23. False
24. True
25. the same
26. the same
27. string
28. fret
29. E, E
30. percussion
31. True
32. percussion clef
33. C-D-G-B   E-A-D-E   F-G-B-E   C-F-A-E
    F-B-G-D   C-A-E-B   D-G-D-A   E-C-F-G
    E-A-D-E   B-E-F-G   F-B-G-D   F-B-G-D
    F-G-B-D   F-G-B-D   C-F-A-E   D-G-D-A
    C-F-A-E   E-A-D-E   E-C-F-G   C-D-G-B

2 - Counting

1. Time
2. (Whole) half, quarter, eighth, sixteenth, thirty-second
3. Whole

4. False
5. False
6. bar
7. twelve
8. 2, 4, 8, 16, 32, 64
9. (Whole) half, quarter, eighth, sixteenth, thirty-second
10. False
11. time signatures
12. False
13. beats
14. note, beat
15. two, half, one beat
16. three-four, three, quarter, one beat
17. four four, four, quarter, one beat
18. common, four, quarter, one beat
19. seven four, seven, quarter, one beat
20. three eight, three, eighth, one beat
21. six eight, eighth, one beat
22. nine eight, nine, one beat
23. twelve eight, twelve, one beat
24. True
25. True
26. True
27. True
28. True
29. False
30. True
31. False
32. Metronome Setting
33. False
34. 60, one minute, quarter, one beat
35. 25, one minute, half, one
36. 100, one minute, eighth, one
37. 50, one minute, quarter, one
38. 40, one minute, half, one
39. NONE
40. 40 to 60
41. 60 to 75
42. 75 to 105
43. 105 to 120
44. 120 to 170
45. 170 to 200
46. 200 to 499
47. False
48. False

49. pickup measure
50. during
51. True
52. False
53. pickup notes

3 - Intervals Part One

1. False
2. False
3. right
4. left
5. higher
6. lower
7. nearest
8. nearest
9. harmonic interval
10. 2nd, 5th, 7th, 4th, 5th, 7th, 3rd, 6th, octave, 2nd, 4th, octave, 5th, 3rd, 5th, 6th, 6th, 7th, 4th, 3rd, octave, 6th, 5th, 2nd
11. melodic interval
12. 7th, 2nd, 5th, 7th, octave, 6th, 2nd, 4th, 7th, octave, 3rd, 5th, 4th, octave, 2nd
13. (column 1) 7th, 6th, 3rd, 2nd, 6th, 3rd, 3rd, 5th, octave, 5th, 7th, 2nd, 2nd, (column 2) 3rd, 6th, 7th, 3rd, 6th, 6th, 4th, octave, 4th, 2nd, 7th, (column 3) octave, octave, 2nd, 4th, 3rd, 5th, 7th, 2nd, 4th, 6th, 3rd, 6th, (column 4) 3rd, 5th, 3rd, 3rd, 6th, 5th, 4th, 6th, 4th, 4th, 2nd, 5th

4 - Intervals Part Two

1. sharp
2. flat
3. half step
4. twelve
5. True
6. higher, one half step
7. lower, one half step
8. enharmonic
9. A sharp, above, B flat
10. C sharp, higher, B flat
11. D sharp, above, E flat
12. F sharp, above, G flat
13. G sharp, above, A flat, below
14. True
15. whole step
16. False
17. half step
18. half step
19. whole step
20. half step
21. half step
22. whole step
23. half step
24. half step
25. half step
26. half step
27. whole step

5 - Intervals Part Three

1. two
2. perfect
3. major
4. decreasing
5. smaller
6. flat, flatted,
7. diminished
8. lower
9. decrease
10. expanding
11. augment
12. sharp
13. raise
14. increase
15. True
16. E
17. G
18. Major 3rd
19. D
20. G
21. 1
22. 2
23. 3
24. 4
25. 5
26. 6
27. 7
28. 8
29. 9
30. 10
31. 11
32. octave
33. octave, tritone
34. major, minor

6 - Scales

1. series of tones
2. Intervals
3. degree, 1, 7
4. alphabetical order
5. seven, no, no

6. whole, whole, half, whole, whole, whole, half
7. G
8. D
9. A flat
10. F sharp
11. Solfege DO RE MI FA SO LA TI
12. False
13. seven, scale
14. Dorian
15. aolian
16. chromatic
17. one half step
18. whole steps, six
19. five
20. 1st, 2nd, 3rd, 5th, 6th
21. 6th, 1st, 2nd, 3rd, 5th
22. True
23. two
24. two
25. three
26. natural, harmonic, melodic

7 - Major and Minor Chords

1. Three or more notes played at the same time.
2. triad
3. scale degree, function
4. root
5. True
6. 3rd, 5th
7. interval, root
8. qualities, Major, minor
9. major 3rd
10. perfect 5th
11. minor 3rd
12. perfect 5th
13. True
14. minor, m, -
15. 3rd
16. change the sequence
17. three
18. root
19. first inversion
20. second inversion
21. False
22. C-E G C-E b -G
23. D-F#-A D-F-A
24. F#-A#-C# F#-A-C#
25. G#-B#-D# G#-B-D#
26. E b -G b -B b E b -G- B b
27. B b -D -F Bb - D b -F
28. C 5th-R-3rd-5th-R-3rd
29. A 5th-R-5th-R-3rd-5th

30. G R-3rd-5th-R-3rd-R
31. E R-5th-R-3rd-5th-R
32. D 3rd-5th-R-5th-R-3rd
33. Cm R- b 3rd-5th-R
34. Am 5th-R-5th-R- b 3rd-5th
35. Gm R- b 3rd-5th-R-5th
36. Em R-5th-R- b 3rd-5th-R
37. Dm 5th-R-5th-R- b 3rd

8 - Beyond Major and Minor Chords

1. extended, adding, triad
2. altered
3. twelve
4. number, letter
5. interval, root
6. left, right
7. True
8. 3rd, 5th, 6th
9. C,E,G. minor, 3rd, flatted. 6th, C
10. 3rd, 5th 7th
11. major 7, maj 7, Δ
12. minor major
13. 3rd, 5th, - b 7th
14. 7, C7
15. 3rd, 5th, b 7th
16. 3rd, 5th, 7th
17. suspended 4th
18. root, 5th, power chords
19. add
20. 7th
21. four
22. C, 9th
23. E, 11th
24. G, 13th
25. C, 3rd,
26. True
27. four
28. 3rd, 5th, 9th four
29. 3rd, 5th, b 7th , 9th, five
30. 3rd, 5th, b 7th , 9th, 11th , six
31. 3rd, 5th, b 7th , 9th, 11th, 13th, seven
32. major
33. 3rd, 5th, 7th, 9th, five
34. 3rd, 5th, 7th, 9th, 11th, six
35. 3rd, 5th, 7th, 9th, 11th, 13th, seven
36. leave some out
37. D, F#
38. A, G
39. Em, G
40. C6, 9th

9 - Augmented, Diminished and (alt.) chords

1. major
2. three
3. eight
4. one
5. major 3rd
6. +
7. C augmented
8. True
9. no
10. C+
11. E+
12. G#+
13. 5th
14. whole tone
15. minor
16. six
17. one
18. minor 3rd
19. four
20. two
21. four
22. minor 3rd
23. C°
24. C diminished seven
25. half diminished
26. C half diminished
27. three
28. flat 7th
29. minor seven flat five
30. minor flat five
31. True

10 - The Key

1. key, chords
2. seven
3. scale tones
4. diatonic
5. seven, major
6. three, three
7. minor, minor, major, major, minor, diminished
8. C. C major.
9. Roman numerals
10. root, I
11. True
12. do-mi-so
13. D minor. re-fa-la
14. 3m. mi, so, ti
15. F. fa, la, do
16. G. so, ti, re

17. A minor. la-do,mi
18. B minor flat 5. ti, re, fa
19. ti, re, fa
20. Dm, G, C
21. C, F, G
22. C, Em, G
23. Transpose, modulate
24. Modulate
25. Transpose
26. True
27. key signature
28. two
29. major, minor
30. lower
31. (C Am)
32. G Em
    (C
    F
    Am)
    Dm
33. D Bm Bb Gm
34. A F#m E b Cm
35. E C#m A b Fm
36. B G#m D b Bb m
37. F# D#m G b E b m
38. True
39. False
40. transposing
41. concert pitch
42. False
43. A
44. E
45. B
46. G b
47. D b
48. D
49. A
50. E
51. B
52. G b
53. True
54. True
55. True
56. True
57. Solfege

13 - Reading The Road Map

1. Intro
2. Verse
3. Chorus/refrain
4. True
5. form

6. True
7. Repeat sign
8. beginning, end
9. three times
10. True
11. first, second
12. 1, 8.
13. 1, 7
14. 8, 9, 13
15. measure repeat
16. 33
17. da capo, D.C.
18. al fine
19. D.C. al fine
20. coda
21. dal segno, D.S.
22. True
23. D.S.
24. D.S. al fine
25. three, two, al coda
26. first, beginning, first, second
27. True
28. D.S. al coda
29. True
30. D.S., D.S.S.
31. coda1, coda2, coda3

Made in the USA
Coppell, TX
10 March 2022

74766719R10326